Microeconomics

Private and Public Choice

18th Edition

James D. Gwartney
†Florida State University

Richard L. Stroup
†Professor Emeritus of Economics at Montana State University

Russell S. Sobel
The Citadel

David A. Macpherson
Trinity University, San Antonio TX

With Assistance of Jane Shaw Stroup

Cengage

Australia • Brazil • Canada • Mexico • Singapore • United Kingdom • United States

The Eight Guideposts to Economic Thinking

These eight guideposts provide the foundation for the economic way of thinking (they are discussed in Chapter 1). To do well in this course you will need to understand and be able to apply these ideas to a wide range of issues.

1. The use of scarce resources is costly; trade-offs must always be made.
2. Individuals choose purposefully — they try to get the most from their limited resources.
3. Incentives matter — choice is influenced in a predictable way by changes in incentives.
4. Individuals make decisions at the margin.
5. Although information can help us make better choices, its acquisition is costly.
6. Beware of the secondary effects: Economic actions often generate indirect as well as direct effects.
7. The value of a good or service is subjective.
8. The test of a theory is its ability to predict.

Special Topics

These Special Topics covered in the "Applying the Basics" section use the basic concepts to analyze important current-day topics.

1. Government Spending and Taxation
2. The Stock Market: Its Function, Performance, and Potential as an Investment Opportunity
3. Keynes and Hayek: Contrasting Views on Sound Economics and the Role of Government
4. The Great Recession of 2008-2009: Causes and Response
5. Lessons from the Great Depression
6. The Economics of Health Care
7. Earnings Differences between Men and Women
8. The Question of Resource Exhaustion
9. Difficult Environmental Cases and the Role of Government

KEYS TO ECONOMIC PROSPERITY

These keys to the economic prosperity of a nation are highlighted throughout the text.

1. **Human Ingenuity.** Economic goods are the result of human ingenuity and action; thus, the size of the economic pie is variable, not fixed. [Chapter 2]
2. **Private Ownership.** Private ownership provides people with a strong incentive to take care of things and develop resources in ways that are highly valued by others. [Chapter 2]
3. **Gains from Trade.** Trade makes it possible for individuals to generate more output through specialization and division of labor, large-scale production processes, and the dissemination of improved products and production methods. [Chapter 2]
4. **Invisible Hand Principle.** Market prices coordinate the actions of self-interested individuals and direct them toward activities that promote the general welfare. [Chapter 3]
5. **Profits and Losses.** Profits direct producers toward activities that increase the value of resources; losses impose a penalty on those who reduce the value of resources. [Chapter 3]
6. **Competition.** Competition motivates businesses to produce efficiently, cater to the views of consumers, and search for innovative improvements. [Chapter 9]
7. **Entrepreneurship.** The entrepreneurial discovery and development of improved products and production processes is a central element of economic progress. [Chapter 10]
8. **Productivity and Earnings.** In a market economy, productivity and earnings are closely linked. In order to earn a large income, one must provide large benefits to others. [Chapter 13]
9. **Innovation and the Capital Market.** If the potential gains from innovative ideas and human ingenuity are going to be fully realized, it must be relatively easy for individuals to try their innovative and potentially ingenious ideas, but difficult to continue if the idea is a bad one. [Chapter 14]

Cengage

Microeconomics: Private and Public Choice, 18e
James D. Gwartney
Richard L. Stroup
Russell S. Sobel
David A. Macpherson
Senior Vice President, Product Management: Cheryl Constantini

Product Director: Joe Sabatino

Senior Portfolio Product Manager: Chris Rader

Senior Content Manager: Nithya Chinnannan

Senior Product Assistant: Autumn Lala-Sonora

Subject Matter Expert: Shannon Aucoin, Andrew DeJong, Eugenia Belova

Senior Product Marketing Manager: Colin Kramer

Intellectual Property Analyst: Rida Syed

Intellectual Property Project Manager: Philominal Susai

Production Service: Straive, Inc.

Art Director: Erin Griffin

Text and Cover Designer: Sarah Cole

Cover Image: Georg Stelzner/imageBROKER/Getty Images

WCN: 01-100-414

Library of Congress Control Number: 2025902291

Student Edition:
ISBN: 979-8-214-04150-6

Loose-leaf:
ISBN: 979-8-214-04151-3

Cengage
5191 Natorp Boulevard
Mason, OH 45040
USA

Printed at CLDPC, USA, 11-25

Dedication

In 1976, James ('Jim') Gwartney published the first edition of *Economics: Private and Public Choice*. In the preface he discusses two goals in creating a new principles of economics textbook: (1) to emphasize the economic way of thinking to help students have a better understanding of the real world–in contrast to the abstract, dull, and overly mathematical approach taken by other textbooks; and (2) to ensure that basic economic tools are applied to both the market and political processes, so that government failure and market failure were presented with equal clarity–in contrast to other textbooks presenting government as an ideal corrective device as if policy was designed and implemented by an omniscient, benevolent central planner.

Gwartney's pioneering integration of public choice theory into a principles textbook enabled students to understand why good politics sometimes conflicts with good economics. Other textbooks compared real world market outcomes with hypothetical ideal government solutions. Gwartney's approach gave students an understanding not only of what government can do to promote a more efficient use of our resources, but also the reasons to expect that public sector action will be counterproductive for certain classes of issues. Approaching the effectiveness of democratic decision making with the same basic tools of economics helped students understand why the outcomes of real-world government action may also be less than ideal, and why in cases of market imperfections government intervention may not always improve the outcome.

The combination of these two novel approaches gave students using the textbook a significant advantage over other students, propelling it to become a market leader with a loyal following that has lasted for decades. In 1996, Gwartney pioneered the creation of the *Economic Freedom of the World Index* which afforded another opportunity to innovate by being the first textbook to include significant coverage of how economic institutions influence economic outcomes and development. In recent editions, the expanded coverage of entrepreneurship has also uniquely differentiated *Economics: Private and Public Choice* from other books that mention it only as an omitted variable–a fitting addition given the entrepreneurial innovations Jim Gwartney himself brought to the principles of economics textbook market.

Richard ('Rick') Stroup became a coauthor starting on the second edition in 1980, Russell Sobel on the ninth edition in 2000, and David Macpherson on the tenth edition in 2003, all after participating in the project in various ways on prior editions. Any discussion of the author team would be incomplete without mentioning Jim's wife Amy Gwartney who contributed significantly over the many editions (as has Rick Stroup's wife Jane Shaw Stroup). We lost Rick in November 2021 and Jim in January 2024. These two esteemed individuals left an indelible mark through their contributions not only to the textbook but also through their scholarly work, contributions to policy, and impact on thousands of students.

The remaining coauthors are forever grateful for the impact these founding authors had on our lives as well. They were both cherished friends and beloved colleagues. Though they may not be here with us physically as we publish this 18th edition, we endeavor to keep their spirit and memory alive–as well as their goal of making economic thinking and the realistic view of government action through the lens of public choice theory the integral and differentiating features of this textbook. We dedicate this edition to Jim and Rick.

Brief Contents

Contents

Part 5

Applying the Basics: Special Topics in Economics 341

Relationship Between Main Edition and the Macro/Micro Editions

In addition to the full length text, Microeconomic and Macroeconomic splits of this text are also available. The chapters and special topics covered by the micro and macro split versions are indicated in this table.

Chapters	Economics	Microeconomics	Macroeconomics
The Economic Approach	1	1	1
Some Tools of the Economist	2	2	2
Demand, Supply, and the Market Process	3	3	3
Demand and Supply: Applications and Extensions	4	4	4
Difficult Cases for the Market, and the Role of Government	5	5	5
The Economics of Political Action	6	6	6
Taking the Nation's Economic Pulse	7		7
Economic Fluctuations, Unemployment, and Inflation	8		8
An Introduction to Basic Macroeconomic Markets	9		9
Dynamic Change, Economic Fluctuations, and the *AD-AS* Model	10		10
Fiscal Policy: The Keynesian View and the Historical Development of Macroeconomics	11		11
Fiscal Policy, Incentives, and Secondary Effects	12		12
Money and the Banking System	13		13
Modern Macroeconomics and Monetary Policy	14		14
Macroeconomic Policy, Economic Stability, and the Federal Debt	15		15
Creating an Environment for Growth and Prosperity	16		16
The Economics of Development	17		17
Gaining from International Trade	18	16	18
International Finance and the Foreign Exchange Market	19		19
Consumer Choice and Elasticity	20	7	
Costs and the Supply of Goods	21	8	
Price Takers and the Competitive Process	22	9	
Price-Searcher Markets with Low Entry Barriers	23	10	
Price-Searcher Markets with High Entry Barriers	24	11	
The Supply of and Demand for Productive Resources	25	12	
Earnings, Productivity, and the Job Market	26	13	
Investment, the Capital Market, and the Wealth of Nations	27	14	
Income Inequality and Poverty	28	15	

Preface

These are interesting times. Our lives have been shaken by a once-in-a-century worldwide pandemic, inflation rates not seen in decades, soaring housing prices, and political uncertainty. Moreover, technology is altering how we communicate, learn, and interact with each other. Students are struggling to understand recent changes and their impact on their lives. Beginning with the first edition 50 years ago, our goal has been to use the tools of economics to explain how the real world works and to do so in a clear and understandable manner. This goal was at the forefront of our minds as we worked on this edition.

We have always used the tools of economics to analyze the operation of both the market and political processes. Both are central to the understanding of today's rapidly changing world. More than any other principles text, we highlight the roles of entrepreneurship, dynamic competition, and public choice analysis. Entrepreneurship is the key to understanding how markets work and the vast improvement in our living standards. Public choice is the key to understanding the structure of incentives confronted by voters, politicians, and bureaucrats and how this impacts political outcomes. This text examines both markets and political decision-making and indicates conditions under which each works well and alternative conditions that cause each to work poorly.

The micro chapters provide extensive coverage of entrepreneurship, innovation, and dynamic competition in the operation of markets. The macro chapters analyze the major alternative theories of both fiscal and monetary policy and provide up-to-date coverage of recent changes in Federal Reserve policy, government debt, and other factors impacting the macroeconomy. The "Beyond the Basics" Special Topics section includes features on micro topics such as the stock market, health care, and environmental economics as well as macro topics like the Great Depression, and the Great Recession of 2008–2009.

Organization and Instructor Flexibility

The organization of *Economics: Private and Public Choice* is designed to provide instructors with maximum flexibility. Those using the full-length text for a two-semester course can cover either microeconomics or macroeconomics first. As in recent editions, the text is divided into core chapters and a concluding special topics section. The 28 core chapters cover all of the material taught in most principles courses, and they are presented in the usual manner. Examples and data from the real world are used to reinforce the analysis. In addition, the "Beyond the Basics" Special Topics section includes 9 relatively short special topic applications covering both micro and macro topics. Features in this section address questions such as these: "Are stocks a good investment for a young person?," "What caused the Great Depression?," "Is discrimination responsible for the earnings differences between men and women?," and "Are we running out of resources?" These features will grab the interest of students and are short enough to cover during a single class period. If you have not integrated the special topic materials into your course, please consider doing so. They will enrich your course and help students better understand the political economy debates that dominate the daily news of our world.

Instructors integrating public choice throughout their course will probably want to cover Chapters 5 and 6 before moving to the core micro or macro material. Others teaching a microeconomics course may want to jump from Chapter 4 directly to the core micro chapters. Correspondingly, some macroeconomics instructors will want to move directly from Chapter 3 or 4 to the core macro material. The chapters have been written so that any of these options will work.

New Material in this edition

New material designed to enliven economics and illustrate its relevance has been integrated into just about every chapter. The following are several of these additions:

The coverage of entrepreneurship and its importance as a source of new goods, services, and production methods that enrich our lives has been expanded in several chapters, as has our series, "Entrepreneurs Who Have Changed Our Lives." This series highlights both the contributions and interesting personal attributes of a diverse set of entrepreneurs including David Steward, Berry Gordy, Taylor Swift, Cathy Hughes, Kendra Scott, Malcom McLean, and Oprah Winfrey. This feature enhances the knowledge of students about how their lives are impacted by entrepreneurs.

Chapter 2 includes an updated feature on "Are Scandinavian Countries Socialist?" The empirical evidence on this question is examined.

In Chapter 4, the analysis of the minimum wage, including the effect of recent increases in city and state minimums, has been updated and expanded.

Chapter 10 contains updated material examining how technological advances that have reduced search and transaction costs, including the growth of the 'sharing economy,' have altered the nature of markets and enabled entrepreneurs to break down traditional barriers to entry and expand competition.

Chapter 11 contains updated material on dynamic competition in the digital age, including the impact of network effects and platform businesses. These two concepts help students understand the changing nature of markets and the growing presence of larger online firms. The impact of the sharing economy and the platform business model based on crowdsourced resources on the competitiveness of markets and choices available to consumers are examined. Improvements in technology, communications, and transportation have lowered transaction and monitoring costs, weakening the forces leading to diseconomies of scale. Marketing, advertising, and information costs have also changed in ways that make it easier to reach a larger customer base more rapidly and cost-effectively.

Additional Text Features

Economics: Private and Public Choice retains several features that make the presentation of economics both more interesting and understandable.

- Keys to Economic Prosperity. Students often fail to appreciate the organizational and institutional factors that are the foundation for economic progress. To help remedy this situation, we have incorporated a "Keys to Economic Prosperity" feature that highlights the importance of factors like gains from trade, secure property rights, competition, and free trade as sources of economic prosperity. These key factors that underlie modern economic prosperity are highlighted at appropriate places throughout the text.
- Applications in Economics. "Applications in Economics" boxes apply economic theory to real-world issues and controversies. These features illustrate the importance and power of the principles covered in the text.
- Outstanding Economists. Boxes throughout the text highlight the lives of major economists and focus on how their work has contributed to the development of economics.
- Entrepreneurs Who Have Changed Our Lives. This expanded series highlights both the economic contribution and personal attributes of key entrepreneurs. It will help students better understand the role of entrepreneurs and how their actions have contributed to the development of various goods and services that are often taken for granted.
- Learning Objectives. A new set of learning objectives are included at the beginning of each chapter. These serve to both direct student reading and provide feedback regarding mastery of the chapter. If students can respond correctly to each of these statements, it indicates they have a good understanding of the items covered in the chapter.
- Key Point Summaries. At the end of each chapter, the Key Points section provides students with a concise statement of the material covered in the chapter (the chapter learning objectives).
- Critical Analysis Questions. Each chapter concludes with a set of analysis and discussion questions designed to test students' ability to analyze economic issues and to apply economic theory to real-world events. Appendix B at the end of the text contains suggested answers for approximately a third of these questions.

For The Instructor

We are sure that many of the features incorporated with this textbook will help you become a better teacher and make your classes more interesting to students. Personally, we have incorporated the Keys to Economic Prosperity series, economics video clips, homework assignments, and online quiz questions into our own classes with great success. The full set of supplements that can accompany the book include the following:

MindTap MindTap is a fully online, highly personalized learning experience built via Cengage Learning content that combines student learning tools—readings, multimedia, activities, and assessments—into a singular Learning Path that guides students through their course. Instructors personalize the experience by customizing authoritative Cengage Learning content and learning tools, including the ability to add their own content in the Learning Path via apps that integrate into the MindTap framework seamlessly with Learning Management Systems.

Interactive eBook In addition to interactive teaching and learning tools, Economic MindTap includes an interactive eBook. Students can take notes, highlight, search, and interact with embedded media specific to their book. Use it as a supplement to the printed text or as a substitute—with MindTap, the choice is up to your students.

Test Banks The test banks for the 18th edition were prepared by the author team with the assistance of Shannon Aucoin and other members of Cengage's excellent team of subject matter experts. Joe Calhoun of Florida State University has also provided valuable assistance in authoring questions for the testbank. The test bank contains approximately 6,000 questions—multiple choice and short answer. Within each chapter, the questions are tied to the major heads and specific topics within the chapter. Instructors who want to motivate their students to study will find online practice quizzes on MindTap that can easily be incorporated into their quizzes and exams. The cloud-based test banks for this edition have been enhanced significantly. Cognero contains all of the questions in the test bank so that you can create and customize tests in minutes. You can easily edit and import your own questions and graphics and edit and maneuver existing questions.

PowerPoint We believe our PowerPoint presentation, is the best you will find in the principles market. The presentation includes chapter-by-chapter lecture notes and hyperlinked slides of the exhibits included in the text. To facilitate classroom discussion and interaction, questions are strategically interspersed throughout the PowerPoint slides to help students develop the economic way of thinking. Instructions explaining how professors can easily add, delete, and modify slides in order to tailor the presentation to their liking are included. If instructors want to make the PowerPoint presentation available to students, they can place it on their website (or the site for their course).

Instructor's Manual Information on how to use and modify the PowerPoint material is contained in the front of the Instructor's Manual. The manual is divided by chapters, and each chapter begins with a detailed chapter outline in lecture-note form. It is designed to help instructors organize their notes to match the 18th edition of the book. Then there are focus questions which cover all the concepts in the chapter. Then the context of each chapter is given followed by important points and teaching suggestions. Each chapter also provides in-class economic games and experiments. Contributed in part by Professor Charles Stull of Kalamazoo College, the games are popular with many instructors. We hope you will try them.

The book companion Web site contains the key supplements designed to aid instructors, including the content from the Instructor's Manual, test banks, and PowerPoint lecture and exhibit slides

A Note to Instructors

As we try to improve the book from one edition to the next, we rely heavily on our experiences as teachers. But our experience using the book is minuscule compared to that of the hundreds of instructors who use it nationwide. If you encounter problems or have suggestions for improving the book, we urge you to let us know by writing to us in care of Cengage Learning, 5191 Natorp Blvd., Mason, OH 45040.

A Note to Students

This textbook contains several features we think will help you maximize (a good economic term) the returns of your study efforts. Here are some of the things that will help you and a few tips for making the most of them.

- Each chapter begins with a set of learning objectives to both direct your reading and provide you with feedback regarding your mastery of the chapter. If you can respond correctly to each of these statements, this indicates that you have a good understanding of the items covered in the chapter.
- The textbook is organized in the form of an outline. The headings within the text (in red) are the major points of the outline. Minor headings are subpoints under the major headings. In addition, important subpoints within sections are often set off and numbered. ***Bold italicized*** type is used to highlight material that is particularly important. Sometimes "thumbnail sketches" are included to recap material and help you keep the important points mentally organized.
- A "Key Points" summary appears at the end of each chapter. Use the summary as a checklist to determine whether you understand the major points of the chapter.

- A review of the exhibits and illustrative pictures will also provide you with a summary of the key points of each chapter. The accompanying captions briefly describe the economic phenomena illustrated by the exhibits.
- The key terms introduced in each chapter are defined in the margins. As you study the chapter, review the marginal definition of each key term as it is introduced. Later, you also may find it useful to review the marginal definitions. If you have forgotten the meaning of a term introduced earlier, consult the glossary at the end of the book.
- The critical analysis questions at the end of each chapter are intended to test your understanding of the economic way of thinking. Answering these questions and solving the problems will greatly enhance your knowledge of the material. Answers to approximately a third of these questions are provided in Appendix B.

If you need more practice, ask your professor about MindTap.

Acknowledgments

A project of this magnitude is a team effort. Through the years, numerous people have assisted us in various ways. Jane Shaw Stroup deserves special recognition for her contribution to this edition. She researched and prepared the initial draft of the material on the "Entrepreneurs Who Have Changed Our Lives" series and assisted the author team with research and proofing. As a result, we listed her name on the title page. Reagan Sobel provided valuable assistance in updating examples, data, and content in many chapters. Signè Thomas, Robert Lawson, and William Trumbull provided valuable comments and assistance with data for exhibits. The text still bears an imprint of the contributions of Woody Studenmund of Occidental College and Gary Galles of Pepperdine University, who assisted us in numerous ways with past editions.

We are also very much indebted to the excellent team of professionals at Cengage Learning, including Chris Rader, Sr. Portfolio Product Manager; Sarah Huber, Sr. Learning Designer; Nithya Chinnannan, Content Project Manager; Colleen Farmer, Sr. Content Manager; Colin Kramer, Sr. Portfolio Marketing Manager; Erin Griffin, Art Director; and Shannon Aucoin, Eugenia Belova, and Andrew DeJong, the inhouse subject matter experts.

We have often revised material in light of suggestions made by reviewers, users, friends, and even a few competitors. In this regard, we would like to express our appreciation to the following people for their reviews and helpful suggestions for recent editions:

Pete Calcagno, College of Charleston; Joseph Calhoun, Florida State University; Cathy Carey, Bowling Green University; Lee Coppock, University of Virginia; Hugo Faría, University of Miami; Tawni Ferrarini, Northern Michigan University; Burton Folsom, Hillsdale College; Seth Gershenson, Michigan State University; Monica Greer, Bellarmine University; Michael Hammock, Florida State University; Robert Higgs, Independent Institute; John Hilston, Eastern Florida State College; Randall Holcombe, Florida State University; Aaron Lowen, Grand Valley State University; Lynn MacDonald, St. Cloud State University; Thomas McCaleb, Florida State University; Barbara Moore, University of Central Florida; Mark Perry, University of Michigan–Flint; Ivan Pongracic, Hillsdale College; Gerry Simons, Grand Valley State University; and Carol Sweeney, Florida Gulf Coast University.

Through the years, many other instructors have provided us with insightful comments and constructive suggestions. We would like to express our appreciation to the following:

Steve Abid, Grand Rapids Community College; Douglas Agbetsiafa, Indiana University, South Bend; James C. W. Ahiakpor, California State University, Hayward; Ali T. Akarca, University of Illinois at Chicago; Ryan C. Amacher, University of Texas at Arlington; Stephen A. Baker, Capital University; Bharati Basu, Central Michigan University; Don Bellante, University of South Florida; Jennis Biser, Austin Peay State University; Donald Boudreaux, George Mason University; George Bowling, St. Charles Community College; Robert Brittingham, Christian Brothers University; Byron Brown, Michigan State University; James Bryan, Manhattanville College; Kathy Clark, Florida Southwestern State College; Mike Cohick, Collin County Community College; David S. Collins, Virginia Highlands Community College; Steven R. Cunningham, University of Connecticut; Jeff Edwards, Lone Star College–CyFair; Ann Eike, University of Kentucky; Christina Esquivel, McLennan Community College; Robert C. Eyler, Sonoma State University; James R. Fain, Oklahoma State University; Andrew W. Foshee, McNeese State University; Mark Funk, University of Arkansas at Little Rock; Gary Galles, Pepperdine University; Marsha Goldfarb, University of Maryland Baltimore County; Richard Gosselin, Houston Community College; Darrin Gulla, University of Kentucky; Barry Haworth, University of Louisville; Ronald Helgens, Golden Gate University; Robert E. Herman, Nassau Community College/SUNY; William D. Hermann, Golden Gate University, San Francisco; Rey Hernandez, Metropolitan State College of Denver; Brad Hobbs, Clemson University; Jim Hubert, Seattle Central Community College; Katherine Huger, Charleston Southern University; Woodrow W. Hughes, Jr., Converse College; Jeffrey Rogers Hummel,

San Jose State University; Tom Jeitschko, Michigan State University; Rob H. Kamery, Christian Brothers University; Derek Kellenberg, University of Montana; Robert Kling, Colorado State University; Frederic R. Kolb, University of Wisconsin–Eau Claire; Barbara Kouskoulas, Lawrence Technological University; Cory Krupp, Duke University; Jean Kujawa, Lourdes University; Randy W. LaHote, Washtenaw Community College; John Larrivee, Mount St. Mary's University; Robert Lawson, Southern Methodist University; Don R. Leet, California State University, Fresno; Joe LeVesque, Northwood University; Andrew T. Light, Liberty University; Edward J. López, Western Carolina University; Dale Matcheck, Northwood University; G. Dirk Mateer, University of Texas; John McArthur, Wofford College; David M. Mitchell, Missouri State University; Hadley Mitchell, Taylor University; Glen A. Moots, Northwood University; Debasri Mukherjee, Western Michigan University; Todd Myers, Grossmont College; Jennifer Pate, Loyola Marymount University; Lloyd Orr, Indiana University, Bloomington; Judd W. Patton, Bellevue University; James Payne, University of New Orleans; Dennis Pearson, Austin Peay State University; Claudiney Pereira, Arizona State University; Jack Phelan, University of New Haven; Jennifer Platania, Elon University; Robert C. Rencher, Jr., Liberty University; Dan Rickman, Oklahoma State University; Karin L. Russell, Keiser University; Allen Sanderson, University of Chicago; Thomas W. Secrest, USC Coastal Carolina; Tim Shaugnessey, Louisiana State University–Shreveport; Gerald Simons, Grand Valley State University; Charles D. Skipton, University of New Haven; Marcia Snyder, College of Charleston; John Solow, University of Iowa; Ken Somppi, Southern Union State Community College; John Sophocleus, Auburn; Joe Stevano, Coker College; Edward Stringham, Trinity College; David Switzer, St. Cloud State University; Alex Tokarev, Northwood University; Richard D.C. Trainer, Warsaw School of Economics; Bich Tran, San Jacinto College; Scott Ward, Trevecca Nazarene University; Christopher Westley, Florida Gulf Coast University; David Wharton, Washington College; Mark Wheeler, Western Michigan University; Edward Wolpert, University of Central Florida; and Janice Yee, Worcester State University.

About the Authors

James D. Gwartney served as Professor of Economics at Florida State University and holder of the Gus A. Stavros Eminent Scholar Chair of Economic Education. His writings have been widely published in both the popular media and scholarly journals such as the *American Economic Review*, *Journal of Political Economy*, *Journal of Economic Education*, *Southern Economic Journal*, and *Journal of Institutional and Theoretical Economics*. He is co-author (with Jane Shaw Stroup, Dwight Lee, Tawni Hunt Ferrarini, and Joseph Calhoun) of *Common Sense Economics: What Everyone Should Know About Wealth and Prosperity*, a primer on economics and personal finance. Dr. Gwartney's research focused on the measurement and determination of factors that influence cross-country differences in income levels and growth rates. Using this research, he developed and co-authors (with Robert Lawson, Joshua Hall, and Ryan Murphy) the annual report, *Economic Freedom of the World*, which provides information on the institutions and policies of 165 countries. This data set, published by a worldwide network of institutes, is widely used by scholars investigating topics ranging from economic growth to peaceful relations among nations. Dr. Gwartney served as chief economist of the Joint Economic Committee of the U.S. Congress during 1999–2000. In 2004, he received the Adam Smith Award of the Association of Private Enterprise Education for his contributions to the advancement of free market ideals. He is a past president of both the Southern Economic Association and the Association for Private Enterprise Education. He earned his Ph.D. in economics from the University of Washington.

Richard L. Stroup served as Professor Emeritus of Economics at Montana State University and Professor Emeritus of Economics at North Carolina State University. He earned his Ph.D. from the University of Washington. From 1982 to 1984, Dr. Stroup served as director of the Office of Policy Analysis at the U.S. Department of the Interior. He published and lectured on topics such as global warming, land use regulation, archaeology and environmental policy improvements. His research helped to develop the approach known as free market environmentalism. Dr. Stroup co-authored the first edition of *Common Sense Economics: What Everyone Should Know About Wealth and Prosperity* with Dr. Gwartney. In addition, he has published *Economics: What Everyone Should Know About Economics and The Environment*, which was sponsored by the Property and Environment Research Center, of which he is a co-founder.

Russell S. Sobel is BB&T Distinguished Professor of Economics and Entrepreneurship in the Baker School of Business at The Citadel in Dr. Sobel's hometown of Charleston, South Carolina. He is co-editor of the *Southern Economic Journal* and editorial board member for the *Journal of Entrepreneurship & Public Policy* and *Public Choice*. He has received numerous awards for both his teaching and research, including the Kenneth G. Elzinga Distinguished Teaching Award from the Southern Economic Association, the Georgescu-Roegen Prize for Best Article of the Year in the *Southern Economic Journal*, the Association of Private Enterprise Education Distinguished Scholar Award, and the Sir Antony Fisher International Memorial Award. He is the author or co-author of over 250 academic journal articles and books, including *Growth and Variability in State Tax Revenue: An Anatomy of State Fiscal Crises*, *The Rule of Law*, *Unleashing Capitalism*, and *The Essential Joseph Schumpeter*. His scholarly publications have appeared in journals such as the *Journal of Political Economy*, *Journal of Law and Economics*, *Public Choice*, *Journal of Business Venturing*, *Small Business Economics,* and *Economic Inquiry*. His recent research focuses on the intersection of entrepreneurship and economic policy. His Ph.D. in economics is from Florida State University.

David A. Macpherson is the E.M. Stevens Distinguished Professor of Economics and Economics Department Chair at Trinity University. Previously, he was Director of the Pepper Institute on Aging and Public Policy and the Rod and Hope Brim Eminent Scholar of Economics at Florida State University, where he received two university-wide awards for teaching excellence. His teaching areas include principles of microeconomics, money and banking, econometrics, and labor economics. Dr. Macpherson is an applied economist whose research focuses on real estate, pensions, discrimination, industry deregulation, labor unions, and the minimum wage. He has published more than 60 articles in leading economics and real estate journals, including *Review of Economics and Statistics, Journal of Labor Economics, Journal of Human Resources, Industrial and Labor Relations Review, and Journal of Real Estate Economics and Finance*. His research has been funded by a variety of entities, including the National Science Foundation, the Florida Legislature, and the National Association of Realtors. He is co-author of the undergraduate labor economics text, *Contemporary Labor Economics*. He is included in *Who's Who In Economics*, 4th edition which includes the 1,200 most frequently cited economists. Dr. Macpherson received his undergraduate degree and Ph.D. from Pennsylvania State University.

Part 1

The Economic Way of Thinking

Life is a series of choices

Economics is about how people choose. The choices we make influence our lives and those of others. Your future will be influenced by the choices you make with regard to education, job opportunities, savings, and investment. Furthermore, changes in technology, demographics, communications, and transportation are constantly altering the attractiveness of various options and the opportunities available to us. The economic way of thinking is all about how incentives alter the choices people make. It can help you make better choices and enhance your understanding of our dynamic world.

Chapter 1 The Economic Approach

> Economist, n.–A scoundrel whose faulty vision sees things as they really are, not as they ought to be.
>
> –Daniel K. Benjamin, after Ambrose Bierce

Welcome to the world of economics. In recent years, economics has often been front-page news, and it affects all of our lives. Inflation and soaring housing prices, climate change and the use of fossil fuel energy sources, artificial intelligence and the changing nature of jobs, volatile cryptocurrency markets, the rise of online work and schooling, and the rising cost of college education–all of these have been in the news and have exerted a major impact on the lives of almost everyone around the world. Economics will enhance your understanding of all of these topics and many more. You will soon discover that economics is about much more than just financial markets and economic policy. In fact, a field trip to the fruits and vegetables section at your local grocery store could well be filled with more economics lessons than a trip to the New York Stock Exchange.

In a nutshell, economics is the study of human behavior, with a particular focus on human decision-making. It will introduce you to a new and powerful way of thinking that will both help you make better decisions and enhance your understanding of how the world works.

You may have heard some of the following statements: The soaring federal debt is mortgaging the future of our children, and it will bankrupt the country if we do not get it under control. Foreign immigrants are stealing our jobs and paralyzing our economy. A move toward socialism would improve outcomes in the United States. A higher minimum wage will help low-income workers. Making college tuition free for all will promote economic growth and lead to higher earnings. Are these statements true? This course will provide you with knowledge that will enhance your understanding of issues like these and numerous others. It may even alter the way you think about them.

Note the learning objectives at the beginning of this chapter. This is a checklist to both direct your reading and provide you with feedback regarding your mastery of the chapter. If you can respond correctly to each of these statements, this indicates that you have a good understanding of the items covered in the chapter. The convention of beginning each chapter with a set of learning objectives will be followed throughout the text.

The origins of economics date back to Adam Smith, a Scottish moral philosopher, who expressed the first economic ideas in his breakthrough book, *An Inquiry into the Nature and Causes of the Wealth of Nations*, published in 1776. As the title of his book suggests, Smith sought to explain why people in some nations were wealthier than those in others. This very question is still a central issue in economics. It is so important that throughout this book we will feature special "Keys to Economic Prosperity" in the margin to highlight sections that focus on this topic. These keys and accompanying discussions will help you understand what factors enable economies, and their citizens, to grow wealthier and prosper.

Learning Objectives

1.1 Explain the concept of scarcity and why it requires people to make choices.

1.2 Differentiate between scarcity and poverty.

1.3 Explain the eight key elements of the economic way of thinking.

1.4 Explain why the basic postulate of economics provides the foundation for the power of economics.

1.5 Differentiate between positive and normative economics.

1.6 Identify the factors that may cause people to arrive at fallacious economic conclusions.

1.7 Identify Adam Smith and his influence on modern economics.

Outstanding Economist

The Importance of Adam Smith, the Father of Economic Science

©Bettmann/CORBIS

Economics is a relatively young science. The foundation of economics was laid in 1776, when Adam Smith (1723-1790) published *An Inquiry into the Nature and Causes of the Wealth of Nations.*

Smith was a lecturer at the University of Glasgow, in his native Scotland. Before economics, morals and ethics were actually his concern. His first book was *The Theory of Moral Sentiments*. For Smith, self-interest and sympathy for others were complementary. However, he did not believe that charity alone would provide the essentials for a good life.

Smith stressed that free exchange and competitive markets would harness self-interest as a creative force. He believed that individuals *pursuing their own interests* would be directed by the "invisible hand" of market prices toward the production of those goods that were most advantageous to society. He argued that the wealth of a nation does not lie in gold and silver, but rather in the goods and services produced and consumed by people. According to Smith, competitive markets would lead to coordination, order, and efficiency without the direction of a central authority.

These were revolutionary ideas at the time, but they had consequences. Smith's ideas greatly influenced not only Europeans but also those who developed the political economy structure of the United States. Further, Smith's notion of the "invisible hand" of the market continues to enhance our understanding of why some nations prosper while others stagnate.[1]

[1]For an excellent biographical sketch of Adam Smith, refer to David Henderson, ed., *The Fortune Encyclopedia of Economics* (New York: Warner Books, 1993), 836-38. The entire text of this useful encyclopedia is now available online, free of charge, at https://oll.libertyfund.org/titles/1064.

1-1 What Is Economics About?

Economics is about scarcity and the choices we have to make because our desire for goods and services is far greater than their availability from nature. Would you like some new clothes, a nicer car, and a larger apartment? How about better grades and more time to watch television, go skiing, and travel? Do you dream of driving your brand-new Porsche into the driveway of your oceanfront house? As individuals, we have a desire for goods that is virtually unlimited. We may want all of these things. Unfortunately, both as individuals and as a society we face a constraint called **scarcity** that prevents us from being able to completely fulfill our desires.

Scarcity
A fundamental concept of economics that indicates that there is less of a good freely available than people would like.

Scarcity is present whenever there is less of a good or resource freely available than people would like. There are some things that are not scarce—seawater comes to mind; nature has provided as much of it as people want. But almost everything else you can think of—even your time—is scarce. In economics, the word *scarce* has a very specific meaning that differs slightly from the way it is commonly used. Even if large amounts of a good have been produced, it is still scarce as long as there is not as much of it *freely available* as we would all like. For example, even though goods like apples and automobiles are relatively abundant in the United States, they are still scarce because we would like to have more of them than nature has freely provided. In economics, we generally wish to determine only if a good is scarce or not, and refrain from using the term to refer to the relative availability or abundance of a good or resource.

Choice
The act of selecting among alternatives.

Resource
An input used to produce economic goods. Land, labor, skills, natural resources, and human-made tools and equipment provide examples. Throughout history, people have struggled to transform available, but limited, resources into things they would like to have–economic goods.

Because of scarcity, we have to make choices. Should I spend the next hour studying or watching TV? Should I spend my last $40 on a new shirt or a dinner out with friends? Should this factory be used to produce clothing or furniture? **Choice**, the act of selecting among alternatives, is the logical consequence of scarcity. When we make choices, we constantly face trade-offs between meeting one desire or another. To meet one need, we must let another go unmet. The basic ideas of *scarcity* and *choice*, along with the *trade-offs* we face, provide the foundation for economic analysis.

Resources are the ingredients, or inputs, that people use to produce goods and services. Our ability to produce goods and services is limited precisely because of the limited nature of our resources.

Capital
Human-made resources (such as tools, equipment, and structures) used to produce other goods and services. They enhance our ability to produce in the future.

Exhibit 1-1 lists a number of scarce goods and the limited resources that might be used to produce them. There are three general categories of resources. First, there are *human resources*—the productive knowledge, skill, and strength of human beings. Second, there are *physical resources*—things like tools, machines, and buildings that enhance our ability to produce goods. Economists often use the term **capital** when referring to these human-made resources. Third, there are *natural resources*—things like land, mineral deposits, oceans, and rivers. The ingenuity of humans is often required to make these natural resources

Exhibit 1-1 A General Listing of Scarce Goods and Limited Resources

History is a record of our struggle to transform available, but limited, resources into goods that we would like to have.

Scarce Goods	Limited Resources
Food (bread, milk, meat, eggs, vegetables, coffee, etc.)	Land (various degrees of fertility)
Clothing (shirts, pants, blouses, shoes, socks, coats, sweaters, etc.)	Natural resources (rivers, trees, minerals, oceans, etc.)
Household goods (tables, chairs, rugs, beds, dressers, televisions, etc.)	Machines and other human-made physical resources
Education	Nonhuman animal resources
National defense	Technology (physical and scientific "recipes" of history)
Leisure time	Human resources (the knowledge, skill, and talent of individual human beings)
Entertainment	
Clean air	
Pleasant environment (trees, lakes, rivers, open spaces, etc.)	
Pleasant working conditions	

useful in production. For example, until recently, the yew tree was considered a "trash tree," having no economic value. Then, scientists discovered that the tree produces taxol, a substance that could be used to fight cancer. Human knowledge and ingenuity made yew trees a valuable resource. Thus, natural resources are important, but knowing how to use them productively is just as important. This knowledge is something that is discovered as a result of the competitive market process.

As economist Thomas Sowell points out, cavemen had the same natural resources at their disposal that we do today. The huge difference between their standard of living and ours reflects the difference in the knowledge they could bring to bear on those resources versus what we can.[1] Over time, human ingenuity, discovery, improved knowledge, and better technology have enabled us to produce more goods and services from the available resources. Nonetheless, our desire for goods and services is still far greater than our ability to produce them. Thus, scarcity is a fact of life today, and in the foreseeable future. As a result, we confront trade-offs and have to make choices. This is what economics is about.

1-1a Scarcity and Poverty Are Not the Same

Think for a moment about what life was like in 1750. People all over the world struggled 50, 60, and 70 hours a week to obtain the basic necessities of life—food, clothing, and shelter. Manual labor was the major source of income. Animals provided the means of transportation. Tools and machines were primitive by today's standards. As the English philosopher Thomas Hobbes stated in the seventeenth century, life was "solitary, poor, nasty, brutish, and short."[2]

Throughout much of South America, Africa, and Asia, economic conditions today continue to make life difficult. In North America, Western Europe, Oceania, and some parts of Asia, however, economic progress has substantially reduced physical hardship and human drudgery. In these regions, the typical family is more likely to worry about financing its summer vacation than about obtaining food and shelter. As anyone who has watched the TV reality show *Survivor* knows, we take for granted many of the items that modern technological advances have allowed us to produce at unbelievably low prices. Contestants on *Survivor* struggle with even basic things like starting a fire, finding shelter, and catching fish. They are thrilled when they win ordinary items like shampoo, rice, and toilet paper. During one episode, a contestant eagerly paid over $125 for a small chocolate bar and spoonful of peanut butter at an auction—and she considered it a great bargain!

It is important to note that scarcity and poverty are not the same thing. Scarcity is an **objective** concept that describes a factual situation in which the limited nature of our resources keeps us from being able to completely fulfill our desires for goods and services. In contrast, poverty is a **subjective** concept that refers to a personal opinion of whether someone meets an arbitrarily defined level of income. This distinction is made even clearer when you realize that different people have vastly different ideas of what it means to be poor. The average family in the United States that meets the federal government's definition of being "in poverty" would be considered wealthy in most any country in Africa. A family in the United States in the 1950s would have been considered fairly wealthy if it had air conditioning, more than one automobile, an automatic dishwasher or clothes dryer, or a television. Today, the majority of U.S. families officially classified as poor have many items that used to be viewed as symbols of great wealth.

Objective
A fact based on observable phenomena that is not influenced by differences in personal opinion.

Subjective
An opinion based on personal preferences and value judgments.

People always want more and better goods for themselves and others about whom they care. Scarcity is the constraint that prevents us from having as much of *all* goods as we would like, but it is not the same as poverty. Even if every individual were rich, scarcity would still be present.

---

[1]Thomas Sowell, *Knowledge and Decisions* (New York: Basic Books, 1980), 47.

[2]Thomas Hobbes, *Leviathan* (1651), Part I, Chapter 13.

Monty Brinton/CBS Photo Archive/Getty Images

The degree to which modern technology and knowledge allow us to fulfill our desires and ease the grip of scarcity is often taken for granted—as the castaways on the CBS reality series *Survivor* quickly find out when they have to struggle to meet even basic needs, such as food, shelter, and cleaning their bodies and clothes.

1-1b Scarcity Necessitates Rationing

Rationing
Allocating a limited supply of a good or resource among people who would like to have more of it. When price performs the rationing function, the good or resource is allocated to those willing to give up the most "other things" in order to get it.

Scarcity makes **rationing** a necessity. When a good or resource is scarce, some criterion must be used to determine who will receive it and who will go without. The choice of which method is used will, however, have an influence on human behavior. When rationing is done through the government sector, a person's political status and ability to manipulate the political process are the key factors. Members of powerful interest groups and those in good favor with influential politicians will obtain more goods and resources. When this method of rationing is used, people will devote time and resources to lobbying and favor seeking with those who have political power, rather than to productive activities.

When the criterion is first-come, first-served, goods are allocated to those who are fastest at getting in line or willing to spend the longest time waiting in line or searching at many different sellers or locations. Many colleges use this method to ration tickets to sporting events, and the result is students waiting in long lines. Sometimes, as at Duke University during basketball season, they even camp out for multiple nights to get good tickets! Imagine how the behavior of students would change if tickets were instead given out to the students with the highest grade point average.

In a market economy, price is generally used to ration goods and resources only to those who are willing and able to pay the prevailing market price. Because only those goods that are scarce require rationing, in a market economy one easy way to determine whether a good or resource is scarce is to ask if it sells for a price. If you have to pay for something, it is scarce.

1-1c The Method of Rationing Influences the Nature of Competition

Competition is a natural outgrowth of scarcity and the desire of human beings to improve their conditions. Competition exists in every economy and every society. But the criteria used to ration scarce goods and resources will influence the competitive techniques employed. When the rationing criterion is price, individuals will engage in income-generating activities that enhance their ability to pay the price needed to buy the goods and services they want. Thus, one benefit of using price as a rationing mechanism is that it encourages individuals to engage in the production of goods and services to generate income. In contrast, rationing on the basis of first-come, first-served encourages individuals to waste a substantial amount of time waiting in line or searching, while rationing through the political process encourages individuals to waste time and other resources in competing with others to influence the political process.

Within a market setting, the competition that results from scarcity is an important ingredient in economic progress. Competition among business firms for customers results in newer, better, and less expensive goods and services. Competition between employers for workers results in higher wages, benefits, and better working conditions. Further, competition encourages discovery and innovation, two important sources of growth and higher living standards.

1-2 The Economic Way of Thinking

It [economics] is a method rather than a doctrine, an apparatus of the mind, a technique of thinking which helps its possessor to draw correct conclusions.

—John Maynard Keynes[3]

One does not have to spend much time around economists to recognize that there is an "economic way of thinking." Admittedly, economists, like others, differ widely in their ideological views. A news commentator once remarked that "any half-dozen economists will normally come up with about six different policy prescriptions." Yet, in spite of their philosophical differences, the approaches of economists reflect common ground.

That common ground is **economic theory**, developed from basic principles of human behavior. Economic researchers are constantly involved in testing and seeking to verify their theories. When the evidence from the testing is consistent with a theory, eventually that theory will become widely accepted among economists. Economic theory, like a road map or a guidebook, establishes reference points indicating what to look for and how economic issues are interrelated. To a large degree, the basic economic principles are merely common sense. When applied consistently, however, these commonsense concepts can provide powerful and sometimes surprising insights.

Economic theory
A set of definitions, postulates, and principles assembled in a manner that makes clear the "cause-and-effect" relationships.

1-2a Eight Guideposts to Economic Thinking

The economic way of thinking requires incorporating certain guidelines—some would say the building blocks of basic economic theory—into your own thought process. Once you incorporate these guidelines, economics can be a relatively easy subject to master. Students who have difficulty with economics have almost always failed to assimilate one or more of these principles. The following are eight principles that characterize the economic way of thinking. We will discuss each of these principles in more depth throughout the book so that you will be sure to understand how and when to apply them.

1. The use of scarce resources is costly, so decision-makers must make trade-offs. Economists sometimes refer to this as the "there is no such thing as a free lunch" principle. Because resources are scarce, the use of resources to produce one good diverts those resources from the production of other goods. A parcel of undeveloped land could be used for a new hospital or a parking lot, or it could simply be left undeveloped. No option is free of cost—there is always a trade-off. A decision to pursue any one of these options means that the decision-maker must sacrifice the others. The highest valued alternative that is sacrificed is the **opportunity cost** of the option chosen. For example, if you use one hour of your scarce time to study economics, you will have one hour less time to watch television, spend on social media, sleep, work at a job, or study other subjects.

Opportunity cost
The highest valued alternative that must be sacrificed as a result of choosing an option.

[3] John Maynard Keynes (1883–1946) was an English economist whose writings during the 1920s and 1930s exerted an enormous impact on both economic theory and policy. Keynes established the terminology and the economic framework that are still widely used when economists study problems of unemployment and inflation.

When a scarce resource is used to meet one need, other competing needs must be sacrificed. The forgone shoe store is an example of the opportunity cost of building the new drugstore.

Whichever one of these options you would have chosen had you *not* spent the hour studying economics is your highest valued option forgone. If you would have slept, then the opportunity cost of this hour spent studying economics is a forgone hour of sleep. In economics, the opportunity cost of an action is the highest valued option given up when a choice is made.

It is important to recognize that the use of scarce resources to produce a good is always costly, regardless of who pays for the good or service produced. In the United States and many other countries, various kinds of schooling are provided free of charge *to students*. However, provision of the schooling is not free *to the community as a whole*. The scarce resources used to produce the schooling—to construct the building, hire teachers, buy equipment, and so on—could have been used instead to produce more recreation, entertainment, housing, medical care, or other goods. The opportunity cost of the schooling is the highest valued option that must now be given up because the required resources were used to produce the schooling.

By now, the central point should be obvious. As we make choices, we always face trade-offs. Using resources to do one thing leaves fewer resources to do another.

Consider one final example. Mandatory air bags in automobiles save an estimated 2500 lives each year. Economic thinking, however, forces us to ask ourselves if the $50 billion spent on air bags could have been used in a better way—perhaps say, for cancer research that could have saved *more* than 2500 lives per year. Most people don't like to think of air bags and cancer research as an "either/or" proposition. It's more convenient to ignore these trade-offs. But if we want to get the most out of our resources, we have to consider all of our alternatives. In this case, the appropriate analysis is not simply the lives saved with air bags versus dollars spent on them but also the number of lives that could have been saved (or other things that could have been accomplished) if the $50 billion had been used differently. A candid consideration of hard trade-offs like this is essential to using our resources wisely.

2. Individuals choose purposefully–they try to get the most from their limited resources. People try not to squander their valuable resources deliberately. Instead, they try to choose the options that best advance their personal desires and goals at the least possible cost. This is called **economizing behavior**. Economizing behavior is the result of purposeful, or rational, decision-making. When choosing among things of equal benefit, an economizer will select the cheapest option. For example, if a pizza, a lobster dinner, and a sirloin steak are expected to yield identical benefits for Mary (including the enjoyment of eating them), economizing behavior implies that Mary will select the cheapest of the three alternatives, probably the pizza. Similarly, when choosing among alternatives of equal cost, economizing decision-makers will select the option that yields the greatest benefit. If the prices of several dinner specials are equal, for example, economizers will choose the one they like the best. Because of economizing behavior, the desires or preferences of individuals are revealed by the choices they make.

Economizing behavior
Choosing the option that offers the greatest benefit at the least possible cost.

Utility
The subjective benefit or satisfaction a person expects from a choice or course of action.

Purposeful choosing implies that decision-makers have some basis for their evaluation of alternatives. Economists refer to this evaluation as **utility**—the benefit or satisfaction that an individual expects from the choice of a specific alternative. Utility is highly subjective, often differing widely from person to person. The steak dinner that delights one person may be repulsive to another (a vegetarian, for example).

The idea that people behave rationally to get the greatest benefit at the least possible cost is a powerful tool. It can help us understand their choices. However, we need to realize that a rational choice is not the same thing as a "right" choice. If we want to understand people's choices, we need to understand their own subjective evaluations of their options *as they understand them*. As we have said, different people have different preferences. If Joan prefers $10 worth of chocolate to $10 worth of vegetables, buying the chocolate would be the rational choice for her, even though some outside observer might say that Joan is making a "bad" decision. Similarly, some motorcycle riders choose to ride without a helmet because they believe the enjoyment they get from riding without one is greater than the cost (the risk of injury). When people weigh the benefits they receive from an activity against its cost, they are making a rational choice—even though it might not be the choice you or I would make in the same situation.

Because consumers respond to incentives, store owners know they can sell off excess inventory by reducing prices.

3. Incentives matter–changes in incentives influence human choices in a predictable way. If the personal cost of an option increases, people will be less likely to choose it. Correspondingly, when an option becomes more attractive, people will be more likely to choose it. Both monetary and nonmonetary incentives matter. This vitally important guidepost, sometimes called the basic postulate of economics, is a powerful tool because it applies to almost everything that we do. Indeed, the predictive power of economics is based on this simple proposition.

When late for an appointment, a person will be less likely to take time to stop and visit with a friend. Fewer people will go picnicking on a cold and rainy day. Higher prices will reduce the number of units consumers will want to purchase. Attendance in college classes will be below normal the day before spring break. During the 2020 COVID-19 pandemic, persons over the age of 70 were far more likely than the young to practice social distancing and avoid public gatherings, because they were at substantially higher risk of contracting and dying from the virus than younger people. In each of these diverse set of cases, the explanation is the same: As the option becomes more costly, less is chosen.

Similarly, when the payoff derived from a choice increases, people will be more likely to choose it. A person will be more likely to bend over and pick up a $5 bill than a penny. Students will attend and pay more attention in class when the material is covered extensively on exams. Customers will buy more from stores that offer low prices, high-quality service, and a convenient location. Senior voters will be more likely to support candidates who favor higher Social Security benefits. All of these outcomes are highly predictable, and they merely reflect the "incentives matter" postulate of economics.

Noneconomists sometimes argue that people respond to incentives only because they are selfish and greedy. This view is false. People are motivated by a variety of goals, some humanitarian and some selfish, and incentives matter equally in both. Even an unselfish individual would be more likely to attempt to rescue a drowning child from a three-foot swimming pool than the rapid currents approaching Niagara Falls. Similarly, people are more likely to give a needy person their hand-me-downs rather than their favorite new clothes.

Just how far can we push the idea that incentives matter? If asked what would happen to the number of funerals performed in your town if the price of funerals rose, how would you respond? The "incentives matter" postulate predicts that the higher cost would reduce the number of funerals. While the same number of people will still die each year, the number of funerals performed will still fall as more people choose to be cremated or buried in cemeteries in other towns. Substitutes are everywhere—even for funerals. Individuals also respond to incentives when committing crimes—precisely the reason why people put signs in their yard saying "This house protected by XYZ Security."

Marginal
Term used to describe the effects of a change in the current situation. For example, a producer's marginal cost is the cost of producing an additional unit of a product, given the producer's current facility and production rate.

4. Individuals make decisions at the margin. When making a choice between two alternatives, individuals generally focus on the *difference* in the costs and benefits between alternatives. Economists describe this process as **marginal** decision-making, or "thinking at the margin." The last time you went to eat fast food, you probably faced a decision that highlights this type of thinking. Will you get the $6.00 cheeseburger and the $2.00 medium drink, or instead get the $9.50 value meal that has the cheeseburger and drink and also comes with a medium order of fries? Naturally, individual decision-making focuses on the difference between the alternatives. The value meal costs $1.50 more (its marginal cost) but will give you one extra food item—the fries (its marginal benefit). Your marginal decision is whether it is worth the extra $1.50 to have the fries. If you pay attention, you'll notice yourself frequently thinking at the margin. Next time you find yourself asking a salesclerk, "How much *more* is this one?" when you are choosing between two items, you are doing a marginal analysis.

Marginal choices always involve the effects of net additions to or subtractions from current conditions. In fact, the word *additional* is often used as a substitute for *marginal*. For example, a business decision-maker might ask, "What is the additional (or marginal) cost of producing one more unit?" Marginal decisions may involve large or small changes. The "one more unit" could be a new factory or a new stapler. It is marginal because it involves additional costs and additional benefits. Given the current situation, what marginal benefits (additional sales revenues, for example) can be expected from the new factory, and what will be the marginal cost of constructing it? What is the marginal benefit versus marginal cost of purchasing a new stapler? The answers to these questions will determine whether building the new factory or buying the new stapler is a good decision.

It is important to distinguish between *average* and *marginal*. A manufacturer's average cost of producing automobiles (which would be the total cost of production divided by the total number of cars the manufacturer produces) may be $30,000, but the marginal cost of producing an additional automobile (or an additional 1,000 automobiles) might be much lower, say, $20,000 per car. Costs associated with research, testing, design, molds, heavy equipment, and similar factors of production must be incurred whether the manufacturer is going to produce 1,000 units, 10,000 units, or 100,000 units. Such costs will clearly contribute to the average cost of an automobile, but they will change very little as additional units are produced. Thus, the marginal cost of additional units may be substantially less than the average cost. Should production be expanded or reduced? That choice should be based on marginal costs, which indicate the *change* in total cost due to the decision.

People commonly ignore the implications of marginal thinking in their comments, but seldom in their actions. Thus, the concept is far better at explaining how people act than what they say. Students are often overheard telling other students that they shouldn't skip class because they have paid to enroll in it. Of course, the tuition is not a factor relevant at the margin—it will be the same whether or not the student attends class on that particular day. The only real marginal considerations are what the student will miss that day (a quiz, information for the exam, etc.) versus what they could do with the extra time by skipping class. This explains why even students who tell others not to skip class because they paid too much for it will ignore the tuition costs when they themselves decide to skip class.

Decisions are made at the margin. That means that they almost always involve additions to, or subtractions from, current conditions. If we are going to get the most out of our resources, activities that generate more benefits than costs should be undertaken, while those that are more costly than they are worth should not be undertaken. This principle of sound decision-making applies to individuals, businesses, governments, and society as a whole.

5. Although information can help us make better choices, its acquisition is costly. Information that helps us make better choices is valuable. However, the time needed to gather it is scarce, making information costly to acquire. As a result, people economize on their search for information just like they do anything else. For example, when you purchase a pair of jeans, you might evaluate the quality and prices of jeans at several different stores. At some point, though, you will decide that additional comparison-shopping is simply not worth the trouble. You will make a choice based on the limited information you already have.

The process is similar when individuals search for a restaurant, a new car, or a roommate. They will seek to acquire some information, but at some point, they will decide that the expected benefit derived from gathering still more information is simply not worth the cost. When differences among the alternatives are important to decision-makers, they will spend more time and effort gathering information. People are much more likely to read the reviews of other consumers before purchasing a new automobile than they are before purchasing a new can opener. Because information is costly for people to acquire, limited knowledge and uncertainty about the outcome generally characterize the decision-making process.

6. Beware of the secondary effects: Economic actions often generate indirect as well as direct effects. In addition to direct effects that are quickly visible, people's decisions often generate indirect, or "secondary," effects that may be observable only with time. Failure to consider **secondary effects** is one of the most common economic errors because these effects are often quite different from initial, or direct, effects. Frédéric Bastiat, a nineteenth-century French economist, stated that the difference between a good and a bad economist is that the bad economist considers only the immediate, visible effects, whereas the good economist is also aware of the secondary effects. The true cause of these secondary effects might not be seen, even later, except by those using the logic of good economics.

Secondary effects
The indirect impact of an event or policy that may not be easily and immediately observable. In the area of policy, these effects are often both unintended and overlooked.

Perhaps a few simple examples that involve both immediate (direct) and secondary (indirect) effects will help illustrate the point. The immediate effect of an aspirin is a bitter taste in one's mouth. The secondary effect, which is not immediately observable, is relief from a headache. The short-term direct effect of drinking twelve cans of beer might be a warm, jolly feeling. In contrast, the secondary effect is likely to be a sluggish feeling the next morning, and perhaps a pounding headache.

Sometimes, as in the case of the aspirin, the secondary effect—headache relief—is actually an intended consequence of the action. In other cases, however, the secondary effects are unintended. Changes in government policy often alter incentives, indirectly affecting how much people work, earn, invest, consume, and conserve for the future. When a change alters incentives, *unintended consequences* that are quite different from the intended consequences may occur.

Sometimes actions change the incentives people face and they respond accordingly, creating secondary effects that were not intended.

Bil Keane, Inc. King Features Syndicate

Let's consider a couple of examples that illustrate the potential importance of unintended consequences in government policy. In an effort to help the environment, many jurisdictions, including San Francisco County, have banned plastic grocery bags. However, reusable grocery bags tend to gather harmful bacteria, such as E. coli, with repeated use. A study published by the University of Pennsylvania found that emergency room visits and deaths related to these bacteria have risen by 25 percent in areas banning plastic bags. Once you consider the harmful secondary effects on human health, these regulations are significantly less beneficial than they might first appear.

Trade restrictions between nations have important secondary effects as well. The proponents of tariffs and quotas on foreign goods almost always ignore the secondary effects of their policies. Import quotas restricting the sale of foreign-produced sugar in the U.S. market, for example, have resulted in domestic sugar prices that have often been two or three times the price in the rest of the world. The proponents of this policy—primarily sugar producers—argue that the quotas "save jobs" and increase employment. No doubt, the employment of sugar growers in the United States is higher than it otherwise would be. But what about the secondary effects? The higher sugar prices mean it's more expensive for U.S. firms to produce candy and other products that use a lot of sugar. As a result, many candy producers, including the makers of Life Savers, Jaw Breakers, Red Hots, and most candy canes, have moved to countries like Canada and Mexico, where sugar can be purchased at its true market price. Thus, employment among sugar-using firms in the United States is reduced. Further, because foreigners sell less sugar in the United States, they have less purchasing power with which to buy products we export to them. This, too, reduces U.S. employment.

Once the secondary effects of trade restrictions like tariffs on imported goods are taken into consideration, we have no reason to expect that U.S. employment will increase as a result. There may be more jobs in favored industries, but there will be less employment in others. Trade restrictions reshuffle employment rather than increase it. But those who unwittingly fail to consider the secondary effects will miss this point. Clearly, consideration of the secondary effects is an important ingredient of the economic way of thinking.

7. The value of a good or service is subjective. Preferences differ, sometimes dramatically, between individuals. How much is a ticket to see a performance of the Nutcracker Ballet worth? Some people would be willing to pay a very high price, while others might prefer to stay home, even if tickets were free! Circumstances can change from day to day, even for a given individual. Makayla, a ballet fan who usually would value the ticket at more than its price of $100, is invited to a party and suddenly becomes uninterested in attending the ballet. Now what is the ticket worth? If she knows a friend who would give her $40 for the ticket, it is worth at least that much. If she advertises the ticket on StubHub and gets $60 for it, a higher value is created. But if someone who doesn't know of the ticket would have been willing to pay even more, then a potential trade creating even more value is missed. If that particular performance is sold out, perhaps someone in town would be willing to pay $120. One thing is certain: The value of the ticket depends on several things, including who uses it and under what circumstances.

Economics recognizes that people can and do value goods differently. Amir may prefer to have a grass field rather than a parking lot next to his workplace and be willing to bear the cost of walking farther from his car each day. Camila, on the other hand, may prefer the parking lot and the shorter walk. As a science, economics does not place any inherent moral judgment or value on one person's preferences over another's—in economics, all individuals' preferences are counted equally. Because the subjective preferences of individuals differ, it is difficult for one person to know how much another will value an item.

Think about how hard it is to know what would make a good gift for even a close friend or family member. Thus, arranging trades, or otherwise moving items to higher valued users and uses, is not a simple task. The entrepreneurial individual, who knows how to locate the right buyers and arranges for goods to flow to their highest valued use, can sometimes create huge increases in value from existing resources. In fact, moving goods toward those who value them most and combining resources into goods that individuals value more highly are primary sources of economic progress.

8. The test of a theory is its ability to predict. Economic thinking is **scientific thinking**. The proof of the pudding is in the eating. How useful an economic theory is depends on how well it predicts the future consequences of economic action. Economists develop economic theories using scientific thinking based on basic principles. The idea is to predict how incentives will affect decision-makers and compare the predictions against real-world events. If the events in the real world are consistent with a theory, we say that the theory has *predictive value* and is therefore valid.

Scientific thinking
Developing a theory from basic principles and testing it against events in the real world. Good theories are consistent with and help explain real-world events. Theories that are inconsistent with the real world are invalid and must be rejected.

If it is impossible to test the theoretical relationships of a discipline, the discipline does not qualify as a science. Because economics deals with human beings who can think and respond in a variety of ways, can economic theories really be tested? The answer to this question is yes, if, on average, human beings respond in predictable and consistent ways to changes in economic conditions. The economist believes that this is the case, even though not all individuals will respond in the specified manner. Economists usually do not try to predict the behavior of a specific individual; instead, they focus on the general behavior of a large number of individuals.

In the 1950s, economists began to do laboratory experiments to test economic theories. Individuals were brought into laboratories to see how they would act in buying and selling situations, under differing rules. For example, cash rewards were given to individuals who, when an auction was conducted, were able to sell at high prices and buy at low prices, thus approximating real-world market incentives. These experiments have verified many of the important propositions of economic theory.

Laboratory experiments, however, cannot duplicate all real economic interactions. How can we test economic theory when controlled experiments are not feasible? This is a problem, but economics is no different from astronomy in this respect. Astronomers can use theories tested in physics laboratories, but they must also deal with the world as it is. They cannot change the course of the stars or planets to see what impact the change would have on the gravitational pull of Earth. Similarly, economists cannot arbitrarily change the prices of cars or unskilled-labor services in real markets just to observe the effects on quantities purchased or levels of employment. However, economic conditions (for example, prices, production costs, technology, and transportation costs), like the location of the planets, do change from time to time. As actual conditions change, an economic theory can be tested by comparing its predictions with real-world outcomes. Just as the universe is the main laboratory of the astronomer, the real-world economy is the primary laboratory of the economist.

1-3 Positive and Normative Economics

As a social science, economics is concerned with predicting or determining the impact of changes in economic variables on the actions of human beings. Scientific economics, commonly referred to as **positive economics**, attempts to determine "what is." Positive economic statements involve potentially verifiable or refutable propositions. For example, "If the price of gasoline rises, people will buy less gasoline." We can statistically investigate (and estimate) the relationship between gasoline prices and gallons sold. We can analyze the facts to determine the correctness of a positive economic statement. Remember, a positive economic statement need not be correct; it simply must be testable.

Positive economics
The scientific study of "what is" among economic relationships.

In contrast, **normative economics** is about "what ought to be," given the preferences and philosophical views of the advocate. Value judgments often result in disagreement about normative economic matters. Two people may differ on a policy matter because one is from one political party and the other is from another, or because one wants cheaper food while the other favors organic farming (which is more expensive), and so on. They may even agree about the expected outcome of altering an economic variable (that is, the positive economics of an issue), but disagree as to whether that outcome is desirable.

Normative economics
Judgments about "what ought to be" in economic matters. Normative economic views cannot be proved false because they are based on value judgments.

Unlike positive economic statements, normative economic statements can neither be confirmed nor proven false by scientific testing. "Business firms should not be concerned with profits." "We should have fewer parking lots and more green space on campus." "The price of gasoline is too high." These normative statements cannot be scientifically tested because their validity rests on value judgments.

Normative economic views can sometimes influence our attitude toward positive economic analysis, however. When we agree with the objectives of a policy, it's easy to overlook the warnings of positive economics. Although positive economics does not tell us which policy is best, it can provide evidence about the likely effects of a policy. Sometimes, proponents unknowingly support policies that are actually in conflict with their own goals and objectives. Positive economics, based on sound economic logic, can help overcome this potential problem.

Economics can expand our knowledge of how the real world operates, in both the private and the public (government) sectors. However, it is not always easy to isolate the impact of economic changes. Let's now consider some pitfalls to avoid in economic thinking.

1-4 Pitfalls to Avoid in Economic Thinking

1-4a Violation of the *Ceteris Paribus* Condition Can Lead One to Draw the Wrong Conclusion

Ceteris paribus
A Latin term meaning "other things constant" that is used when the effect of one change is being described, recognizing that if other things changed, they also could affect the result. Economists often describe the effects of one change, knowing that in the real world, other things might change and also exert an effect.

Economists often qualify their statements with the words ***ceteris paribus***. *Ceteris paribus* is a Latin term meaning "other things constant." An example of a *ceteris paribus* statement would be the following: "*Ceteris paribus*, an increase in the price of housing will cause buyers to reduce their purchases of housing." However, we live in a dynamic world, so things seldom remain constant. For example, as the price of housing rises, the income of consumers might also increase for unrelated reasons. Each of these factors—higher housing prices and increasing consumer income—will have an impact on housing purchases. In fact, we would generally expect them to have opposite effects: Higher prices are likely to reduce housing purchases, whereas higher consumer incomes are likely to increase them. We point out this pitfall because sometimes statistical data (or casual observations) appear inconsistent with economic theories. In most of these cases, the apparent contradictions reflect the effects of changes in other factors (violations of the *ceteris paribus* conditions). The observed effects are the result of the combination of the changes.

The task of sorting out the effects of two or more variables that change at the same time is difficult. However, with a strong grip on economic theory, some ingenuity, and enough data, it can usually be done. This is, in fact, precisely the day-to-day work of many professional economists.

1-4b Good Intentions Do Not Guarantee Desirable Outcomes

There is a tendency to believe that if the proponents of a policy have good intentions, their proposals must be sound. This is not necessarily the case. Proponents may be unaware of some of the adverse secondary effects of their proposals, particularly when they are indirect and observable only over time. Even if their policies would be largely ineffective, politicians may still find it advantageous to call attention to the severity of a problem and propose a program to deal with it. In other cases, proponents of a policy may actually be seeking a goal other than the one they espouse. They may tie their arguments to objectives that are widely supported by the general populace. Thus, the fact that an advocate says a program will help the economy, expand employment, reduce the poverty rate, increase wages, improve health care, or achieve some other highly desirable objective does not necessarily make it so.

Let's begin with a couple of straightforward examples. Federal legislation has been introduced that would require all children, including those under age two, to be fastened in a child safety seat when traveling by air. Proponents argue the legislation will increase the survival rate of children in the case of an airline crash and thereby save lives. Certainly, saving lives is a highly desirable objective, but will this really be the case? *Some* lives will probably be saved by the airline child safety seats. But what about the secondary effects? The legislation would mean that a parent traveling with a small child would have to purchase an additional ticket, which will make it more expensive to fly. As a result, many families will choose to travel by auto rather than by air. Because the likelihood of a serious accident per mile traveled in an automobile is several times higher than for air travel, more automobile travel will result in more injuries and fatalities. In fact, studies indicate that the increase in injuries and fatalities from additional auto travel will exceed the number of lives saved by airline safety seats.[4] Thus, even though the intentions of the proponents may well be lofty, there is reason to believe that the net impact of their proposal will be more fatalities and injuries than would be the case in the absence of the legislation.

The stated objective of the Endangered Species Act is to protect various species that are on the verge of extinction. Certainly, this is an admirable objective, but there is nonetheless reason to question the effectiveness of the act itself. The Endangered Species Act allows the government to regulate the use of individual private property if an endangered species is found present on or near an individual's land. To avoid losing control of their property, many landowners have taken steps to make their land less attractive as a natural habitat for these endangered species. For example, the endangered red-cockaded woodpecker nests primarily in old trees within southern pine ecosystems. Landowners have responded by cutting down trees the woodpeckers like to nest in to avoid having one nest on their land, which would result in the owner losing control of this part of their property. The end result is that the habitat for these birds has actually been disappearing more rapidly.

As these examples demonstrate, good intentions are not enough. An unsound proposal will lead to undesirable outcomes, even if it is supported by proponents with good intentions. Sound economic reasoning can help us better anticipate the secondary effects of policy changes and avoid the pitfall of thinking that good intentions are enough.

1-4c Association Is Not Causation

In economics, identifying cause-and-effect relationships is very important. But statistical association alone cannot establish this causation. Perhaps an extreme example will illustrate the point. Suppose that each November, a witch doctor performs a voodoo dance designed to summon the gods of winter, and that soon after the dance is performed, the weather in fact begins to turn cold. The witch doctor's dance is associated with the arrival of winter, meaning that the two events appear to have happened in conjunction with one another. But is this really evidence that the witch doctor's dance actually caused the arrival of winter? Most of us would answer no, even though the two events seemed to happen in conjunction with one another.

Those who argue that a causal relationship exists simply because of the presence of statistical association are committing a logical fallacy known as the *post hoc propter ergo hoc* fallacy. Sound economics warns against this potential source of error.

1-4d The Fallacy of Composition: What's True for One Might Not Be True for All

What is true for the individual (or subcomponent) may not be true for the group (or the whole). If you stand up for an exciting play during a football game, you will be better able to see. But what happens if everyone stands up at the same time? Will everyone be better able to see? The answer is, of course, no. Thus, what is true for a single individual does not necessarily apply to the group as a whole. When everyone stands up, the view for individual spectators fails to improve; in fact, it may even become worse.

People who mistakenly argue that what is true for the part is also true for the whole are said to be committing the **fallacy of composition**. What is true for the individual can be misleading and is often fallacious when applied to the entire economy. The fallacy of

Fallacy of composition
Erroneous view that what is true for the individual (or the part) will also be true for the group (or the whole).

[4]For a detailed analysis of this subject, refer to Thomas B. Newman, Brian D. Johnston, and David C. Grossman, "Effects and Costs of Requiring Child-Restraint Systems for Young Children Traveling on Commercial Airplanes," *Archives of Pediatrics and Adolescent Medicine* 157 (October 2003): 969–74.

Microeconomics
The branch of economics that focuses on how human behavior affects the conduct of affairs within narrowly defined units, such as individual households or business firms.

Macroeconomics
The branch of economics that focuses on how human behavior affects outcomes in highly aggregated markets, such as the markets for labor or consumer products.

composition highlights the importance of considering both a micro view and a macro view in the study of economics. **Microeconomics** focuses on the decision-making of consumers, producers, and resource suppliers operating in a narrowly defined market, such as that for a specific good or resource. Because individual decision-makers are the moving force behind all economic action, the foundations of economics are clearly rooted in a micro view.

As we have seen, however, what is true for a small unit may not be true in the aggregate. **Macroeconomics** focuses on how the aggregation of individual micro-units affects our analysis. Like microeconomics, it is concerned with incentives, prices, and output. Macroeconomics, however, aggregates markets, lumping together all 131 million households in this country. Macroeconomics involves topics like total consumption spending, saving, and employment, in the economy as a whole. Similarly, the nation's 33 million business firms are lumped together in "the business sector." What factors determine the level of aggregate output, the rate of inflation, the amount of unemployment, and interest rates? These are macroeconomic questions. In short, macroeconomics examines the forest rather than the individual trees. As we move from the microcomponents to a macro view of the whole, it is important that we beware of the fallacy of composition.

Key Points

- Scarcity and choice are the two essential ingredients of economic analysis. A good is scarce when the human desire for it exceeds the amount freely available. As a result of scarcity, both individuals and societies must choose among the available alternatives. Every choice entails a trade-off.
- Every society will have to devise some method of rationing scarce resources among competing uses. Markets generally use price as the rationing device. Competition is a natural outgrowth of the need to ration scarce goods.
- Scarcity and poverty are not the same thing. Absence of poverty implies that some basic level of need has been met. An absence of scarcity implies that our desires for goods are fully satisfied. We may someday eliminate poverty, but scarcity will always be with us.
- Economics is a way of thinking that emphasizes eight points:
  1. The use of scarce resources to produce a good always has an opportunity cost.
  2. Individuals make decisions purposefully, always seeking to choose the option they expect to be most consistent with their personal goals.
  3. Incentives matter. The likelihood of people choosing an option increases as personal benefits rise and personal costs decline.
  4. Economic reasoning focuses on the impact of marginal changes because it is the marginal benefits and marginal costs that influence choices.
  5. Information helps individuals make better decisions, but it is costly to acquire; therefore, choices are generally made based on limited information.
  6. In addition to their direct impact, economic changes often generate secondary effects.
  7. The value of a good or service is subjective and varies with individual preferences and circumstances.
  8. The test of an economic theory is its ability to predict and explain events in the real world.
- Economic science is positive; it attempts to explain the actual consequences of economic actions or "what is." Normative economics goes further, applying value judgments to make suggestions about what "ought to be."
- Microeconomics focuses on narrowly defined units, while macroeconomics is concerned with highly aggregated units. When shifting focus from micro to macro, one must beware of the fallacy of composition: What's good for the individual may not be good for the group as a whole.
- The origin of economics as a science dates to the publication of *An Inquiry into the Nature and Causes of the Wealth of Nations* by Adam Smith in 1776. Smith believed a market economy would generally bring individual self-interest and the public interest into harmony.

Critical Analysis Questions

1. Indicate how each of the following changes would influence the incentive of a decision-maker to undertake the action described.

a. A reduction in the temperature from 80° to 50° on one's decision to go swimming

b. A change in the meeting time of the introductory economics course from 11:00 A.M. to 7:30 A.M. on one's decision to attend the lectures

c. A reduction in the number of exam questions that relate directly to the text on the student's decision to read the text

d. An increase in the price of beef on one's decision to buy steak

e. An increase in the rental rates of apartments on one's decision to build additional rental housing units

2. "The government should provide such goods as health care, education, and highways because it can provide them for free." Is this statement true or false? Explain your answer.

3. **a.** What method is used to ration goods in a market economy? How does this rationing method influence the incentive of individuals to supply goods, services, and resources to others?

b. How are grades rationed in your economics class? How does this rationing method influence student behavior? Suppose the highest grades were rationed to those whom the teacher liked best. How would this method of rationing influence student behavior?

4. *In recent years, the child tax credit has been increased in the United States. According to the basic principles of economics, how will the birthrate be affected by policies that reduce the taxes imposed on those with children?

5. *"The economic way of thinking stresses that good intentions lead to sound policy." Is this statement true or false? Explain your answer.

6. Self-interest is a powerful motivator. Does this necessarily imply that people are selfish and greedy? Do self-interest and selfishness mean the same thing?

7. A restaurant offers an "all you can eat" lunch buffet for $15. Lamont has already eaten three servings, and is trying to decide whether to go back for a fourth. Describe how Lamont can use marginal analysis to make his decision.

8. *"Individuals who economize are missing the point of life. Money is not so important that it should rule the way we live." Evaluate this statement.

9. *"Positive economics cannot tell us which agricultural policy is better, so it is useless to policy makers." Evaluate this statement.

10. *"I examined the statistics for our basketball team's wins last year and found that, when the third team played more, the winning margin increased. If the coach played the third team more, we would win by a bigger margin." Evaluate this statement.

11. Which of the following are positive economic statements, and which are normative?

a. The speed limit should be lowered to 55 miles per hour on interstate highways.

b. Higher gasoline prices cause the quantity of gasoline that consumers buy to decrease.

c. A comparison of costs and benefits should not be used to assess environmental regulations.

d. Higher taxes on alcohol result in less drinking and driving.

12. Why can't we consume as much of each good or service as we would like? If we become richer in the future, do you think we will eventually be able to consume as much of everything as we would like? Why or why not?

13. Suppose that in an effort to help low-skill workers the government raises the legal minimum wage to $25 per hour. Can you think of any unintended secondary effects that will result from this action? Will all low-skill workers be helped by the minimum wage law?

14. Should the United States attempt to reduce air and water pollution to zero? Why or why not?

*Asterisk denotes questions for which answers are given in Appendix B.

Chapter 2

Some Tools of the Economist

> The key insight of Adam Smith's *Wealth of Nations* is misleadingly simple: if an exchange between two parties is voluntary, it will not take place unless both believe they will benefit from it. Most economic fallacies derive from the neglect of this simple insight, from the tendency to assume that there is a fixed pie, that one party can gain only at the expense of another.
>
> –Milton and Rose Friedman[1]

In the preceding chapter, you were introduced to the economic way of thinking. We will now begin to apply that approach. This chapter focuses on five topics: opportunity cost, trade, property rights, the potential output level of an economy, and the creation of wealth. These seemingly diverse topics are in fact highly interrelated. For example, the opportunity cost of goods determines which ones an individual or a nation should produce and which should be acquired through trade. In turn, the ways in which trade and property rights are structured influence the amount of output and wealth an economy can create. These tools of economics are important for answering the basic economic questions: what to produce, how to produce it, and for whom it will be produced.

Learning Objectives

- 2.1 Explain the concept of opportunity cost and its importance to the choices made by individuals.
- 2.2 Explain why people engage in trade and how it affects their well-being.
- 2.3 Explain how transaction costs affect exchange and the role of middlemen.
- 2.4 Explain how the incentives created by private ownership impact the use of resources.
- 2.5 Explain how a production possibilities curve illustrates the trade-offs associated with the use of scarce resources.
- 2.6 Indicate how, over time, output can be expanded and higher incomes achieved.
- 2.7 Identify the major sources of gains from trade that provide the foundation for our modern living standards.
- 2.8 Compare and contrast the two major methods of economic organization.

[1]Milton Friedman and Rose Friedman, *Free to Choose* (Harcourt Brace, 1990), 13.

2-1 What Shall We Give Up?

Because of scarcity, we can't have everything we want. As a result, we constantly face choices that involve trade-offs between our competing desires. Most of us would like to have more time for leisure, recreation, vacations, hobbies, education, and skill development. We would also like to have more wealth, a larger savings account, and more consumable goods. However, all these things are scarce, in the sense that they are limited. Our efforts to get more of one will conflict with our efforts to get more of others.

2-1a Opportunity Cost

The choice to do one thing is, at the same time, a choice *not* to do something else. Your choice to spend time reading this book is a choice not to spend the time watching Netflix, posting on social media, or hanging out with friends. These things must be given up because you decided to read this book instead. As we indicated in Chapter 1, the highest valued alternative sacrificed in order to choose an option is called the *opportunity cost* of that choice.

Opportunity costs are subjective; they depend on the value the decision-maker places on alternative options. Because of this, opportunity costs can never be directly measured by someone other than the decision-maker. Only the person choosing can know the value of what is given up.[2] This makes it difficult for someone other than the decision-maker—including experts and elected officials—to make choices on that person's behalf. Moreover, not only do people differ in the trade-offs they prefer to make, but their preferences also change with time and circumstances. Thus, the decision-maker is the only person who can properly evaluate the options and decide which is the best, given his or her preferences and current circumstances.

Monetary costs reflect opportunities foregone, and they can be measured objectively in terms of dollars and cents. If you spend $40 on a student ticket to a college football game, you must now forgo the other items you could have purchased with the $40—a new pair of jeans, for example. However, it is important to recognize that monetary costs do not represent the total opportunity cost of an option. The total cost of attending the football game, for example, is the highest valued opportunity lost as a result of both the time you spend at the game and the amount of money you pay for your ticket. In cases like buying and downloading a game from an app store, for which there is minimal outlay of time, effort, and other resources to make the purchase, the monetary cost will approximate the total cost. Contrast this with a decision to sit on your sofa and play your new game on your cell phone, which involves little or no monetary cost, but has a clear opportunity cost of your time. In this second case, the monetary cost is a poor measure of the total cost.

LeBron James understands opportunity cost. As a high school player, James was already one of the best basketball players in the nation. He had received numerous scholarship offers. However, after high school graduation, LeBron decided to go directly into the NBA because the opportunity cost of college was simply too high. He was selected as the first pick in the 2003 NBA draft, signing a three-year contract worth almost $13 million, with an option for a fourth year at $5.8 million. Would you have skipped college if your opportunity cost was $19 million?

Cal Sport Media/Alamy Stock Photo

2-1b Opportunity Cost and the Real World

Is real-world decision-making influenced by opportunity costs? Consider your own decision to attend college. Your opportunity cost of going to college is the value of the next best alternative, which could be measured as the salary you would earn if you had chosen to go directly into full-time work instead. Every year you stay in college, you give up what you could have earned by working that year. Typically, students incur opportunity costs of $120,000 or more in forgone income during their stay in college.

But what if the opportunity cost of attending college changes? How will it affect your decision? Suppose, for example, that you received a job offer today

[2]Refer to James M. Buchanan, *Cost and Choice* (Chicago: Markham, 1969), for a classic work on the relationship between cost and choice.

Outstanding Economist

Thomas Sowell (1930-)

CHUCK KENNEDY/KRT/Newscom

Thomas Sowell, a long-time senior fellow at the Hoover Institution at Stanford University, recognizes the critical importance of the institutions–the "rules of the game"–that shape human interactions. His book *Knowledge and Decisions* stresses the role of knowledge in the economy and how different institutional arrangements compare at using scarce information. Sowell is the author of many books and journal articles and for 25 years wrote a nationally syndicated column that appeared in more than 150 newspapers. His writings address subjects ranging from race preferences and cultural differences to the origins and ideology of political conflict.

for $500,000 per year as an athlete or an entertainer, but the job would require so much travel that school would be impossible. Would this change in the opportunity cost of going to college affect your choice as to whether to continue in school? It likely would. Going to college would mean you would have to say good-bye to the huge salary you've been offered. (Refer to the accompanying illustration on LeBron James for a good example.) You can clearly tell from this example that the monetary cost of college (tuition, books, and so forth) isn't the only factor influencing your decision. Your opportunity cost plays a part, too.

Consider another decision made by college students—whether to attend a particular class lecture. The monetary cost of attending class (bus fare, parking, gasoline costs, and so on) remains fairly constant from day to day. Why then do students choose to attend class on some days and not on others? Even though the monetary cost of attending class is fairly constant, a student's opportunity cost can change dramatically from day to day. Some days, the next best alternative to attending class may be sleeping in or streaming a movie. Other days, the opportunity cost may be substantially larger, perhaps the value of attending a big football game, getting an early start on spring break, or having additional study time for a crucial exam in another class. As options like these increase the cost of attending class, more students will decide not to attend.

Failure to consider opportunity cost often leads to unwise decision-making. Suppose that your community builds a beautiful new civic center. The mayor, speaking at the dedication ceremony, tells the world that the center will improve the quality of life in your community. People who understand the concept of opportunity cost may question this view. If the center had not been built, the resources might have funded construction of a new hospital, improvements to the educational system, or housing for low-income families. Will the civic center contribute more to the well-being of people in your community than would these other facilities? If so, it was a wise investment. If not, your community will be worse off than it would have been if decision-makers had chosen a higher valued project.

2-2 Trade Creates Value

Why do individuals trade with each other, and what is the significance of this exchange? We have learned that value is subjective. It is wrong to assume that a particular good or service has a fixed objective value just because it exists.[3] The value of goods and services

[3]An illuminating discussion of this subject, termed the "physical fallacy," is found in Thomas Sowell, *Knowledge and Decisions* (New York: Basic Books, 1980), 67–72.

generally depends on who uses them, and on circumstances, such as when and where they are used, as well as on the physical characteristics. Some people love onions, whereas others dislike them. Thus, when we speak of the "value of an onion," this makes sense only within the context of its value to a specific person. Similarly, to most people an umbrella is more valuable on a rainy day than on a sunny one.

Consider the case of Janet, who loves tomatoes but hates onions, and Brad, who loves onions but hates tomatoes. They go out to dinner together, and the waiter brings their salads. Brad turns to Janet and says, "I'll trade you the tomatoes on my salad for the onions on yours." Janet gladly agrees to the exchange. This simple example will help us illustrate two important aspects of voluntary exchange.

1. When individuals engage in a voluntary exchange, both parties are made better off. In the previous example, Janet has the option of accepting or declining Brad's offer of a trade. If she accepts his offer, she does so *voluntarily*. Janet would agree to this exchange only if she expects to be better off as a result. Because she likes tomatoes better than onions, Janet's enjoyment of her salad will be greater with this trade than without it. On the other side, Brad has voluntarily made this offer of an exchange to Janet because Brad believes he will also be better off as a result of the exchange.

People tend to think of making, building, and creating things as productive activities. Agriculture, software development, and manufacturing are like this. On the one hand, they create something genuinely new, something that was not there before. On the other hand, trade—the mere exchange of one thing for another—does not create new material items. It is tempting to think that if nothing new is created, the action cannot generate gain. But this is a fallacy, and the motivation for trade illustrates why. An exchange will not occur unless both parties agree to it, and they will not do so unless the exchange makes them better off. As the chapter-opening quotation of Milton and Rose Friedman illustrates, many errors in economic reasoning happen when we forget that voluntary trades, like the one between Janet and Brad, make both parties better off.

2. By channeling goods and resources to those who value them most, trade creates value and increases the wealth created by a society's resources. Because preferences differ among individuals, the value of an item can vary greatly from one person to another. Therefore, trade can create value by moving goods from those who value them less to those who value them more. The simple exchange between Janet and Brad also illustrates this point. Imagine for a moment that Brad and Janet had never met and instead were both eating their salads alone. Without the ability to engage in this exchange, both would have eaten their salads but would not have had as much enjoyment from them. When goods are moved to individuals who value them more, the total value created by a society's limited resources is increased. The same two salads create more value when the trade occurs than when it doesn't.

It is easy to think of material things as wealth, but material things are not wealth until they are in the hands of someone who values them. A highly technical medical reference book that is of no value to an art collector may be worth several hundred dollars to a doctor. Similarly, a painting that is unappreciated by a doctor may be of great value to an art collector. Therefore, a voluntary exchange that moves the medical reference book to the doctor and the painting to the art collector will increase the value of both goods. By channeling goods and resources toward those who value them most, trade creates wealth for both the trading partners and for the nation.

2-2a Transaction Costs–A Barrier to Trade

Have you ever been sitting at home late at night, hungry, wishing you could have some food from your favorite restaurant, but felt it wasn't worth the time and effort to get dressed and make the drive? Have you ever wanted an item that was advertised as part of a Black Friday

Bloomberg/Bloomberg/Getty Images

Are items less costly during Black Friday sales once you factor in the transaction costs of dealing with the lines and crowds? To some people, it isn't, and they find it cheaper to simply pay full price on a different day.

sale but didn't feel like dealing with the lines and crowds just to get the lower price? The costs of the time, effort, and other resources necessary to search out, negotiate, and conclude an exchange are called **transaction costs**. High transaction costs can be a barrier to potentially productive exchange.

Transaction costs
The time, effort, and other resources needed to search out, negotiate, and complete an exchange.

Transaction costs are sometimes high because of physical obstacles, such as oceans, rivers, and mountains, that make it difficult to get products to customers. Investment in roads and improvements in transportation and communications can reduce these transaction costs. In other instances, transaction costs may be high because of the lack of information. For example, you may want a new coat in a particular style, color, and size but don't know which store has it at an attractive price. The time and energy you spend gathering this information are part of your transaction costs. In still other cases, transaction costs are high because of political obstacles, such as taxes, licensing requirements, government regulations, price controls, tariffs, or quotas. Regardless of whether the roadblocks are physical, informational, or political, high transaction costs reduce the potential gains from trade.

Because of transaction costs, we should not expect all potentially valuable trades to take place, any more than we expect all useful knowledge to be learned, all safety measures to be taken, or all potential "A" grades to be earned. The cost of information, transportation, and other elements of transaction costs will sometimes be so great that potential gains from trade will go unrealized.

Reductions in transaction costs will increase the gains from trade. In recent years, technology has reduced the transactions costs of numerous exchanges. With just a few swipes on a touch screen, buyers can now acquire information about potential sellers and virtually any product. Phone apps are routinely used to shop, book travel, obtain event tickets, order food, or even get a ride home. These reductions in transaction costs have increased the volume of trade and have enhanced living standards.

Moreover, reductions in transaction costs can be profitable, and they can even make it possible for us to achieve more value from our existing assets. Examples abound. Uber and Lyft have grown rapidly by reducing the transaction costs of arranging for ground transportation. Airbnb has become a sizable business by reducing the transaction costs between apartment and housing owners and those seeking short-term living quarters. In turn, these reductions in transaction costs have increased the value generated by our cars, houses, and apartments.

2-2b The Middleman as a Cost Reducer

Middlemen
People who buy and sell goods or services or arrange trades. A middleman reduces transaction costs.

Because it is costly for buyers and sellers to find each other and to negotiate the exchange, an entrepreneurial opportunity exists for people to become **middlemen**. Middlemen provide buyers and sellers information at a lower cost and arrange trades between them. Many people think middlemen just add to the buyer's expense without performing a useful function. However, because of transaction costs, without middlemen, many trades would never happen (nor would the gains from them be realized). Services like Uber Eats and DoorDash are middlemen that, for a fee, are willing to solve the problem of getting food from your favorite restaurant to you when you don't feel like making the drive.

Grocers are also middlemen. Each of us could deal with farmers directly to buy our food—probably at a lower monetary cost. But that would have a high opportunity cost. Finding and dealing with different farmers for every product we wanted to buy would take a lot of time. Stockbrokers, realtors, publishers, and merchants of all sorts are other kinds of middlemen. For a fee, they reduce transaction costs for both buyers and sellers. By making exchanges cheaper and more convenient, middlemen expand the number of trades. In so doing, they themselves create value.

2-3 The Importance of Property Rights

The buyer of an orange, a laptop, a television, or an automobile generally takes the item home. The buyer of a cargo ship, satellite, or an office building, though, may never touch it. When exchange occurs, it's really the **property rights** of the item that change hands.

Private property rights involve three things:

1. the right to exclusive use of the property and to the income or benefits it produces (that is, the owner has sole possession, control, and use of the property, including the right to exclude others);
2. legal protection against invasion from other individuals who would seek to use or abuse the property without the owner's permission; and
3. the right to transfer, sell, exchange, rent, lease, or mortgage the property.

Private owners can do anything they want with their property as long as they do not use it in a manner that invades or infringes on the rights of another. For example, I cannot throw the hammer that I own through the television that you own. If I did, I would be violating your property right to your television. The same is true if I operate a factory spewing out pollution harming you or your land.[4] Because an owner has the right to control the use of property, the owner also must accept responsibility for the outcomes of that control. Private property rights represent a bundle of legal rights that are often separable, as an owner may lease the usage rights to another individual.

In contrast to private ownership, common-property ownership occurs when multiple people simultaneously have or claim ownership rights to a good or resource. If the resource is open to all, none of the common owners can prevent the others from using or damaging the property. Most beaches, rivers, and roads are examples of commonly owned property. The distinction between private- and common-property ownership is important because common ownership does not create the same powerful incentives for conservation and efficient use as private ownership. Economists are fond of saying that when everybody owns something, nobody owns it.

Clearly defined and enforced private property rights are a key to economic progress because of the powerful incentive effects that private ownership generates. The following four incentives are particularly important:

1. Private owners can gain by employing their resources in ways that are beneficial to others, and they bear the opportunity cost of ignoring the wishes of others. Realtors often advise homeowners to use neutral colors for countertops and walls in their house because they will improve the resale value of the home. As a private owner, you could install bright green fixtures and paint your walls deep purple, but you will bear the cost (in terms of a lower selling price) of ignoring the wishes of others who might want to buy your house later. Conversely, by fixing up a house and doing things to it that others find beneficial, you can reap the benefit of a higher selling price. Similarly, you could spray paint orange designs all over the outside of your brand-new car, but private ownership gives you an incentive not to do so because the resale value of the car depends on the value that *others* place on it.

Property rights
The rights to use, control, and obtain the benefits from a good or resource.

Private property rights
Property rights that are exclusively held by an owner and protected against invasion by others. Private property can be transferred, sold, leased, or mortgaged at the owner's discretion.

Keys to Economic Prosperity

Private Ownership

Private ownership provides people with a strong incentive to take care of things and develop resources in ways that are highly valued by others.

[4]For a detailed explanation of how property rights protect the environment, with several real-world examples, refer to Roger E. Meiners and Bruce Yandle, *The Common Law: How It Protects the Environment* (Bozeman, MT: PERC, 1998), available online at www.perc.org.

The Wall Street Journal/Cartoon Features Syndicate

A private owner has a strong incentive to do things with his or her property that increase its value to others.

Consider a parcel of undeveloped, privately owned land near a university. The private owner of the land can do many things with it. For example, she could leave it undeveloped, turn it into a metered parking lot, erect a restaurant, or build rental housing. Will the wishes and desires of the nearby students be reflected in her choice, even though they are not the owners of the property? Yes. Whichever use is more highly valued by potential customers will earn her the highest investment return. If housing is relatively hard to find but there are plenty of other restaurants, the profitability of using her land for housing will be higher than the profitability of using it for a restaurant. Private ownership gives her a strong incentive to use her property in a way that will also fulfill the wishes of others. If she decides to leave the property undeveloped instead of erecting housing that would benefit the students, she will bear the opportunity cost of forgone rental income from the property.

Consider a second example: the incentive structure confronted by the owner of an apartment complex near your campus. The owner may not care much for swimming pools, workout facilities, study desks, washers and dryers, or green areas. Nonetheless, private ownership provides the owner with a strong incentive to provide these items if students and other potential customers value them more than the costs of their provision. Why? Because tenants will be willing to pay higher rents to live in a complex with amenities that they value. The owners of rental property can profit by providing an additional amenity that tenants value as long as the tenants are willing to pay enough additional rent to cover their cost.

2. Private owners have a strong incentive to care for and properly manage what they own. Will Pablo regularly change the oil in his car? Will he see to it that the seats don't get torn? Probably so, because being careless about these things would reduce the car's value, both to him and to any future owner. The car and its value—the sale price if he sells it—belong just to Pablo, so he would bear the burden of a decline in the car's value if the oil ran low and ruined the engine, or if the seats were torn. Similarly, he would capture the value of an expenditure that improved the car, like a new paint job. As the owner, Pablo has both the authority and the incentive to protect the car against harm or neglect and even to enhance its value. Private property rights give owners a strong incentive for good stewardship.

Do you take equally good care not to damage an apartment you rent as you would your own house? If you share an apartment with several roommates, are the common areas of the apartment (such as the kitchen and living room) as neatly kept as the bedrooms? Based on economic theory, we guess that the answer to both of these questions is probably "No."

3. Private owners have an incentive to conserve for the future–particularly if the property is expected to increase in value. People have a much stronger incentive to conserve privately owned property than they do commonly owned property. For example, when Steven was in college, the general rule among his roommates was that any food or drink in the house was common property—open game for the hungry or thirsty mouth of anyone who stumbled across it. There was never a reason for Steven to conserve

AirCam.PRO/Shutterstock.com

iStock.com/StefaNikolic

When apartments and other investment properties are owned privately, the owner has a strong incentive to provide amenities that others value highly relative to their cost.

food or drinks in the house because it would be quickly consumed by a roommate coming in later that night. When Steven first started living alone, he noticed a dramatic change in his behavior. When he ordered a pizza, he would save some for the next day's lunch rather than eating it all that night. Steven began counting his drinks before he had one to make sure there were enough left for the next day. When Steven was the sole owner, he began delaying his current consumption to conserve for the future because he was the one, not his roommates, who reaped the benefit from his conservation.

Similarly, when more than one individual has the right to drill oil from an underground pool of oil, each has an incentive to extract as much as possible, as quickly as possible. Any oil conserved for the future will probably be taken by someone else. In contrast, when only one owner has the right to drill, the oil will be extracted more slowly. The same applies to the common-property problems involved in overfishing of the sea compared with fisheries that use privately owned ponds.

Someone who owns land, a house, or a factory has a strong incentive to bear costs now, if necessary, to preserve the asset's value for the future. The owner's wealth is tied up in the value of the property, which reflects nothing more than the net benefits that will be available to a future owner. Thus, the wealth of private owners is dependent upon their willingness and ability to look ahead, maintain, and conserve those things that will be more highly valued in the future. This is why private ownership is particularly important for the optimal conservation of natural resources.

4. Private owners have an incentive to lower the chance that their property will cause damage to the property of others. Private ownership links responsibility with the right of control. Private owners can be held accountable for damage done to others through the misuse of their property. A car owner has a right to drive his car, but will be held accountable if the brakes aren't maintained and the car damages someone else's property. Similarly, a chemical company has control over its products, but, exactly for that reason, it is legally liable for damages if it mishandles the chemicals. Courts of law recognize and enforce the authority granted by ownership, but they also enforce the responsibility that goes with that authority. Because private property owners can be held accountable for damages they cause, they have an incentive to use their property responsibly and take steps to reduce the likelihood of harm to others. A property owner, for example, has an incentive to cut down a dying tree before it falls into a neighbor's house and to leash or restrain his or her dog if it's likely to bite others.

2-3a Private Ownership and Markets

Private ownership and competitive markets provide the foundation for cooperative behavior among individuals. When private property rights are protected and enforced, the permission of the owner must be sought before anyone else can use the property. Put another way, if you want to use a good or resource, you must either buy or lease it from the owner. This means that each of us must face the cost of using scarce resources. Furthermore, market prices give private owners a strong incentive to consider the desires of others and use their resources in ways others value highly relative to cost.

Friedrich Hayek, a Nobel Prize winner in economics, used the expression "the extended order" to refer to the tendency for markets to lead perfect strangers from different backgrounds around the world to cooperate with one another. Let's go back to the example of the property owner who has the choice of leaving her land idle or building housing to benefit students. The landowner might not know any students in her town nor particularly care about providing them housing. However, because she is motivated by market prices, she might build an apartment complex and eventually do business with a lot of students she never intended to get to know. In the process, she will purchase materials, goods, and services produced by other strangers.

Applications in Economics

Protecting Endangered Species with Private Property Rights and Trade

Robert Harding Video/Shutterstock.com

Have you ever wondered why the wild tiger is endangered in much of the world but domestic cats are thriving? Or why the northern spotted owl is threatened in the western United States but chickens are not? Why have elephant and rhinoceros populations declined in number but not cattle or hogs? The incentives accompanying private ownership and freedom to trade provide the answer.

Consider what happens with animals that provide food, such as cattle, that are privately owned. If people decided to eat more beef, beef prices would rise. The higher prices would provide an incentive for individuals to dedicate more land and other resources to raising cattle, so they could sell more (and earn more income). The result would be more cows. Because cattle are privately owned, the market demand for beef creates a strong incentive for suppliers to maintain herds of cattle and to protect them.

In some ways, the rhinoceros is like a cow. A rhino, like a large bull in a cattle herd, may charge if disturbed. At 3,000 pounds, a charging rhino can be very dangerous to humans. Also, like cattle, rhinos can be valuable to people—a single rhino horn, used for artistic carvings and medicines, can sell for many thousands of dollars.

But rhinos are endangered. Even though a rhino horn can be harvested without killing the animal, the Convention on International Trade in Endangered Species (CITES) forbids selling the horn. People who want a rhino horn—and demand for it has persisted over many years—cannot obtain it legally. When hunting rhinos and selling their horns are illegal, trade goes underground. Rhinos become a favorite target of poachers—that is, people who kill animals illegally. They are sometimes assisted by local people or even the government officials who are supposed to protect the animals, eager to reap a financial gain.

With the intention of stemming poaching, many nations forbid trade in rhino parts. This has not reduced the number of rhino killings. After the government banned domestic trade in rhino horns in South Africa in 2009, the number of illegal killings went up to over 1,000 rhinos annually compared to fewer than 100 prior to the ban. In 2017, 21 government officials were arrested for poaching-related crimes. Most of the poaching occurred in the country's government parks, including the famed Kruger National Park.[1]

In some African countries, however, the numbers of wild animals, such as elephants, lions, and rhinos, have gone up. This growth has occurred in regions where private owners and local communities are allowed to own and control them. South Africa started giving ownership rights to private landholders in the 1980s, and Namibia extended rights to communal lands in the mid-1990s. With these policy changes, local farmers and tribal communities enjoyed rights over the wildlife in their areas and were able to earn revenues from these animals. This transformed the incentives in both countries. Because the revenues come primarily from trophy hunting and tourism, local communities have a strong incentive to protect the animals and their habitat. These new incentives led to a natural resurgence in wildlife numbers. For example, the number of black rhinos in Namibia rose from 580 in 1992 to 3,390 in 2021.[2]

Clearly, property rights to ownership or use, plus freedom to trade, are among the keys to conservation. Ownership can spur protection, care, and population growth, just as it does with cattle. Trade could provide farmers and communities that own rhinos with an added incentive to protect them. But where ownership and trade are prohibited, the protection will be missing, and poaching is likely to continue.

[1]See Rachael Bale, "More Than 1,000 Rhinos Killed by Poachers in South Africa Last Year," *National Geographic*, January 25, 2018, news.nationalgeographic.com/2018/01/wildlife-watch-rhino-poaching-crisis-continues-south-africa/.

[2]Michael 't Sas-Rolfes, Richard Emslie, Keryn Adcock, and Michael Knight, "Legal Hunting for Conservation of Highly Threatened Species: The Case of African Rhinos," *Conservation Letters*, March 3, 2022, https://doi.org/10.1111/conl.12877.

Things are different in countries that don't recognize private-ownership rights or enforce them. In his book *The Mystery of Capital*, economist Hernando de Soto argues that the lack of well-defined and enforced property rights explains why some underdeveloped countries (despite being market based) have made little economic progress. He points out that in many of these nations, generations of people have squatted on the land without any legal deed giving them formal ownership. These squatters cannot borrow against the land or the homes they built on it to generate capital because they don't have a deed to it, nor can they prevent someone else from arbitrarily taking the land away from them. Private ownership and markets can also play an important role in environmental protection and natural-resource conservation. Ocean fishing rights, tradable rights to pollute, and private ownership of endangered species are just some examples. The accompanying Applications in Economics feature, "Protecting Endangered Species with Private Property Rights and Trade," explores some of these issues.

2-4 Production Possibilities Curve

People try to get the most from their limited resources by making purposeful choices and engaging in economizing behavior. This can be illustrated using a conceptual tool called the **production possibilities curve**. The production possibilities curve shows the maximum amount of any two products that can be produced from a fixed set of resources and the possible trade-offs in production between them. The real economy obviously produces more than just two products, but this concept can help us understand a number of important economic ideas.

Production possibilities curve
A curve that outlines all possible combinations of total output that could be produced, assuming (1) a fixed amount of productive resources, (2) a given amount of technical knowledge, and (3) full and efficient use of those resources. The slope of the curve indicates the amount of one product that must be given up to produce more of the other.

Exhibit 2-1 illustrates the production possibilities curve for Susan, an intelligent economics major. This curve indicates the combinations of English and economics grades that she thinks she can earn if she spends a total of ten hours per week studying for the two subjects. Currently, she is choosing to study the material in each course that she expects will help her grade the most for the time spent, and she is allocating five hours of study time to each course. She expects that this amount of time, carefully spent on each course, will allow her to earn a B grade in both, indicated at point *T*. But if she were to take some time away from studying one of the two subjects and spend it studying the other, she could raise her grade in the course receiving more study time. However, it would come at the cost

Exhibit 2-1 Production Possibilities Curve for Susan's Grades in English and Economics

The production possibilities for Susan, in terms of grades, are illustrated for ten hours of total study time. If Susan studied ten hours per week in these two classes, she could attain a D in English and an A in economics (point *S*), a B in English and a B in economics (point *T*), or an A in English and a D in economics (point *U*).

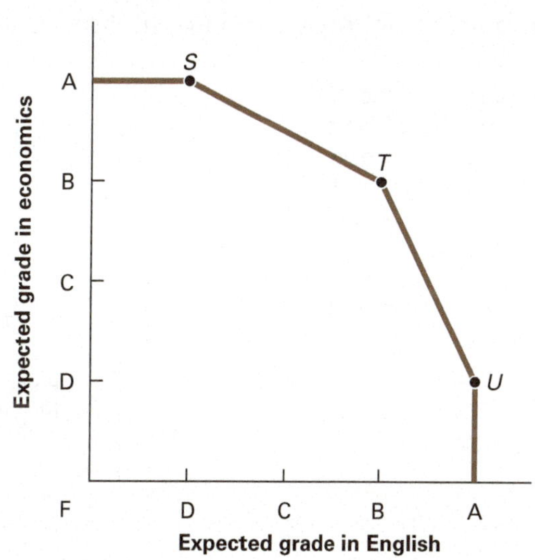

of a lower grade in the course. If she were to move to point *S* by spending more hours on economics and fewer on English, for example, her expected economics grade would rise, while her expected English grade would fall. This illustrates an important point: the idea of trade-offs in the use of scarce resources. Whenever more of one thing is produced, there is an opportunity cost in terms of something else that now must be forgone.

You might notice that Susan's production possibilities curve indicates that the additional study time required to raise her economics grade by one letter, from a B to an A (moving from point *T* to point *S*), would require giving up two letter grades in her English class, not just one, reducing her English grade from a B to a D. If, alternatively, Susan were to move from point *T* to point *U*, the opposite would be true—she would improve her English grade by one letter at the expense of two letter grades in economics. You can understand this by thinking about your own studying behavior. When you have only a limited amount of time to study a subject, you begin by studying the most important (grade-increasing) material first. As you spend additional time on that subject, you begin studying topics that are of decreasing importance for your grade. Thus, adding an hour of study time to the subject Susan studies least will have a larger impact on her grade than will taking away an hour from the subject on which she currently spends more time.

This idea of increasing opportunity cost is reflected in the slope of the production possibilities curve. The curve is flatter to the left of point *T* and steeper to the right, showing that, as Susan takes more and more of her resources (time, in this case) from one course and puts it into the other, she must give up greater and greater amounts of productivity in the course getting fewer resources.

Of course, Susan could study more economics *without* giving up her English study time, if she gave up some leisure, or study time for other courses, or her part-time job in the campus bookstore. If she gave up leisure or her job and added those hours to the ten hours of study time for economics and English, the entire curve in Exhibit 2-1 would shift outward. She could get better grades in both classes by having more time to study.

Can the production possibilities concept be applied to the entire economy? Yes. We can grow more soybeans if we grow less corn, because both can be grown on the same land. Beefing up the nation's military would mean we would have to produce fewer nonmilitary goods than we could otherwise. When scarce resources are being used efficiently, getting more of one requires that we sacrifice others.

Exhibit 2-2 shows a hypothetical production possibilities curve for an economy with a limited amount of resources that produces only two goods: food and clothing. The points

Exhibit 2-2 Concept of Production Possibilities Curve for an Economy

When an economy is using its limited resources efficiently, production of more clothing requires that the economy give up some other goods–such as food in this example. In time, improved technology, more resources, or improvement in its economic organization could make it possible to produce more of both goods by shifting the production possibilities curve outward.

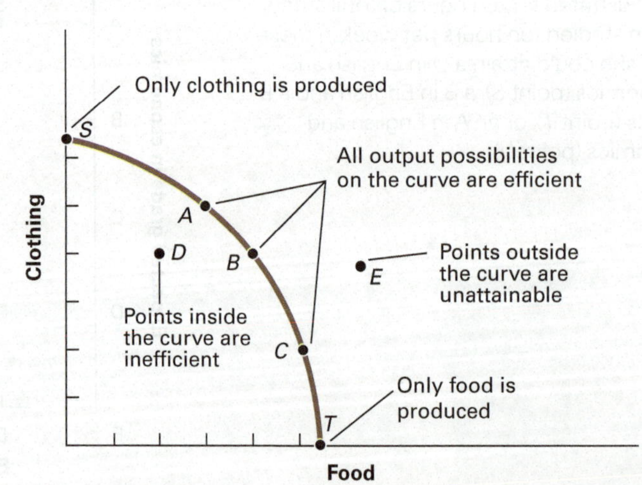

along the curve represent all possible combinations of food and clothing that could be produced with the current level of resources and technology in the economy (assuming the resources are being used efficiently). A point outside the production possibilities curve (such as point *E*) would be considered unattainable at the present time. A point inside the production possibilities curve (such as point *D*) is attainable, but producing that amount would mean that the economy is not making maximum use of its resources (some resources are being underutilized). Thus, point *D* is considered inefficient.

More specifically, the production possibilities curve shows all of the maximum combinations of two goods that an economy will be able to produce: (1) given a fixed quantity of resources, (2) holding the level of technology constant, and (3) assuming that all resources are used efficiently.

When these three conditions are met, the economy will be at the edge of its production possibilities frontier (where points *A*, *B*, and *C* lie), and producing more of one good will necessitate producing less of others. If condition 3 above is not met, and resources are being used inefficiently, an economy would be operating inside its production possibilities curve. If the quantity of resources increases or the level of technology improves (conditions 1 and 2), this will result in an outward shift in the production possibilities curve. We will return to these factors that can shift the production possibilities curve in a moment.

Notice that the production possibilities curve is concave (or bowed out) to the origin, just as Susan's was in Exhibit 2-1 because of the concept of increasing opportunity cost. Here, the curved shape reflects the fact that an economy's resources are not equally well suited to produce food and clothing. If an economy were using all its resources to produce clothing (point *S*), transferring those resources least suited for producing clothing toward food production would reduce clothing output a little but increase food output a lot. Because the resources transferred would be those better suited for producing food and less suited for producing clothing, the opportunity cost of producing additional food (in terms of clothing forgone) is low near point *S*. However, as more and more resources are devoted to food production and successively larger amounts of food are produced (moving the economy from *S* to *A* to *B* and so on), the opportunity cost of food will rise. This is because, as more and more food is produced, additional food output can be achieved only by using resources that are less and less suitable for the production of food relative to clothing. Thus, as food output is expanded, successively larger amounts of clothing must be forgone per unit of additional food. This is similar to what happened to Susan when she diverted study hours from one course to another. Only this time, we are talking about an entire economy.

2-4a Shifting the Production Possibilities Curve Outward

What restricts an economy—once its resources are fully utilized—from producing more of everything? Why can't we get more of something produced without having to give up the production of something else? The same constraint that kept Susan from simultaneously making a higher grade in both English and economics: a lack of resources. As long as all current resources are being used efficiently, the only way to get more of one good is to sacrifice some of the other. Over time, however, it is possible for a country's production possibilities curve to shift outward, making it possible for more of all goods to be produced. There are four factors that could potentially shift the production possibilities curve outward.

1. An increase in the economy's resource base would expand our ability to produce goods and services. If we had more or better resources, we could produce a greater amount of all goods. Resources such as machinery, buildings, tools, and education are human-made, and thus we can expand our resource base by devoting some of our efforts to producing them. This **investment** would provide us with better tools and skills and increase our ability to produce goods and services in the future. However, like

Investment
The purchase, construction, or development of resources, including physical assets, such as plants and machinery, and human assets, such as better education. Investment expands an economy's resources. The process of investment is sometimes called capital formation.

Technology
The technological knowledge available in an economy at any given time. The level of technology determines the amount of output we can generate with our limited resources.

Invention
The creation of a new product or process, often facilitated by the knowledge of engineering and science.

Innovation
The successful introduction and adoption of a new product or process; the economic application of inventions and marketing techniques.

Entrepreneur
A person who decides what resources will be used, how they will be combined, and what goods and services they will be utilized to produce. Typically, entrepreneurs will undertake these activities within a business enterprise. A successful entrepreneur's actions will increase the value of resources and expand the size of the economic pie.

with the production of other goods, devoting effort and resources toward producing these long-lasting physical assets means fewer resources are available to produce other things, in this case goods for current consumption. Thus, the choice between using resources to produce goods for current consumption and using them to produce investment goods for the future can also be illustrated within the production possibilities framework. The two economies illustrated in **Exhibit 2-3** begin with identical production possibilities curves (*RS*). Notice that Economy A dedicates more of its output to investment (shown by I_A) than does Economy B (shown by I_B). Economy B, on the other hand, consumes more than Economy A. Because Economy A allocates more of its resources to investment and less to consumption, A's production possibilities curve shifts outward over time by a greater amount than B's. In other words, the growth rate of Economy A—the expansion of its ability to produce goods—is enhanced by this investment. But more investment in machines and human skills requires a reduction in current consumption.

2. Advancements in technology can expand the economy's production possibilities.

Technology determines the maximum amount of output an economy can produce given the resources it has. New and better technology makes it possible for us to get more output from our resources. An important form of technological change is **invention**—the use of science and engineering to create new products or processes. In recent years, for example, inventions have allowed us to download music faster and more cheaply, process data more rapidly, get more oil and natural gas from existing fields, and send information instantly and cheaply by satellite. Such technological advances increase our production possibilities, shifting our economy's entire production possibilities curve outward.

The production possibilities of an economy can also be expanded by technological change through **innovation**—the practical and effective adoption of new techniques. Such innovation is commonly carried out by an **entrepreneur**—a person who decides what resources will be used, how they will be combined, and what goods and services they will be utilized to produce. In order to succeed, entrepreneurs must produce goods and services that increase the value of resources. Sometimes this can be achieved by introducing new products, new technologies, and lower cost production methods. When an entrepreneur produces goods that are highly valued relative to cost, their actions will both generate personal

Exhibit 2-3 Investment and Production Possibilities in the Future

Here we illustrate two economies (A and B) that initially confront identical production possibilities curves (*RS*). Economy A allocates a larger share of its output to investment (I_A, compared to I_B for Economy B). As a result, the production possibilities curve of the high-investment economy (Economy A) will tend to shift outward by a larger amount over time than the low-investment economy's will.

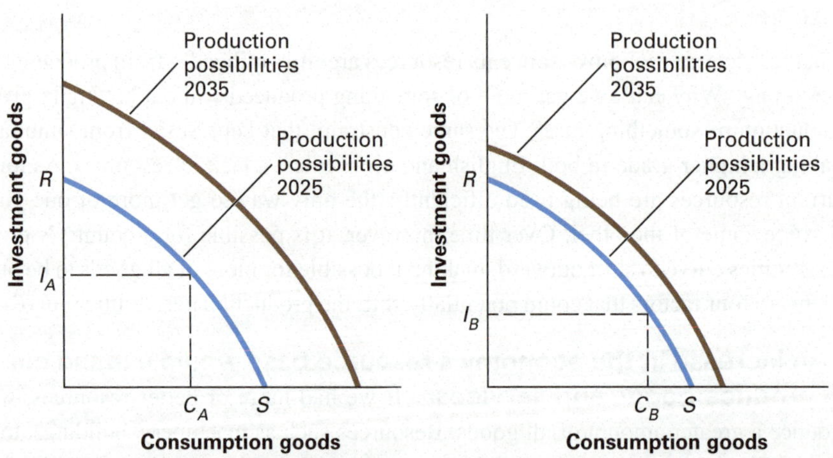

(a) Economy A, high investment **(b) Economy B, low investment**

success and expand the economy's production possibilities. Take, for example, Henry Ford, an entrepreneur who changed how cars were made by pioneering the assembly line. With the same amount of labor and materials, Ford made more cars more cheaply. Entrepreneurs like Bill Gates and Steve Jobs helped develop the personal computer and software programs that dramatically increased their usefulness to businesses and households. More recently, entrepreneurs such as Jeff Bezos (Amazon), Jack Dorsey (Twitter, now X), and Mark Zuckerberg (Facebook, now Meta) have enhanced our ability to transact, interact, and communicate online with the innovative businesses they started.

Through entrepreneurial discovery and innovation, new products and methods of production are continuously replacing old ones. The great Harvard economist Joseph Schumpeter called this process **creative destruction**. Digital music has largely replaced CDs and vinyl records, while the automobile caused the demise of the horse and buggy industry. A modern cell phone can replace more than $2,500 worth of products from the past that would fill a small room, including a portable music player, alarm clock, watch, camera, flashlight, calendar, address book, car GPS system, pedometer, level, ruler, calculator, dictionary, guitar tuner, video recorder, gaming system, and many more. Artificial intelligence (AI) is now revolutionizing jobs, companies, and entire industries. Although this process destroys some businesses or industries, it creates new and more valuable ones in their place. Creative destruction is a powerful force leading to economic growth and prosperity.

Creative destruction
The replacement of old products and production methods by innovative new ones that consumers judge to be superior. The process generates economic growth and higher living standards.

3. An improvement in the rules under which the economy functions can also increase output. The legal system of a country influences the ability of people to cooperate with one another and produce goods. Changes in legal institutions that promote social cooperation and motivate people to produce what others want will also push the production possibilities curve outward. Since the collapse of the Soviet Union in 1991, many countries around the world have reformed their economies in ways that have expanded the use of private ownership and markets, for example. However, poor institutions can reduce both the level of resources used (shifting the curve inward) and how efficiently they are used (causing the economy to operate inside its production possibilities curve).

Historically, legal innovations have been an important source of economic progress. During the eighteenth century, a system of patents was established in Europe and North America, giving inventors private property rights to their ideas. At about the same time, laws were passed allowing businesses to establish themselves legally as corporations, reducing the cost of forming large firms that were often required for the mass production of manufactured goods. Both of these legal changes allowed improved forms of economic organization and accelerated the growth of output by shifting the production possibilities curve outward more rapidly.

4. By working harder and giving up current leisure, we could increase our production of goods and services. Hypothetically, the production possibilities curve would shift outward if everyone worked more hours and took less leisure time. Strictly speaking, however, leisure is also a good, so we would simply be giving up leisure to have more of other things. If we were to construct a production possibilities curve for leisure versus other goods, this would be shown as simply a movement along the curve. However, if we restrict our model to only material goods and services, a change in the amount we work would be shown as a shift in the curve.

How much people work depends not only on their personal preferences but also on public policy. For example, high tax rates on personal income may cause people to work less. This is because high tax rates reduce the payoff from working. When this happens, people spend more time doing other, untaxed activities—like leisure activities. This will move the production possibilities curve for material goods inward because the economy can't produce as much when people work less.

Entrepreneurs Who Have Changed Our Lives

New products and better ways of doing things do not just happen; they must be discovered. This is the function of the entrepreneur. Successful entrepreneurs exert an impact—often a huge impact—on our lives. However, their contributions are often either overlooked or misunderstood. Everyone knows that highly successful entrepreneurs make a lot of money. But their innovative ideas and product improvements enhance the lives of others. If they did not, people would not buy their products and services. Various chapters of this text will include a feature, "Entrepreneurs Who Have Changed Our Lives." Although you will recognize several of the entrepreneurs in this series, others are relatively unknown. As the series will illustrate, successful entrepreneurs come from diverse backgrounds. Some are ordinary individuals who developed and acted on a great idea. Others are truly unique. Many experienced failure prior to their success. These elements are all part of entrepreneurship.

Jeff Bezos

Kristoffer Tripplaar/Alamy

Jeff Bezos, founder of Amazon, dreamed of harnessing the Internet to transform retailing and expand the value of his company to more than a billion dollars. Instead, he has turned Amazon into something close to a trillion-dollar company, while becoming perhaps the world's richest person.

Amazon, which started with the sale of books in 1995, has revolutionized buying and selling products online. More than 200 million people subscribe to its Prime service, which lets them obtain quicker delivery on millions of products, online music, and videos. Often, they can receive their product within a day or two.

Amazon has drastically reduced retail transaction costs. Buyers no longer have to trudge from store to store to find the right book, gadget, or even food item; they can order it with the click of a button after seeing it on the Internet and reading reviews by previous purchasers. Amazon delivers products without the complex transaction cost of sending them to retail stores, where they might linger for months or never be bought at all.

Bezos was born in Albuquerque, New Mexico, but moved around the country; his father was a petroleum engineer. He was always interested in how things worked. When he was very young, he didn't like sleeping in a baby crib, so he took it apart with a screwdriver. When he was older, he devised a buzzer on his bedroom door to warn him if his little brother or sister was about to enter. In high school, he was an outstanding student and popular with classmates, becoming both valedictorian and president of his class.

At Princeton he tried physics, but switched to computer science. (He thought the students in physics were smarter and he wouldn't do well in that field.) After graduation he had a series of Wall Street jobs in which he created or managed computer systems. But once he learned how fast the Internet was growing, he recognized its potential for retailing. His entrepreneurial talents built a great company, but they also improved the lives of millions of consumers throughout the world.

Sources: Josepha Sherman, *Jeff Bezos: King of Amazon* (Brookfield, CT: Twenty-First Century Books, 2001).

Karen Weise "Amazon's Profit Falls Sharply as Company Buys Growth," *New York Times*, October 24, 2019.

G. Bruce Knecht, "Wall Street Whiz Finds Niche Selling Books on the Internet," *Wall Street Journal*, May 16, 1996.

2-4b Production Possibilities and Economic Growth

Within the production possibilities framework, economic growth is simply an outward shift in the curve through time. The more rapidly the curve shifts outward, the more rapid is economic growth. There are other economic models that are used to analyze economic growth; however, they all share the production possibilities curve as a foundation. Economic growth is one of the most important topics in modern economics for good reason. On the one hand, an economic growth rate of 3 percent per year will result in living standards doubling approximately every 23 years. On the other hand, in a country experiencing an economic growth rate of only 1 percent, it will take approximately 70 years for living standards to double.

2-5 Trade, Output, and Living Standards

As we previously discussed, trade creates value by moving goods from people who value them less to people who value them more. However, this is only part of the story. Trade also makes it possible for people to expand their output through specialization and **division of labor**, large-scale production, and the dissemination of better products and production methods.

2-5a Gains from Specialization and Division of Labor

Businesses can achieve higher output levels and greater productivity from their workers through specialization and division of labor. About 250 years ago, Adam Smith noted the importance of this factor. Observing the operation of a pin manufacturer, Smith noted that when each worker specialized in a separate function needed to make pins, 10 workers together were able to produce 48,000 pins per day, or 4,800 pins per worker. Smith doubted an individual worker could produce even 20 pins per day working alone from start to finish on each pin.[5]

The division of labor separates production tasks into a series of related operations. Each worker performs one or a few of perhaps hundreds of tasks necessary to produce something. This process makes it possible to assign different tasks to those individuals who are able to accomplish them most efficiently (that is, at the lowest cost). Furthermore, a worker who specializes in just one narrow area becomes more experienced and more skilled in that task over time.

Trading partners can also benefit from specialization and the division of labor. The **law of comparative advantage**, developed in the early 1800s by the great English economist David Ricardo, explains why this is true. ***The law of comparative advantage states that the total output of a group of individuals, an entire economy, or a group of nations will be greatest when the output of each good is produced by the person (or firm) with the lowest opportunity cost for that good.***

Comparative advantage applies to trade among individuals, business firms, regions, and even nations. When trading partners are able to use more of their time and resources to produce the things each is best at, they will be able to produce more together than would otherwise have been possible. In turn, the mutual gains they get from trading will result in higher levels of income for each. It's a win–win situation for both.

If a good or service can be obtained more economically through trade, it makes sense to get it that way rather than producing it for yourself. When you think about it, the law of comparative advantage is common sense. If someone else is willing to supply you with a good at a lower cost than you can produce it yourself, doesn't it make sense to trade for it and use your time and resources to produce more of the things you can produce most efficiently? Consider the situation of Andrea, an attorney who earns $300 per hour providing legal services. She has several documents that need to be typed, and she is thinking about hiring a typist earning $25 per hour to do it. Andrea is an excellent typist, much faster than the prospective employee. She could do the job in 20 hours, whereas the typist would take 40 hours.

Keys to Economic Prosperity

Gains from Trade

Trade makes it possible for people to generate more output through specialization and division of labor, large-scale production processes, and the dissemination of improved products and production methods.

Division of labor
A method that breaks down the production of a product into a series of specific tasks, each performed by a different worker.

Law of comparative advantage
A principle that states that individuals, firms, regions, or nations can gain by specializing in the production of goods that they produce cheaply (at a low opportunity cost) and exchanging them for goods they cannot produce cheaply (at a high opportunity cost).

[5]Refer to Adam Smith, *An Inquiry into the Nature and Causes of the Wealth of Nations* (1776; Cannan's ed., Chicago: University of Chicago Press, 1976), 7–16, for additional detail on the importance of the division of labor.

CARLOSBARRIA/Reuters/Corbis

Trade channels goods to those who value them most. Trade also helps disseminate ideas for improved products and makes production methods such as specialization, the division of labor, and mass production more feasible. Over the years, trade has enabled us to produce more with our limited resources, dramatically improving our living standards.

Because of her greater typing speed, some might think Andrea should handle the job herself. This is not the case. If she types the documents, the job will cost her \$6,000—the opportunity cost of 20 hours of practicing law at \$300 per hour. Alternatively, the cost of having the documents typed by the typist is only \$1,000 (40 hours at \$25 per hour). Andrea's comparative advantage lies in practicing law. By hiring the typist, she will increase her own productivity for clients and will make more money.

The implications of the law of comparative advantage are universal. Any group will be able to produce more output from its available resources when each good or service is produced by the person with the lowest opportunity cost. This insight is particularly important in understanding the way a market economy works. Buyers will try to get the most for their money. They will not knowingly choose a high-cost option when a lower-cost alternative of the same value is available. This places low-cost suppliers at a competitive advantage. Thus, low-cost producers will generally survive and prosper in a market economy. As a result, the production of goods and resources will naturally tend to be allocated according to comparative advantage.

Most people recognize that Americans benefit from trade among the nation's 50 states. For example, the residents of Nebraska and Florida are able to produce a larger joint output and achieve higher income levels when Nebraskans specialize in producing corn and other grain products and Floridians specialize in producing oranges and other citrus products. The same is true for trade among nations. Like Nebraskans and Floridians, people in different nations will be better off if they specialize in the goods and services they can produce at a low cost and trade them for goods they produce at a high cost. Refer to the addendum to this chapter for additional evidence on this point.

2-5b Gains from Mass Production Methods

Trade also promotes economic progress by making it possible for firms to lower their per-unit costs with mass production. Suppose a nation isolated itself and refused to trade with other countries. In an economy like this, self-sufficiency and small-scale production would be the norm. If trade were allowed, however, the nation's firms could sell their products to customers around the world. This would make it feasible for the firms to adopt more efficient, large-scale production processes. Mass production often leads to labor and machinery efficiencies that increase output per worker. But without trade, these gains could not be achieved.

2-5c Gains from Innovation

Trade also makes it possible to realize gains from the discovery and dissemination of innovative products and production processes. Economic growth involves brain power, innovation, and the application of technology. Without trade, however, the gains derived from the discovery of better ways of doing things would be stifled. Furthermore, observing and interacting with other people using different and better technologies often encourage others to copy successful approaches. People also modify the technology they observe, adapting it for their own purposes. This sometimes results in new, and even better, technologies. Again, gains from these sources would be far more limited in a world without trade.

The importance of trade in our modern world can hardly be exaggerated. Trade makes it possible for most of us to consume a bundle of goods and services far beyond what we would be able to produce for ourselves.

Can you imagine the difficulty involved in producing your own housing, clothing, and food, to say nothing of computers, televisions, dishwashers, automobiles, and cell phones? Yet most families in North America, Western Europe, Japan, and Australia enjoy all these conveniences. They are able to do so largely because their economies are organized in such a way that individuals can cooperate, specialize, and trade, thereby reaping the benefits of the enormous increases in output—in both quantity and diversity—that can be generated. In contrast, countries that impose obstacles that restrict exchange—either domestic or international—hinder their citizens from achieving these gains and more prosperous lives.

2-6 Human Ingenuity, Entrepreneurship, and the Creation of Wealth

Keys to Economic Prosperity

Human Ingenuity

Economic goods are the result of human ingenuity and action; thus, the size of the "economic pie" is variable, not fixed.

The size of a country's "economic pie" is most easily thought of as the total dollar value of all goods and services produced during some period of time. This economic pie is the grand total of the wealth (or value) created by each member of the society. It is not some fixed total waiting to be divided up among people. On the contrary, the size of the economic pie reflects the physical effort and ingenuity of human beings. It is not an endowment from nature.

Economic output expands as entrepreneurs discover new and better ways of doing things. So over time, it is human knowledge and ingenuity—perhaps more than anything else—that limit our economic progress. If Jim, a local farmer who normally produces \$150,000 worth of corn each year, finds a better growing method enabling him to produce \$160,000 of corn per year, he has created additional wealth. But Jim has actually created more than the \$10,000 in extra wealth. The \$10,000 is only his share of the gains from the additional trades made possible by the extra corn he grew. Exchange makes both buyer and seller better off, so the total wealth created by Jim includes not only his \$10,000 but also the gains of all of the buyers who purchased his additional output of corn.

This highlights an important point: in a market economy, a larger income for one person does not mean a smaller income for a trading partner. In fact, it is just the opposite. When a person earns income, he or she expands the economic pie by more than the amount of the slice that he or she gets, making it possible for the rest of us to have a bigger slice, too. When an entrepreneur, such as Chuck Hull, the inventor of the 3D printer, earns income through voluntary exchanges in the marketplace, he has enlarged the economic pie by an even larger amount. Here's why: Suppose that Linda, a freelance graphic artist, pays \$2,000 for a new 3D printer developed by Chuck Hull. As a result, she can do twice as much work in the same amount of time. Because she's more productive, Linda can earn more than enough additional income with the printer to justify her purchase. In addition, the businesses she serves are also better off because the printer makes it possible for her to give them quicker service and a lower price. More is produced in total. Thus, while Chuck Hull gained, so, too, did Linda and her customers.

The same is true for other successful entrepreneurs such as Jeff Bezos or Mark Zuckerberg. Amazon and Facebook (now Meta) have expanded the size of the entire economic pie by enhancing the ability of businesses to market and sell products to willing consumers. Even a successful writer such as J.K. Rowling enriches the lives of millions through her novels. When income is acquired through voluntary exchange, people who earn income also help others earn more income and live better, too.

2-7 Economic Organization

Every economy faces three basic questions: (1) What will be produced? (2) How will it be produced? and (3) For whom will it be produced? These questions are highly interrelated. Throughout the book, we will consider how different types of economies solve them. There are two broad ways that an economy can be organized: markets or government (political) planning. Let us briefly consider each.

2-7a Market Organization

Market organization
A method of organization in which private parties make their own plans and decisions with the guidance of unregulated market prices. The basic economic questions of consumption, production, and distribution are answered through these decentralized decisions.

Private ownership of productive assets, voluntary exchange, and market prices are the distinguishing features of **market organization**. Under market organization, private parties are permitted to buy and sell ownership rights of their assets at mutually acceptable prices. The government plays the limited role of rule maker and referee. It develops the rules, or the legal structure, that recognizes, defines, and protects private ownership rights. It helps individuals enforce contracts and protects people from violence and fraud. But in this role, the government is not an active player in the economy. Ideally, it avoids modifying market outcomes in an attempt to favor some people at the expense of others. For example, it doesn't prevent sellers from slashing prices or improving the quality of their products to attract customers from other competitors. Nor does it prevent buyers from outbidding others for products and productive resources. No legal restraints limit potential buyers or sellers from producing, selling, or buying in the marketplace.

Capitalism
An economic system in which productive resources are owned privately and goods and resources are allocated through market prices.

The term **capitalism** is often used to refer to an economic system based on market organization.[6] However, the term is also widely used to describe the economic systems of countries that make extensive use of regulations, trade restrictions, taxes and subsidies, and price controls to alter the operation of markets as long as property is generally privately owned and operated for profit. Therefore, economists generally prefer using market organization instead of capitalism because of the ambiguity of the latter.

Under market organization, no single individual or group of individuals guides the economy. There is no central planning authority, only individual planning. The three basic questions are solved independently in the marketplace by individual buyers and sellers making their own decentralized decisions. Buyers and sellers decide on their own what to produce, how to produce it, and whom to trade it to, based on the prices they themselves decide to charge.

Collective decision-making
The use of the political process (voting, taxes, government spending, regulation, political bargaining, lobbying, and so on) to make decisions and allocate resources. In a democratic setting, the votes of citizens and their representatives will determine the actions undertaken.

2-7b Political Organization

Socialism
A system of economic organization in which (1) the ownership and control of the basic means of production rest with the state and (2) resource allocation is determined by centralized planning rather than by market forces.

The major alternative to market organization is **collective decision-making**, whereby the government, through the political process, makes decisions for buyers and sellers in an attempt to solve the basic economic questions facing the economy. Sometimes, the government will maintain private ownership but uses taxes, subsidies, and regulations to resolve the basic economic questions. Alternatively, an economic system in which the government also owns the income-producing assets (machines, buildings, and land) and directly determines what goods will be produced is called **socialism**. Either way, individual planning and decisions are replaced by central planning and decisions made through the political process. These decisions can be made by a single dictator or a group of experts, or through

[6]*Capitalism* is a term coined by Karl Marx.

Applications in Economics

Are Scandinavian Countries Socialist?

Venezuela, Cuba, North Korea, and the former Soviet Union provide examples of socialist economies. These countries are characterized by low living standards and authoritarian political regimes. Are there any socialist success stories? During his 2016 and 2020 presidential campaigns, Bernie Sanders, a self-proclaimed democratic socialist, pointed to Scandinavian countries like Denmark and Sweden as socialist countries he would like the United States to emulate.

Are the Scandinavian countries really socialist? Scandinavian countries do have a high level of government expenditures, including large income transfer programs. But socialism involves government ownership of enterprises in major industries and allocation of resources via government planning rather than markets. Market economies are characterized by legal protection of private property, unbiased enforcement of contracts, free trade, and minimal business regulation. On the other hand, socialist economies are characterized by government ownership, trade restrictions, and imposition of mandates and regulations on the activities of business. In socialist countries, the means of production, including factories, banks, and agricultural land, are generally owned or controlled by the government.

Let's examine the institutions and policies of Scandinavian countries in order to determine where they stand on the market versus socialism spectrum. The annual *Economic Freedom of the World* report published by the Fraser Institute provides data for 165 countries on legal protection of property rights, freedom of exchange, and regulation of business.[1] These data can be used to determine whether the institutions and policies of Scandinavian countries are market oriented or predominately socialist. Higher rankings indicate more market-oriented policies and institutions.

Examination of the economic freedom subarea data for legal protection of private property rights and enforcement of contracts indicates that the Scandinavian countries rank quite high compared to predominantly market economies such as the United States and the United Kingdom. Among the 165 countries examined in 2021, Denmark ranked 2nd, Norway 3rd, Finland 5th, and Sweden 12th in this area, compared to 15th for the United Kingdom and 18th for the United States. Thus, the protection of private property and contracting in Scandinavian countries is highly reflective of market institutions.

In the subarea of free trade and international exchange, the Scandinavian countries also compare quite favorably with predominantly market economies. In the free trade area, Sweden ranked 10th, Denmark 31st, Norway 33rd, and Finland 51st, compared to 5th for the United Kingdom and 45th for the United States in 2021.

Socialist countries are known for their mandates and regulations imposed on business. However, again, the imposition of business regulations in Scandinavian countries is similar to that of market economies. In the subarea of business regulation, the Fraser Institute data ranked Finland 7th, Sweden 14th, Norway 16th, and Denmark 20th, compared to 31st for the United States and 33rd for the United Kingdom.

The World Bank's *Doing Business* report covering 190 countries provides additional data on the regulation of business.[2] This measure examines how the regulatory environment impacts the ease of entry into markets, cost of regulatory compliance, and regulations that make it difficult to operate a business. Free market economies rank high on this list, whereas heavily regulated, government-directed economies earn lower ratings. Again, the summary rankings of Scandinavian countries are similar to those of predominately market economies. In 2020, Denmark ranked 4th, Norway 9th, Sweden 10th, and Finland 20th, compared to 6th for the United States and 8th for the United Kingdom. By way of comparison, two other high-income market-directed economies—Belgium and Italy—ranked 46th and 58th, respectively, whereas socialist Venezuela placed 188th among the 190 countries rated. (Note: Neither Cuba nor North Korea is included because of insufficient data.)

In summary, the economic institutions of Scandinavian countries are those of a market economy. The protection of private property rights, openness of markets, and regulation of business in Scandinavian countries are similar to those of market-oriented economies. Thus, it should not be surprising that Danish Prime Minister Lars Løkke Rasmussen in a speech at Harvard stated, "Denmark is far from a socialist planned economy. Denmark is a market economy. The Nordic model is an expanded welfare state which provides a high level of security for its citizens, but it is also a successful market economy with much freedom to pursue your dreams and live your life as you wish."[3]

[1]James Gwartney, Robert Lawson, and Ryan Murphy, *Economic Freedom of the World: 2023 Annual Report* (Vancouver: The Fraser Institute, 2023). Refer to Exhibits 1.2 and 1.3.

[2]The World Bank, *Doing Business 2020*, at www.doingbusiness.org.

[3]Lars Løkke Rasmussen, "Denmark Is Not Socialist," Speech at Harvard University Kennedy School of Government, November 2015, at www.thelocal.dk/20151101/danish-pm-in-us-denmark-is-not-socialist.

democratic voting. Political rather than market forces direct the economy, and government officials and planning boards hand down decisions to expand or contract the output of education, medical services, automobiles, electricity, steel, consumer durables, and thousands of other commodities.

While the market and political process can be used to address the same basic economic questions, there are fundamental differences between the two. The market system relies on voluntary exchange, price signals, and freedom of entry. This results in a wider variety of products, a more competitive environment, and more dynamic change. On the other hand, the democratic political process responds primarily to the votes of the majority. In varying degrees, all economies use a combination of the two main methods of economic organization. Even predominantly market economies will still use taxes, subsidies, and some government ownership to direct and control resources. Similarly, predominantly socialist economies will, to some degree, use markets to allocate certain goods and services. As examples, countries such as Venezuela, Zimbabwe, Angola, Cuba, and North Korea rely predominantly on socialism and government planning to organize economic activity. In contrast, countries such as Singapore, New Zealand, Switzerland, Canada, and Australia rely predominantly on market organization. Countries with mixed economies that have significant aspects of both systems include Portugal, Turkey, Mexico, Italy, and Greece.

As we proceed, the tools of economics will be used to analyze both the market and political sectors. We think this approach is important and that you will find it both interesting and enlightening.

Key Points

- The highest valued activity sacrificed when a choice is made is the opportunity cost of the choice; differences (or changes) in opportunity costs help explain human behavior.
- Mutual gain is the foundation of trade. When two parties engage in voluntary exchange, they are both made better off. Trade creates value because it channels goods and resources to those who value them the most.
- Transaction costs—the time, effort, and other resources necessary to search out, negotiate, and conclude an exchange—hinder the gains from trade in an economy. Middlemen perform a productive function by reducing transaction costs.
- Private property rights motivate owners to use their resources in ways that benefit others and avoid doing harm to them. Private ownership also motivates owners to maintain and care for items they own and conserve valuable resources for the future.
- The production possibilities curve shows the maximum combination of any two products that can be produced with a fixed quantity of resources.
- Over time, the production possibilities curve of an economy can be shifted outward by (1) investment, (2) technological advances, (3) improved institutions, and (4) greater work effort (forgoing leisure).
- The law of comparative advantage indicates that the joint output of individuals, regions, and nations will be maximized when each productive activity is undertaken by the low-opportunity-cost supplier. When a good can be acquired through trade more economically than it can be produced directly, it makes sense to trade for it.
- In addition to the gains that occur when goods are moved toward those who value them most, trade also makes it possible to expand output through specialization, division of labor, mass production processes, and innovation. These improved production techniques have contributed greatly to our modern living standards.
- The size of the economic pie is variable, not fixed. Human ingenuity can expand output by discovering lower cost methods of production and new products that are highly valued relative to cost.
- Economies can either be organized by decentralized markets or be centrally planned by government through political decision-making. In varying degrees, all economies use a combination or mixture of these two methods.

Critical Analysis Questions

1. "If Jones trades a used car to Smith for $5,000, nothing new is created. Thus, there is no way the transaction can improve the welfare of people." Is this statement true? Why or why not?
2. *Why do people engage in trade? If one trading partner gains, must the others involved in the transaction lose an equal amount? Why or why not?
3. What are transaction costs, and why do they reduce the number of trades? How have companies such as eBay (and the Internet more generally) lowered transaction costs?
4. "People in business get ahead by exploiting the needs of their consumers. The gains of business are at the expense of suffering imposed on their customers." Evaluate this statement.
5. What is the major function of the middleman? Would people be better off if there were no middlemen? Why or why not?
6. If you have a private-ownership right to something, what does this mean? Does private ownership give you the right to do anything you want with the things that you own? Explain. How does private ownership influence the incentive of individuals to (a) take care of things, (b) conserve resources for the future, and (c) develop and modify things in ways that are beneficial to others? Explain.
7. What is the law of comparative advantage? According to the law of comparative advantage, what should be the distinguishing characteristics of the goods a nation produces? What should be the distinguishing characteristics of the goods a nation imports? How will international trade influence people's production levels and living standards? Explain.
8. *Does a 60-year-old tree farmer have an incentive to plant and care for Douglas fir trees that will not reach optimal cutting size for another 50 years?
9. *What forms of competition does a private property, market-directed economy authorize? What forms does it prohibit?
10. Why is exchange important to a nation's prosperity? How does trade influence the quantity of output that trading partners are able to produce? In a market economy, will there be a tendency for both resources and products to be supplied by low-cost producers? Why or why not? Does this matter? Explain.
11. Chick-fil-A's "Eat Mor Chikin" advertising campaign features three cows holding signs that say things like "Save the cows, eat more chicken." If consumers began eating more chicken and less beef, would the cattle population increase or decrease? Explain.
12. *In many states, ticket scalping, or reselling tickets to entertainment events at prices above the original purchase price, is prohibited. Who is helped and who is hurt by such prohibitions? How can owners who want to sell their tickets get around the prohibition? Do you think it would be a good idea to prohibit the resale of other things—automobiles, books, works of art, or stock shares—at prices higher than the original purchase price? Why or why not?
13. Two centuries ago, there were more buffalo than cattle in the United States. Even though millions of cattle are killed for beef consumption each year, the cattle population continues to grow while the buffalo are virtually extinct. Why?
14. Consider the following questions:
    a. Do you think that your work effort is influenced by whether there is a close link between personal output and personal compensation (reward)? Explain.
    b. Suppose the grades in your class were going to be determined by a random drawing at the end of the course. How would this influence your study habits?
    c. How would your study habits be influenced if everyone in the class was going to be given an A grade? How about if grades were based entirely on examinations composed of the end of chapter questions in the textbook?
    d. Do you think the total output of a nation will be influenced by whether or not there is a close link between the productive contribution of individuals and their personal reward? Why or why not?
15. In this chapter, it was stated that a private property right also involves having the right to transfer or exchange what you own with others. However, selling your organs is a violation of federal law, a felony punishable by up to five years in prison or a $50,000 fine. In fact, eBay intervened when a person put one of his kidneys up for sale on the auction site (the bidding reached $5.7 million before the auction was halted). Does this lack of legal ability to exchange mean that individuals do not own their own organs? Explain.
16. During the last four decades, entrepreneurs like Steve Jobs, Jeff Bezos, and Elon Musk have earned billions of dollars. Do you think the average American is better or worse off as the result of the economic activities of these individuals? Explain your response.

17. *As the skill level (and therefore earnings rate) of, say, an architect, computer specialist, or chemist increases, what happens to his or her opportunity cost of doing other things? How is the time spent on leisure likely to change?

18. *This question pertains to the addendum to* Chapter 2. The following tables show the production possibilities for two hypothetical countries, Italia and Nire. Which country has the comparative advantage in producing butter? Which country has the comparative advantage in producing guns? What would be a mutually agreeable rate of exchange between the countries?

Italia		Nire	
Guns	Butter	Guns	Butter
12	0	16	0
8	2	12	1
4	4	8	2
0	6	4	3
		0	4

*Asterisk denotes questions for which answers are given in Appendix B.

Addendum

Comparative Advantage, Specialization, and Gains from Trade

This addendum is for instructors who want to assign a more detailed numerical example demonstrating comparative advantage, specialization, and mutual gains from trade. Students who are uncertain about their understanding of these topics may also find this material enlightening. The international trade chapter later in the text provides still more information on trade and how it affects our lives.

We begin with hypothetical production possibilities curves for two countries, Slavia and Lebos, shown in **Exhibit A-1**. The numerical tables represent selected points from each country's production possibilities curve. To make calculations easier, we have assumed away increasing opportunity costs in production so that the production possibilities curves are linear.

Without trade, each country would be able to consume only what it can produce for itself. Let's arbitrarily assume that for survival, Slavia requires three units of food and Lebos

Exhibit A-1 Production Possibilities for Slavia and Lebos

For Slavia, the opportunity cost of producing one unit of clothing is equal to three units of food (1C = 3F). For Lebos, the opportunity cost of producing three units of clothing is equal to three units of food (3C = 3F or 1C = 1F). The difference in the opportunity costs of production will make possible mutually beneficial trade between the countries, with each specializing in its area of comparative advantage.

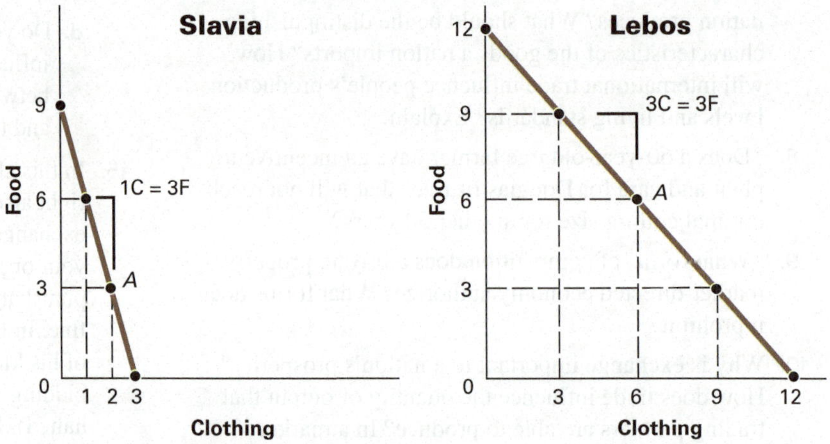

Slavia

Food	Clothing
9	0
6	1
3	2
0	3

3F = 1C

Lebos

Food	Clothing
12	0
9	3
6	6
3	9
0	12

3F = 3C

requires six units of food. Refer to point *A* in the exhibit, if Slavia were to produce the three units of food it requires, it would have enough resources remaining to produce two units of clothing. Similarly, if Lebos were to produce the six units of food it requires, it would have enough resources left to produce six units of clothing, again shown by point *A* in the exhibit. As we proceed, we will use this outcome as our benchmark outcome that occurs in the absence of specialization and trade between the countries.

Economic analysis suggests that both countries could gain if each were to specialize in the production of the good for which it has the comparative advantage and then trade for the other. First, let's figure out which country has a comparative advantage in the production of clothing. Doing so requires calculating the opportunity cost of producing clothing for each country. Because, in this example, the opportunity costs are constant at all points along the production possibilities curve, rather than increasing, this can be found by first selecting any two points on the production possibilities curve (or equivalently by comparing any two rows of numbers in the numerical tables given in the exhibit). For Slavia, moving from the point of producing six food units and one clothing unit to the alternative point of producing three food units and two clothing units, two clothing units, Slavia gains one clothing unit but must give up three units of food. For simplicity, the opportunity cost for Slavia can be written as 1C = 3F, where C stands for clothing and F for food. You might note that this same numerical trade-off is true for Slavia anywhere along its production possibilities curve (for example, beginning from nine food units and zero clothing units, it would also have to give up three food units to gain one unit of clothing).

Using a similar approach (taking any two points or two rows in the table) for Lebos shows that for every three units of clothing the country wishes to produce, it must give up three units of food (3C = 1F). This can be treated as any other mathematical equation, and can be simplified by dividing both sides by three, resulting in an opportunity cost of one clothing unit equals one food unit (1C = 1F). Now, compare this to the opportunity cost for Slavia (1C = 3F). Slavia must give up the production of three units of food for every one unit of clothing it produces, whereas Lebos must give up only one unit of food for every one unit of clothing it produces. Thus, Lebos gives up the production of *less* food for every unit of clothing. Lebos is the low-opportunity-cost producer of clothing, and thus, it has a comparative advantage in the production of clothing.

Because comparative advantage is a relative comparison, if one country has the comparative advantage in the production of one of the products, the other country must have the comparative advantage for the other good. Thus, because Lebos has the comparative advantage in clothing, it will be true that Slavia has the comparative advantage in food. However, it is worthwhile to show this here as well. To produce one unit of food, Lebos must give up one unit of clothing (recall the 1C = 1F opportunity cost). To produce one unit of food, Slavia must give up the production of only one-third of a unit of clothing (recall the 1C = 3F opportunity cost and rewrite the equation as 1 / 3C = 1F by dividing both sides of the equation by 3). Thus, Slavia gives up the production of *less* clothing for every unit of food produced. Slavia is the low-opportunity-cost producer of food, and thus has a comparative advantage in the production of food.

Suppose that, according to their comparative advantages, Lebos specializes in producing clothing and Slavia in food. From the last row of the table, Lebos can produce twelve units of clothing (and zero food) if it specializes in producing only clothing. From the top row of the table, Slavia can produce nine units of food (and zero clothing) if it specializes in producing only food. Note that this joint output (nine food and twelve clothing) is greater than the benchmark joint output (nine food and eight clothing) produced and consumed without trade.

If they are to trade, the countries now must find a mutually agreeable rate of exchange. Any rate of exchange *between* the two opportunity costs of 1C = 3F and 3C = 3F would be mutually agreeable. Here we will use 2C = 3F.

Recall that Slavia requires three units of food for survival. Now, however, they are specializing and producing nine units of food. Using this rate of exchange, Slavia would send its extra six units of food to Lebos in exchange for four units of clothing. After trade, Slavia would then have three units of food and four units of clothing. Compare this to the situation that existed before specialization and trade, in which Slavia had only three units of food and two units of clothing to consume. Specialization and trade have created two additional units of clothing for Slavia that it would not have had without trade.

With specialization, Lebos is producing twelve units of clothing. In the trade with Slavia, Lebos gave up four units of clothing to obtain six units of food. After trade, Lebos has eight units of clothing remaining and six units of food imported from Slavia. Compare this to the situation that existed before specialization and trade, in which Lebos had only six units of food and six units of clothing to consume. For Lebos, specialization and trade have also created two additional units of clothing that it would not have had without trade.

As this simple example shows, total output is greater and *both* countries are better off when they specialize in the area in which they have a comparative advantage. By doing so, each is able to consume a bundle of goods and services that exceeds what it could have achieved in the absence of trade. This concept applies equally to individuals, states, or nations. The typical worker could not begin to produce alone all of the things he or she can afford to buy with the money earned in a year by specializing and working in a single occupation. As our world has become more integrated over the past several hundred years, the gains that have occurred from specialization and trade are at the root of the significant improvements in well-being that we have experienced.

Part 2

Markets and Government

There are two primary methods of allocating scarce resources: markets and government

Economics has a great deal to say about how both markets and governments allocate scarce resources. It gives us insight about the conditions under which each will likely work well (and each will likely work poorly). The next four chapters will focus on this topic.

Market allocation of resources

Business firms purchase resources like materials, labor services, tools, and machines from households in exchange for income, bidding the resources away from their alternate uses. The firms then transform the resources into products like shoes, automobiles, food products, and medical services and sell them to households. In a market economy, businesses will continue to supply a good or service only if the revenues from the sale of the product are sufficient to cover the cost of the resources required for its production.

Entrepreneurs play an important role in the operation of markets. Their discovery of new products that are highly valued relative to cost and better (or lower cost) methods of production are a central element leading to higher income levels and living standards.

Government allocation of resources

Resource allocation by the government involves a more complex, three-sided exchange. In a democratic political setting, a legislative body levies taxes on voter-citizens, and these revenues are subdivided into budgets, which are allocated to government bureaus and agencies. In turn, the bureaus and agencies use the funds from their budgets to supply goods, services, and income transfers to voter-citizens. The legislative body is like a board of directors elected by the citizens. Legislators have an incentive to take action that will attract votes. Voters have an incentive to support legislators who provide them with goods, services, and transfers that are highly valued relative to their tax payments. When decisions are made democratically, political action will require the approval of a legislative majority.

This section will first analyze the operation of markets and then turn to the political process.

Chapter 3 Demand, Supply, and the Market Process

> I am convinced that if [the market system] were the result of deliberate human design, and if the people guided by the price changes understood that their decisions have significance far beyond their immediate aim, this mechanism would have been acclaimed as one of the greatest triumphs of the human mind.
>
> –Friedrich Hayek, Nobel Laureate[1]

> From the point of view of physics, it is a miracle that [8 million New Yorkers are fed each day] without any control mechanism other than sheer capitalism.
>
> –John H. Holland, scientist, Santa Fe Institute[2]

To those who study art, the *Mona Lisa* is much more than a famous painting of a woman. Looking beyond the overall picture, they see and appreciate the brush strokes, colors, and techniques embodied in the painting. Similarly, studying economics can help you to gain an appreciation for the details behind many things in your everyday life. During your last visit to the grocery store, you probably noticed the fruit and vegetable section. Next time, take a moment to ponder how potatoes from Idaho, oranges from Florida, apples from Washington, bananas from Honduras, kiwi fruit from New Zealand, and other items from around the world got there. Literally thousands of different individuals, *working independently*, were involved in the process. Their actions were so well coordinated, in fact, that the amount of each good was just about right to fill exactly the desires of your local community. Furthermore, even the goods shipped from halfway around the world were fresh and reasonably priced.

Media Home/Shutterstock.com

The produce section of your local grocery store is a great place to observe economics in action. Literally millions of individuals from around the world have been involved in the process of getting these goods to the shelves in just the right quantities. Market prices underlie this feat.

How does all this happen? The short answer is that it is the result of market prices and the incentives and coordination

[1]Friedrich Hayek, "The Use of Knowledge in Society," *American Economic Review* 35 (September 1945): 519–30.

[2]As quoted by Russell Ruthen in "Adapting to Complexity," *Scientific American* 268 (January 1993): 132.

that flow from them. To the economist, the operation of markets–including your local grocery market–is like the brush strokes underlying a beautiful painting. Reflecting on this point, Friedrich Hayek speculates that if the market system had been deliberately designed, it would be "acclaimed as one of the greatest triumphs of the human mind." Similarly, computer scientist John H. Holland argues that, from the viewpoint of physics, the feeding of millions of New Yorkers day after day with very few shortages or surpluses is a miraculous feat (refer to the chapter-opening quotations).

Amazingly, markets coordinate the actions of millions of individuals *without* central planning. There is no individual, political authority, or central planning committee in charge. Considering that there are more than 340 million Americans with widely varying skills and desires, and roughly 33 million businesses producing a vast array of products ranging from diamond rings to toilet paper, the coordination derived from markets is indeed an awesome achievement.

This chapter focuses on demand, supply, and the determination of market prices. For now, we will analyze the operation of competitive markets–that is, markets in which buyers and sellers are free to enter and exit. We will also assume that the property rights are well defined. Later, we will consider what happens when these conditions are absent.

The buyers' and sellers' desires and incentives determine prices and make markets work. We will begin with the demand (buyer's) side, then turn to the supply (seller's) side of the market.

Learning Objectives

3.1 Explain how consumers decide whether or not to purchase a good and how producers decide whether or not to supply it.

3.2 State the laws of demand and supply.

3.3 Explain the difference between a "change in demand" and a "change in quantity demanded" and distinguish it graphically.

3.4 Graph the demand and supply curves for a good and identify the corresponding market equilibrium price.

3.5 Explain the difference between a highly elastic and highly inelastic demand curve and distinguish it graphically.

3.6 Explain the role of profits and losses in a market economy and how they relate to the willingness to pay of consumers and the opportunity cost of production.

3.7 Explain the role of an entrepreneur in a market economy and how entrepreneurial success is related to economic progress.

3.8 Analyze the impact on the market price and equilibrium quantity of a good or service for each shift factor of the demand and supply curves.

3.9 Explain how the invisible hand of market prices guides self-interested individuals toward activities that benefit society.

3-1 Consumer Choice and the Law of Demand

Law of demand
A principle that states there is an inverse relationship between the price of a good and the quantity of it buyers are willing to purchase. As the price of a good increases, consumers will wish to purchase less of it. As the price decreases, consumers will wish to purchase more of it.

Clearly, prices influence our decisions. As the price of a good increases, we have to give up more of *other* goods if we want to buy it. Thus, as the price of a good rises, its opportunity cost increases (in terms of other goods that must be forgone to purchase it). This basic principle underlies the **law of demand**. ***The law of demand states that there is an inverse (or negative) relationship between the price of a good or service and the quantity of it that consumers are willing to purchase***. This inverse relationship means that price and the quantity consumers wish to purchase move in opposite directions. As the price increases, buyers purchase less—and as the price decreases, buyers purchase more.

The availability of **substitutes**—goods that help people achieve similar objectives—helps explain this inverse relationship. No single good is absolutely essential; everything can be replaced with something else. A chicken sandwich can be substituted for a cheeseburger. Wood, aluminum, bricks, and glass can take the place of steel. Going to the movies, playing tennis, watching television, and going to a football game are substitute forms of entertainment. When the price of a good increases, people cut back on their purchases of it and turn to substitute products.

Substitutes
Products that serve similar purposes. An increase in the price of one will cause an increase in demand for the other (examples include hamburgers and tacos, butter and margarine, Chevrolets and Fords).

3-1a The Market Demand Schedule

The lower portion of **Exhibit 3-1** shows a hypothetical *demand schedule* for pizza delivery in a city. A demand schedule is simply a table listing the various quantities of something consumers are willing to purchase at different prices. When the price of a large pizza delivery is $35, only 4,000 people per month order pizza delivery. As the price falls to $25, the quantity of pizza deliveries demanded rises to 8,000 per month; when the price falls to $10, the quantity demanded increases to 14,000 per month.

The upper portion of Exhibit 3-1 uses a graph to illustrate what would happen if we plotted the various prices and corresponding quantities from a demand schedule on a graph

Exhibit 3-1 Law of Demand

As the demand schedule shown in the table indicates, the number of people ordering pizza delivery (just like the consumption of other products) is inversely related to price. The data from the table are plotted as a demand curve in the graph. The inverse relationship between price and amount demanded reflects the fact that consumers will substitute away from a good as it becomes more expensive.

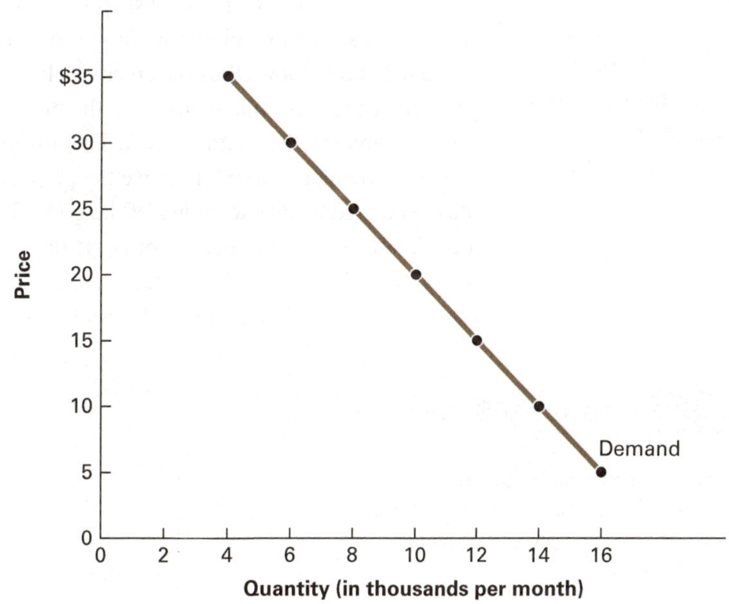

Price	Quantity (in thousands per month)
$35	4
30	6
25	8
20	10
15	12
10	14
5	16

and connected these points with a line. This is called the *demand curve*. When representing the demand schedule graphically, economists measure price on the vertical or *y*-axis and the amount demanded on the horizontal or *x*-axis. Because of the inverse relationship between price and amount purchased, the demand curve will have a negative slope—that is, it will slope downward to the right. More of a good will be purchased as its price decreases. This is the law of demand.

Read horizontally, the demand curve shows how much of a particular good consumers are willing to buy at a given price. Read vertically, the demand curve shows how much consumers value the good. The height of the demand curve at any quantity shows the maximum price consumers are willing to pay for an additional unit. If consumers value highly an additional unit of a product, they will be willing to pay a large amount for it. Conversely, if they place a low value on the additional unit, they will be willing to pay only a small amount for it.

Because the amount a consumer is willing to pay for a good is directly related to the good's value to them, the height of the demand curve indicates the marginal benefit (or value) consumers receive from additional units. (Recall that we briefly discussed marginal benefit in Chapter 1.) When viewed in this manner, the demand curve reveals that as consumers have more and more of a good or service, they value additional units less and less.

3-1b Consumer Surplus

Previously, we indicated that voluntary exchanges make both buyers and sellers better off. The demand curve can be used to illustrate the gains to consumers. Suppose you value a particular good at \$50, but you are able to purchase it for only \$30. Your net gain from buying the good is the \$20 difference. Economists call this net gain of buyers **consumer surplus**. Consumer surplus is simply the difference between the maximum amount consumers would be willing to pay and the amount they actually pay for a good.

Consumer surplus
The difference between the maximum price consumers are willing to pay and the price they actually pay. It is the net gain derived by the buyers of the good.

Exhibit 3-2 shows the consumer surplus for an entire market. The height of the demand curve measures how much buyers in the market value each unit of the good. The price indicates the amount they actually pay. The difference between these two—the triangular area below the demand curve but above the price paid—is a measure of the total consumer surplus generated by all exchanges of the good. The size of the consumer surplus, or triangular area, is affected by the market price. If the market price for the good falls, more of it will be purchased, resulting in a larger surplus for consumers. Conversely, if the market price rises, less of it will be purchased, resulting in a smaller surplus (net gain) for consumers.

Exhibit 3-2 Consumer Surplus

Consumer surplus is the area below the demand curve but above the actual price paid. This area represents the net gains to buyers from market exchange.

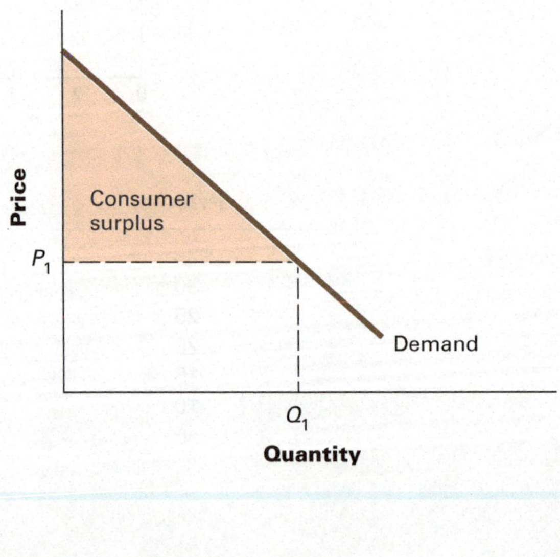

Because the value a consumer places on a particular unit of a good is shown by the corresponding height of the demand curve, we can use the demand curve to clarify the difference between the *marginal value* and *total value* of a good—a distinction we introduced briefly in Chapter 1. Returning to Exhibit 3-2, if consumers are currently purchasing Q_1 units, the marginal value of the good is indicated by the height of the demand curve at Q_1—the last unit consumed (or purchased). So at each quantity, the height of the demand curve shows the marginal value of that unit, which declines along a demand curve. The *total value* of the good, however, is equal to the combined value of all units purchased. This is the sum of the value of each unit (the heights along the demand curve) on the x-axis, out to and including unit Q_1. This total value is indicated graphically as the entire area under the demand curve out to Q_1 (the triangular area representing consumer surplus *plus* the unshaded rectangular area directly below it).

The total value to consumers of a good can be far greater than the marginal value of the last unit consumed. When additional units are available at a low price, the marginal value of a good may be quite low, even though its total value to consumers is exceedingly high. This is usually the case with water. The value of the first few units of water consumed per day will be exceedingly high. The consumer surplus derived from these units will also be large when water is plentiful at a low price. As more and more units are consumed, however, the *marginal value* of even something as important as water will fall to a low level. When water is cheap, then, people will use it not only for drinking, cleaning, and cooking but also for washing cars, watering lawns, flushing toilets, and maintaining fish aquariums. Thus, although the total value of water is rather large, its marginal value is quite low.

Consumers will tend to expand their consumption of a good until its price and *marginal value* are equal (which occurs at Q_1 in Exhibit 3-2 at a price of P_1). Thus, the price of a good (which equals marginal value) reveals little about the *total value* derived from the consumption of it. This is the reason that the market price of diamonds (which reflects their high marginal value) is greater than the market price of water (which has a low marginal value), even though the total value of diamonds is far less than the total value of water. Think of it this way: Beginning from your current levels of consumption, if you were offered a choice between one diamond or one gallon of water right now, which would you take? You would probably take the diamond, because at the margin it has more value to you than additional water. However, if given a choice between giving up *all* of the water you use or *all* of the diamonds you have, you would probably keep the water over diamonds, because water has more total value to you.

3-1c Responsiveness of Quantity Demanded to Price Changes: Elastic and Inelastic Demand Curves

As we previously noted, the availability of substitutes is the main reason why the demand curve for a good slopes downward. As the price of tacos rises, most consumers find hamburgers a reasonable substitute. Because of the ease of substitutability, the quantity of tacos demanded is quite sensitive to a change in their price. Economists would say that the demand for tacos is relatively *elastic* because a small price change will cause a rather large change in the amount purchased. Alternatively, goods like gasoline and electricity have fewer close substitutes. When their prices rise, it is harder for consumers to find substitutes for these products. When close substitutes are unavailable, even a large price change may not cause much of a change in the quantity demanded. In this case, an economist would say that the demand for such goods is relatively *inelastic*.

Graphically, this different degree of responsiveness is reflected in the steepness of the demand curve, as shown in **Exhibit 3-3**. The flatter demand curve (D_1, left frame) is for a product like tacos, for which the quantity purchased is highly responsive to a change in price. As the price increases from \$2.00 to \$4.00, the quantity demanded falls sharply from ten to four units. The steeper demand curve (D_2, right frame) is for a product like gasoline,

Exhibit 3-3 Elastic and Inelastic Demand Curves

The responsiveness of consumer purchases to a change in price is reflected in the steepness of the demand curve. The flatter demand curve (D_1) for tacos shows a higher degree of responsiveness and is called relatively elastic, while the steeper demand curve (D_2) for gasoline shows a lower degree of responsiveness and is called relatively inelastic.

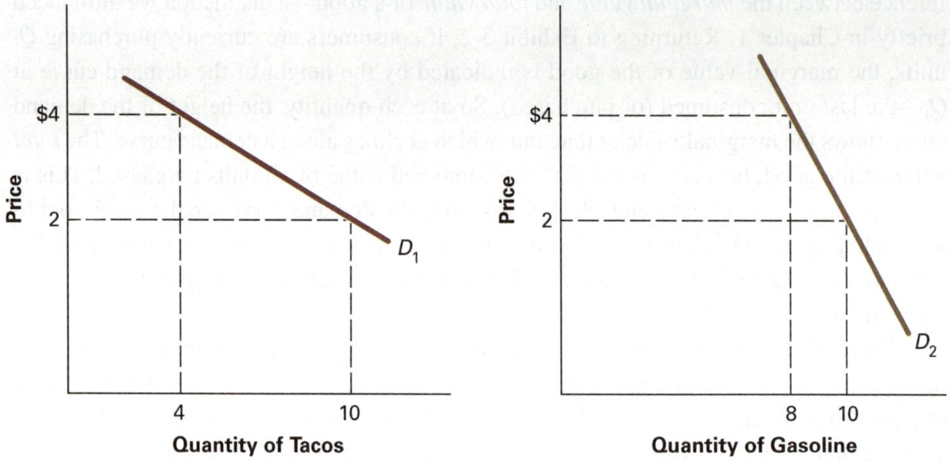

for which the quantity purchased is much less responsive to a change in price. For gasoline, an increase in price from $2.00 to $4.00 results in only a small reduction in the quantity purchased (from ten to eight units). An economist would say that the flatter demand curve D_1 is "relatively elastic," whereas the steeper demand curve D_2 is "relatively inelastic." The availability of substitutes is the main determinant of a product's elasticity or inelasticity and thus how flat or steep its demand curve is.

3-2 Changes in Demand versus Changes in Quantity Demanded

The purpose of the demand curve is to show what effect a price change will have on the quantity demanded (or purchased) of a good. Economists refer to a change in the quantity of a good purchased in response solely to a price change as a "change in *quantity demanded*." A change in quantity demanded is simply a movement along a demand curve from one point to another.

Changes in factors other than a good's price—such as consumers' income and the prices of closely related goods—will also influence the decisions of consumers to purchase a good. If one of these other factors changes, the entire demand curve will *shift* inward or outward. Economists refer to a shift in the demand curve as a "change in *demand*."

Failure to distinguish between a change in demand and a change in quantity demanded is one of the most common mistakes made by beginning economics students.[3] ***A change in demand is a shift in the entire demand curve. A change in quantity demanded is a movement along the same demand curve.*** The easiest way to distinguish between these two concepts is the following: If the change in consumer purchases is caused by a change in the price of the good, it is a change in quantity demanded—a movement along the demand curve; if the change in consumer purchases is due to a change in anything other than the price of the good (a change in consumer income, for example), it is a change in demand—a shift in the demand curve.

[3]Questions designed to test the ability of students to make this distinction are favorites of many economics instructors. A word to the wise should be sufficient.

Let us now examine some of the factors that cause a "change in demand"—an inward or outward shift in the entire demand curve.

1. Changes in consumer income. An increase in consumer income makes it possible for consumers to purchase more goods. If you were to win the lottery, or if your boss were to give you a raise, you would respond by increasing your spending on many products. Alternatively, when the economy goes into a recession, falling incomes and rising unemployment cause consumers to reduce their purchases of many items. A change in consumer income will result in consumers buying more or less of a product at all possible prices. When consumer income increases, in the case of most goods, individuals will purchase more of the good even if the price is unchanged. This is shown by a shift to the right—an outward shift—in the demand curve. Such a shift is called an *increase in demand*. A reduction in consumer income generally causes a shift to the left—an inward shift—in the demand curve, which is called a *decrease in demand*. Note that the appropriate terminology here is an increase or a decrease in demand, not an increase or a decrease in quantity demanded.

Exhibit 3-4 highlights the difference between a change in demand and a change in quantity demanded. The demand curve D_1 indicates the initial demand curve for tablet computers. At a price of \$300, consumers will purchase Q_1 units. If the price were to decline to \$100, the *quantity demanded* would increase from Q_1 to Q_3. The arrow in panel (a) indicates the change in *quantity demanded*—a movement along the original demand curve D_1 in response to the change in price. Now, alternatively suppose there were an increase in income that caused the *demand* for tablet computers to shift from D_1 to D_2. As indicated by the arrows in panel (b), the entire demand curve would shift outward. At the higher income level, consumers would be willing to purchase more tablet computers than before. This is true at a price of \$300, \$200, \$100, and every other price. The increase in income leads to an increase in *demand*—a shift in the entire curve.

2. Changes in the number of consumers in the market. Businesses that sell products in college towns are greatly saddened when summer arrives. As you might expect in these towns, the demand for many items—from pizza delivery to beer—falls during the summer.

Exhibit 3-4 Change in Demand versus Change in Quantity Demanded

Panel (a) shows a change in quantity demanded, a movement along the demand curve D_1, in response to a change in the price of tablet computers. Panel (b) shows a change in demand, a shift of the entire curve, in this case due to an increase in consumer income.

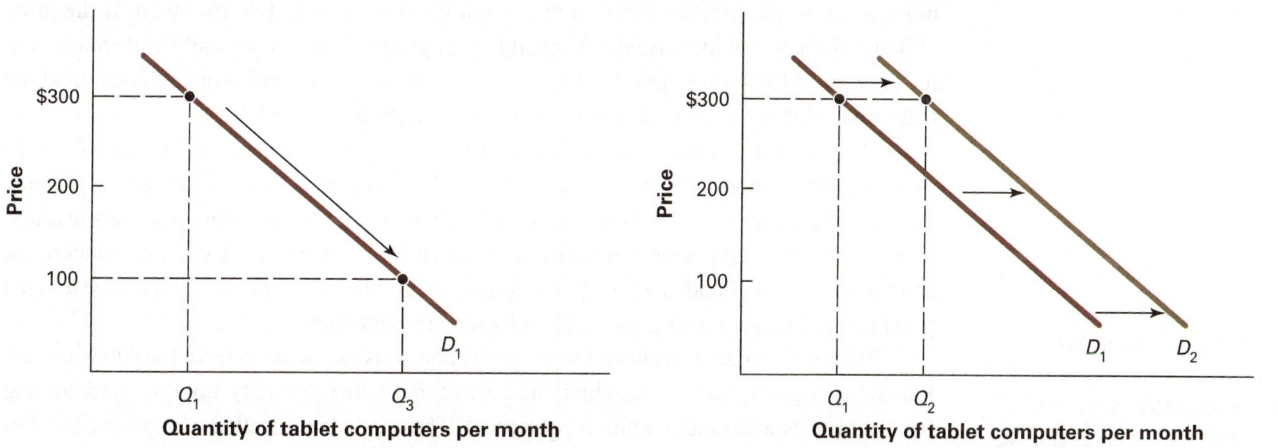

(a) Increase in quantity demanded

(b) Increase in demand

Exhibit 3-5 A Decrease in Demand

In college towns, the demand for pizza delivery decreases substantially when students go home for the summer. A decrease in demand is a leftward shift in the entire demand curve. Fewer pizzas are demanded at every price.

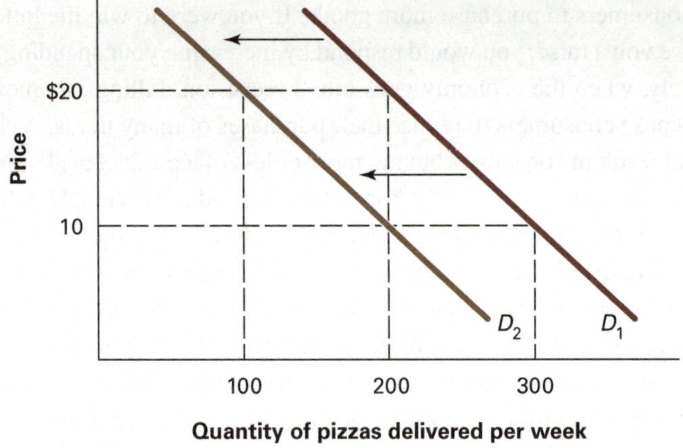

Exhibit 3-5 shows how the falling number of consumers in the market caused by students going home for the summer affects the demand for pizza delivery. With fewer customers, the demand curve shifts inward from D_1 to D_2. There is a decrease in demand; pizza stores sell fewer pizzas than before regardless of what price they originally charged. Had their original price been $20, then demand would fall from 200 pizzas per week to only 100. Alternatively, had their original price been $10, then demand would fall from 300 pizzas to 200. When autumn arrives and the students come back to town, there will be an increase in demand that will restore the curve to about its original position. As cities grow and shrink, and as international markets open up to domestic firms, changes in the number of consumers affect the demand for many products.

3. Changes in the price or availability of a related good. Changes in prices or availability of closely related products also influence the choices of consumers. Related goods may be either substitutes or complements. When two products perform similar functions or fulfill similar needs, they are substitutes. Economists define goods as substitutes when there is a direct relationship between the price of one and the demand for the other—meaning an increase in the price of one leads to an increase in demand for the other (they move in the same direction). For example, margarine is a substitute for butter. If the price of butter rises, it will increase the demand for margarine as consumers substitute margarine for the more expensive butter. Conversely, lower butter prices will reduce the demand for margarine, shifting the entire demand curve for margarine to the left.

When restaurants were closed during the COVID-19 pandemic, the demand for substitutes such as food delivery services and food to prepare at home from grocery stores dramatically increased. Gasoline and hybrid cars provide another example of a substitute relationship. When gasoline prices rise, the demand for gas–electric hybrid cars increases, and vice versa. Beef and chicken, pencils and pens, apples and oranges, and coffee and tea provide other examples of goods with substitute relationships.

Complements
Products that are usually consumed jointly (for example, bread and butter, hot dogs and hot dog buns). A decrease in the price of one will cause an increase in demand for the other.

Other products are consumed jointly, so the demands for them are linked together as well. Examples of goods that "go together" include peanut butter and jelly, hot dogs and hot dog buns, and tents and other camping equipment. These goods are called **complements**. For complements, a decrease in the price of one will not only increase its quantity demanded; it will also increase the demand for the other good. The reverse is also true. As a complement becomes more expensive, the quantity demanded of it will fall, and so will the demand for its complements. For example, if the price of steak rises, grocery stores can expect to sell fewer bottles of steak sauce, even if the price of steak sauce remains unchanged.

The process of entrepreneurial innovation also frequently results in the introduction of new substitute or complementary products that affect the demand for existing products. The introduction of the automobile reduced the demand for horses and buggies, while the rise in online shopping has increased the demand for shipping and packaging.

4. Changes in expectations. Consumers' expectations about the future also can affect the current demand for a product. If consumers begin to expect that a major hurricane will strike their area, the current demand for batteries and canned food will rise. Expectations about the future direction of the economy can also affect current demand. If consumers are pessimistic about the economy, they start spending less, causing the current demand for goods to fall. Perhaps most important is how a change in the expected future price of a good affects current demand. When consumers expect the price of a product to rise in the near future, their current demand for it will increase. Gasoline is a good example. If you expect the price to increase soon, you'll want to fill up your tank now before the price goes up. In contrast, consumers will delay a purchase if they expect the item to decrease in price. No doubt you have heard someone say, "I'll wait until it goes on sale." When consumers expect the price of a product to fall, current demand for it will decline.

5. Demographic changes. The demand for many products is strongly influenced by the demographic composition of the market. An increase in the elderly population in the United States in recent years has increased the demand for medical care, retirement housing, and vacation travel. The demand curves for these goods have shifted to the right. During the 1980s, the number of people aged 15 to 24 fell by more than 5 million. Because young people are a major part of the U.S. market for jeans, the demand for jeans fell by more than 100 million pairs over the course of the decade.[4] More recently, the increased use of cell phones has led to a dramatic reduction in the demand for digital cameras and alarm clocks.

6. Changes in consumer tastes and preferences. Why do preferences change? Preferences change because people change, because circumstances change, and because people acquire new information. The demand for high-carbohydrate foods like white bread has fallen substantially, whereas the demand for low-carbohydrate foods like beef has risen in response to changing trends in diet programs and eating habits. During the COVID-19 pandemic, knowledge of the effectiveness of face masks in preventing spread of the disease led to large increases in demand for the product. Trends in the markets for clothing, toys, collectibles, and entertainment are constantly causing changes in the demand for these products as well. Firms may even try to change consumer preferences for their own products through advertising and information brochures.

The accompanying **Thumbnail Sketch** summarizes the major factors that cause a change in *demand*—a shift of the entire demand curve—and points out that quantity *demanded* (but not demand) will change in response to a change in the price of a good.

3-3 Producer Choice and the Law of Supply

Now let's shift our focus to producers and the supply side of the market. How does the market process determine the amount of each good that will be produced? As we discussed in the last chapter, entrepreneurs, generally using a business firm, decide how resources

[4]These figures are from Suzanne Tregarthen, "Market for Jeans Shrinks," *The Margin* 6, no. 3 (January–February 1991): 28.

Thumbnail Sketch

Factors That Cause Changes in Demand and Quantity Demanded

This factor changes the quantity demanded of a good:

1. The price of the good: A higher price decreases the quantity demanded; a lower price increases the quantity demanded.

These factors change the demand for a good:

1. Consumer income: Lower consumer income will generally decrease demand; higher consumer income will generally increase demand.
2. Number of consumers in the market: Fewer consumers decreases demand; more consumers increases demand.

3a. Price or availability of a substitute good: A decrease in the price (or increase in the availability) of a substitute decreases the demand for the original good; an increase in the price (or decrease in the availability) of a substitute increases the demand for the original good.

3b. Price or availability of a complementary good: An increase in the price (or decrease in the availability) of a complement decreases the demand for the original good; a decrease in the price (or increase in the availability) of a complement increases the demand for the original good.

4. Expected future price of the good: If the price of a good is expected to fall in the future, the current demand for it will decrease; if the price of a good is expected to rise in the future, the current demand for it will increase.
5. Demographic changes: Population trends in age, gender, race, and other factors can increase or decrease demand for specific goods.
6. Consumer preferences: Changes in consumer tastes and preferences can increase or decrease demand for specific goods.

will be combined and what goods and services they will be used to produce. The producer–entrepreneur converts resources into goods and services by doing the following:

1. organizing productive inputs and resources, like land, labor, capital, natural resources, and intermediate goods;
2. transforming and combining these inputs into goods and services; and
3. selling the final products to consumers.

Producers have to purchase the resources at prices determined by market forces. Predictably, the owners of these resources will supply the resources only at prices at least equal to what they could earn elsewhere. Put another way, each resource the producers buy to make their product has to be bid away from all other potential uses. Its owner has to be paid its opportunity cost. The sum of the producer's cost of each resource used to produce a good will equal the **opportunity cost of production**.

Opportunity cost of production
The total economic cost of producing a good or service. The cost component includes the opportunity cost of all resources, including those owned by the firm. The opportunity cost is equal to the value of the production of other goods sacrificed as the result of producing the good.

There is an important difference between the opportunity cost of production and standard accounting measures of cost. Accountants generally do not count the cost of assets owned by the firm or services provided by its owners when they calculate the firm's cost. But economists do. Economists consider the fact that these resources could be used some other way—in other words, that they have an opportunity cost. Unless these opportunity costs are covered, the resources will eventually be used in other ways.

The opportunity cost of the assets owned by the firm is the earnings these assets could have generated if they were used in another way. Consider a manufacturer that invests \$100 million in buildings and equipment to produce shirts. Instead of buying buildings and equipment, the manufacturer could simply put the \$100 million in the bank and let it draw interest. If the \$100 million were earning, say, 5 percent interest, the firm would make \$5 million on that money in a year's time. This \$5 million in forgone interest is part of the firm's opportunity cost of producing shirts. Unlike an accountant, an economist will take that $5 million opportunity cost into account. If the firm plans to invest the money in shirt-making equipment, it had better earn more from making the shirts than the $5 million it could earn by simply putting the money in the bank. If the firm can't generate enough to cover all of its costs, including the opportunity cost of assets owned by the firm, it will not continue in business. If the firm were earning only $3 million producing shirts, it might be earning profit on its accounting statement, but it would be suffering a $2 million economic loss relative to simply putting the money in the bank. Additional economic costs to consider include the opportunity cost of the labor and entrepreneurial services provided by the owner and rent foregone on assets owned by the firm.

3-3a The Role of Profits and Losses

Firms earn a **profit** when the revenues from the goods and services that they supply exceed the opportunity cost of the resources used to make them. Consumers will not buy goods and services unless they value them at least as much as their purchase price. For example, Susan would not be willing to pay $40 for a pair of jeans unless she valued them by at least that amount. At the same time, the seller's opportunity cost of supplying a good will reflect the value consumers place on *other* goods that could have been produced with those same resources. This is true precisely because the seller has to bid those resources away from other producers wanting to use them.

Think about what it means when, for example, a firm is able to produce jeans at a cost of $30 per pair and sell them for $40, thereby earning a profit of $10 per pair. The $30 opportunity cost of the jeans indicates that the resources used to produce the jeans could have been used to produce other items worth $30 to consumers (perhaps a denim backpack). In turn, the profit indicates that consumers value the jeans more than other goods that might have been produced with the resources used to supply the jeans.

The willingness of consumers to pay a price greater than a good's opportunity cost indicates that they value the good more than other things that could have been produced with the same resources. Viewed from this perspective, profit is a reward earned by entrepreneurs who use resources to produce goods consumers value more highly than the other goods those resources could have produced. In essence, this profit is a signal that an entrepreneur has increased the value of the resources under his or her control.

Producer–entrepreneurs will seek to undertake production of goods and services that will generate profit. However, things do not always turn out as expected. Sometimes, business firms are unable to sell their products at prices that will cover their costs. **Loss** occurs when the revenue derived from sales is insufficient to cover the opportunity cost of the resources used to produce a good or service. Losses indicate that the firm has reduced the value of the resources it has used. In other words, consumers would have been better off if those resources had been used to produce something else. In a market economy, losses will eventually cause firms to go out of business, and the resources they previously utilized will be directed toward other things valued more highly, or to other firms that can produce those same goods at a lower cost.

Profits and losses play a very important role in a market economy. They determine which products (and firms) will expand and survive and which will contract and be driven from the market. Clearly, there is a positive side to business failures. As our preceding discussion highlights, losses and business failures free up resources being used unwisely so they can be put to use by other firms providing consumers with more value.

Keys to Economic Prosperity

Profits and Losses

Profits direct producers toward activities that increase the value of resources; losses impose a penalty on those who reduce the value of resources.

Profit
An excess of sales revenue relative to the opportunity cost of production. The cost component includes the opportunity cost of all resources, including those owned by the firm. Therefore, profit accrues only when the value of the good produced is greater than the value of the resources used for its production.

Loss
A deficit of sales revenue relative to the opportunity cost of production. Losses are a penalty imposed on those who produce goods even though they are valued less than the resources required for their production.

3-3b Market Supply Schedule

How will producer–entrepreneurs respond to a change in product price? Other things constant, a higher price will increase the producer's incentive to supply the good. Established producers will expand the scale of their operations, and over time new entrepreneurs,

Exhibit 3-6 Supply Curve

As the price of a product increases, other things constant, producers will increase the amount of the product supplied to the market.

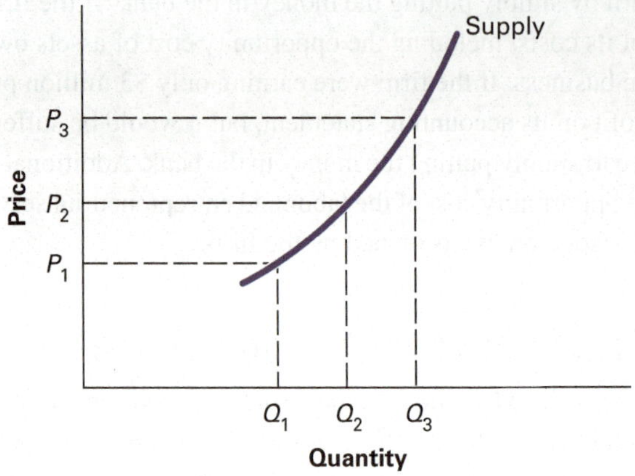

Law of supply
A principle that states there is a direct relationship between the price of a good and the quantity of it producers are willing to supply. As the price of a good increases, producers will wish to supply more of it. As the price decreases, producers will wish to supply less.

seeking personal gain, will enter the market and begin supplying the product, too. ***The* law of supply *states that there is a direct (or positive) relationship between the price of a good or service and the amount of it that suppliers are willing to produce. This direct relationship means that the price and the quantity producers wish to supply move in the same direction. As the price increases, producers will supply more—and as the price decreases, they will supply less*.**

Like the law of demand, the law of supply reflects the basic economic principle that incentives matter. Higher prices increase the reward entrepreneurs get from selling their products. Other things constant, as the price of a product rises, the more of it entrepreneurs will be willing to supply. Conversely, as the price of a product falls, entrepreneurs will supply fewer units. Just think about how many hours of tutoring services you would be willing to supply for different prices. Would you be willing to spend more time tutoring students if instead of $25 per hour, tutoring paid $50 per hour? The law of supply suggests you would, and producers of other goods and services are no different.

Exhibit 3-6 illustrates the law of supply. The curve shown in the exhibit is called a *supply curve*. Because there is a direct relationship between a good's price and the amount offered for sale by suppliers, the supply curve has a positive slope. It slopes upward to the right. Read horizontally, the supply curve shows how much of a particular good producers are willing to produce and sell at a given price. Read vertically, the supply curve reveals important information about the cost of production. The height of the supply curve indicates both (1) the minimum price necessary to induce producers to supply that additional unit and (2) the opportunity cost of producing that additional unit. These are both measured by the height of the supply curve because the minimum price required to induce a supplier to sell a unit is precisely the marginal cost of producing it.

Producer surplus
The difference between the price that suppliers actually receive and the minimum price they would be willing to accept. It measures the net gains to producers and resource suppliers from market exchange. It is not the same as profit.

3-3c Producer Surplus

We previously used the demand curve to illustrate consumer surplus, the net gains of buyers from market exchanges. The supply curve can be used in a similar manner to illustrate the net gains of producers and resource suppliers. Suppose that you are an aspiring musician and are willing to perform a two-hour concert for $500. If a promoter offers to pay you $750 to perform the concert, you will accept and receive $250 more than your minimum price. This $250 net gain represents your **producer surplus**. In effect, producer surplus is the difference between the amount a supplier actually receives (based on the market price) and the minimum price required to induce the supplier to produce the given units (their

Exhibit 3-7 Producer Surplus

Producer surplus is the area above the supply curve but below the actual sales price. This area represents the net gains to producers and resource suppliers from production and exchange.

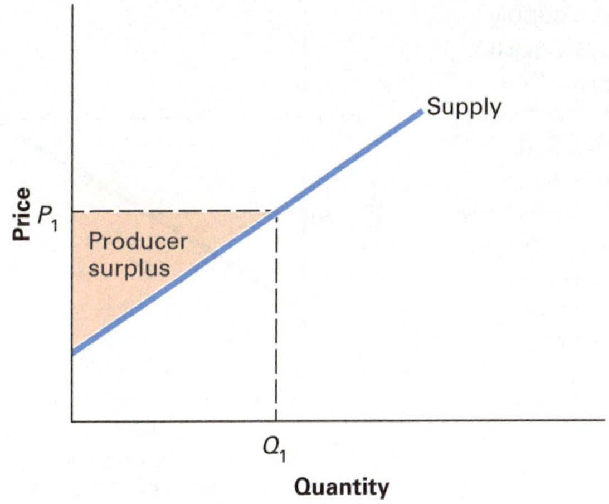

marginal cost). The shaded area of **Exhibit 3-7** illustrates the measurement of producer surplus for an entire market.

It's important to note that producer surplus represents the gains received by all parties contributing resources to the production of a good. In this respect, producer surplus is fundamentally different from profit. Profit accrues to the owners of the business firm producing the good, whereas producer surplus encompasses the net gains derived by all people who help produce the good, including those employed by or selling resources to the firm.

3-3d Responsiveness of Quantity Supplied to Price Changes: Elastic and Inelastic Supply Curves

Like the quantity demanded, the responsiveness of the quantity supplied to a change in price is different for different goods. The supply curve is said to be relatively elastic when a modest change in price leads to a large change in quantity supplied. This is generally true when the additional resources needed to expand output can be obtained with only a small increase in their price. Consider the supply of soft drinks. The contents of soft drinks—primarily carbonated water, sugar, and flavoring—are abundantly available. A sharp increase in the use of these ingredients by soft drink producers is unlikely to push up their price much. Therefore, as **Exhibit 3-8** illustrates, if the price of soft drinks were to rise from $1.50 to $2.25, producers would be willing to expand output sharply from 100 million to 200 million cans per month. A 50 percent increase in price leads to a 100 percent expansion in quantity supplied. The larger the increase in quantity in response to a higher price, the more elastic the supply curve. The flatness of the supply curve for soft drinks reflects the fact that it is highly elastic.

In contrast, when the quantity supplied is not very responsive to a change in price, supply is said to be relatively inelastic. In this case, the supply curve has a very steep slope. Physicians' services are an example. If the earnings of doctors increase from $100 to $150 per hour, there will be some increase in the quantity of the services they provide. Some physicians will work longer hours; others may delay retirement. Yet these adjustments are likely to result in only a small increase in the quantity supplied because it takes a long time to train a physician and the number of qualified doctors who are working in other occupations or who are outside of the labor force is small. Therefore, as panel (b) of Exhibit 3-8 shows, a 50 percent increase in the price of physician services leads to only a 20 percent expansion in the quantity supplied. Unlike soft drinks, higher prices for physician services do not generate much increase in quantity supplied. Economists would say that the supply of physician services is relatively inelastic.

Exhibit 3-8 Elastic and Inelastic Supply Curves

Panel (a) illustrates a supply curve that is relatively elastic and therefore the quantity supplied is highly responsive to a change in price. Soft drinks provide an example. Panel (b) illustrates a relatively inelastic supply curve, one in which the quantity supplied increases by only a small amount in response to a change in price. This is the case for physician services.

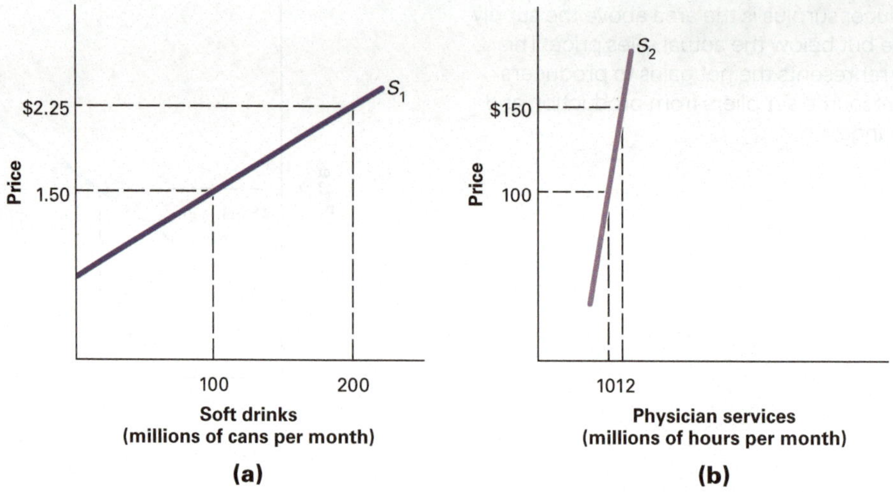

Outstanding Economist

Alfred Marshall (1842–1924)

Historic Collection/Alamy Stock Photo

British economist Alfred Marshall was one of the most influential economists of his era. Many concepts and tools that form the core of modern microeconomics originated with Marshall in his famous *Principles of Economics*, first published in 1890. Marshall introduced the concepts of supply and demand, equilibrium, elasticity, consumers' and producers' surplus, and the idea of distinguishing between short-run and long-run changes.

3-4 Changes in Supply versus Changes in Quantity Supplied

Like demand, it is important to distinguish between a change in the *quantity supplied* and a change in *supply*. When producers change the number of units they are willing to supply in response to a change in price, this movement along the supply curve is called a "change in *quantity supplied*." A change due to any factor *other than the price* that shifts the supply curve is called a "change in *supply*."

As we previously discussed, profit-seeking entrepreneurs will produce a good only if its sales price is expected to exceed its opportunity cost of production. Therefore, changes that affect the opportunity cost of supplying a good will also influence the amount of it producers are willing to supply. These other factors, such as the prices of resources used to make the good and the level of technology available, are held constant when we draw the supply curve. The supply curve itself reflects quantity changes only in response to price changes. Changes in these other factors shift the supply curve. Factors that increase the opportunity

Exhibit 3-9 A Decrease in Supply

Crude oil is a resource used to produce gasoline. When the price of crude oil rises, it increases the cost of producing gasoline and results in a decrease in the supply of gasoline.

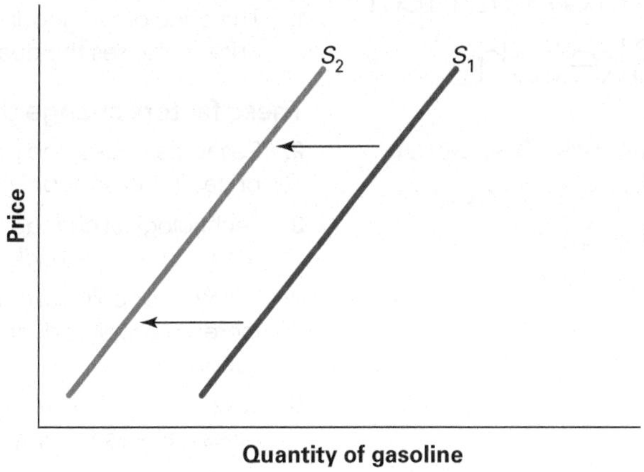

cost of providing a good will discourage production and decrease supply, shifting the entire curve inward to the left. Conversely, changes that lower the opportunity cost of producers will encourage production and increase supply, shifting the entire curve outward to the right.

Let us now examine the primary factors that will cause a change in supply and shift the entire curve right or left.

1. Changes in resource prices. How will an increase in the price of a resource, such as wages of workers or the materials used to produce a product, affect the supply of a good? Higher resource prices will increase the cost of production, reducing the profitability of firms supplying the good. The higher cost will induce firms to reduce their output. With time, some may even be driven out of business. As **Exhibit 3-9** illustrates, higher resource prices will reduce the supply of the good, causing a shift to the left in the supply curve from S_1 to S_2. Alternatively, a reduction in the price of a resource used to produce a good will cause an increase in supply—a rightward shift in the supply curve—as firms expand output in response to the lower costs and increased profitability of supplying the good.

2. Changes in technology. Like lower resource prices, technological improvements—the discovery of new, lower-cost production techniques—reduce production costs, and thereby increase supply. Technological advances have affected the cost of almost everything. Before the invention of the printing press, books had to be handwritten. Just imagine the massive reduction in cost and increase in the supply of books caused by this single invention. Similarly, improved farm machinery has vastly expanded the supply of agricultural products through the years. The field of robotics has reduced the cost of producing airplanes, automobiles, and other types of machinery. Better computer chips have drastically reduced the cost of producing electronics. In the 1980s, a simple calculator cost more than $100, a microwave oven almost $500, and a cell phone more than $4,000. Even the prices of televisions have fallen substantially in recent decades. Again, technological advances explain these changes.

3. Elements of nature and political disruptions. Natural disasters and changing political conditions can also alter supply, sometimes dramatically. In some years, good weather leads to "bumper crops," increasing the supply of agricultural products. At other times, freezes or droughts lead to poor harvests, reducing supply. War and political unrest in the Middle East region have had a major impact on the supply of oil several times during the past few decades. The COVID-19 pandemic resulted in worldwide disruptions

Thumbnail Sketch

Factors That Cause Changes in Supply and Quantity Supplied

This factor changes the quantity supplied of a good:

1. The price of the good: A lower price decreases the quantity supplied; a higher price increases the quantity supplied.

These factors change the supply of a good:

2. Resource prices (the prices of things used to make the good): Lower resource prices increase supply; higher resource prices decrease supply.
3. Technological change: A technological improvement increases supply; a technological setback decreases supply.
4. Weather or political conditions: Favorable weather or good political conditions increase supply; adverse weather conditions or poor political conditions decrease supply.
5. Taxes imposed on the producers of a good: Lower taxes increase supply; higher taxes decrease supply.

to production, temporarily reducing the supply of many goods and services. Factors such as these will alter supply.

4. Changes in taxes. If the government increases the taxes on the sellers of a product, the result will be the same as any other increase in the cost of doing business. The added tax that sellers have to pay will reduce their willingness to sell the product at any given price. Each unit must now be sold for a price that covers not only the opportunity cost of production but also the tax. For example, a special tax is levied on commercial airline tickets, partially to cover the cost of airport security. This tax increases the cost of air travel and thereby reduces the supply (a shift to the left in the supply curve).

The accompanying **Thumbnail Sketch** summarizes the major factors that change *supply* (a shift of the entire supply curve) and quantity supplied (a movement along the supply curve).

3-5 How Market Prices Are Determined: Demand and Supply Interact

Market
An abstract concept encompassing the forces of demand and supply and the interaction of buyers and sellers with the potential for exchange to occur.

Equilibrium
A state in which the conflicting forces of demand and supply are in balance. When a market is in equilibrium, the decisions of consumers and producers are brought into harmony with one another, and the quantity demanded will equal the quantity supplied.

Consumer–buyers and producer–entrepreneurs make decisions independent of each other, but market prices coordinate their choices and influence their actions. To the economist, a **market** is not a physical location but an abstract concept that encompasses the forces generated by the decisions of buyers and sellers. A market may be quite narrow (for example, the market for grade A jumbo eggs), or it may be quite broad like when we lump diverse goods into a single market, such as the market for all "consumer goods." There is also a wide range of sophistication among markets. The New York Stock Exchange is a highly formal, computerized market. Each weekday, buyers and sellers, who seldom meet, electronically exchange corporate shares they own worth billions of dollars. In contrast, a neighborhood market for babysitting services or tutoring in economics may be highly informal, bringing together buyers and sellers primarily by word of mouth.

Equilibrium ***is a state in which the conflicting forces of demand and supply are in balance. When a market is in equilibrium, the decisions of consumers and producers are brought into harmony with one another, and the quantity demanded will equal the quantity supplied.*** In equilibrium, it is possible for both buyers and sellers to realize their choices simultaneously. What could bring these diverse interests into harmony? The answer is market prices.

3-5a Market Equilibrium

As we have learned, a higher price will reduce the quantity of a good demanded by consumers. Conversely, a higher price will increase the quantity of a good supplied by producers. The market price of a good will tend to change in a direction that will bring the quantity of a good consumers want to buy into balance with the quantity producers want to sell. If the price is too high, the quantity supplied by producers will exceed the quantity demanded. Producers will be unable to sell as much as they would like unless they reduce their price. Alternatively, if the price is too low, the quantity demanded by consumers will exceed the quantity supplied. Some consumers will be unable to get as much as they would like, unless they are willing to pay a higher price to bid some of the good away from other potential customers. Thus, there will be a tendency for the price in a market to move toward the price that brings the two into balance.

People have a tendency to think of consumers wanting lower prices and producers wanting higher prices. Although this is true, price changes frequently trend toward the middle of the two extremes. When a local store has an excess supply of a particular item, how does it get rid of it? By having a sale or otherwise lowering its price. Firms often lower their prices in order to get rid of excess supply.

In contrast, excess demand is solved by consumers bidding up prices. For example, at initial box office prices, the quantity of tickets demanded for a World Series game or a popular band's upcoming concert often exceeds the quantity offered for sale. As a result, the immediate value of a ticket on the resale market can be much higher than the original price. This sometimes occurs with popular Christmas toys as well. Rather than going without, consumers attempt to outbid other purchasers. When excess demand is present, market prices tend to rise, bringing the quantity demanded in line with the quantity supplied.

As these examples illustrate, whenever quantity supplied and quantity demanded are not in balance, there is a tendency for price to change in a manner that will correct the imbalance. It is possible to show this process graphically with the supply and demand curves we have developed in this chapter. **Exhibit 3-10** shows hypothetical supply and demand curves in the market for a basic calculator. At a high price—$12, for example—producers will plan to supply 600 calculators per day, whereas consumers will choose to purchase only 450. An excess supply of 150 calculators (shown by distance *ab* in the graph) will result. Unsold calculators will push the inventories of producers upward. To get rid of some of their calculators in inventory, some producers will cut their price to increase their sales. Other firms will have to lower their price, too, as a result, or sell even fewer calculators. This lower price will make supplying calculators less attractive to producers. Some of them will go out of business. Others will reduce their output or perhaps produce other products. How low will the price of calculators go? As the figure shows, when the price has declined to $10, the quantity supplied by producers and the quantity demanded by consumers will be in balance at 550 calculators per day. At this price ($10), the quantity demanded by consumers just equals the quantity supplied by producers, and the choices of the two groups are brought into harmony.

What will happen if the price per calculator is lower—$8, for example? In this case, the amount demanded by consumers (650 units) will exceed the amount supplied by producers (500 units). An excess demand of 150 units (shown by the distance *cd* in the graph) will be the result. Some consumers who are unable to purchase the calculators at $8 per unit because of the inadequate supply would be willing to pay a higher price. Recognizing this fact, producers will raise their price. As the price increases to $10, producers will expand their output and consumers will cut down on their consumption. At the $10 price, equilibrium will be restored.

Exhibit 3-10 Supply and Demand

The table indicates the supply and demand conditions for calculators. These conditions are also illustrated by the graph. When the price exceeds $10, an excess supply is present, which places downward pressure on price. In contrast, when the price is less than $10, an excess demand results, which causes the price to rise. Thus, the market price will tend toward $10, at which point the quantity demanded will be equal to the quantity supplied.

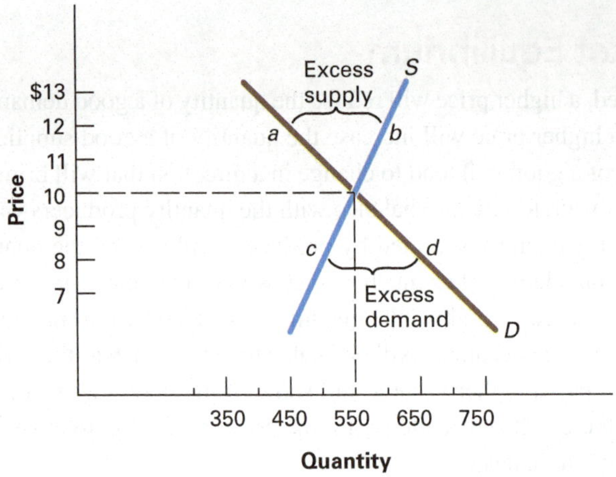

Price of Calculators (dollars)	Quantity Supplied (per day)	Quantity Demanded (per day)	Condition in the Market	Direction of Pressure on Price
$13	625	400	Excess supply	Downward
12	600	450	Excess supply	Downward
11	575	500	Excess supply	Downward
10	550	550	Balance	Equilibrium
9	525	600	Excess demand	Upward
8	500	650	Excess demand	Upward
7	475	700	Excess demand	Upward

3-5b Efficiency and Market Equilibrium

Economic efficiency
A situation in which all of the potential gains from trade have been realized. An action is efficient only if it creates more benefit than cost. With well-defined property rights and competition, market equilibrium is efficient.

When a market reaches equilibrium, all the gains from trade have been fully realized and **economic efficiency** is present. Economists often use economic efficiency as a standard to measure outcomes under alternative circumstances. The central idea of efficiency is a cost-versus-benefit comparison. On the one hand, undertaking an economic action will be efficient only if it generates more benefit than cost. On the other hand, undertaking an action that generates more cost than benefit is inefficient. For a market to be efficient, all trades that generate more benefit than cost need to be undertaken. In addition, economic efficiency requires that no trades creating more cost than benefit be undertaken.

A deeper examination of the way that markets work can help us understand the concept of efficiency. The supply curve reflects producers' opportunity cost. Each point along the supply curve indicates the minimum price for which the units of a good could be produced without a loss to the seller. Assuming no other third parties are affected by the production of this good, the height of the supply curve represents the opportunity cost to society of producing and selling the good. On the other side of the market, each point along the demand curve indicates how consumers value an extra unit of the good—that is, the maximum amount the consumer is willing to pay for the extra unit. Again assuming that no other third parties are affected, the height of the demand curve represents the benefit to society of producing and selling the good. Any time the consumer's valuation of a unit (the benefit) exceeds the producer's minimum supply price (the cost), producing and selling the unit is consistent with economic efficiency. The trade will result in mutual gain to both parties. When property rights are well defined and only the buyers and sellers are affected by production and exchange, competitive market forces will automatically guide a market toward an equilibrium level of output that satisfies economic efficiency.

Exhibit 3-11 Economic Efficiency

When markets are competitive and property rights are well defined, the equilibrium reached by a market satisfies economic efficiency. All units that create more benefit (the buyer's valuation shown by the height of the demand curve) than cost (opportunity cost of production shown by the height of the supply curve) are produced. This maximizes the total gains from trade, the combined area represented by consumer and producer surplus.

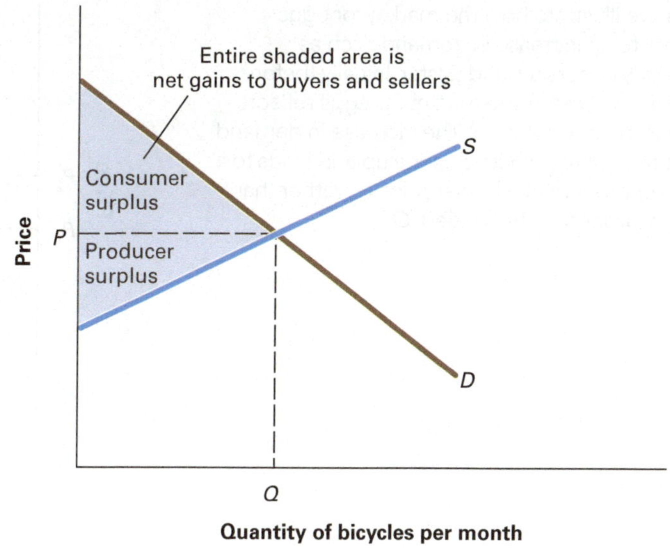

Exhibit 3-11 illustrates why this is true. Suppliers of bicycles will produce additional bicycles as long as the market price exceeds their opportunity cost of production (shown by the height of the supply curve). Similarly, consumers will continue to purchase additional bikes as long as their benefit (shown by the height of the demand curve) exceeds the market price. Eventually, market forces will result in an equilibrium output level of Q and a price of P. At this point, all the bicycles providing benefits to consumers that exceed the costs to suppliers will be produced. Economic efficiency is met because all of the potential consumer and producer gains from exchange (shown by the shaded area) have occurred. The point of market equilibrium is also the point where the combined area showing consumer and producer surplus is the greatest.

When fewer than Q bicycles are produced, some bicycles valued more by consumers than the opportunity cost of producing them are not being produced. This is not consistent with economic efficiency. On the other hand, if output is expanded beyond Q, inefficiency will also result because some of the bicycles cost more to produce than consumers are willing to pay for them. Prices in competitive markets will direct producers and consumers toward the level of output consistent with economic efficiency.

3-6 How Markets Respond to Changes in Demand and Supply

How will a market adjust to a change in demand? **Exhibit 3-12** shows the market adjustment to an increase in the demand for eggs around Easter. Demand D_1 and supply S are typical throughout much of the year. During the two weeks before Easter, however, consumer demand for eggs rises because people purchase them to decorate, too. This shifts egg demand from D_1 to D_2 during that time of year. The increase in demand pushes the price upward from P_1 to P_2 (typically by about 20 cents per dozen) and results in a larger equilibrium quantity traded (Q_2 rather than Q_1—an increase of typically around 600 million eggs). There is a new equilibrium at point b around Easter (versus point a during the rest of the year).

Although consumers may not be happy about paying a higher price for eggs around Easter, the higher price serves two essential purposes. First, it encourages consumers to

Exhibit 3-12 Market Adjustment to Increase in Demand

Here, we illustrate how the market for eggs adjusts to an increase in demand such as generally occurs around Easter. Initially (before the Easter season), the market for eggs reflects demand D_1 and supply S. The increase in demand (shift from D_1 to D_2) pushes price up and leads to a new equilibrium at a higher price (P_2 rather than P_1) and larger quantity traded (Q_2).

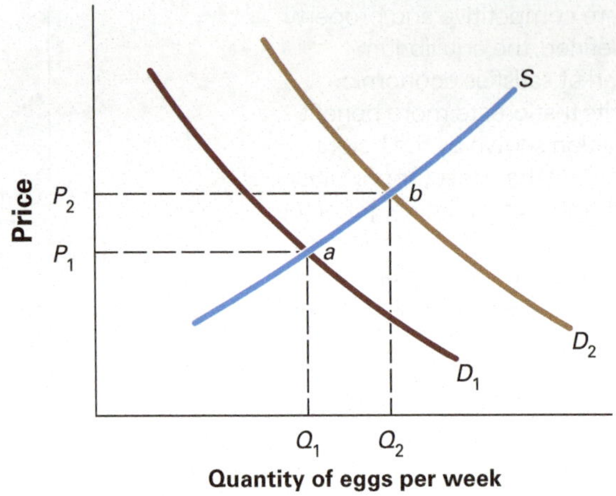

Hub.-Wilh. Domröse/Shutterstock.com

The tradition of coloring and hunting for eggs causes an increase in demand for eggs around Easter. As Exhibit 3-12 illustrates, this leads to higher egg prices and costly actions by producers to supply a larger quantity during this period.

conserve on their usage of eggs. Some consumers may purchase only two dozen eggs to color, rather than three; other consumers may skip having an omelet for breakfast and have yogurt instead. These steps on the consumer side of the market help make the eggs that are available around Easter go further. Second, the higher price is precisely what results in the additional 600 million eggs being supplied to the market to satisfy this increased consumer demand. Without the price increase, excess demand would be present, and many consumers would simply be unable to find eggs to purchase around Easter. If the price remained at P_1 (the equilibrium price throughout most of the year), consumers at Easter time would want to purchase more eggs than producers would be willing to supply. At the higher P_2 price, however, the quantity suppliers are willing to sell is again in balance with the quantity consumers wish to purchase.

Why were suppliers unwilling to supply the additional 600 million eggs at the original price of P_1? Because at the original equilibrium price of P_1, suppliers were already producing and selling all the eggs that cost less to produce than that price. The additional eggs desired by consumers around Easter all cost more to produce than the old market price of P_1. The higher price of P_2 is what allows suppliers to cover their higher production costs associated with these extra eggs. Around Easter, farmers take costly steps to avoid having the hens molt because hens lay fewer eggs when they are molting. They do this by changing the quantity and types of feed and by increasing the lighting in the birds' sheds—both of which mean higher production costs. Farmers also try to build up larger than normal inventories of eggs before Easter. Eggs are typically about two days old when consumers buy them at the store, but can be up to seven days old around Easter time. Building up and maintaining this additional inventory are costly, too.

In a market economy, when the demand for a good increases, its price will rise, which will (1) motivate consumers to search for substitutes and cut back on additional purchases of the good and (2) motivate producers to supply more of the good. These two forces will eventually bring the quantity demanded and quantity supplied back into balance.

It's important to note that this response on the supply side of the egg market is not a shift in the supply curve. The supply curve remains unchanged. Rather, there is a movement along the original supply curve—a change in *quantity* supplied. The only reason suppliers are willing to alter their behavior (produce more eggs) is that the increased demand has pushed up the price of eggs. Notice that it is the change in demand (a shift of the demand curve) that leads to the change in quantity supplied (a movement along the supply curve). Producers are simply responding to the price movement caused by the change in demand. A movement along one curve (a change in quantity supplied *or* a change in quantity demanded) happens in response to a shift in the other curve (a change in demand or a change in supply).

When the demand for a product declines, the adjustment process sends buyers and sellers just the opposite signals. A decline in demand (a shift to the left in the demand curve) will lead to a lower price and a lower quantity traded. What's going on is that the lower price (caused by lower consumer demand) is reducing the incentive of producers to supply the good. When consumers no longer want as much of a good, falling market prices signal producers to cut back production. The reduced output allows these resources to be freed up to go into the production of other goods consumers want more.

How will markets respond to changes in supply? **Exhibit 3-13** shows the market's adjustment to a decrease in the supply of lemons (for example, when freezing temperatures in California destroy a large portion of the lemon crop). A reduction in supply (shift from S_1 to S_2) will cause the price of lemons to increase sharply (P_1 to P_2). Because of the higher price, consumers will cut back on their consumption of lemons (the movement along the demand curve from *a* to *b*). Some will switch to substitutes—in this case, probably other varieties of citrus. The higher price also encourages the remaining lemon suppliers to take additional steps—like more careful harvesting techniques or using more fertilizer—that allow them to produce more lemons than otherwise would be the case. The higher prices will rebalance the quantity demanded and quantity supplied.

As the lemon example illustrates, a decrease in supply will lead to higher prices and a lower equilibrium quantity. How do you think the market price and quantity would adjust to an increase in supply, as might be caused by a breakthrough in the technology used to harvest the lemons? Again, try to draw the appropriate supply and demand curves to illustrate this case. If you do it correctly, the graph you draw will show an increase in supply (a shift to the right in the supply curve) leading to a lower market price and a larger equilibrium quantity.

Exhibit 3-13 Market Adjustment to a Decrease in Supply

Here, using lemons as an example, we illustrate how a market adjusts to a decrease in supply. Assume adverse weather conditions substantially reduce the supply (shift from S_1 to S_2) of lemons. The reduction in supply leads to an increase in the equilibrium price (from P_1 to P_2) and a reduction in the equilibrium quantity traded (from Q_1 to Q_2).

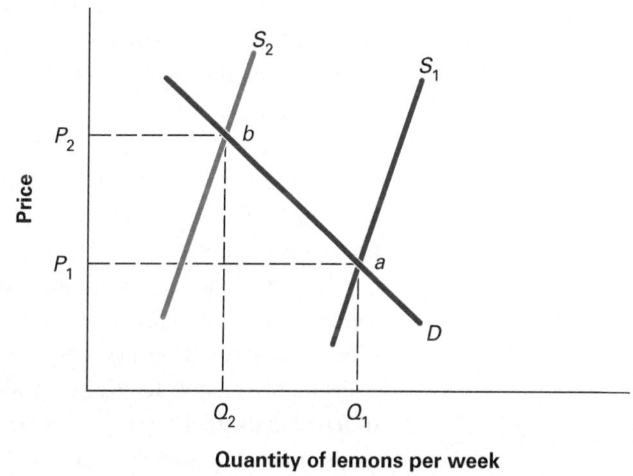

Thumbnail Sketch

How Changes in Demand and Supply Affect Market Price and Quantity

Changes in Demand

1. An increase in demand–shown by a rightward shift of the demand curve–will cause an increase in both the equilibrium price and the equilibrium quantity.
2. A decrease in demand–shown by a leftward shift of the demand curve–will cause a decrease in both the equilibrium price and the equilibrium quantity.

Changes in Supply

3. An increase in supply–shown by a rightward shift of the supply curve–will cause a decrease in the equilibrium price and an increase in the equilibrium quantity.
4. A decrease in supply–shown by a leftward shift of the supply curve–will cause an increase in the equilibrium price and a decrease in the equilibrium quantity.

The accompanying **Thumbnail Sketch** summarizes the effect of changes—both increases and decreases—in demand and supply on the equilibrium price and quantity. The cases listed in the sketch, however, are for when only a single curve shifts. But sometimes market conditions simultaneously shift both demand and supply. For example, consumer income might increase at the same time that a technological advance in production occurs. These two changes will cause both demand and supply to increase at the same time—both curves will shift to the right. The new equilibrium will definitely be at a larger quantity, but the direction of the change in price is indeterminate. The price may either increase or decrease, depending on whether the increase in demand or increase in supply is larger—which curve shifted the most, in other words.

What will happen if supply increases but demand falls at the same time? Price will definitely fall, but the new equilibrium quantity may either increase or decrease. Draw the supply and demand curves for this case and make sure that you understand why.

3-7 Entrepreneurship, Profit, and the Dynamics of Market Competition

While focusing on demand, supply, and the determination of market prices, the important role of entrepreneurs must not be overlooked. Profit opportunities and better ways of doing things do not just happen; they must be discovered. Profit provides entrepreneurs with the incentive to search for, discover, and act upon opportunities to increase the value of resources. As they do so, there will be two effects on markets. First, the actions of entrepreneurs will move some markets toward equilibrium. An unexpected increase in demand for an existing product will create a temporary increase in profit. Perceptive entrepreneurs who discover and act on this opportunity will increase the supply of the product, returning profit rates back to normal levels. In contrast, an unexpected reduction in demand for a product will lead to lower prices and economic losses. In this case, entrepreneurs will respond by reducing output and exiting the market, causing profit rates to return to normal levels. This process is discussed in more detail in principles of microeconomics courses.

However, the search for profit opportunities by entrepreneurs may also lead to a disruptive impact on markets when it involves the discovery of a new product, production process, or form of business organization that generates a good or service that consumers value highly relative to cost. Consider how the introduction of the iPhone disrupted many different markets. This multidimensional product reduced the demand for cameras, watches, maps, portable gaming devices, and several other products for which the iPhone is a good substitute. At the same time, the success of the iPhone increased the demand for cell phone

Entrepreneurs Who Have Changed Our Lives

Kendra Scott

Backgrid/Alamy Stock Photo

The road to entrepreneurial success is often rocky. At the age of 19, Kendra Scott dropped out of college to help her stepfather when he was diagnosed with cancer. At the MD Anderson Cancer Center in Houston, she discovered many women who had lost their hair while going through chemotherapy. So, she started the Hat Box to sell attractive hats to those and other women. But the business didn't draw enough customers. After five years and the loss of both her life savings and that of her stepfather, she had to close her store. As she did so, she thought she was "the biggest failure on the planet."

From the time she was a child, Kendra loved fashion. As an adult, she wanted to wear jewelry made of gemstones but couldn't find anything between cheap casual jewelry and fine pieces priced beyond her means. So she started her own jewelry business in Austin, Texas, in 2002. Taking $500 out of the bank, she designed medium-priced gemstone jewelry in a spare bedroom in her home. Then, carrying her infant son, she walked from shop to shop to sell her designs.

Initially selling her jewelry wholesale, she opened her first Kendra Scott retail store in 2010. She had learned an important lesson from her prior business failure: retailers need to give people a reason to come into their store. Unlike stiff and formal jewelry stores with their locked cases, says *Success* magazine, Scott has made her stores sites of exciting "bridal-shower parties, cupcake and champagne evenings, and other partnership events that not only draw foot traffic but also inspire engagement with the brand as a whole."

She describes her initial business failure as "an MBA in the school of hard knocks. It's an incredible university." She learned a lot from it. Today, in her mid-forties, Kendra Scott has a business worth a billion dollars and has received numerous entrepreneurship awards. She also pursues her philanthropic interest with "Kendra Gives Back" parties that allow nonprofit organizations to raise money by having in-store selling events where 10 percent of the proceeds go to the charity.

Sources: Amy Anderson, "Meet Kendra Scott, Homemade Millionaire," *Success*, March 7, 2016, at https://www.forbes.com/profile/kendra-scott/#643c4a0762f7.

"America's Self-made Women," *Forbes*, June 3, 2019, at https://www.forbes.com/profile/kendra-scott/#643c4a0762f7.

Elana Lyn Gross, "How Kendra Scott Built a Billion-dollar Jewelry Company," *Forbes*, March 1, 2018, at https://www.forbes.com/sites/elanagross/2018/03/01/how-kendra-scott-built-a-billion-dollar-jewelry-company/#3cfeb18e161.

"Kendra Scott," Wikipedia, at https://en.wikipedia.org/wiki/Kendra_Scott (for her birth date).

chargers, protective cases, and software development for apps to achieve specialized objectives. Think about the disruptive impact of other products introduced in recent decades. Streaming online movies from firms such as Netflix provided more convenient access and lower cost, reducing the demand for movie cassette rentals and the eventual demise of firms such as Blockbuster and Pic-a-Flick Video. Amazon and other online shopping firms have substantially reduced the demand for shopping at brick-and-mortar stores. Google and the personal computer have virtually eliminated the demand for encyclopedias, dictionaries, and thesauruses. As these cases indicate, competition often arises from the discovery and introduction of an innovative new product or distribution method rather than from other firms producing similar products.[5] While this form of entrepreneurial action is disruptive, it is also a powerful source of economic progress.

Of course, not all innovative actions by entrepreneurs will be successful in the marketplace. It is a process of discovery, one of trial and error. We must find a way to sort the good

[5]The writings of two prominent scholars, Israel Kirzner and Joseph Schumpeter, highlight the dual role of entrepreneurs in the market process. Kirzner stresses the role of the entrepreneur in directing market prices toward equilibrium, while Schumpeter argues that the innovative, disruptive acts of entrepreneurs are the primary source of economic growth and higher living standards.

ideas from the bad ones. The profit and loss system in a competitive market performs this function quite well—it both incentivizes innovation and provides feedback to entrepreneurs. In a market economy, it is relatively easy for entrepreneurs to try out their new ideas. All they have to do is to provide financing or convince investors to do so. This is important because no one knows either the source or the nature of the next good or service that will improve the quality of our lives. But markets also hold entrepreneurs accountable. If an entrepreneur's innovative new product or service fails to provide consumers with value greater than cost, losses will result, reducing the wealth of both the entrepreneur and the investors who financed the project. With time, losses and business failures will bring counterproductive activities to a halt, freeing up the resources for other entrepreneurs to employ in a more productive manner.

Although this chapter has focused on how market prices coordinate the actions of buyers and sellers, it is important to recognize that markets also coordinate the actions of entrepreneurs. If markets are going to direct entrepreneurs toward productive actions, open competition and avoidance of artificial barriers limiting access are vitally important. The following section highlights this point and summarizes the content of this chapter.

Keys to Economic Prosperity

Invisible Hand Principle

Market prices coordinate the actions of self-interested individuals and direct them toward activities that promote the general welfare.

3-8 Invisible Hand Principle

About 250 years ago, Adam Smith, the father of economics, stressed that personal self-interest *when directed by market prices* is a powerful force promoting economic progress. In a famous passage in his book *An Inquiry into the Nature and Causes of the Wealth of Nations*, published in 1776, Smith put it this way:

> Every individual is continually exerting himself to find out the most advantageous employment for whatever [income] he can command. It is his own advantage, indeed, and not that of the society which he has in view. But the study of his own advantage naturally, or rather necessarily, leads him to prefer that employment which is most advantageous to society.... He intends only his own gain, and he is in this, as in many other cases, led by an invisible hand to promote an end which was not part of his intention. By pursuing his own interest he frequently promotes that of the society more effectually than when he really intends to promote it.[6]

The "invisible hand" to which Smith referred was the pricing system—prices determined by the forces of supply and demand. Smith's fundamental insight was that market prices tend to bring the self-interest of individuals into harmony with the betterment of society. Moreover, when it is directed by market prices, personal self-interest is a powerful force promoting growth and prosperity.

The tendency of market prices to channel the actions of self-interested individuals into activities that promote the prosperity of the society is now known as the **invisible hand principle**. Let's examine this important principle.

Invisible hand principle
The tendency of market prices to direct individuals pursuing their own interests to engage in activities promoting the economic well-being of society.

3-8a Prices and Market Order

The invisible hand principle can be difficult to grasp because there is a natural tendency to associate order with central direction and control. Surely some central authority must be in charge. But this is not the case. The pricing system, reflecting the choices of literally millions of consumers, producers, and resource owners, provides the direction. Moreover, the market process works so automatically that most of us give little thought to it. We simply take it for granted.

[6]Adam Smith, *An Inquiry into the Nature and Causes of the Wealth of Nations* (New York: Modern Library, 1937), 423.

Perhaps an example from your everyday life will help you better understand the invisible hand principle. Visualize a busy retail store with 10 checkout lanes. No one is assigning shoppers to checkout lanes. Shoppers are left to choose for themselves. Nonetheless, they do not all try to get in the same lane. Why? Individuals are always alert for adjustment opportunities that offer personal gain. When the line at one lane gets long or is held up by a price check, some shoppers will shift to other lanes and thereby smooth out the flow among the lanes. Even though central planning is absent, this process of mutual adjustment by self-interested individuals results in order and social cooperation. A similar phenomenon occurs on busy interstate highways as drivers switch between lanes for personal gain, with the end result being the quickest flow of traffic for everyone and for the group as a whole.

The incentive structure generated by markets is a lot like that accompanying the checkout at a busy retail store or driving on the freeway. Like the number of people in a lane, profits and losses provide market participants with information about the advantages and disadvantages of different economic activities. Losses indicate that an economic activity is congested, and, as a result, producers are unable to cover their costs. In such a case, successful market participants will shift their resources away from such activities toward other, more valuable uses. Conversely, profits are indicative of an open lane, the opportunity to experience gain if one shifts into an activity in which the price is high relative to the per-unit cost. As producers and resource suppliers shift away from activities characterized by congestion and into those characterized by the opportunity for profit, they enlarge the flow of economic activity.

Consider the following three vitally important functions performed by market prices.

1. Market prices communicate information to both buyers and sellers that will promote efficient resource use and a proper response to changing conditions. Prices provide producers with up-to-date information about which goods consumers most intensely desire and with important information about the abundance of the resources used in the production process. The cost of production, driven by the opportunity cost of resources, tells the producer–entrepreneur the relative importance others place on the alternative uses of those resources. A boom in the housing market might cause lumber prices to rise. In turn, furniture-makers seeing these higher lumber prices will utilize substitute raw materials such as metal and plastic in their production processes. Because of market prices, furniture-makers will conserve on their use of lumber, just as if they had known that lumber was now more urgently needed for constructing new housing.

Consider another example. Suppose a drought in Brazil severely reduces the supply of coffee. Coffee prices will rise. Even if consumers do not know about the drought, the higher prices will provide them with all the information they need to know—it's time to cut back on coffee consumption. ***Market prices register information derived from the choices of millions of consumers, producers, and resource suppliers and provide them with everything they need to know to make wise decisions.***

2. Market prices coordinate the actions of market participants. Market prices also coordinate the choices of buyers and sellers, bringing their decisions into line with each other. Excess supply will lead to falling prices, which discourage production and encourage consumption until the excess supply is eliminated. Alternatively, excess demand will lead to price increases, which encourage consumers to economize on their use of the good and producer–entrepreneurs to supply more of it, eliminating the excess demand. Changing market prices induce responses on both sides of the market that will correct imbalances.

3. Market prices motivate economic players. Market prices establish a reward–penalty (profit–loss) structure that encourages people to work, cooperate with others, use efficient production methods, supply goods that are intensely desired by others, and invest for the future. Self-interested entrepreneurs will seek to produce only the goods consumers value enough to pay a price sufficient to cover production cost. Self-interest will also encourage entrepreneurs to use efficient production methods, adopt cost-saving technologies, and discover new products and distribution methods that improve the well-being of consumers. Such actions will improve profitability and provide a competitive advantage relative to rival producer–entrepreneurs.

At the beginning of this chapter, we asked you to reflect on why the grocery stores in your local community generally have on hand about the right amount of milk, bread, vegetables, and other goods. Likewise, how is it that refrigerators, automobiles, and clothing, produced at different places around the world, make their way to stores near you in approximately the same numbers that they are demanded by consumers? The invisible hand principle provides the answer, and it leads to an amazing degree of social cooperation.

Is the concept of the invisible hand really valid? Next time you sit down to have a nice dinner, think about all the people who help make it possible. It is unlikely that any of them, from the farmer to the truck driver to the grocer, was motivated by a concern that you have an enjoyable meal. Market prices, however, bring their interest into harmony with yours. Farmers who raise the best beef or turkeys receive higher prices, truck drivers and grocers earn more money if their products are delivered fresh and in good condition, and so on. An amazing degree of cooperation and order is created by market exchanges—all without the central direction of any government official.

3-8b Competition and Property Rights

As we noted earlier in this chapter, our focus so far has been on markets in which rival firms can freely enter and exit, and private-property rights are clearly defined and enforced. ***The efficiency of market organization is, in fact, dependent upon these two things: (1) competitive markets and (2) well-defined and enforced private-property rights.***

Competition, the great regulator, can protect both buyer and seller. It protects consumers from sellers who would charge a price substantially above the cost of production or withhold a vital resource for an exorbitant amount of money. Similarly, it protects employees (sellers of their labor) from the power of any single employer (the buyers of labor). When markets are competitive, both buyers and sellers have alternatives and these alternatives provide them with protection against ill treatment by others.

When property rights are well defined, secure, and tradable, suppliers of goods and services have to pay resource owners for their use. They will not be permitted to seize and use scarce resources without compensating the owners. Neither will they be permitted to use violence (for example, to attack or invade the property of another) to get what they want. The efficiency of markets hinges on the presence of property rights—after all, people can't easily exchange or compete for things they cannot own. Without well-defined property rights, markets simply cannot function effectively.

Key Points

- The law of demand states that there is an inverse (or negative) relationship between the price of a good or service and the quantity of it that consumers are willing to purchase. The height of the demand curve at any quantity shows the maximum price that consumers are willing to pay for that unit.
- The elasticity of a demand curve reflects the responsiveness of consumers to a change in price. The larger the change in quantity purchased by consumers in response to a change in price, the more elastic (or flatter) the demand curve will be.

- A movement along a demand curve is called a change in quantity demanded. A shift of the entire curve is called a change in demand. A change in *quantity demanded* is caused by a change in the price of the good (generally in response to a shift of the supply curve). A change in *demand* can be caused by several things, including a change in consumer income or a change in the price of a closely related good.
- The opportunity cost of producing a good is equal to the cost incurred by bidding the required resources away from alternative uses. Profit indicates that the producer has increased the value of the resources used, whereas a loss indicates that the producer has reduced the value of the resources used.
- The law of supply states that there is a direct (or positive) relationship between the price of a good or service and the quantity of it that producers are willing to supply. The height of the supply curve at any quantity shows the minimum price necessary to induce suppliers to produce that unit—that is, the opportunity cost of producing it.
- A movement along a supply curve is called a change in quantity supplied. A change in *quantity supplied* is caused by a change in the price of the good (generally in response to a shift of the demand curve). A shift of the entire supply curve is called a change in supply. A change in *supply* can be caused by several factors, such as a change in resource prices or an improvement in technology.
- The responsiveness of supply to a change in price is shown by the steepness of the supply curve. The more willing producers are to alter the quantity supplied in response to a change in price, the flatter, or more elastic, the supply curve. Conversely, the less willing producers are to alter the quantity supplied in response to a change in price, the steeper, or less elastic, the supply curve.
- Prices bring the conflicting forces of supply and demand into balance. There is an automatic tendency for market prices to move toward the equilibrium price, at which the quantity demanded equals the quantity supplied.
- Consumer surplus represents the net gain to buyers from market trades. Producer surplus represents the net gain to producers and resource suppliers from market trades. In equilibrium, competitive markets maximize these gains, a condition known as economic efficiency.
- Changes in the prices of goods are caused by changes in supply and demand. An increase in demand will cause the price and quantity supplied to rise. Conversely, a decrease in demand will cause the price and quantity supplied to fall. An increase in supply, however, will cause the price to fall and quantity demanded to rise. Conversely, a decrease in supply will cause the price to rise and quantity demanded to fall.
- The actions of entrepreneurs are central to the operation of markets. Entrepreneurs move prices toward equilibrium by expanding supply when profits are present, but contracting it when losses exist. But entrepreneurs also disrupt markets when they discover new products, production processes, or forms of organization that generate a good or service that consumers value highly relative to cost. Innovative actions of this type are a driving force underlying improvements in living standards.
- Market prices communicate information, coordinate the actions of buyers and sellers, and motivate decision-makers to act. As the invisible hand principle indicates, market prices are generally able to bring the self-interest of individuals into harmony with the general welfare of society. The efficiency of the system is dependent upon two things, however: (1) competitive market conditions and (2) well-defined and secure property rights.

Critical Analysis Questions

1. *Which of the following do you think would lead to an increase in the current demand for beef?

a. higher pork prices

b. higher consumer income

c. higher prices of feed grains used to feed cattle

d. widespread outbreak of mad cow or hoof-and-mouth disease among cattle

e. an increase in the price of beef

2. What is being held constant when a demand curve for a specific product (shoes or apples, for example) is constructed? Explain why the demand curve for a product slopes downward to the right.

3. What is the law of supply? How many of the following "goods" do you think conform to the general law of supply? Explain your answer in each case.

a. gasoline

b. cheating on exams

c. political favors from legislators

d. the services of heart specialists

e. children

f. legal divorces

4. *Are prices an accurate measure of a good's total value? Are prices an accurate measure of a good's marginal value? What's the difference? Can you think of a good that has high total value but low marginal value? Use this concept to explain why professional wrestlers earn more than nurses, despite the fact that it is virtually certain that nurses create more total value for society than do wrestlers.

5. What is being held constant when the supply curve is constructed for a specific good like pizza or automobiles? Explain why the supply curve for a good slopes upward to the right.
6. Define consumer surplus and producer surplus. What is meant by economic efficiency, and how does it relate to the gains of consumers and producers?
7. How is the market price of a good determined? When the market for a product is in equilibrium, how will consumers value an additional unit compared to the opportunity cost of producing that unit? Why is this important?
8. *"The future of our industrial strength cannot be left to chance. Somebody has to develop notions about which industries are winners and which are losers." Is this statement by a newspaper columnist true? Who is the "somebody"?
9. What factors determine the cost of producing a good or service? Will producers continue to supply a good or service if consumers are unwilling to pay a price sufficient to cover the cost?
10. *"Production should be for people and not for profit." Answer the following questions concerning this statement:
    a. If production is profitable, are people helped or harmed? Explain.
    b. Are people helped more if production results in a loss than if it leads to profit? Is there a conflict between production for people and production for profit?
11. What must an entrepreneur do to earn a profit? How do the actions of firms earning profits influence the value of resources? What happens to the value of resources when losses are present? If a firm making losses goes out of business, is this bad? Why or why not?
12. *What's wrong with this way of thinking? "Economists claim that when the price of something goes up, producers increase the quantity supplied to the market. But last year, the price of oranges was really high and the supply of them was really low. Economists are wrong!"
13. What is the invisible hand principle? Does it indicate that self-interested behavior within markets will result in actions that are beneficial to others? What conditions are necessary for the invisible hand to work well? Why are these conditions important?
14. In a market economy, will there be a tendency for both resources and products to be supplied by low-cost producers? Why or why not? Does this matter? Explain.
15. What is the difference between substitutes and complements? Indicate two goods that are substitutes for each other. Indicate two goods that are complements.
16. Do business firms operating in competitive markets have a strong incentive to serve the interest of consumers? Are they motivated by a strong desire to help consumers? Are "good intentions" necessary if individuals are going to engage in actions that are helpful to others? Discuss.
17. What must an entrepreneur do in order to be successful? If an entrepreneur is successful, how will the lives of others be affected? Explain.
18. How has entrepreneurial activity altered the goods and services available to consumers in recent years? Provide examples.
19. What determines whether a new product will be a success or failure? Why is the profit and loss system important to guide entrepreneurial efforts in a competitive market economy?

*Asterisk denotes questions for which answers are given in Appendix B.

Chapter 4 Demand and Supply: Applications and Extensions

> The division of labour, from which so many advantages are derived, is not originally the effect of any human wisdom, which foresees and intends that general opulence to which it gives occasion. It is the necessary, though very slow and gradual consequence of a certain propensity in human nature . . .; the propensity to truck, barter, and exchange one thing for another.
>
> –Adam Smith[1]

Markets are everywhere. They exist in many different forms and degrees of sophistication. In elementary schools, children trade their lunch box items; in households, individuals trade chores ("I'll clean the bathroom, if you'll clean the kitchen"); and in the stock market, individuals who have never met exchange shares of corporate stock and other financial assets worth billions of dollars each business day. Even making an activity illegal does not eliminate the market for it. Instead, the market is merely pushed underground. The exchange of illegal drugs or tickets to a big game at illegal prices illustrates this point.

As Adam Smith put it about 250 years ago, human beings have a natural propensity "to truck, barter, and exchange one thing for another" (quotation at the chapter opening). We all want to improve our standard of living, and trade with others helps us achieve this goal–by allowing us to get the goods and services we really want and giving us the opportunity to earn the income necessary to buy them.

Market prices coordinate the actions of buyers and sellers, but sometimes the "price" of a good or service in a particular market is called something different. For example, in the labor market, the price is often called the "wage rate." In the loanable funds market, the price is generally referred to as the "interest rate." However, as Juliet observes in Shakespeare's Romeo and Juliet, "What's in a name? That which we call a rose by any other name would smell as sweet." The same is true for prices. When the price of something is referred to by another term, such as the wage or interest rate, it will still play the same role. Therefore, when these special terms are used, we put them along the vertical axes of supply and demand diagrams, just as we do "price"–because that's what they are.

In the previous chapter, we saw how the forces of supply and demand determine market prices and coordinate the actions of buyers and sellers in the absence of government intervention. In this chapter, we turn our attention to using the supply and demand model to understand more fully what happens when governments intervene in markets by implementing price controls, taxes, and subsidies.

[1]Adam Smith, *An Inquiry into the Nature and Causes of the Wealth of Nations* (New York: Modern Library, 1937), 13.

Learning Objectives

4.1 Explain how an increase in the demand for a good will affect the market for resources used to produce the good.

4.2 Analyze the impact of government-imposed price floors and price ceilings on markets.

4.3 Compare and contrast how underground markets function relative to legal markets.

4.4 Explain the concept of tax incidence and why taxes impose an excess burden on buyers and sellers.

4.5 Indicate the impact of a tax on a good and what determines the burden of the tax between buyers and sellers.

4.6 Graph the Laffer curve and use it to explain why high tax rates are generally counterproductive.

4.7 Analyze the impact of a subsidy on the market for a specific good or service.

4-1 The Link between Resource and Product Markets

Understanding the interrelationship among markets is vitally important. A change in one market will also lead to changes in other markets. This section addresses the link between the resource and product markets.

The production process generally involves (1) the purchase of resources—like raw materials, labor services, tools, and machines; (2) transformation of the resources into products (goods and services); and (3) sale of the goods and services in a product market. Production is generally undertaken by business firms. Typically, business firms will demand resources, and households will supply them. Firms demand resources *because* they contribute to the production of goods and services. In turn, households supply them in order to earn income.

Resource market
The market for inputs used to produce goods and services.

Just as in product markets, the demand curve in a **resource market** is typically downward-sloping and the supply curve upward-sloping. The inverse relationship between the amount of a resource demanded and its price exists because businesses will substitute away from a resource as its price rises. In contrast, there will be a direct relationship between the amount of a resource supplied and its price because a higher price means greater rewards to those who provide more. As in product markets, prices will coordinate the choices of buyers and sellers in resource markets, bringing the quantity demanded into balance with the quantity supplied.

The labor market is a large component of the broader resource market. Actually, there is not just one market for labor, but rather there are many labor markets, one for each different skill-experience-occupational category. Let's examine the labor market for waitstaff (waiters and waitresses). **Exhibit 4-1** shows how resource and product markets are linked. The supply of young workers in many occupations, including waitstaff, has declined in recent years in many areas of the United States. This lower supply has caused the wages (tip-inclusive wages) of waitstaff to increase (for example, from \$15 to \$17 in Exhibit 4-1a). The higher price of this resource increases the cost of producing restaurant meals. This higher cost, in turn, reduces the supply (shifting S_1 to S_2) of restaurant meals, pushing the price upward (Exhibit 4-1b). When the price of a resource increases, it will lead to higher production costs, lower supply, and higher prices for the goods and services produced with the resource.

Of course, lower resource prices have the opposite effect. Lower resource prices reduce costs and expand the supply of consumer goods made with the lower-priced resources (shifting the supply curve to the right). The increase in supply will lead to a lower price in the product market. ***Thus, when the price of a resource—such as labor—changes, the prices of goods and services produced with that resource will change in the same direction.***

Exhibit 4-1 Resource Prices, Opportunity Cost, and Product Markets

When the supply of young workers falls, it pushes the wage rates of waiters and waitresses upward (a). In the product market (b), the higher wage rates will increase the opportunity costs of restaurants, reducing supply (shift from S_1 to S_2), thus leading to higher meal prices.

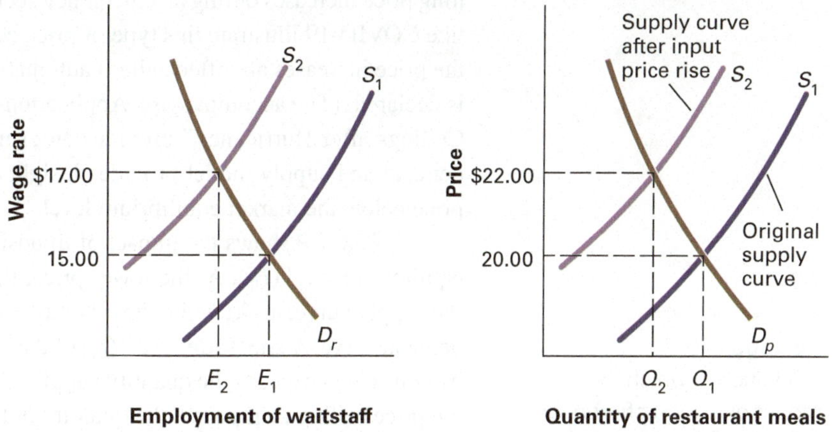

(a) Resource market

(b) Product market

Changes in product markets will also influence resource markets. There is a close relationship between the demand for products and the demand for the resources required for their production. An increase in demand for a consumer good—automobiles, for example—will lead to higher auto prices, which will increase the profitability of producing automobiles and give automakers an incentive to expand output. But the expansion in automobile output will require additional resources, causing an increase in the demand for, and prices of, the resources required for their production (steel, rubber, plastics, and the labor services of autoworkers, for example). The higher prices of these resources will cause other industries to conserve on their use, freeing them up for more automobile production.

The process will work in reverse if demand for a product falls. A decrease in demand will not only reduce the price of the product but will also reduce the demand for and prices of the resources used to produce it. ***Thus, when the demand for a product changes, the demand for (and prices of) the resources used to produce it will change in the same direction.***

4-2 The Economics of Price Controls

Buyers often complain that prices are too high, while sellers complain that they are too low. Unhappy with the prices established by market forces, various groups might try to persuade the government to intervene and impose **price controls**. Price controls force buyers or sellers to alter the prices of certain products. Price controls may be either price ceilings, which set a maximum legal price for a product, or price floors, which impose a minimum legal price. Imposing price controls may look like a simple, easy way for the government to help buyers at the expense of sellers (or vice versa). However, price controls reduce the gains from trade, and they generate secondary effects that often harm even the intended beneficiaries. Let's consider this issue in more detail.

Price controls
Government-mandated prices that are generally imposed in the form of maximum or minimum legal prices.

4-2a The Impact of Price Ceilings

A **price ceiling** establishes a maximum legal price that can be charged for a good, service, or resource. Exchanges at prices above the ceiling are prohibited. Sometimes price ceilings reflect political forces wanting to keep the price of a specific item low. The rent controls

Price ceiling
A legally established maximum price sellers can charge for a good, service, or resource.

adopted by some cities provide examples of this type of price ceiling. In other cases, the price ceiling is designed to prohibit temporary increases in the price of goods. Laws prohibiting price increases during an emergency such as a hurricane or spread of a contagious virus like COVID-19 illustrate this type of price ceiling. These laws against "price gouging" (as the price increases are often called) automatically go into effect once a state of emergency is declared. (The accompanying Applications in Economics box, "The Imposition of Price Ceilings after Hurricanes," provides an example.) Regardless of the reason adopted, the demand and supply model provides insight on what happens when a price ceiling forces price below the market equilibrium level.

Shortage
A condition in which the amount of a good offered for sale by producers is less than the amount demanded by buyers at the existing price. An increase in price would eliminate the shortage.

Exhibit 4-2 shows the impact of imposing a price ceiling (P_1) for a product below its equilibrium level (P_0). At the lower price, the quantity supplied by producers is lower on the supply curve, at Q_S, while the quantity demanded by consumers is greater, at Q_D, on the demand curve. A **shortage** ($Q_D - Q_S$) of the good will result because the quantity demanded by consumers exceeds the quantity supplied by producers at the new controlled price. After the price ceiling is imposed, the quantity of the good exchanged declines from the equilibrium quantity to Q_S, and the gains from trade (consumer and producer surplus) fall as well.

Normally, a higher price would ration the good to the buyers most willing to pay for it and encourage consumers to conserve on their purchases. Because the price ceiling keeps this from happening, though, other means must be used to allocate the smaller quantity Q_S among consumers wanting to purchase Q_D. The situation may be worsened as consumers anticipating the shortages may hoard the item when they do find it available. Predictably, nonprice factors will become more important in the rationing process. Sellers will ration their goods and services to eager buyers on the basis of factors other than their willingness to pay. For example, sellers will be more inclined to sell their products to their friends, to buyers who do them favors, and even buyers willing to make illegal "under-the-table" payments. Time might also be used as the rationing device, with those willing to wait in line the longest being the ones able to purchase the good. Sellers may also impose quantity limits on consumer purchases. In addition, the below-equilibrium price reduces the incentive of sellers to expand the future supply of the good. At the lower price, suppliers will direct resources away from production of the good and into other, more profitable areas. As a result, the product shortage will worsen over time.

What other secondary effects can be expected? ***In the real world, there are two ways that sellers can raise prices. First, they can raise their money price, holding quality constant. Or, second, they can hold the money price constant while reducing the quality of***

Exhibit 4-2 The Impact of a Price Ceiling

When a price ceiling like P_1 pushes the price of a product (rental housing, for example) below the market equilibrium, a shortage will develop. Because prices are not allowed to direct the market to equilibrium, nonprice elements will become more important in rationing the good.

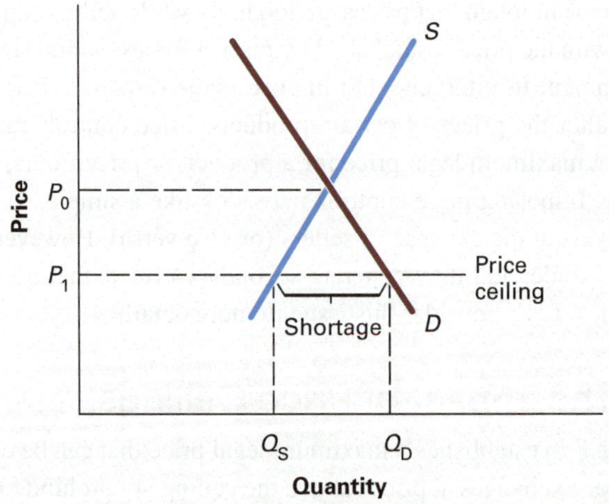

Applications in Economics

The Imposition of Price Ceilings after Hurricanes

AP Images/Eric Gay

Major hurricanes not only cause massive property damage and widespread power outages but also dramatically increase the local demand for items such as lumber, gasoline, ice, batteries, chain saws, and gasoline-powered generators. As a result, the prices of these items rise significantly.

The higher prices play three important roles. First, they encourage suppliers to bring more of these items quickly to the disaster area. Second, they allocate the supplies to those deriving the greatest value from their use. Third, they encourage consumers to conserve on their purchases, helping to discourage hoarding of supplies. The higher prices will begin to subside as additional quantities of critically needed supplies flow into the disaster area, but it is precisely these higher prices that encourage this response.

It is a natural reaction to think that the higher prices are unfair and that price controls should be imposed to prevent "price gouging." State and local officials have often imposed price controls for precisely these reasons. While price ceilings may be motivated by a desire to help consumers by keeping prices low, they exert secondary effects that hinder both the evacuation and recovery process. At the lower mandated prices, increased consumer demand quickly outstrips the available supplies creating artificial shortages. The artificial shortages created by price controls in turn encourage consumers to hoard items when they do locate them. The controls also slow the flow of supplies into the area.

The price controls result in serious misallocation of resources. Electric generators provide one of the best examples. The lack of electric power after a hurricane means that gasoline pumps, refrigerators, cash registers, credit card processors, ATMs, and other electrical equipment do not work. Grocery stores can't open, and thousands of dollars' worth of food spoils. Although gas stations have gasoline in their underground storage tanks, it can't be pumped out. ATMs and banks can't operate without electricity, so people can't get to their money, which is critical because almost all transactions in post-hurricane environments are made with cash.

Hardware stores that sell gasoline-powered electric generators typically have only a few in stock, but after a hurricane suddenly hundreds of businesses and residents want to buy them. In the absence of price controls, the price of these generators would rise and individual homeowners would generally be outbid by businesses, which can put the generators to use operating stores, gas stations, and ATMs. It is these uses that would yield enough revenue to cover the high price of the generators because they facilitate the provision of other goods and services that people desperately want.

Market prices would allocate generators and other urgently needed supplies to those most willing to pay for them. Price ceilings keep this from happening. In the absence of price rationing people keep their generators at home, and it is commonplace for hardware store owners with a few generators on hand to take one home for their family and then sell the others to their close friends, neighbors, and relatives to run televisions and household appliances. Moreover, the incentive of people to take action and bring generators in from other areas is slowed. For example, John Shepperson of Kentucky took time away from his normal job to buy 19 generators, rent a truck, and drive it 600 miles to the Hurricane Katrina-damaged area of Mississippi. He thought he would be able to sell the generators at high enough prices to cover his cost and earn a profit. Instead his generators were confiscated, Shepperson was arrested for price gouging, held by police for four days, and the generators kept in police custody. They never made it to consumers with urgent needs who desperately wanted to buy them.

The dramatic change in conditions that often accompany a hurricane highlights the role prices play. It also illustrates how the secondary effects accompanying price controls can magnify the damage and suffering generated by hurricanes and stand in the way of evacuation efforts.

the good. (The latter might also include reducing the size of the product, say, for example, a smaller candy bar or a shorter loaf of bread.) Faced with a price ceiling, sellers will use quality reductions as a way to raise their prices. Because of the government-created shortage, many consumers will buy the lower-quality good rather than do without it.

It is important to note that a shortage is not the same as scarcity. ***Scarcity is inescapable.*** Scarcity exists whenever people want more of a good than nature has provided. This means, of course, that almost everything of value is scarce. ***Shortages, on the other hand, are a result of prices being set below their equilibrium values—a situation that is avoidable if prices are permitted to rise.*** Removing the price ceiling will allow the price to rise to its equilibrium level (P_0 rather than P_1 in Exhibit 4-2). This will stimulate additional production, discourage consumption, and increase the incentive of entrepreneurs to search for and develop substitute goods. This combination of forces will eliminate the shortage.

4-2b Rent Control: A Closer Examination of a Price Ceiling

Rent controls are a price ceiling intended to protect residents from high housing prices. Rent controls are currently in place in over 100 U.S. cities; a large number of which are in New Jersey, New York, and California. Most of these measures were enacted during either World War II or the 1970s, when inflation was high. Rent controls peaked in the mid-1980s. At that time, more than 200 cities, encompassing about 20 percent of the nation's population, imposed rent controls. Currently, 37 states prohibit cities within their state from enacting rental control laws.[2]

Because rent controls push the price of rental housing below the equilibrium level, the amount of rental housing demanded by consumers will exceed the amount landlords will make available. Initially, if the mandated price is only slightly below equilibrium, the impact of rent controls may be barely noticeable. Over time, however, the effects will worsen. Inevitably, rent controls that continue will lead to the following results.

1. Shortages and underground markets will develop. Because the quantity of housing demanded will exceed the quantity supplied, some people who value rental housing highly will be unable to find it. Frustrated by the shortage, they will try to induce landlords to rent to them. Some will agree to prepay their rent, including a substantial damage deposit. Others might agree to rent or buy the landlord's furniture at exorbitant prices in order to get an apartment. Still others will make under-the-table payments to secure housing.

2. The future supply of rental housing will decline. The below-equilibrium price will discourage entrepreneurs from constructing new rental housing units, and private investment will flow elsewhere. A recent study of rent control in San Francisco found that the controls decreased the supply of rental units by 15 percent, primarily as the result of the sale of units to occupants and the conversion of apartment buildings to condominiums.[3] In contrast, removal of rent controls will often lead to a sharp increase in rental housing construction, as builders seek to expand the supply that lagged behind as the result of the controls. This happened in both Boston and Santa Monica following repeal of rent controls.

3. The quality of rental housing will deteriorate. When apartment owners are not allowed to raise their prices, they will use quality reductions to achieve this objective. Normal maintenance and repair service will deteriorate. Tenant parking lots will be eliminated (or rented out). Eventually, the quality of the rental housing will reflect the controlled

[2]Prasanna Rajasekaran, Mark Treskon, and Solomon Greene, "Rent Control: What Does the Research Tell Us about the Effectiveness of Local Action?" Urban Institute *Research to Action Lab*, January 2019, at https://www.urban.org/sites/default/files/publication/99646/rent_control._what_does_the_research_tell_us_about_the_effectiveness_of_local_action_1.pdf.

[3]Rebecca Diamond, Tim McQuade, and Franklin Qian, "The Effects of Rent Control Expansion on Tenants, Landlords, and Inequality: Evidence from San Francisco," *American Economic Review* 109 (September 2019): 3365–94.

price. Cheaper housing will be of cheaper quality.

Denis Tangney Jr/Getty Images

Rent controls lead to shortages, poor maintenance, and deterioration in the quality of rental housing.

4. Nonprice methods of rationing will become more important. Because price no longer rations rental housing, other forms of competition will develop. Landlords will rely more heavily on nonmonetary discriminating devices. They will favor friends, people of influence, and those whose lifestyles resemble their own. In contrast, applicants with many children or unconventional lifestyles, and perhaps racial minorities, will find fewer landlords who will rent to them. In New York City, where rent controls are in force, a magazine article suggested that "joining a church or synagogue" could help people make the connections they need to get an apartment. Can you imagine having to devote this amount of effort to finding an apartment? If your city enacts rent controls, you just might have to.

5. Inefficient use of housing space will result. The tenant in a rent-controlled apartment will think twice before moving. Why? Even though the tenant might want a larger or smaller space or an apartment closer to work, they will be less likely to move because it will be much more difficult to find a unit that's vacant. Turnover will be lower, and many people will find themselves in locations and in apartments not well suited to their needs.[4]

Imposing rent control laws may sound like a simple way to deal with high housing prices. However, the secondary effects are so damaging that many cities have begun repealing them. In the words of Swedish economist Assar Lindbeck: "In many cases, rent control appears to be the most efficient technique presently known to destroy a city—except for bombing."[5] Though this may overstate the case, both economics and experience show that the controls adversely impact the quantity and quality of rental housing.

4-2c The Impact of Price Floors

A **price floor** establishes a minimum price that can legally be charged. The government imposes price floors on some agricultural products, for example, in an effort to artificially increase the prices that farmers receive. When a price floor is imposed above the current market equilibrium price, it will alter the market's operation. **Exhibit 4-3** illustrates the impact of imposing a price floor (P_1) for a product above its equilibrium level (P_0). At the higher price, the quantity supplied by producers increases along the supply curve to Q_S, while the quantity demanded by consumers decreases along the demand curve to Q_D. A **surplus** ($Q_S - Q_D$) of the good will result, as the quantity supplied by producers exceeds the quantity demanded by consumers at the new controlled price. Just like a price ceiling, a price floor reduces the quantity of the good exchanged and reduces the gains from trade.

Price floor
A legally established minimum price buyers must pay for a good, service, or resource.

Surplus
A condition in which the amount of a good offered for sale by producers is greater than the amount that buyers will purchase at the existing price. A decline in price would eliminate the surplus.

As in the case of the price ceiling, nonprice factors will play a larger role in the rationing process. But because there is a surplus rather than a shortage, this time buyers will be in a position to be more selective. Buyers will purchase from sellers willing to offer them

[4]Ibid.

[5]Assar Lindbeck, *The Political Economy of the New Left* (New York: Harper & Row, 1972), 39.

Exhibit 4-3 The Impact of a Price Floor

When a price floor such as P_1 keeps the price of a good or service above the market equilibrium, a surplus will result.

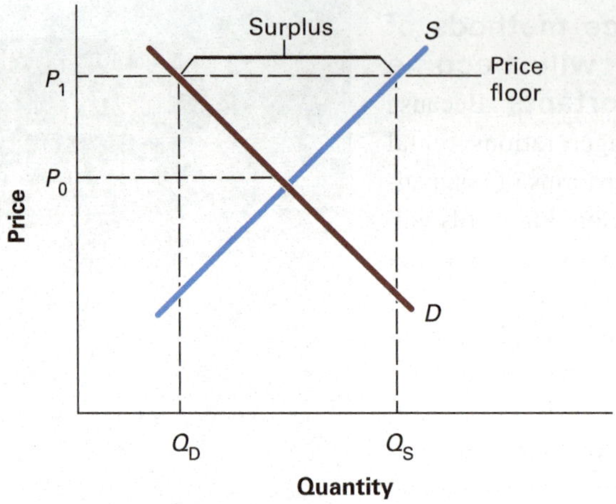

nonprice favors—better service, discounts on other products, or easier credit terms, for example. When it's difficult to alter the product's quality—in this case, improve it to make it more attractive for the price that must be charged—some producers will be unable to sell it.

It is important to note that a surplus doesn't mean the good is no longer scarce. People still want more of the good than is freely available from nature, even though they want less of it at the controlled price than sellers want to bring to the market. A decline in price would eliminate the surplus, but the item will be scarce in either case.

4-2d Minimum Wage: A Closer Examination of a Price Floor

Minimum wage
Legislation requiring that workers be paid at least the stated minimum hourly rate of pay.

A **minimum wage** is a price floor. The federal minimum wage is currently $7.25 per hour. Some states and cities have adopted minimum wage rates higher than the federal level. For example, San Francisco, Denver, and Seattle all have minimum wage rates of $18 or more. Because most employees in the United States earn wages in excess of the minimum, their employment opportunities are largely unaffected by minimum wage laws. However, low-skilled and inexperienced workers whose equilibrium wage rates are lower than the minimum wage will be affected.

Exhibit 4-4 shows the direct effect of a $17 per-hour minimum wage on the employment opportunities of a group of low-skilled workers. Without a minimum wage, the supply of and demand for these low-skilled workers would be in balance at some lower wage rate; here we use $12. Because the minimum wage makes low-skilled labor more expensive, employers will substitute machines and more highly skilled workers for the now more expensive low-skilled employees. Fewer low-skilled workers will be hired when the minimum wage pushes their wages up. Graphically, this is reflected in the movement up along the demand curve in Exhibit 4-4 from the equilibrium point to the point associated with the higher, $17 wage rate (point *A*). The result will be a reduction in employment of low-skilled workers from E_0 to E_1.

On the supply side of the market, as the wages of low-skilled workers are pushed above equilibrium, there will be more unskilled workers looking for jobs. Graphically, this is reflected in the movement up along the supply curve in Exhibit 4-4 from the equilibrium point to the point associated with the higher, $17 wage rate (point *B*). At the $17 wage rate, the quantity of workers searching for jobs will exceed the quantity of jobs available, causing excess supply.

Exhibit 4-4 Employment and the Minimum Wage

If the market wage of a group of employees is \$12 per hour, a \$17 per-hour minimum wage will increase the earnings of workers able to retain their jobs, but reduce the employment opportunities of others as the number of jobs available shrinks from E_0 to E_1.

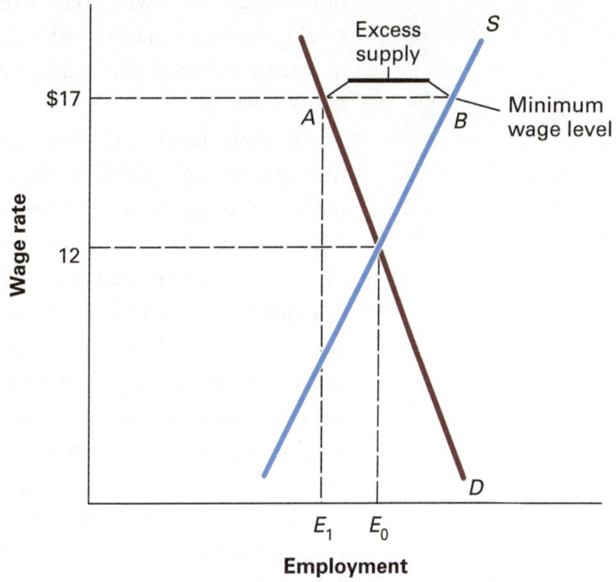

In a labor market, an excess supply will take the form of an abnormally high rate of unemployment. Thus, ***economic analysis indicates that minimum wage legislation will lead to high unemployment rates among low-skilled workers***. The exceedingly high unemployment rate of teenagers in the United States (a group with limited skills because they lack work experience) is consistent with this analysis. In recent years, the unemployment rate of teenagers has generally been about four times the rate for workers aged 25 and older. Of course, the higher unemployment rate of teenagers reflects their shifts back and forth between schooling and the labor force, but detailed studies indicate that the minimum wage is also a contributing factor.

It is important to remember that the market price—the wage rate—is only one dimension of the transaction. When a price floor pushes the wage rate above equilibrium, employers will have less incentive to offer nonwage benefits to employees because they will have no trouble hiring low-skilled workers. Predictably, a higher minimum wage will lead to a deterioration of the nonwage attributes of minimum wage jobs, and so workers in these jobs will experience less convenient working hours, fewer training opportunities, and less continuous employment. Moreover, minimum wage legislation prohibits employers and employees from entering into agreements for mutually advantageous job opportunities that offer attractive work experiences at a wage below the minimum. As a result, employment opportunities such as internships that open doors and enhance future earnings are more difficult to arrange.

The adverse impact of minimum wage laws on the work experience and training opportunities of youthful workers is particularly important. Low-paying, entry-level jobs often provide workers with experience that will help them move up the job ladder to higher-paying positions. Employment experience obtained at an early age, even on menial tasks, can help people acquire self-confidence, good work habits, and skills that make them more valuable to future employers. Mandated minimum wages will make it more difficult for youthful workers to acquire work experience and jobs with training opportunities.[6]

[6]For evidence that the minimum wage limits training opportunities, refer to David Neumark and William Wascher, "Minimum Wages and Training Revisited," *Journal of Labor Economics* 19 (July 2001): 563–95.

Workers who are able to maintain their employment at the higher minimum wage rate—most likely the better qualified among those with low skill levels—gain from a minimum wage. However, some firms will respond to the higher minimum by reducing the weekly hours of the low-skill workers who remain employed. Thus, part of the increase in weekly earnings due to a higher hourly wage rate will be offset by a decrease in weekly hours worked.

Proponents of minimum wage laws argue that they help reduce poverty. Is this really true? According to the U.S. Department of Labor, most minimum wage earners are young, part-time workers and relatively few live below the poverty line. Nearly one-half of minimum wage workers are between the ages of 16 and 24 years, and approximately three-fifths hold a part-time job. Fewer than 20 percent of minimum wage workers (at the effective state or federal minimum wage) are from families below the poverty line, and only about one out of every four workers at the federal minimum wage is married. Only 15 percent are a sole earner providing support for a family with one or more children. Therefore, even if the adverse effects of a higher minimum wage on employment and training opportunities are small, a higher minimum wage does little to help reduce the poverty rate, making it a much less attractive antipoverty program than other alternatives.[7]

How does the minimum wage affect the employment of low-skilled workers? Numerous studies have been conducted on the minimum wage's impact on employment levels. It is challenging to isolate the effect of the minimum wage since other factors such as economic conditions also affect the number of workers employed. As a result, some studies find little or no effect of the minimum wage on employment levels. However, a comprehensive survey of 70 studies reported that about 80 percent of the statistical estimates found that a higher minimum wage reduces employment. These studies indicate that a 10 percent increase in the minimum wage reduces the employment of low-skilled workers by about 1.5 percent (range is 1–3 percent).[8] Minimum wage supporters argue that the higher wages for low-skilled workers are worth this reduction in employment and job-training opportunities. The critics disagree, arguing that if permitted to work, the low-skill workers would gain experience and training, which would facilitate their movement up the job ladder to higher wage positions.

Because of its rapid increase in recent years, the Seattle minimum wage has been studied extensively. A team of economists from the University of Washington found that as two hikes increased the minimum rate from $9.47 in April 2015 to $13 per hour by January 2016, the percent reduction in employment was approximately equal to the percent wage increase for workers with low work experience who were impacted by the mandated hikes.[9] This means that the labor income of this group of employees was unchanged. Further, the increased minimum wage decreased the rate of new entrants into the workforce. Together, these results indicate that the minimum wage increases did not help those starting out in their careers. The employment reductions of the Seattle minimum wage hike were substantially larger than those accompanying federal and state minimum wage increases. This is not surprising. Compared to state and federal minimums, it is much easier for at least some of the employers to shift their business location away from the geographically smaller areas of cities.

[7]For evidence on this point, refer to David Neumark and William Wascher, *Minimum Wages*. (Cambridge, MA: MIT Press, 2008); and Richard V. Burkhauser, Drew McNichols, and Joseph J. Sabia, "Minimum Wages and Poverty: New Evidence from Dynamic Difference-in-Differences Estimates." National Bureau of Economic Research Working Paper Number 31182, April 2023.

[8]Refer to David Neumark and Peter Shirley, "Myth or Measurement: What Does the New Minimum Wage Research say About Minimum Wages and Job Loss in the United States?" *Industrial Relations* 61 (October 2022): 384–417.

[9]Ekaterina Jardim, Mark C. Long, Emma van Inwegen, Jacob Vigdor, and Hilary Wething, "Minimum Wage Increases and Individual Employment Trajectories," *American Economic Journal: Economic Policy* 14 (May 2022): 263–314.

4-3 Underground Markets and the Importance of the Legal Structure

When price controls are imposed, exchanges at prices outside of the range set by the government are illegal. Governments may also make it entirely illegal to buy and sell certain products. This is the case with drugs like heroin and cocaine in the United States. Similarly, prostitution is illegal in all states except Nevada. However, controlling prices and making a good or service illegal doesn't eliminate market forces. When gains from trade can be had, markets will develop and exchanges will occur in spite of the restrictions. People will also engage in illegal exchanges in order to evade taxes. For example, the $6.85 per-pack cigarette tax in New York City has made cigarette smuggling into that city a thriving business.

Markets that operate outside the legal system are called **underground markets**. How do underground markets work? Can markets function without the protection of the law? As in other markets, supply and demand will determine prices in these markets, too. However, because underground markets operate outside the official legal structure, enforcement of contracts and the dependability of quality will be less certain. The need to escape detection eliminates the use of brand names, packaging, advertising, and labeling—the factors that normally help inform consumers about a product and hold sellers accountable for its quality and consumer satisfaction. Furthermore, participation in these illegal underground markets involves greater risk, particularly for suppliers. Prices in these markets will have to be higher than they otherwise would be to compensate suppliers for the risks they are taking—the threat of arrest, possibility of a fine or prison sentence, and so on. Perhaps most important, in underground markets buyers and sellers are unable to use normal legal channels for the peaceful settlement of disputes. When a buyer or a seller fails to deliver, it is the other party who must try to enforce the agreement, usually through the use or threat of physical force.

Underground market
A market that operates outside the legal system in which either illegal goods or services are sold, or legal ones are sold at illegal prices or terms.

Compared with normal markets, economic analysis indicates that underground markets will be characterized by a higher incidence of defective products, higher profit rates (for those who do not get caught), and more violence. The incidence of phony concert tickets and deaths caused by toxic, illicit drugs are reflections of the high presence of defective goods in these markets (see the boxed feature, "Entrepreneurs Who Have Changed Our Lives: Taylor Swift," for an example). The expensive clothes and automobiles of many drug dealers provide evidence of the high monetary profits present in underground markets. Crime statistics indicate that violence is often used to settle disputes arising from underground-market transactions. In urban areas, a high percentage of the violent crimes, including murder, are associated with illegal trades gone bad and competition among dealers in the illegal drug market.

The prohibition of alcohol in the United States from 1920 to 1933 provides additional evidence that violence, deception, and fraud plague markets that operate outside the law. When the production and sale of alcohol were illegal during the Prohibition era, gangsters dominated the alcohol trade, and the murder rate soared to record highs. There were also problems with product quality (tainted or highly toxic mixtures, for example) similar to the ones present in modern-day illegal-drug markets. When Prohibition was repealed and the market for alcoholic beverages began operating once again within the legal framework, these harmful secondary effects disappeared.

Similarly, in states that have legalized marijuana, products sold at legal dispensaries use brand names and labeling to help ensure product quality and inform consumers about

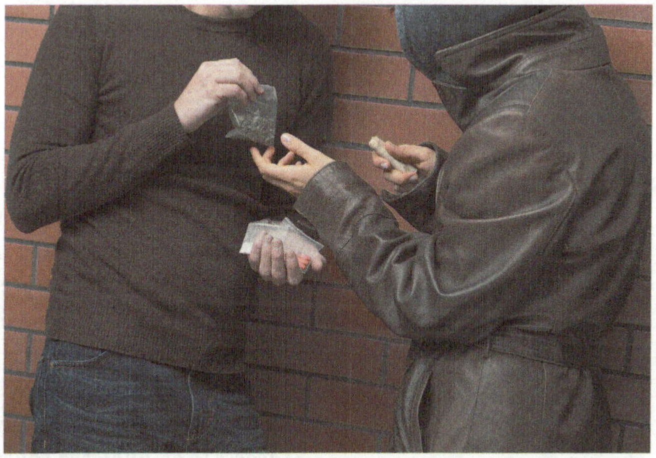

Underground markets like those for illegal drugs are characterized by less dependable product quality and the greater use of violence to settle disputes between buyers and sellers.

KatarzynaBialasiewicz/Getty Images

Entrepreneurs Who Have Changed Our Lives

Taylor Swift

Kim Chen/Alamy Stock Photo

Taylor Swift is more than a musical superstar–she's a savvy entrepreneur whose record-breaking *Eras Tour* in 2023 and 2024 led to an estimated $5 billion in economic activity. Her tour boosted tourism and economic activity in the cities where she performed, often for multiple nights, in sold-out stadiums. The demand for her concert tickets was so strong it not only broke the record for the highest single-day ticket sales ever by an artist but also overwhelmed the Ticketmaster online sales platform.

The underground resale market for her concert tickets flourished, and it resulted in some fans purchasing fake or nonexistent tickets–a problem, which we discuss in this chapter, that often plagues these markets. Her appeal spans generations, and her fans (known as "Swifties") even help boost the revenues of the fashion brands she wears.

Swift began her musical career at the age of 14 and aspired to be a country music artist before pivoting to become a pop icon and a billionaire–the first to do so solely based on income from music and performances alone. Aware of the high price her concert tickets command, Swift took steps to ensure her customers received value for their money. She played for hours, sometimes in pouring rain to avoid canceling her shows. She filled the performances with special effects, outfit changes, pyrotechnics, special effects, and "surprise songs." Fans who could not find or afford tickets often gathered outside the concert venues singing along in the surrounding streets.

A movie version of her *Eras Tour* was released in 2023 and became the highest grossing domestic concert film ever. For the first time since *The Rocky Horror Picture Show* in the late 1970s, moviegoers were encouraged to stand up and participate along with the movie while it was playing.

Her business acumen incorporated not only innovative uses of social media, agreements with major streaming and on-demand video services, and a partnership with UPS for shipping but also innovative strategies to protect her intellectual property rights. After a dispute regarding the rights to her original music, she began re-recording her old albums. In many cases these new versions (indicated by the term "Taylor's Version") actually broke chart records set by the original releases. Re-recording the older albums had a high opportunity cost for Swift as the time spent re-recording music could have been used to create and record new music. Swift has also been innovative in her usage of trademark applications to protect her catchphrases and keywords, including related terms like "Merry Swiftmas."

Sources:

Brian Edmondson, "Don't 'Shake Off' These 5 Business, Brand and Legal Lessons from Taylor Swift," *Entrepreneur*, December 16, 2023, at https://www.entrepreneur.com/starting-a-business/how-taylor-swift-became-a-billionaire-and-business-icon/465256.

Jeff Haden, "Why Taylor Swift Is My Entrepreneur of the Year," *Inc.*, December 29, 2023, at https://www.inc.com/jeff-haden/why-taylor-swift-is-my-2023-entrepreneur-of-year.html.

Kate Taylor, "9 Reasons Taylor Swift Is a Savvy Business Leader," *Entrepreneur*, April 1, 2015, at https://www.entrepreneur.com/leadership/9-reasons-taylor-swift-is-a-savvy-business-leader/244614.

Hilary Weaver, "What's the New Taylor Swift All About? Just Look at the Trademarks," *Vanity Fair*, September 5, 2017, at https://www.vanityfair.com/style/2017/09/taylor-swift-trademarks-reputation-album.

Susan Tompor, "Taylor Swift Ticket Scams Are Breaking Fans' Hearts: How to Verify Tickets Are Real," *USA Today*, June 18, 2023, at https://www.usatoday.com/story/money/2023/06/18/taylor-swift-tickets-eras-tour-scam/70334063007/.

potency. This is in stark contrast to the unlabeled bags of unknown origin and potency found previously in illegal drug markets. However, the ongoing federal marijuana prohibition, complex state licensing procedures, and high tax rates on legal purchases have resulted in continued large underground markets and other problems such as the inability of sellers to use the banking system.

The operation of illegal underground markets highlights a point often taken for granted: ***A legal system that provides for secure private-property rights, contract enforcement, and access to an unbiased court system for settling disputes is vitally important for the smooth***

operation of markets. Markets will exist in any environment, but they can be counted on to function efficiently only when property rights are secure and contracts are impartially enforced.

4-4 The Impact of a Tax

How do taxes affect market exchange? When governments tax goods, who bears the burden? Economists use the term **tax incidence** to indicate how the burden of a tax is *actually* shared between buyers (who pay more for what they purchase) and sellers (who receive less for what they sell). When a tax is imposed, the government can make either the buyer or the seller legally responsible for payment of the tax. The legal assignment is called the *statutory incidence* of the tax. However, the person who writes the check to the government—that is, the person statutorily responsible for the tax—is not always the one who bears the tax burden. The *actual incidence* of a tax may lie elsewhere. If, for example, a tax is placed statutorily on a seller, the seller might simply increase the price of the product. In this case, the buyers end up bearing some, or all, of the tax burden through the higher price.

Tax incidence
The way the burden of a tax is distributed among economic units (consumers, producers, employees, employers, and so on). The actual tax burden does not always fall on those who are statutorily assigned to pay the tax.

To illustrate, **Exhibit 4-5** shows how a $1,000 tax placed on the sale of used cars would affect the market. (To simplify this example, let's assume all used cars are identical.) Here, the tax has statutorily been placed on the seller. When a tax is imposed on the seller, it shifts the supply curve upward by exactly the amount of the tax—$1,000, in this example. To understand why, remember that the height of the supply curve at a particular quantity shows the minimum price required to cause enough sellers to offer that quantity of cars for sale. Suppose you were a potential seller, willing to sell your car for any price over $26,000, but you would keep it unless you could pocket at least $26,000 from the sale. Because you now have to pay a tax of $1,000 when you sell your car, the minimum price you will accept

Exhibit 4-5 The Impact of a Tax Imposed on Sellers

When a $1,000 tax is imposed statutorily on the sellers of used cars, the supply curve shifts vertically upward by the amount of the tax. The price of used cars to buyers rises from $27,000 to $27,400, resulting in buyers bearing $400 of the burden of this tax. The price received by a seller falls from $27,000 to $26,400 ($27,400 minus the $1,000 tax), resulting in sellers bearing $600 of the burden.

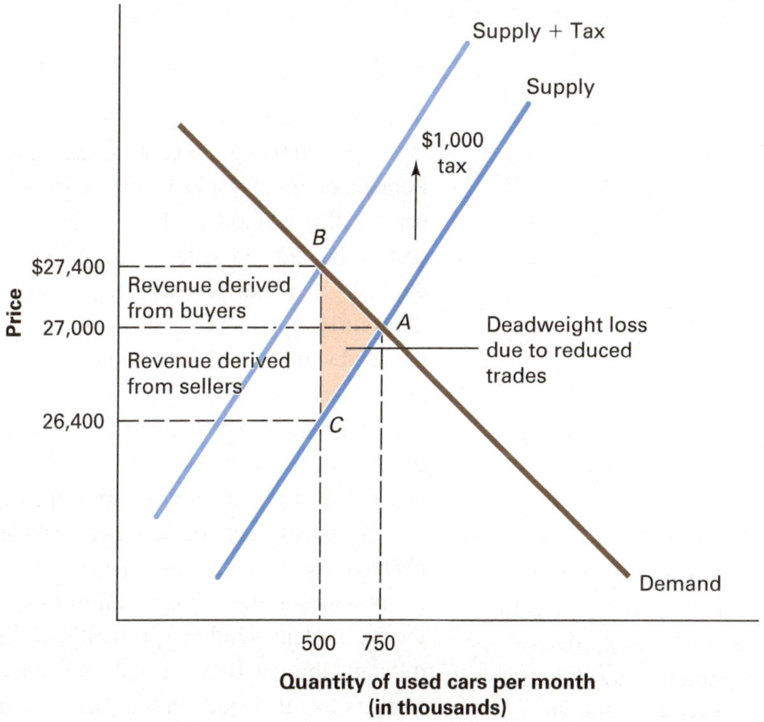

from the buyer will rise to \$27,000, so that after paying the tax, you will retain \$26,000. Other potential sellers will be in a similar position. The tax will push the minimum price each seller is willing to accept upward by \$1,000. Thus, the after-tax supply curve will shift vertically by this amount.

Sellers would prefer to pass the entire tax on to buyers by raising prices by the full amount of the tax, rather than paying any part of it themselves. However, as sellers begin to raise prices, customers respond by purchasing fewer units. At some point, to avoid losing additional sales, some sellers will find it more profitable to accept part of the tax burden themselves (in the form of a lower price net of tax), rather than to raise the price by the full amount of the tax. This process is shown in Exhibit 4-5.

Before the tax was imposed, used cars sold for a price of \$27,000 (at the intersection of the original supply and demand curves shown by point *A*). After the \$1,000 tax is imposed, the equilibrium price of used cars will rise to \$27,400 (to point *B*, the intersection of the new supply curve including the tax, and the demand curve). Thus, despite the tax being statutorily imposed on sellers, the higher price shifts some of the tax burden to buyers. Buyers will now pay \$400 more for used cars. Sellers now receive \$27,400 from the sale of their used cars. However, after sending \$1,000 in taxes to the government, they retain only \$26,400. This is exactly \$600 less than the seller would have received had the tax not been imposed. Because the distance between the supply curves is exactly \$1,000, this net price can be found in Exhibit 4-5 by following the vertical line down from the new equilibrium (point *B*) to the original supply curve (point *C*) and over to the price axis. In this case, each \$1,000 of tax revenue transferred to the government imposes a burden of \$400 on buyers (in the form of higher used-car prices) and a \$600 burden on sellers (in the form of lower net receipts from a car sale), even though sellers are responsible for actually sending the \$1,000 tax payment to the government.

Tax base
The level or quantity of an economic activity that is taxed. Higher tax rates reduce the level of the tax base because they make the activity less attractive.

Tax rate
The per-unit amount of the tax or the percentage rate at which the economic activity is taxed.

The tax revenue derived from a tax is equal to the **tax base** (in this case, the number of used cars exchanged) multiplied by the **tax rate**. After the tax is imposed, the quantity exchanged will fall to 500,000 cars per month because some buyers will choose not to purchase at the \$27,400 price, and some sellers will decide not to sell when they are able to net only \$26,400. Given the after-tax quantity sold, the monthly revenue derived from the tax will be \$500 million (500,000 cars multiplied by \$1,000 tax per car).

4-4a The Deadweight Loss Caused by Taxes

Deadweight loss
The loss of gains from trade to buyers and sellers that occurs when a tax is imposed. The deadweight loss imposes a burden on both buyers and sellers over and above the actual payment of the tax.

Excess burden of taxation
Another term for deadweight loss. It reflects losses that occur when beneficial activities are forgone because they are taxed.

As Exhibit 4-5 shows, a \$1,000 tax on used cars causes the number of units exchanged to fall from 750,000 to 500,000. It reduces the quantity of units exchanged by 250,000 units. Remember, trade results in mutual gains for both buyers and sellers. The loss of the mutual benefits that would have been derived from these additional 250,000 units also imposes a cost on buyers and sellers. But this cost—the loss of the gains from trade eliminated by the tax—does not generate any revenue for the government. Economists call this the **deadweight loss** of taxation. In Exhibit 4-5, the size of the triangle *ABC* measures the deadweight loss. The deadweight loss is a burden imposed on buyers and sellers over and above the cost of the revenue transferred to the government. Sometimes it is referred to as the **excess burden of taxation**. It is composed of losses to both buyers (the lost consumer surplus consisting of the upper part of the triangle *ABC*) and sellers (the lost producer surplus consisting of the lower part of the triangle *ABC*).

The deadweight loss to sellers includes an indirect cost imposed on the people who supply resources to that industry (such as its suppliers and employees). The federal luxury-boat tax provides a vivid illustration of this point. Supporters of the luxury-boat tax assumed the tax burden would fall primarily on wealthy yacht buyers. The actual effects were quite different, though. Because of the tax, luxury-boat sales fell sharply and an estimated 25,000 workers lost their jobs in the yacht-manufacturing industry. The deadweight loss triangle might seem like an abstract concept, but it wasn't so abstract to the employees in the boating industry who lost their jobs! Their losses are part of what is reflected in the triangular area. Moreover, because luxury-boat sales declined so sharply, the tax generated only a meager amount of revenue. The large deadweight loss (or excess burden) combined with meager revenue for the government eventually led to the repeal of the tax.

4-4b Actual versus Statutory Incidence

Economic analysis indicates that the actual burden of a tax—or more precisely, the split of the burden between buyers and sellers—does not depend on whether the tax is statutorily placed on the buyer or the seller. Let's examine how the market responds to a tax statutorily placed on the buyer. Continuing with the auto tax example, let's suppose that the government places the $1,000 tax on the buyer of the car, rather than the seller. After making a used-car purchase, the buyer must send a check to the government for $1,000. Imposing a tax on buyers will shift the demand curve downward by the amount of the tax, as shown in **Exhibit 4-6**. This is because the height of the demand curve represents the maximum price a buyer is willing to pay for the car. If a particular buyer is willing and able to pay only $25,000 for a car, the $1,000 tax would mean that the most the buyer would be willing to pay *to the seller* would be $24,000. This is because the total cost to the buyer is now the purchase price plus the tax.

As Exhibit 4-6 shows, the price of used cars falls from $27,000 (point *A*) to $26,400 (point *B*) when the tax is statutorily placed on the buyer. Even though the tax is placed on buyers, the reduction in demand that results causes the price received by sellers to fall by $600. Thus, $600 of the tax is again borne by sellers, just as it was when the tax was placed statutorily on them. From the buyer's standpoint, a car now costs $27,400 ($26,400 paid to the seller plus $1,000 in tax to the government). Just as when the tax was imposed on the seller, the buyer now pays $400 more for a used car.

Exhibit 4-6 The Impact of a Tax Imposed on Buyers

When a $1,000 tax is imposed statutorily on the buyers of used cars, the demand curve shifts vertically downward by the amount of the tax. The price of used cars falls from $27,000 to $26,400, resulting in sellers bearing $600 of the burden. The buyer's total cost of purchasing the car rises from $27,000 to $27,400 ($26,400 plus the $1,000 tax), resulting in buyers bearing $400 of the burden of this tax. The incidence of this tax on used cars is the same regardless of whether it is statutorily imposed on buyers or sellers.

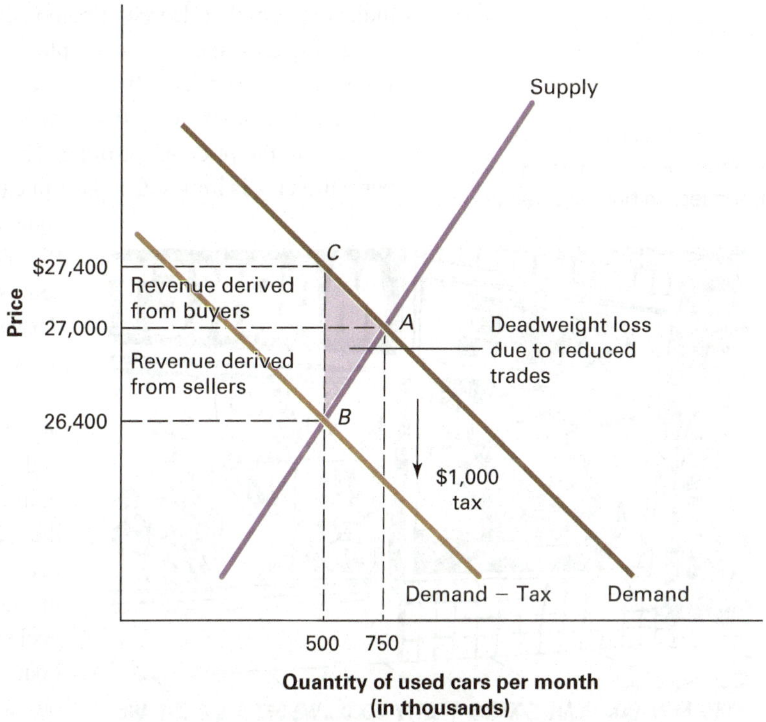

A comparison of Exhibits 4-5 and 4-6 makes it clear that the actual burden of the $1,000 tax is independent of its statutory incidence. In both cases, buyers pay a total price of $27,400 for the car (a $400 increase from the pretax level), and sellers receive $26,400 from the sale (a $600 decrease from the pretax level). Correspondingly, the revenue derived by the government, the number of sales eliminated by the tax, and the size of the deadweight loss are identical whether the law requires payment of the tax by the sellers or by the buyers. A similar phenomenon occurs with any tax. The 15.3 percent FICA (Social Security and Medicare) payroll tax, for example, is statutorily levied as 7.65 percent on the employee and 7.65 percent on the employer. The impact is to drive down the net pay received by employees and raise the employers' cost of hiring workers. Economic analysis tells us that the actual burden of this tax will probably differ from its legal assignment and that it will be the same regardless of how the tax is statutorily assigned. Because market prices (here, workers' gross wage) will adjust, the incidence of the tax will be identical regardless of whether the 15.3 percent is levied on employees or on employers or is divided between the two parties.

4-4c Elasticity and the Incidence of a Tax

If the actual incidence of a tax is independent of its statutory assignment, then what does determine the incidence? The answer: The incidence of a tax depends on the responsiveness of buyers and of sellers to a change in price. When buyers respond to even a small increase in price by leaving the market and buying other things, they will not be willing to accept a price that is much higher than it was prior to the tax. Similarly, if sellers respond to a small reduction in what they receive by shifting their goods and resources to other markets, or by going out of business, they will not be willing to accept a much smaller payment, net of tax. The burden of a tax—its incidence—tends to fall more heavily on whichever side of the market has the least attractive options elsewhere—the side of the market that is less sensitive to price changes, in other words.

In the preceding chapter, we saw that the steepness of the supply and demand curves reflects how responsive producers and consumers are to a price change. Relatively inelastic demand or supply curves are steeper (more vertical), indicating less responsiveness to a change in price. Relatively elastic demand or supply curves are flatter (more horizontal), indicating a higher degree of responsiveness to a change in price.

Using gasoline as an example, panel (a) of **Exhibit 4-7** illustrates the impact of a tax when demand is relatively inelastic and supply is relatively elastic. It will not be easy for gasoline consumers to shift—particularly in the short run—to other fuels in response to an increase in the price of gasoline. The inelastic demand curve shows this. When a 50-cent per-gallon tax is imposed on gasoline (roughly the current average of combined federal and state taxes), buyers end up paying 40 cents more per gallon ($3.00 instead of $2.60), while the net price received by sellers is only 10 cents less ($2.50 instead of $2.60). ***When demand is relatively inelastic, or supply is relatively elastic, buyers will bear the larger share of the tax burden.***

The actual burden of a tax is independent of whether it is imposed on buyers or sellers.

"THIS NEW TAX PLAN SOUNDS PRETTY GOOD... WE GET A 9% CUT AND BUSINESS PICKS UP THE BURDEN...."

Conversely, when demand is relatively elastic and supply is inelastic, more of the tax burden will fall on sellers and resource suppliers. The luxury-boat tax illustrates this point. As we mentioned earlier, Congress imposed a tax on the sale of luxury boats in 1990. Later, the tax was repealed because of its adverse impact on sales and employment in the industry. There are many things wealthy potential yacht owners can spend their money on other than luxury boats *sold in the United States.* For one thing, they can buy a yacht someplace else, perhaps in Mexico, England, or the Bahamas. Or they can spend more time on the golf

Exhibit 4-7 How the Burden of a Tax Depends on the Elasticities of Demand and Supply

In panel (a), when demand is relatively more inelastic than supply, buyers bear a larger share of the burden of the tax. In panel (b), when supply is relatively more inelastic than demand, sellers bear a larger share of the tax burden.

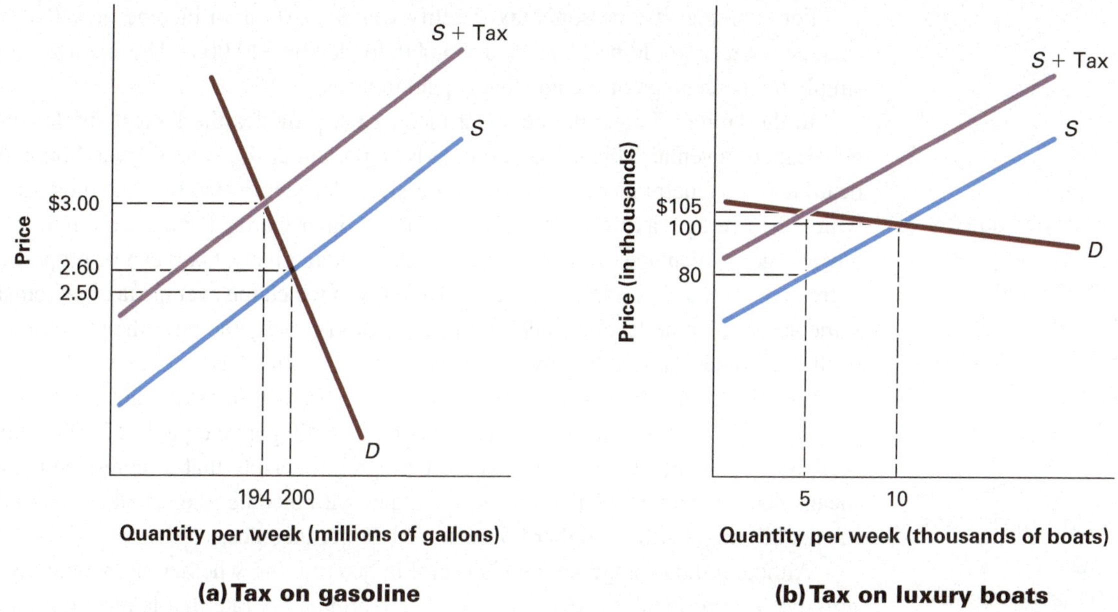

course, travel to exotic places, or purchase a nicer car or a vacation home. Because there are attractive substitutes, the demand for domestically produced luxury boats is relatively elastic compared with supply. Therefore, as panel (b) of Exhibit 4-7 illustrates, when a $25,000 tax is imposed on luxury boats, prices rise by only $5,000 (from $100,000 to $105,000), but output falls substantially (from 10,000 to 5,000 boats). The net price received by sellers falls by $20,000 (from $100,000 to $80,000 per boat). ***When demand is relatively elastic, or supply is relatively inelastic, sellers (including resource suppliers) will bear the larger share of the tax burden.***

4-4d Elasticity and the Deadweight Loss

The elasticities of supply and demand determine how the burden of a tax is distributed between buyer and seller. They also influence the size of the deadweight loss caused by the tax because they determine the total reduction in the quantity exchanged. When either demand or supply is highly inelastic, fewer trades will be eliminated by the tax, so the deadweight loss will be smaller. From a policy perspective, the excess burden of a tax system will therefore be lower if taxes are levied on goods and services for which either demand or supply is highly inelastic.

4-5 Tax Rates, Tax Revenues, and the Laffer Curve

It is important to distinguish between the average and marginal rates of taxation. They can be very different, and both provide important information. The average tax rate is generally used to examine how different income groups are burdened by a tax, whereas the marginal tax rate is the key to understanding the negative economic effects created by a tax. Both

Average tax rate (ATR)
Tax liability divided by taxable income. It is the percentage of income paid in taxes.

can be computed with simple equations. The **average tax rate (ATR)** can be expressed as follows:

$$\text{ATR} = \frac{\textbf{Tax liability}}{\textbf{Taxable income}}$$

For example, if a person's tax liability was $6,000 on an income of $40,000, their average tax rate would be 15 percent ($6,000 divided by $40,000). The average tax rate is simply the percentage of income that is paid in taxes.

In the United States, the personal income tax provides the largest single source of government revenue. This tax is particularly important at the federal level. You may have heard that the federal income tax is "progressive." A **progressive tax** is defined as a tax in which the average tax rate rises with income. In other words, people with higher income pay a larger percentage of their income in taxes. Alternatively, taxes can be proportional or regressive. A **proportional tax** is defined as a tax in which the average tax rate remains the same across income levels. Under a proportional tax, everyone pays the same percentage of their income in taxes. Finally, a **regressive tax** is defined as a tax in which the average tax rate falls as income rises. If someone making $100,000 per year paid $30,000 in taxes (an ATR of 30 percent), while someone making $30,000 per year paid $15,000 in taxes (an ATR of 50 percent), the tax code would be regressive. Note that a regressive tax merely means that the percentage paid in taxes declines with income; the actual dollar amount of the tax bill might still be higher for those with larger incomes.

Progressive tax
A tax in which the average tax rate rises with income. People with higher incomes will pay a higher percentage of their income in taxes.

Proportional tax
A tax in which the average tax rate is the same at all income levels. Everyone pays the same percentage of income in taxes.

Regressive tax
A tax in which the average tax rate falls with income. People with higher incomes will pay a lower percentage of their income in taxes.

Although the average tax rate is useful in determining whether an income tax is progressive, proportional, or regressive, it is the marginal tax rate that is most relevant when individuals are making choices. It is the marginal tax rate that determines how much of an additional dollar of income must be paid in taxes (and thus, also, how much one gets to keep). An individual's marginal tax rate can be very different from his or her average tax rate. The **marginal tax rate (MTR)** can be expressed as follows:

Marginal tax rate (MTR)
The additional tax liability a person faces divided by his or her additional taxable income. It is the percentage of an extra dollar of income earned that must be paid in taxes. It is the marginal tax rate that is relevant in personal decision-making.

$$\text{MTR} = \frac{\textbf{Change in tax liability}}{\textbf{Change in taxable income}}$$

The marginal tax rate (MTR) reveals both how much of one's *additional* income must be turned over to the tax collector and how much is retained by the individual taxpayer. For example, when the marginal tax rate is 25 percent, $25 of every $100 of additional earnings must be paid in taxes. The individual is permitted to keep only $75 of his or her additional income, in other words. The marginal tax rate is vitally important because it affects the incentive to earn additional income. The higher the marginal tax rate, the less incentive individuals have to earn more income. At high marginal rates, for example, many spouses will choose to stay home rather than take a job, and others will choose not to take on second jobs or extra work. **Exhibit 4-8** shows the calculation of both the average and marginal tax rates within the framework of the 2023 federal income tax tables. In addition to the federal income tax, there are also state and local income taxes and payroll taxes. The taxpayer's marginal tax rate will reflect the combined impact of all taxes that reduce the take-home pay derived from additional earnings.

Governments generally levy taxes to raise revenue. The revenue derived from a tax is equal to the tax base multiplied by the tax rate. As we previously noted, taxes will reduce the level of the activity. When an activity is taxed more heavily, people will choose to do less of it. The higher the tax rate, the greater the shift away from the activity. If taxpayers can easily escape the tax by altering their behavior (perhaps by shifting to substitutes), the tax base will shrink significantly as rates are increased. This erosion in the tax base in response to higher rates means that an increase in tax rates will generally lead to a less-than-proportional increase in tax revenue.

Economist Arthur Laffer popularized the idea that, beyond some point, higher tax rates will shrink the tax base so much that tax revenue will eventually decline as tax rates are pushed

Exhibit 4-8 Average and Marginal Tax Rates in the Income Tax Tables

This excerpt from the 2023 federal income tax table shows that in the 22 percent federal marginal income tax bracket, each $100 of additional taxable income a single taxpayer earns ($45,000 versus $45,100, for example) causes his or her tax liability to increase by $22 (from $5,213 to $5,235). Note that the average tax rate for a single taxpayer at $45,000 is about 11.6 percent ($5,213 divided by $45,000), even though the taxpayer's marginal rate is 22 percent.

2023 Tax Table–*Continued*

If line 11b (taxable income) is–		And you are–			
AT LEAST	BUT LESS THAN	SINGLE	MARRIED FILLING JOINTLY	MARRIED FILLING SEPARATELY	HEAD OF A HOUSEHOLD
		Your tax is–			
45,000	45,050	5,213	4,963	5,213	5,089
45,050	45,100	5,224	4,969	5,224	5,095
45,100	45,150	5,235	4,975	5,235	5,101
45,150	45,200	5,246	4,981	5,246	5,107

$100 of additional income. . . . . . results in $22 of additional tax liability.

to higher and higher levels. The curve illustrating the relationship between tax rates and tax revenues is called the **Laffer curve. Exhibit 4-9** illustrates the concept of the Laffer curve as it applies to income taxes. Obviously, tax revenue would be zero if the income tax rate were zero. What isn't so obvious is that tax revenue would also be zero (or at least very close to zero) if the tax rate were 100 percent. Confronting a 100 percent tax rate, most individuals would go fishing or find something else to do rather than engage in taxable productive activity, since the 100 percent tax rate would eliminate all personal reward derived from earning taxable income. Why work when you have to give every penny of your earnings to the government?

Laffer curve
A curve illustrating the relationship between the tax rate and tax revenues. Tax revenues will be low at both very high and very low tax rates. When tax rates are quite high, lowering them can increase tax revenue.

As tax rates are reduced from 100 percent, the incentive to work and earn taxable income increases, income expands, and tax revenue rises. Similarly, as tax rates increase from zero, tax revenue expands. Clearly, at some rate greater than zero but less than 100 percent, tax revenue will be maximized (point *B* in Exhibit 4-9). This revenue-maximizing rate is hypothetically shown in Exhibit 4-9 as 50 percent. This is not to imply that the tax rate that maximizes revenue is the ideal, or optimal, tax rate from the standpoint of the economy as a whole. Although it might be the tax rate that generates the most revenue for government, we must also consider the welfare reductions imposed on individuals by the deadweight loss created by the tax. As rates are increased and the maximum revenue point (*B*) is approached, relatively large tax rate increases will be necessary to expand tax revenue by even a small amount. In this range, the deadweight loss of taxation in the form of reductions in gains from trade will be exceedingly large relative to the additional tax revenue. Far from being ideal, the revenue maximizing tax rate will be highly inefficient.

The Laffer curve shows that it is important to distinguish between changes in tax rates and changes in tax revenues. Higher rates will not always lead to more revenue for the government. Similarly, lower rates will not always lead to less revenue. ***When tax rates are already high, a rate reduction may increase tax revenues. Correspondingly, increasing high tax rates may lead to less tax revenue.***

Evidence from the sharp reduction in marginal tax rates imposed on those with high incomes during the 1980s supports the Laffer curve. The top marginal rate was reduced from 70 percent at the beginning of the decade to 33 percent by the end of the decade. Even though the top rates were cut sharply, tax revenues and the share of the personal income tax

Exhibit 4-9 Laffer Curve

Because taxing an activity affects the amount of it people will do, a change in tax rates will not lead to a proportional change in tax revenues. As the Laffer curve indicates, beyond some point (*B*), an increase in tax rates will cause tax revenues to fall. At high tax rates, revenue can be increased by lowering tax rates. The tax rate that maximizes tax revenue is higher than the ideal tax rate for the economy as a whole because of the large deadweight loss of taxation as tax rates increase toward point *B*.

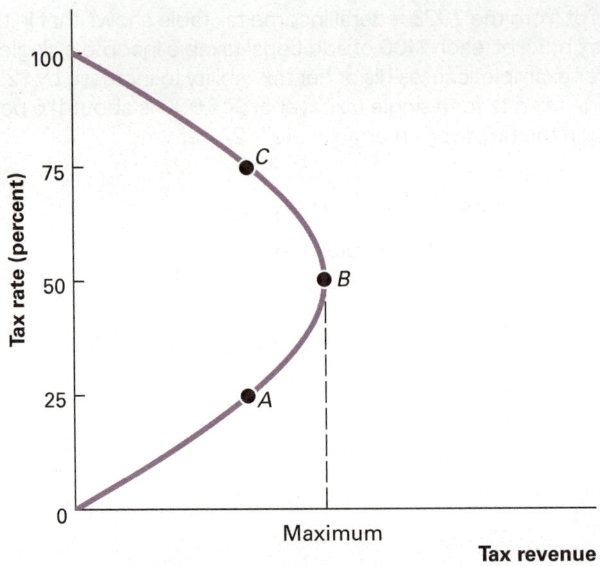

paid by high-income earners actually rose as a result. During the decade, revenue collected from the top 1 percent of earners rose a whopping 51.4 percent (after adjusting for inflation). In 1980, 19 percent of the personal income tax was collected from the top 1 percent of earners. By 1990, at the lower tax rates, the top 1 percent of earners accounted for more than 25 percent of income tax revenues. The top 10 percent of earners paid just over 49 percent of total income taxes in 1980, but by 1990 the share paid by these earners had risen to 55 percent. Thus, the reduction in the exceedingly high rates increased the revenue collected from high-income taxpayers. Additional evidence on the impact of these tax changes in the 1980s is provided in Special Topic 1.

4-6 The Impact of a Subsidy

Subsidy
A payment the government makes to either the buyer or the seller, usually on a per-unit basis, when a good or service is purchased or sold.

The supply and demand framework can also be used to analyze the impact of a government **subsidy**. A subsidy is a payment to either the buyer or seller of a good or service, usually on a per-unit basis. When a subsidy is granted to buyers, proponents typically argue that the subsidy will make the purchase of the good more affordable. Correspondingly, subsidies to sellers are generally thought to improve the profitability of the producers in the industry. As we have discovered in other cases, however, the effect of government programs often differ substantially from the stated intentions of their proponents. Because prices change when subsidies are imposed (just as when taxes are imposed), the benefit of a subsidy can be partially, or totally, shifted from buyer to seller, or vice versa.

Suppose that the government, in an effort to make the cost of college more affordable, granted full-time students a subsidy of $4,000 per year. What impact would this subsidy have on the price and quantity in the market for a college education? **Exhibit 4-10** provides insight on the answer to this question. Prior to the subsidy, the market price was determined by the intersection of the initial demand and supply curves. Thus, the pre-subsidy equilibrium price for a year of college was $10,000. The subsidy to the student-buyers increases demand, causing the demand curve to shift upward by $4,000. A new equilibrium will occur at a higher price ($12,000 in our example) and larger output (Q_2 rather than Q_1). The net price to students will fall to $8,000, the $12,000 new market price minus the $4,000.

Exhibit 4-10 The Impact of a Subsidy Granted to Buyers

Here we illustrate how a $4,000 subsidy granted to full-time college students would impact the price and quantity of a year of college education. Prior to the subsidy, the equilibrium price of a year of college was $10,000 and Q_1 students attended college. The subsidy to students would cause demand to shift vertically upward by the amount of the subsidy, pushing the equilibrium price of a year of college to $12,000. Students would gain $2,000 in the form of a lower net cost of a year of college (the new net price after the subsidy is $8,000), but the suppliers would also gain $2,000 in the form of higher prices for their services. If the supply curve was more inelastic relative to the demand curve, the gains of the students would be smaller and those of the suppliers larger.

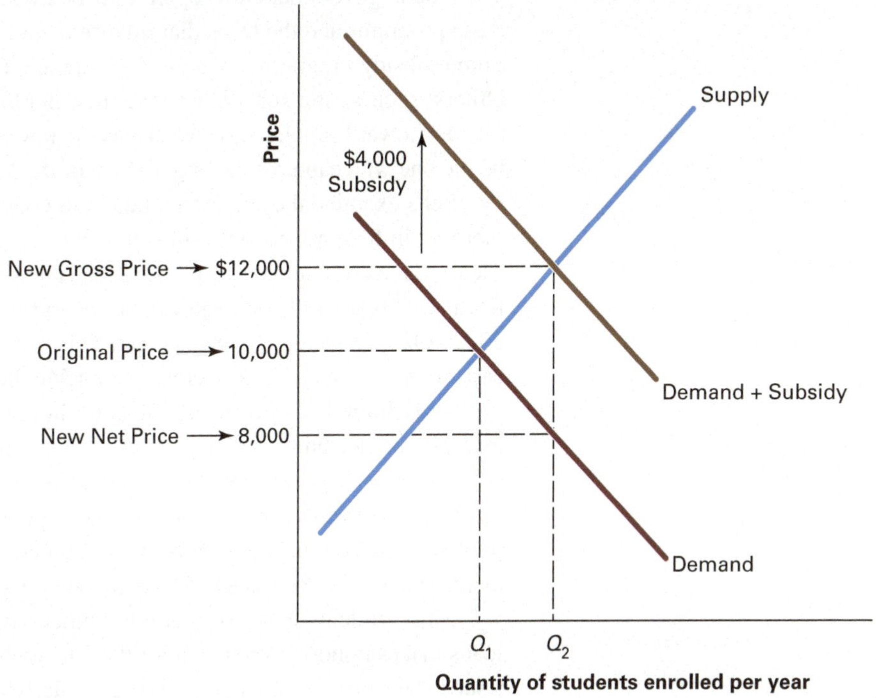

Interestingly, even though the students received an educational subsidy of $4,000, their net gain was only $2,000. The rest of the benefits went to the educational suppliers in the form of higher prices for their services.

As we previously discussed, the burden of a tax does not necessarily fall entirely or even primarily on the party writing out the check to the taxing authority. The same is true for subsidies. Parties other than the direct subsidy recipients may benefit substantially from the subsidies. Moreover, the direct recipients of the subsidy may gain less, and often substantially less, than their grant from the government.

4-6a Elasticity and the Benefit of Government Subsidy Programs

What determines the allocation of the benefits derived from a subsidy? In the example of Exhibit 4-10, the benefit of the $4,000 subsidy granted to students was split evenly between buyers and sellers. However, the actual distribution of this benefit will depend on the elasticity of supply and demand—just as it does with a tax. Consider the case where the subsidy is granted to the buyers, causing the demand curve for the product to shift upward by the amount of the subsidy. If the supply curve is highly inelastic relative to demand, the increase in demand will lead primarily to higher prices and most of the benefits will be derived by the suppliers of the good or service. In contrast, if the supply curve is elastic and the demand curve inelastic, the increase in demand will lead to only a small increase in price and the primary beneficiaries of the subsidy will be consumers in the form of lower prices.

The greater share of the benefit of a subsidy will always be shifted toward the more inelastic side of the market. Thus, the more inelastic the supply, the larger the share of the benefit that will accrue to sellers. Conversely, the more inelastic the demand, the larger the share of the benefit that will accrue to buyers. Sometimes the subsidies will be granted to sellers rather than buyers. Nonetheless, the benefits will still flow primarily toward the more inelastic side of the market.

4-6b Real-World Subsidy Programs

The federal government now operates over 2,000 separate subsidy programs. Spending on these programs and the taxes that finance them are major items in the government budget. Some subsidy programs, such as Medicare and food stamps, provide payments to buyers. Others, such as the subsidies to the arts, public broadcasting, and sports stadiums, are directed toward suppliers. As we discussed, however, the party granted the subsidy may not be the one who captures the larger share of the actual benefit from the subsidy.

Let's examine the subsidies granted to college students. There has been a substantial increase in federal and state subsidies to college students over the past several decades. Measured in constant 2022 dollars, federal and state grants directly to college students rose from $5,900 per full-time equivalent undergraduate student in 2002–2003 to $10,680 in 2022–2023, an increase of 81 percent. This is a continuation of the trend that began in the early 1990s, with a similar increase occurring throughout the 1990–2002 period.

As Exhibit 4-10 illustrates, subsidies in the form of grants and loans to students will increase the demand for college education and thereby push up its price. Indeed, this has been the case. Between 1993–1994 and 2023–2024, after adjusting for inflation to constant 2023 dollars, the average price of college at public four-year institutions based on average published tuition and fees more than doubled, from $5,380 to $11,260 (with a similar increase from $23,300 to $41,540 at private nonprofit four-year institutions).[10]

Most students perceive that government aid in the form of grants and low-interest loans makes it more economical for them to attend college. But there is another side to this issue: The subsidies are a driving force underlying the soaring cost of a college education and rising student loan debt. Moreover, colleges themselves are major beneficiaries of the student subsidies. Thus, it is not surprising that college administrators are at the forefront of those lobbying for additional subsidies.

Subsidies for medical care have had a similar impact. The Medicare and Medicaid programs were introduced in the mid-1960s. Since the large subsidies accompanying these programs were initiated, prices of medical services have persistently increased at twice the rate of the general level of prices. Again, this suggests that the suppliers of these services derived a substantial share of the benefits in the form of higher prices for their services. Given that the supply of most medical services is highly inelastic, this is precisely what one would expect from an increase in the subsidies granted to buyers.

Both the educational and medical care subsidies are allocated to a subset of the population. For example, the Medicare program subsidizes the healthcare purchases of senior citizens, and the Medicaid program provides subsidies to low-income households. These subsidies increase the demand for health care and drive up the prices of medical service for all consumers, including those ineligible for either program. When only some of the buyers in a market are subsidized, groups that are ineligible for the subsidies will generally be harmed because they will have to pay higher prices than would be the case in the absence of the subsidies.

Proponents of the health care and higher education subsidies argue they would make these items more affordable, but their impact has been nearly the opposite. This is not a surprising result. The prices of health care and higher education, including the cost of tuition, textbooks, and on- and off-campus housing, have increased substantially. Subsidies mean that a third party, the taxpayer, pays part of the cost. When someone else is paying for all or part of the cost, the consumer has less incentive to economize. Recognizing that consumers are less sensitive to price, producers are better able to raise their prices. Thus, the price of the

[10]The figures presented here are from "Trends in College Pricing and Student Aid 2023," The College Board, New York, NY, 2023, Figures SA–1 and CP–3. For additional details on the impact of subsidies to students on the cost of college, refer to Robert E. Martin and Andrew Gillen, "How College Pricing Undermines Financial Aid," The Center for College Affordability and Productivity, Washington, DC, March 2011.

subsidized good will rise more rapidly than otherwise would be the case. This is precisely what has happened in the health care and higher education sectors.

Many subsidy programs are driven by political considerations—the desire of politicians to favor various groups, particularly those that are well organized, in exchange for their votes and other forms of political support. Moreover, the subsidies often generate harmful secondary effects. Subsidized firms are encouraged to spend more time lobbying politicians and less time pleasing customers. They are also encouraged to undertake wasteful projects that fail to generate revenue sufficient to cover costs. As we proceed, we will consider the nature of favoritism and its relationship to the political process in more detail.

Key Points

- Resource markets and product markets are closely linked. A change in one will generally result in changes in the other.
- Legally imposed price ceilings result in shortages, and legally imposed price floors will cause surpluses. Both also cause other harmful secondary effects. Rent controls, for example, will lead to shortages, less investment, poor maintenance, and deterioration in the quality of rental housing.
- The minimum wage is a price floor for low-skilled labor. It increases the earnings of some low-skilled workers but also reduces employment and leads to fewer training opportunities and nonwage job benefits for many low-skilled workers.
- Because underground markets operate outside the legal system, they are often characterized by deception, fraud, and the use of violence as a means of enforcing contracts. A legal system that provides secure private-property rights and unbiased enforcement of contracts enhances the operation of markets.
- The division of the actual tax burden between buyers and sellers is determined by the relative elasticities of demand and supply rather than on whom the tax is legally imposed.
- In addition to the cost of the tax revenue transferred to the government, taxes will reduce the level of the activity taxed, eliminate some gains from trade, and thereby impose an excess burden, or deadweight loss.
- As tax rates increase, the size of the tax base will shrink. Initially, rates and revenues will be directly related—revenues will expand as rates increase. However, as higher and higher rates are imposed, eventually an inverse relationship will develop—revenues will decline as rates are increased further. The Laffer curve illustrates this pattern.
- The division of the benefit from a subsidy is determined by the relative elasticities of demand and supply rather than to whom the subsidy is actually paid. For example, when the buyers of a good are subsidized, the subsidy will increase demand and lead to higher prices. If the supply is more inelastic than the demand, the providers of the services will derive most of the benefits even though the subsidy was granted to the purchasers.

Critical Analysis Questions

1. *How will a substantial increase in demand for housing affect the wages and employment of carpenters, plumbers, and electricians?
2. Suppose that college students in your town persuaded the town council to enact a law setting the maximum price for rental housing at $400 per month. Will this help or hurt college students who rent housing? In your answer, address how this price ceiling will affect (a) the quality of rental housing; (b) the amount of rental housing available; (c) the incentive of landlords to maintain their properties; (d) the amount of racial, gender, and other types of discrimination in the local rental housing market; (e) the ease with which students will be able to find housing; and, finally, (f) whether an underground market for housing would develop.
3. What is the difference between a price ceiling and a price floor? If a price ceiling for a good is set below the market equilibrium, what will happen to the quality and future availability of the good? Explain.

4. *To be meaningful, a price ceiling must be below the market price. Conversely, a meaningful price floor must be above the market price. What impact will a meaningful price ceiling have on the quantity exchanged? What impact will a meaningful price floor have on the quantity exchanged? Explain.
5. The tax on cigarettes in New York City is one of the highest in the nation—$6.85 per pack. Does this tax raise a lot of revenue for New York City? Why or why not? What are some of the secondary effects of this tax?
6. Analyze the impact of an increase in the minimum wage from the current level to $25 per hour. How would the following be affected?
   a. employment of people previously earning less than $25 per hour
   b. the unemployment rate of teenagers
   c. the availability of on-the-job training for low-skilled workers
   d. the demand for high-skilled workers who are good substitutes for low-skilled workers
7. What is an illegal underground market? What are some of the main differences in how these markets operate relative to legal markets?
8. What is the Laffer curve? What are the important implications of the Laffer curve?
9. What is meant by the incidence of a tax? Explain why the statutory and actual incidence of a tax often differ.
10. What impact do government grants and loans to college students have on the cost of going to college? Are students the primary beneficiary of these subsidies? Discuss.
11. What is the nature of the deadweight loss accompanying taxes? Why is it often referred to as an "excess burden"?
12. *Suppose Congress were to pass legislation requiring that businesses employing workers with three or more children pay these employees at least $30 per hour. How would this legislation affect the employment level of low-skilled workers with three or more children? Do you think some workers with large families might attempt to conceal the fact? Why?
13. "We should impose a 20 percent luxury tax on expensive automobiles (those with a sales price of $75,000 or more) in order to collect more tax revenue from the wealthy." Will the burden of the proposed tax fall primarily on the wealthy? Why or why not?
14. *Should policy makers seek to set the tax on an economic activity at a rate that will maximize the revenue derived from the tax? Why or why not? Explain.
15. Suppose the government subsidizes the production and sale of spinach. What impact would this have on the price and output of spinach? Who would benefit and who would lose from this subsidy?
16. Several states have laws prohibiting businesses from increasing prices in response to a natural disaster such as a hurricane or during a declared state of emergency like the COVID-19 pandemic. In what ways is this legislation like a price control? Do these laws increase or decrease the quantity of needed supplies available in the affected areas? How do they affect the efficiency with which the limited supplies are allocated?

*Asterisk denotes questions for which answers are given in Appendix B.

Chapter 5

Difficult Cases for the Market, and the Role of Government

The principal justification for public policy intervention lies in the frequent and numerous shortcomings of market outcomes.

–Charles Wolf, Jr.[1]

As we previously discussed, market allocation and political decision-making are the two main alternatives for the organization of economic activity. Chapters 3 and 4 introduced you to how markets work and analyzed the impact of government intervention in the form of price controls, taxes, and subsidies. We noted that when property rights are well defined, and competition present, markets will tend to direct self-interested individuals into activities that promote the general welfare. But this will not always be the case. In this chapter, we turn our attention to potential problem areas when a conflict arises between personal self-interest and getting the most out of the available resources. We will also consider the implications of these problem areas with regard to the role of government. In the following chapter, we will analyze how the political process works and will compare it more directly with markets.

Learning Objectives

5.1 Explain the concept of economic efficiency and how it can be used to evaluate markets.

5.2 Differentiate the protective and productive functions of government.

5.3 Explain the concept of externalities and the reasons why they are most likely to occur.

5.4 Identify how market output will compare with the efficient ideal when external costs or external benefits are present.

5.5 Explain private or government actions that may improve economic efficiency when external costs or external benefits are present.

5.6 Describe the two characteristics of a public good that sometimes make it difficult for markets to efficiently produce these goods.

5.7 Identify the exchanges most likely to suffer from information problems and the ways in which markets help to alleviate them.

5.8 Explain the concept of government failure, including why political action will not necessarily improve efficiency when market failure is present.

[1]Charles Wolf, Jr., *Markets or Government* (Cambridge, MA: MIT Press, 1988), 17.

5-1 A Closer Examination of Economic Efficiency

Economic efficiency
A situation that occurs when (1) all activities generating more benefit than cost are undertaken and (2) no activities are undertaken for which the cost exceeds the benefit.

Economists use the standard of **economic efficiency** to assess the desirability of economic outcomes. We briefly introduced the concept in Chapter 3. We now want to explore it in more detail. The central idea of economic efficiency is straightforward. For any given level of cost, we want to obtain the largest possible benefit. Alternatively, we want to obtain any particular benefit for the least possible cost. Economic efficiency means getting the most value from the available resources—making the largest pie from the available set of ingredients, so to speak.

Economists acknowledge that individuals generally do not regard the efficiency of the entire economy as a primary goal for themselves. Rather, each person is interested in enlarging the size of their own slice. But if resources are used more efficiently, the overall size of the pie will be larger, and therefore, at least potentially, *everyone* could have a larger slice. For an outcome to be consistent with ideal economic efficiency, two conditions are necessary:

Rule 1. *Undertaking an economic action is efficient if it produces more benefits than costs.* To satisfy economic efficiency, all actions generating more benefits than costs must be undertaken. Failure to undertake all such actions implies that a potential gain has been forgone.

Rule 2. *Undertaking an economic action is inefficient if it produces more costs than benefits.* To satisfy economic efficiency, no action that generates more costs than benefits should be undertaken. When such counterproductive actions are taken, society is worse off because even better alternatives were forgone.

Economic efficiency results only when both of these conditions have been met. ***Either failure to undertake an efficient action (Rule 1) or the undertaking of an inefficient action (Rule 2) will result in economic inefficiency.*** To illustrate, consider **Exhibit 5-1**, which shows the benefits and costs associated with expanding the amount of any particular activity. We have avoided using a specific example here to ensure you understand the general idea of efficiency without linking it to a specific application. As we will show, the concept has wide-ranging applications, from the evaluation of government policy to how long you choose to brush your teeth in the morning.[2]

In Exhibit 5-1, the marginal benefit curve shows the additional benefit associated with expanding the activity. The marginal cost curve shows the cost—including any opportunity costs—of spending additional time, effort, and resources on the activity. At Q_1, the height of the marginal benefit curve exceeds the height of the marginal cost curve. Thus, at that point, the additional benefits of expanding the activity past Q_1 exceed the additional costs. According to Rule 1 of economic efficiency, we should continue to expand the activity until we reach Q_2. Beyond Q_2 (at Q_3, for example), the height of the marginal benefit curve is less than the height of the marginal cost curve. The additional benefits of expanding the activity beyond Q_2 to Q_3 are smaller than the additional costs. According to Rule 2, at Q_3, we have

[2]Note to students who may pursue advanced study in economics: Using the concept of efficiency to compare alternative policies typically requires that the analyst estimate costs and benefits that are difficult or impossible to measure. Costs and benefits are the values of opportunities forgone or accepted by individuals, *as evaluated by those individuals*. Then, these costs and benefits must be added up across all individuals and compared. But does a dollar's gain for one individual really compensate for a dollar's sacrifice by another? Some economists simply reject the validity of making such comparisons. They say that neither the estimates by the economic analyst of subjectively determined costs and benefits nor the adding up of these costs and benefits across individuals is meaningful. Their case may be valid, but most economists today nevertheless use the concept of efficiency as we present it. No other way to use economic analysis to compare policy alternatives has been found.

Exhibit 5-1 Economic Efficiency

As we use more time and resources to expand the level of an activity, the marginal benefits will generally decline and the marginal costs rise. From the viewpoint of efficiency, the activity should be expanded as long as the marginal benefits exceed the marginal costs. Therefore, quantity Q_2 is the economically efficient level of this activity. Q_1 is inefficient because some production that could generate more benefits than costs is not undertaken. Q_3 is also inefficient because some units are produced even though their costs exceed the benefits they create. Thus, either too much or too little of an activity will result in inefficiency.

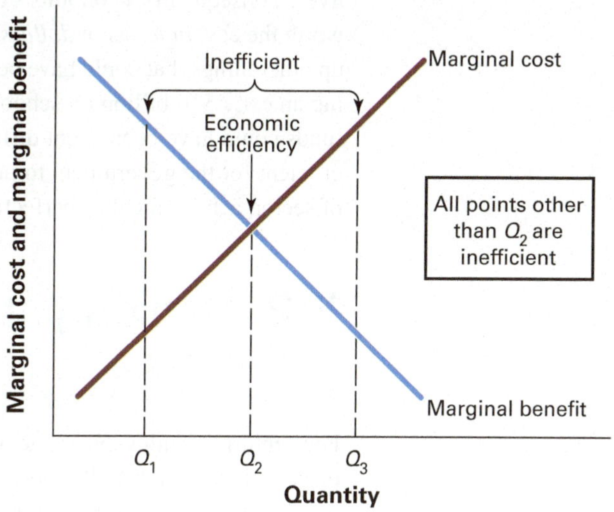

gone too far and should cut back on the activity. Q_2 is the only point consistent with both rules of economic efficiency.

5-1a If It's Worth Doing, It's Worth Doing Imperfectly

Eliminating pollution. Earning straight As. Being completely organized. Cleaning your apartment until it sparkles. Making automobiles completely safe. Making airplanes fully secure against terrorist attacks. All of these are worthwhile goals, right? Well, they are until you consider the costs of actually achieving them. The heading for this section is, of course, a play on the old saying "If it's worth doing, it's worth doing to the best of your ability." Economics suggests, however, that this is not a sensible guideline. At some point, the gains from doing something even better will not be worth the cost. It will make more sense to stop short of perfection.

Exhibit 5-1 can also be used to illustrate this point. As more resources are dedicated to an activity, the marginal improvements (benefits) will become smaller and smaller, while the marginal costs will rise. The optimal time and effort put into the activity will be achieved at Q_2, and this will nearly always be well below one's best effort. Note that inefficiency results when either too little (for example, Q_1) or too much (for example, Q_3) time and effort are put into the activity.

Do you make decisions this way? Last time you cleaned your car or apartment, why did you decide to leave some things undone? Once the most important areas were clean, you likely began to skip over other areas (like on top of the refrigerator or under the bed), figuring that the benefits of cleaning these areas were simply not worth the cost. Very few people live in a perfectly organized and clean house, wash their hands enough to prevent all colds, brush their teeth long enough to prevent all cavities, or make their home as safe as Fort Knox. They recognize that the benefit of perfection in these, and many other areas, is simply not worth the cost.

Economics is about trade-offs; it is possible to pursue even worthy activities beyond the level that is consistent with economic efficiency. People seem to be more aware of this in their personal decision-making than when evaluating public policy. It is not uncommon to hear people say things like "We ought to eliminate all pollution" or "No price is too high to save a life."

If we want to get the most out of our resources, we need to think about both marginal benefits and marginal costs and recognize that there are alternative ways of pursuing objectives. Consequently, economists do not ask whether eliminating pollution or saving lives is worth the cost *in terms of dollars* per se, but whether it is worth the cost in terms of giving up other things that could have been done with those dollars—the opportunity cost. Spending an extra $10 billion on school safety requirements to save 50 lives isn't efficient if the funds could have been spent differently and saved the lives of 500 children. It is no more efficient for the government to pursue perfection than for individuals to do so. Regardless of sector, achievement of perfection is virtually never worth the cost.

5-2 Thinking about the Economic Role of Government

For centuries, philosophers, economists, and other scholars have debated the proper role of government. While the debate continues, there is substantial agreement that at least two functions of government are legitimate: (1) protecting individuals and their property against invasions by others and (2) providing goods that cannot easily be provided through private markets. These two functions correspond to what Nobel laureate James M. Buchanan conceptualizes as the protective and productive functions of government.

5-2a Protective Function of Government

The most fundamental function of government is the protection of individuals and their property against acts of aggression. As John Locke wrote more than three centuries ago, individuals are constantly threatened by "the invasions of others." Therefore, each individual "is willing to join in society with others, who are already united, or have a mind to unite, for the mutual preservation of their lives, liberties, and estates."[3] ***The protective function of government involves the maintenance of a framework of security and order—an infrastructure of rules within which people can interact peacefully with one another.*** Protection of person and property is crucial. It entails providing police protection and prosecuting aggressors who take things that do not belong to them. It also involves providing for a national defense designed to protect against foreign invasions. The legal enforcement of contracts and rules against fraud are also central elements of the protective function. People and businesses that write bad checks, violate contracts, or knowingly supply others with false information, for example, are therefore subject to legal prosecution.

It is easy to recognize the economic importance of the protective function. When it is performed well, the property of citizens is secure, freedom of exchange is present, and contracts are legally enforceable. When people are assured that they will be able to enjoy the benefits of their efforts, they will be more productive. In contrast, when property rights are insecure and contracts unenforceable, productive behavior is undermined. Plunder, fraud, and economic chaos result. Governments set and enforce the "rules of the game" that enable markets to operate smoothly.

5-2b Productive Function of Government

The nature of some goods makes them difficult to provide through markets. Sometimes it is difficult to establish a one-to-one link between the payment and receipt of a good. If this link cannot be established, the incentive of market producers to supply these goods is weak.

---

[3]John Locke, *Treatise of Civil Government*, 1690, ed. Charles Sherman (New York: Appleton-Century-Crofts, 1937), 82.

In addition, high transaction costs—particularly, the cost of monitoring use and collecting fees—can sometimes make it difficult to supply a good through the market. When either of these conditions is present, it may be more efficient for the government to supply the good and impose taxes on its citizens to cover the cost.

One of the most important productive functions of government is providing a stable monetary and financial environment. If markets are going to work well, individuals have to know the value of what they are buying or selling. For market prices to convey this information, a stable monetary system is needed. This is especially true for the many market exchanges that involve a time dimension. Houses, cars, consumer durables, land, buildings, equipment, and many other items are often paid for over a period of months or even years. When the purchasing power of money fluctuates wildly, previously determined prices do not represent their intended values. Under these circumstances, exchanges involving long-term commitments are hampered, and the smooth operation of markets is undermined.

The government's tax, spending, and monetary policies exert a powerful influence on the stability of the overall economy. If properly conducted, these policies contribute to economic stability, full and efficient utilization of resources, and stable prices. However, improper stabilization policies can cause massive unemployment, rapidly rising prices, or both. For those pursuing a course in macroeconomics, these issues will be central to that analysis.

Bettmann/Getty Images

The English philosopher John Locke argued that people own themselves and, as a result of this self-ownership, they also own the fruits of their labor. Locke stressed that individuals are not subservient to governments. On the contrary, the role of governments is to protect the "natural rights" of individuals to their person and property. This view, also reflected in the "unalienable rights" section of the U.S. Declaration of Independence, is the basis for the protective function of government.

5-3 Potential Shortcomings of the Market

As we previously discussed, the invisible hand of market forces generally gives resource owners and business firms a strong incentive to use their resources efficiently and undertake projects that create value. Will this always be true? The answer to this question is "No." There are four major factors that can undermine the invisible hand and reduce the efficiency of markets: (1) lack of competition, (2) externalities, (3) public goods, and (4) poorly informed buyers or sellers. We will now consider each of these factors and explain why they may justify government intervention.

5-3a Lack of Competition

Competition is vital to the proper operation of the pricing mechanism. The existence of competing buyers and sellers reduces the power of both to rig or alter the market in their own favor. Although competition is beneficial from a social point of view, individually each of us would prefer to be loosened from its grip. Students do not like stiff competitors in their romantic lives, at exam time, or when they're trying to get into graduate school. Buyers in online auctions hope for few competing bidders so they can purchase the items they're bidding on at lower prices. Similarly, sellers prefer fewer competing sellers so they can sell at higher prices. This is precisely why taxi companies are quick to protest and seek bans against ride-sharing services like Uber and Lyft when they come to an area.

Exhibit 5-2 illustrates how sellers can gain from restricting competition. In the absence of any restrictions on competition in the market, the price P_1 and output Q_1 associated with the competitive supply curve (S_1) will prevail. Here, Q_1 is the level of output consistent with economic efficiency. If a group of sellers is able to restrict competition, perhaps by forcing some firms out of the market and preventing new firms from entering, the group would be able to gain by raising the price of the product. This is illustrated by the price P_2 and output Q_2 associated with the restricted supply (S_2). Even though the output is smaller, the total revenue (price P_2 times quantity Q_2) derived by the sellers at the restricted output level is

Exhibit 5-2 Lack of Competition and Problems for the Market

If a group of sellers can restrict competition, the group may be able to gain by reducing supply (to S_2, for example) and raising the price (to P_2, for example) rather than charging the competitive market price of P_1. Under these circumstances, output will be less than the economically efficient level.

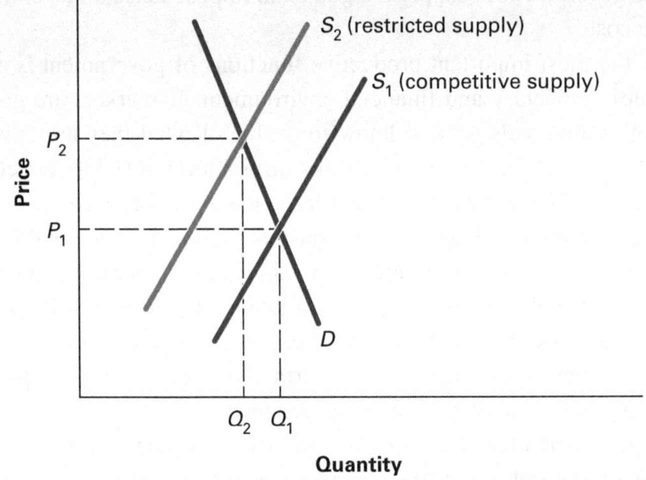

greater than at the competitive price P_1. Clearly, the sellers gain because, at the higher price, they are being paid more to produce less.

The restricted output level, however, is clearly less efficient. At the competitive output level Q_1, all units that were valued more than their cost are produced and sold. But this is not the case at Q_2. The additional units between Q_2 and Q_1 are valued more than their cost. Nonetheless, they will not be produced if suppliers are able to limit competition and restrict output. When competition is absent, there is a potential conflict between the interests of sellers and the efficient use of resources.

What can the government do to ensure that markets are competitive? The first guideline might be borrowed from the medical profession: Do no harm. A productive government will refrain from using its powers to impose licenses, discriminatory taxes, price controls, tariffs, quotas, and other entry and trade restraints that lessen the intensity of competition. In the vast majority of markets, sellers will find it difficult or impossible to limit the entry of rival firms (including rival producers from other countries). Thus, most suppliers will not be able to limit competition unless they get the government to impose various types of entry restrictions or mandates that provide them with an advantage relative to rivals. Predictably, private firms and interest groups will lobby for government action of this type. When governments succumb to these pressures and engage in actions that limit competition, however, economic inefficiency will result.

When entering a market is very costly and there are only a few existing sellers, it may be possible for these sellers by themselves to restrict competition. In an effort to deal with cases like this, the United States has enacted a series of "antitrust laws," most notably the Sherman Antitrust Act (1890) and the Clayton Act (1914), making it illegal for firms to collude or attempt to monopolize a market.

Virtually all economists favor competitive markets, but there is considerable debate about the impact of government action in this area. Many economists believe that, by and large, government policy in this area has been ineffective. Others stress that government policies have often been misused to actually limit competition, rather than promote it. Laws are often adopted that restrict entry into markets, protect existing producers from competitors, and limit price competition. For those taking a microeconomics course, noncompetitive markets and related policy alternatives will be analyzed in greater detail later.

5-3b Externalities–a Failure to Account for All Costs and Benefits

When property rights are unclear or poorly enforced, the actions of an individual or group may "spill over" onto others and thereby affect their well-being without their consent. These spillover effects are called **externalities**. You are probably familiar with externalities. For example, when your neighbor's loud music makes it hard for you to study, you are experiencing an externality firsthand. Although your neighbors do not have a right to come in to your apartment and create a disturbance, they do have a right to listen to their music, and if they play it loudly, this may interfere with the quietness of your apartment. Their actions impose a cost on you, and they also raise an issue of property rights. Do your neighbors have a property right to play their music as loudly as they please? Or do you have a property right to quietness in your own apartment? When questions like these arise, how should the boundaries of property rights be determined, and what steps should be taken to ensure adequate enforcement? Although the volume of your neighbor's music may not be a major economic issue, it nonetheless illustrates the nature of the problems that arise when property rights are unclear and externalities are present.

Externalities
Spillover effects of an activity that influence the well-being of nonconsenting parties.

The spillover effects may either impose a cost or create a benefit for external parties—people not directly involved in the transaction, activity, or exchange. Economists use the term **external cost** to describe a situation in which the spillover effects harm external parties. If the spillover effects enhance the welfare of the external parties, an **external benefit** is present. We will analyze both external costs and external benefits and consider why both of them can lead to problems.

External cost
Spillover effects that reduce the well-being of nonconsenting parties.

External benefit
Spillover effects that generate benefits for nonconsenting parties.

5-3c External Costs

Economists worry about external costs because they may result in economic inefficiency. For example, resources may be used to produce goods that are valued less than their production costs, including the costs imposed on the nonconsenting parties. Consider the production of paper. The firms in the market operate mills and purchase labor, trees, and other resources to produce the paper. But they also emit pollutants into the atmosphere that impose costs on residents living around the mills. The pollutants cause paint on buildings to deteriorate more rapidly. They make it difficult for some people to breathe normally, and perhaps cause other health hazards. If the residents living near a pulp mill can prove they have been harmed, they could take the mill to court and force the paper producer to cover the cost of their damages. But it might be difficult to prove that they were harmed and that the pulp mill is responsible for the damage. The residents' property rights to clean air may be difficult to enforce, particularly if there are many parties emitting pollutants into the air.

If the residents are unable to enforce their property rights, the production of paper will result in an external cost that will not be registered through markets. **Exhibit 5-3** illustrates the implications of these external costs within the supply and demand framework. As the result of the external cost generated in paper production, the market supply curve S_1 will understate the true cost of producing paper. It reflects only the cost actually paid by the firms and ignores the uncompensated costs imposed on the nearby residents. Under these circumstances, the

External costs resulting from poorly defined and enforced property rights underlie the problems of excessive air and water pollution.

Inu/Shutterstock.com

Exhibit 5-3 External Costs and Output That Is Greater than the Efficient Level

When an activity such as paper production imposes external costs on nonconsenting parties, these costs will not be registered by the market supply curve (S_1). As a result, output will be beyond the economically efficient level. The units between Q_2 and Q_1 will be produced, even though their cost exceeds the value they provide to consumers.

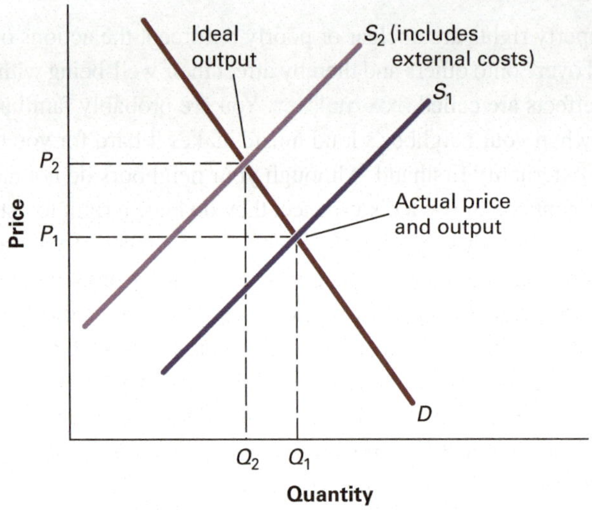

firm will expand output to Q_1 (the intersection of the demand curve D and supply curve S_1) and the market price P_1 will emerge. Is this price and output consistent with economic efficiency? The answer is clearly "No." If all of the costs of producing the paper, including those imposed on external parties, were taken into account, the supply curve S_2 would result. From an efficiency standpoint, only the smaller quantity Q_2 should be produced. The units beyond Q_2 on out to Q_1 cost more than their value to consumers. People would be better off if the resources used to produce those units (beyond Q_2) were used to produce other things. Nonetheless, profit-maximizing firms will expand output into this range. Thus, when external costs are generated in production, the market supply curve will understate production costs, and output will be expanded beyond the quantity consistent with economic efficiency. Moreover, resources for which property rights are poorly enforced will be overutilized and sometimes polluted. This is often the case with air and water when the property rights to these resources are poorly enforced.

5-3d What Should Be Done about External Costs?

External costs often arise because property rights are poorly defined or imperfectly enforced. Initially, therefore, it makes sense to think seriously about how property rights might be better defined and enforced. However, the nature of some goods will make the defining and enforcement of property rights extremely difficult. This will certainly be the case for resources like clean air and many fish species in the ocean. In cases that involve a relatively small number of people, the parties involved may be able to agree to rules and establish procedures that will minimize the external effects. For example, property owners around a small lake will generally be able to control access to the lake and prevent each other, as well as outsiders, from polluting or overfishing the lake.

However, in cases that involve large numbers of people, the transaction costs of arriving at an agreement will generally be prohibitively high, so it is unrealistic to expect that private contracts among the parties will handle the situation satisfactorily. For example, this will be the case when a large number of automobiles and firms emit pollutants into the atmosphere. In the case of pollution from a large number of emitters, government regulations requiring devices that limit the level of emissions may be the best option.

Sometimes creative arrangements can be devised to reduce the harmful side effects of external cost even in cases involving large numbers of people. Consider the case of ocean

Outstanding Economist

Elinor Ostrom (1933-2012)

John Sommers/Reuters

In 2009, Elinor Ostrom became the first woman to earn the Nobel Prize in Economics, an award she shared with Oliver Williamson. Ostrom had a lengthy career as a distinguished professor and director of the Workshop in Political Theory and Policy Analysis at Indiana University. She was awarded the Nobel Prize for her research on the "tragedy of the commons"–the idea that when a resource is owned in common it will be overused because each person has an incentive to use it before others do. Ostrom examined numerous real-world cases and discovered that communities were often able to develop rules for the successful private management of common-pool resources. If the rules were going to work well, they must clearly define who gets what, provide for conflict resolution, and assign the duty of individuals to maintain the resource in proportion to the benefits received. Ostrom's research found that community management and rulemaking was often superior to top-down central planning by governmental authorities. Her work provides insight on how cooperative arrangements can sometime lead to efficient solutions even when a resource is owned in common.

fisheries. Because the ocean is an open-access resource, each fisherman has an incentive to catch as many fish as possible. But their actions impose an external cost on others, because the population of many fish species will be reduced to levels that are insufficient for reproduction to sustain the species in the future. Many governments responded to this situation by shortening the fishing season. But this option was ineffective because fishermen countered with bigger boats, more advanced technology, and taking greater risk such as fishing even when weather conditions were highly unfavorable. Thus, this option was dangerous for the fishermen and did little to improve sustainability.

Recognizing the nature of the problem, fishing interests have cooperated with governments to develop a property rights system to help ensure the sustainability of the fish population. These systems provide individual fishermen with transferable quotas, representing a property right to a share of the season's total catch. A fisheries management authority determines the sustainable limit prior to each season. The quotas can be bought, sold, or leased at unregulated market prices. With the tradable quota system, the fish population is sustainable and the race to catch fish before someone else does is eliminated. Individuals know they will be permitted to keep fishing until they catch their quota. These arrangements have now been adopted in more than 200 fishing areas throughout the world. The research of Elinor Ostrom, the 2009 Nobel laureate in economics, provides insight on both the operation and structure of effective arrangements designed to reduce the harmful side effects of common ownership and externalities in a broad range of areas. However, despite the development of innovative arrangements, failure of markets to register fully costs that are external to decision-makers is nonetheless a continuing source of economic inefficiency.

5-3e External Benefits

As we mentioned, sometimes the actions of individuals and firms generate external benefits for others. The homeowner who keeps a house in good condition and maintains a neat lawn improves the beauty of the entire community. A flood-control dam built by upstream residents for their benefit might also generate gains for those who live downstream. Scientific theories benefit their authors, but the knowledge can also help others who did not contribute to the development of them.

From the standpoint of efficiency, why might external benefits be a problem? Here, inefficiency may arise because potential producers may fail to undertake productive activities because they are unable to fully capture the benefits their actions create for others. Suppose a pharmaceutical company develops a vaccine protecting users against a contagious virus or some other communal disease. Of course, the vaccine can easily be marketed to users who will benefit directly from it. However, because of the communal nature of the virus, as people take the vaccine, nonusers who are unvaccinated will also be less likely to get the virus. But these external benefits accruing to other individuals will not be reflected in the market demand curve. Individuals will make the decision to get vaccinated based upon their own personal benefit, and the pharmaceutical companies will be unable to capture revenue reflecting the benefit to the nonusers. As a result, too few individuals will get the vaccine, and too little of it will be supplied, relative to economic efficiency.

Exhibit 5-4 illustrates the impact of external benefits in consumption like those generated by the vaccine within the framework of supply and demand. The market demand curve reflects the benefits derived by the users of the vaccine, while the supply curve reflects the opportunity cost of providing it. Market forces result in an equilibrium price of P_1 and output of Q_1. Is this outcome consistent with economic efficiency? Again, the answer is "No." The market demand curve D_1 will register only the benefits derived by the users. Those benefits that accrue to unvaccinated nonusers, who are now less likely to contract the flu, will not be taken into account by decision-makers. The vaccine makes it more likely that these people will not get sick, but the producer doesn't derive any benefit (sales revenue) from having done so. Thus, market demand D_1 understates the total benefits derived from the use of the vaccine. Demand D_2 provides a measure of these total benefits, including those that accrue to the nonusers. The units between Q_1 and Q_2 are valued more highly than what it costs to produce them. Nonetheless, they will not be consumed or supplied. Thus, when external benefits are present, market forces may result in less output than the amount consistent with economic efficiency.

Exhibit 5-4 External Benefits and Output That Is Less than the Efficient Level

A vaccine that protects users against the flu will also help nonusers by making it less likely that they will catch it. But this benefit will not be registered by the market demand curve (D_1). In cases where external benefits like this are present, output will be less than the economically efficient level. Even though the units between Q_1 and Q_2 generate more benefits than costs, they will not be consumed or supplied, and sellers will be unable to capture the value of these external benefits.

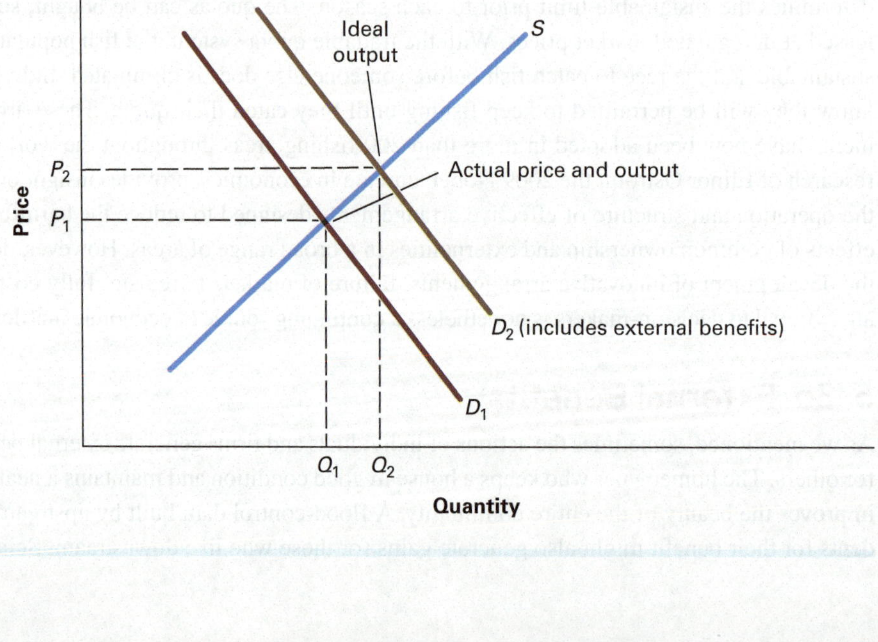

Entrepreneurs Who Have Changed Our Lives

Walt Disney

HO Images/Alamy Stock Photo

Although it did not open until five years after Walt Disney's death, Disney World was the culmination of a career of innovation. Disney pushed the boundaries of technology to create unusual products that appealed to the imagination and drew enormous crowds, especially families. Most of Disney's achievements were in film, particularly animated movies, as he created iconic cartoon figures such as Mickey Mouse, Donald Duck, and Goofy.

Born in Chicago in 1901, Disney was the son of a struggling businessman. His family—Walt, his parents, and three siblings—moved around the Midwest, as his father tried one business after another, and most failed. As a child, Disney loved to draw cartoons, to listen to his mother tell fairy tales, and to read the books of Charles Dickens and Mark Twain. His love of fantasy and fiction served him well over time.

Disney, along with his brother Roy and a friend, Ubbe Iwerks, began to develop animated cartoon movies in Kansas City. They moved to Los Angeles when the animated film industry was still in its early stages of development. In 1937, in the depths of the Great Depression, Disney's first full-length animated film, *Snow White and the Seven Dwarfs*, earned nearly $1.5 million at the box office and won eight Academy Awards. Animated features such as *Bambi* and *Fantasia* followed.

But he didn't stop there. As television became popular in the 1950s, Disney created such popular programs as *Zorro*, *Davy Crockett*, and *The Mickey Mouse Club*. And in 1955 he opened the most exciting amusement park of its time, Disneyland, in Anaheim, California. Disney's restless mind, supported by his brother and a friend, created joy for generations of children—and adults, too.

Sources: "Walt Disney," *Biography*, biography.com, https://www.biography.com/business-figure/walt-disney.

Marc Eliot, *Walt Disney: Hollywood's Dark Prince* (New York: HarperPaperbacks, 1993).

5-3f Expanding the Scope of a Project and Capturing External Benefits

External benefits result in a misallocation of resources if entrepreneurs fail to undertake potentially wealth-creating projects because of their inability to fully capture the benefits of their actions. However, when entrepreneurs can figure out a way to more fully capture these benefits, some otherwise unprofitable projects can be transformed into profitable ones. Entrepreneurs have an incentive to figure out ways to do this. In some cases, they can do so by extending the scope of the project.

The development of golf courses provides an example. Because of the beauty and openness of the courses, many people find it attractive to live nearby. Thus, constructing a golf course typically generates an external benefit—an increase in the value of the nearby property. In recent years, golf course developers have figured out how to capture this benefit. Now, they typically purchase a large tract of land around the planned course *before it is built.* This lets them resell the land at a higher price after the golf course has been completed and the surrounding land has increased in value. By extending the scope of their activities to include real estate as well as golf course development, they are able to capture what would otherwise be external benefits. As a result, some wealth-creating projects are undertaken that would have otherwise gone unrealized.

The development of Florida's Walt Disney World provides another interesting case study in entrepreneurial ingenuity designed to capture external benefits more fully. When Walt Disney developed Disneyland in California, the market value of the land in the immediate area soared as a result of the increase in demand for services (food, lodging, gasoline, and so on). Because the land in the area was owned by others, the developers of Disneyland were unable to capture these external benefits. In addition, Disney felt as if some of the adult nightclubs that had opened around his existing Disneyland park were imposing external costs on him by detracting from the family image his park was trying to attain.

Because of his experience with these externalities, when Walt Disney World was developed outside of Orlando, Florida, in the mid-1960s, Walt Disney purchased far more land than was needed for the amusement park. This enabled him to capture the increased land value surrounding his development (when he resold the land for a higher price) and reduce the negative externalities imposed on him via his control of the surrounding property.

The purchases were made as secretly as possible to prevent speculators from driving up the land prices if Disney's actions were detected. Disney even created a handful of smaller companies, with names like the Latin-American Development and Managers Corporation and the Reedy Creek Ranch Corporation, to purchase the land. After his first major land purchase of 12,400 acres, Walt Disney was at a meeting at which he was offered an opportunity to purchase an additional 8,500 acres. Walt Disney's assistant was rumored to have said, "But Walt, we already own 12,000 acres, enough to build the park." Disney replied, "How would you like to own 8,000 acres around our existing Disneyland facility right now?" His assistant immediately responded, "Buy it!"

By June 1965, Disney had purchased 27,400 acres, or about 43 square miles—an area 150 times larger than his existing Disneyland park, and about twice as big as Manhattan. In October 1965, when an Orlando newspaper finally broke the story that Disney was behind the land purchases, the remaining land prices around his property jumped from $183 an acre to $1,000 an acre overnight. Just as Disney expected, the value of the land surrounding Walt Disney World soared as the demand for hotels, restaurants, and other businesses increased along with the development of the amusement park. After the park's construction, the resale of nearby land was a major source of revenue for the company. To a large degree, the success of the Disney Corporation reflects Walt Disney's entrepreneurial ability to figure out how to capture external benefits by expanding the scope of the project.

5-3g Public Goods and Why They Pose a Problem for the Market

Public goods
Goods for which rivalry among consumers is absent and exclusion of nonpaying customers is difficult.

What are public goods? **Public goods** have two distinguishing characteristics; they are (1) nonrival in consumption and (2) nonexcludable. Let's examine both of these characteristics in more detail.

Nonrivalry in consumption means that making the good available to one consumer does not reduce its availability to others. In fact, providing it to one person simultaneously makes it available to other consumers, so these goods are considered joint-in-consumption. A radio broadcast signal provides an example. The same signal can be shared by everyone within the listening range. Having additional listeners tune in does not detract from the availability of the signal. Clearly, most goods do not have this shared consumption characteristic, but are instead rival-in-consumption. For example, two individuals cannot simultaneously consume the same pair of jeans. Further, a pair of jeans purchased by one person does not make jeans more readily available to others.

The second characteristic of a public good—nonexcludability—means that it is impossible (or at least very costly) to exclude nonpaying customers from receiving the good. Suppose an antimissile system were being built around the city in which you live. How could some people in the city be protected by the system and others excluded? Most people will realize there is no way the system can protect their neighbors from incoming missiles without providing similar protection to other residents. Thus, the services of the antimissile system have the nonexcludability characteristic.

It is important to note that it is the characteristic of the good, not the sector in which it is produced, that determines whether it qualifies as a public good. There is a tendency to think that if a good is provided by the government, then it is a public good. This is not the case. Many of the goods provided by governments clearly do not have the characteristics of public goods. Medical services, education, mail delivery, trash collection, and electricity come to mind. Although these goods are often supplied by governments, they do not have either nonrivalry or nonexcludability characteristics. Thus, they are not public goods.

Why are public goods difficult for markets to allocate efficiently? The nonexcludability characteristic provides the answer. Because those who do not pay cannot be excluded, sellers are generally unable to establish a one-to-one link between the payment and receipt of these goods. Realizing they cannot be excluded, potential consumers have little incentive to pay for these goods. Instead, they have an incentive to become **free riders**, people who receive the benefits of the good without helping to pay for its cost. But, when a large number of people become free riders and revenues thus are low, not very much of the good is supplied. This is precisely the problem: Markets will tend to undersupply public goods, even when the population in aggregate values them highly relative to their cost.

Free riders
People who receive the benefit of a good without paying for it. Because it is often virtually impossible to restrict the consumption of public goods to those who pay, these goods are subject to free-rider problems.

Suppose national defense were provided entirely through the market. Would you voluntarily help to pay for it? Your contribution would have little impact on the total supply of defense available to each of us, even if you made a large personal contribution. Many citizens, even though they might value defense highly, would become free riders, and few funds would be available to finance national defense.

For most goods, it is easy to establish a link between payment and receipt. If you do not pay for a gallon of ice cream, an automobile, a laptop, and literally thousands of other items, suppliers will not provide them to you. Thus, there are very few public goods. National defense is the classic example of a public good. Radio and TV signals, software programs, flood-control projects, mosquito abatement programs, and perhaps some scientific theories also have public good characteristics. But beyond this short list, it is difficult to think of additional goods that qualify.

Just because a good is a public good does not necessarily mean that markets will fail to supply it. When the benefit of producing these goods is high, entrepreneurs will attempt to find innovative ways to gain by overcoming the free-rider problem. For example, radio and television broadcasts, which have both of the public good characteristics, are still produced well by the private sector. The free-rider problem is overcome through the use of advertising (which generates indirect revenue from listeners), rather than by directly charging listeners or viewers. Private entrepreneurs have developed things like copy limitations on digital music and movies as well as computer software, and tie-in purchases (for example, tying the inclusion of operating system software with the purchase of a computer) to overcome the free-rider problem.

In spite of the innovative efforts of entrepreneurs, however, the quantity of public goods supplied strictly through market allocation might still be smaller than the quantity consistent with economic efficiency. This creates a potential opportunity for government action to improve the efficiency of resource allocation.

5-3h Potential Information Problems

Like other goods, information is scarce. Thus, when making purchasing decisions, people are sometimes poorly informed about the price, quality, durability, and side effects of alternative products. Imperfect knowledge is not the fault of the market. In fact, the market provides consumers with a strong incentive to acquire information. If they mistakenly purchase a "lemon," they will suffer the consequences. Furthermore, sellers have a strong incentive to inform consumers about the benefits of their products, especially in comparison with competing products. However, circumstances will influence the incentive structure confronted by both buyers and sellers.

The consumer's information problem is minimal if the item is purchased regularly. Consider the purchase of soap. There is little cost associated with trying different brands. Because soap is a regularly purchased product, trial and error is an economical means of determining which brand is most suitable to one's needs. Regularly purchased items such as toothpaste, most food products, lawn service, and gasoline provide additional examples of **repeat-purchase items**. When purchasing items like these, the consumer can use past experience to acquire accurate information and make wise decisions.

Repeat-purchase items
An item purchased often by the same buyer.

Furthermore, the sellers of repeat-purchase items also have a strong incentive to supply consumers with accurate information about them because failing to do so will adversely affect future sales. Because future demand is directly related to the satisfaction level of current customers, sellers of repeat-purchase items will want to help their customers make satisfying long-run choices. This helps harmonize the interests of buyers and sellers.

But harmony will not always occur. Conflicting interests, inadequate information, and unhappy customers can arise when goods are either (1) difficult to evaluate on inspection and seldom repeatedly purchased from the same producer or (2) potentially capable of serious and lasting harmful side effects that cannot be predicted by a typical consumer. Under these conditions, consumers might make decisions they will later regret.

When customers are unable to distinguish between high-quality and low-quality goods, business entrepreneurs have an incentive to cut costs by reducing quality. Businesses that follow this course may survive and even prosper. Consider the information problem when an automobile is purchased. Are consumers capable of properly evaluating the safety equipment? Most are not. Of course, some consumers will seek the opinion of experts, or consult the online reviews by prior customers, but this information will be costly and difficult to evaluate. In this case, it might be more efficient to have the government regulate automobile safety and require certain safety equipment.

Similar issues arise with regard to product effectiveness. Suppose a new wonder drug promises to reduce the probability a person will be stricken by cancer or heart disease. Even if the product is totally ineffective, many consumers will waste their money trying it. Verifying the effectiveness of the drug will be a complicated and lengthy process. Consequently, it may be better to have experts certify its effectiveness. The federal Food and Drug Administration was established to perform this function. However, letting the experts decide is also a less than ideal solution. The certification process is likely to be costly and lengthy. As a result, the introduction of products that are effective may be delayed for years, and they are likely to be more costly than they would be otherwise.

5-3i Information as a Profit Opportunity

Consumers are willing to pay for and invest their time in acquiring information that will help them make better decisions. This presents a profit opportunity. Entrepreneurial providers of information help consumers find what they seek by offering product evaluations by experts. For example, dozens of sources provide independent expert opinions about automobiles and computers at a low cost to potential purchasers. Laboratory test results and detailed product evaluations on a wide variety of goods are provided by firms such as Consumer Reports and J.D. Power.

The online reviews written by bloggers and other customers are helping to even better overcome potential information problems than was possible prior to the widespread use of cell phones and the internet. The reviews of previous customers on Etsy, Amazon, and Google Maps, for example, help buyers make better-informed choices. In effect, this online review process holds a seller's future sales hostage to the quality with which they satisfy even a one-time buyer, creating the same incentives present for sellers of repeat-purchase items. Failure to satisfy just a few customers can result in many other buyers not being willing to purchase from that seller. The ability of buyers and sellers to leave online reviews for others to consider in their decision process is part of the value proposition that makes these companies successful ventures.

Franchise
A right or license granted to an individual to market a company's goods or services or use its brand name. The individual firms are independently owned but must meet certain conditions to continue to use the name.

Franchises are another way entrepreneurs have responded to the need of consumers for more and better information. A **franchise** is a right or license granted to an individual to market a company's goods or services (or use their brand name). Fast-food restaurants like

McDonald's and Wendy's are typically organized as franchises. The individual restaurants are independently owned, but the owner pays for the right to use the company name and must offer specific products and services in a manner specified by the franchiser. Franchises help give consumers reliable information. The tourist traveling through an area for the first time with very little time to search out alternatives may find that eating at a franchised restaurant and sleeping at a franchised motel are the cheapest ways to avoid annoying and costly mistakes that might come from patronizing an unknown local establishment. The franchiser sets the standards for all firms in the chain and establishes procedures, including continuous inspections, designed to maintain the standards. Franchisers have a strong incentive to maintain their reputation for quality, because if it declines, their ability to sell new franchises and to collect ongoing franchise fees is adversely affected. Even though the tourist may visit a particular establishment only once, the franchise turns that visit into a "repeat purchase" because the reputation of the entire national franchise operation is at stake.

Similarly, advertising a brand name nationally puts the brand's reputation at stake each time a purchase is made. How much would the Coca-Cola Company pay to avoid the sale of a dangerous bottle of Coke? Surely, it would be a large sum. Coca-Cola's brand name was worth an estimated $106 billion in 2023. The value of that brand name is a hostage to quality control. The firm would suffer enormous damage if it failed to maintain the quality of its product. For example, in 2000 and 2001, Firestone's brand name suffered an immense reduction in value after only a few Firestone tires were suspected of being defective. In 2018, amid concerns over user privacy issues, Facebook's brand value declined by 6 percent. More recently, a controversial marketing campaign by Bud Light in 2023 resulted in its

NetPhotos/Alamy Stock Photo

ferdyboy/Shutterstock.com

McDonalds

360b/Shutterstock.com

Ingram Publishing/Newscom

Brand names (like Coca-Cola), franchises (like McDonald's or Best Western), consumer-ratings organizations (like Consumer Reports), and private-sector certification firms (like Underwriters Laboratories, Inc.) are ways the private sector helps buyers overcome potential information problems.

parent company (AB InBev) experiencing a 20 percent decline in its stock price, and the beer losing its place as the best-selling brand in the United States after 20 years at the top.

Creative entrepreneurs have found ways to assure buyers that products meet high standards of quality, even when the producer is small and not so well known. Consider the case of Best Western Motels.[4] Best Western owns no motels; however, building on the franchise idea, it publishes rules and standards with which motel owners must comply if they are to use the Best Western brand name and the reservation service that the company also operates. To protect its brand name, Best Western sends out inspectors to see that each Best Western Motel meets these standards. Every disappointed customer harms the reputation and reduces the value of the Best Western name, which reduces the willingness of motel owners to pay for use of the name. The standards are designed to keep customers satisfied. Even though each motel owner has only a relatively small operation, renting the Best Western name provides the small operator with the kind of international reputation formerly available only to large firms. In effect, Best Western acts as a regulator of all motels bearing its name. It profits by requiring efficient standards—those that produce maximum visitor satisfaction for every dollar spent by the motels utilizing the franchise name. As it does so, it helps eliminate problems in the market that result from imperfect information.

Underwriters Laboratories Inc. (UL) is another example of private-sector regulation aimed at overcoming potential information problems. UL is a private-sector corporation that has been testing and certifying products for more than 100 years based on its own set of quality standards. Many of your household appliances probably have an UL mark. Sellers pay a fee to have UL evaluate their products for possible certification. The value of the UL brand depends on its careful evaluation of every product it certifies. If UL allows defective products to carry its mark, its brand value will diminish.

Information published by reliable sources, franchising, and brand names can help consumers make better-informed decisions. Although these options are effective, they will not always provide an ideal solution. Government regulation may sometimes be able to improve the situation, but this, too, has some predictable shortcomings. As with other things, there is no general solution to imperfect information problems.

5-4 Market and Government Failure

Market failure
A situation in which the structure of incentives is such that markets will encourage individuals to undertake activities that are inconsistent with economic efficiency.

As we have shown in this chapter, a lack of competition, externalities, public goods, and information problems often pose challenges and sometimes undermine the efficient operation of markets. Economists use the term **market failure** to describe the situation where there is reason to believe that markets will fail to achieve the conditions implied by idealized economic efficiency. Private entrepreneurs can profit, however, from solving these problems, so markets can sometimes overcome these potential challenges on their own.

Government failure
A situation in which the structure of incentives is such that the political process, including democratic political decision-making, will encourage individuals to undertake actions that conflict with economic efficiency.

It is tempting to jump to the conclusion that if the market fails to achieve economic efficiency, then the government can intervene and improve the situation. Indeed, even professional economists often make this error. But we must not forget that government directed by political decision-making is merely an alternative form of economic organization. It is not a corrective device that can be counted on to make choices that will promote economic efficiency. There is government failure, as well as market failure. **Government failure** is present when political choices lead to outcomes that conflict with the efficient allocation of resources. In order to evaluate the potential of political decision-making to improve on the shortcomings of the market and allocate resources efficiently, we need better knowledge about how the political process works. This will be the focal point of the next chapter.

[4]This section draws from Randall G. Holcombe and Lora P. Holcombe, "The Market for Regulation," *Journal of Institutional and Theoretical Economics* 142, no. 4 (1986): 684–96.

Key Points

- Economists use the standard of economic efficiency to assess the desirability of economic outcomes. Efficiency requires (1) that all actions generating more benefit than cost be undertaken and (2) that no actions generating more cost than benefit be undertaken.
- Although perfection is a noble goal, it is rarely worth achieving because additional time and resources devoted to an activity generally yield smaller and smaller benefits and cost more and more. Inefficiency can result when either too little or too much effort is put into an activity.
- Governments can enhance economic well-being by performing both protective and productive functions. The protective function involves (1) the protection of individuals and their property against aggression and (2) the provision of a legal system for the enforcement of contracts and settlement of disputes. The productive function of government can help people obtain goods that would be difficult to supply through markets.
- When markets fail to meet the conditions for ideal economic efficiency, the problem can generally be traced to one of four sources: absence of competition, externalities, public goods, or poor information.
- Externalities generally reflect a lack of fully defined and enforced property rights. When external costs are present, output may be too large—units are produced even though their costs exceed the benefits they generate. In contrast, external benefits may lead to an output that is too small—some units are not produced even though the benefits of doing so would exceed the cost.
- Public goods are goods for which (1) rivalry in consumption is absent and (2) it is difficult to exclude those who do not pay. Because of the difficulties involved in establishing a one-to-one link between payment and receipt of such goods, the market supply of public goods will often be less than the economically efficient quantity.
- Entrepreneurs in markets have an incentive to find solutions to each market problem, and new solutions are constantly being discovered. But problems remain that can potentially be improved through government action.
- Both markets and government can have problems in achieving the efficient allocation of resources. The term *market failure* describes the situation where markets will fail to achieve the conditions implied by idealized economic efficiency. But political action may also result in outcomes that are inefficient, a situation known as *government failure*.

Critical Analysis Questions

1. *Why is it important for producers to be able to prevent nonpaying customers from receiving a good?
2. In response to the terrorist attacks of September 11, 2001, airline security screening increased dramatically. As a result, the travel time of airline passengers has increased substantially. Would it make economic sense to devote enough resources to completely prevent any such future attacks? Why or why not?
3. What are the distinguishing characteristics of "public goods"? Give two examples of a public good. Why are public goods difficult for markets to allocate efficiently?
4. Which of the following are public goods? Explain, using the definition of a public good.
   - **a.** an antimissile system surrounding Washington, D.C.
   - **b.** a fire department
   - **c.** tennis courts
   - **d.** Yellowstone National Park
   - **e.** elementary schools
5. Explain in your own words what is meant by external costs and external benefits. Why may market outcomes be less than ideal when externalities are present?
6. English philosopher John Locke argued that the protection of each individual's person and property (acquired without the use of violence, theft, or fraud) was the primary function of government. Why is this protection important to the efficient operation of an economy?
7. "If it's worth doing, it's worth doing to the best of your ability." What is the economic explanation for why this statement is frequently said but rarely followed in practice? Explain.
8. "Unless quality and price are regulated by government, travelers would have no chance for a fair deal. Local people would be treated well, but the traveler would have no way to know, for example, who offers a good night's lodging at a fair price." Is this true or false? Explain.
9. *If sellers of toasters were able to organize themselves, reduce their output, and raise their prices, how would economic efficiency be affected? Explain.

10. What are external costs? When are they most likely to be present? When external costs are present, what is likely to be the relationship between the market output of a good and the output consistent with ideal economic efficiency?

11. *"Elementary education is obviously a public good. After all, it is provided by the government." Evaluate this statement.

12. What are the necessary conditions for economic efficiency? In what four situations might a market fail to achieve ideal economic efficiency?

13. What is market failure? If market failure is present, does this imply that government intervention will lead to a more efficient allocation of resources? Why or why not?

14. Apply the economic efficiency criterion to the role of government. When would a government intervention be considered economically efficient? When would a government intervention be considered economically inefficient?

*Asterisk denotes questions for which answers are given in Appendix B.

Chapter 6 The Economics of Political Action

> [Public choice] analyzes the motives and activities of politicians, civil servants and government officials as people with personal interests that may or may not coincide with the interest of the general public they are supposed to serve. It is an analysis of how people behave in the world as it is.
>
> -Arthur Seldon[1]

As we have previously discussed, the protection of property rights, evenhanded enforcement of contracts, and provision of a stable monetary environment are vital for the smooth and efficient operation of markets. Governments that perform these functions well will help their citizens prosper and achieve higher levels of income. Governments may also help allocate goods difficult for markets to handle. However, it is crucially important to recognize that government is simply an alternative form of economic organization. In most industrialized nations, the activities of governments are directed by the democratic political process. In this chapter, we will use the tools of economics to analyze how this process works.

Learning Objectives

6.1 Discuss the size of government expenditures as a share of the U.S. economy and how it has changed through time.

6.2 Describe the similarities and differences between market and political allocation.

6.3 Explain the methodology of public choice and the objective of research in this area.

6.4 Indicate the three major categories of political decision-makers and the incentive structure confronted by each.

6.5 Identify when democratic political decision-making is most likely to allocate resources efficiently.

6.6 Explain why the special interest effect, the shortsightedness effect, rent-seeking, and the inefficiency of government operations reduce the ability of the democratic political process to produce and allocate goods efficiently.

6.7 Describe crony capitalism and why it is likely to increase as the size and scope of government expands.

6.8 List the major reasons why both market and political allocation will fail to achieve economic efficiency.

[1] Preface to Gordon Tullock, *The Vote Motive* (London: Institute of Economic Affairs, 1976), x.

6-1 The Size and Growth of the U.S. Government

What exactly does government do? Has its role in the economy shrunk or grown over time? Data on government spending shed light on these questions. As **Exhibit 6-1** illustrates, total government expenditures (federal, state, and local combined) were only 9.9 percent of the U.S. economy in 1930. (*Note:* GDP, or Gross Domestic Product, is generally how economists measure the size of the economy. The term will be explained more fully in a macroeconomics course.) In that year, federal government spending by itself was only about 3 percent of the economy. At the time, this made the federal government about half the size of all state and local governments combined.

Between 1930 and 1980, the size of government grew very rapidly. By 1980, government expenditures had risen to 33.7 percent of the economy, *more than three times* the level of 1930. Moreover, the federal government grew to about twice the size of all state and local

Exhibit 6-1 The Growth of Government Spending between 1930 and 2023

U.S. government expenditures as a share of the economy's gross domestic product have risen dramatically since 1930. In 2023, the ratio was 37.1 percent, almost four times the value for 1930.

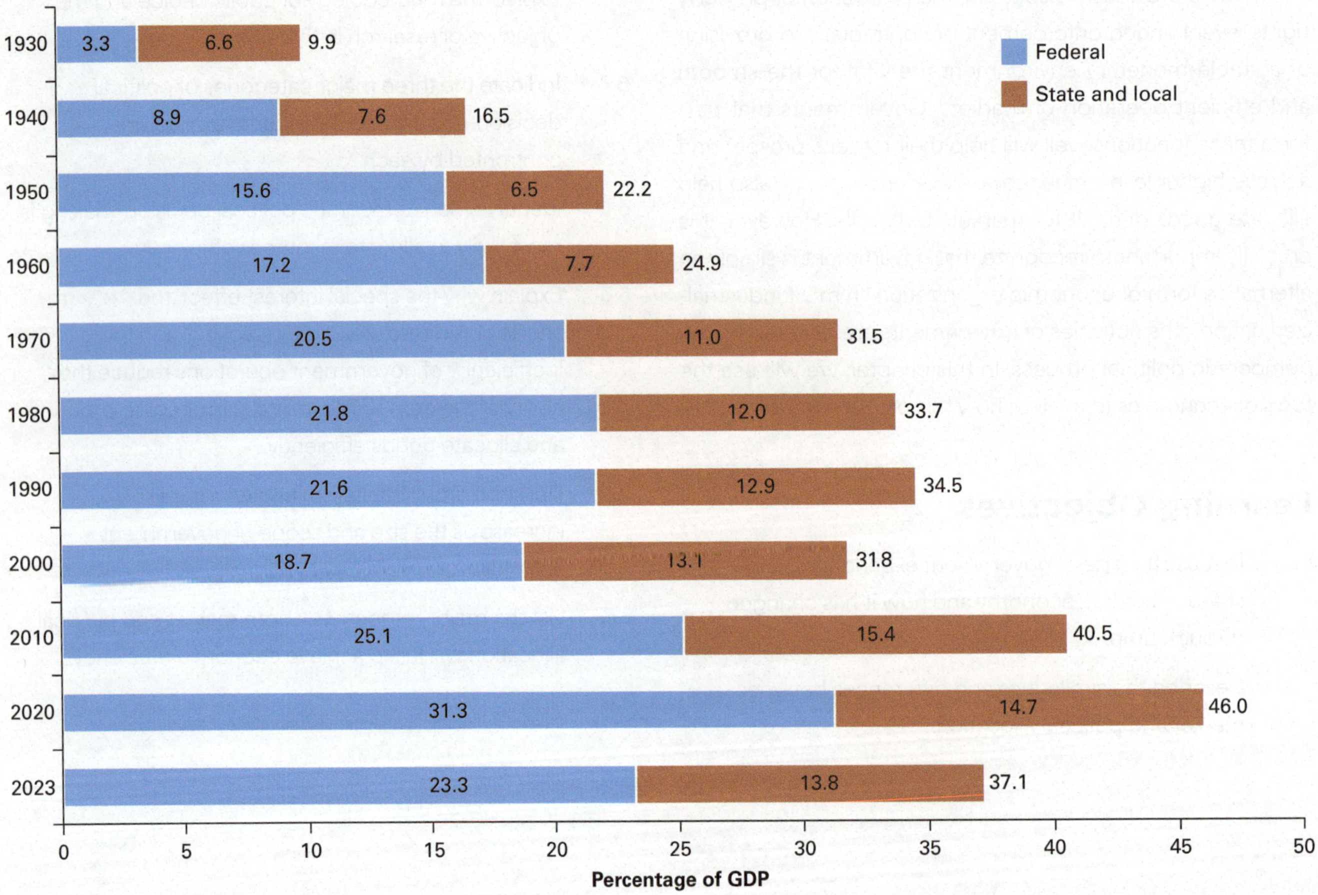

Source: Bureau of Economic Analysis, http://www.bea.gov. Grants to state and local governments are included in federal expenditures. Individual data may not add to total due to rounding.

Exhibit 6-2 Government Spending by Category

The major categories of federal government spending are health care, Social Security, national defense, and income security (welfare transfers). The major categories of state and local government spending are education, health and welfare programs, and administration.

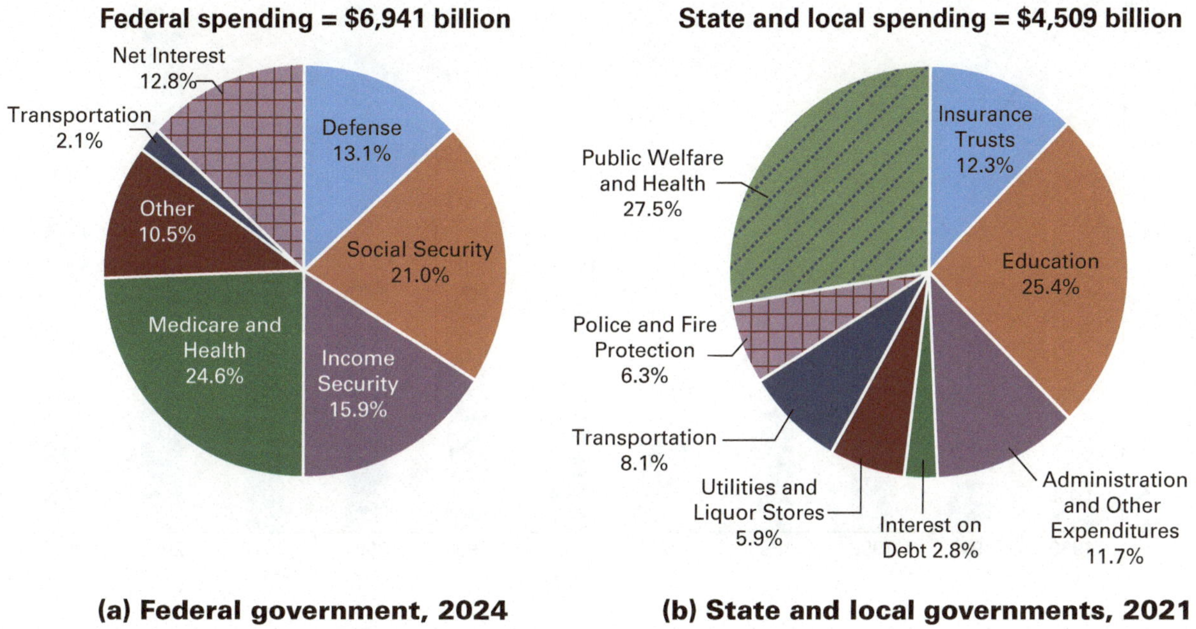

Source: *Economic Report of the President* (Washington, DC: Government Printing Office, 2024) and U.S. Census Bureau, State and Local Government Finances, 2021.

governments combined, despite the fact that they were growing rapidly, too. After remaining fairly constant between 1980 and 2000, the size of government increased substantially to 40 percent by 2010. While government spending soared to 46 percent during the COVID-19 pandemic in 2020, it was near 37 percent in 2023.

Exhibit 6-2 shows the major categories of government spending for both the federal government and state and local governments. The major categories of federal spending are health care, Social Security, national defense, and other income transfers. Education, administration, and public welfare and health constitute the largest areas of spending for state and local governments.

Transfer payments are transfers of income from some individuals (who pay taxes) to others (who receive government payments). Social Security, unemployment benefits, and welfare are examples of transfer payments. Direct income transfers now account for almost half of the total spending of the government. As **Exhibit 6-3** illustrates, federal, state, and local government spending on income transfers has grown rapidly. In 1930, income transfers summed to only 1.1 percent of total income. By 1970, the figure had jumped to 8.2 percent; by 2010, it had risen to 18.5 percent of national income. In 2020, during the COVID-19 pandemic, it rose to 23.9 and was 19.0 percent in 2023. Obviously, the government has become much more involved in tax-transfer activities during the past nine decades.

Transfer payments
Payments to individuals or institutions that are not linked to the current supply of a good or service by the recipient.

Given the size and growth of government, understanding how the political process works and how it is likely to affect the economy is vitally important. The remainder of this chapter will address this issue.

Exhibit 6-3 The Growth of Government Transfer Payments

The government takes almost 20 percent of national income away from some people and transfers it to others. Means-tested income transfers—those directed toward people with low income—account for only about one-sixth of all income transfers. Government income-transfer activities have grown substantially since 1930.

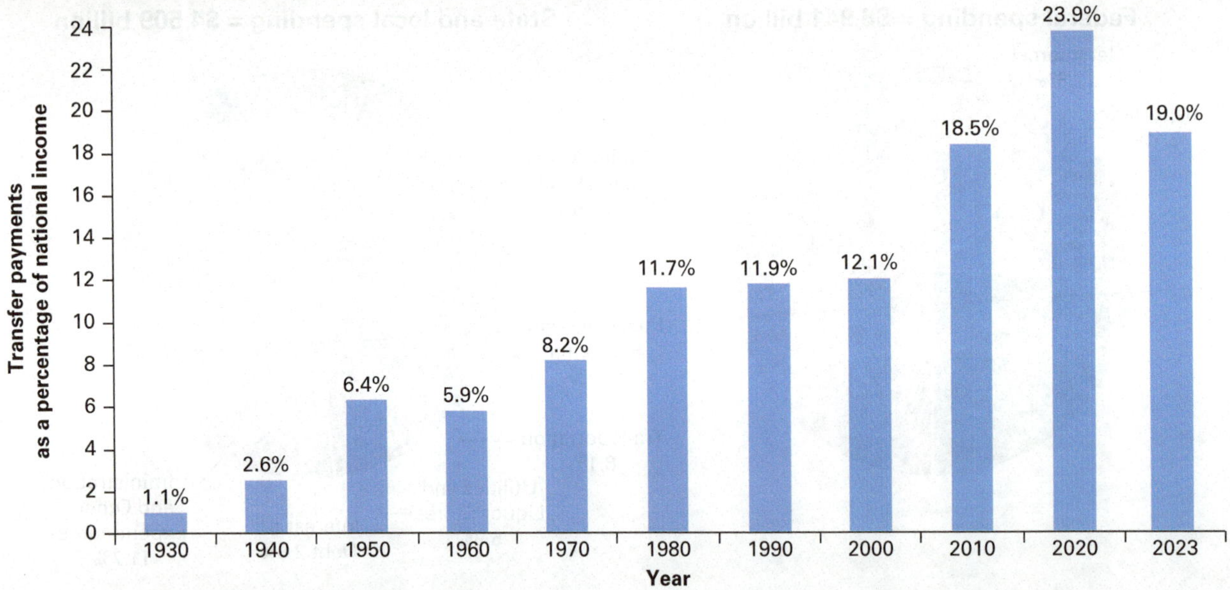

Source: Bureau of Economic Analysis, http://www.bea.gov.

6-2 Similarities and Differences between Political and Market Allocation

Let's begin our analysis of how the political process works by considering some of the major similarities and differences between the two sectors. Competition is present in the government sector, just as it is in the market sector. The nature of the competition and criteria for success differ, but intense competition is present in both. In the government sector, politicians compete for elective office. Bureau chiefs and agency heads compete for larger budgets. Government employees compete for promotions and higher pay rates. Perhaps most importantly, business, labor, and other special-interest groups compete for program funding, favorable bureaucratic rulings, and other political favors that serve their narrow interests.

Scarcity and the opportunity cost of resource use are present in both sectors. If the government uses resources to achieve one goal, those resources are unavailable to achieve others. Thus, just as in the market sector, provision of goods through government is costly, and this is true even if the good is provided free of charge to certain consumers.

But there are also important differences between market and political allocation, and these differences shed light on how the two processes allocate resources. Let's consider four of the key differences.

First, public sector organization can break the linkage between payment and consumption of a good. In the market sector, goods are allocated to those who are willing to pay the price: there is a one-to-one relationship between a person's payment and receipt of a good. This is often not the case when decisions are made politically. Sometimes goods are allocated to people even if they have paid little or nothing to cover their cost. In other instances, however, individuals are required to pay dearly for a government program even though they derive few, if any, benefits from it.

Second, private-sector action is based on mutual agreement; public-sector action is based on majority rule. In the market sector, when two parties engage in trade, their actions are voluntary and motivated by the expectation of mutual gain. Corporations like Exxon and Microsoft, no matter how large or powerful, cannot take income from you or force you to buy their products. Mutual gain is the foundation for market exchange. In contrast, political action is based on majority rule, either through direct voting or through legislative procedures involving elected representatives. If a legislative majority decides on a particular policy, the minority must accept the policy and help pay for it, even if they strongly object. Political action, even when it is democratic, creates "losers" as well as "winners." Further, as we will explain, there is no assurance that the gains the winners derive from a project will exceed the losses imposed on the losers.

Third, when choices are made politically, voters face a "bundle purchase" problem. They must choose among candidates who represent a bundle of positions on issues. On election day, the voter cannot choose the views of one politician on healthcare and agricultural subsidies, for example, and simultaneously choose the views of a different politician on social security reform and national defense. This greatly limits the voter's power to make their preferences count on specific issues. The situation in markets is quite different. A buyer can purchase some groceries or clothing from one store, while choosing related items from different suppliers. There is seldom a bundle-purchase problem in markets.

Fourth, income and influence are distributed differently in the two sectors. People who supply more highly valued resources in the marketplace have larger incomes. The number of these dollar "votes" earned by a person in the marketplace will reflect their abilities, ambitions, skills, past savings, inheritance, good fortune, and willingness to produce for others, among other things. In contrast, in a democratic setting, one citizen, one vote is the rule. But there are ways other than voting to influence political outcomes. People can donate their money and time to help a campaign. They can also try to influence friends and neighbors, write letters to legislators, and speak in public on behalf of a candidate or cause. The greatest rewards of the political process go to those best able and most willing to use their time, persuasive skills, organizational abilities, and financial contributions to help politicians get votes. People who have more money and skills of this sort—and are willing to spend them in the political arena—can expect to benefit themselves and their favorite causes more handsomely. Thus, while the sources of success and influence differ between sectors, the allocation of income and influence is unequal in both.

6-3 Political Decision-Making: An Overview

When political decisions are made democratically, or in a representative democracy, as we assume in this chapter, the choices of individuals will influence outcomes in the government sector, just as they do in the market sector. **Public-choice analysis** is a branch of economics that applies the principles and methodology of economics to the operation of the political process. Public-choice analysis links the theory of *individual* behavior to political action, analyzes the implications of the theory, and tests them against events in the real world. Since the mid-1960s, research in this area has greatly enhanced our understanding of how the political process works and the structure of the outcomes it generates.[2] Just as economists

Public-choice analysis
The study of decision-making as it affects the formation and operation of collective organizations, like governments. In general, the principles and methodology of economics are applied to political science topics.

[2]The contributions of Kenneth Arrow, James Buchanan, Duncan Black, Anthony Downs, William Niskanen, Mancur Olson, Robert Tollison, and Gordon Tullock have been particularly important. Public choice is something of a cross between economics and political science. Thus, advanced courses are generally offered in both departments.

use self-interest and the structure of incentives to analyze markets, public-choice economists use them to analyze political choices and the operation of government. After all, the same people make decisions in both sectors. If self-interest and the structure of incentives influence market choices, there is good reason to expect that they will also influence choices in a political setting.

The collective decision-making process can be thought of as a complex interaction among voters, legislators, and bureaucrats. Voters elect a legislature, which levies taxes and allocates budgets and regulatory authority to various government agencies and bureaus. The bureaucrats in charge of these agencies utilize the funds to supply government services and income transfers, and to exercise regulatory authority as well. In a representative democracy, voter support determines who is elected to the legislature. A majority vote of the legislature is generally required for the passage of taxes, budget allocations, and regulatory legislation. Let's examine the incentive structure confronting the three primary political players—voters, legislators, and bureaucrats—and consider how they affect the operation of the political process.

6-3a Incentives Confronted by the Voter

How do voters decide whom to support? Self-interest dictates that voters, like market consumers, will ask, "What can you do for me and my goals, and how much will it cost me?" The greater the voter's perceived net personal gain from a particular candidate's election, the more likely it is that the voter will favor that candidate. In contrast, the greater the perceived net economic cost imposed on the voter by the positions of a candidate, the less inclined the voter will be to support the candidate. Other things being equal, voters will tend to support those candidates who they believe will provide the most government services and transfer benefits to them and their favorite causes, net of costs.

How well will voters be informed about political issues and candidates? When decisions are made collectively, the choices of a single person will not be decisive. The

Outstanding Economist

James Buchanan (1919–2013)

Wally McNamee/Corbis Historical/Getty Images

The 1986 winner of the Nobel Prize in Economics, James Buchanan might properly be called the "father of public choice economics." Rather than assuming that voters, elected political officials, and bureaucrats are "saints" seeking to promote the common good, Buchanan assumed that the key political players responded to the structure of incentives. His work illustrated that, like the market, the political process has deficiencies that often result in counterproductive government actions and misallocation of resources. As he put it, public-choice analysis is "government without the romance." Buchanan's most famous work, *The Calculus of Consent* (1962), coauthored with Gordon Tullock, argues that unless constitutional rules are structured in a manner that will bring the self-interests of the political players into harmony with the wise use of resources, government action will often be counterproductive.[1] Given the continued growth of government, Buchanan's work is now perhaps more relevant than at any time in American history.

[1]J. M. Buchanan and G. Tullock, *The Calculus of Consent* (Ann Arbor: University of Michigan Press, 1962).

MANDEL NGAN/AFP/Getty Images

AP Images/Sipa

Spencer Grant/AGE Fotostock

Voters, politicians, and bureaucrats are the primary decision-makers in the political arena.

probability that an individual vote will decide a city, state, or national election is virtually zero. Realizing that their votes will not affect the outcome, individual voters have little incentive to spend much effort seeking the information needed to cast an informed ballot. Economists refer to this lack of incentive as the **rational ignorance effect**.

Rational ignorance effect
Because it is highly unlikely that an individual vote will decide the outcome of an election, a rational individual has little or no incentive to search for and acquire the information needed to cast an informed vote.

As the result of the rational ignorance effect, most voters simply rely on information supplied to them freely by candidates (via political advertising) and the mass media, as well as conversations with friends and coworkers. Surveys, in fact, indicate that huge numbers of voters are unable even to identify their own congressional representatives, much less know where they stand on issues like Social Security reform, tariffs, and agricultural price supports. Given that voters gain little from casting a more informed vote, their meager knowledge of political candidates and issues is not surprising.

When people can put information to good use in serving their own goals, they will put forth more effort to acquire it. Consider the incentive of auto purchasers to make well-informed choices. They often shop at several dealerships, take different models for test drives, review consumer publications, and consult with various car experts as they make their purchasing decisions. Most important, if an auto buyer makes a bad choice, they will personally bear the consequences. In contrast, voters gain little or nothing if they cast a more informed vote. It is a virtual certainty that their vote will not decide the outcome of an election, and therefore there will be no adverse consequences of casting a poorly informed vote. Thus, it is actually *reasonable* to expect people to be far better informed when choosing a car than a senatorial, congressional, or other political candidate.

The fact that citizens recognize that their individual vote will not sway the outcome also helps explain why many do not vote. Even in a presidential election, only about half of all voting-age Americans take the time to register and vote. The turnout for state and local elections is generally still lower. Given the low probability that one's vote will be decisive, low voter turnout is an expected result.

6-3b Incentives Confronted by the Politician

What motivates political candidates and officeholders? Economics indicates that their actions and political positions will be heavily affected by the pursuit of votes. No doubt, many of them genuinely care about the "public interest" and the quality of government, but they need to be elected to achieve their objectives, whatever they may be. Clearly, politicians have a strong incentive to give voters a reason to support their candidacy. One way of doing so is to convince voters that they will provide valuable goods either free of charge or at a very low cost. Predictably, politicians will exaggerate the benefits their programs will provide to voters while understating and concealing the cost. As Stanford economist Thomas Sowell puts it:

The first lesson of economics is scarcity: there is never enough of anything to fully satisfy all those who want it. The first lesson of politics is to disregard the first lesson of economics.[3]

Moreover, if a candidate is going to be successful, their positive attributes must be brought to the attention of rationally ignorant voters focused on their families, jobs, various civic activities, and local sports teams (which are probably more entertaining). The successful candidate needs an expert staff, sophisticated polling techniques to uncover popular issues and positions, and high-quality advertising to shape their image favorably. This, of course, will be costly. It is not unusual for an incumbent candidate for the U.S. Senate to spend $15 million or more seeking to win an election. In other words, votes are the necessary objective of politicians, but money helps them get those votes. Predictably, the pursuit of campaign contributions then shapes the actions of politicians, too.

Are we implying that politicians are selfish, caring only for their pocketbooks and reelection chances? The answer is "No." Factors other than personal political gain, narrowly defined, may well influence their actions. Sometimes an elected official may feel so strongly about an issue that they will knowingly take a position that is politically unpopular and damaging to their future electoral prospects. None of this is inconsistent with the economic view of the political process. Over time, however, the politicians most likely to remain in office are the ones who focus on how their actions will influence their reelection prospects. Just as profits are the lifeblood of the market entrepreneur, votes are the lifeblood of the politician.

Politicians face competition for elected office from other candidates. Like market suppliers, political suppliers have an incentive to find ways to gain an advantage over their competitors. Catering to the strongly held views of voters and contributors is one way of doing that. Enacting rules that put potential challengers at a disadvantage is another. When geographic political districts are redrawn, for example, politicians frequently manipulate the process to increase their chances (and those of their party) of winning elections—a process known as "gerrymandering." Incumbents can also attempt to use government resources for their reelection campaigns, an advantage challengers do not have. Campaign finance "reforms" that make it more difficult for a challenger to raise funds may also provide incumbents with an additional advantage.

6-3c Incentives Confronted by the Government Bureaucrat

Like other people, bureaucrats who staff government agencies, especially those who rise to senior decision-making levels, have narrowly focused interests. They usually want to see their own agency's goals furthered. Doing so, however, requires larger budgets or greater authority to regulate or both. In turn, larger budgets and more authority lead to more satisfaction, prestige, and career opportunities for the bureaucrats. Economic analysis suggests there is a strong tendency for government bureaucrats and employees to want to expand their budgets and their authority well beyond what would be economically efficient. Indeed, analysts recognize that bigger programs often have strong, organized political backing. In contrast "efficiency has no political constituency."

Legislative bodies are in charge of overseeing these bureaus, but the individual legislators themselves generally know little about the true costs of agency decisions, especially the costs to those regulated. This makes it even more likely that bureaucrats will be able to get funding and authority beyond what's economically efficient.

In summary, the political process, which begins with voter-driven elections and proceeds to legislative decisions and bureaucratic actions, brings about results that please some voters and displease others. The goals of the three major categories of participants—voters,

[3]Thomas Sowell, *Is Reality Optional? And Other Essays* (Stanford, CA: Hoover Institution Press, 1993), 131.

King Features Syndicate, Inc.

Just as the general does not want his Camp Swampy budget cut, most heads of agencies want expanded budgets to help them do more and do it more comfortably.

politicians, and bureaucrats—frequently conflict with one another. Each group wants more of the government's limited supply of resources. Coalitions form and the members of each coalition hope to enhance their ability to get the government to do what they want. Sometimes this results in productive activities on the part of the government, and sometimes it does not.

6-4 When the Political Process Works Well

Under what conditions are voting and representative government most likely to result in productive actions? People have a tendency to believe that support by a majority makes a political action productive. However, if a project is truly productive, it will always be possible to allocate its costs such that *all* voters gain. This would mean that, even if voting rules required unanimity or near unanimity, all truly productive government projects would pass if the costs were allocated in the right manner. **Exhibit 6-4** helps illustrate this point. Column 1 presents hypothetical data on the distribution of benefits from a government road construction project. These benefits sum to $40, which exceeds the $25 cost of the road, so the project is productive. But if the project's $25 cost were allocated equally among the voters (plan A), Adams and Chan gain substantially, but Green, Lee, and Diaz lose. If the fate of the project is decided by majority vote, the project will be defeated by the "no" votes of Green, Lee, and Diaz. This productive government project fails to obtain a majority vote in this case because of the way that the costs have been allocated.

Because the project is indeed productive, there is an alternative way to allocate its costs so that Adams, Chan, Green, Lee, and Diaz all benefit. This can be accomplished by

Exhibit 6-4 The Benefits Derived by Voters from a Hypothetical Road Construction Project

When taxes are levied in proportion to benefits received (tax plan B), any efficient project can pass unanimously (and any inefficient project will fail unanimously). When taxes are not levied in accordance with benefits received (tax plan A), efficient projects can fail to win a majority vote (or inefficient projects can pass in a majority vote).

		Tax Payment	
Voter	Benefits Received (1)	Plan A(2)	Plan B (3)
Adams	$20	$5	$12.50
Chan	12	5	7.50
Green	4	5	2.50
Lee	2	5	1.25
Diaz	2	5	1.25
Total	**$40**	**$25**	**$25.00**

allocating the cost of the project among voters in proportion to the benefits that they receive (plan B). Under this arrangement, Adams would pay half ($12.50) of the $25 cost, because he receives half ($20) of the total benefits ($40). The other voters would all pay in proportion to the benefits they receive. Under this plan, all voters would gain from the proposal. Even though the proposal could not secure a majority when the costs were allocated equally among voters, it will be favored by all five voters when they are taxed in proportion to the benefits they receive (plan B).

This simple illustration highlights an extremely important point about voting and the efficiency of government action. ***When voters pay in proportion to benefits received, all voters will gain if the government action is productive, and all will lose if it is unproductive.***[4] ***When the benefits and costs derived by individual voters are closely related, the voting process will enact efficient projects while rejecting inefficient ones. When voters pay in proportion to the benefits they receive, there will tend to be harmony between good politics and sound economics.***

User Charges
Payments users (consumers) are required to make if they want to receive certain services provided by the government.

How might the cost of a government service be linked to the benefits received? **User charges**, which require people who use a service more to pay a larger share of the cost, provide one way. User charges are most likely to be levied at the local level. Local services such as electricity, water, and garbage collection are generally financed with user charges. Sometimes the intensity of the use of a service and the amount paid for it can be linked by specifying that the revenue from a specific tax be used for a designated purpose. For example, many states finance road construction and maintenance with the revenue collected from taxes on gasoline and other motor fuels. The more an individual drives—getting more benefits from the roads—the more that individual pays.

Exhibit 6-5 provides a useful way to look at the possible linkage between the benefits and costs of government programs. The benefits from a government action may be either widespread among the general public or concentrated among a small subgroup (for example,

Exhibit 6-5 Distribution of Benefits and Costs among Voters

It is useful to visualize four possible combinations for the distribution of benefits and costs among voters to consider how the alternative distributions affect the operation of representative governments. When the distribution of benefits and costs is both widespread among voters (type 1) or both concentrated among voters (type 3), representative government will tend to undertake projects that are productive and reject those that are unproductive. In contrast, when the benefits are concentrated and the costs are widespread (type 2), representative government is biased toward the adoption of inefficient projects. Finally, when benefits are widespread but the costs concentrated (type 4), the political process may reject projects that are productive.

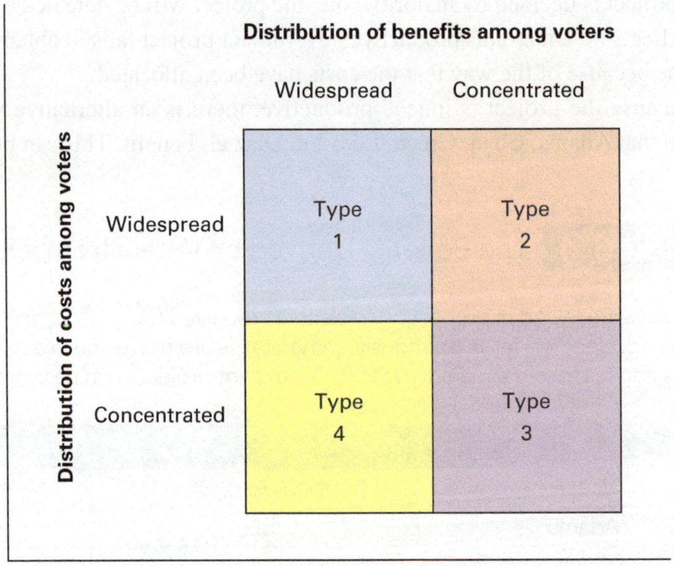

[4]The principle that productive projects generate the potential for political unanimity was initially articulated by Swedish economist Knut Wicksell in 1896. Refer to Wicksell, "A New Principle of Just Taxation," in *Public Choice and Constitutional Economics*, James Gwartney and Richard Wagner (Greenwich, CT: JAI Press, Inc., 1988). Nobel laureate James Buchanan stated that Wicksell's work provided him with the insights that led to his large role in the development of modern public-choice theory.

farmers, students, business interests, senior citizens, or members of a labor union). Similarly, the costs may be either widespread or highly concentrated among voters. Thus, as the exhibit shows, there are four possible patterns of voter benefits and costs: (1) widespread benefits and widespread costs, (2) concentrated benefits and widespread costs, (3) concentrated benefits and concentrated costs, and (4) widespread benefits and concentrated costs.

When both the benefits and costs are widespread among voters (type 1 issue), essentially everyone benefits and everyone pays. Although the costs of type 1 measures may not be precisely proportional to the benefits individuals receive, there will be a rough relationship. When type 1 measures are productive, almost everyone gains more than they pay. There will be little opposition, and political representatives have a strong incentive to support such proposals. In contrast, when type 1 proposals generate costs in excess of benefits, almost everyone loses, and representatives will face pressure to oppose such issues. Thus, for type 1 projects, the political process works pretty well. Productive projects will tend to be accepted and unproductive ones rejected.

Similarly, there is reason to believe that the political process will work fairly well for type 3 measures—those for which both benefits and costs are concentrated on one or more small subgroups. In some cases, the concentrated beneficiaries may be the same group of people paying for the government to provide them a service. In other cases, the subgroup of beneficiaries may differ from the subgroup footing the bill. Even in this case, however, when the benefits exceed the costs, the concentrated group of beneficiaries will have an incentive to expend more resources lobbying for the measure than those harmed by it will expend opposing it. Thus, when the benefits and costs are both concentrated, there will be a tendency for productive projects to be adopted and unproductive ones to be rejected.

6-5 When the Political Process Works Poorly

Although the political process yields reasonable results when there is a close relationship between the receipt of benefits and the payment of costs, the harmony between good politics and sound economics breaks down when the beneficiaries differ from those bearing the costs (type 2 and type 4 projects). Inefficiency may also arise from other sources when governments undertake economic activities. In this section, we consider four major reasons why the political allocation of resources will often result in inefficiency.

6-5a Special-Interest Effect

Trade restrictions that limit the import of steel and lumber from abroad; subsidies for sports stadiums, the arts, and various agricultural products; federal spending on an indoor rain forest in Iowa; special tax breaks for NASCAR track owners and Hollywood movie studios; and special grants and loans to a business producing expensive electric sports cars: These seemingly diverse programs funded by tax dollars from the federal government have one thing in common—they reflect the attractiveness of special-interest issues to vote-seeking politicians. A **special-interest issue** is one that generates substantial personal benefits for a small number of constituents while the costs are spread widely across the bulk of citizens (type 2 projects). Individually, a few people gain a great deal, but many others lose a small amount. In aggregate, the losses may exceed the benefits.

Special-interest issue
An issue that generates substantial individual benefits to a small minority while imposing a small individual cost on many other citizens. In total, the net cost to the majority might either exceed or fall short of the net benefits to the special-interest group.

How will a vote-seeking politician respond to special-interest issues? Because their personal stake is large, members of the interest group (and lobbyists representing their interests) will feel strongly about such issues. Many of the special-interest voters will vote for or against candidates strictly on the basis of whether they are supportive of their positions. In addition, interest groups are generally an attractive source of campaign resources, including financial contributions. In contrast, most of the other, largely rationally ignorant, voters will either not know or will care little about special-interest issues. Even if voters know about some of these programs, it will be difficult for them to punish their legislators because each politician represents a bundle of positions on many different issues. While politicians would gain little from support of the rationally ignorant and unorganized majority, organized interest groups are eager to provide cooperative politicians with vocal supporters, campaign workers, and, most important, financial contributions.

As a result, politicians have a strong incentive to support legislation that provides concentrated benefits to special-interest groups at the expense of disorganized groups (like the bulk of taxpayers and consumers). Consider the cotton subsidy program. This program, which dates back to the New Deal era, has provided cotton farmers with subsidies averaging more than $1.5 billion per year since 2000. Moreover, because the subsidies are linked to production, the overwhelming bulk of these transfers go to well-off large farmers. Five percent of the recipients collect about two-thirds of the subsidies, and more than 80 percent of this federal largess is bestowed on the largest 10 percent of growers. The top 1 percent of cotton farmers received an average subsidy of about $150,000 per year. What explains the political popularity of this program? The special-interest effect provides the answer. The subsidy recipients feel strongly about the program and congressional supporters can count on them for political contributions. In contrast, the taxpayers and consumers of cotton products are almost totally unaware of the cost the program imposes on them. Thus, there is a strong incentive for congressional representatives to support the interests of the cotton farmers even though the program promotes inefficient use of resources and redistributes income from the less well-off to those with higher incomes.

The sugar subsidy program provides a similar example of concentrated benefits and widespread costs. For many years, the price of sugar in the United States has been 50 to 100 percent higher than the world price. Why? Because the federal government's price support program and highly restrictive quotas limiting the import of sugar keep the domestic price of sugar high. As a result, the roughly 20,000 sugar growers in the United States gain about $1.7 billion, or approximately $85,000 per grower! In contrast, sugar consumers pay between $3.4 billion and $4.0 billion, or a little more than $25 per household, in the form of higher prices each year.[5]

The artificially high sugar prices have resulted in a steady stream of candy manufacturers exiting the United States for countries such as Canada and Mexico, where sugar can be purchased at the lower, world market price. It is estimated that three jobs are lost in candy manufacturing for every job saved in the sugar production sector. Some heavy users of sugar have shifted to substitutes. The producers of Coca-Cola and Pepsi now use corn syrup rather than the more expensive sugar in their products. As the result of the sugar program, consumers living in the country where Coca-Cola was invented drink a modified version. If Americans want to enjoy a coke the way it was initially invented, they have to import it from abroad. Many are doing just that. In recent years, there has been a surge in imports of Coca-Cola bottled in Mexico.

The cotton and sugar programs are not unusual. Numerous government programs reflect this same pattern of incentives. These programs provide politicians with an opportunity to support policies favored by special interests, solicit those parties for political contributions, and use the funds to attract the support of other voters. Even when these programs are counterproductive, they may be still a political winner.

Logrolling
The exchange between politicians of political support on one issue for political support on another.

The power of special interests is further strengthened by logrolling and pork-barrel legislation. **Logrolling** involves the practice of vote trading by politicians in order to get the

---

[5]Refer to Jared Meyer and Preston Cooper, "Sugar Subsidies Are a Bitter Deal for American Consumers," *Economic Policies for the 21st Century at the Manhattan Institute*, Manhattan Institute (June 23, 2014); and John Beghin and Amani Elobeid, "Analysis of the US Sugar Program," American Enterprise Institute, November 2017, p. 1, http://www.aei.org/wp-content/uploads/2017/11/Analysis-of-the-US-Sugar-Program.pdf.

Exhibit 6-6 Trading Votes and Passing Counterproductive Legislation

All three projects are inefficient and would not pass majority vote individually. However, representatives from districts A, B, and C could trade votes (logrolling) or put together pork-barrel legislation that would result in all three projects passing.

	Net Benefits (+) or Costs (-) to Voters in District			
Voters of District[a]	Construction of Post Office in A	Dredging Harbor in B	Construction of Stadium in C	Total
A	+$10	−$ 3	−$ 3	−$4
B	− 3	+ 10	− 3	+ 4
C	− 3	− 3	+ 10	+ 4
D	− 3	− 3	− 3	− 9
E	− 3	− 3	− 3	− 9
Total	**−$ 2**	**−$ 2**	**−$ 2**	**−$6**

[a]We assume the districts are of equal size.

necessary support to pass desired legislation. **Pork-barrel legislation** is the term used to describe the bundling of unrelated projects benefiting many interests into a single bill. Both logrolling and pork-barrel legislation will often make it possible for special-interest projects to gain legislative approval, even though each project is counterproductive and individually could not muster the needed votes.

Pork-barrel legislation
A package of spending projects bundled into a single bill. It is often used as a device to obtain funding for a group of projects intensely desired by regional or interest groups that would be unlikely to pass if voted on separately.

Exhibit 6-6 provides a numeric illustration of the forces underlying logrolling and pork-barrel legislation. Here we analyze the operation of a five-member legislature considering three projects: construction of a post office in district A, dredging of a harbor in district B, and spending on a stadium in district C. For each district, the net benefit or cost is shown—that is, the benefit to the district minus the tax cost imposed on it. The total cost of each of the three projects exceeds the benefits (as shown by the negative number in the total row at the bottom of the table); therefore, each is counterproductive. If the projects were voted on separately, each would lose by a 4-to-1 vote because only one district would gain, and the other four would lose. However, when the projects are bundled together through either logrolling (representatives A, B, and C could agree to trade votes) or pork-barrel legislation (all three programs put on the same bill), they can all pass, despite the fact that all are inefficient.[6] This can be seen by noting that the total combined net benefit is positive for representatives A, B, and C.

The political incentive to support special-interest projects, including those that are counter-productive, is even stronger than the simple numeric example of **Exhibit 6-6** implies. As the result of the rational ignorance effect, those harmed by pork-barrel and other special-interest policies will often be unaware of the adverse impact the projects exert on their welfare. Moreover, the incentive to cater to special interests often deters entry of innovative firms and weakens the competitive process. Older, more established businesses have built a stronger record of political contributions, have more knowledge of lobbying techniques, and have developed a closer relationship with powerful political figures. Predictably, the more mature firms generally have more political clout than newer upstarts and will use it to deter innovative rivals.

[6]Logrolling and pork-barrel policies can sometimes lead to the adoption of productive measures. However, if a project is productive, there would always be a pattern of finance that would lead to its adoption even if logrolling and pork-barrel policies were absent. Thus, the tendency for logrolling and pork-barrel policies to result in the adoption of inefficient projects is the more significant point.

Consider the experience of Uber, which uses technology to bring willing drivers together with potential ground transportation passengers. Consumers searching for ground transportation request cars via their smartphones, and the Uber app immediately gives them a wait time. Uber also provides feedback about drivers to potential passengers, and vice versa. The technology reduces transaction costs, and the process is often faster and cheaper than traditional taxi service. As Uber has sought to enter markets in large cities throughout the world, the traditional taxi industry has fought for and often achieved legislation prohibiting the use of the technology employed by Uber and similar firms seeking to enter this market.[7] As a result, the gains from the innovative technology and expansion in the volume of exchange have been slowed.

The experience of Tesla, an electric car manufacturer, provides another example of existing producers using the political process to deter the entry of a newcomer. Tesla's business model is based on the sale of its autos directly to consumers. But a well-organized interest group, the established auto dealers, has lobbied state legislatures demanding passage of laws making it illegal for an auto manufacturer to sell cars directly to consumers. Nearly 20 states have adopted such legislation. These laws have made it more difficult for Tesla to enter the automobile market successfully.

Why don't representatives oppose measures that force their constituents to pay for projects that benefit others? There is some incentive to do so, but the constituents of any one elected representative would capture only a tiny portion of the benefits of tax savings from improved efficiency. The savings, after all, would be spread nationwide among all taxpayers. We would not expect the president of a corporation to devote any significant amount of the firm's resources toward projects that chiefly benefit other firms. Neither should we expect an elected representative to devote political resources to projects like defeating pork-barrel programs when the bulk of the benefits derived from spending reductions and tax savings will accrue to constituents in other districts. Instead, representatives have a strong incentive to fight for more spending for their constituents and not worry much about the spending pushed by other members of Congress.

When the benefits of a governmental action are spread far and wide among the unorganized, and the costs are highly concentrated (type 4 of **Exhibit 6-5**), special-interest groups—those who stand to bear the cost—are likely to oppose and lobby strongly against even an efficient project. Most other voters will be largely uninformed and uninterested. Once again, politicians will have an incentive to respond to the views of the concentrated interests. A proposal to reduce or eliminate a tariff (tax) on an imported good would be an example of this type of legislation. Although many thousands of consumers would benefit from the lower prices that result, the domestic firms that compete with the imported good would devote substantial resources toward lobbying to keep the tariff in place. Projects of this type will tend to be rejected even when they are productive, that is, when they would generate larger benefits than costs.

There is a tendency to believe that if a project or program can muster a political majority, it will be good for the society. ***However, the special-interest effect indicates this is not necessarily the case***. The special-interest effect helps explain the presence of numerous government programs that increase the size of government but reduce the overall size of the economic pie. As we discuss diverse topics throughout this text, counterproductive political action that has its foundation in the special-interest effect will arise again and again.

6-5b Shortsightedness Effect

Current economic conditions will have a major impact on the choices of voters on election day. As a result, incumbent politicians will want to institute programs that will provide visible results prior to the next major election. Thus, legislators have a strong incentive to favor

[7]Refer to Holman W. Jenkins Jr., "How Uber Won the Big Apple," *Wall Street Journal*, July 24, 2015. http://www.wsj.com/articles/how-uber-won-the-big-apple-1437778176.

projects that yield highly visible current benefits at the expense of costs that will be difficult to identify and mostly observable in the future. In contrast, politicians will find projects unattractive when they generate visible costs now with the expectation of future gain. Economists refer to this bias inherent in the political process as the **shortsightedness effect**.

Shortsightedness effect
The misallocation of resources that results because public-sector action is biased (1) in favor of proposals yielding clearly defined current benefits in exchange for difficult-to-identify future costs and (2) against proposals with clearly identifiable current costs that yield less concrete and less obvious future benefits.

As the result of the shortsightedness effect, elected political officials will have a strong incentive to spend on programs designed to provide highly visible benefits before the next election, but they will be reluctant to levy the taxes for their finance. Borrowing provides politicians with an alternative to current taxes: it makes it possible for them to spend now and push the visible taxes into the future. Thus, the political process is biased toward debt finance. The experience of the United States during the past six decades illustrates this bias. During the past 60 years, the federal government of the United States has run 55 budget deficits but only five surpluses. The federal debt as a share of the economy has now surpassed the levels experienced even during World War II. Moreover, the experience of Greece and several other European countries indicates that elected political officials will sometimes continue with a borrow-and-spend political strategy until they drive their country into virtual economic collapse.

The shortsightedness effect also explains why vote-seeking politicians find it attractive to promise future benefits without levying the taxes that are sufficient for their finance. This has been the case with both the Social Security and Medicare programs. The unfunded liabilities of these two programs are now about *six times* the size of the outstanding federal debt held by the public. By the time the higher taxes (or benefit cuts) for these programs are confronted, the politicians who gained votes from the promised benefits will be long gone.

6-5c Rent-Seeking

There are two ways individuals can acquire wealth: production and plunder. When individuals produce goods or services and exchange them for income, they not only enrich themselves, but they also enhance the wealth of the society. Sometimes the rules—or lack of rule enforcement—also allow people to get ahead by taking, or plundering, from others. This method not only fails to generate additional income—the gain of one is a loss to another—but it also consumes resources and thereby reduces the wealth of the society.

Rent-seeking is the term economists use to describe actions taken by individuals and groups seeking to use the political process to take the wealth of others.[8] Perhaps "favor seeking" would be a more descriptive term for this type of activity, which generally involves "investing" resources in lobbying and other activities designed to gain favors from the government. The incentive for individuals to spend time and effort in rent-seeking will be determined by how rewarding it is. Rent-seeking will be unattractive when constitutional constraints prevent politicians from taking the property of some and transferring it to others (or forcing some to pay for things desired by others).

Rent-seeking
Actions by individuals and groups designed to restructure public policy in a manner that will either directly or indirectly redistribute more income to themselves or the projects they promote.

To get elected (or reelected), politicians have a strong incentive to provide spending programs to important interest groups to secure their support.

[8]Refer to the classic work of Charles K. Rowley, Robert D. Tollison, and Gordon Tullock, *The Political Economy of Rent-Seeking* (Boston: Kluwer Academic Publishers, 1988) for additional details on rent-seeking.

However, when the government becomes heavily involved in income transfer activities and the granting of favors to some at the expense of others (instead of simply acting as a neutral force protecting property rights and enforcing contracts), people will spend more time rent-seeking and less time producing. Rather than competing by offering consumers more for their money, rent-seekers compete by using resources to obtain more funds from taxpayers. Rent-seeking is a natural outgrowth of government activism. When the government is heavily involved in the granting of contracts, subsidies, tax credits, low-interest loans, regulatory favors, and other forms of government intervention, business firms, labor organizations, and other well-organized interests will compete for the government favors. The result will be a shift of resources away from productive activities and into rent-seeking. Economic efficiency will decrease and output and income levels will fall below their potential.

6-5d Inefficiency of Government Operations

Will government enterprises and agencies be operated efficiently? The incentive to keep costs low and provide customers with highly valued goods and services differs substantially between the market and government sectors. In the market sector, there is a strong incentive to produce efficiently because lower costs mean higher profits. The profit motive also provides private firms with a strong incentive to supply goods and services that are highly valued relative to their cost. Bankruptcy weeds out private sector firms that have high costs and serve their customers poorly.

In the public sector, the structure of incentives is much different. There is nothing like profit and loss that might be used to evaluate the performance of agencies, enterprises, and managers. Neither is there a mechanism like bankruptcy that can be counted on to eventually bring inefficient public sector operations to a halt. In fact, failure to achieve a targeted objective (for example, a lower crime rate or improvement in student achievement scores) is often used as an argument for *increased* public-sector funding of an agency or its programs. Furthermore, public-sector managers are seldom in a position to gain personally from measures that reduce costs. The opposite is often true, in fact. If an agency fails to spend its entire budget for a given year, not only does it have to return the extra money, but its budget for the next year is likely to be cut. Because of this, government agencies typically go on a spending spree near the end of a budget period if they discover they have failed to spend all the current year's allocated funds.

It is important to note that the argument of internal inefficiency is not based on the assumption that employees of a bureaucratic government are lazy or less capable. Many agency managers are highly capable, diligent, and focused strongly on their mission within the agency. Rather, the inefficiency stems from the incentives and opportunities that such managers and workers face. Government enterprises do not have owners that are risking their wealth on the future success of the firm. No decision-maker in the firm can reap substantial economic gain if the firm produces more efficiently or incorporates a new product or service highly valued relative to its costs. In the public sector, there is no test like profit and loss that might be used to measure inefficiency, much less eliminate it. Given this incentive structure, inefficient use of resources is the predicted result.

The empirical evidence is consistent with this view. Economies dominated by government control, like those of the former Soviet bloc, Argentina, Venezuela, and Zimbabwe (and many other African countries), have performed poorly. The level of output per unit of resource input in countries dominated by government agencies and enterprises is low. Similarly, when private firms are compared with government enterprises providing the same goods or services (like garbage collection, hospitals, electric and water utilities, weather forecasting, and public transportation), studies indicate that private firms generally provide the services more economically.

6-6 Political Favoritism, Crony Capitalism, and Government Failure

Goodwill suffered greatly from restrictions imposed on the sale of items containing lead that were pushed by toy-maker Mattel.

Public-choice analysis indicates that as government spending, subsidies, income transfers, loan guarantees, financial bailouts, targeted tax credits, and regulatory favors grow, businesses and other well-organized groups have a greater incentive to expend resources seeking to obtain the government favors. As a result, crony capitalism tends to expand relative to market allocation. **Crony capitalism** is the situation where the allocation of resources and winners and losers in business are determined by political favors rather than by consumer preferences translated through the market profit-and-loss system. Under crony capitalism, rather than providing equal treatment of individuals and businesses under the law, government uses spending, subsidies, and regulations to favor those most willing to provide political decision-makers with campaign contributions and other forms of political support. In essence, crony capitalism reflects the intermingling of government and business. The politicians use the favoritism to obtain political resources (for example, campaign contributions, support of organized interest groups) while the businesses use the government favors to enhance their profitability.

Crony capitalism
A situation where the institutions of markets are maintained, but to a large degree the allocation of resources and the profit and loss of businesses are determined by political decision-making rather than consumer purchases and market forces. Many of the business firms will use contributions and other forms of political support to compete for government favors.

Is crony capitalism an emerging problem in the United States? There is reason to believe that it is. As was illustrated in **Exhibits 1** and **3**, federal, state, and local expenditures, as well as transfers and subsidies, have risen substantially over the past few decades. Social Security and healthcare comprise the bulk of the transfers, but there are now more than 2,300 federal subsidy programs, compared to 1,425 in 2000.

A substantial portion of government spending is driven by what economist Bruce Yandle calls the "bootleggers and Baptists" coalition.[9] During the era when many states and counties had bans on the sale of alcoholic beverages, the bootleggers and Baptists both supported the bans, the former because it increased the demand for their product and the latter for moral reasons. Like the bootleggers, opportunistic rent-seekers often frame their programs in a manner designed to attract support from naïve idealists. They argue their programs will enhance child safety, promote energy independence, save family farms, or some other widely supported goal. But when one looks below the surface, you note that the programs provide favoritism that generates handsome profits for the rent-seekers.

Let's consider some examples that illustrate special-interest politics, rent-seeking, and bootlegger–Baptist-type coalitions at work. The Consumer Product Safety Improvement Act of 2008 (CPSIA) and the role played by giant toy manufacturer Mattel in its passage provide an example. The bill imposed new lead testing requirements on manufacturers of products ranging from apparel to home furnishings and toys. Between 1998 and 2007, Mattel had 36 costly recalls, which both damaged its reputation and added to its legal expenses. By 2008, however, it had completed its own product-testing lab. Mattel played a central role in the writing of the CPSIA, and the act permitted Mattel to test its own products because, unsurprisingly, its lab met the specifications of the legislation it helped to formulate. The act also provided Mattel with a sizeable advantage relative to its smaller rivals, who had to submit their products for costly testing at independent laboratories. Equally important, the testing virtually eliminated the secondhand toy and children's clothing market. Clearly, Goodwill and other retailers of used toys and clothing with zippers, buttons, or other accessories with even a touch of paint could not afford to test these products and still make them available at economical prices. Literally, tens of millions of dollars of used

[9]Refer to Adam Smith and Bruce Yandle, *Bootleggers and Baptists: How Economic Forces and Moral Persuasion Interact to Shape Regulatory Politics* (Washington, DC: Cato Institute, 2014); and Bruce Yandle, "Bootleggers and Baptists in Retrospect," *Regulation* 22, no. 3 (1999): 5–7.

toys and clothing were rendered useless and eliminated from the market. This made it possible for Mattel to charge higher prices than would have otherwise been the case. Like many other rent-seekers, Mattel used the bootlegger–Baptist strategy to achieve its goals. They argued that the requirement would protect children from suffering great harm and benefitted from the support of consumer lobby groups. Controversy over these claims helped to divert attention away from the cost that the program was sure to impose on taxpayers and consumers. There was no evidence that even one child had suffered health damage from lead paint on toys or clothing. Nonetheless, Mattel was able to reap substantial benefits from the child safety legislation.[10]

Since 2005, the federal government has mandated that gasoline must contain a corn-based ethanol blend, currently at 10 percent. The mandate also reflects the bootlegger and Baptist incentive structure at work. The ethanol producers stress that the mandate will reduce U.S. dependency on imported oil and non-renewable energy. In 2000, about 5 percent of the corn crop went to the production of ethanol, but by 2023, the figure had risen to more than 30 percent. The huge increase in demand for ethanol generated by the mandate has resulted in a doubling of corn prices. Essentially, this program involves a huge income transfer from consumers to ethanol producers, particularly corn farmers, including those in the important presidential primary state of Iowa. According to the U.S. Department of Agriculture, the doubling of the corn price generates $32 billion of additional revenue for the nation's 400,000 corn farmers, an average of $80,000 per farmer. On the other hand, the nation's 330 million consumers are forced to pay about $100 per person in the form of higher prices for ethanol and other products containing corn. Even the livestock industry has faced significantly higher costs due to the higher price of corn, which is used for animal feed. The special-interest effect explains why the political process tends to favor the concentrated interest of the ethanol producers relative to consumers. But the bootlegger–Baptist factor is also present here. The ethanol producers (the bootleggers) use those concerned about oil imports and the exhaustion of non-renewable resources (the Baptists) when lobbying for the mandate while downplaying their personal gains at the expense of consumers.

While cronyism is bad for the economy, there is evidence that it is quite lucrative for the politically connected business firms and the lobbyists who represent them. In a recent study, Jeffrey Brown and Jiekun Huang of the University of Illinois used a novel data set of White House visitor logs to examine this issue. Top corporate executives from S&P 1500 firms who had face-to-face meetings with high-level White House officials were associated with significantly higher stock returns during a 50-day window surrounding their meetings. They also found evidence suggesting that after meetings with federal government officials, firms received more government contracts and were more likely to receive regulatory favors. The authors concluded that, overall, their "results provide evidence suggesting that political access is of significant value to corporations."[11]

Both political officials in a position to provide favoritism and the lobbyists representing business firms and other rent-seekers are heavily represented in Washington. There are now over 12,500 registered federal lobbyists and over $4 billion spent per year lobbying for political favors from the federal government.

It is interesting to consider the difference in the incentive structure confronted by business firms directed by markets compared to crony capitalists directed by political decision-making. In both cases, pursuit of profit will direct the actions of the firm. Market entrepreneurs have a strong incentive to serve the interests of consumers spending their own money. In order to be successful, market entrepreneurs must produce goods and services that consumers value more than the resources required for their production. When they do

[10]Timothy P. Carney, "Mattel Exempted from Toy Safety Law It Helped Write," *Washington Examiner*, September 4, 2009.

[11]Jeffrey R. Brown and Jiekun Huang, "All the President's Friends: Political Access and Firm Value," *Journal of Financial Economics* 138, no. 2 (2020): 415–431.

so, their actions are productive. In contrast, crony capitalists have a strong incentive to serve the interests of political decision-makers spending someone else's money. Crony capitalists succeed by providing political players with campaign contributions and other political resources in exchange for government contracts, subsidies, tax benefits, and other forms of political favoritism. Their activities will often be counterproductive.

While the cozy relationship between government contractors and political leaders is nothing new, the expanded role of the government provides reason for additional concern. Can political decision-makers really be evenhanded when they derive substantial political support from those benefiting from their spending, regulatory, and tax policies? The answer to this question exerts an impact on not only economic efficiency but also the legitimacy of the democratic political process.

6-7 The Economic Way of Thinking about Markets and Government

When analyzing the operation of markets and government, it is vitally important to keep two points in mind. First, the government's protective role provides the foundation for the smooth operation of markets. A government that protects private property, enforces contracts evenhandedly, maintains monetary stability, and refrains from regulations that restrict voluntary exchange and entry into markets is central to the efficient operation of markets.

Second, both the market and the political process have shortcomings. As explained in Chapter 5, economic analysis indicates that there are cases where markets will fail to allocate resources efficiently. However, as the analysis of this chapter indicates, there are also reasons the political process will lead to the inefficient allocation of resources. There is government failure as well as market failure. As in the case of market failure, government failure reflects the situation where the structure of incentives encourages individuals to engage in counterproductive rather than productive use of resources. The accompanying **Thumbnail Sketch** lists the major sources of both market failure and government failure.

There is a tendency to idealize democratic governance—to focus on the stated objectives of political officials rather than the actual effects of their policies. Public-choice analysis warns against this naïve view. It focuses on how the political process really works, even if that is not how we might like for it to work. Public-choice analysis also indicates that the presence of government failure will grow as government becomes larger and more intrusive. A larger government will mean more grants, contracts, subsidies, and regulatory favors.

Thumbnail Sketch

Market Failure and Government Failure

Major sources of market failure:

1. lack of competition
2. externalities
3. public goods
4. poor information

Major sources of government failure:

1. the special-interest effect
2. the shortsightedness effect
3. rent-seeking
4. weak incentives for operational efficiency

This will create more special-interest spending, rent-seeking, and crony capitalism. Public choice also highlights the importance of institutions, constitutional rules, and procedures that encourage productive political actions and restrain those that are counter-productive. Higher income levels *and* living standards can be achieved if institutions more consistent with economic progress are adopted. This will be a recurring theme throughout this book.

Key Points

- In recent years, government spending has increased, and in 2023 it was 37 percent of the U.S. economy. Government now takes almost 20 percent of national income away from some people and transfers it to others, and only about one-sixth of these transfers are directed toward people with low income.
- There are both similarities and differences between market and political allocation. Competition is present in both, but its nature differs between the two sectors. While the government can use its taxing power to break the link between payment and receipt of a good for an individual, it cannot do so for the economy as a whole. In the public sector, voters face a "bundle"-purchase problem; they are unable to vote for some policies favored by one candidate and other policies favored by the candidate's opponent. Power and income are unequal in both sectors, but the factors influencing their distribution differ between the two.
- In a representative democracy, government is controlled by voters who elect politicians to set policy and hire bureaucrats to run government agencies. The incentives faced by all three classes of participants influence political outcomes.
- Voters have a strong incentive to support the candidate who offers them the greatest gain relative to their personal costs. Because collective decisions break the link between the choice of the individual and the outcome of the issue, voters are likely to be poorly informed on most political matters.
- Politicians have a strong incentive to follow a strategy that will enhance their chances of getting elected (and reelected). Political competition more or less forces them to focus on how their actions influence their support among voters and potential contributors.
- The distribution of the benefits and costs among voters influences how the political process works. When voters pay in proportion to the benefits they receive from a public-sector project, productive projects tend to be approved and counterproductive ones rejected. When the costs of a policy are distributed among voters differently than are the benefits, democratic decision-making will tend to be less efficient.
- Government actions will often lead to economic inefficiency as the result of (1) the special-interest effect, (2) the shortsightedness effect, (3) rent-seeking, and (4) weak incentives to keep costs low within government enterprises and agencies. Thus, just as the market sometimes fails to allocate goods efficiently, so, too, will the political process.
- As the size and scope of government grows, public-choice analysis indicates that political activity involving the exchange of government favors for political support will become more widespread. More resources will be channeled into rent-seeking and inefficient government programs, particularly those favored by special-interest groups.

Critical Analysis Questions

1. Are voters likely to be well informed on issues and the positions of candidates? Why or why not?
2. What is public-choice analysis? What are economists and others involved in public-choice analysis attempting to do?
3. What is rent-seeking? When is it likely to be widespread? How does it influence economic efficiency? Explain.
4. *"The political process sometimes leads to economic inefficiency because we elect the wrong people to political office. If the right people were elected, a democracy governed by majority rule would allocate resources efficiently." Evaluate this statement.
5. What are "bootleggers and Baptists" coalitions? Why are "bootleggers and Baptists" coalitions highly attractive to rent-seekers and politicians?

How do these coalitions impact government spending, regulation, and favoritism?

6. "The average person is more likely to make a well-informed choice when purchasing a personal computer than when voting for a congressional candidate." Is this statement true? Why or why not?
7. "Government action is based on majority rule, whereas market action is based on mutual consent. The market allows for proportional representation of minorities, but minorities must yield to the views of the majority when activities are undertaken through government." In your own words, explain the meaning of this statement. Is the statement true? Why or why not?
8. *"Voters should simply ignore political candidates who play ball with special-interest groups and vote instead for candidates who will represent all the people when they are elected. Government will work far better when this happens." Evaluate this view.
9. If a project is efficient (its total benefits exceed its total costs), would it be possible to allocate the cost of the project in a manner that would provide net benefits to each voter? Why or why not? Explain. Will efficient projects necessarily be favored by a majority of voters? Explain.
10. *"When an economic function is turned over to the government, social cooperation replaces personal self-interest." Is this statement true? Why or why not?
11. What is the shortsightedness effect? How does it influence the attractiveness of government borrowing? Explain.
12. *"Public policy and government intervention are necessary to protect the average citizen from the power of special interest groups and big businesses." Evaluate this statement.
13. "Because government-operated firms do not have to make a profit, they can usually produce at a lower cost and charge a lower price than privately owned enterprises." Evaluate this view.
14. If a senator trades his or her vote on an issue for a $10,000 payment, would you consider this corruption? If a senator votes a certain way in "exchange" for a $10,000 contribution to his or her political campaign, would you consider this corruption? Is there a major difference between the two? Discuss.
15. The United States imposes highly restrictive sugar import quotas that result in a domestic price that is generally 50 percent to 100 percent higher than the world price. The quotas benefit sugar growers at the expense of consumers. Given that there are far more sugar consumers than growers, why aren't the quotas abolished? Has government action in this area improved the living standards of Americans? Why or why not?
16. The federal Food and Drug Administration will not approve new pharmaceutical products unless the developer can prove that its product is both safe and effective as a remedy for specified ailments. Do you think the "safe and effective" criterion would be a good one for Congress to adopt for the passage of new legislation? Why or why not? Do you think most government action would meet this criterion? Discuss.
17. "When politicians decide what is bought and sold, the first thing that will be bought and sold is politicians." What is the central point of this statement? Is it true?

*Asterisk denotes questions for which answers are given in Appendix B.

Part 3

Core Microeconomics

Microeconomics focuses on the choices of consumers, the operation of firms, the structure of markets, and the choices of resource suppliers and employers.

Consumers are the ultimate judge of both products and business firms. Their choices determine which survive and which fail. The competitive process is highly dynamic. Numerous businesses come and go. Each year, newly incorporated businesses account for approximately 10 percent of the total. However, about 53 percent of the new businesses will fail within the first six years, 20 percent of which fail within their first year. Microeconomics analyzes the dynamic interaction among consumers, business firms, and resource suppliers, and how it affects the quality of our lives.

Chapter 7 Consumer Choice and Elasticity

The most famous law in economics, and the one economists are most sure of, is the law of demand. On this law is built almost the whole edifice of economics.

—David R. Henderson[1]

A thing is worth whatever a buyer will pay for it.

—Publilius Syrus, first century B.C.[2]

The statement of David Henderson highlights the central position of the law of demand in economics. As Publilius Syrus noted more than 2,000 years ago, demand reflects the willingness of individuals to pay for what is offered in the marketplace. In this section, we begin our examination of microeconomic markets for specific products with an analysis of the demand side of markets. In essence, we will be going "behind" the market demand curve to discover how it is made up of individual consumer demands and what factors determine the choices of individual consumers.[3]

Learning Objectives

7.1 Indicate the fundamental postulates underlying consumer choice.

7.2 Explain the relationship between the law of diminishing marginal utility and the law of demand.

7.3 Describe how a consumer's marginal benefit and the substitution and income effects from a price change relate to the downward sloping nature of a demand curve.

7.4 Explain the relationship between the demand curve of individuals for a good and the market demand curve.

7.5 Indicate what the price elasticity of demand measures and how it is calculated.

7.6 Explain how the values of the price elasticity of demand differ for demand curves that are elastic and inelastic.

7.7 Explain how the availability of substitutes and the time of the adjustment process will impact the elasticity of demand for a good.

7.8 Analyze how a price change will impact the total expenditures on a good and how it is influenced by whether the demand for the good is elastic or inelastic.

7.9 Explain the meaning of income elasticity and how it is calculated.

[1]David R. Henderson, "Demand," in *The Concise Encyclopedia of Economics*, ed. David R. Henderson (https://www.econlib.org/library/Enc1/Demand.html).

[2]Quoted in Michael Jackman, ed., *Macmillan Book of Business and Economic Quotations* (New York: Macmillan, 1984), 150.

[3]You may want to review the section on demand in Chapter 3 before proceeding with this chapter.

7-1 Fundamentals of Consumer Choice

Each of us must decide how to allocate our limited income among the many possible things we would like to buy. The prices of goods, *relative to each other,* are important determining factors. If your favorite cereal doubled in price, would you switch to a different brand? Would your decision be different if all cereals, not just yours, doubled in price? Your choice *between* brands of cereal will be affected only by the change in relative prices. If the prices of all cereals rose by a proportional amount, you might quit purchasing cereal, but this would not give you a strong reason to switch to a different brand. Relative prices measure opportunity cost. If cereal is $5 per box when movie tickets are $10, you must give up two boxes of cereal to purchase one movie ticket.

Entrepreneurs Who Have Changed Our Lives

Rick Diamond/Getty Images

Sara Blakely

In 2000, Sara Blakely started the company Spanx with two years of part-time research, $5,000 of personal savings, and a lot of innovative ideas and marketing savvy. Spanx succeeded because Blakely updated an old apparel category–girdles and corsets–into the cool category of "shapewear." Spanx now has hundreds of different products, stores in over 50 countries, and has even expanded into men's clothing and activewear. Along the way, Blakely became the youngest female self-made billionaire in the United States.

Blakely, who grew up in Clearwater, Florida, always had an entrepreneurial streak. After high school, she ran a babysitting service at the Clearwater Beach Hilton–until the hotel management found out she was unlicensed, inexperienced, and didn't carry insurance. She wanted to be a lawyer but scored so poorly on the LSAT (twice) that she got a job at nearby Disney World instead. She had hoped to dress up as Goofy but was too short to fit the costume, so a few months later, she left Disney and began selling fax machines. One day, she wanted to wear a new pair of slacks to a party but didn't want her panty line to show. She wore her pantyhose, cutting off the feet so they wouldn't show seams under open-toed shoes. As she told *Forbes,* "I cut the feet off my pantyhose and wore them underneath. But they rolled up my legs all night. I remember thinking, 'I've got to figure out how to make this'."

It took her a couple of years, but she did it. Once she had a design for a slimming underwear product, she tried to find a hosiery company to produce it. She was continually turned down, but one manager in Asheboro, North Carolina, changed his mind after learning that his daughters thought the product was great.

Blakeley was a one-woman marketing department. She sent samples to a stylist for Oprah Winfrey, who named Spanx her favorite product of 2000. She spent three months on a reality TV show, *Rebel Billionaire*, doing stunts like climbing up a hot air balloon on a rope ladder. She persuaded stores to sell Spanx near the trend-setting women's and shoes departments, not hidden in the lingerie or underwear departments.

Spanx succeeded in part because its products appealed to young women. But attitudes about women's bodies have been changing: maybe women shouldn't try to slim and shape themselves so much, after all. So, as is pointed out by *The New York Times,* the company has been subtly "softening" its approach, noting how good the product feels, not just what it does. Even the most successful companies must adjust to changing preferences and market forces.

Sources: Simona Covel, "A Dated Industry Gets a Modern Makeover," *Wall Street Journal*, August 7, 2008, https://www.wsj.com/articles/SB121804932355517723.

Clare O'Connor, "How Sara Blakely of Spanx Turned $5,000 into $1 Billion," *Forbes*, March 14, 2012, https://www.forbes.com/global/2012/0326/billionaires-12-feature-united-states-spanx-sara-blakely-american-booty.html#189c2a8d7ea0.

Hiroko Tabuchi, "Spanx Tries to Loosen Up Its Image," *The New York Times*, April 24, 2015, https://www.nytimes.com/2015/04/25/business/spanx-tries-to-loosen-up-its-image.html.

quartetworld/Shutterstock.com

Consumers will seek to spend their income in a manner that will provide them with the maximum value (total utility).

Consumer choice theory analyzes how the information, incentives, and constraints individuals face affect their consumption decisions. In economics, the preferences of consumers are generally taken as a given. These preferences do change through time for a variety of reasons, and those also alter the consumption choices individuals make (refer to the boxed feature, "Entrepreneurs Who Have Changed Our Lives: Sara Blakely," for an example). Several fundamental principles underlie the choices of consumers. Let's take a closer look at the key factors influencing consumer behavior.

1. Limited income necessitates choice. Because of scarcity, we all have limited incomes. The limited nature of our income requires us to make choices about which goods we will and will not buy. When more of one good or service is bought, we must buy less of some other goods if we are to stay within our budget.

2. Consumers make decisions purposefully. The goals that underpin consumer choice can usually be met in alternative ways. If two products cost the same, a consumer will choose to buy the one expected to have the higher benefit. Conversely, if two products yield equal benefits, the consumer will choose to buy the less expensive one. Fundamentally, economics assumes that consumers are rational—that they are able to weigh the costs and benefits of alternative choices.

3. One good can be substituted for another. Consumers can achieve *utility*—that is, satisfaction—from many different alternatives. Either a hamburger or a taco might satisfy your hunger, whereas going either to a movie or to a football game might satisfy your desire for entertainment. With $1,000, you might either buy a new laptop or take a short vacation. No single good is so precious that some of it will not be given up in exchange for a large enough quantity of other goods. Even seemingly unrelated goods are sometimes substituted one for another. For example, high water prices in the western United States have led residents there to substitute cactus gardens for water.

4. Consumers must make decisions without perfect information, but knowledge and past experience will help. In Chapter 1, we noted that information is costly to acquire. Asking family and friends, searching through *Consumer Reports,* and reading online reviews are all ways of gathering information about products and potential sellers. The time and effort consumers spend acquiring information will be directly related to the value derived from it. Predictably, consumers will spend more time and money to inform themselves when they are buying "big ticket" items such as automobiles or air-conditioning systems than when they are buying pencils or paper towels.

While no one has perfect foresight, your own experiences—and those of others—will help you make better-informed choices. You have a pretty good idea of what to expect when you buy a cup of coffee and a bagel at your favorite café. Your expectations might not always be fulfilled precisely the same way every time (for example, the coffee may be weak or the bagel too crispy), but even then, you will gain valuable information that will help you project the outcome of future choices more accurately.

5. The law of diminishing marginal utility applies: As the rate of consumption increases, the marginal utility gained from consuming additional units of a good will decline. Utility is a term economists use to describe the subjective personal benefits that result from taking an action. The **law of diminishing marginal utility** states that the **marginal utility** (or additional utility) derived from consuming successive units of a product will eventually decline as the rate of consumption increases. For example, the law says that even though you might like ice cream, your marginal satisfaction from additional ice cream will eventually decline as you eat more and more of it. Ice cream at lunchtime might be great. An additional helping for dinner might also be good. However, after you have had it for lunch and dinner, another serving as a midnight snack will be less attractive. When the law of diminishing marginal utility sets in, the additional utility derived from still more units of ice cream declines.

Law of diminishing marginal utility
The basic economic principle that as the consumption of a product increases, the marginal utility derived from consuming more of it (per unit of time) will eventually decline.

Marginal utility
The additional utility, or satisfaction, derived from consuming an additional unit of a good.

The law of diminishing marginal utility explains why, even if you really like a certain product, you will not spend your entire budget on it. As you increase your consumption of any good, the utility you derive from each additional unit will become smaller and smaller, eventually becoming less than the price. At that point, you will not want to purchase any more units of the good.

7-2 Marginal Utility, Consumer Choice, and the Demand Curve of an Individual

The law of diminishing marginal utility helps us understand the law of demand and the shape of the demand curve. The height of an individual's demand curve at any specific unit is equal to the maximum price the consumer would be willing to pay for that unit—its **marginal benefit** to the consumer—given the number of units they have already purchased. Although marginal benefit is measured in dollars, the dollar amount reflects the opportunity cost of the unit in terms of other goods forgone. If a consumer is willing to pay, at most, \$5 for an additional unit of the product, this indicates a willingness to give up, at most, \$5 worth of other goods. ***Because a consumer's willingness to pay for a unit of a good is directly related to the utility derived from consuming the unit, the law of diminishing marginal utility implies that a consumer's marginal benefit, and thus the height of the demand curve, falls as the quantity consumed increases.***

Marginal benefit
The maximum price a consumer will be willing to pay for an additional unit of a product. It is the dollar value of the consumer's marginal utility from the additional unit, and therefore it falls as consumption increases.

Exhibit 7-1 shows this relationship for a hypothetical consumer Jones, relative to her weekly consumption of pizza. Because of the law of diminishing marginal utility, each additional pizza consumed per week will generate less marginal utility for Jones than did the previous pizza. For this reason, Jones's maximum willingness to pay—her marginal benefit—will fall as the quantity consumed increases. In addition, the steepness of Jones's demand curve, or its responsiveness to a change in price—its elasticity—is a reflection of how rapidly Jones's marginal utility diminishes with additional consumption. An individual's demand curve for a good whose marginal value declines more rapidly will be steeper.

Exhibit 7-1 Diminishing Marginal Utility and the Individual's Demand Curve

An individual's demand curve, Jones's demand for pizzas in this case, reflects the law of diminishing marginal utility. Because marginal utility (*MU*) falls with increased consumption, so does the consumer's maximum willingness to pay–marginal benefit (*MB*). A consumer will purchase until *MB* = Price, so at a price of \$12.50 per pizza, Jones would purchase three pizzas and receive a consumer surplus shown by the shaded triangle.

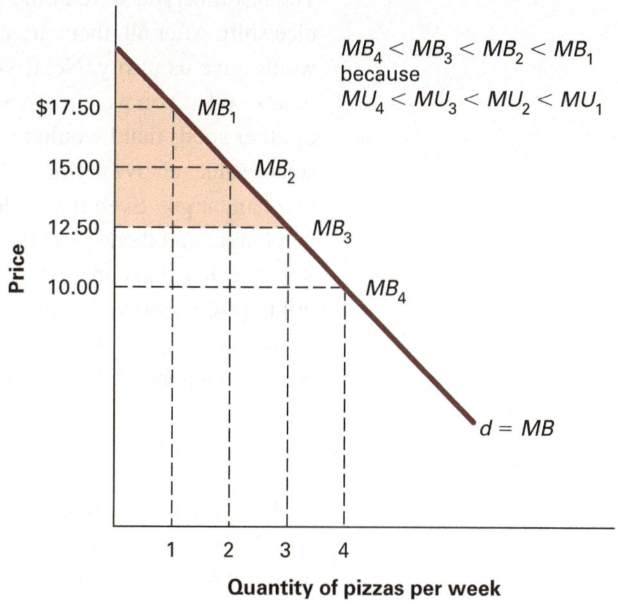

Given what we now know about a consumer's maximum willingness to pay for additional units of a good, we are in a position to discuss how many units the consumer will choose to purchase at various prices. ***At any given price, consumers will purchase all units of a good for which their maximum willingness to pay—their marginal benefit—is greater than the price.*** They will stop at the point at which the marginal benefit of the next unit would be less than the price. Although there are some problems related to dividing up certain kinds of goods (for example, it is hard to purchase half a car), we can generally say that a consumer will purchase all units of a good up to the point at which the marginal benefit from it equals the price of the good ($MB = P$).

Returning to Exhibit 7-1, if the price of pizza were \$12.50, Jones would purchase three pizzas per week.[4] Remember from Chapter 3 that consumer surplus is defined as the difference between the maximum price the consumer is willing to pay and the price actually paid, summed over all units consumed. Because the height of the demand curve reflects Jones's maximum willingness to pay for pizza, the shaded triangle that lies above the price shows the total consumer surplus derived from her consumption of the three pizzas. When a consumer has purchased all units to the point at which $MB = P$, total consumer surplus is maximized.

Within this framework, how would a consumer respond to a decrease in the price of a good? The consumer will increase purchases to the point at which marginal benefit diminishes to the level of the new lower price. If marginal utility declines rapidly with consumption, the consumer will expand his or her purchases only slightly. If marginal utility declines less rapidly, it will take a larger expansion in purchases to reach this point. The law of diminishing marginal utility underlies a person's demand curve for a product. The shape and steepness of the curve, for example, depend on his or her marginal utility.

---

[4]Jones would certainly purchase the first and second pizzas because $MB > P$. For the third pizza, $MB = P$, so Jones would be indifferent to buying the unit or not purchasing it. For a good that is easily divisible, say, pounds of roast beef, the consumer could continue purchasing up to 2.9999 pounds at a deli counter. Thus, economists are comfortable with simply concluding that the consumer will purchase this final unit, implying that Jones will purchase three pizzas.

7-2a Consumer Equilibrium with Many Goods

The last time you were at the mall, you probably saw something that you liked, perhaps a nice shirt. After all, there are many things we would like—many different alternatives that would give us utility. Next, you looked at the price tag: "Fifty dollars, wow! That's too much." What you were really saying was, "I like the shirt, but not as much as the $50 worth of other goods that I would have to give up for it." Consumer choice is a constant comparison of value relative to price. Consider another example: Perhaps you prefer expensive steak to a hamburger. Even if you do, your happiness may often be better served if you buy the hamburger and then spend the savings on something else.

The idea that consumers choose among products by comparing their relative marginal utility (*MU*) to price (*P*) can be expressed more precisely. A consumer with a limited amount of income to spend on a group of products is not likely to do the following math, but will act as though they had, and will end up consuming a bundle of goods and services such that

$$\frac{MU_A}{P_A} = \frac{MU_B}{P_B} = \cdots = \frac{MU_n}{P_n}$$

In this formula, *MU* represents the marginal utility derived from the last unit of a product, and *P* represents the price of the good. The subscripts $_{A,\, B, \ldots, n}$ indicate the different products available to the consumer. ***This formula implies that the consumer will maximize his or her satisfaction (or total utility) by ensuring that the last dollar spent on each good purchased yields an equal degree of marginal utility.*** Alternatively stated, the last unit of each item purchased should provide the same marginal utility *per dollar spent on it*. Thus, if the price of a gallon of ice cream is twice as high as the price of a smoothie, the ice cream should provide twice the marginal benefits to justify its purchase. Thus, a consumer will purchase these items to the point at which the marginal utility of the last gallon of ice cream is exactly twice as high as the marginal utility derived from the last smoothie.

Perhaps the best way to grasp this point is to think about what happens when your ratios of marginal utility to price are not equal for two goods. Suppose that you are at a local restaurant eating buffalo chicken wings and drinking Coke. For simplicity, assume that a large Coke and an order of wings each costs $4. With your $20 budget, you decide to purchase four orders of wings and one large Coke. When you finish your Coke, there are still lots of wings left. You have already eaten so many wings, though, that those remaining do not look as attractive. You could get more utility with fewer wings and another Coke, but it is too late. You have not spent your $20 in a way that gets you the most for your money. Instead of satisfying the preceding condition, you find that the marginal utility of wings is lower than the marginal utility of a Coke, and because they both have the same price ($4), this implies that

$$\frac{MU_{WINGS}}{P_{WINGS}} < \frac{MU_{COKE}}{P_{COKE}}$$

If you had purchased fewer wings and more Coke, your total utility would have been higher. Consuming the added Coke would have lowered its marginal utility, decreasing the value of the right side of the equation. Simultaneously, spending less on wings would have raised the marginal utility of wings, increasing the value of the left side of the equation. You will maximize your utility—and get the most "bang for the buck" from your budget—when you make these values (the ratios) equal.

The equation can also be used to illustrate the law of demand. Beginning with a situation in which the two sides were equal, suppose that the price of wings increased. It would lower the value of *MU/P* for wings below the *MU/P* for Coke. In response, you would reallocate your budget, purchasing fewer of the more costly wings and more Coke. Thus, we have the law of demand—as the price of wings rises, you will purchase less of them. When people try to spend their money in a way that gives them the greatest amount of satisfaction, the consumer decision-making theory outlined here is difficult to question. In the next section, we will take the theory a little further.

7-2b Price Changes and Consumer Choice

The demand curve or schedule shows the amount of a product that consumers are willing to buy at alternative prices during a specific time period. The law of demand states that the amount of a product bought is inversely related to its price. We have explained how the law of demand can be derived from fundamental principles of consumer behavior. Now, we go further and distinguish two different phenomena underlying a consumer's response to a price change. First, as the price of a product declines, the lower opportunity cost will induce consumers to buy more of it—even if they have to give up some other products, whose price has not fallen. This tendency to substitute a product that has become cheaper for goods that are now relatively more expensive is called the **substitution effect** of a price change.

Substitution effect
That part of an increase (decrease) in amount consumed that is the result of a good being cheaper (more expensive) in relation to other goods because of a reduction (increase) in price.

Second, if a consumer's money income is unchanged, a reduction in the price of a product they consume will increase their real income—the amount of goods and services the consumer is able to purchase with that fixed amount of money income. If your rent were to decline by $100 per month, for example, that would allow you to buy more of many other goods. This increase in your real income has the same effect as if the rent had remained the same but your income had risen by $100 per month. As a result, this second way in which a price change affects consumption is called the **income effect**. Typically, consumers will respond to the income effect by buying more of the cheaper product and other products as well because they can better afford to do so. Substitution and income effects generally work in the same direction: They both cause consumers to purchase more of a good as its price falls and less of a good as its price rises.[5]

Income effect
That part of an increase (decrease) in amount consumed that is the result of the consumer's real income being expanded (contracted) by a reduction (rise) in the price of a good.

7-2c Time Costs and Consumer Choice

You may have heard the saying that "time is money." It is certainly true that time has value and that this value can sometimes be measured in dollars. As we have learned, the monetary price of a good is not always a complete measure of its cost to the consumer. Consuming most goods requires not only money but also time; and time, like money, is scarce to the consumer. So a lower time cost, like a lower money price, will make a product more attractive. For example, one study showed that patients in a dentist's office are willing to pay more than $5 per minute saved to shorten their time spent in waiting rooms.[6] Similarly, fast food and air travel are demanded mainly for the time savings they offer.

Time costs, unlike money prices for goods, differ among individuals. They are higher for people with higher wage rates, for example. Other things being equal, high-wage consumers choose more time-saving commodities than do people with lower time costs and wages. For example, high-wage consumers are overrepresented among airplane and taxicab passengers but underrepresented among television watchers, chess players, and long-distance bus travelers.

Failure to account for time costs can lead to bad decisions. For example, which is cheaper for consumers: (1) waiting in line three hours on Black Friday to purchase an inkjet printer on sale for $69 or (2) buying the same printer for $99 without standing in line? A consumer whose time is worth more than $10 per hour will find that $99 without the wait in line is less costly. Obviously, time costs matter. For example, when government-imposed price ceilings (discussed in Chapter 4) create shortages, rationing by waiting or searching occurs. For many consumers, the benefit of the lower price due to the ceiling will be largely, if not entirely, offset by their increased time cost of having to wait in line or search across multiple stores or sellers attempting to find the item in stock. During the COVID-19

[5]The substitution effect will always work in this direction. The income effect, however, may work in the reverse direction for some types of goods known as inferior goods. These will be addressed later in this chapter.

[6]Rexford E. Santerre and Stephen P. Neun, *Health Economics: Theories, Insights and Industry Studies* (Orlando, FL: Harcourt, 2000), 113.

Exhibit 7-2 Individual and Market Demand Curves

The market demand curve is merely the horizontal sum of the individual demand curves. It will slope downward to the right just as individual demand curves do.

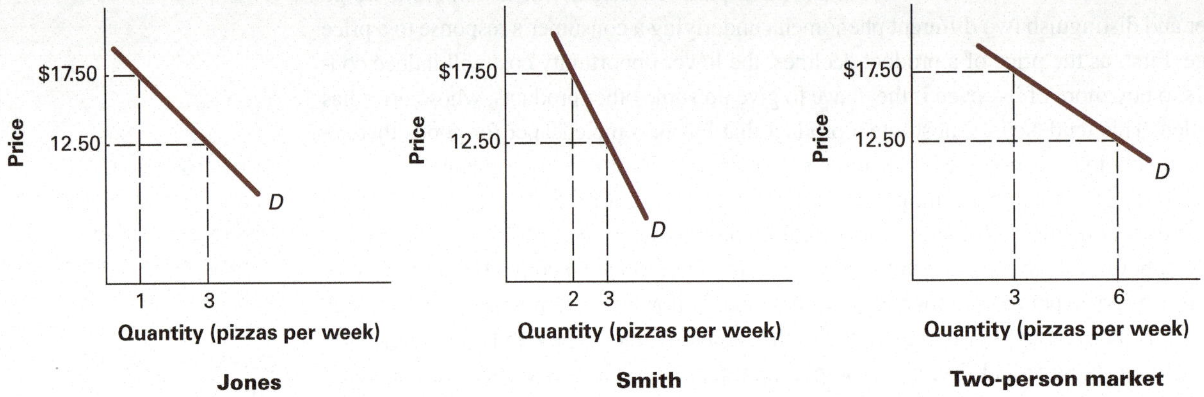

pandemic, for example, it was not unusual for consumers to spend days searching at multiple stores for items like toilet paper and hand sanitizer due to state laws that prevented prices from rising on these items during the state-of-emergency declarations.

7-2d Market Demand Reflects the Demand of Individual Consumers

The market demand schedule is the relationship between the market price of a good and the amount demanded by all the individuals in the market area. Because individual consumers purchase less at higher prices, the amount demanded in a market area as a total is also inversely related to price.

Exhibit 7-2 shows the relationship between individual demand and market demand for a hypothetical two-person market. The individual demand curves for both Jones and Smith are shown. Jones and Smith each consume three pizzas per week at a price of $12.50. The quantity demanded in the two-person market is six pizzas. If the price rises to $17.50 per pizza, the amount demanded in the market will fall to three pizzas, one demanded by Jones and two by Smith. ***The market demand is simply the horizontal sum of the individual demand curves of consumers—in this case, Smith and Jones.***

In the real world, there can be millions of consumers in a market. But the relationship between the demand curves of individuals and the market demand curve will still be just like the one shown in Exhibit 7-2. At any given price, the amount purchased in the market will be the sum of the amounts purchased by each consumer in the market. Furthermore, the total amount demanded in the market will decline as price increases because individual consumers will purchase fewer units at the higher prices. The market demand curve reflects the collective choices of the individual consumers.

7-3 Elasticity of Demand

Although it is important to recognize that consumers will buy less of a product as its price increases, it is also often important to know whether the increase will lead to a large or small reduction in the amount purchased. Economists have designed a tool called the price elasticity of demand to measure this sensitivity of amount purchased in response to a change in price. The equation for the **price elasticity of demand** is as follows:

Price elasticity of demand
The percentage change in the quantity of a product demanded divided by the percentage change in the price that caused the change in quantity. The price elasticity of demand indicates how responsive consumers are to a change in a product's price.

$$\textbf{Price elasticity of demand} = \frac{\textbf{Percentage change in quantity demanded}}{\textbf{Percentage change in price}} = \frac{\%\Delta Q}{\%\Delta P}$$

This ratio is often called the *elasticity coefficient*. To express it more briefly, we use the notation $\%\Delta Q$ to represent percentage change in quantity and $\%\Delta P$ to represent percentage change in price. (The Greek letter delta [Δ] means "change in.") The law of demand states that an increase in a product's price lowers the quantity of it purchased, whereas a decrease in price raises it. ***Because a change in price causes the quantity demanded to change in the opposite direction, the price elasticity coefficient is always negative, although economists often ignore the sign and use the absolute value of the coefficient.***

To illustrate how the concept of elasticity works, suppose that the price of the Ford Explorer rises 10 percent, while other prices remain the same. Ford could expect Explorer sales to fall substantially—perhaps 30 percent—as sport-utility vehicle (SUV) buyers respond by switching to other SUVs whose prices have not changed. This strong response by buyers means that the demand for the Explorer is elastic.

Now consider a different situation. Suppose that, because of a new tax, the price of not only the Explorer *but of all new SUVs* rises 10 percent. In this case, consumers' options are much more limited. They can't simply switch to a cheaper close substitute as they could when the price of the Explorer alone rose. They might either simply pay the extra money for a new SUV or settle for a used SUV instead. Because of this, the 10 percent rise in the price of all new SUVs will lead to a smaller consumer response, perhaps a 5 percent decline in sales of new SUVs.

To calculate the elasticity coefficient for the Explorer in the initial example, we begin with the 30 percent decline in quantity demanded and divide it by the 10 percent increase in the price. Thus, the elasticity of demand for the Explorer would be

$$\frac{\%\Delta Q}{\%\Delta P} = \frac{-30\%}{+10\%} = -3$$

(or 3.0 if we ignore the minus sign). This means that the percentage change in quantity demanded is three times the percentage change in price.

To calculate the demand elasticity for *all* SUVs (our second example), we take the percentage change in quantity, 5 percent, divided by the percentage change in price, 10 percent, gives us –1/2, or –0.5. When it comes to the price elasticity of demand for all SUVs, the percentage change in quantity demanded (using our hypothetical numbers) is only half the percentage change in price, not three times the percentage change in price as it was with the Explorer.

Often, we will have to derive the percentage change in quantity and price. If you know the quantities that will be purchased at two different prices, you can then derive the percentage change in both the price and the quantity. For example, suppose that a price change from P_0 to P_1 causes a change in quantity demanded from Q_0 to Q_1. The change in quantity demanded would therefore be $Q_0 - Q_1$. To calculate the percentage change in quantity, we divide the actual change by the midpoint (or average) of the two quantities.[7] Although it is often easy to find the midpoint without a formula (halfway between \$4 and \$6 is \$5), it can also be found as $(Q_0 + Q_1)/2$. Finally, because 0.05 is simply 5 percent, we multiply by 100. Thus, we can express the percentage change in quantity demanded as

$$\frac{(Q_0 - Q_1)}{[(Q_0 + Q_1)/2]} \times 100$$

[7]This formula uses the average of the starting point and the ending point of the change so that it will give the same result whether we start from the lower or the higher price. This arc elasticity formula is not the only way to calculate elasticity, but it is the most frequently used.

Similarly, when the change in price is $P_0 - P_1$, the *percentage* change in price is

$$\frac{(P_0 - P_1)}{[(P_0 + P_1)/2]} \times 100$$

Dividing the resulting percentage change in quantity by the percentage change in price gives us the elasticity.

Using substitution, it is possible to derive a version of the elasticity formula that incorporates these two percentage calculations. Because each term is multiplied by 100 and the denominator of each term contains a 2, these factors cancel out of the final expression. After simplification this version is

$$\frac{\left[(Q_0 - Q_1)/(Q_0 + Q_1)\right]}{\left[(P_0 - P_1)/(P_0 + P_1)\right]}$$

A numerical example will help you understand this. Suppose that Trina's Cakes can sell 50 specialty cakes per week at \$7 each, or it can sell 70 specialty cakes per week at \$6 each. The percentage difference in quantity is the difference in the quantity demanded (50 – 70 = –20) divided by the midpoint (60) times 100. The result is a –33.33 percent change in quantity (–20 ÷ 60 × 100 = –33.33).

Now that we've calculated the percentage change in quantity demanded of cakes, let's calculate the percentage change in the price. The percentage change in price is the difference in the two prices (\$7 – \$6 = \$1) divided by the midpoint price (\$6.50) times 100, or a 15.38 percent change in price (1 ÷ 6.5 × 100 = 15.38). Dividing the percentage change in quantity by the percentage change in price (–33.33 ÷ 15.38) gives an elasticity coefficient of –2.17. Alternatively, we could have expressed this directly as

$$\frac{\left[(50-70)/(50+70)\right]}{\left[(7-6)/(7+6)\right]} = \frac{(-20/120)}{(1/13)} = \frac{(-1/6)}{(1/13)} = \frac{-13}{6} = -2.17$$

The same result is obtained either way. The elasticity of 2.17 (ignoring the minus sign) indicates that the percentage change in quantity is just over twice the percentage change in price.

The elasticity coefficient lets us make a precise distinction between elasticity and inelasticity. When the elasticity coefficient is greater than 1 (ignoring the minus sign), as it was for the demand for Trina's Cakes, demand is elastic. When it is less than 1, demand is inelastic. Demand is said to be of *unitary elasticity* if the price elasticity is exactly 1.

7-3a Graphic Representation of Price Elasticity of Demand

Exhibit 7-3 presents demand curves of varying elasticity. A demand curve that is completely vertical is said to be *perfectly inelastic*, shown in panel (a) of Exhibit 7-3. In the real world, such demand does not exist because the substitutes for a good become more attractive as the price of that good rises. Moreover, because of the income effect, we should expect that a higher price will always reduce the quantity demanded, other things remaining the same.

The more inelastic the demand, the steeper the demand curve *over any specific price range*. The demand for electronic cigarettes (e-cigarettes) (shown in panel b of Exhibit 7-3) is highly inelastic; a big change in price doesn't change quantity demanded much. People who crave nicotine will be willing to pay the higher price. Conversely, the demand for apples (shown in panel d) is relatively elastic. People will find it easy to switch to oranges or bananas, for example, if the price of apples increases dramatically.

When demand elasticity is unitary, as panel (c) shows, a demand curve that is convex to the origin will result. When a demand curve is completely horizontal, an economist would say that it is *perfectly elastic*. Demand for the wheat marketed by a single wheat farmer, for example, would approximate perfect elasticity (panel e).

Exhibit 7-3 Price Elasticity of Demand

(a) Perfectly inelastic: Despite an increase in a product's price, consumers still purchase the same amount of it. Substitution and income effects prevent this from happening in the real world, though.
(b) Relatively inelastic: A percentage increase in a product's price results in a smaller percentage reduction in its sales. The demand for e-cigarettes has been estimated to be highly inelastic.
(c) Unit elastic: The percentage change in quantity demanded of a product is equal to the percentage change in its price. A curve with a decreasing slope results. Sales revenue (price times quantity sold) is constant.
(d) Relatively elastic: A percentage increase in a product's price leads to a larger percentage reduction in purchases of it. When good substitutes are available for a product (as in the case of apples), the amount of it purchased will be highly sensitive to price changes.
(e) Perfectly elastic: Consumers will buy all of Farmer Jones's wheat at the market price, but none will be sold above the market price.

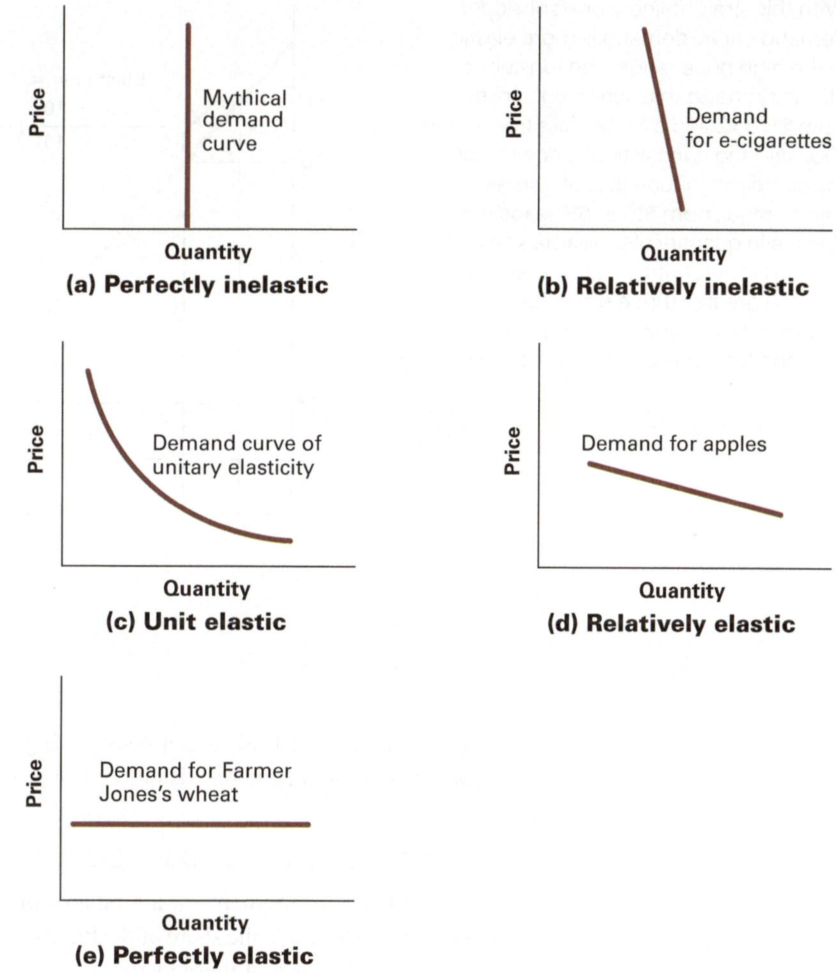

Because elasticity is a relative concept, the elasticity of a straight-line demand curve will differ at each point along the demand curve. As **Exhibit 7-4** shows, the elasticity of a straight-line demand curve (one with a constant slope) will range from highly elastic to highly inelastic. In this exhibit, when the price rises from \$10 to \$11, sales decline from 20 to 10. According to the formula, the price elasticity of demand is –7.0. Demand is very elastic in this region. In contrast, demand is quite inelastic in the \$1 to \$2 price range. As the price increases from \$1 to \$2, the amount demanded declines from 110 to 100. The ten-unit change in quantity is the same, but it is a smaller *percentage* change. And the \$1 change in price is the same, but it is now a larger *percentage* change. The elasticity of demand in this range is only –0.14; demand in this case is highly inelastic.

7-3b How Large Are the Demand Elasticities of Various Products?

Economists have estimated the price elasticity of demand for many products. As **Exhibit 7-5** shows, the elasticity of demand varies substantially among products. The demand is highly inelastic for several products—salt, toothpicks, matches, coffee, and gasoline (short-run)—in their normal price range. In contrast, the demand curves for fresh tomatoes, Chevrolet

Exhibit 7-4 Slope of the Demand Curve Versus Price Elasticity

With this straight-line (constant slope) demand curve, demand is more elastic in the high price range. The formula for elasticity shows that, when price rises from $1 to $2 and quantity falls from 110 to 100, demand is inelastic. A price rise of the same magnitude (but of a smaller percentage), from $10 to $11, leads to a decline in quantity of the same size (but of a larger percentage), so that elasticity is much greater. (Price elasticities are negative, but economists often ignore the sign and look only at the absolute value.)

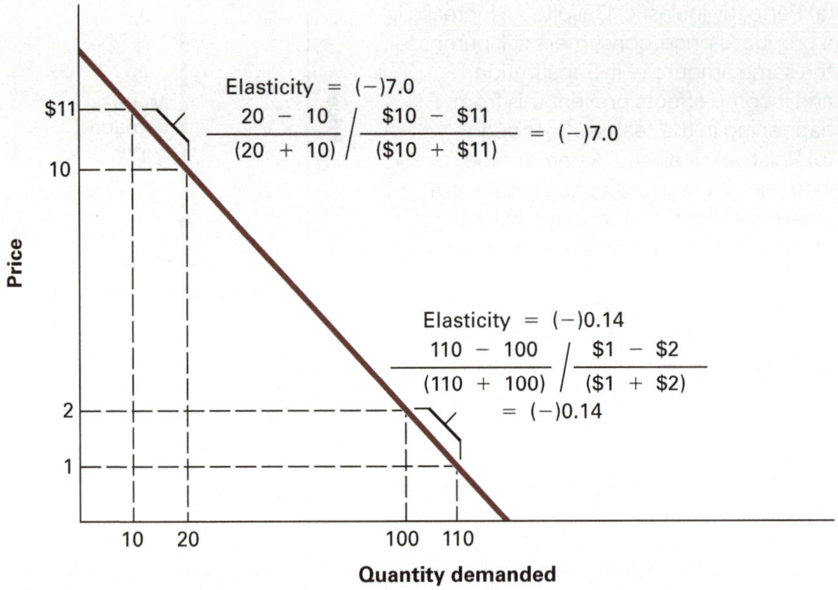

automobiles, and fresh green peas are highly elastic. The demand for movies, housing, private education, and televisions is near 1.0 (unitary).

7-3c Why Do the Price Elasticities of Demand Vary?

The primary determinants of a product's price elasticity of demand are the availability of good substitutes and the share of the typical consumer's total budget expended on a product. Let's consider each of these factors.

Availability of substitutes ***The most important determinant of the price elasticity of demand is the availability of substitutes. When good substitutes for a product are available, a price increase induces many consumers to switch to other products.*** Demand is elastic. For example, if the price of apples increases, consumers might substitute oranges or bananas.

When good substitutes for a product are unavailable, the demand for it will tend to be inelastic. Medical services are an example. When we are sick, most of us find witch doctors, faith healers, palm readers, and aspirin to be highly imperfect substitutes for the services of a physician. Not surprisingly, the demand for physician services is inelastic.

The availability of substitutes increases as the product class becomes more specific, thus increasing price elasticity. For example, as Exhibit 7-5 shows, the price elasticity of Chevrolets, a narrow product class, exceeds that of the broad class of automobiles in general. If the price of Chevrolets alone rises, many substitute cars are available. But if the prices of all automobiles rise together, consumers have fewer good substitutes.

Product's share of the consumer's total budget If the expenditures on a product are quite small relative to the consumer's budget, the income effect will be small even if there is a substantial increase in the price of the product. This will make demand less elastic. Compared to one's total budget, expenditures on some commodities are minor. Matches, toothpicks, and salt are good examples. Most consumers spend less than a couple of dollars per year on each of these items. A doubling of their price would exert little influence on a

Exhibit 7-5 Estimated Price Elasticity of Demand for Selected Products

Inelastic		Approximately unitary elasticity	
Salt	−0.1	Movies	−0.9
Matches	−0.1	Housing, owner occupied, long run	−1.2
Toothpicks	−0.1	Shellfish, consumed at home	−0.9
Airline travel, short run	−0.1	Oysters, consumed at home	−1.1
Gasoline, short run	−0.2	Private education	−1.1
Gasoline, long run	−0.7	Tires, short run	−0.9
Residential natural gas, short run	−0.1	Tires, long run	−1.2
Residential natural gas, long run	−0.5	Televisions	−1.2
Coffee	−0.25	**Elastic**	
Fish (cod), consumed at home	−0.5	Restaurant meals	−2.3
Electronic cigarettes (e-cigarettes), disposable	−0.37	Foreign travel, long run	−4.0
Cigarettes	−0.21	Airline travel, long run	−2.4
Legal services, short run	−0.4	Fresh green peas	−2.8
Physician services	−0.6	Automobiles, short run	−1.2–1.5
Dental services	−0.7	Chevrolet automobiles	−4.0
Taxi, short run	−0.6	Fresh tomatoes	−4.6
UberX rides, short run	−0.55	Hospital care in California	−4.8
Automobiles, long run	−0.2	iPhone Apps (Apple App Store)	−2.0
		Android Apps (Google Play Store)	−3.7

Sources: Hendrick S. Houthakker and Lester D. Taylor, *Consumer Demand in the United States, 1929–1970* (Cambridge, MA: Harvard University Press, 1966, 1970); Douglas R. Bohi, *Analyzing Demand Behavior* (Baltimore: Johns Hopkins University Press, 1981); Hsaing-tai Cheng and Oral Capps Jr., "Demand for Fish," *American Journal of Agricultural Economics* 70, no. 3 (1988): 533–42; Rexford E. Santerre and Stephen P. Neun, *Health Economics: Theories, Insights and Industry Studies* (Orlando, FL: Harcourt, 2000); Martin Gaynor and William Vogt, "Competition among Hospitals," *The RAND Journal of Economics* (Winter 2003): 764–85; Anindya Ghose and Sang Pil Han, "Estimating Demand for Mobile Applications in the New Economy," *Management Science* 60, no. 6 (June 2014): 1470–1488; Peter Cohen, Robert Hahn, Jonathan Hall, Steven Levitt, and Robert Metcalfe, "Using Big Data to Estimate Consumer Surplus: The Case of Uber," *NBER Working Paper 22627* (2016); and Tingting Yao, Hai-Yen Sung, Jidong Huang, Lela Chu, Gideon St. Helen, and Wendy Max, "The impact of e-cigarette and cigarette prices on e-cigarette and cigarette sales in California," *Preventive Medicine Reports* 20 (December 2020): 101244.

family's budget. Therefore, even if the price of such a product were to rise sharply, consumers would still not find it worthwhile to spend much time and effort looking for substitutes.

Exhibit 7-6 provides a graphic illustration of both elastic and inelastic demand curves. In panel (a), the demand curve for fast-food hamburgers is elastic because there are good substitutes—for example, tacos, burritos, salads, chicken, and other sandwiches. Therefore, when the price of the hamburgers increases from $5.00 to $7.50, the quantity purchased declines sharply from 100 million to only 25 million. The calculated price elasticity equals −3.0. The fact that the absolute value of the coefficient is greater than 1 confirms that the demand for hamburgers is elastic over the price range shown.

Panel (b) of Exhibit 7-6 shows the demand curve for disposable electronic cigarettes (e-cigarettes). Because most users do not find other products to be a good substitute, the demand for e-cigarettes is highly inelastic. As the price of e-cigarettes increases from $5.00 to $7.50, the number purchased falls by only a small amount (from 100 million to 86 million). The price elasticity coefficient is −0.37, substantially less in absolute value than 1, confirming that the demand for e-cigarettes is inelastic. (*Exercise:* Use the price elasticity formula to verify the values of these elasticity coefficients.)

Exhibit 7-6 Inelastic and Elastic Demand

As the price of fast-food hamburgers (a) rose from $5.00 to $7.50, the quantity purchased fell sharply from 100 million to 25 million. The percentage reduction in quantity is larger than the percentage increase in price. Thus, the demand for the hamburgers is elastic. In contrast, an increase in the price of disposable e-cigarettes from $5.00 to $7.50 leads to only a small reduction in the number purchased from 100 million to 86 million (b). Because the percentage reduction in quantity is smaller than the percentage increase in price, demand is inelastic.

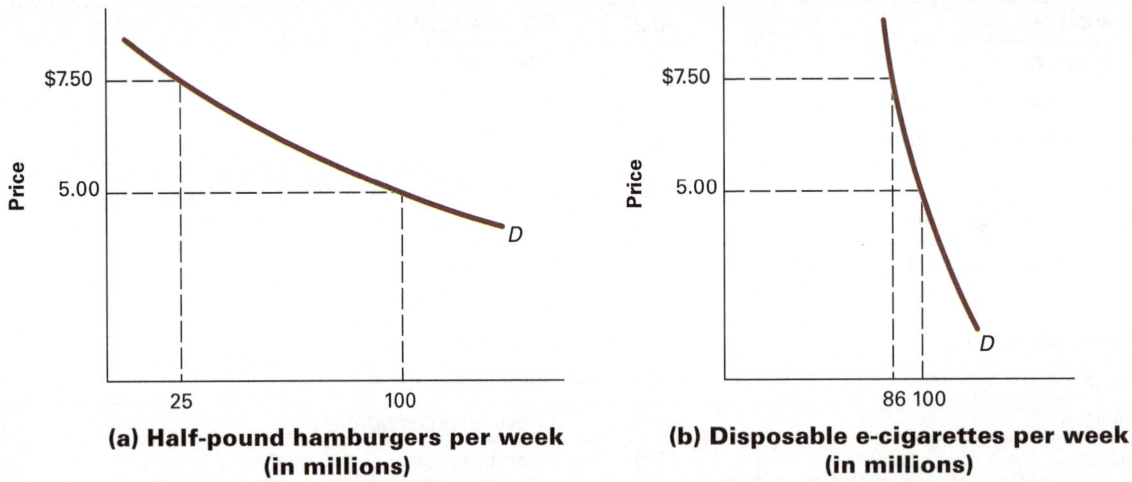

7-3d Time and Demand Elasticity

As changing market conditions raise or lower the price of a product, both consumers and producers will respond. However, the response will not be instantaneous, and it is likely to become larger over time. ***In general, when the price of a product increases, consumers will reduce their consumption by a larger amount in the long run than in the short run. Thus, the demand for most products will be more elastic in the long run than in the short run. This relationship between elasticity and the length of the adjustment period is sometimes referred to as the second law of demand.***

The first law of demand says that buyers will respond predictably to a price change, purchasing more when the price is lower than when the price is higher, if other things remain the same. The second law of demand says that the response of buyers will be greater after they have had time to adjust more fully to a price change.

7-4 How Demand Elasticity and Price Changes Affect Total Expenditures (or Revenues) on a Product

By looking at demand elasticity, we can determine changes in total consumer spending on a product when its price changes. We can do this in three different ways: by looking at (1) changes in an individual's total spending, using the demand elasticity from his or her demand curve for the product; (2) changes in the total combined spending of all consumers, using the elasticity from the total market demand curve; or (3) changes in total consumer spending on the product, using the demand curve facing the firm that produces it. This third method allows us to look at elasticity based not on what consumers spend, but on what the producer receives from selling the product.

Total expenditures (or revenues) simply amount to the price of the product times the number of units of it purchased (or sold). Because total expenditures are equal to the price times the quantity, and because the price and the quantity move in opposite directions, the net effect of a price change on the total spending on a product depends on whether the (percentage) price change or the (percentage) quantity change is greater.

Change in Total Expenditures	=	Price	×	Quantity
?	=	↑	×	↓
?	=	↓	×	↑

When demand is inelastic, the price elasticity coefficient is less than 1. This means that the percentage change in price is greater than the percentage change in quantity. ***Therefore, when demand is inelastic, the change in the price will dominate and, as a result, the price and total expenditures will change in the same direction.*** In other words, when the price of an inelastic product (say, disposable e-cigarettes) increases, spending on it will increase, too—and vice versa. Conversely, when demand is elastic, the change in quantity will be greater than the change in the price. ***As a result, the impact of the change in quantity will dominate, and therefore the price and expenditures will move in opposite directions.*** In other words, when the price of a product with an elastic demand (say, fast-food hamburgers) increases, spending on it will decrease.

When demand elasticity is unitary, the change in quantity demanded will be equal in magnitude to the change in price. With regard to their impact on total expenditures, these two effects will exactly offset each other. ***Thus, when price elasticity of demand is equal to 1, total expenditures will remain unchanged as price changes.***

Exhibit 7-7 summarizes the relationship between changes in the price of a product and changes in total spending on it when demand is elastic, inelastic, and unit elastic. The demand curves shown in Exhibit 7-6 can also be used to show the link between elasticity and changes in total spending. When the price of e-cigarettes (panel b) increases from $5.00 to $7.50, the price elasticity of demand is 0.37, indicating that demand is inelastic. This increase in cigarette prices leads to an increase in spending on the product from $500 million ($5.00 × 100 million units) to $645 million ($7.50 × 86 million units). If the change had occurred in the opposite direction, with the price falling from $7.50 to $5.00, total expenditures would have declined.

The price elasticity of demand for fast-food hamburgers when the price increases from $5.00 to $7.50 (panel a of Exhibit 7-6) is 3.0, indicating that demand is elastic. In this case, price and expenditures will move in the opposite direction. The increase in the price of hamburgers lowers total consumer spending on the product from $400 million ($5.00 × 100 million hamburgers) to $187.5 million ($7.50 × 25 million hamburgers). If the price change had been in the opposite direction, with the price falling from $7.50 to $5.00, total expenditures would have risen.

Exhibit 7-7 Demand Elasticity and How Changes in Price Affect Total Consumer Expenditures or a Firm's Total Revenue

Price Elasticity of Demand	Numerical Elasticity Coefficient (in absolute value)	Impact of Raising Price on Total Consumer Expenditures or a Firm's Total Revenue	Impact of Lowering Price on Total Consumer Expenditures or a Firm's Total Revenue
Elastic	1 to ∞	decrease	increase
Unit Elastic	1	unchanged	unchanged
Inelastic	0 to 1	increase	decrease

When a firm increases the price of its product, its revenues may rise, fall, or remain the same. If the demand for the firm's product is inelastic, the higher price will expand the firm's total revenue. However, if the demand for the firm's product is elastic, a price increase will lead to substantially lower sales and a decline in total revenue. In the case of unitary elasticity, the price increase will leave total revenue unchanged.

Beyond the price elasticity of demand, two other elasticity relationships are important. We therefore end this chapter with a brief discussion of income elasticity of demand and price elasticity of supply.

Income elasticity
The percentage change in the quantity of a product demanded divided by the percentage change in consumer income that caused the change in quantity demanded. It measures the responsiveness of the demand for a good to a consumer's change in income.

7-5 Income Elasticity

Increases in consumer income will increase the demand (the quantity demanded at each price) for most goods. Income elasticity tells us how responsive the demand for a product is to income changes. **Income elasticity** is defined as

$$\textbf{Income elasticity} = \frac{\textbf{Percentage change in quantity demanded}}{\textbf{Percentage change in income}}$$

Normal good
A good that has a positive income elasticity, so that as consumer income rises, demand for the good rises, too.

As **Exhibit 7-8** shows, although the income elasticity coefficients for products vary from one good to another, they are normally positive. In fact, the term **normal good** refers to any good with a positive income elasticity of demand. Some normal goods have lower income elasticities than others, however. In general, goods that people regard as "necessities" will have low income elasticities (between 0 and 1). Significant quantities are purchased even at low incomes, and, as income increases, spending on these items will increase by less than a proportional amount. It is understandable that items such as fuel, electricity, bread, tobacco, economy clothing, and potatoes have a low income elasticity.

Goods that consumers regard as "luxuries" generally have a high (greater than 1) income elasticity. For example, private education, new automobiles, swimming pools, and vacation travel are all highly income-elastic. As the consumer's income increases, the

Exhibit 7-8 Estimated Income Elasticity of Demand for Selected Products

Low income elasticity		High income elasticity	
Margarine	−0.20	Private education	2.46
Fuel	0.38	New cars	2.45
Electricity	0.20	Recreation and amusements	1.57
Fish (haddock)	0.46	Alcohol	1.54
Food	0.51		
Lottery tickets	0.13		
Tobacco	0.64		
Hospital care	0.69		
Tablet computer/iPad, for college students	0.24		

Sources: Hendrick S. Houthakker and Lester D. Taylor, *Consumer Demand in the United States, 1929–1970* (Cambridge, MA: Harvard University Press, 1966); L. Taylor, "The Demand for Electricity: A Survey," *Bell Journal of Economics* 6, no. 1 (1975): 74–110; F. W. Bell, "The Pope and the Price of Fish," *American Economic Review* 58, no. 5 (1968): 1346–50; Rexford E. Santerre and Stephen P. Neun, *Health Economics: Theories, Insights and Industry Studies* (Orlando, FL: Harcourt, 2000); Martijn B. W. Kobus, Piet Rietveld, and Jos N. van Ommeren, "Ownership Versus On-campus Use of Mobile IT Devices by University Students," *Computers & Education* 68 (October 2013): 29–41; and Thomas A. Garrett and Cletus C. Coughlin, "Intertemporal Differences in the Income Elasticity of Demand for Lottery Tickets," *National Tax Journal* 62, no. 1 (2009): 77–99.

demand for these goods expands even more rapidly, and therefore spending on these items increases as a proportion of income.

A few commodities, such as margarine, low-quality meat cuts, ramen noodles, and bus travel, actually have a negative income elasticity. Economists refer to goods with a negative income elasticity as **inferior good**. As income expands, the demand for inferior goods will decline. Conversely, as income declines, the demand for inferior goods will increase.

Inferior good
A good that has a negative income elasticity, so that as consumer income rises, the demand for the good falls.

7-6 Price Elasticity of Supply

The **price elasticity of supply** is the percentage change in quantity supplied divided by the percentage change in the price causing the supply response. Because this measures the responsiveness of sellers to a change in price, it is analogous to the price elasticity of demand. However, the price elasticity of supply will be positive because the quantity producers are willing to supply is directly related to price. As in demand elasticity, time plays a role. In the next two chapters, we will discuss more fully the factors that determine supply elasticity. For now, it is important simply to recognize the concept of supply elasticity and the fact that suppliers (like buyers) will be more responsive to a price change when they have had more time to adjust to it.

Price elasticity of supply
The percentage change in quantity supplied divided by the percentage change in the price that caused the change in quantity supplied.

Key Points

- Consumers will try to allocate their limited incomes among a multitude of goods in a way that maximizes their utility. The role of relative prices, information, and preferences, as well as the law of diminishing marginal utility, help explain the choices consumers make and the downward slope of a person's demand curve for products.
- The market demand curve for a product is the horizontal sum of the demand curve of the individuals for the product.
- The price elasticity of demand measures the responsiveness of the quantity of a product purchased to a change in its price.
- The availability of substitutes is the primary determinant of the price elasticity of demand for a product. When there are good substitutes available, and the item is a sizable component of the consumer's budget, its demand will tend to be elastic. When only poor substitutes are available, demand will tend to be inelastic.
- Typically, the price elasticity of a product will increase as consumers have had more time to adjust to a change in its price. This direct relationship between the size of the elasticity coefficient and the length of the adjustment period is often referred to as the *second law of demand*.
- The concept of elasticity helps us determine how a change in price will affect total consumer expenditures on a product or a firm's total revenues derived from it. When the demand for a product is elastic, a price change will cause total spending on it to change in the opposite direction. When demand for a product is inelastic, a change in price will cause total spending on it to change in the same direction.
- The concept of elasticity can also be applied to consumer income (which is called the income elasticity of demand) and supply (which is called the price elasticity of supply).

Critical Analysis Questions

1. Suppose that, in an attempt to raise more revenue, Nowhere State University (NSU) increases its tuition. Will this necessarily result in more revenue? Under what conditions will revenue (a) rise, (b) fall, or (c) remain the same? Explain this, focusing on the relationship between the increased revenue from students who enroll at NSU despite the higher tuition and the lost revenue from lower enrollment. If the true price elasticity were –1.2, what would you suggest the university do to expand revenue?

2. *A bus ticket between two cities costs $150 and the trip will take 25 hours, whereas an airplane ticket costs $450 and takes five hours. Kathy values her time at $12 per hour, and Rachel values her time at $18 per hour. Will Kathy take the bus or the plane? Which will Rachel take? Explain.
3. *Recent research confirms that the demand for e-cigarettes is not only inelastic, but it also indicates that users with incomes in the lower half of all incomes respond to a given price increase by reducing their purchases by amounts that are more than four times as large as the purchase reductions made by users in the upper half of all incomes. How can the income and substitution effects of a price change help explain this finding?
4. Dominique is currently purchasing three pairs of jeans and five T-shirts per year. The price of jeans is $60, and T-shirts cost $20. At the current rate of consumption, her marginal utility of jeans is 120, and her marginal utility of T-shirts is 60. Is Dominique maximizing her utility? Would you suggest that she buy more jeans and fewer T-shirts, or more T-shirts and fewer jeans?
5. Estimates presented in Exhibit 7-5 show that Android users have a higher price elasticity of demand for apps in the Google Play Store than do iPhone users in the Apple App Store. Why might Android users tend to be more sensitive to app prices than iPhone users? What categories or types of apps (for example, games/social media) do you think have the highest price elasticities?
6. *People who are wealthy are widely believed to have more leisure time than people who are poor. However, even though we are a good deal wealthier today than our great-grandparents were 100 years ago, we appear to live more hectic lives and have less free time. Can you explain why?
7. What are the major determinants of a product's price elasticity of demand? Studies indicate that the demand for Florida oranges, Chevrolet automobiles, fresh tomatoes, and airfares to Europe are elastic. Why?
8. Most systems of medical insurance substantially lower the out-of-pocket costs consumers have to pay for additional units of physician services and hospitalization. Some reduce these costs to zero. How does this method of payment affect the consumption levels of medical services? Might this method of organization result in "too much" consumption of medical services? Discuss.
9. Are the following statements true or false? Explain your answers.
   a. A 10 percent reduction in price that leads to a 5 percent increase in the amount purchased indicates a price elasticity of more than 1.
   b. A 10 percent reduction in price that leads to a 2 percent increase in total expenditures (or total revenue) indicates a price elasticity of more than 1.
   c. If the percentage change in price is less than the resultant percentage change in quantity demanded, demand is inelastic.
10. *Respond to the following questions: If you really like pizza, should you try to consume as much pizza as possible? If you want to succeed, should you try to make the highest possible grade in your economics class?
11. *Sue loves ice cream but cannot stand frozen-yogurt desserts. In contrast, Carole likes both foods and can hardly tell the difference between the two. Who will have the more elastic demand for yogurt?
12. *Jill's Sausage Dog Stand projects the following demand for Jill's sausage dogs:

Price	Quantity Purchased (per day)
$2	50
4	40
6	20

   a. Calculate the price elasticity of demand between $2 and $4. Is demand in this range elastic or inelastic?
   b. Calculate the price elasticity of demand between $4 and $6. Is demand in this range elastic or inelastic?
13. Suppose Kira, the owner-manager of a local hotel, projects the following demand for her rooms:

Price	Quantity Purchased (per Night)
$90	100
110	90
130	70

   a. Calculate the price elasticity of demand between $90 and $110.
   b. Is the price elasticity of demand between $90 and $110 elastic, unit elastic, or inelastic?
   c. Will Kira's total revenue rise if she increases the price from $90 to $110?
   d. Calculate the price elasticity of demand between $110 and $130.
   e. Is the price elasticity of demand between $110 and $130 elastic, unit elastic, or inelastic?
   f. Will Kira's total revenue rise if she increases the price from $110 to $130?

*Asterisk denotes questions for which answers are given in Appendix B.

Chapter 8

Costs and the Supply of Goods

> From the standpoint of society as a whole, the "cost" of anything is the value that it has in alternative uses.
>
> –Thomas Sowell[1]

Demand and supply interact to determine the market price of a product. In the preceding chapter, we showed that the demand for a product reflects the strength of consumer desire for that product. In this chapter, we will focus on the cost of production. The resources needed to produce one good could be used to produce other goods instead. As Thomas Sowell says in the quotation that begins this chapter, the cost to society of anything is the value that it has in alternative uses. The market price for resources makes that cost clear to producers as they must bid resources away from alternative uses. The maker of soccer balls, for example, must compete against producers of other goods when purchasing the machines, raw materials, and labor needed to produce the balls.

Costs carry an important message: They tell producers the value of the resources if left in their alternative uses. If the per-unit cost of producing a good exceeds its price, producers will suffer losses, reduce output, and some may go out of business. Only when a producer can generate enough value for consumers to allow the price to exceed production costs will the firm be profitable and survive. This chapter lays the foundation for a detailed investigation of the links between costs, business output, and market supply.

Learning Objectives

8.1 Explain why business firms are used to organize production.

8.2 Explain why residual claimants have an incentive to develop incentive structures that minimize principal-agent problems and shirking.

8.3 Compare and contrast the three types of business firms.

8.4 Differentiate between economic profit and accounting profit, including the role of implicit and explicit costs.

8.5 Explain the difference between the short-run and long-run time periods in production.

8.6 Calculate and illustrate graphically a firm's per-unit (average) costs, including fixed and variable costs per unit, and marginal cost.

8.7 Explain the reasoning behind a firm's U-shaped short-run average total cost curve.

8.8 Explain the law of diminishing returns and its significance for a firm's marginal cost in the short run.

8.9 Indicate how economies of scale, constant returns to scale, and diseconomies of scale will impact long-run average total cost.

8.10 List the major factors that will cause a firm's cost curves to shift.

8.11 Define sunk costs and indicate their relevance to the decision-making of an individual or firm.

[1]Thomas Sowell, *Basic Economics* (New York: Basic Books, 2000), 10.

8-1 The Organization of the Business Firm

The business firm is an entity designed to organize raw materials, labor, and machines with the goal of producing goods and/or services. Firms (1) purchase productive resources from households and other firms, (2) transform them into a different commodity, and (3) sell the transformed product or service to consumers. In market economies, business firms choose their own price, output level, and methods of production. They not only reap the benefits of sales revenues, but they also must pay the costs of the resources they use.

8-1a Incentives, Cooperation, and the Nature of the Firm

In privately owned firms, owners risk their wealth on the success of the business. If the firm is successful and earns profits, the owners earn a financial gain. Conversely, if the firm suffers losses, the owners must bear the consequences.

Residual claimants
Individuals who personally receive the excess, if any, of revenues over costs. Residual claimants gain if the firm's costs are reduced or revenues increase.

The property right of owners to the residual income of the firm plays a very important role: It provides owners with a strong incentive to organize and operate their business in a manner that will maximize the value of their output to consumers while keeping the cost of producing output low. The wealth of these **residual claimants** is directly influenced by the success or failure of the firm. Thus, they have both the authority and a strong incentive to ensure that resources under their direction are used efficiently and directed toward production of goods that are valued more highly than their costs.

Team production
A production process in which employees work together under the supervision of the owner or the owner's representative.

There are two ways of organizing productive activity: contracting and **team production**. In principle, all production could be accomplished solely through contracting. For example, a builder might have a house built by contracting with one person to pour the concrete, another to construct the wooden part of the house, a third to install the roofing, a fourth to do the electrical wiring, and so on. No employees would have to be involved in such a project. More commonly, though, goods and services are produced with some combination of contracting and the use of team production.

Shirking
Working at less than the expected rate of productivity, which reduces output. Shirking is more likely when workers are not monitored, so that the cost of lower output falls on others.

Team production involves the employment of workers operating under the supervision of the owner, or the owner's representative—a manager. While team production can often reduce transaction costs, it leads to another set of problems. Team members—the employees working for the firm—must be monitored and given incentives to avoid **shirking**, or working at less than the expected rate of productivity. Taking long work breaks, paying more attention to their own convenience than to work results, and wasting time when diligence is called for are examples of shirking. Hired managers, even including those at the top, must be monitored and given incentives to avoid shirking.

Principal-agent problem
The incentive problem that occurs when the purchaser of services (the principal) lacks full information about the circumstances faced by the seller (the agent) and cannot know how well the agent performs the purchased services. The agent may to some extent work toward objectives other than those sought by the principal paying for the service.

Imperfect monitoring and imperfect incentives are always a problem with team production. It is part of a larger class of what economists call **principal-agent problems**. If you have ever taken a car to an auto mechanic, you may have confronted this problem. The mechanic wants to get the job done quickly and make as much money as possible. The car owner not only wants to get the job done quickly but also wants the problem fixed in a lasting way, at the lowest possible cost. Because the mechanic typically knows far more about the job than the customer, it is hard for the customer to monitor the mechanic's work. Therefore, the mechanic (the agent) may not act in the best interest of the customer (the principal).

The owner of a firm is in a similar situation. It is often difficult to monitor the performance of individual employees and motivate them to work together productively. If it is going to keep costs low and the value of output high, a firm must discover and adopt an incentive structure that motivates executives, managers, and workers to cooperate productively and discourages shirking. An effective incentive structure will align the costs and benefits faced by employees making decisions with those of the firm as a whole. Ultimately, it is the job of the owners, as residual claimants, to develop an effective incentive structure that will minimize the principal–agent problem.

8-1b Three Types of Business Firms

Business firms can be organized in one of three primary ways: as a proprietorship, a partnership, or a corporation. The structure chosen determines how the owners share the risks and liabilities of the firm and how they participate in making decisions.

A **proprietorship** is a business firm owned by a single individual who is fully liable for the debts of the firm. In addition to assuming the responsibilities of ownership, the proprietor often works directly for the firm, providing managerial and other labor services. Many small businesses, including restaurants, barbershops, and farms, are business proprietorships. As **Exhibit 8-1** shows, proprietorships account for 72 percent of the business firms in the United States. Because most proprietorships are small, however, they account for only 4 percent of all business revenues.

Proprietorship
A business firm owned by an individual who possesses the ownership right to the firm's profits and is personally liable for the firm's debts.

A **partnership** consists of two or more people who are co-owners of a business firm. The partners share risks and responsibilities in an agreed-upon manner. There is no difference between a proprietorship and a partnership in terms of owner liability. In both cases, the owners are fully liable for all business debts incurred by the firm. Many law, medical, and accounting firms are organized along partnership lines. However, this form of business structure accounts for only 11 percent of the total number of firms and 14 percent of all business revenues.

Partnership
A business firm owned by two or more individuals who possess ownership rights to the firm's profits and are personally liable for the debts of the firm.

The business firms that are **corporations** account for 82 percent of total business revenue, even though they constitute only 17 percent of all firms. What accounts for the attractiveness of this business structure? From its start, by an act of the British Parliament in 1862, the corporation, or "joint stock company," as it is also called, grew in importance for two main reasons. First, although the stockholders of the corporation are the legal owners, their liability is limited to the value of their shares of the corporation. If a corporation owes you money, you cannot directly sue the stockholders. Of course, you can sue the corporation. However, if a corporation goes bankrupt, you and others to whom the firm owes money may simply be out of luck. This limited liability makes it possible for corporations

Corporations
A business firm owned by shareholders who possess ownership rights to the firm's profits, but whose liability is limited to the amount of their investment in the firm.

Exhibit 8-1 How Business Firms Are Organized

Nearly three out of every four firms are proprietorships, but only 4 percent of all business revenue is generated by proprietorships. Corporations account for about one out of every six firms but generate 82 percent of all revenues.

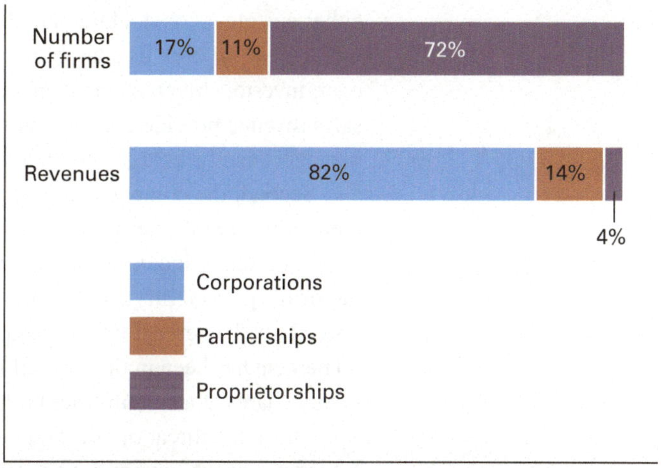

Source: *Statistics of Income Tax Stats Integrated Business Data*, Internal Revenue Service, Table 1. (The latest available data are for 2015.)

to attract investment funds from a large number of "owners" who do not participate in the day-to-day management of the firm.

Second, ownership can easily be transferred under the corporate structure. The shares, or ownership rights, of an owner who dies can be sold by the heirs to another owner without disrupting the business firm. Because of this, the corporation is an ongoing concern. Similarly, stockholders who become unhappy with the way a corporation is run can bail out simply by selling their stock.

While there are advantages to the corporate form of business organization, large corporations with many stockholders—millions in some cases—are also more likely to suffer from principal–agent problems. The stockholders elect a board of directors, which in turn appoints the company's high-level managers. Internal corporate policies and competition for control of the firm by outsiders can be used to reduce these principal–agent problems.

Another disadvantage of the corporate form of business organization is higher taxation. While the incomes of sole proprietors and partnerships are taxed as ordinary personal income, the income of corporations is taxed twice—once as corporate income and again as personal income when it accrues to the owners in the form of dividends or capital gains. Since 1977, individual states have passed laws creating a hybrid form of business organization called the *limited liability company* (LLC), which gives business owners the advantages of limited liability of a corporation but retains the tax advantages of a sole proprietorship or partnership. LLCs are registered at the state level, and the rules governing LLCs differ across states. They remain classified as either sole proprietorships or partnerships for federal tax purposes and are thus reflected in those categories in national data, such as is presented in Exhibit 8-1. In 2021, LLCs made up approximately 72 percent of all partnerships and 10 percent of all non-farm sole proprietorships.

8-2 How Well Does the Corporate Structure Work?

Do corporations serve the interests of consumers? Are corporate managers in a position to serve themselves at the expense of their customers and stockholders? When thinking about these questions, keep three points in mind.

First, in a market economy, firms must compete for investment funds and for customers. Investors are free to buy and sell the shares of corporations. Similarly, consumers are free to choose among firms, including both corporate and noncorporate businesses. This competitive process greatly limits the ability of managers to benefit personally at the expense of either customers or stockholders. If a business firm is not managed in a manner that serves the interests of both its shareholders and customers, they will choose other options. Moreover, investor-driven changes in a company's stock price and consumer-driven changes in sales revenue provide channels through which managerial performance can be judged, and managers can be held accountable, by shareholders and the board of directors.

Second, the compensation of managers can be structured in a manner that will bring their interests into harmony with those of the shareholder-owners. This is generally the case. The salary increases and bonuses of most high-level managers are directly related to the firm's profitability and the price of its shares. In recent years, salaries have constituted only about 10 percent of the compensation of chief executive officers (CEOs). The other 90 percent has been in the form of bonuses, often stock awards and stock options (the right to buy shares at a certain price) related to company performance.

Third, the threat of corporate takeover helps keep current managers from straying too far from a profit-maximization strategy. Managers who do not serve the interests of their shareholders leave the firm vulnerable to a takeover, a move by an outside person or group to gain control of the firm. Poor management will cause market value of the firm's stock

Zamrznuti tonovi/Shutterstock.com

Corporate managers have a strong incentive to serve the interests of customers and stockholders because of the following: competition for investment funds and consumer sales, the linkage of their compensation to company performance, and the threat of takeover if the company is run poorly.

to decline, making it an attractive prospect for takeover specialists shopping for a poorly run business, the value of which could be substantially increased by a new and better management team.

The prevalence of the corporate form of business organization provides strong evidence that it is an effective form of business organization in many sectors of the economy. Rival forms of business organization, including proprietorships, partnerships, consumer cooperatives, employee ownership, and mutually owned companies, can and do compete in the marketplace for investment funds and customers. Nonetheless, the corporate structure is the dominant form of business organization (refer to Exhibit 8-1). If the corporation was not generally a cost-efficient and consumer-sensitive form of organization, this would not be the case.

8-3 The Economic Role of Costs

Consumers would like to have more economic goods, but resources to produce them are scarce. How much of each desired good should be produced? In a market economy, consumer demand and production costs are central to performing this balancing function. ***The demand for a product represents the voice of consumers instructing firms to produce the good. Conversely, a firm's costs represent the desire of consumers not to sacrifice goods that could be produced if the same resources were employed elsewhere.*** A profit-seeking firm will try to produce only those units of output for which buyers are willing to pay full cost. Proper measurement and interpretation of costs by the firm are critical to both the firm's profitability and its efficient use of resources.

8-3a Calculating Economic Costs and Profits

Profit directs the actions of business firms. Profit is simply the firm's total revenue minus its total costs. But to calculate profit correctly, costs must be measured properly. Most people think of costs as amounts paid for raw materials, labor, machines, and similar inputs. However, this concept of cost, which stems from accounting procedures, excludes some important components.

The key to understanding the economist's concept of profit is to remember the idea of *opportunity cost*—the highest valued alternative forgone by the resource owner when the resource is used. These costs may be either explicit or implicit. **Explicit costs** result when the firm makes a monetary payment to resource owners. Money wages, interest, and rental payments are a measure of what the firm gives up to employ the services of labor and capital resources. These are relatively easy to track. But firms also incur **implicit costs**—those associated with the use of resources owned by the firm. For example, the owners of small proprietorships often work for their own businesses, and provide their services as entrepreneurs, for little or no pay. These businesses incur an implicit cost—an opportunity cost—associated with the use of this resource (the owners' labor and entrepreneurial services). The highest valued alternative forgone in this case is the maximum amount of money the owners could have earned doing something else. The **total cost** of production is the sum of these explicit and implicit costs incurred by the employment of all resources involved in the production process.

Explicit costs
Payments by a firm to purchase the services of productive resources.

Implicit costs
The opportunity costs associated with a firm's use of resources that it owns. These costs do not involve a direct money payment. Examples include wage income and interest forgone by the owner of a firm who also provides labor services and equity capital to the firm.

Total cost
The costs, both explicit and implicit, of all the resources used by the firm. Total cost includes a normal rate of return for the firm's equity capital.

Accounting statements also generally omit the implicit cost of equity capital—the cost of funds supplied by the firm's owners. If a firm borrows financial capital from a bank or other private source, it will have to pay interest. Accountants properly record this interest expense as a cost. In contrast, when the firm acquires financial capital by issuing shares of stock, accountants don't record this as an expense. Essentially, this is because the stockholders *are* the firm's owners. Either way, acquiring capital has an opportunity cost. Banks will demand interest payments, and shareholders will expect a return from their investment in the form of dividend payments or rising share value.

Economists use the normal return on financial capital as a basis for determining the implicit **opportunity cost of equity capital**. If the normal rate of return on financial capital is 10 percent, for example, investors will not continue to supply equity capital unless they can earn this normal return. Thus, it is an opportunity cost of equity capital. Owners may also provide physical assets such as buildings that have associated opportunity costs (forgone rental income, for example).

Opportunity cost of equity capital
The rate of return that must be earned by investors to induce them to supply financial capital to the firm.

8-3b How Do Economic and Accounting Profit Differ?

Economic profit is total revenues minus total costs, including both the explicit and implicit cost components. Economic profit will be positive only if the earnings of the business exceed the opportunity cost of all the resources used by the firm, *including the opportunity cost of assets owned by the firm and any unpaid labor and entrepreneurial services supplied by the owner*. In contrast, economic losses result when the earnings of the firm are insufficient to cover explicit and implicit costs. That is why the **normal profit rate** is zero economic profit, yielding just the competitive rate of return on the capital (and labor) of owners. A higher rate would draw more competitors and their investors into the market; a lower rate would cause competitors and their investors to exit the market.

Economic profit
The difference between the firm's total revenues and its total costs, including both the explicit and implicit cost components.

Normal profit rate
Zero economic profit, providing just the competitive rate of return on the capital (and labor) of owners. An above-normal profit will draw more entry into the market, whereas a below-normal profit will lead to an exit of investors and capital.

Remember, zero economic profits do not imply that the firm is about to go out of business. On the contrary, they indicate that the owners are receiving exactly the normal profit rate, or the competitive market rate of return on their investment.

Whenever accounting procedures omit implicit costs, like those associated with owner-provided labor services or equity capital, the firm's opportunity costs of production will be understated. This understatement of cost leads to an overstatement of profits. Therefore, the **accounting profits** of a firm are generally greater than the firm's economic profits (refer to the Applications in Economics feature on accounting costs). For most large corporations, though, omitting the implicit costs of services provided by an owner isn't an issue. In this case, the accounting profits approximate the returns to the firm's equity capital. High accounting profits (measured as a rate of return on a firm's assets), relative to those of other firms, suggest that a firm is earning an economic profit. Correspondingly, a low rate of accounting profit implies economic losses. Either positive or negative economic profits, of course, call for a change in output. Such a change, however, will take time.

Accounting profits
The sales revenues minus the expenses of a firm over a designated time period, usually one year. Accounting profits typically make allowances for changes in the firm's inventories and depreciation of its assets. No allowance is made, however, for the opportunity cost of the equity capital of the firm's owners, or other implicit costs.

8-4 Short-Run and Long-Run Time Periods

Time plays an important role in the production process. All of a firm's resources can be expanded (or contracted) over time, but for specialized equipment, expanding (and contracting) availability quickly is likely to be very expensive or even impossible. Economists often speak of the **short run** as a time period so short that the firm is unable to alter its present plant size. In the short run, the firm is typically stuck with its existing plant and heavy equipment. These assets are "fixed" for a given time period, in other words. The firm can alter output, however, by applying larger or smaller amounts of "variable" resources, like labor and raw materials. In this way, the existing plant capacity can be used more or less intensively in the short run.

Short run (in production)
A time period so short that a firm is unable to vary some of its factors of production. The firm's plant size typically cannot be altered in the short run.

How long is the short run? *The short run is that period of time during which at least one factor of production, usually the size of the firm's plant, cannot be changed.* The length varies across industries and firms. A trucking firm might be able to hire more drivers and buy or rent more trucks and double its hauling capacity in a few months. In other industries,

Applications in Economics

Economic and Accounting Costs: A Hypothetical Example

The revenue-cost statement for a corner grocery store owned and operated by Destiny Rodriguez is presented here.

TOTAL REVENUE	
Sales (groceries)	$170,000
Costs (explicit)	
Groceries, wholesale	$76,000
Utilities	4,000
Taxes	6,000
Advertising	2,000
Labor services (employees)	12,000
Total (explicit) costs	$100,000
Net (accounting) profit	$70,000
Additional (implicit) costs	
Interest (personal investment)	$7,000
Rent (Destiny's building)	18,000
Salary (Destiny's labor)	50,000
Total (implicit) costs	$75,000
TOTAL EXPLICIT AND IMPLICIT COSTS	$175,000
ECONOMIC PROFIT (TOTAL REVENUE MINUS EXPLICIT AND IMPLICIT COSTS)	–$5,000

Destiny works full-time as the manager, chief cashier, and janitor. She has $140,000 worth of refrigeration and other equipment invested in the store. Last year, her total sales were $170,000, and suppliers and employees were paid $100,000. Destiny's revenues therefore exceeded explicit costs by $70,000. This is what was recorded on the accounting statements as profit.

But did Destiny really make a profit last year? Let's examine her opportunity costs and see: If Destiny didn't have $140,000 of her own money invested in equipment, she could be earning 5 percent interest on the money in the bank, which would add up to $7,000 each year. Similarly, if the building she owns weren't being used as a grocery store, it could be rented to someone else for $1,500 per month. Rental income forgone is therefore $18,000 per year. In addition, because Destiny is tied up working in the grocery store, a $50,000 managerial position she could hold at another local grocery store is forgone. Considering the interest, rental, and salary income that Destiny had to forgo to operate the grocery store last year, her implicit costs were $75,000. This makes her total costs–both explicit and implicit–$175,000. (Recall that explicit costs were $100,000.) That's $5,000 *less* than her actual revenues of $170,000. As a result, Destiny incurred an economic loss of $5,000, despite the accounting profit of $70,000 recorded on the store's books.

particularly those that use assembly lines and mass-production techniques, increasing production capacity may take several years.

Long run (in production)
A time period long enough to allow the firm to vary all of its factors of production.

The **long run** is a time period long enough for existing firms to alter the size of their plants and for new firms to enter (or exit) the market. *All of the firm's resources are variable in the long run.* In the long run, firms can expand their output by increasing the sizes of their plants—perhaps by adding on to them or by constructing entirely new facilities.

An example may help you understand the distinction between the short- and long-run time periods: If a cell phone manufacturer hired 200 additional workers and ordered more raw materials in order to squeeze more production out of its existing plant, it would be making a short-run adjustment. In contrast, if the manufacturer built an additional plant (or expanded the size of its current facility) and installed additional heavy equipment, it would be making a long-run adjustment.

8-5 Categories of Costs

In the short run, we can break a firm's costs into two categories—fixed and variable. Each category of costs behaves differently. Illustrating this graphically will help us understand how the profit-maximizing level of the firm's output is determined. It will also be important to distinguish between a firm's total costs and its per-unit costs, which we call "average" costs.

Total fixed cost
The sum of the costs that do not vary with output. They will be incurred as long as a firm continues in business and the assets have alternative uses.

Average fixed cost
Total fixed cost divided by the number of units produced. It always declines as output increases.

Each of the firm's fixed costs, and their sum, called **total fixed cost** (*TFC*), will remain unchanged when output rises or falls in the short run. For example, a firm's insurance premiums; its property taxes; and, most significantly, the opportunity cost of using its fixed assets will be present whether the firm produces a large or small amount of output. These costs will not vary with output. They can be avoided only if the firm goes out of business.

What will happen to **average fixed cost** (*AFC*), which is fixed cost *per unit*, as output expands? Remember that the firm's fixed cost will be the same whether output is 1, or 100, or 1,000. The *AFC* is simply fixed cost divided by output. As output increases, *AFC* declines because the fixed cost will be spread over more and more units, as is illustrated in panel (a) of **Exhibit 8-2**.

Some costs vary with output. For example, additional output can usually be produced by hiring more workers and buying more raw materials. The sum of those and other costs

Exhibit 8-2 The General Characteristics of Short-Run Cost Curves

Average fixed costs (a) will be high for small rates of output, but they will always decline as output expands. Marginal cost (b) will rise sharply as the plant approaches its production capacity, *q*. As panel (c) shows, *ATC* will be a U-shaped curve because *AFC* will be high for small rates of output, and *MC* will be high as the plant's production capacity is approached.

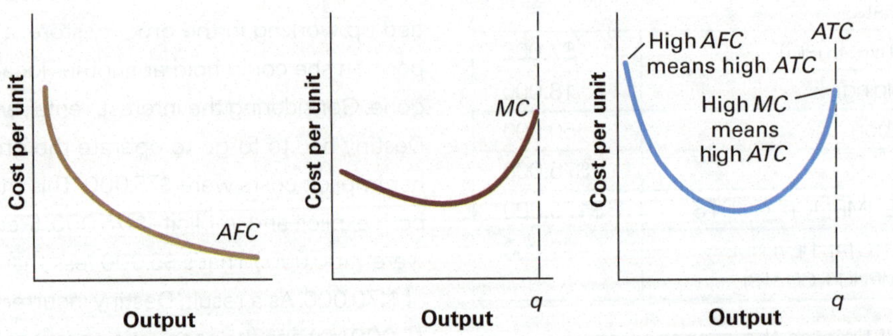

(a) Average fixed cost **(b) Marginal cost** **(c) Average total cost**

that rise as output increases is the firm's **total variable cost** (*TVC*). At any given level of output, the firm's **average variable cost** (*AVC*), which is variable cost *per unit*, is the total variable cost divided by output.

A firm's total cost (*TC*) is the sum of the fixed and variable costs. At zero output a firm has no variable costs, thus total cost will be equal to total fixed cost. As output expands from zero, variable costs begin to increase, causing total cost to rise with output even though fixed costs are remaining unchanged. **Average total cost** (*ATC*), sometimes referred to as unit cost, can be found by dividing total cost by the total number of units produced. *ATC* is also equal to the sum of the average fixed and average variable costs. One way to look at ATC is that it is the amount of revenue needed per unit of output to cover total cost.

The economic way of thinking focuses on what happens "at the margin." How much does it cost to produce an additional unit? **Marginal cost** (*MC*) is the change in total cost that results from the production of one additional unit. The profit-conscious decision-maker recognizes *MC* as the addition to cost that must be covered by additional revenue if producing the marginal unit is to be profitable. In the short run, as illustrated by panel (b) of Exhibit 8-2, *MC* will generally decline at first if output is increased, reach a minimum, and then increase. The rising *MC* simply reflects the fact that it becomes increasingly difficult to squeeze additional output from a plant as the facility's maximum capacity (the dashed line at output level *q* in Exhibit 8-2) is approached. The accompanying Thumbnail Sketch summarizes how the firm's various costs are related to one another.

Total variable cost
The sum of those costs that rise as output increases. Examples of variable costs are wages paid to workers and payments for raw materials.

Average variable cost
The total variable cost divided by the number of units produced.

Average total cost
Total cost divided by the number of units produced. It is sometimes called per-unit cost.

Marginal cost
The change in total cost required to produce an additional unit of output.

8-6 Output and Costs in the Short Run

As a firm changes its rate of output in the short run, how will its unit cost be affected? In the short run, the firm can vary its output by using its fixed plant size more (or less) intensively. Exhibit 8-2 shows two ways that this can result in high unit costs. First, when the output rate of a plant is small relative to its capacity, the facility is being underutilized, causing *AFC* to be high and *ATC* to be high, too. It will be costly to operate a large plant, with its high fixed costs, substantially below its production capacity. Alternatively, overutilization can also cause high unit costs. An overutilized plant will mean congestion—time spent by workers waiting for machines and similar costly delays. Requiring output beyond the least-cost, or designed, output level of a plant will lead to high *MC* and therefore to high *ATC*.

Thus, the* ATC *curve will be U-shaped, as pictured in part (c) of Exhibit 8-2.* ATC *will be high for both an underutilized plant and an overutilized plant. It will be high for an underutilized plant because average fixed cost will be high. It will be high for an overutilized plant because marginal cost will be high.

8-6a Diminishing Returns and Production in the Short Run

Our analysis of the changes in unit cost as the output rate rises reflects a long-established economic law. This **law of diminishing returns** states that, as more and more units of a variable factor are applied to a fixed amount of other resources, output will eventually increase by smaller and smaller amounts. Therefore, the impact on output of additional units of the variable factor will diminish. The cost per unit of adding the variable factor may be the same, but the added output per dollar spent falls. The impact on cost per unit of output is clear: When the returns to the variable factor are rising, marginal costs (the additions to total variable cost needed to add a unit of output) are falling. Similarly, when the returns to the variable factor are falling, marginal cost is rising.

The law of diminishing returns is as famous in economics as the law of gravity is in physics. It is based on common sense and real-life observation. Have you ever noticed that as you apply a single resource more intensively, the resource eventually tends to accomplish

Law of diminishing returns
The postulate that as more and more units of a variable resource are combined with a fixed amount of other resources, using additional units of the variable resource will eventually increase output only at a decreasing rate. Once diminishing returns are reached, it will take successively larger amounts of the variable factor to expand output by one unit.

Thumbnail Sketch

Compact Glossary on Cost

Term	Symbol	Equation	Definition
Fixed cost			Cost that is independent of the output level
Variable cost			Cost that varies with the output level
Total fixed cost	*TFC*		Cost of the fixed inputs (equals sum of quantity times unit price for each fixed input)
Total variable cost	*TVC*		Cost of the variable inputs (equals sum of quantity times unit price for each variable input)
Total cost	*TC*	$TC = TFC + TVC$	Cost of all inputs (equals fixed costs plus variable costs)
Marginal cost	*MC*	$MC = \Delta TC \div \Delta q$	Change in total cost resulting from a one-unit rise in output (*q*) (equals the change in total cost divided by the change in output)
Average fixed cost	*AFC*	$AFC = TFC \div q$	Total fixed cost per unit of output (equals total fixed cost divided by total output)
Average variable cost	*AVC*	$AVC = TVC \div q$	Total variable cost per unit of output (equals total variable cost divided by total output)
Average total cost	*ATC*	$ATC = AFC + AVC$	Total cost per unit of output (equals average fixed cost plus average variable cost)

less and less? Consider a wheat farmer who applies fertilizer (a variable resource) more and more intensively to an acre of land (a fixed factor). At some point, the application of additional 100-pound units of fertilizer will expand the wheat yield by successively smaller amounts.

Essentially, the law of diminishing returns is a constraint imposed by nature. If it were not valid, it would be possible to raise all the world's food in a flowerpot. We would be able to increase output simply by applying another unit of labor and fertilizer to the world's most fertile flowerpot! In the real world, of course, this is not the case; the law of diminishing returns is valid, reflecting a constraint we all must face.

Total product
The total output of a good that is associated with each alternative utilization rate of a variable input.

Marginal product
The increase in the total product resulting from a unit increase in the employment of a variable input. Mathematically, it is the ratio of the change in total product to the change in the quantity of the variable input.

Exhibit 8-3 illustrates the law of diminishing returns numerically. Column 1 indicates the quantity of the variable resource, labor in this example, which is combined with a specified amount of the fixed resource. Column 2 shows the **total product** that will result as the utilization rate of labor increases. Column 3 provides data on the **marginal product**, the change in total output associated with each additional unit of labor. Without the application of labor, output will be zero. As additional units of labor are applied, total product (output) rises. As the first three units of labor are applied, total product increases by successively larger amounts (8, then 12, then 14). Beginning with the fourth unit, however, diminishing returns are confronted. When the fourth unit of labor is added, marginal product—the change in the total product—declines to 12 (down from 14, when the third unit was applied). As additional units of labor are applied, marginal product continues to decline. It is increasingly difficult to squeeze a larger total product from the fixed resources (for example, plant size and equipment). Eventually, marginal product becomes negative (beginning with the tenth unit).

Exhibit 8-3 The Law of Diminishing Returns (Hypothetical Data)

(1) Units of the Variable Resource, Labor (per day)	(2) Total Product (output)	(3) Marginal Product	(4) Average Product
0	0		—
1	8	8	8.0
2	20	12	10.0
3	34	14	11.3
4	46	12	11.5
5	56	10	11.2
6	64	8	10.7
7	70	6	10.0
8	74	4	9.3
9	75	1	8.3
10	73	–2	7.3

Column 4 of Exhibit 8-3 provides data for the **average product** of labor, which is simply the total product divided by the units of labor applied. Note that the average product increases as long as the marginal product is greater than the average product. Whenever the marginal unit's contribution is greater than the average, it must cause the average to rise. (A good analogy would be your grade point average. If the grade you get in this course is higher than your overall grade point average, your grade in this class will increase your overall average.) Here, marginal product rises through the first four units. The marginal product of the fifth unit of labor, though, is 10, less than the average product for the first four units of labor (11.5). Therefore, beginning with the fifth unit, the average product declines as additional labor is applied. When marginal productivity is below the average, it brings down the average product.

Average product
The total product (output) divided by the number of units of the variable input required to produce that output level.

Using the data from Exhibit 8-3, **Exhibit 8-4** illustrates the law of diminishing returns graphically. Initially, the total product curve (panel a) increases quite rapidly. As diminishing marginal returns are confronted (beginning with the fourth unit of labor), total product increases more slowly. Eventually, a maximum output (75) is reached with the application of the ninth unit of labor. The marginal product curve (panel b) reflects the total product curve. Geometrically, marginal product is the slope—the rate of increase—of the total product curve. That slope, the marginal product, reaches its maximum here with the application of three units of labor. Beyond three units, diminishing returns are present. Eventually, at ten units of labor, the marginal product becomes negative. When marginal product becomes negative, total product is necessarily declining. The average product curve rises as long as the marginal product curve is above it, because each added unit of labor is raising the average. The average product reaches its maximum at four units of labor. Beyond that, each additional unit of labor brings down the average product, and the curve slopes downward.

8-6b Diminishing Returns and the Shape of the Cost Curves

What impact will diminishing returns have on a firm's costs? Once a firm confronts diminishing returns, larger and larger additions of the variable factor are required to expand output by one unit. This will cause marginal cost (MC) to rise. As MC continues

Exhibit 8-4 The Law of Diminishing Returns

As units of variable input (labor) are added to a fixed input, total product will increase, first at an increasing rate and then at a declining rate (a). This will cause both marginal and average product curves (b) to rise at first and then decline. Note that the marginal product curve intersects the average product curve at its maximum (when four units of labor are used). The smooth curves indicate that labor can be increased by amounts of less than a single unit.

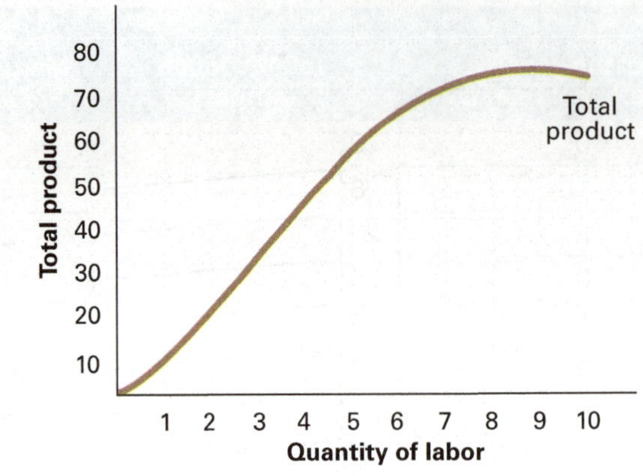

(a) Total product curve

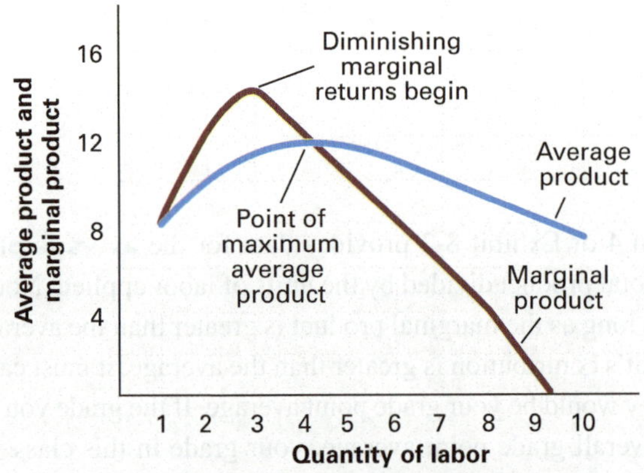

(b) Average and marginal product curve

to increase, eventually it will exceed average total cost. Until that point,* MC *is below* ATC, *bringing* ATC *down. When* MC *is greater than* ATC, *the additional units cost more than the average, and* ATC *must increase. Think about what happens when you get a grade on an exam above your current class average. Your class average goes up. What happens if a unit of above-average cost is added to output? Average total cost rises. The firm's *MC* curve therefore crosses the *ATC* curve at the *ATC*'s lowest point. For output rates beyond the minimum *ATC*, the rising *MC* causes *ATC* to increase.

Exhibit 8-5 numerically illustrates the effect of the law of diminishing returns on a firm's short-run cost curve. Here, we assume that Super Sunglasses, Inc., combines units of a variable input with a fixed factor to produce units of output (pairs of sunglasses). Columns 2, 3, and 4 indicate how the total cost schedules vary as output is expanded. Total fixed costs (*TFC*), representing the opportunity cost of the fixed factors of production, are $50 per day at all levels of output. For the first four units of output, total variable costs (*TVC*) increase at a decreasing rate—by $15 with the production of the first unit, $10 with the production of the second unit, $9 with the third, and so on. Why? In this range, there are increasing returns to the variable input. Beginning with the fifth unit of output, however, diminishing marginal returns are present. From this point on, *TVC* and *TC* increase by successively larger amounts as output is expanded.

Columns 5 through 8 of Exhibit 8-5 are the average and marginal cost schedules. For small output rates, the *ATC* of producing sunglasses is high, primarily because of the high

Exhibit 8-5 The Numerical Short-Run Cost Schedules of Super Sunglasses, Inc.

Total Cost Data (Per Day)				Average/Marginal Cost Data (Per Day)			
(1) Output Per Day	(2) TFC	(3) TVC	(4) TC (2) + (3)	(5) AFC (2) ÷ (1)	(6) AVC (3) ÷ (1)	(7) ATC (4) ÷ (1)	(8) MC Δ(4) ÷ Δ(1)
0	$50	$0	$50	—	—	—	—
1	50	15	65	$50.00	$15.00	$65.00	$15
2	50	25	75	25.00	12.50	37.50	10
3	50	34	84	16.67	11.33	28.00	9
4	50	42	92	12.50	10.50	23.00	8
5	50	52	102	10.00	10.40	20.40	10
6	50	64	114	8.33	10.67	19.00	12
7	50	79	129	7.14	11.29	18.43	15
8	50	98	148	6.25	12.25	18.50	19
9	50	122	172	5.56	13.56	19.11	24
10	50	152	202	5.00	15.20	20.20	30
11	50	202	252	4.55	18.36	22.91	50

AFC. Initially, *MC* is less than *ATC*, so *ATC* is falling. When diminishing returns set in for output rates beginning with five units, however, *MC* rises. Beginning with the sixth unit of output, *MC* exceeds *AVC*, causing *AVC* to rise. Beginning with the eighth unit of output, *MC* exceeds *ATC*, causing it also to rise. *ATC* thus reaches its minimum at seven units of output. Look carefully at the data of Exhibit 8-5 to be sure that you fully understand the relationships among the various cost curves. Do you understand how columns 4 to 8 are derived from columns 1 to 3?

Using the numeric data of Exhibit 8-5, **Exhibit 8-6** graphically illustrates the total, the average, and the marginal cost curves. Note that the *MC* curve intersects both the *AVC* and *ATC* curves at their minimum points (panel b). As *MC*, driven up by diminishing returns, continues to rise above *ATC*, unit costs rise higher and higher as output increases beyond seven units.

In sum, the firm's short-run cost curves reflect the law of diminishing marginal returns. Assuming that the price of the variable resource is constant, *MC* declines so long as the marginal product of the variable input is rising. This results because, in this range, smaller and smaller additions of the variable input are required to produce each extra unit of output. The situation is reversed, however, when diminishing returns are confronted. Once diminishing returns set in, more and more units of the variable factor are required to generate each additional unit of output. *MC* will rise because the marginal product of the variable resource is declining. Eventually, *MC* exceeds *AVC* and *ATC*, causing these costs also to rise. A U-shaped, short-run average total cost curve results.

8-7 Output and Costs in the Long Run

The short-run analysis relates costs to output *for a specific size of plant*. Firms, though, are not committed forever to their existing plants. In the long run, all resources used by the firm are variable, thus there are no long-run fixed costs.

Exhibit 8-6 Costs in the Short Run

Using data from Exhibit 8-5, this exhibit shows the general shape of the firm's short-run total cost curves (a) and average and marginal cost curves (b). Note that when output is small (for example, two units), *ATC* will be high because the *AFC* is so high. Similarly, when output is large (for example, 11 units), per-unit cost (*ATC*) will be high because additional units will be extremely costly to produce at this point. Thus, the short-run *ATC* curve will be U-shaped.

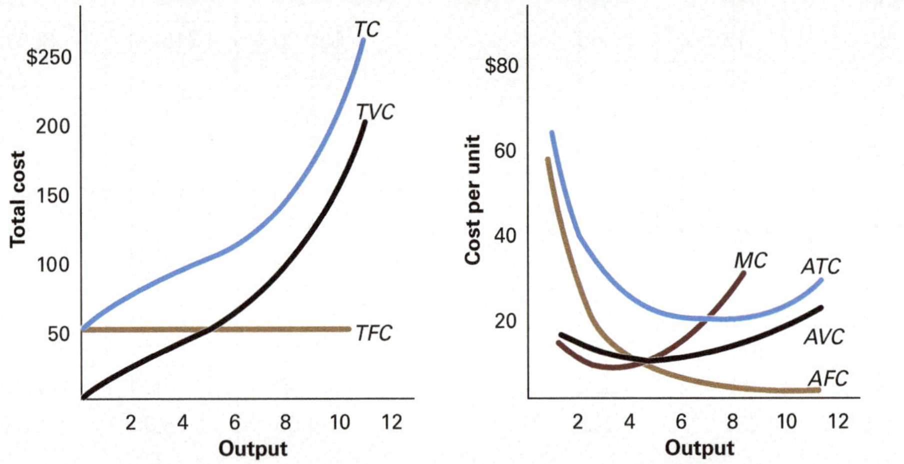

(a) Total cost data **(b) Average and marginal cost data**

How will the firm's choice of plant size affect per-unit production costs? **Exhibit 8-7** illustrates the short-run *ATC* curves for three different plant sizes, ranging from small to large. If these three plant sizes were the only possible choices, which one should the firm choose as it plans for the future? The answer depends on the rate of output the firm expects to produce from the plant. The smallest plant would have the lowest cost if an output rate of less than q_1 were produced. The medium-size plant would provide the least cost method of producing output rates between q_1 and q_2. For any output level greater than q_2, the largest plant would be the most cost efficient.

Exhibit 8-7 Long-Run Average Total Cost

The short-run average total cost curves are shown for three alternative plant sizes. If these three were the only possible plant sizes, the long-run average total cost curve would be *ABCD*.

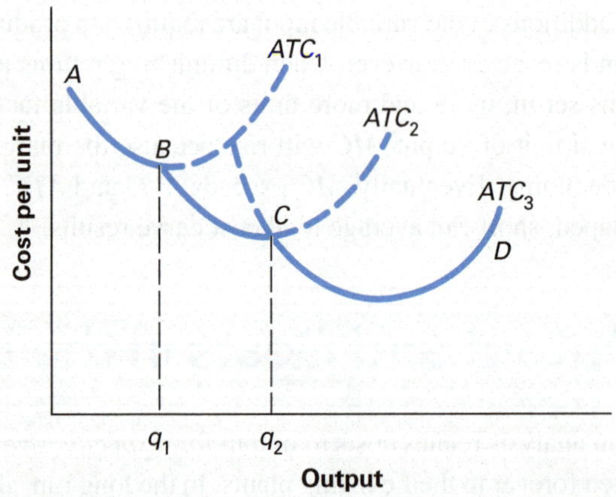

Exhibit 8-8 The Planning Curve (LRATC)

When many different plant sizes are possible, the long-run average total cost (*LRATC*) curve can be mapped out. When firms are able to plan large volumes of output, using mass-production methods will generally lead to lower per-unit costs. This helps explain why the *LRATC* has a downward-sloping portion.

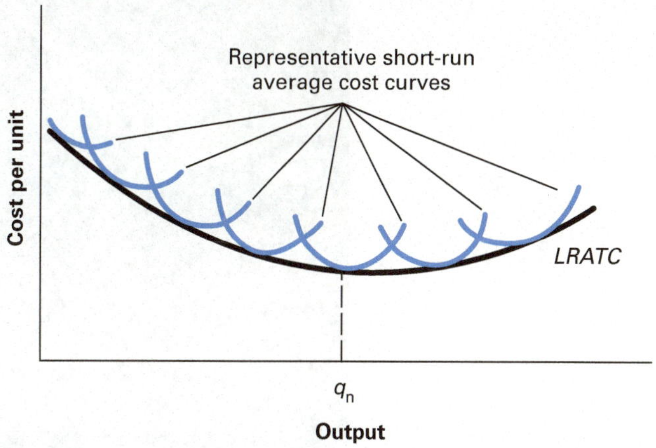

The long-run* ATC *curve shows the minimum average cost of producing each output level when the firm is free to choose among all possible plant sizes. It can best be thought of as a planning curve because it reflects the expected per-unit cost of producing alternative rates of output while plants are still in the blueprint stage.

Exhibit 8-7 illustrates the long-run *ATC* curve when only three plant sizes are possible, and the planning curve *ABCD* is thus mapped out. Of course, given sufficient time, firms can usually choose among many plants of various sizes. **Exhibit 8-8** presents the long-run planning curve under these circumstances. It is a smooth curve, with each short-run *ATC* curve tangent to it.

It is important to keep in mind that no single plant size could produce the alternative output rates at the costs indicated by the planning curve *LRATC* in Exhibit 8-8. Any of the planning curve options are, of course, available to the firm before a plant size is chosen and the plant is built. But it can *operate* in the short run only *after* a plant size has been chosen and put in place. The *LRATC* curve outlines the *possibilities* available in the planning stage. It shows the expected output and average total costs of production for the firm depending on the plant size it chooses.

8-7a Economies and Diseconomies of Scale

Do larger firms have lower minimum unit costs than smaller ones?[2] There are three major reasons why planning a larger volume of output generally reduces, at least initially, unit costs: (1) economies accompanying the use of mass-production methods, (2) higher productivity as a result of specialization and "learning by doing," and (3) economies in promotion and purchasing.[3] Let's consider each of these factors.

Mass-production techniques usually are economical only when large volumes of output are planned, because they tend to involve large development and setup costs. Once the

---

[2]Throughout this section, we assume that firms with larger plants necessarily plan a larger volume of output than do their smaller counterparts. Reality approximates these conditions. Firms choose large plants because they are planning to produce a large volume.

[3]Note the distinction between rate and volume of output. Rate of output is the number of units produced during a specific period (for example, the next six months). Volume is the total number of units produced during all time periods. For example, Boeing might produce two 787 airplanes per month (rate of output) while planning to produce a volume of two hundred 787s during the expected life of the model. Increasing the rate (reducing the time period during which a given output is produced) tends to raise costs, whereas increasing the volume (total amount produced) tends to lower costs per unit.

SUKREE SUKPLANG/REUTERS

Mass-production methods can often reduce average costs for firms planning higher output volumes.

production methods are established, though, marginal costs are low. For example, the use of die cast molds and assembly line production methods reduce the per-unit cost of automobiles only when the planned volume of output is in the millions. High-volume methods, although cheaper to use for high rates of output and high volumes, will typically require high fixed costs and therefore cause unit costs to be far higher for low volumes of production.

Large-scale operation also allows the specialized use of labor and machines. In a giant auto plant, hundreds of different jobs must be done, and many of them require a training period for each worker. In a small plant, a single worker might do ten or twenty of these jobs, so each worker would have a much longer, more costly training period. Even then, the worker doing so many tasks might never fully develop the same level of proficiency of the more specialized worker. Baseball players improve by playing baseball, and pianists by playing the piano. Similarly, the employees of a firm improve their skills as they experience "learning by doing" in their jobs. Even better, concentration on a narrower range of tasks can help workers discover or develop cost-reducing techniques. The result of greater size and specialization is often more output per unit of labor.

Large firms are also able to achieve lower costs by spreading fixed costs (like the costs of advertising, developing specialized equipment, and searching out and negotiating better input prices, for example) over many more units. For example, both McDonald's and General Motors are able to spread these costs over a large number of stores and volume of sales. The cost advantages of scale come in many forms.

Economies of scale Reductions in the firm's per-unit costs associated with the use of large plants to produce a large volume of output.

Diseconomies of scale Increases in the firm's per-unit costs associated with increases in firm size due to inefficiencies and monitoring problems.

Economic theory explains why, at least initially, larger firms have lower unit costs than comparable smaller firms. Declining unit costs mean that **economies of scale** are present over the initial range of outputs. The long-run *ATC* curve is falling.

What about **diseconomies of scale?** As output continues to expand, is there reason to believe that larger firms will eventually have higher average total costs than smaller ones? The underlying causes of diseconomies of scale are less obvious, but they do occur. As a firm gets bigger and bigger, beyond some point bureaucratic inefficiencies *may* result. Inflexible procedures tend to replace managerial genius. Innovation requires clearance from more levels of management and becomes more difficult and costly. Motivating the workforce, carrying out managerial directives, and monitoring results of plans are also more complex when the firm is larger, and principal–agent problems grow as the number of employees increases and more levels of communication and monitoring are needed.

Circumstances vary, so diseconomies of scale set in at smaller firm sizes for some kinds of firms than for others. For example, firms in the fast-food industry can be very large and remain efficient; economies of scale apparently outweigh the diseconomies, even for giants like McDonald's. But in the fine-dining segment of the restaurant industry, the best restaurants seem to be small. Customers demand individual attention, and a constantly changing, innovative menu that takes advantage of the continually changing array of locally available fresh ingredients—with consistently high quality as the only constant—is important. There are few truly gourmet restaurant chains because diseconomies seem to set in at a much smaller size at these firms. The bottom line for diseconomies of scale is this: For some firms, bureaucratic inefficiencies, principal–agent problems, difficulties with innovation, and similar problems that increase with firm size cause long-run average total costs to rise beyond some output level. However, there is considerable variation among industries and even among firms in the same industry concerning the precise output level at which diseconomies of scale begin to occur.

It is important to note that scale economies and diseconomies stem from sources different from those of increasing and diminishing returns. Economies and diseconomies of scale are long-run concepts. They relate to conditions of production when all factors are variable. In contrast, increasing and diminishing returns are short-run concepts, applicable only when the firm has at least one fixed factor of production.

8-7b Alternative Shapes of the *LRATC*

Exhibit 8-9 outlines three different long-run average total cost (*LRATC*) curves, each describing real-world conditions in differing industries. For a firm described by the cost curve in panel (a), both economies and diseconomies of scale are present. Higher per-unit costs will result if the firm chooses a plant size other than the one that minimizes the cost of producing output *q*. If each firm in an industry faces the same cost conditions, we can generalize and say that all plants larger or smaller than this ideal size will experience higher unit costs. A very narrow range of plant sizes would be expected in industries with the *LRATC* depicted by panel (a). Some agricultural products and retail lines approximate these conditions.

Panel (b) demonstrates the general shape of the *LRATC* that economists believe is present in most industries. Initially, economies of scale exist, but once a minimum efficient scale is reached, wide variation in firm size is possible. Firms smaller than the minimum efficient size would have higher per-unit costs, but firms larger than that would not gain a cost advantage. **Constant returns to scale** are present for a broad range of output rates (between q_1 and q_2), in other words. This situation is consistent with real-world conditions in many industries. For example, small firms can be as efficient as larger ones in the apparel, lumber, and publishing industries, as well as in several retail industries.

Constant returns to scale
Unit costs that are constant as the scale of the firm is altered. Neither economies nor diseconomies of scale are present.

In panel (c) of Exhibit 8-9, economies of scale exist for all relevant output levels. The larger the firm size, the lower the per-unit cost. The *LRATC* for local telephone service can approximate the curve shown here.

8-8 What Factors Cause Cost Curves to Shift?

When we drew the general shapes of a firm's cost curves in both the long run and short run, we assumed that certain other factors—resource prices, taxes, regulations, and technology—remained constant as the firm altered its rate of output. Let's now consider how changes in these factors affect the firm's costs.

Exhibit 8-9 Three Different Types of Long-Run Average Total Cost Curves

For one type of *LRATC* curve, economies of scale are present for output levels less than q, but immediately beyond q, diseconomies of scale occur (a). In another instance, economies of scale are important until some minimum output level (q_1) is attained. Once the minimum level has been attained, there is a wide range of output levels (q_1 to q_2) consistent with the minimum *LRATC* for the industry (b). In the third situation, economies of scale exist for all relevant output levels (c). Later we will explain how this type of *LRATC* curve has important implications for how industries are structured.

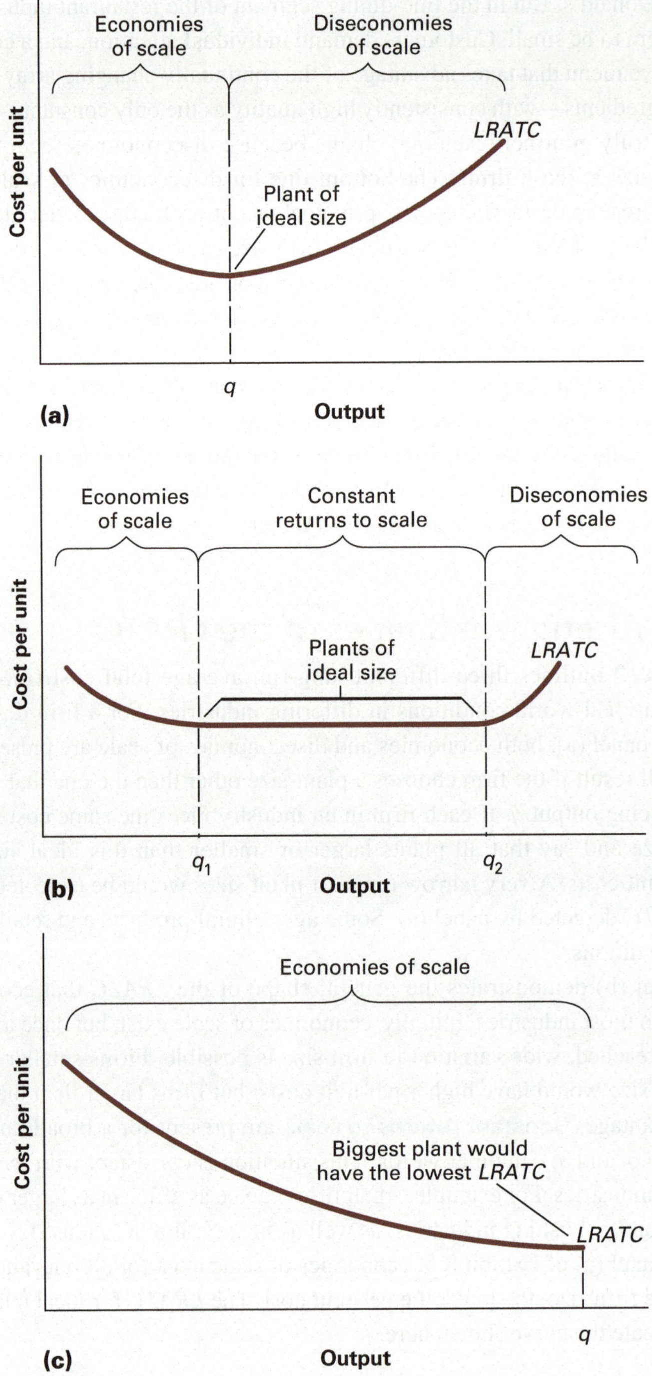

8-8a Prices of Resources

If the price of resources used should rise, the firm's cost curves will shift upward, as **Exhibit 8-10** shows. Higher resource prices will increase the cost of producing each alternative output level. For example, what happens to the cost of producing automobiles when the price of steel rises? The cost of producing automobiles also rises. Conversely,

Exhibit 8-10 Higher Resource Prices and Cost

An increase in resource prices will cause the firm's cost curves to shift upward.

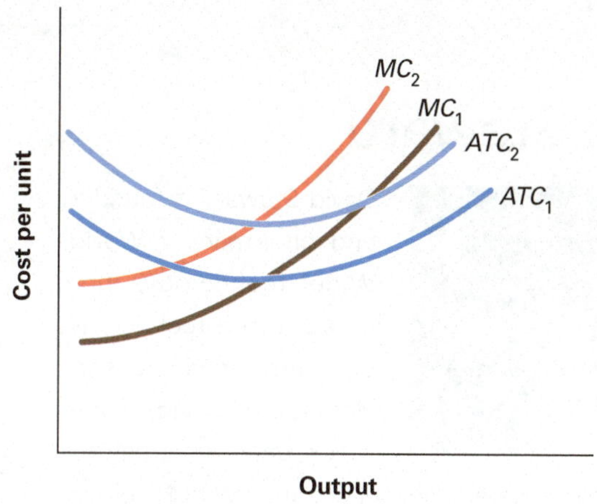

lower resource prices will reduce costs and shift the cost curves downward at each level of output.

8-8b Taxes

Taxes are a component of a firm's cost. Suppose that an excise tax of 20 cents were levied on the seller for each gallon of gasoline sold. What would happen to the seller's costs? They would increase, just as they did in Exhibit 8-10. The firm's average total and marginal cost curves would shift upward by the amount of the tax. If the tax were an annual business license fee instead, it would raise the average cost, but not the variable cost. Can you explain why?

8-8c Regulations

The government often imposes health, safety, environmental, and production regulations on business firms. For example, regulations compel firms to provide certain benefits to employees, mandate and restrict the usage of productive inputs or locations, and force firms to build certain features into their products. Although regulations provide benefits, they are also costly. Just processing the paperwork that must be submitted to regulators is costly, and so are the compulsory changes themselves. Like tax increases, increases in regulatory compliance costs will shift cost curves upward. In some cases, only fixed costs will be affected; in other instances, variable costs will be altered as well. In both cases, the firm's *ATC* will be higher.

8-8d Technology

Improvements in technology often make it possible to produce a specific amount of output with fewer resources. Advancements in robotics, 3D printing, cloud computing, data analytics, and artificial intelligence have lowered costs in many industries. The Internet has made it easy to find and outsource many business-to-business services, including building maintenance, bookkeeping, software development, and the purchase of manufacturing components. As **Exhibit 8-11** shows, a technological improvement will shift the firm's cost curves downward, reflecting the lower amount of resources needed to produce different levels of output.

Entrepreneurs Who Have Changed Our Lives

David Steward

AP Photo/Michael Allio/Icon Sportswire

David Steward is founder and chairman of World Wide Technology, Inc., an advanced technology company providing services such as cloud optimization, data infrastructure, artificial intelligence, and network security. With $17 billion in annual revenue, World Wide Technology is one of the largest minority-owned businesses in the United States, and Steward is now estimated to be worth close to $8 billion.

World Wide Technology has helped many other firms reduce their production costs through the implementation of new technologies. It has done so by developing key partnerships with large technology manufacturers, such as Cisco Systems, Dell, Hewlett Packard, Intel, and Microsoft.

Born in Chicago in 1951, Steward grew up on a farm in rural Missouri that did not even have indoor plumbing. He and his seven siblings worked on the farm, helping to feed the animals and clean the barn. Steward, the first in his family to graduate from college, received a bachelor's degree in business administration from Central Missouri State College. He worked at a variety of different jobs after graduation, including as a salesperson for both the Missouri Pacific Railroad and Federal Express, where he was named salesperson of the year.

In 1984, with $2,000 from his father, he started two companies providing price audits and reviews for railroads, using the expertise he had developed working for Missouri Pacific. Then, in 1990, he started World Wide Technology with a 4,000-square-foot office and a few employees. Today, it is not only a leading technology company with 9,000 employees but also a great place to work. The company has remained on Fortune's "100 Best Companies to Work For" for more than a decade. Steward's focus on an innovative and inclusive culture has been a key to the company's success, as has their strategy of embracing change and turning technological disruption into opportunity.

What made Steward so successful? He gives a lot of credit to his teachers, Boy Scout leaders, and his parents, who provided role models for him. His father was an entrepreneur and a hard worker–in addition to working as a mechanic, he took jobs hauling trash, working as a janitor, and being a bartender at parties. Steward is now a role model himself and takes an active role in organizations that help to develop minority entrepreneurs. He and his wife, Teresa, are also philanthropists, who donate money to a variety of causes including community projects in St. Louis and jazz music education.

Sources: "About David," World Wide Technology, at https://www.wwt.com/profile/dave-steward/bio.

"David L. Steward," Horatio Alger Association, at https://horatioalger.org/members/detail/david-l-steward/.

"David L. Steward," The Org.Com, at https://theorg.com/org/washington-university-in-st-louis/org-chart/david-l-steward.

8-9 The Economic Way of Thinking About Costs

Think for a moment about what the cost curves developed in this chapter really mean. The firm's short-run *MC* curve represents the opportunity cost of expanding output, *given the firm's current plant size*. The firm's long-run *ATC* curve represents the opportunity cost per unit of output associated with varying plant sizes and rates of output, *given that the alternative plants are still on the drawing board*. Costs are associated with choices, and they are forward-looking. At the time decisions must be made, neither the short-run *MC*

Exhibit 8-11 Egg Production Costs and Technological Change

Suppose an egg producer discovers (or develops) a "super" mineral water that makes it possible to get more eggs from the same number of chickens. Because of this technological improvement, various output levels of eggs can now be produced with less feed, space, water, and labor. Costs will be reduced. The egg producer's *ATC* and *MC* curves will shift downward.

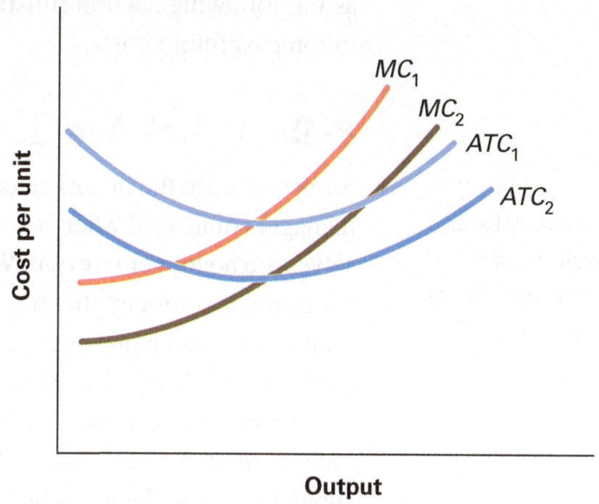

Applications in Economics

Ignore Sunk Costs to Make Better Decisions: Why You Shouldn't Cry over Spilled Milk

Suppose you paid a $75 non-refundable fee to attend an upcoming cooking class, but right before it starts a better opportunity arises–an old friend is in town and wants to get together. Should you tell your friend "no" simply because you already paid for the class?

The $75 already spent is an example of a sunk cost. It should not factor into your decision. That evening, assuming both activities require zero additional (marginal) expenditure, you should do whichever has the higher marginal benefit–the one you prefer. If that's seeing your old friend you should do it, regardless of the cost already incurred for the cooking class.

Consider another example. Erin paid $100 for a share of stock and the price has fallen to $60. She expresses unwillingness to sell the stock until it goes back up to at least $100. Should the original price influence her current decision to hold or sell the stock? No. She should hold the stock if she expects the price to rise in the future and sell if she expects the price to fall further, regardless of the original price. Similarly, should a grocer refuse to sell oranges that are about to spoil at a reduced price that is below the wholesale cost paid? Because the alternative would be to throw them in the garbage, almost any price, even one far below cost, will be better than letting the oranges spoil.

Lastly, consider a road construction project expected to cost $50 million and create $65 million in benefits. Near completion, after $50 million is spent, an unexpected cost results in an additional $25 million needed to complete the project or the road is unusable. Should it be completed even though the new total cost of $75 million is greater than the total benefit? The answer is yes, because the $50 million already spent is a sunk cost. It should be disregarded and the additional $15 million should be spent to generate the $65 million in benefits from completing the road.

This last example highlights the struggle some decision-makers have with sunk costs. A good decision-maker will not undertake a project knowing the cost exceeds the benefit. However, this overlooks the time dimension of the undertaking as well as the uncertainty associated with most decisions. In retrospect, the road should not have been built. But one cannot go back in time. Whether the road is currently worth finishing is an entirely new and different decision. Past mistakes provide useful lessons for the future, but they cannot be reversed. Bygones are bygones, even if they result in loss. There is no need to fret over spilt milk, burnt toast, or yesterday's business losses.

nor the long-run *ATC* can be determined from accounting records, because accounting costs look backward. Accounting figures yield valuable information about historical costs, but, as the following section illustrates, they must be interpreted carefully when they are used to forecast future costs.

8-9a What Are Sunk Costs?

Sunk costs
Costs that have already been incurred as a result of past decisions. They are sometimes referred to as historical costs.

Sunk costs are the historical costs of past decisions that cannot be reversed. Sunk costs give managers hindsight when it comes to making current decisions, but the specific costs themselves are no longer relevant. When past choices cannot be reversed—no refund is available, for example—money that has been spent is gone for good. Today's choices must be based on the costs and benefits expected under *current and future* market conditions, if mistakes are to be avoided (refer to the accompanying Applications in Economics box).

To minimize costs, business decision-makers need to realize that sunk costs are, indeed, *sunk*. A simple example will emphasize this point. Suppose that the firm producing sunglasses considered earlier in this chapter pays $100,000 to purchase and install a new machine that is expected to last ten years. The company's books record the cost of the machine as $10,000 each year under the heading of depreciation. The machine can be used only to make sunglasses, though. Because dismantling and reinstallation costs are high, it cannot be leased or sold to another firm. Also, it has no scrap value. In other words, there are no alternative uses for the machine. The machine's annual production of sunglasses will generate $50,000 of revenues for the firm when it is employed with raw materials and other factors of production that cost $46,000. Thus, the net revenue generated by the machine is $4,000.

Should the firm continue to use the machine? Its depreciation figures suggest that the machine is costing the firm $10,000 annually, compared to the $4,000 net revenue it generates. Put another way, accounting costs indicate that the machine is reducing the firm's profit by $6,000 annually. The machine's depreciation cost, however, is a sunk cost. It was incurred when the machine was purchased and installed, which is over and done with now. The *current* opportunity cost of the machine is therefore precisely zero. Because using the machine generates $4,000 of additional net revenue, the firm can gain by continuing with its operation. Of course, if market conditions are not expected to improve, the firm will not purchase a similar machine or replace the machine when it wears out, but this should not influence its decision whether to continue operating the one it already has.

8-9b How Will Cost Influence Supply?

Costs underpin the firm's supply decisions. A strictly profit-maximizing firm will compare the expected revenues derived from a decision or a course of action with the expected costs. If the anticipated revenues exceed costs, then the course of action will be chosen because it is expected to expand profits (or reduce losses).

For short-run supply decisions, the marginal cost of producing additional units is the relevant cost to consider. To maximize profits, the decision-maker should compare the expected marginal costs with the expected additional revenue from larger sales. If the latter exceeds the former, output (the quantity supplied) should be expanded.

While marginal costs are central in the short run, average total costs are the relevant cost consideration in the long run. Before entering an industry (or purchasing capital assets for expansion or replacement), a profit-maximizing decision-maker will compare the expected market price with the expected long-run average total cost. Profit-seeking potential entrants will supply the product if, and only if, they expect the market price to exceed their long-run average total cost. Similarly, existing firms will continue to supply a product in the long run only if they expect that the market price will enable them at least to cover their long-run average total cost.

Key Points

- The business firm is used to organize productive resources and transform them into goods and services. There are three major types of business structure—proprietorships, partnerships, and corporations.
- The principal–agent problem tends to reduce efficiency within the firm. Monitoring and the structure of incentives can be used to minimize inefficiencies arising from this source.
- The demand for a product indicates the intensity of consumers' desires for the item. The (opportunity) cost of producing the item indicates the intensity of consumers' desires for other goods that could have been produced instead, with the same resources.
- In economics, total cost includes not only explicit payments for resources employed by the firm but also the implicit costs associated with the use of productive resources owned by the firm (like the opportunity cost of the firm's equity capital or owner-provided services) that could be used elsewhere.
- Because accounting methods omit the cost of equity capital (and sometimes other implicit costs), they tend to understate the opportunity cost of producing a good and overstate the firm's economic profit.
- Economic profit (or loss) results when a firm's sales revenues exceed (or are less than) its total costs, both explicit and implicit. Firms that are earning the market (or "normal") rate of return on their assets will therefore make zero economic profit.
- The firm's short-run average total cost (*ATC*) curve will tend to be U-shaped.
- The law of diminishing returns explains why a firm's short-run marginal and average total costs will eventually rise. When diminishing marginal returns are present, successively larger amounts of the variable input will be required to increase output by one more unit. As this happens, marginal cost will rise.
- The long-run *ATC* (*LRATC*) reflects the costs of production for plants of various sizes. When economies of scale are present, *LRATC* will decline. When constant returns to scale are experienced, *LRATC* will be constant. When diseconomies of scale are present, *LRATC* will rise.
- Changes in (1) resource prices, (2) taxes, (3) regulations, and (4) technology will cause the cost curves of firms to shift.
- Sunk costs are costs that have already been incurred and cannot be recovered. Sunk costs give managers hindsight when it comes to making current decisions, but the specific costs themselves are no longer directly relevant for current and future decisions.

Critical Analysis Questions

1. The owners of a firm are residual income claimants. How does their property right to the residual income affect their incentive to (a) produce efficiently and keep cost low and (b) supply goods that consumers value highly relative to cost? Why is this important?
2. Which of the following statements do you think reflect sound economic thinking? Explain your answer.
   a. "I paid $1,800 for this economics course. Therefore, I'm going to attend the lectures even if they are useless and boring."
   b. "Because we own rather than rent, and the house is paid for, housing doesn't cost us anything."
   c. "I own 100 shares of stock that I can't afford to sell until the price goes up enough for me to get back at least my original investment."
   d. "Private education is costly to produce, whereas public schooling is free."
3. Suppose a firm produces bicycles. Will the firm's accounting statement reflect the opportunity cost of the bicycles? Why or why not? What costs would an accounting statement reveal? Should current decisions be based on accounting costs? Explain.
4. What is the principal–agent problem? When will the principal–agent problem be most severe? Why might there be a principal–agent problem between the stockholder owners and the managers of a large corporation?
5. *"If a firm maximizes profit, it must minimize the cost of producing the profit-maximizing output." Is this statement true or false? Explain your answer.
6. What are some of the advantages of the corporate business structure of ownership for large business firms? What are some of the disadvantages? Is the corporate form of business ownership cost-efficient? In a market economy, how would you tell whether the corporate structural form was efficient?
7. Explain the factors that cause a firm's short-run average total costs initially to decline but eventually to increase as the rate of output rises.

8. Which of the following are relevant to a firm's decision to increase output: (a) short-run average total cost, (b) short-run marginal cost, (c) long-run average total cost? Justify your answer.

9. Economics students often confuse (a) diminishing returns related to the variable factors of production and (b) diseconomies of scale. Explain the difference between the two, and give one example of each.

10. "Firms that make a profit have increased the value of the resources they used; their actions created wealth. In contrast, the actions of firms that make losses reduce wealth. The discovery and undertaking of profit-making opportunities are key ingredients of economic progress." Evaluate the statement.

11. *Is profit maximization consistent with the self-interest of corporate owners? Is it consistent with the self-interest of corporate managers? Is there a conflict between the self-interests of owners and those of managers?

12. *What is the opportunity cost of (a) borrowed funds and (b) equity capital? Under current tax law, firms can record as an expense the opportunity cost of borrowed funds, but not equity capital. How does this tax law affect the amount of debt the firm wants to incur, compared with the amount of money it raises by selling equity?

13. Why do economists consider normal returns to capital to be a cost? How does economic profit differ from normal profit?

14. *Draw a U-shaped, short-run *ATC* curve for a firm. Construct the accompanying *MC* and *AVC* curves.

15. What is shirking? If the managers of a firm are attempting to maximize its profits, will they have an incentive to limit shirking? How might they go about doing so?

16. What are implicit costs? Do implicit costs contribute to the opportunity cost of production? Should an implicit cost be counted as cost? Give three examples of implicit costs. Does the firm's accounting statement take implicit costs into account? Why or why not?

17. *Consider a machine purchased one year ago for $12,000. The machine is being depreciated $4,000 per year over a three-year period. Its current market value is $5,000, and the expected market value of the machine one year from now is $3,000. If the interest rate is 10 percent, what is the expected cost of holding the machine during the next year?

18. *Investors seeking to take over a firm often bid a positive price for the business even though it is currently experiencing losses. Why would anyone ever bid a positive price for a firm operating at a loss?

19. Fill in the blanks in the accompanying table shown at the bottom of the page and answer the following questions:

   a. What happens to total product when marginal product is negative?
   b. What happens to average product when marginal product is greater than average product?
   c. What happens to average product when marginal product is less than average product?
   d. At what point does marginal product begin to decrease?
   e. At what point does marginal cost begin to increase?
   f. Summarize the relationship between marginal product and marginal cost.
   g. What happens to marginal costs when total product begins to fall?
   h. What happens to average variable costs when they equal marginal costs?
   i. Marginal costs equal average variable costs between what output levels?
   j. What happens to average total costs when they equal marginal costs?
   k. Marginal costs equal average total costs between what output levels?

*Asterisk denotes questions for which answers are given in Appendix B.

Units of Variable Input	Total Product	Marginal Product	Average Product	Price of Input	Total Variable Cost	Average Variable Cost	Total Fixed Cost	Total Cost	Average Total Cost	Marginal Cost
0	0	______	______	$1	______	______	$2	______	______	______
1	6	______	______	$1	______	______	$2	______	______	______
2	15	______	______	$1	______	______	$2	______	______	______
3	27	______	______	$1	______	______	$2	______	______	______
4	37	______	______	$1	______	______	$2	______	______	______
5	45	______	______	$1	______	______	$2	______	______	______
6	50	______	______	$1	______	______	$2	______	______	______
7	52	______	______	$1	______	______	$2	______	______	______
8	50	______	______	$1	______	______	$2	______	______	______

Chapter 9

Price Takers and the Competitive Process

Competition means decentralized planning by many separate persons.

—Friedrich A. von Hayek[1]

[I]t is competition that drives down costs and prices, induces firms to produce the goods consumers want, and spurs innovation and the expansion of new markets . . .

—President's Council of Economic Advisers[2]

In the previous chapter, we focused on cost conditions of business firms. In this chapter and the next two, we will examine the price and output decisions of the firm, and how they are influenced by costs and market conditions. The importance of profits, losses, and competition will be addressed. As we proceed, we will also analyze how the structure of a market—for example, the number of firms, the control they have over price, and the ease of entry into the market—influences both the decision-making of firms and the operation of markets.

Learning Objectives

9.1 Differentiate between firms that are price takers and those that are price searchers.

9.2 Describe the characteristics of a price-taker market.

9.3 Indicate how a firm that is a price taker decides what quantity of output to produce to maximize profit.

9.4 Construct a graph of the average total cost, marginal cost, and demand curves for a firm making profit, loss, and zero economic profit in a price-taker market.

9.5 Indicate when a firm making losses will decide to (a) continue operating, (b) shutdown, or (c) go out of business.

9.6 Explain why firms in a price-taker market can earn profit in the short run but not in the long run.

9.7 Describe how time affects the elasticity of the market supply curve for a price-taker market and how the cost structure of the industry determines the shape of the long-run market supply curve.

9.8 Explain why competition and the profit and loss system provide a strong incentive for producers to innovate and supply goods that consumers want at a low cost.

[1]Friedrich A. von Hayek, "The Use of Knowledge in Society," *American Economic Review* 35 (September 1945): 521.

[2]President's Council of Economic Advisers, *Economic Report of the President, 1996* (Washington, DC: U.S. Government Printing Office, 1996), 155.

9-1 Price Takers and Price Searchers

Price takers
Sellers who must take the market price in order to sell their product. Because each price taker's output is small relative to the total market, price takers can sell all their output at the market price, but they are unable to sell any of their output at a price higher than the market price.

Price searchers
Firms that face a downward-sloping demand curve for their product. The amount the firm is able to sell is inversely related to the price it charges.

Competition as a dynamic process
Rivalry or competitiveness between or among parties (for example, producers or input suppliers) to deliver a better deal to buyers in terms of quality, price, and product information.

Pure competition
A market structure characterized by a large number of small firms producing an identical product in an industry (market area) that permits complete freedom of entry and exit. Also called price-taker markets.

Barriers to entry
Obstacles that limit the freedom of potential rivals to enter and compete in an industry or market.

This chapter will focus on markets in which the firms are **price takers**: They simply take the price that is determined in the market. ***In a price-taker market, the firms all produce identical products (for example, wheat, eggs, or regular unleaded gasoline), and each seller is small relative to the total market. Thus, the output of any single firm has no effect on the market price. Each firm can sell all its output at the market price but cannot sell any of its output at a higher price.*** When a firm is a price taker, there is no pricing decision to be made. Price takers try to choose the output level that will maximize profit, given their costs and the price determined by the market.

In the real world, most firms are not price takers. They are usually able to increase their prices, at least a little, without losing all their customers. For example, if Nike increased the price of its athletic shoes by 10 percent, the number of shoes sold would decline, but it would not fall to zero. Firms like Nike are not price takers. They are **price searchers**: They choose the price that they will charge for their product, but the quantity that they are able to sell is very much related to that price. To maximize their profits, price searchers must not only decide how much to produce but also what price to charge. Price-taker markets and price-searcher markets have differing methods of competition, differing ease of entry for competitors, and perhaps differing scale economies, too. We will examine markets in which the firms are price searchers in the next two chapters.

If most real-world firms are price searchers, why is it important to analyze price-taker markets? There are several reasons. First, even though most firms are not price takers, there are a number of important markets, particularly in agriculture and mining, in which the firms do essentially take the price determined in the market. Second, the price-taker model helps clarify the relationship between the decision-making of individual firms and the market supply. Finally, and perhaps most important, the study of markets in which firms are price takers enhances our knowledge of **competition as a dynamic process**, ***including its operation in markets other than those that are price takers***.

Historically, the term **pure competition** has been used to refer to markets in which firms are price takers. However, the expression "price-taker market" is more descriptive. Furthermore, this label avoids the implication that competitive forces are necessarily less pure or less intense in price-searcher markets. Often, this is not the case. When **barriers to entry** are low, the competitive process is just as important in price-searcher markets as it is when the firms are price takers.

Nonetheless, it should be noted that price-taker markets and purely competitive markets are really alternative names for the same thing. So when you hear people talk about pure competition or purely competitive markets, they mean markets with characteristics like those analyzed in this chapter.

9-2 What Are the Characteristics of Price-Taker Markets?

Consider the situation of Jerell, a Texas cattle rancher. Even if his ranch is quite large, there is little that Jerell can do to change the market price of beef cattle. After all, there are tens of thousands of farmers who raise cattle. Thus, Jerell supplies only a small portion of the total cattle market. The amount that he sells will exert little or no effect on the market price of cattle. Jerell is a price taker.

©smereka/Shutterstock.com

Ron Niebrugge/Alamy

Producers in the wheat-farming and beef cattle markets are price takers. If they are going to sell their output, they must do so at the price determined by the market. Because individual producers are small relative to the total market, they can sell as many units as they like at the market price.

The firms in a market will be price takers when the following four conditions are met:

1. All the firms in the market are producing an identical product (for example, beef or eggs of a given grade).
2. A large number of firms exist in the market.
3. Each firm supplies only a very small portion of the total amount supplied to the market.
4. No barriers limit the entry or exit of firms in the market.

Exhibit 9-1 illustrates the relationship between the market forces (panel b) and the demand curve facing the price-taking firm (panel a). If the firm sets a price above the market level, consumers will simply buy from other sellers. Why pay the higher price when the identical good is abundantly available elsewhere at the lower market price? For example, if the market price of wheat were \$6.50 per bushel, a farmer would be unable to find buyers for wheat if he tried to sell his at \$7.00 per bushel. A firm would gain nothing by setting its price below the market level, because any small firm in the market can already sell as much as it wants at the market price. A price reduction would only reduce revenue and profit. A firm that is a price taker thus faces a perfectly elastic demand for its product. (In Exhibit 9-1, note that a lowercase *d* is used to denote the demand curve faced by the *firm,* whereas an uppercase *D* indicates the *market* demand curve.)

Exhibit 9-1 The Price Taker's Demand Curve

The market forces of supply and demand determine price (b). Price takers have no control over price. Thus, the demand for the product of the firm is perfectly elastic (a).

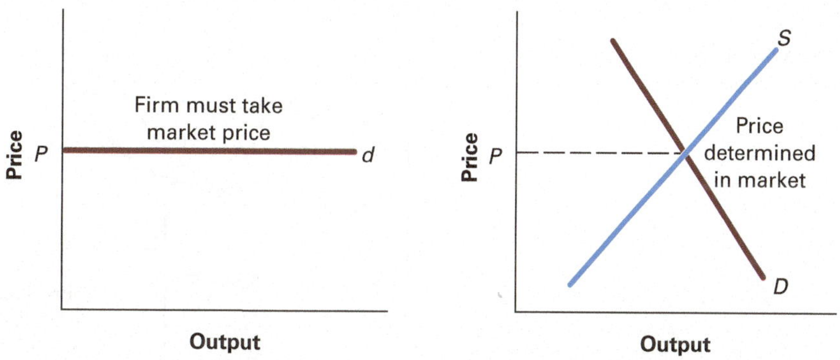

(a) Firm **(b) Market**

9-3 How Does the Price Taker Maximize Profit?

The firm's output decision is based on maximizing profit, which requires comparing revenue with cost. A firm will continue to expand output as long as the additional revenues from the production and sales of the additional units exceed their marginal costs, thereby increasing profit. In the preceding chapter, we discovered that the law of diminishing returns assures that a firm's short-run marginal costs will eventually increase as the firm expands its output. As the firm continues to add additional variable resources to its fixed plant facilities, marginal productivity falls, and marginal costs rise, and eventually increase to the point where it is no longer profitable to further expand output.

Marginal revenue (*MR*) The incremental change in total revenue derived from the sale of one additional unit of a product.

What about the benefits or additional revenues from output expansion? **Marginal revenue (*MR*)** is the change in the firm's total revenue per unit of output. It is the additional revenue derived from the sale of an additional unit of output. Mathematically,

$$MR = \frac{\textbf{Change in total revenue}}{\textbf{Change in output}}$$

Because the price taker sells all units at the same price, its marginal revenue will be equal to the market price. That is, producing and selling one more unit of output increases the firm's revenue by exactly the amount of the current market price. The firm's marginal revenue curve is a horizontal line at the market price. For a price-taker firm the marginal revenue curve is also the demand curve faced by the price-taker firm, as is shown in Exhibit 9-1.

To maximize profits the price taker will expand its output until marginal cost just equals marginal revenue (price). **Exhibit 9-2** illustrates this decision. The firm will continue to expand output as long as the marginal revenue curve (*MR*) lies above the marginal cost (*MC*) curve. The profit of the price taker is maximized at the output rate at which $P = MR = MC$. In Exhibit 9-2, this occurs at output q. The firm will not expand output beyond q because those units would add more to the firm's costs than to its revenue, thus reducing profit.

Using Exhibit 9-2 it is also possible to illustrate the firm's total revenue, total cost, and profit as areas in the diagram. The total revenue of the firm would be the sales price of each unit, *P*, multiplied by output sold, q. Total revenue is represented by the area *P0qB*. The firm's total cost, in contrast, can be found by multiplying the average total cost (*ATC*) by the output level. Total cost is represented by the area *C0qA*. Because the firm's total revenues

Exhibit 9-2 Profit Maximization When the Firm Is a Price Taker

The price taker will maximize profits by producing the output level q, where $P = MC$.

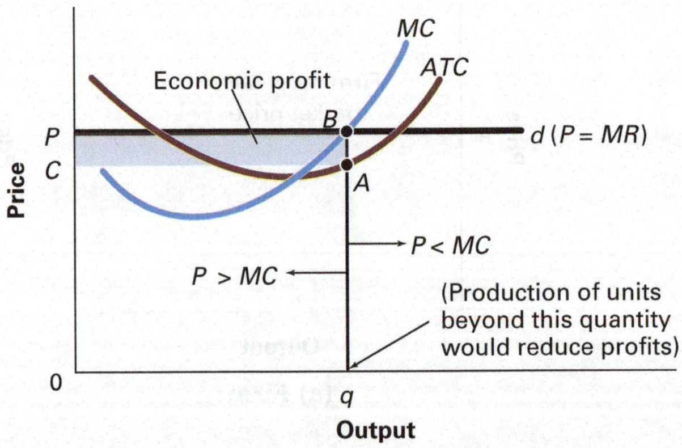

exceed its total costs, it is making short-run economic profit, shown by the area of excess revenue over cost (the shaded area *PCAB*).

In the real world, of course, decisions are not made by entrepreneurs who spend time drawing demand and marginal cost curves. However, business firms do attempt to maximize their profits, producing units only when it is profitable to do so. Experimentation, trial and error, and strong competitive forces will eventually lead firms to seek out the level of output consistent with this rule for profit maximization.

9-3a Profit Maximizing: A Numeric Example

Exhibit 9-3 uses numeric data to illustrate profit-maximizing decision-making for a firm that is a price taker. As column 6 of Exhibit 9-3 shows, the firm maximizes profit at an output of 15 units.

There are two ways to determine this profit-maximizing output rate. First, profit is equal to the difference between total revenue and total cost. Thus, profit will be maximized at the output rate where this difference (*TR* minus *TC*) is greatest. For output rates less than 11 units the firm would actually experience losses. But at 15 units of output, an $11 profit is earned ($75 total revenue minus $64 total cost). The profit figures in column 6 show that it's impossible to earn a profit larger than $11 at any other rate of output.

Exhibit 9-3 Profit Maximization for a Price Taker: A Numeric Illustration

(1) Output (per Day)	(2) Total Revenue (*TR*)	(3) Total Cost (*TC*)	(4) Marginal Revenue (*MR*)	(5) Marginal Cost (*MC*)	(6) Profit (*TR* – *TC*)
0	$0.00	$25.00	—	—	$–25.00
1	5.00	29.80	$5.00	$4.80	–24.80
2	10.00	33.75	5.00	3.95	–23.75
3	15.00	37.25	5.00	3.50	–22.25
4	20.00	40.25	5.00	3.00	–20.25
5	25.00	42.75	5.00	2.50	–17.75
6	30.00	44.75	5.00	2.00	–14.75
7	35.00	46.50	5.00	1.75	–11.50
8	40.00	48.00	5.00	1.50	–8.00
9	45.00	49.25	5.00	1.25	–4.25
10	50.00	50.25	5.00	1.00	–0.25
11	55.00	51.50	5.00	1.25	3.50
12	60.00	53.25	5.00	1.75	6.75
13	65.00	55.75	5.00	2.50	9.25
14	70.00	59.25	5.00	3.50	10.75
15	75.00	64.00	5.00	4.75	11.00
16	80.00	70.00	5.00	6.00	10.00
17	85.00	77.25	5.00	7.25	7.75
18	90.00	85.50	5.00	8.25	4.50
19	95.00	95.00	5.00	9.50	0.00
20	100.00	108.00	5.00	13.00	–8.00
21	105.00	125.00	5.00	17.00	–20.00

In **Exhibit 9-4**, panel (a) presents the total revenue and total cost approach in graph form. (However, the curves are drawn smoothly, as though output could be increased by tiny amounts, not just in whole-unit increments like those shown in Exhibit 9-3.) Profits will be greatest when the total revenue line lies above the total cost curve by the largest vertical amount, at 15 units of output.

You can also use the marginal approach to determine the profit-maximizing rate of output for the firm. Remember, as long as price (marginal revenue) exceeds marginal cost, production and sale of additional units will add to the firm's profit (or reduce its losses). Columns 4 and 5 of Exhibit 9-3 reveal that *MR* is greater than *MC* for the first 15 units of output. Producing these units will expand the firm's profit. In contrast, producing any unit beyond 15 adds more to cost than to revenue. Profit will therefore decline when output is expanded beyond 15 units. Given the firm's cost and revenue schedule, profits are maximized by producing 15, and only 15, units per day.

Panel (b) of Exhibit 9-4 graphically illustrates the marginal approach. Note here that the output rate at which the marginal cost and marginal revenue curves intersect (15 units) coincides with the output rate in panel (a) at which the total revenue curve exceeds the total cost curve by the largest amount. Beyond that output rate, *MR* is less than *MC*, so profit will decline.

Exhibit 9-4 The Firm's Profit-Maximizing Output Level–Total and Marginal Approaches

Using the data of Exhibit 9-3, we can find the profit-maximizing output of a price taker using either the total approach or the marginal approach. Using the total approach, we find that profits are maximized when the firm's total revenues exceed its total costs by the greatest amount (a). Using the marginal approach, we find that profits are maximized by comparing marginal revenue and marginal costs (b).

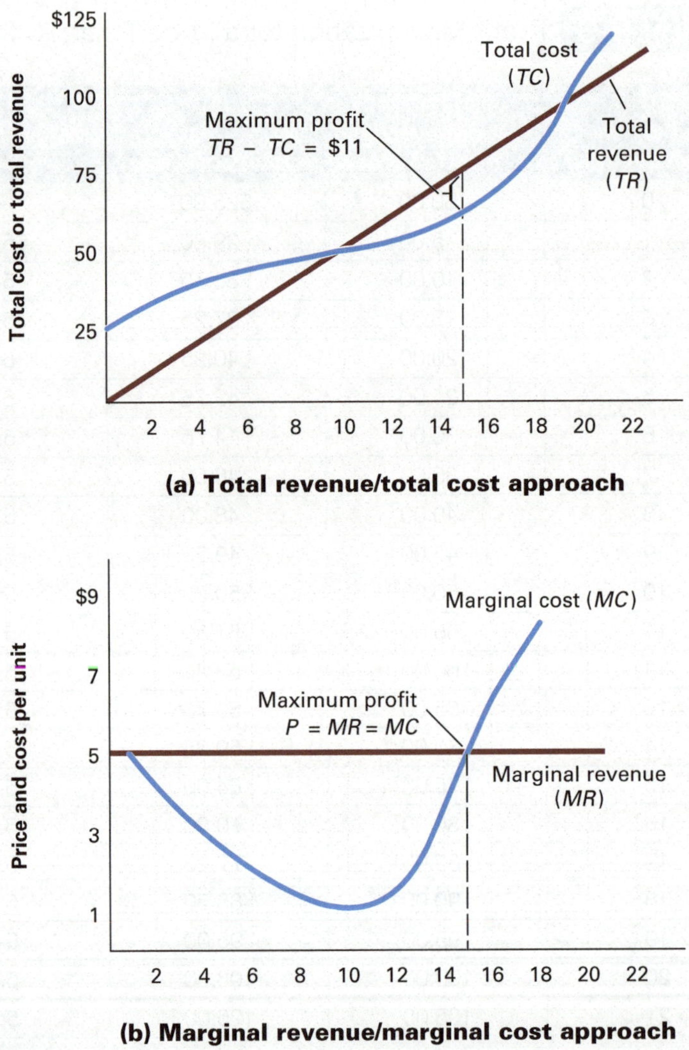

Exhibit 9-5 Operating with Short-Run Losses

A firm making losses will operate in the short run if it (1) can cover its variable costs now and (2) expects price to be high enough in the future to cover all its costs.

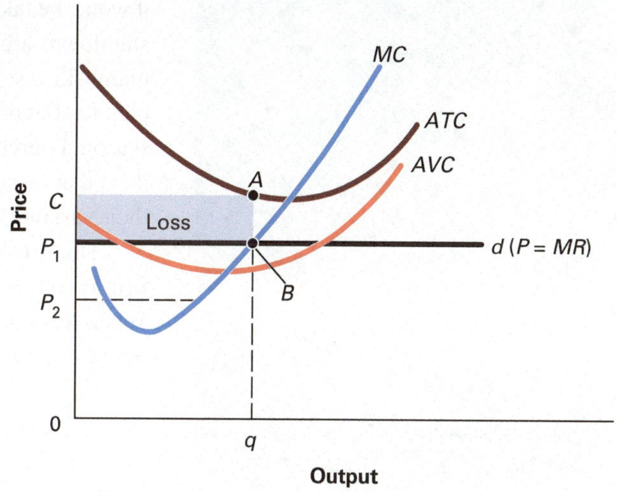

9-3b Losses and When to Go Out of Business

Suppose that changes in the bigger marketplace cause the price to drop below a firm's average total cost at all possible output levels. How will a profit-maximizing firm respond to this situation? The answer to this question depends both on the firm's revenues relative to its *variable* cost and on its expectations about the future. The firm's owner has three options: (1) continue to operate in the short run, (2) shut down temporarily, or (3) go out of business.

If the firm anticipates that the lower market price is temporary, it may want to continue operating in the short run as long as it can cover its variable cost.[3] **Exhibit 9-5** illustrates why. The firm shown in this exhibit would minimize its loss at output level q, where $P = MR = MC$. But at q, total revenues ($0qBP_1$) are less than total costs ($0qAC$). The firm faces short-run economic losses. Even if it shuts down completely, it will still incur fixed costs, *unless the firm goes out of business.* If it anticipates that the market price will increase enough to allow the firm to cover its average total costs in the future, it may not want to terminate operations and sell its assets. It may choose to produce q units in the short run, even though it will incur losses. At price P_1, producing output q is more advantageous than shutting down, because the firm is able to cover its variable costs and have revenue remaining to pay some of its fixed costs. If it were to shut down but not sell out, the firm would lose the entire amount of its fixed cost.

What if the market price drops below the firm's average variable cost (for example, to P_2)? When this happens, not only is the firm not covering its fixed costs, it's not fully covering its variable costs either. In other words, if the firm operates, it will lose even more money. Under these circumstances, a temporary **shutdown** is preferable to short-run operation. Even if the firm's owner expects the market price to increase later, enabling the

Shutdown
A temporary halt in the operation of a firm. Because the firm anticipates operating in the future, it does not sell its assets and go out of business. The firm's variable cost is eliminated by the shutdown, but its fixed costs continue.

---

[3]Keep in mind the opportunity-cost concept. The firm's fixed costs are opportunity costs that do not vary with the level of output. They can be avoided if, and only if, the firm goes out of business. To specify fixed costs, we need to know (1) how much the firm's fixed assets would bring if they were sold or rented to others and (2) any other costs, such as operating license fees and debts, that could be avoided if the firm declared bankruptcy and/or went out of business. Because fixed costs can be avoided if the firm goes out of business, the firm will foresee greater losses from operating even in the short run if it does not expect conditions to improve.

Arterra Picture Library/Alamy Stock Photo

A firm will temporarily shut down if it cannot cover its variable cost but does not want to go out of business because it expects to be able to operate profitably in the future. Ski resorts, for example, generally close for several months each summer and reopen during the winter. During these short-run shutdowns, the ski resort still pays its fixed costs, such as its rent, taxes, and insurance. The ski resort avoids only variable costs during the summer months.

firm to survive and prosper in the future, shutting down in the short run will minimize its losses. The firm will still have to pay its fixed costs, but it won't be taking an additional loss on each unit it produces. Temporary shutdowns are actually regularly planned in some markets. For example, many ski resorts, golf courses, hotels, and restaurants in vacation areas plan to shut down in slow seasons, operating only when tourists or other seasonal purchasers provide enough demand. The price-taker model predicts that these firms will operate only when they expect to cover at least their variable costs.

The firm's third option is **going out of business** immediately. If the firm is sold, even the losses resulting from its fixed costs can be avoided. When market conditions are not expected to change for the better, going out of business is the preferred option.

Going out of business
The sale of a firm's assets and its permanent exit from the market. By going out of business, a firm is able to avoid its fixed costs, which would continue during a shutdown.

9-4 The Firm's Short-Run Supply Curve

The price taker that intends to stay in business will maximize profits (or minimize losses) when it produces the output level at which P = MR = MC ***and variable costs are covered. Therefore, the portion of the firm's short-run marginal cost curve that lies above its average variable cost is the short-run supply curve of the firm.***

Exhibit 9-6 illustrates that, as the market price increases, the firm will expand output along its *MC* curve. If the market price were less than P_1, the firm would shut down immediately and produce zero output. If the market price is P_1, a price equal to the firm's minimum average variable cost, the firm may supply output q_1 in the short run. Economic losses will result, but the firm would incur similar losses if it shut down completely. As the market price increases to P_2, the firm will happily expand output along its *MC* curve to q_2. At P_2, price is equal to average total costs. At this point, the firm is making a "normal rate of return," or zero economic profits. Higher prices will result in a still larger short-run output. For example, when the price rises to P_3, the firm will supply q_3 units. At this price, economic profits will result. As long as price exceeds average variable cost, higher prices will cause the firm to expand output along its *MC* curve, which therefore becomes the firm's short-run supply curve.

9-5 The Short-Run Market Supply Curve

The short-run market supply curve shows the total quantity supplied at alternative market prices. ***When the firms are price takers, the short-run market supply curve is the horizontal summation of the marginal cost curves (ΣMC) above the level of average variable cost for all of the firms in the market. Because individual firms will supply a larger amount at a higher price, the short-run market supply curve will slope upward to the right.***

Exhibit 9-6 illustrates this relationship. As the price of the product rises from P_1 to P_2 to P_3, the individual firms expand their output along their marginal cost curves. Because the individual firms supply a larger output as the market price increases, the total amount supplied to the market also expands.

Exhibit 9-6 The Short-Run Supply Curve for the Firm and the Market

As price increases, firms will expand output along their *MC* curve. Thus, the firm's *MC* curve is also its supply curve (a). When resource prices are constant, the short-run market supply (a) is merely the sum of the supply produced by all the firms in the market (b).

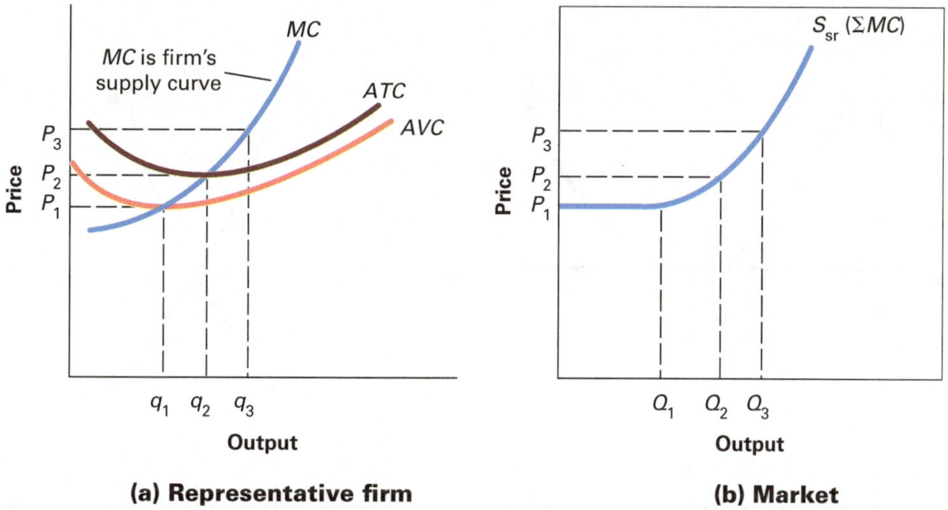

9-6 Price and Output in Price-Taker Markets

The short-run market supply curve, together with the demand curve for the industry's product, will determine the market price. At the short-run equilibrium market price, each firm will have expanded output until marginal costs are equal to the market price, and they may be earning either economic profits or losses.

9-6a Long-Run Equilibrium

In the long run, existing firms will have the opportunity to expand (or contract) the sizes of their plants, and firms will also be able to enter and exit the industry. As these long-run adjustments are made, output in the whole industry may either expand or contract. If economic profit is present, new firms will enter the industry to capture some of those profits. Current producers will have an incentive to expand the scale of their operations to capture some of the additional profits, too. This increase in supply will put downward pressure on prices. In contrast, if firms in the industry are suffering economic losses, they will leave the market. This decrease in supply will put upward pressure on prices. This process of entry and exit will continue until the profit rate in the industry has returned to a normal level ("zero economic profit") consistent with the profit rates in other competitive industries. Therefore, as **Exhibit 9-7** shows, when a price-taker market is in long-run equilibrium, the quantity supplied and the quantity demanded will be equal at the market price (panel b) and each firm in the industry will be earning normal (zero) economic profit (that is, its minimum *ATC* will just equal the market price [panel a]).

Exhibit 9-7 Long-Run Equilibrium in a Price-Taker Market

The two conditions necessary for long-run equilibrium in a price-taker market are depicted here. First, quantity supplied and quantity demanded must be equal in the market (b). Second, the firms in the industry must earn zero economic profit (the "normal rate of return") at the established market price (a).

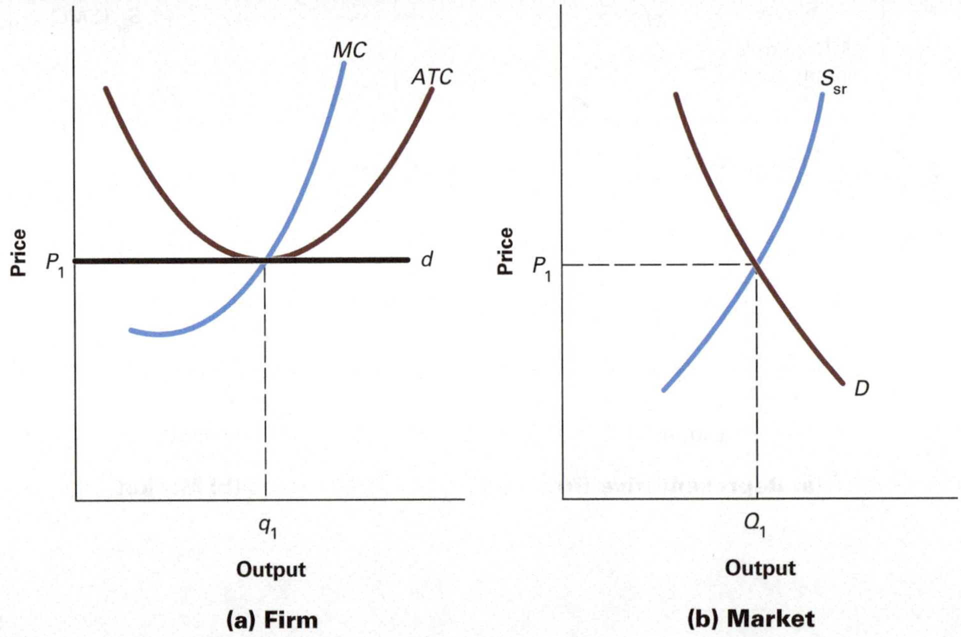

In price-taker markets, a single price will emerge and all of the potential gains from trade between the buyer-consumers and seller-suppliers will be realized. Does the price-taker model really work in the real world? As the Applications in Economics feature on experimental economics and the significance of competition indicates, the general implications of the price-taker model are approximated even when the restrictive assumptions of the model are not fully met.

When long-run equilibrium is present, firms will have no incentive to alter either their output levels or their plant sizes. Neither will there be incentive for net investment to flow into or away from the industry. Thus, the market price and output will persist into the future. This is why it is referred to as a long-run equilibrium.

9-6b How Will the Market Respond to an Increase in Demand?

Suppose that a price-taker market is in long-run equilibrium. What will happen if there is an increase in demand? **Exhibit 9-8** shows us. When the market demand increases from D_1 to D_2, the market price will rise from P_1 to P_2. The higher price will induce firms to expand output (from q_1 to Q_2 in panel a of the exhibit) along their *MC* curves. In the short run, producers will make economic profits. The profits will attract new firms to the industry and cause the existing firms to expand the scale of their plants. Hence, the market supply will increase (shift from S_1 to S_2) and eventually eliminate the short-run profits. If the prices of resources supplied to the industry are unchanged, the market supply will continue to expand (shift to the right) until the price returns to its initial level (P_1), even though output has expanded to Q_3.

Applications in Economics

Experimental Economics and the Significance of Competition

In fields like physics and chemistry, scientists use controlled laboratory experiments to test and verify the basic principles on which their science is built. Historically, it was thought that experiments of this type were not an option for economists. But this changed during the middle part of the twentieth century, and economists now routinely conduct experiments investigating key elements of economic theory.

Vernon Smith, currently at Chapman University, won the 2002 Nobel Prize in Economics for his path breaking work in experimental economics. In one of his early experiments, Smith brought individuals into a laboratory setting and arbitrarily assigned them roles as buyers and sellers in a game-like activity. Each buyer was assigned a maximum value representing the maximum price they would be willing to pay for a hypothetical commodity. If the buyer could purchase the commodity at a price less than their maximum value, they would receive a cash payment equal to the difference between the two. Each buyer gained financially by purchasing at lower prices—just as buyers do in real markets. The sellers were treated similarly. All sellers were assigned a minimum value representing their cost, and if they were able to sell the commodity for more than this minimum, they would receive a cash payment for the difference. Buyers and sellers were free to make verbal offers and enter into exchanges at any mutually agreeable price.

The competitive price-taker model predicts that all mutually advantageous trades among buyers and sellers will be undertaken and that, as trades occur, the price will tend to converge toward a single price—the market price. Smith and other experimental researchers confirmed that this was indeed the case. After the experiments, participants often describe the experience as disorganized and chaotic. Thus, many are startled when shown that their actions (trades) achieved the maximum income for the group and that a sealed envelope, given to them prior to the experiment, approximated both the price of most trades and the maximum joint gains achieved by the group. The competitive model presented in this chapter provided the foundation for these predictions.

Prior to the work in experimental economics, many economists thought this model was relevant only under highly restrictive conditions. Experimental researchers, however, have found that outcomes approximating those of the competitive price-taker model generally emerge even when the strict assumptions of the model are not fully met. For example, even if the number of sellers is relatively small, say 10 to 15, outcomes similar to those predicted by the price-taker model generally occur.

At first, Smith himself was surprised that efficient outcomes were achieved under a wide variety of conditions, but after numerous experiments, he stated that:

> *In many experimental markets, poorly informed, error-prone, and uncomprehending human agents interact through the trading rules to produce social algorithms which demonstrably approximate the wealth maximizing outcomes traditionally thought to require complete information and cognitively rational actors.*[1]

In addition to analyzing the exchange process, experimental research has addressed numerous other topics, including the impact of alternative auction rules, the likelihood of a stock market or real estate bubble, and the provision of public goods. Experimental economics is one of the most exciting and fruitful areas of economic research.

[1] Vernon L. Smith, "Economics in the Laboratory," *Journal of Economic Perspectives* 8, no. 1 (Winter 1994): 118.

9-6c How Will the Market Respond to a Decrease in Demand?

Economic profits attract new firms to an industry. In contrast, economic losses encourage firms to move out of the industry and into other areas where the profitability potential is more favorable. Economic losses mean firms are earning less than a normal market rate of return. The opportunity cost of continuing in the industry exceeds the gain.

Exhibit 9-8 Market Response to Increased Demand

When demand increases from D_1 to D_2, the market price rises from P_1 to P_2, inducing firms to expand output (b). Firms make short-run profits (a), which draw new competitors into the industry. The supply then expands (shifts from S_1 to S_2). If cost conditions are unchanged, the expansion in supply will continue until the market price declines to its initial level of P_1.

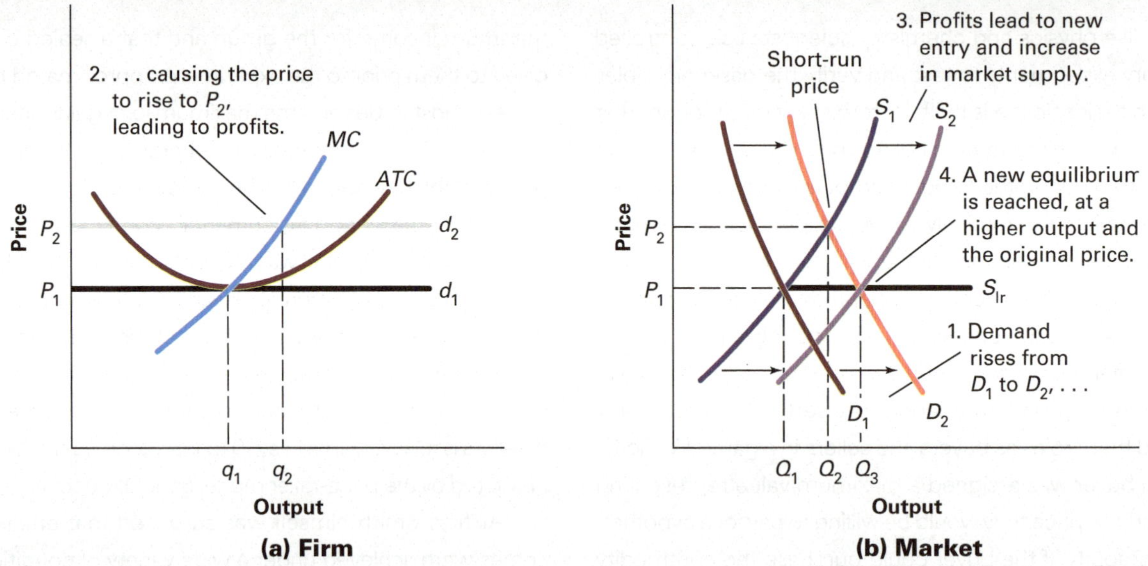

Exhibit 9-9 shows market forces reacting to economic losses. Initially, assume that an equilibrium price exists in the industry. The firms are able to cover their average costs of production. Now suppose that consumer incomes fall, lowering the product's demand and its market price. At the new, lower price, firms in the industry will not be able to cover their costs of production. In the short run, they will reduce output along their *MC* curves. The lower output by the individual firms results in a lower quantity supplied in the market.

In the face of short-run losses, some firms will leave the industry, causing the industry supply to decline, indicated by the shift from S_1 to S_2. Firms will continue to exit until the price rises enough that the firms remaining in the industry can once again earn a normal rate of return, or zero economic profit. At that point, a new long-run equilibrium is established.

9-6d The Long-Run Market Supply Curve

The *long-run market supply curve* shows how the quantity supplied in an industry varies with the market price, given enough time for firms to adjust the sizes of their plants (or other fixed factors) and to enter or exit the industry. Because the curve is constructed from points of long-run equilibrium, at each point the market price is equal to the minimum average total cost for firms in the industry. Therefore, the shape of the curve depends on what happens to the cost of production as the *industry's* output is altered; there are three possibilities.

Constant-cost industry
An industry for which factor prices and costs of production remain constant as market output is expanded. The long-run market supply curve is therefore horizontal in these industries.

Long-run supply in constant-cost industries. If resource prices remain unchanged, the long-run market supply curve will be horizontal, or perfectly elastic. In terms of economics, this describes a **constant-cost industry**. Exhibits 9-8 and 9-9 both depict constant-cost industries. As Exhibit 9-8 shows, in these industries an increase in market demand for the product results in only a temporary increase in the price of the product. With time, the higher price and profits will stimulate expansion and additional production, which will push the market price back down precisely to its initial level (and profitability back to its normal rate).

Similarly, Exhibit 9-9 illustrates the impact of a decline in demand in a constant-cost industry. Here, market price falls, inducing losses and the exit of firms. Assuming resource

Exhibit 9-9 The Impact of a Fall in Demand

Lower market demand will cause the price to fall and short-run losses to occur. The losses will cause some firms to go out of business and others to reduce their output. In the long run, the market supply will fall, causing the market price to rise. The supply will continue to decline and price will continue to rise until the short-run losses have been eliminated.

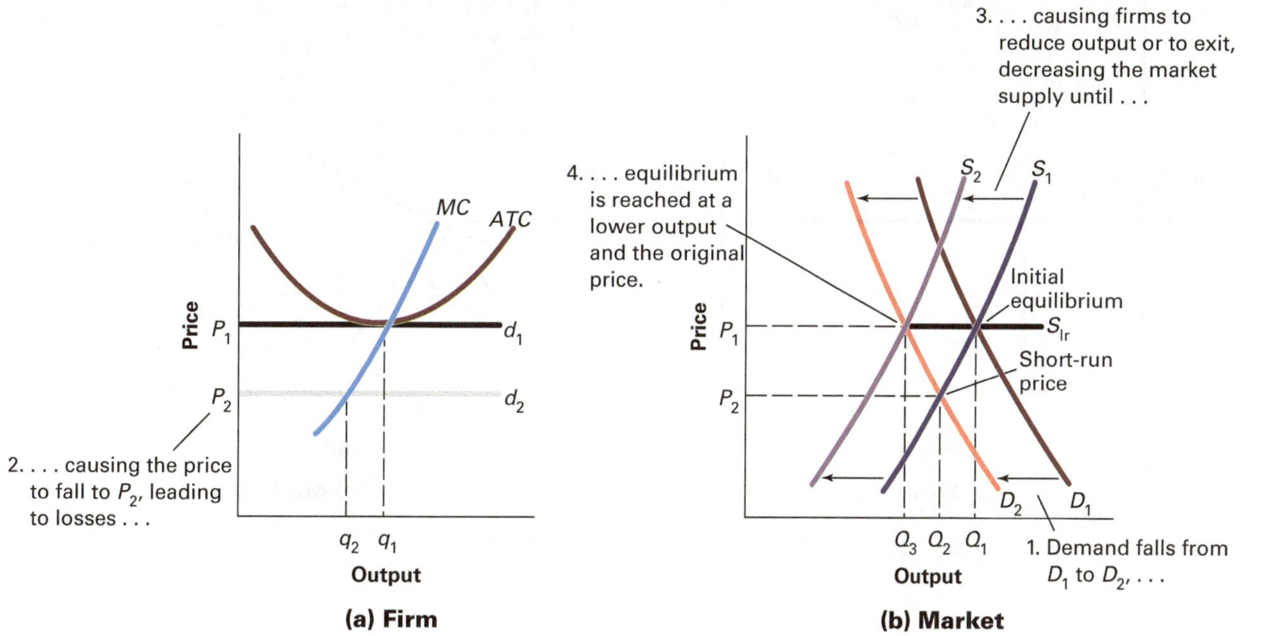

prices and production costs are unaffected by the change in market output, the reduction in demand lowers the price in the short run, but it returns to its original level in the long run. Thus, in a constant-cost industry, the *long-run market supply curve* (S_{lr}) is perfectly elastic.

Long-run supply in increasing-cost industries. In most industries, an increase in *industry* output will lead to higher resource prices and per-unit production costs for all the firms in the industry. Economists refer to such industries as **increasing-cost industries**. **Exhibit 9-10** depicts an increasing-cost industry. The rising resource costs cause the firms' average and marginal cost curves to shift upward (to ATC_2 and MC_2) as the industry expands. For an increasing-cost industry, the market price necessary to result in zero economic profit (long-run equilibrium) will have to be higher as the industry gets larger (now P_2). The long-run market supply curve for the product will therefore slope upward to the right.

Increasing-cost industry An industry for which costs of production rise as output is expanded. In these industries, even in the long run, higher market prices will be needed to induce firms to expand total output. As a result, the long-run market supply curve in these industries will slope upward to the right.

Long-run supply in decreasing-cost industries. Sometimes, resource prices will decline when an industry expands, causing the cost curves to shift downward as new firms enter the industry. For example, as the electronics industry expands, suppliers of certain components may be able to adopt large-scale production techniques that will lead to lower component prices. In such **decreasing-cost industries**, the long-run (but not the short-run) market supply curve will slope downward to the right. Decreasing-cost industries are rare.

Decreasing-cost industry An industry for which costs of production decline as the industry expands. The market supply is therefore inversely related to price. Such industries are atypical.

9-6e Supply Elasticity and the Role of Time

The short- and long-run supply curve distinction offers a convenient two-stage analysis, but in the real world there are many intermediate production "runs." The delivery rates for some factor inputs that could not be easily increased in a one-week time period can be increased over a two-week period. It might take two weeks, for example, to hire reliable workers who need no special skills. Expanding other factors might take a month, and still others, six months. More precisely, the cost penalty for quicker availability is greater for some

Exhibit 9-10 Increasing Costs and Long-Run Supply

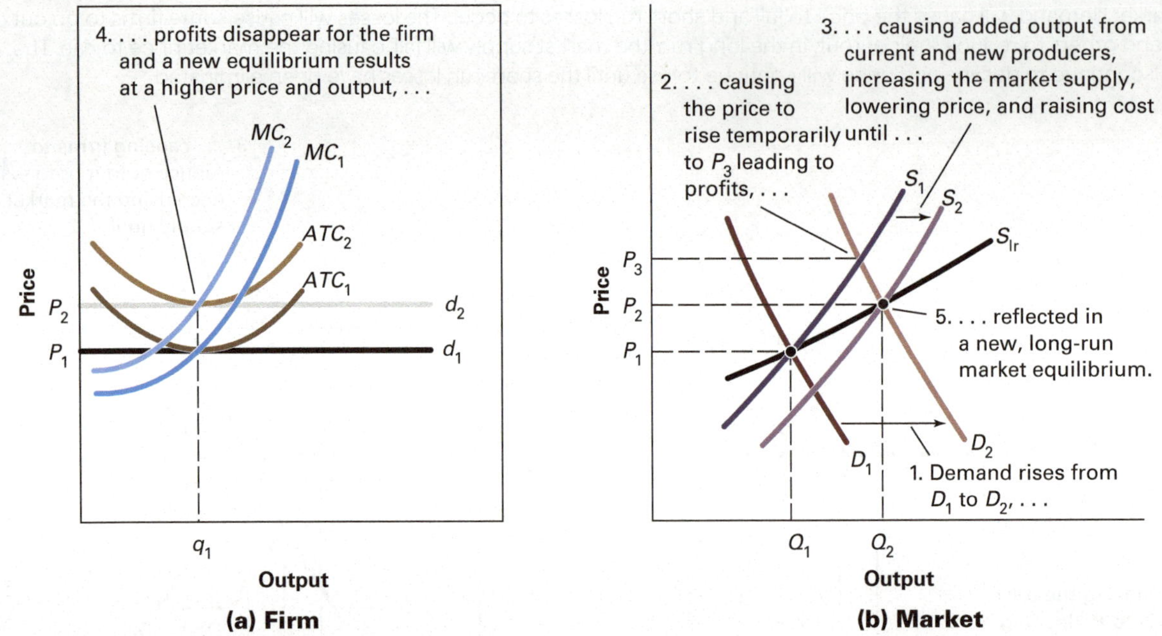

productive resources than others. In any case, a faster expansion usually means that greater cost penalties are encountered in order to obtain the earlier availability of the resources needed to expand production.

As a result, the supply curve for products is typically more inelastic the shorter the time frame of the response to a price change. **Exhibit 9-11** illustrates this point. When the price of a product increases from P_1 to P_2, the immediate supply response of the firms is small, reflecting the high cost of hasty expansion. After one week, firms are willing to expand output only from Q_1 to Q_2. After one month, cost reductions made possible by the longer production-planning period allow firms to offer Q_3 units at the price P_2. After three

Exhibit 9-11 Time and the Elasticity of Supply

The elasticity of the market supply curve usually increases when suppliers have more time to adjust to a change in the price.

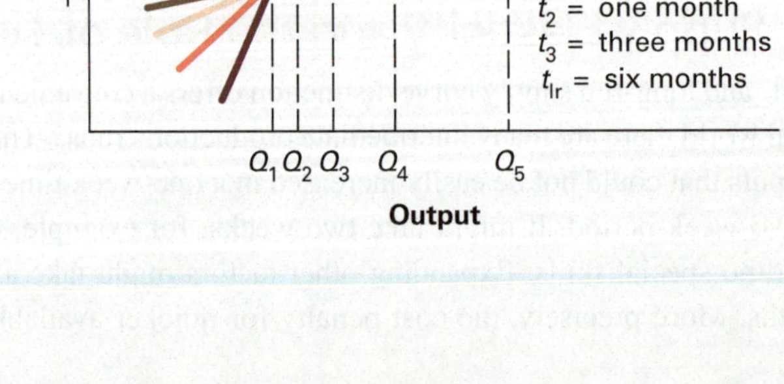

months, the rate of output expands to Q_4. In the long run, when it is possible to adjust all inputs to the desired utilization levels (after a six-month time period, for example), firms are willing to supply Q_5 units of output at the market price of P_2.

9-7 The Role of Profits and Losses

Profit is a reward that business owners will earn if they produce a good that consumers value more (as measured by their willingness to pay) than the alternative goods that could have been produced with those same resources (as measured by the cost of bidding the resources away from their alternative uses). In contrast, losses are a penalty imposed on businesses that reduce the value produced from resources. Losses are a signal that the other goods that could have been produced with those same resources were of greater value than what is currently being produced. Losses and bankruptcies are the market's way of providing signals and incentives to bring such wasteful activities to a halt, releasing those resources for use in other more highly valued uses.

The price-taker model also highlights the role of profits and losses in directing the actions of entrepreneurs and resource suppliers in an economy. When consumer demand for a product increases, higher economic profits result in the entry of new firms to satisfy this increased demand. Additional resources flow into the production of the now more highly valued good and away from other industries. In contrast, when consumer demand for a product decreases, economic losses result in firms going out of business and reallocation of resources toward other industries where they are now more valuable. It is the profit and loss mechanism, driven by consumer demand and the costs of production that steers the allocation of resources in a market economy.

We live in a world of changing tastes and technology, imperfect knowledge, and uncertainty. Entrepreneurs can never be certain in advance if their ideas will be successful in the marketplace, and business decision-makers cannot be sure of future market prices or costs. Economics Nobel laureate Friedrich von Hayek (refer to the accompanying Outstanding Economist Box) viewed the competitive market system itself as a discovery process that

Tetra Images/Alamy

In central areas of large cities, the supply of parking spaces can be expanded only by using higher-cost space and higher-cost techniques, such as taller parking garages that use a large portion of the building for access ramps. As a result, the unit cost of parking spaces increases as the total number is expanded. Thus, provision of parking space is an increasing-cost industry.

Outstanding Economist

Friedrich A. von Hayek (1899-1992)

Apic/Getty Images

The writings of this 1974 Nobel Prize recipient spanned seven decades. Friedrich von Hayek's analysis of knowledge and markets greatly enhanced the understanding of how the competitive market process works. Hayek also made important contributions in the areas of monetary theory, law and economics, business cycles, and capital theory. He is also well known for the idea that market exchanges create an "extended order" in which perfect strangers who never meet nonetheless cooperate with one another to achieve their individual goals. Hayek stressed the role of the competitive market process as a procedure that helps us discover the best use of resources, the costs of production, and the prices of goods and services.

helps to identify and determine what the prices of goods and costs of resources are, as well as which products are more highly valued than their costs (and which are not). Just like a football game is a process that allows us to discover which team is better, the market is a process that helps us to discover the best uses for our resources. Without the process taking place, the answers would not be known. The answers are, rather, a result of discoveries that occur as the process unfolds.

Nonetheless, the reward–penalty structure of a market economy is clear. ***Firms that anticipate correctly the products and services for which future demand will be most urgent (relative to production costs) and produce and market them efficiently will make economic profits. Those that are inefficient and allocate resources incorrectly to areas of weak demand (relative to costs) will be penalized with losses.***

The firms most adept at giving consumers value for their money thrive and expand. Those less successful in doing so tend to shrink or even to disappear from the market. Free entry and the competitive process will protect the consumer from arbitrarily high prices. When profits are present, profit-seeking entrepreneurs will put more resources into these markets, supply will expand, and eventually the price will be driven down to the unit cost.

9-8 Competition Promotes Prosperity

Keys to Economic Prosperity

Competition

Competition motivates businesses to produce efficiently, cater to the views of consumers, and search for innovative improvements.

The price-taker model highlights the importance of the competitive process. Competition puts pressure on producers to operate efficiently and use resources wisely. Holding quality constant, lower costs will mean more profit. Therefore, pursuit of profit will encourage each firm to minimize its cost of production—to use the set of resources least valued in other uses to produce the desired output. Firms that fail to keep costs low will be driven from the market.

Similarly, firms in competitive markets have a strong incentive to discover and produce goods and services that consumers value highly relative to cost. Thus, resources will be drawn to those uses where they are most productive, as judged by the consumers' willingness to pay. The ability of firms freely to expand or contract their businesses and enter or exit markets means that resources will not be trapped unproductively in a particular industry when they're valued more highly elsewhere.

If firms are going to be successful in competitive markets, they must also be innovative and forward-looking. The production techniques and product offerings that lead to success

Entrepreneurs Who Have Changed Our Lives

Sam Walton

ZUMA Press, Inc./Alamy Stock Photo

Innovation, low prices, quality products, and customer service are key attributes of market success. During the past half century, perhaps no retailer has followed this prescription better than Sam Walton and the Walmart stores he founded.

Prior to opening his first Walmart store in Rogers, Arkansas, in 1962, Walton owned and operated multiple franchise locations of a five-and-dime variety store named Ben Franklin across the state of Arkansas. Walton had graduated from the University of Missouri with a degree in economics and began working in retail right out of college.

Walton was always watching his competitors, and he made no bones about copying what they did well. In the late 1950s, he learned about the discount stores that had shown up in New England. Owners were buying merchandise at low prices in large quantities and selling them at low prices in threadbare outlets. They earned lower profits on each item but made up for it by selling so many items.

Walton's versatility and determination were essential to his success. Soon, he was opening one Walmart after another, around the country and then the world. By the 1980s, Walmart was the largest retailer in the world, a position it continued to occupy until 2019 when it was eclipsed by Amazon. For many years, Walton was the richest man in the United States, and his heirs are now one of the world's richest families.

What was Walton's secret? He focused on smaller cities and towns–markets other major retailers had avoided–and emphasized logistics. Walton developed a network of regional warehouses and started his own trucking service, enabling him to provide consumers with discounted name-brand merchandise. Through hard work and innovation, Walton and his company have lowered the prices of goods to consumers around the world.

Sources: Lauren Debter, "Amazon Surpasses Walmart as the World's Largest Retailer," *Forbes*, May 15, 2019.

Vance H. Trimble, *Sam Walton: The Inside Story of America's Richest Man* (New York: Dutton, 1990).

"Sam Walton," *Biography*, biography.com, https://www.biography.com/business-figure/sam-walton.

today will not necessarily pass the competitive market test tomorrow. Producers who survive in a competitive environment cannot become complacent. On the contrary, they must be willing to experiment and quick to adopt improved methods.

In competitive markets, business firms must serve the interests of consumers. As Adam Smith noted about 250 years ago, competition harnesses personal self-interest and channels it into activities that enhance our living standards. Smith stated that

> It is not from the benevolence of the butcher, the brewer, or the baker, that we expect our dinner, but from their regard to their own self-interest. We address ourselves, not to their humanity but to their self-love, and never talk to them of our own necessities, but of their advantages.[4]

Sellers profit when they supply products valued more highly than the resources needed to make them. But their actions also help the rest of us get more value from those resources than we would otherwise. As Smith properly noticed, personal self-interest is a powerful source of economic progress when it is directed by the competitive market process.

[4]Adam Smith, *An Inquiry into the Nature and Causes of the Wealth of Nations* (1776; Cannan's ed., Chicago: University of Chicago Press, 1976), 18.

Key Points

- A firm facing a perfectly elastic demand for its product is a price taker. A firm that can raise its price without losing all of its customers (and that must lower its price in order to sell more units) is a price searcher.
- To maximize profit, a price taker will expand its output as long as the sale of additional units adds more to revenues than to costs. Therefore, the profit-maximizing price taker will produce the output level at which marginal revenue (and price) equals marginal cost.
- A firm that experiences losses but that anticipates being able to cover its costs in the long run will operate in the short run if it can cover its average variable costs. Conversely, the firm will shut down if it cannot cover its average variable costs. A firm that does not anticipate being able to cover its average total cost even in the long run will minimize losses by immediately going out of business.
- The price taker's short-run marginal cost curve (above its average variable cost) is its supply curve. The short-run market supply curve is the horizontal summation of the marginal cost curves (above *AVC*) of the firms in the industry.
- When the market price exceeds the firm's average total cost, it will earn an economic profit. When entry barriers are absent, profits will attract new firms into the industry and stimulate the existing firms to expand. This increasing market supply continues and puts downward pressure on the price until it reaches the level of average total cost, eliminating the economic profit.
- When the market price is less than the firm's average total cost, the resulting losses imply that the resources could be used elsewhere to produce more value. Losses will cause firms to leave the industry or to reduce the scale of their operations. This declining market supply continues and puts upward pressure on price until the firms remaining in the market are once again able to earn normal returns (zero economic profit).
- As the output of an industry expands in response to rising demand, "fixed" resources like the size of the firm's plant will make it costly for firms to expand output quickly. The diminishing returns and rising marginal costs of firms explain why the short-run market supply curve slopes upward to the right.
- Normally, as industry output expands, rising factor prices push the costs of each firm upward, causing the long-run market supply curve to slope upward to the right also. However, in the long run, firms can alter the size of their plants and other resources that are fixed in the short run. As a result, the market supply curve is generally more elastic in the long run than the short run.
- Firms earn economic profit by producing goods that can be sold for more than the cost of the resources required to produce them. Profit is a reward people get for increasing the value of resources. Conversely, losses are a penalty imposed on those who use resources in a way that reduces their value.
- Competition motivates producers to operate efficiently, heed the views of consumers, and discover better products and lower-cost production methods. In competitive markets, self-interested producers will be directed toward wealth-creating activities that generate economic progress.

Critical Analysis Questions

1. Farmers are often heard to complain about the high costs of machinery, labor, and fertilizer, suggesting that these costs drive down their profits. Does it follow that if, for example, the price of fertilizer fell by 10 percent, farming (a highly competitive industry with low barriers to entry) would be more profitable? Explain.
2. *If the firms in a price-taker market are making short-run profits, what will happen to the market price in the long run? Explain.
3. "In a price-taker market, if a business operator produces efficiently—that is, if the cost of producing the good is minimized—the operator will be able to make at least a normal profit." True or false? Explain.
4. What is the shape of the demand curve confronted by a price-taker firm? Does the price-taker firm have to decide what price to charge?
5. If coffee suppliers are price takers, how will an unanticipated increase in demand for their product affect each of the following, in a market that was initially in long-run equilibrium?
   a. the short-run market price of the product
   b. industry output in the short run
   c. profitability in the short run
   d. the long-run market price in the industry
   e. industry output in the long run
   f. profitability in the long run

6. *Suppose that the development of a new drought-resistant hybrid seed corn leads to a 50 percent increase in the average yield per acre without increasing the cost to the farmers who use the new technology. If the producers in the corn production industry were price takers, what would happen to the following?
   a. the price of corn
   b. the profitability of corn farmers who quickly adopt the new technology
   c. the profitability of corn farmers who are slow to adopt the new technology
   d. the price of soybeans, a substitute product for corn
7. If a price-taker firm is making losses, how does it decide whether or not to go out of business? What is the difference between shutting down in the short run and going out of business in the long run?
8. Why does the short-run market supply curve for a product slope upward to the right? Why does the long-run market supply curve generally slope upward to the right? Why is the long-run market supply curve generally more elastic than the short-run supply curve?
9. *How does competition among firms affect the incentive of each firm to (a) operate efficiently (produce at a low per-unit cost) and (b) produce goods that consumers value? What happens to firms that fail to do these two things?
10. Will firms in a price-taker market be able to earn profits in the long run? Why or why not? What determines profitability? Discuss.
11. *Occasionally, drought conditions substantially reduce the size of the corn, wheat, and soybean crops, three commodities for which demand is inelastic. Use the price-taker model to determine how a drought would affect (a) prices of the three commodities, (b) revenue from the three crops, and (c) the profitability of those farming the three crops.
12. What is a price-taker firm? What is a price-searcher firm? Provide some examples of both.
13. New York City licenses taxicabs, and the number of licenses was increased only once (by 2,000 in 1996 to around 14,000) since the system was created in 1937. The licenses are tradable, and the market price of the licenses was more than a million dollars in 2016 prior to the entry of Uber and Lyft. Why did the licenses sell for such a high price? Did the limitations on the number of taxis in New York City make the operation of taxis more profitable? Who benefited from this system? What impact did the entry of Uber and Lyft have on taxi fares and the market price of the licenses?
14. Government policies mandating the use of ethanol in gasoline have led to a sharp increase in the demand for corn. What impact did this increase in demand for corn have on (a) the price of corn; (b) the quantity of corn supplied; (c) the cost of producing soybeans and wheat, crops that are often produced on land suitable for production of corn; (d) the price of cereals, tortillas, and other products produced from corn; and (e) the price of beef, chicken, and pork, meats produced from animals that are generally fed large quantities of corn? Explain each of your answers.
15. *The accompanying table presents the expected cost and revenue data for the Tucker Tomato Farm. The Tuckers produce tomatoes in a greenhouse and sell them wholesale in a price-taker market.
   a. Fill in the firm's marginal cost, average variable cost, average total cost, and profit schedules.
   b. If the Tuckers are profit maximizers, how many tomatoes should they produce when the market price is $500 per ton? Indicate their profits.
   c. Indicate the firm's output level and maximum profit if the market price of tomatoes increases to $550 per ton.
   d. How many units would the Tucker Tomato Farm produce if the price of tomatoes fell to $450 per ton? What would be the firm's profits? Should the firm stay in business? Explain.

Cost and Revenue Schedules for Tucker Tomato Farm, Inc.

Output (Tons per Month)	Total Cost	Price per Ton	Marginal Cost	Average Variable Cost	Average Total Cost	Profits (Monthly)
0	$1,000	$500	n/a	n/a	n/a	—
1	1,200	500	—	—	—	—
2	1,350	500	—	—	—	—
3	1,550	500	—	—	—	—
4	1,900	500	—	—	—	—
5	2,300	500	—	—	—	—
6	2,750	500	—	—	—	—
7	3,250	500	—	—	—	—
8	3,800	500	—	—	—	—
9	4,400	500	—	—	—	—
10	5,150	500	—	—	—	—

16. In the accompanying table, you are given information about two firms that compete in a price-taker market. Assume that fixed costs for each firm are $20.

a. Complete the table.

b. What is the lowest price at which firm A will produce?

c. How many units of output will it produce at that price? (Assume that it cannot produce fractional units.)

d. What is the lowest price at which firm B will produce?

e. How many units of output will it produce?

f. How many units will firm A produce if the market price is $20?

g. How many units will firm B produce at the $20 price? (Assume that it cannot produce fractional units.)

h. If each firm's total fixed costs are $20 and the price of output is $20, which firm would earn a higher net profit or incur a smaller loss?

i. How much would that net profit or loss be?

*Asterisk denotes questions for which answers are given in Appendix B.

Firm A				Firm B			
Quantity	Total Variable Cost	Marginal Cost	Average Variable Cost	Quantity	Total Variable Cost	Marginal Cost	Average Variable Cost
1	$24	—	—	1	$8	—	—
2	30	—	—	2	10	—	—
3	38	—	—	3	16	—	—
4	48	—	—	4	24	—	—
5	62	—	—	5	36	—	—
6	82	—	—	6	56	—	—
7	110	—	—	7	86	—	—

Chapter 10
Price-Searcher Markets with Low Entry Barriers

> [T]he price to the price searcher is not determined for him as if by some impersonal market mechanism. Instead he must search out the optimal (wealth-maximizing) price. And, not knowing the demand schedule exactly, he will have to resort to retrial-and-error search processes.
>
> –Armen A. Alchian and William R. Allen[1]

As we noted in the previous chapter, price-taker firms decide what output to produce, but they do not have a pricing decision to make. They must take the market-determined price for their output, and they operate in a market with low entry barriers. In this chapter, we will focus on markets in which entry barriers are also low, but firms can instead decide the price they charge. These firms differ in that they face a downward sloping demand curve. If they increase their price they will sell fewer units, and if they reduce their price they will sell more units. This is in contrast to a price-taker firm whose horizontal demand curve means they lose all their sales if they raise price.

Learning Objectives

10.1 Identify the characteristics of competitive price-searcher markets.

10.2 List some of the strategies a price searcher can use in order to gain an advantage relative to rivals.

10.3 Indicate how a price searcher decides what price to charge and what quantity to produce to maximize profits.

10.4 Explain why firms in competitive price-searcher markets can earn profits in the short run, but not in the long run, using the concept of contestable markets.

10.5 Explain why some economists argue that competitive price-searcher markets are inefficient, while others argue this is not the case.

10.6 State the conditions necessary for a price searcher to increase profits through price discrimination.

10.7 Explain the incentive of entrepreneurs in price-searcher markets to innovate and develop new products that improve our living standards.

[1]Armen A. Alchian and William R. Allen, *University Economics*, 2nd ed. (Belmont, CA: Wadsworth Publishing, 1967), 113.

10-1 Competitive Price-Searcher Markets

Competitive price-searcher market
A market in which the firms have a downward-sloping demand curve, and entry into and exit from the market are relatively easy.

Differentiated products
Products distinguished from similar products by characteristics like quality, design, location, and method of promotion.

Monopolistic competition
A term often used by economists to describe markets characterized by a large number of sellers that supply differentiated products to a market with low barriers to entry. Essentially, it is an alternative term for a competitive price-searcher market.

Markets that are characterized by (1) low entry barriers and (2) firms that face a downward-sloping demand curve are called **competitive price-searcher markets.**[2] The low entry barriers ensure that these markets are competitive, and the firm's downward-sloping demand curve means that the sellers in these markets have to search for the price and output combination that will maximize their profits.

In contrast with price-taker markets, in which the firms produce identical products, price searchers produce **differentiated products**. For example, a hamburger from Burger King is not identical to one from McDonald's or Five Guys. The products supplied by the alternative sellers may differ in their design, dependability, location, packaging, and a multitude of other factors. This product differentiation explains why the firms confront a downward-sloping demand curve. Because some consumers are willing to pay more to get the specific product they like best, the firm will lose some but not all its customers to rivals if it raises its price.

Rival firms, however, supply products that are quite similar. Because good substitutes are readily available from other suppliers, the demand curve faced by the firms in competitive price-searcher markets will be downward sloping, but highly elastic.

Given the low entry barriers, new entrants will be attracted if an activity is profitable. Thus, sellers in competitive price-searcher markets face competition from both firms already in the market and potential new firms that might be attracted.

Sometimes economists use the term **monopolistic competition** to describe markets quite similar to those of the competitive price-searcher model, but because there is nothing "monopolistic" about these markets, we believe that this term is misleading. Competitive price searcher is much more descriptive of the conditions in these markets. However, students should be aware that the expression "monopolistic competition" is often used to describe markets like those analyzed in this chapter.

PHOVOIR/Alamy Stock Photo

In the highly competitive market for custom-fitted golf clubs, firms use competitive weapons such as style, swingweight, variable length and club-shaft flexibility, advertising, and celebrity endorsements. Firms in this market are price searchers.

For the price searcher, demand is not simply a given. Price searchers must try to estimate how buyers will respond to the various prices that might be charged. In essence, the firm must try to figure out what the demand curve for its product looks like. The firm, by changing product quality, style, location, and service (among many other factors), and by advertising, can also alter the demand for its products. It can increase demand by drawing customers from rivals if it can convince consumers that its products provide more value. In the real world, most firms occupy the complex and risky territory of the price searcher.

10-1a Price and Output in Competitive Price-Searcher Markets

How does a price searcher decide what price to charge and what level of output to produce? For the price searcher, reducing price in order to expand output and sales has two conflicting influences on total revenue, illustrated by areas in **Exhibit 10-1**. First, the increase in sales (from q_1 to Q_2) due to the lower price will, by itself, add to the revenue of the price searcher as revenue is obtained on the additional units sold. Second, the price reduction, because it applies to all units sold—*including those that could otherwise have been sold at a higher price* (P_1, rather than the lower price, P_2)—reduces the revenue received on the original q_1 units of output.

[2]It is important to distinguish between the demand curve faced by the firm and the market demand curve. The competitive price-searcher model focuses on the *firm's* demand curve.

Exhibit 10-1 Marginal Revenue of a Price Searcher

When a firm faces a downward-sloping demand curve, a price reduction that increases sales will exert two conflicting influences on total revenue. First, total revenue will rise because of an increase in the number of units sold (from q_1 to q_2). However, revenue losses from the lower price (P_2) on units that could have been sold at a higher price (P_1) will at least partially offset the additional revenues from increased sales. Therefore, the marginal revenue curve will lie inside the firm's demand curve.

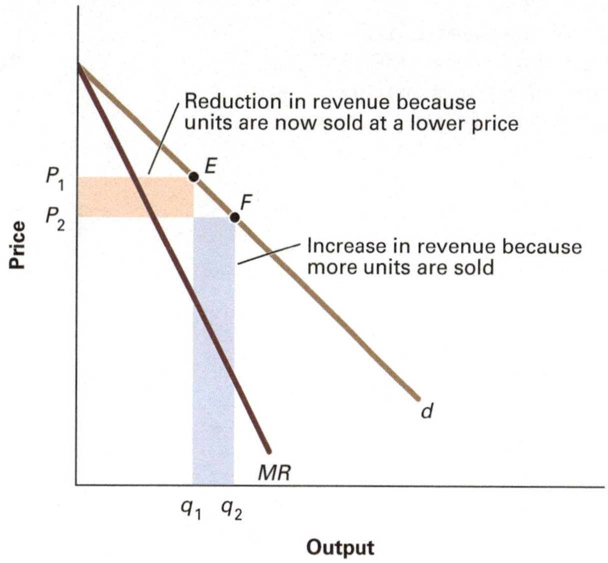

A numerical example will help to illustrate. Suppose a firm could sell three units at $5 for a total revenue of $15, or at a reduced price of $4 it could sell 4 units for a total revenue of $16. When the firm lowers price to $4 to sell the fourth unit, this additional unit sold adds $4 to revenue. But there is an offsetting factor: The three units that could have been sold at $5 now only sell for $4, so the firm loses $1 in revenue on each of those original three units. Thus, the net addition to the firm's revenue (the marginal revenue from the sale of the fourth unit) is only $1, as the loss of $3 is deducted from the gain of $4. This can also be seen in the firm's total revenue, which was $15 at an output of three units (sold at $5) and only $16 at an output of four units (sold at $4).

As price is lowered, these two conflicting forces will result in marginal revenue (a change in total revenue) that is less than the selling price of the additional units. The price searcher's marginal revenue will always be less than price because the prices of units that could have been sold for more will be reduced as price is lowered in order to expand sales. Therefore, as Exhibit 10-1 shows, the price searcher's marginal revenue curve will always lie below the firm's demand curve.[3] (Remember, the lowercase *d* is used when the reference is to the *firm's* demand curve.)

All firms maximize profits by producing all units for which marginal revenue is greater than marginal cost. Therefore, a price searcher will continue to lower price and expand output until marginal revenue is equal to marginal cost.

Exhibit 10-2 illustrates the profit-maximizing price and output. The price searcher will maximize profit by producing the level of output *q*, where marginal revenue is equal to marginal cost ($MC = MR$). For any output level less than *q* (for example, *R*), a price reduction and resulting sales expansion will add more to revenues than to costs, increasing profit. In contrast, all units beyond *q* (for example, *S*) add more to costs than to revenues, reducing profit. Profits will therefore be maximized by producing the output level *q*. The price the firm should charge is simply the price that will result in exactly *q* units being sold, which is a price of *P*. This price can be found by going up to the demand curve (to point A) at the profit-maximizing level of output.

[3]For a straight-line demand curve, the marginal revenue curve will bisect any line from the *y*-axis to the demand curve, drawn parallel to the *x*-axis.

Exhibit 10-2 The Price Searcher's Price and Output

A price searcher maximizes its profits by producing output *q*, for which *MR* = *MC*, and charging price *P*. The firm is making economic profits. What impact will these profits have if this is a typical firm?

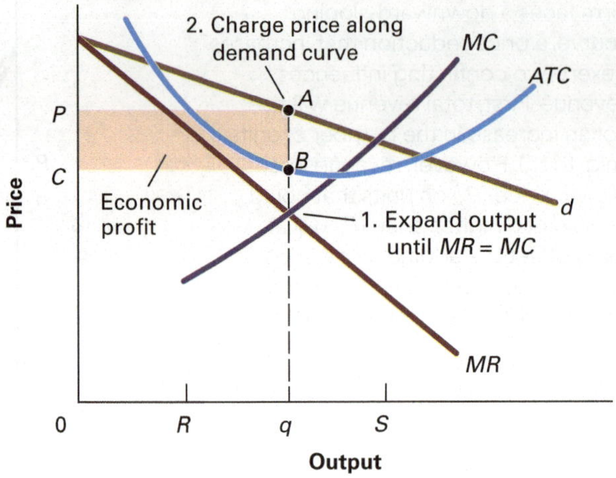

The firm in Exhibit 10-2 is making an economic profit in the short run. Total revenues *PAq*0 exceed the firm's total costs *CBq*0 at the profit-maximizing output level *q*. Given low barriers to entry in these markets, in the long run economic profits will result in other firms entering the market. These new rivals will draw customers away from existing firms and thereby reduce their demand. This entry of new firms into the market will continue until competition among rivals shifts the demand curve in far enough to eliminate the economic profit earned by the firms in the industry.

As **Exhibit 10-3** illustrates, when long-run equilibrium is present in a competitive price-searcher market, the price will equal per-unit cost. Firms will produce at the *MR* = *MC* output level, but they will be unable to earn economic profits because competitive pressures will force the price down to the per-unit cost level.

If losses are present in a specific market, with time, some of the firms in the market will go out of business. As firms leave, some of their previous customers will buy from other firms. The demand curve facing the remaining firms in the industry will then shift outward

Exhibit 10-3 Competitive Price-Searcher and Long-Run Normal Profit

Because firms are free to enter and exit the market, competition will eventually drive down prices to the level of average total cost for price searchers.

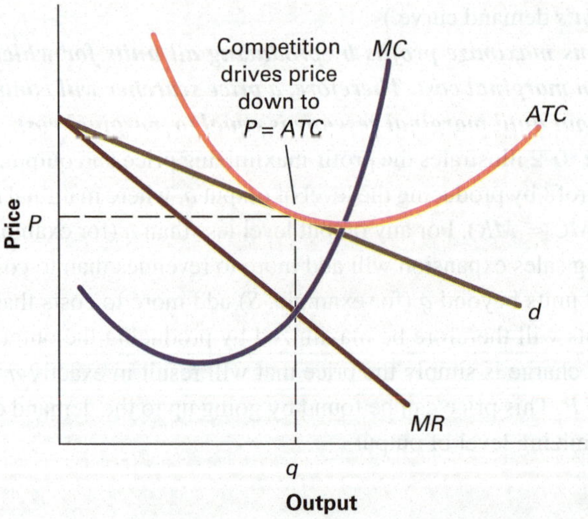

until the economic losses are eliminated and the long-run, zero-profit equilibrium illustrated by Exhibit 10-3 is restored.

Consider the role of profits and losses in competitive price-searcher markets. Profits will attract both new firms and additional investment capital into the market. In turn, the increased availability of the product (and similar products) will drive down the price until the profits are eliminated. Conversely, economic losses will cause competitors to exit the market and investment capital to move elsewhere. This will reduce the supply of the product and eventually make it possible for the firms remaining in the market to charge a price sufficient to cover their unit costs. ***Thus, firms in competitive price-searcher markets can make either economic profits or losses in the short run. But, after long-run adjustments occur, only a normal profit (that is, zero economic profit) will be possible because entry barriers are low and competition is strong.***

10-2 Contestable Markets and the Competitive Process

If firms can easily enter a market with little risk of suffering a substantial loss if they later exit the market, competition is likely to be intense, even if there are only a few firms operating within it. Markets in which firms can enter and exit with minimal risk are known as **contestable markets**.[4] Even if entering a contestable market requires a substantial amount of capital, this won't be a major deterrent if the funds can largely be recovered should the firm need to exit. This will be the case when the assets necessary to compete in a market can be either leased for short time periods or resold at something near their original purchase price.

Contestable market
A market in which the costs of entry and exit are low, so a firm risks little by entering. Efficient production and zero economic profits should prevail in a contestable market.

When airport landing rights and facilities are available, an airline route is a classic example of a contestable market. Even if only one airline currently serves a particular route, it faces the threat that other airlines will enter the market. Indeed, airlines often enter and exit on certain routes as prices, and profitability, change over time with demand. Because it is a contestable market, the threat of competitors entering the market makes the market effectively competitive even if only one airline currently serves the route.

Dushlik/Shutterstock.com

Airliners are extremely expensive, so their cost might be a barrier to entry. But airplanes can also be leased and are highly mobile among markets, as are pilots, flight attendants, and office workers. These highly mobile resources allow firms to enter and exit a given transportation market with relative ease. Such a market is contestable.

[4]The classic article on this topic is William J. Baumol's "Contestable Markets: An Uprising in the Theory of Industry Structure," *American Economic Review* 72 (March 1982): 1–15.

In a contestable market, potential competition, as well as actual entry, will discipline sellers. When entry and exit are not expensive, even a firm alone in a market faces the serious prospect of competition. Two important conditions will be present in contestable markets: (1) Prices above the level necessary to achieve zero economic profits will not be sustained, and (2) the costs of production will be kept to a minimum. This is because production inefficiencies and prices that are above costs present a profitable opportunity for new entrants. Predictably, profit-seeking rivals will enter and drive the price down to the level of per-unit costs.

The contestable market model has important policy implications. If policy-makers are concerned that a market is not sufficiently competitive, they should examine its entry barriers and what might be done to make it contestable. Much of economists' enthusiasm for deregulation can be traced to the fact that regulation often impedes market entry. Many economists believe that deregulating markets to make entry easier can lead to lower prices and better performance than other alternatives, including directly regulating prices.

10-3 Evaluating Competitive Price-Searcher Markets

Because the long-run equilibrium conditions in price-taker markets are generally consistent with ideal economic efficiency, it is useful to compare and contrast them with long-run conditions in competitive price-searcher markets.

First, let us consider the similarities. Because of the low entry barriers, both price takers and competitive price searchers will have a strong incentive to serve the interests of consumers. Neither will be able to earn long-run economic profits. In the long run, competition will drive prices down to the level of average total cost in both price-taker and competitive price-searcher markets. Furthermore, entrepreneurs in both price-taker and price-searcher markets have a strong incentive to manage and operate their businesses efficiently. In both cases, operational inefficiency will lead to higher costs, losses, and forced exit from the market. Similarly, price takers and competitive price searchers alike will be motivated to develop and adopt new, cost-reducing procedures and techniques because lower costs will lead to higher short-run profits (or at least smaller losses).

The responses to changing demand conditions in price-taker and competitive price-searcher markets are also similar. In both cases, any increase in market demand that was not already expected leads to higher prices, short-run profits, expanded output, and the entry of new firms. With the entry of new producers and the expanded output of existing firms, the market supply will increase, putting downward pressure on the price. Profits drive this process until the market price falls to the level of average total cost, squeezing out all economic profit. Correspondingly, lower demand will lead to lower prices and short-run losses, causing output to fall and some firms to exit. As the market supply declines, prices will rise until the short-run losses are eliminated and the firms remaining in the market can again cover their costs. Thus, profits and losses direct the output decisions and market supply in both price-taker and competitive price-searcher markets.

What are some of the differences between the two market structures? As **Exhibit 10-4** shows, the price taker confronts a horizontal demand curve, while the demand curve of the price-searcher firm is downward sloping. This is important: It means that the marginal revenue of the price-searcher will be less than, not equal to, the price charged for the product sold. So, when the price searcher expands output until *MR* = *MC*, the price will still exceed the marginal cost (panel b). In contrast, the price charged by a profit-maximizing price taker will equal the marginal cost (panel a). In addition, when a price searcher is in long-run equilibrium, the firm's output rate will be less than the rate that minimizes average total cost. The price searcher would have a lower per-unit cost ($0.97 rather than $1.00) if a larger output were produced, but *MR* would be even less.

Exhibit 10-4 Comparing Price-Taker and Price-Searcher Markets

Here, we illustrate the long-run equilibrium conditions of a price taker and a price searcher when entry barriers are low. In both cases, the price is equal to the average total cost, and economic profit is zero. However, because the price searcher confronts a downward-sloping demand curve for its product, its profit-maximizing price exceeds marginal cost, and output is not large enough to minimize average total cost when the market is in long-run equilibrium. For identical cost conditions, the price of the product in a price-searcher market will be slightly higher than in a price-taker market. Some argue that this higher price is indicative of inefficiency, whereas others believe that it merely reflects the higher cost accompanying greater variety and convenience.

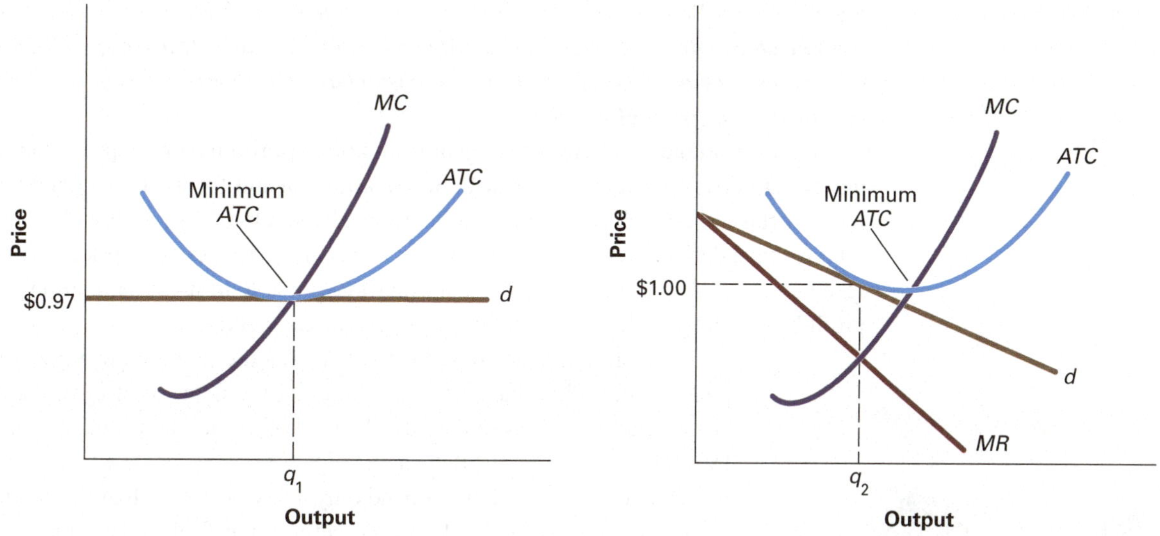

(a) Price taker **(b) Price searcher**

Some argue that the slightly higher prices (and unit costs) in competitive price-searcher markets indicate that these markets allocate goods and services inefficiently. However, it is important to recognize that the higher prices reflect the fact that it is costly to provide the greater product variety and diversity found in competitive price-searcher markets. But a broader range of choices also provides benefits. The greater variety makes it possible for a wider range of consumers to obtain the quality, style, and accompanying service that best fit their preferences and specific situation.

Are the higher prices accompanying the greater diversity worth the cost? This question can't be answered with certainty, but in some cases it is clear that consumers are willing to pay for it. For example, many consumers patronize small, conveniently located stores, even though they know that the same items are available at lower prices at large supermarkets.

The two market structures also differ with regard to advertising: Price searchers often advertise, but price takers do not. Like variety, advertising is costly, and in the long run, consumers cover this cost in the form of higher prices. Do advertised products provide enough information and variety to justify the higher cost from the consumer's viewpoint? We cannot know for certain. However, we do know that producers are always free to use low-priced, more uniform, and less-advertised products to lure buyers away from firms that advertise and provide variety at a higher price. Some firms do, and sometimes the strategy works; yet many consumers choose to buy advertised goods and pay the higher prices. This result suggests that many customers do find that advertised products and greater variety are worth the added cost.

10-4 A Special Case: Price Discrimination

So far, we have assumed that all sellers of a product will charge each customer the same price. Sometimes, though, price searchers can increase their revenues (and profits) by charging different prices to different groups of consumers. Businesses like hotels, restaurants, and drugstores often charge senior citizens less than other customers. Students and children are often given discounts at movie theaters and athletic events. Bars offer "ladies' night" discounts on drinks for women. Colleges often give financial aid (reduced tuition) to students from low-income families, or scholarships to students with good grades. These practices are called **price discrimination**. ***To gain from such a practice, price searchers must be able to do two things: (1) identify and separate at least two groups with differing elasticities of demand and (2) prevent those who buy at the low price from reselling to the customers charged higher prices.***

Price discrimination
A practice whereby a seller charges different consumers different prices for the same product or service.

Let us examine how sellers may gain from price discrimination. Suppose that a seller has two groups of customers: one with an inelastic demand for its product and the other with an elastic demand. An increase in the price charged the first group will increase the total revenue derived from that group. At the same time, a reduction in price will increase revenues derived from the latter. Thus, a seller may be able to increase total revenue and profit by charging the first group a higher price than the second.

The pricing of airline tickets illustrates the potential of price discrimination. The airline industry has found that the demand of business fliers is substantially less elastic than the demand of vacationers, students, and other travelers. Thus, airlines often charge higher fares to people who are unwilling to stay over a weekend, who spend only a day or two at their destination, and who make reservations a short time before their flight. These high fares fall primarily on business travelers, who are less sensitive to price. In contrast, discount fares are offered to fliers willing to make reservations well in advance, travel during off-peak hours, and stay at their destinations over a weekend before returning home. Such travelers are likely to be vacationers and students, who are highly sensitive to price.

Lisa F. Young/Shutterstock.com

Students from low-income families are likely to be more sensitive to tuition charges than those from high-income families. Colleges often make scholarships and other forms of financial aid more readily available to low-income students. This price discrimination makes it possible for them to generate larger revenues from tuition than would otherwise be the case.

Exhibit 10-5 illustrates the logic of this policy. Panel a shows what would happen if a single price were charged to all customers. Given the demand, the profit-maximizing firm expands output to 100, where *MR* equals *MC*. The profit-maximizing price on coast-to-coast flights is \$400, which generates \$40,000 of revenue per flight. Because the marginal cost per passenger is \$100, this provides the airline with net operating revenue of \$30,000 with which to cover other costs.

However, as panel b shows, although the market demand schedule is unchanged, the airline can do even better if it uses price discrimination. When it charges business travelers \$500, most of these passengers continue to use the airline, because their demand is highly inelastic. Conversely, a \$100 price cut generates substantial additional ticket sales from price-sensitive vacationers, students, and others whose demands are more elastic. Therefore, with price discrimination, the airline can sell sixty tickets (primarily to business travelers) at \$500 and sixty additional tickets to others at \$300. Total revenue jumps to \$48,000 and leaves the airline with \$36,000 (\$48,000 minus 120 times the \$100 marginal cost per passenger) of revenue in excess of variable cost. Compared with the single-price outcome (panel a), the price-discrimination strategy expands profit by \$6,000.

When sellers can segment their market (at a low cost) into groups with differing price elasticities of demand, price discrimination can increase profits. For *each group*, the seller will maximize profit by equating marginal cost and marginal revenue. This rule will lead to higher prices for groups with a less elastic demand and lower prices for those with a more

Exhibit 10-5 Price Discrimination

As panel (a) illustrates, a $400 ticket price will maximize profits on coast-to-coast flights if an airline charges a single price. However, the airline can do still better if it raises the price to $500 for passengers with a highly inelastic demand (business travelers) and reduces the price to $300 for travelers with a more elastic demand (for example, students and vacationers). When sellers can segment their market, they can gain by (1) charging a higher price to consumers with a less elastic demand and (2) offering discounts to customers whose demand is more elastic.

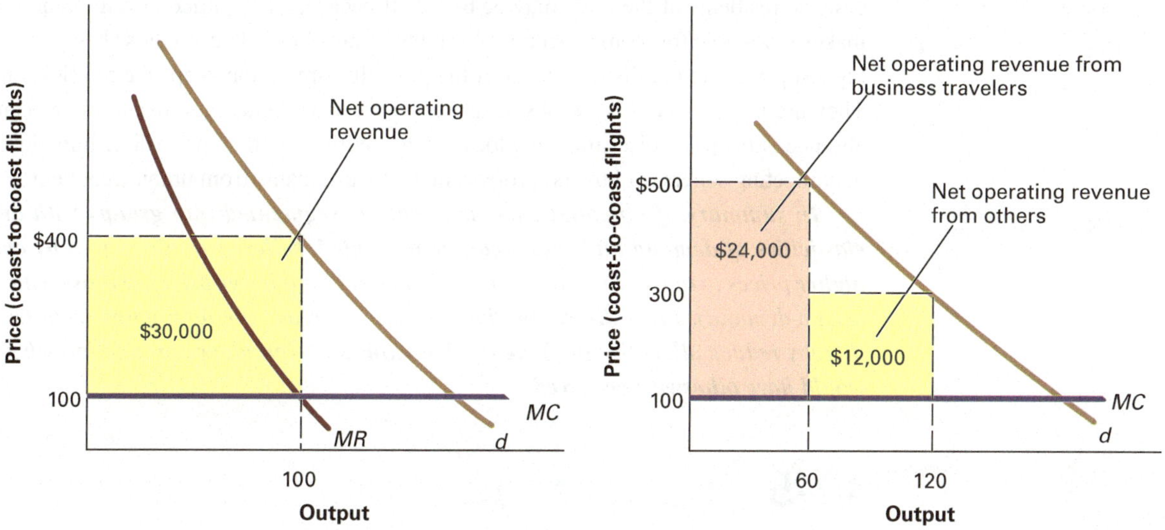

(a) Seller charges a single price **(b) Seller uses price discrimination**

elastic demand. Compared with the single-price situation, price discrimination increases profitability because a higher price increases the net revenue from groups with an inelastic demand, while a lower price increases the net revenue from price-sensitive customers. With price discrimination, the total quantity of units sold also increases (compare panel a with panel b) because the lower price charged to price-sensitive groups increases the quantity sold to them by more than the reduction in the quantity sold to the less price sensitive group that results from charging them higher prices.

Of course, this will work only if the two groups can't trade with each other. Movie theaters sell children's tickets to kids, and the tickets cannot be used by adults. Notice, though, that they don't try to sell popcorn at lower prices to children because popcorn could be too easily resold to adults.

How do buyers fare when a seller can price discriminate? Some buyers pay more than they would if a single, intermediate price were offered. They purchase fewer units, and they are worse off. In contrast, those for whom the price-discrimination process lowers the price are better off. Of course, with some products, such as airline transportation, a single buyer might be better off with some purchases and worse off with others.

On balance, however, we can expect that output will be greater with price discrimination than it would be with a single price. The market is not as understocked as it would have been in the absence of the price discrimination. So from an allocative efficiency standpoint, price discrimination gets high marks; it allows more trades, reducing the inefficiency due to price being set above marginal cost. Some of the gains that would accrue to consumers with an inelastic demand are transferred to the price searcher as increased revenue, but additional gains from trade are created by the increased output of goods that would be lost if price discrimination were absent.

In some markets, there is an additional gain from price discrimination: Production may occur that would be lost entirely if only a single price could be charged. With price discrimination, some otherwise unprofitable firms may be able to generate enough additional revenue to operate successfully in the marketplace. For example, some small towns might not provide enough revenue at a single price to enable a local physician to cover their opportunity costs. However, if the physician is able to discriminate on the basis of income, charging higher-income patients more than normal rates and lower-income patients less, the resulting revenues from practicing in the small town may enable the physician to stay in the community. In this case, all residents of the town may be better off because of the price discrimination, since it makes it possible for them to access a local physician. After all, even those being charged the highest prices are not disadvantaged if the price discrimination keeps the physician in town. They are just as able to seek physician services elsewhere as they would have been in the absence of the price-discriminating local doctor. With or without price discrimination, access to competing sellers (or buyers) protects market participants from unfair treatment.

In summary, if potential customers can be segmented into groups with different elasticities of demand and resale can be prevented, sellers can often gain by charging higher prices to those with the less elastic demand (and lower prices to those with a more elastic demand). Price discrimination can also increase the total gains from trade and thereby reduce allocative inefficiency. Sometimes it even allows production where none would have otherwise occurred.

10-5 Entrepreneurship and Economic Progress

Keys to Economic Prosperity

Entrepreneurship

Entrepreneurial discovery and the development of improved products and production processes provide a central element of economic progress.

Economic models like the price-taker and price-searcher models simplify conditions in order to help us understand complex relationships. But these models are not rich enough to fully capture all aspects of the dynamic process of competition. Competitive markets provide entrepreneurs with a strong incentive to innovate and discover better ways of doing things. However, if we are going to get the most from the available resources, they must be directed toward the activities that create the most value. This target, however, is an ever-shifting one. Discovery of new products, technologies, and organizational structures creates opportunities for some and diminishes them for others. To a large degree, market economies are successful because they provide entrepreneurs with a strong incentive to search for and act on opportunities to move resources toward higher-valued uses in a world of constant change.[5]

Entrepreneurs must make choices about how much and what kind of output to produce, what resources to employ, and what price to charge. They also must figure out the type of business structure, scale of operation, and combination of jointly supplied goods and services that will keep per-unit costs low. The entry of firms into an industry earning short-run economic profit also reflects the decisions and behavior of entrepreneurs searching for profit opportunities. Moreover, all of these choices must be made with imperfect information under conditions of uncertainty. While the assumptions and operational elements of the price-taker and price-searcher models incorporate these elements, they do not reflect the central role of entrepreneurial decision-making. Therefore, the picture is incomplete.

The role of the entrepreneur cannot be fully captured by the profit maximization assumption of a model. Better ways of doing things do not just happen; they must be discovered and developed by entrepreneurs. Further, the actions of entrepreneurs often cause

[5]For a more complete overview of entrepreneurship, refer to Mark Crosson, "Entrepreneurship," in *The New Palgrave: A Dictionary of Economics,* ed. John Eatwell et al. (New York: Stockton Press, 1987), 151–53; and Russell S. Sobel, "Entrepreneurship," in *The Concise Encyclopedia of Economics*, 2nd ed., ed. David R. Henderson (Indianapolis: Liberty Fund, 2007, available online at https://www.econlib.org/library/Enc/Entrepreneurship.html).

entirely new markets to appear, and others to disappear. A hypothetical newspaper ad to hire an entrepreneur might read something like this:

> Entrepreneur
> Diverse Skills Required
>
> **WANTED**
>
> Must be (1) alert to new business opportunities and new problems before they become obvious; (2) willing to back judgments with hard work and creative effort before others recognize the correctness of judgments; (3) able to make correct decisions and convince others of their validity, so as to attract additional financial backing; and (4) able to recognize own inevitable mistakes and to back away from incorrect decisions without wasting additional resources. Exciting, exhausting, high-risk position. Pay will be very good for success and very poor for failure.

Entrepreneurship is a process in which individual entrepreneurs discover previously unnoticed profit opportunities and act on them. In this framework profit opportunities always exist in the marketplace, but they must be discovered. The rate of discovery will depend on the reward. In economies where it is attractive to discover better ways of doing things, the discovery rate of wealth-creating opportunities will be higher and human progress more rapid.

Entrepreneurship and discovery can happen within existing business firms (often called "intrapreneurship") or from new entrants into the marketplace. Research shows that large existing corporations are more likely to make marginal improvements on existing products, while breakthrough ideas are more likely to come from new start-up firms.

An entrepreneur is someone who finds new combinations of resources and creates products and production methods that did not previously exist. Sifting through these many combinations is a complex task fraught with uncertainty because the number of ways of combining resources is almost limitless. A growing, vibrant economy will be characterized by the constant introduction of new products and services. Think of the new products that have been introduced during the last fifty years: computers, cell phones, 3D printers, video games, better coronary artery bypass techniques, and online social networks come to mind. Innovations like these have had an enormous impact on our lives.

But no one knows what the next innovative breakthrough will be or who will discover and develop it. Even smart professors, business leaders, and government officials are unable to pre-evaluate business ideas and differentiate between those that will succeed and the ones destined for failure. Not even entrepreneurs themselves can know for certain in advance whether their business idea will be profitable. The only real test is to try it out within the framework of the competitive market process.

10-5a Technology, Entrepreneurship, and Dynamic Competition

Over the past few decades technological advances have greatly increased the competitiveness of markets. By reducing search and transaction costs, and breaking down traditional barriers to entry, new technologies have revolutionized the way we shop, travel, and communicate.

Entrepreneurs Who Have Changed Our Lives

Fred Smith

Chip Somodevilla/Getty Images

Have you ever urgently needed to get an item from one place to another quickly? If so, FedEx founder and CEO Fred Smith has exerted an impact on your life.

When he was in college during the 1960s, Smith recognized that computers were going to play a central role in the future operation of business. Given their importance, the computers would have to be in good working order every day. If something went wrong, it would need to be fixed immediately. In turn, this would create a strong demand for a delivery system that could quickly get parts and materials to where they were needed.

Smith was convinced he knew how this could be done. In 1973, he founded FedEx to achieve this objective. His chief innovation was the development of a transportation system with a "central switch" or "central junction." For FedEx, this was Memphis, Tennessee. When one looks at moving an item from Detroit to Minneapolis via Memphis, it seems inefficient, says Smith. "But when you take all of the transactions on the network together, it's tremendously efficient."

While a student at Yale, Smith developed and explained the system in a paper for a business course. As Smith recounted later, the professor gave him a "C" because he thought the idea was infeasible. In the following decade, however, Smith founded FedEx and created the overnight delivery network of airplane and truck transportation outlined in his paper.

FedEx has revolutionized the express mail and package delivery system. It has forced competitors, from the U.S. Postal Service to United Parcel Service, to become more efficient and to make major changes in their operations. In 2023, FedEx had nearly 540,000 employees and generated over $90 billion in revenues. Smith can take great pride in the fact that the market gave him a much higher grade than his old professor.

Source: Revenue and employee figures from *Wall Street Journal*, at https://www.wsj.com/market-data/quotes/FDX/company-people

Diego Thomazini/Shutterstock.com

Technological advances and the sharing economy have increased dynamic competition in markets by reducing search and transaction costs.

In the early 1990s, if you wanted to purchase a book or a new backpack, you would have been limited to the selections offered by your local retailers, and you would have had to drive to each store or use your home phone to call around to see what was available and at what prices. Today, with a few simple clicks on a phone or computer, you can view the selections and prices of hundreds or thousands of sellers from all over the world and have the item shipped directly to your home. Websites such as Google, Amazon, and eBay have greatly reduced search and transaction costs for consumers and have allowed even smaller local businesses to have internet storefronts and sell their products to consumers in other geographic locations.

The rise of the "sharing economy," as it is sometimes called, is another example of how entrepreneurs have used technology to break down traditional barriers to entry and expand competition. Uber and Airbnb are two such examples. In the past, if you were to travel to a different city, you would have been limited to taking a traditional taxi and probably staying in one of the local hotels. In many cities the local taxi markets were anything but competitive, with governments limiting the number of cabs through licensing or medallions to increase the profitability of the politically powerful cab companies and driver unions. Today, ride-sharing services like Uber and Lyft allow virtually anyone with a car to become a driver, offer their services, and compete in this market. This has not only reduced the price of ground transportation, it also often increases the speed with which passengers can acquire the service. Similarly, Airbnb enhances the ability of those willing to provide short-term housing to communicate with potential customers seeking overnight accommodations. Again, the result is a more competitive market and more efficient use of resources.

The open and competitive nature of the app stores for the two major phone brands itself is a key source of these advances. In fact, a large proportion of the value of a cell phone to a typical user is created by the apps they have installed rather than the hardware itself. The programs and software on early cell phones were tightly controlled by the manufacturer of the phone. Today, individuals can invent apps and easily place them in the app stores, giving consumers thousands of choices for new apps to download. Open and competitive app marketplaces allow entrepreneurs to innovate and compete in new ways that enhance the value of what a cell phone can do for a user.

Dynamic competition is a key source of progress and prosperity. The technological advances pioneered by entrepreneurs over the past few decades have helped to increase the competitiveness of markets, thereby promoting prosperity and improving our standard of living.

10-5b Dynamic Competition, Innovation, and Business Failures

Business failures are often painful for the parties directly involved. From the standpoint of the entire economy, however, business failures and the shrinkage of other firms play an important role: They weed out less efficient, high-cost producers and production, and release resources to be employed more productively elsewhere. The assets and workers of firms that shrink or fail become available for use by others, supplying goods that are more highly valued by consumers, relative to their costs. Without this release of resources, the expansion of both profitable firms and the entire economy would be slowed. Viewed from this perspective, business failures are often the flip side of consumers shifting their spending toward firms offering improved products and/or lower prices.

While business failures occur for a variety of reasons, including poor management and misjudgment of market conditions, innovative actions by rivals is also a major contributing factor. When a firm introduces a new, improved product or comes up with a lower-cost method of supplying a good, it will attract buyers away from other firms. Entrepreneurship is inherently a disruptive force in an economy because the introduction of new products leads to the obsolescence of others, a process known as "creative destruction." As we discussed in Chapter 2, creative destruction is the term noted economist Joseph Schumpeter used to refer to the replacement of old products and production methods by innovative new ones that consumers judge to be superior. The process is one of the key sources of economic growth. Examples abound. The digital camera has virtually eliminated the use and production of film. The introduction of digital music resulted in the closure of stores selling CDs like Tower Records and Music Den. The innovations of streaming services and on-demand movies, Netflix, and Redbox have driven traditional movie rental stores like Blockbuster into bankruptcy.

Even giant firms can be brought down by innovative rivals. During the 1990s, Microsoft's dominance of the computer industry was overwhelming. Between January 1990 and January 2000, Microsoft's stock price rose by about 8,000 percent. Apple lagged far behind Microsoft in both market share and brand-name recognition. But things soon began to change. Apple introduced the iPod in 2001, which revolutionized how consumers purchased and listened to music, and gained substantial brand-name recognition among consumers, especially younger consumers. In 2007, Apple introduced the iPhone, again changing the game, but this time in the market for cell phones. The innovative behavior of Apple continued; in 2008 the MacBook Air was introduced, and in 2010 the iPad again unleashed a wave of creative destruction, altering the way consumers receive news, read books, and play games. By 2010, the market value of Apple eventually grew to rival and even surpass that of the previously dominant Microsoft.

In a competitive economy, numerous businesses come and go. Each year, newly incorporated businesses account for about 10 percent of the total, but about 53 percent of them will fail within six years, 20 percent of which will fail within their first year. Even during good economic times, approximately 1 percent of businesses file for bankruptcy each year, and many others close their doors or sell their assets to other, more successful (or at least more optimistic) operators.

From an economic standpoint then, business failure has a positive side; it gets rid of bad or outdated ideas, freeing up resources to be used in other endeavors. A vibrant economy will have both a large number of new business start-ups and a large number of business failures. However, as more ideas are tried, it will be more likely that we will stumble on to that one-in-a-million new innovation that will substantially improve our lives.

Consumers are the ultimate beneficiaries from the process of entrepreneurship and dynamic competition that results in the introduction of new goods and services, lower-cost production methods, increased specialization and variety, and reductions in transaction costs. Moreover, this dynamic change is indicative of a healthy, competitive economy. Firms that are more successful at providing consumers with value relative to cost will expand, while those that are less successful will contract. As a result, there will be constant movement of firms up and down the ladder of success. When comparing the list of the 500 largest firms from fifty years ago with the list today, 90 percent of these firms have fallen off the list and have been replaced by new firms. Among the top ten largest firms today, about half didn't even exist fifty years ago, and only one was in the top ten as recently as three decades ago!

Let's summarize the importance of entrepreneurship. Discovery of new products and better ways of doing things is an important source of economic growth and improved living standards. These discoveries often come from unexpected sources, and there is no way to tell in advance which will succeed and which will fail. Thus, it is vitally important that new ideas can be tested. Many will fail, but a few will succeed and transform our lives. This discovery process is too complex to be captured, at least not fully, by models, but it is nonetheless a central ingredient of a healthy, growing economy.

Key Points

- Firms in price-searcher markets with low barriers to entry face a downward-sloping demand curve. They are free to set the prices for the products that they sell but face strong competitive pressure from existing and potential rivals.
- Firms in price-searcher markets with low entry barriers use product quality, style, convenience of location, advertising, and price as competitive weapons. Because each firm competes with rivals offering similar products, each confronts a highly elastic demand curve for its products.
- A profit-maximizing price searcher will expand output as long as marginal revenue exceeds marginal cost, lowering its price in the process, until $MR = MC$. The price charged by the profit-maximizing price searcher will be greater than its marginal cost.
- Firms in competitive price-searcher markets can experience either profits or losses in the short run. Profits will attract rival firms into the market until supply increases and the profit-maximizing price falls to the level of per-unit price. Losses will cause firms to exit the market until the price increases enough that

the remaining firms can once again cover their per-unit costs. Because of the low entry barriers, the firms in competitive price-searcher markets will earn only normal returns (zero economic profit) in long-run equilibrium.

- Competition can come from potential as well as actual rivals. If entry and exit can be arranged at low cost, and if there are no legal barriers to entry, the theory of contestable markets indicates that competitive results will be approximated, even if there are only a few firms actually in the market.
- Competitive price-searcher markets provide more variety but may raise costs relative to price-taker markets because (1) price exceeds marginal cost at the profit-maximizing output level, (2) long-run average cost is not minimized, and (3) advertising is costly. When barriers to entry are low, however, price searchers have an incentive to (1) produce efficiently; (2) undertake production if, and only if, their actions are expected to increase the value of the resources used; and (3) be innovative in offering new product options.
- When a price searcher can (1) identify groups of customers that have different price elasticities of demand and (2) prevent customers from retrading the product, price discrimination may emerge. Sellers may be able to gain by charging higher prices to groups with a less elastic demand and lower prices to those with a more elastic demand. The practice generally leads to a larger output and more gains from trade than would otherwise occur.
- Entrepreneurs discover previously unnoticed profit opportunities and act on them. By discovering and developing new products that are highly valued relative to cost, entrepreneurs promote economic progress. The profit and loss system provides entrepreneurs with quick and persuasive feedback on the merit of their idea.
- Entrepreneurship is an inherently disruptive force in an economy as new products often cause the failure of old ones. But this creative destruction is an important source of improved products, lower-cost production methods, and higher living standards.

Critical Analysis Questions

1. Why do the demand curves of the firms in competitive price-searcher markets slope downward to the right? What is the relationship between price and marginal revenue of the firms in a competitive price-searcher market. Explain the relationship between the two answers.
2. Because price searchers can set their prices, does this mean that their prices are unaffected by market conditions? In price-searcher markets with low barriers to entry, will the firms be able to make economic profit in the long run? Why or why not?
3. *What determines the *variety* of styles, designs, and sizes of different products? Why do you think there are only a few different varieties of toothpicks but lots of different types of napkins on the market?
4. What is a contestable market? What conditions must be present for a market to be contestable? Will a firm in a contestable market be able to earn economic profit? Why or why not?
5. What must an entrepreneur do in order to introduce a new innovative product? What determines whether the new product will be a success or failure? Why is the role of the entrepreneur an important source of economic growth and improvement of living standards?
6. Is quality and style competition as important as price competition? Would you like to live in a country where government regulation restricted the use of quality and style competition? Why or why not? Do you think you would get more or less for your consumer dollar under restrictions like these? Discuss.
7. Suppose that a price searcher is currently charging a price that maximizes the firm's total revenue. Will this price also maximize the firm's profit? Why or why not? Explain.
8. a. *What determines whether corporations, individual proprietorships, employee-owned firms, consumer cooperatives, or some other form of business structure will dominate in a market?

   b. What determines whether small firms, medium-size firms, or large firms will dominate in a market?
9. Would our standard of living be higher if the government "bailed out" troubled businesses? If a firm goes out of business, what happens to the firm's assets, workers, and customers? Are business failures bad for the economy? Why or why not?
10. *Suppose that a group of investors wants to start a business operated out of a popular Utah ski area. The group is considering either building a new hotel complex or starting a new local airline serving that market. Each new business would require about the same amount of capital and personnel hiring. The group believes each endeavor has the same profit potential. Which is the safer (less likely to result in a substantial capital loss) investment? Why? Is there an offsetting advantage to the other investment?
11. Is price discrimination harmful to the economy? How does price discrimination affect the total amount of gains from exchange? Explain. Why do colleges often charge students different prices based on their family income?
12. *"When competition is intense, only the big firms survive. The little guy has no chance." True or false? Explain.

13. What is the primary requirement for a market to be competitive? Is competition necessary for markets to work well? Why or why not? How does competition influence the following: (a) the cost efficiency of producers, (b) the quality of products, and (c) the discovery and development of new products? Explain your answers.

14. *What keeps McDonald's, Walmart, General Motors, or any other business firm from raising prices, selling shoddy products, and providing lousy service?

15. What role do profits and losses play in competitive price-taker and competitive price-searcher markets? Why do some economists argue that competitive price-searcher markets are inefficient, while others argue this is not the case?

16. The accompanying graph shows the short-run demand and cost situation for a price searcher in a market with low barriers to entry.

a. What level of output will maximize the firm's profit level?

b. What price will the firm charge?

c. How much revenue will the firm receive in this situation? How much is total cost? Total profit?

d. How will the situation change over time?

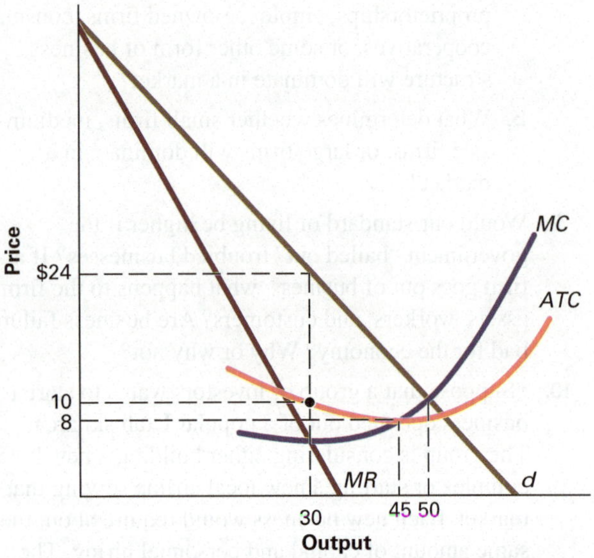

17. Rod N. Reel owns a dealership that sells fishing boats in an open, price-searcher market. To develop his pricing strategy, Rod hired an economist to estimate his demand curve. Columns (1) and (2) of the accompanying chart provide the data for the expected weekly quantity demanded for Rod's fishing boats at alternative prices. Rod's marginal (and average) cost of supplying each boat is constant at $5,000 per boat no matter how many boats he sells per week in this range. This cost includes all opportunity costs and represents the economic cost per boat.

a. Find Rod's economic profits at each alternative price by calculating the difference between total revenue and total cost.

b. Find Rod's marginal revenue and marginal cost from the sale of each additional boat.

c. If Rod wants to maximize his profits, what price should he charge per boat?

d. How many boats will Rod sell per week at the profit-maximizing price?

e. What will Rod's profits be per week at this price and sales volume?

f. At the price and sales level where profits are maximized, has Rod sold all boats that have higher marginal revenue than marginal cost?

g. If Rod's profits are typical of all firms in the boat sales business, what might be expected to happen in the future? Will more boat dealers open in the area, or will some of the existing ones go out of business? What will happen to the profitability of the boat dealers in the future once the entry/exit has occurred?

h. Challenge Question: Recall the relationship between elasticity of demand, price changes, and their impact on total revenues. As Rod lowers his price from $9,000 to $5,000, his total revenues keep increasing. Is demand in this price range elastic, inelastic, or unit elastic? When Rod lowers his price from $5,000 to $4,000, his total revenues stay the same. Is demand in this price range elastic, inelastic, or unit elastic? Can you guess what might happen at prices below $4,000? Explain.

*Asterisk denotes questions for which answers are given in Appendix B.

Price of Fishing Boats (1)	Number of Fishing Boats Sold per Week (2)	Total Revenue per Week (3)	Total Cost per Week (4)	Economic Profit per Week (5)	Marginal Revenue (6)	Marginal Cost (7)
$9,000	0	—	—	—	n/a	n/a
8,000	1	—	—	—	—	—
7,000	2	—	—	—	—	—
6,000	3	—	—	—	—	—
5,000	4	—	—	—	—	—
4,000	5	—	—	—	—	—

Chapter 11 Price-Searcher Markets with High Entry Barriers

> "When the monopolist raises prices above the competitive level in order to reap his monopoly profits, customers buy less of the product, less is produced, and society as a whole is worse off. In short, monopoly reduces society's income." "... [C]ompetition is a tough weed, not a delicate flower."
>
> –George Stigler[1]

In the previous two chapters, we analyzed the way firms behave in markets with low barriers to entry. In those markets, short-run economic profits lead to the entry of new firms and expansion in supply that drive profits down to a normal level (zero economic profit). We now turn to the analysis of firm behavior when entry barriers are high and there are few, if any, rival firms offering the same or similar products. This chapter focuses on factors that make entry into a market more difficult, and how this can reduce the ability of markets to keep firms in check. We will also consider policy alternatives that might improve the efficiency of these markets.

Learning Objectives

- 11.1 List the four factors that can cause high barriers to entry, limiting the competitiveness of markets.
- 11.2 Define monopoly and indicate why the definition involves some subjectivity.
- 11.3 Indicate how a monopolist decides what price to charge and what quantity to produce to maximize profits.
- 11.4 Define oligopoly and indicate the characteristics of an oligopolistic market.
- 11.5 Analyze how an oligopolist decides what price to charge and what quantity to produce.
- 11.6 Indicate when collusion among oligopolists to increase profits is most likely and least likely to be successful.
- 11.7 Analyze the problems that arise when entry barriers are high and the major policy alternatives under such circumstances.

[1]Both quotes are from George J. Stigler, "Monopoly," in *The Concise Encyclopedia of Economics*, 2nd ed., ed. David R. Henderson (Indianapolis, Ind.: Liberty Fund, Inc., 2007), available online at http://www.econlib.org/library/Enc/Monopoly.html.

11-1 Why Are Entry Barriers Sometimes High?

What makes it difficult for potential competitors to enter a market? Under certain conditions, four factors can be important: economies of scale, government licensing, patents, and control over an essential resource. Let's consider each.

11-1a Economies of Scale

When the fixed costs in an industry are large, bigger firms can generally achieve lower average total per-unit costs than can smaller ones. As our discussion of contestable markets indicated in the last chapter, however, economies of scale and high fixed costs are not a significant barrier to entry when the assets needed to enter the market can be leased, transferred to another location, or resold later without a major loss of value.

In some markets, however, this will not be the case. Airline routes may be contestable, but airplane manufacturing is not, because much of the equipment used to produce airplanes is of little use in the production of other things. Once it is in place, most of the equipment cannot be shifted to other uses. The cost of the equipment is a sunk cost. Under these circumstances, if necessary, the incumbent firm will continue operating for a lengthy period of time as long as it can cover its variable (operating) costs. Potential new entrants will recognize that this incentive structure will make it extremely difficult to displace the current incumbent. Thus, they will be reluctant to attempt entry, even if the current incumbent is earning economic profit. A dominant firm will tend to emerge in the industry, and if the market is not contestable, the cost advantages resulting from its size will protect it from potential rivals.

11-1b Government Licensing and Other Legal Barriers to Entry

Government-imposed legal barriers are the oldest and most prevalent method of protecting a business firm from potential competitors. Kings once granted exclusive business rights to favored citizens or groups. To compete in certain parts of the communications industry in the United States (for example, to operate a radio or television station), one must obtain a government license. Similarly, local governments often grant exclusive licenses for the local operation of utilities or cable television systems. Each of these measures reduces competition and protects the profits of favored firms, and often in effect provides a local monopoly franchise.

Licensing
A requirement that one obtain permission from the government in order to perform certain business activities or work in various occupations.

Licensing can also limit entry and reduce competitiveness even without the monopoly franchise feature. States and cities often require the operators of liquor stores, hairstyling shops, taxicabs, funeral homes, and many other businesses to obtain a license. Sometimes, these licenses cost little and are designed to ensure certain minimum standards. Often, however, they are costly to obtain and a major deterrent to the entry of potential rivals.

Similarly, in the healthcare industry, government-imposed "certificate of need" (CON) laws that exist in 35 states and Washington, DC, serve as a barrier to entry or expansion, limiting competition. These laws require potential new entrants to get permission from incumbent firms or to otherwise prove that there is an excess demand in the marketplace that existing firms cannot supply.

11-1c Patents

Most countries have patent laws to give inventors a property right to their inventions. A patent grants the owner the exclusive legal right to the commercial use of a newly invented product or process for a limited period of time—20 years in the United States. Others are not

Entrepreneurs Who Have Changed Our Lives

Catherine ("Cathy") Hughes

NurPhoto/Getty Images

Catherine ("Cathy") Hughes is the founder and chairperson of one of the largest Black-owned media companies in the nation, Urban One (formerly Radio One). She started the company with a single radio station in Washington, D.C., directed at the local urban audience. Due to the FCC (Federal Communications Commission) regulatory limiting and control of radio station licenses, Hughes was only able to expand by buying existing radio stations from their owners. Her company eventually grew to own 70 stations at its peak, and with the help of her son (who is now the CEO of the company), it has expanded into TV and online platforms. Cathy Hughes's estimated net worth was almost half of a billion dollars in 2024.

Hughes was born in 1947, into a large family in a housing project in Omaha, Nebraska. After marrying her first husband and having a child, she went to work for Omaha's only Black-owned radio station. While attending the University of Nebraska at Omaha, she met Tony Brown—a well-known TV personality at the time—who invited her to come work at Howard University in Washington, D.C., where he was setting up a school of communications. Hughes soon became sales manager for the university's radio station, and her success led to her becoming the station's general manager.

After struggling to secure a loan, Hughes and her second husband bought the AM radio station WOL 1450 in Washington, D.C., in 1980. After going through a divorce and falling deeply in debt, Hughes with her son moved into the radio station's studio. She slept on the floor in a sleeping bag, never losing sight of her goal to build the radio station—which would eventually become a large media company. Hughes hosted a morning talk show on the station for 11 years. As her success grew, Hughes began to buy up other radio stations. In 1988 her company Radio One went public, becoming the largest Black-owned publicly traded company in the United States. In 2017, Howard University named the Cathy Hughes School of Communications in her honor.

Sources:

Ericka Blount Danois, "Media Mogul Cathy Hughes Is in It for the Long Run," *The Root*, Oct. 23, 2016, at https://www.theroot.com/media-mogul-cathy-hughes-is-in-it-for-the-long-run-1790857366.

Saflon Floyd, "How Cathy Hughes Stays on Top of the Entertainment Industry," *Black Enterprise*, February 5, 2017, at https://www.blackenterprise.com/cathy-hughes-entertainment-industry/.

Reco McCambry, "Business Lessons from Successful Black Entrepreneurs (Part 3): Tenacity Is Needed to Succeed," *Forbes*, Dec. 7, 2021, at https://www.forbes.com/sites/forbesbusinesscouncil/2021/12/07/business-lessons-from-successful-black-entrepreneurs-part-3-tenacity-is-needed-to-succeed/?sh=5c73067f353f/.

"Cathy Hughes," *The History Makers*, March 2, 2005, at https://www.thehistorymakers.org/biography/cathy-hughes-39

allowed to copy the product or procedure without the permission of the patent holder. For example, when a pharmaceutical company is granted a patent for a newly developed drug, other potential suppliers must obtain permission from the patent holder before producing and selling the product during the life of the patent. Others might be able to supply the drug more economically. During that time period though, if they want to do so while the patent is in effect, they will have to purchase the production and marketing rights from the originating firm.

Both costs and benefits for consumers come with a patent system. The entry barrier created by the grant of a patent generally leads to higher consumer prices for several years, for products that have already been developed. On the positive side, however, patents increase the potential returns to inventive activity, thus encouraging scientific research and technological improvements. As we noted in the previous chapter, entrepreneurial discovery will

Vince Bucci/Getty Images

Both the Keurig coffee maker and the pods (K-Cups) were protected by patents, so companies like Starbucks and Dunkin' Donuts had to pay licensing fees to sell coffee in the patented K-Cups. In 2012, patents on the K-Cups expired, so other companies can now produce and sell K-Cups that are compatible with the Keurig machine. The increased competition resulted in lower prices for consumers.

occur at a faster rate when it is more profitable. The average cost of developing and testing a new pharmaceutical drug can be in excess of $2 billion. Without the profit potential accompanying patents, the incentive to engage in research and develop new products would be reduced.

11-1d Control over an Essential Resource

Control over a resource essential to produce a product may also insulate a firm from direct competitors. An example often cited is the Aluminum Company of America, which before World War II controlled the known supply of bauxite conveniently available to American firms. Without this critical raw material, potential competitors could not produce aluminum. Over time, however, other supplies of bauxite were discovered, and the Aluminum Company of America lost its advantage. Resource monopolies are seldom complete or long lasting. Profit opportunities provide potential competitors with an incentive to search for mineral deposits, new technologies, and substitute resources. Over time, they are usually found.

Barriers to entry like the different ones we've just described are often temporary, but they do exist. Let's examine what happens when, at least temporarily, there is a barrier to entry high enough to limit the market to only one seller.

11-2 Characteristics of a Monopoly

The word *monopoly*, derived from two Greek words, means "single seller." We will define **monopoly** as a market characterized by (1) high barriers to entry and (2) a single seller of a well-defined product for which there are no good substitutes. Even this definition is ambiguous, because "high barriers" and "good substitutes" are both relative terms. Are the barriers to entry into the automobile or steel industries high? Many observers would argue that they are. After all, it takes a great deal of capital to operate at the least-cost scale of output in both of these industries. However, there are no *physical* or *legal* restraints that prevent an entrepreneur from producing automobiles or steel. If price is well above cost and profit potential is present, it should not be too difficult to find the necessary investment capital. Thus, some would argue that entry barriers into these industries are not particularly high.

Monopoly
A market structure characterized by (1) a single seller of a well-defined product for which there are no good substitutes and (2) high barriers to the entry of any other firms into the market for that product.

"Good substitute" is also a subjective term. There is always some substitutability among products, even those produced by a single seller. Is a letter a good substitute for a phone call or an e-mail message? For some purposes—correspondence between law firms, for example—a letter delivered by mail is a very good substitute. In other cases, when the speed of communication and immediacy of response are important, the telephone and e-mail are far superior forms of communication.

Monopoly, then, is a matter of degree. Only a small fraction of all markets are served by just one seller. In a few markets, governments have allocated specific markets to a single seller. In many communities, this is the case with cable television and providers of electricity. The monopoly model we discuss next will illuminate the operation of these markets. It will also help us understand markets in which there are just a few sellers and little active rivalry. When there are only two or three producers in a market, firms may seek to collude rather than compete, and thus, together, they may behave much like a monopoly.

Exhibit 11-1 The Short-Run Price and Output of a Monopolist

The monopolist will reduce its price and expand its output as long as *MR* exceeds *MC*. Output *Q* will result. When the price exceeds the average total cost at any output level, a profit will be earned.

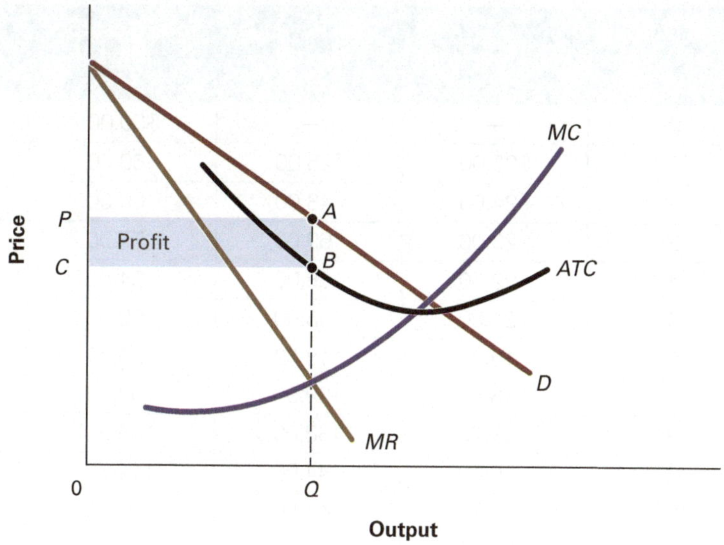

11-2a Price and Output Under Monopoly

Because a monopolist is a price searcher like the firms we examined in the previous chapter, the graphical analysis is similar. The main difference is that because the monopolist is the only seller in the market, the demand curve facing the firm (*d*) is the entire market demand curve (*D*), and the firm's output (*q*) is the entire market output (*Q*). ***Like other price searchers, the monopolist will expand its output until marginal revenue equals marginal cost. This profit-maximizing output rate can be sold at the price indicated on the firm's demand curve.***

Exhibit 11-1 graphically illustrates how a monopolist derives the profit-maximizing output rate.[2] Output will be expanded to *Q*, where *MR* = *MC*. The monopolist will set a price of *P* to sell exactly the desired profit-maximizing level of output *Q* (the height of the demand curve at *Q*). Thus, output rate *Q* and price *P* will maximize the firm's profit.

The profits earned by the monopolist are also shown in Exhibit 11-1. At output *Q* and price *P*, the firm's total revenue is equal to *PAQ*0, the price times the number of units sold. The firm's total cost would be *CBQ*0, the average per-unit cost multiplied by the number of units sold. The firm's profits are total revenue less total cost, the shaded area of Exhibit 11-1 (*PABC*).

Exhibit 11-2 provides a numeric illustration of decision-making by a profit-maximizing monopolist. At low output rates, marginal revenue exceeds marginal cost. The monopolist will expand output as long as *MR* is greater than *MC*. Thus, an output rate of eight units per day will be chosen. (*Note:* If tiny portions of a unit could be produced and sold, then production would increase to where *MR* = *MC*.) Given the demand for the product, the monopolist can sell eight units at a price of $17.25 each. Total revenue will be $138, compared with a total cost of $108.50. The monopolist will make a profit of $29.50. The profit rate will be smaller at all other output rates. For example, if the monopolist reduces the price to $16 in

[2]In this chapter, we assume that firms are unable to use price discrimination to increase their revenues. If they could, the analysis of price discrimination from the previous chapter would be relevant to their decision-making.

Exhibit 11-2 Profit Maximization for a Monopolist

Rate of Output (per Day) (1)	Price (per Unit) (2)	Total Revenue (1) × (2) (3)	Total Cost (per Day) (4)	Profit (3) – (4) (5)	Marginal Cost (6)	Marginal Revenue (7)
0	—	—	$50.00	$–50.00	—	—
1	$25.00	$25.00	60.00	–35.00	$10.00	$25.00
2	24.00	48.00	69.00	–21.00	9.00	23.00
3	23.00	69.00	77.00	–8.00	8.00	21.00
4	22.00	88.00	84.00	4.00	7.00	19.00
5	21.00	105.00	90.50	14.50	6.50	17.00
6	19.75	118.50	96.75	21.75	6.25	13.50
7	18.50	129.50	102.75	26.75	6.00	11.00
8	17.25	138.00	108.50	29.50	5.75	8.50
9	16.00	144.00	114.75	29.25	6.25	6.00
10	14.75	147.50	121.25	26.25	6.50	3.50
11	13.50	148.50	128.00	20.50	6.75	1.00
12	12.25	147.00	135.00	12.00	7.00	–1.50
13	11.00	143.00	142.25	.75	7.25	–4.00

order to sell nine units per day, revenue will increase by $6. However, the marginal cost of producing the ninth unit is $6.25. Because the cost of producing the ninth unit is greater than the revenue it brings in, profits will decline.

When high barriers to entry are present, they will insulate the monopolist from competition from new entrants producing a similar product. Thus, in markets with high entry barriers, short-run monopoly profits will not be competed away through the process of entry.

Protected by high entry barriers, a monopolist may be able to continue earning a profit, even in the long run. Does this mean that monopolists can charge as high a price as they want? Monopolists are often accused of price gouging. In evaluating this charge, however, it is important to recognize that, like other sellers, monopolists will seek to maximize *profit*, not *price*. Consumers will buy less as the price increases. Thus, a higher price is not always better for a monopolist. Exhibit 11-2 illustrates this point. What would happen to the profit of the monopolist if the price were increased from $17.25 to $18.50? At the higher price, only seven units would be sold, and total revenue would equal $129.50. The cost of producing seven units would be $102.75. Thus, when the price is $18.50 and output seven units, profit is only $26.75—less than it would be at the lower price ($17.25) and larger output (eight units). The highest price is not usually the best price for the monopolist.

Will a monopolist always earn a profit? The ability of a monopolist to cover cost and make a profit is limited by the demand for the product that it produces. In some cases, a monopolist—even one protected by high barriers to entry—may be unable to sell its product for a profit. For example, there are thousands of clever, patented items that are never produced because demand–cost conditions are not favorable. **Exhibit 11-3** illustrates this possibility. Here, the monopolist's average total cost curve is above its demand curve at every level of output. Even when operating at the $MR = MC$ rate of output, economic losses (shaded area) will occur. While output Q could be sold at price P, this price and quantity yield too little revenue to cover cost for the monopolist. This model explains why many small towns lack even a single gourmet coffee shop, or any number of other specialty stores,

Exhibit 11-3 How a Monopolist Can Lose Money

Even a monopolist will lose money if its average total cost curve lies everywhere above the demand curve.

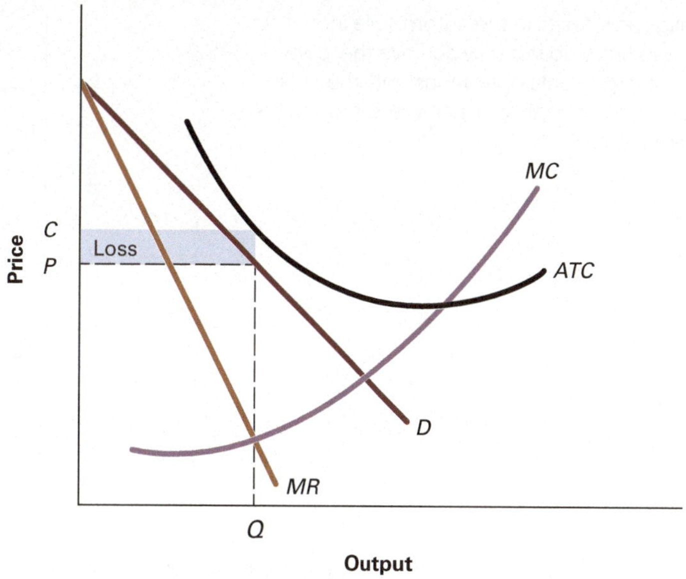

even though if one opened up it would be the only one in town. Under these circumstances, not even a monopolist would want to operate—at least not for long.

11-3 The Characteristics of an Oligopoly

In the United States, the domestic output in certain industries, such as the automobile, cigarette, and aircraft industries, is produced by five or fewer dominant firms. These industries are characterized by **oligopoly**. *Oligopoly* means "few sellers." ***The distinguishing characteristics of an oligopolistic market are (1) a small number of rival firms, (2) interdependence among the sellers because each is large relative to the size of the market, (3) substantial economies of scale, and (4) high entry barriers to the market.***

Oligopoly
A market situation in which a small number of sellers constitutes the entire industry. It is competition among the few.

11-3a Interdependence Among Oligopolistic Firms

Because the number of sellers in an oligopolistic industry is small, the supply decisions of any one firm will significantly influence the demand, price, and profit of rival firms. This adds to the complexity of the firm's decision-making. A firm that is deciding what price to charge, output to produce, or quality of product to offer must consider not only the currently available substitutes but also the potential reactions of rival producers. The business decisions of each firm depend on the policies it expects its major rivals to follow because those will influence the demand for all the rivals' products.

11-3b Substantial Economies of Scale

In an oligopolistic industry, large-scale production (relative to the total market) is generally required to achieve minimum per-unit cost. Economies of scale are present, so a small number of large-scale firms can produce enough of the product to meet the entire market demand. Using the passenger-car segment of the automobile industry in the recent past as an example, **Exhibit 11-4** illustrates the importance of economies of scale as a source of oligopoly. It has been estimated that each firm must produce approximately 1 million automobiles

Exhibit 11-4 Economies of Scale and Oligopoly

An oligopoly exists in the automobile industry because firms do not fully achieve the lower costs of large-scale operations until they are able to produce approximately one-sixth of the total market.

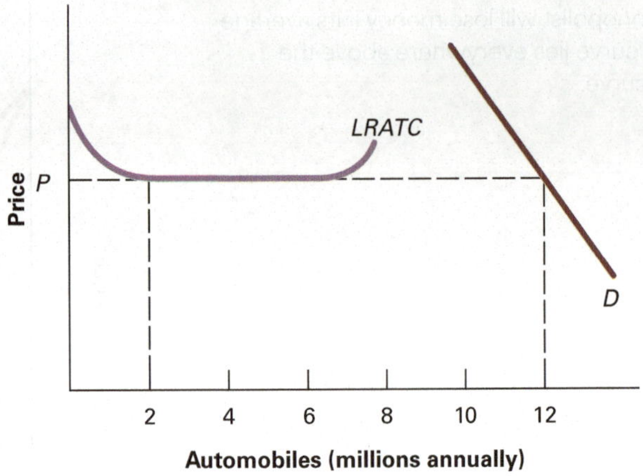

annually before its per-unit cost of production is minimized. However, when the selling price of passenger cars is barely sufficient to cover costs, the total quantity demanded from these producers is only 6 million. To minimize costs, then, each firm must produce at least one-sixth (1 million of the 6 million) of the output demanded. If this is true, the industry can support no more than five or six domestic firms of cost-efficient size.

11-3c Significant Barriers to Entry

As with monopoly, barriers to entry limit the ability of new firms to compete effectively in oligopolistic industries. Except where a market is contestable, economies of scale are probably the most significant entry barrier protecting firms in an oligopolistic industry. A potential competitor may be unable to start out small and gradually grow to the optimal size, because it must gain a large share of the market before it can minimize its per-unit cost. The manufacture of refrigerators, diesel engines, and automobiles seems to fall into this category. Other factors, including patent rights, control over an essential resource, and government-imposed entry restraints, can also prevent new competitors from entering profitable oligopolistic industries.

11-3d Identical or Differentiated Products

The products of sellers in an oligopolistic industry may be either similar or differentiated. On the one hand, when firms produce identical products, like milk or gasoline, there is less opportunity for nonprice competition. On the other hand, when rival firms produce differentiated products, they are more likely to use style, quality, and advertising as competitive weapons. Each firm attempts to convince buyers that other products are poor substitutes.

11-4 Price and Output Under Oligopoly

Unlike the other firms we have examined, an oligopolist cannot determine the product price that will deliver maximum profit simply by estimating only its own costs and the *existing* market demand. The demand facing an oligopolistic firm depends also on the pricing behavior of its rivals. Suppose, for example, that Ford is considering how to price a new car model when it comes on the market next year. The number of cars it can sell at each price will depend not only on buyer preferences but also on the prices (and quality) of substitutes available from Toyota, General Motors, and other rival firms. What pricing strategy will each rival use if Ford puts a low price on its new model? How will each rival firm react to a higher Ford price?

Economic models cannot predict these complex interactions among rivals without making some strong, simplifying assumptions about how each firm reacts when another firm makes a change in price or quality. These simplifying assumptions will not be realistic for the general case, and therefore we cannot precisely predict the price and output that will emerge in an oligopoly. We can, however, zero in on a potential range of prices and the factors that will determine whether prices in the industry will be high or low relative to costs of production.

Consider a typical oligopolistic industry in which seven or eight rival firms produce the entire market output because substantial economies of scale are present. The firms produce nearly identical products and have similar costs of production. **Exhibit 11-5** depicts the market demand conditions and long-run costs of production of the individual firms for such an industry.

What price will prevail? We can answer this question for two extreme cases. First, suppose that each firm sets its price independently of the other firms. There is no **collusion** (no agreement among the firms to limit output and keep the price high), so each competitive firm is free to seek additional customers and profits by offering buyers a slightly better deal than its rivals. Under these conditions, the market price would be driven down to P_c. Firms would be just able to cover their per-unit costs of production. If a single firm raised its price, its customers would switch to rival firms, which would now expand to accommodate the new customers. It would be self-defeating for any one firm to raise its price if the other firms didn't also raise theirs.

Collusion
Agreement among firms to avoid various competitive practices, particularly price reductions. It may involve either formal agreements or merely tacit recognition that competitive practices will be self-defeating in the long run. Tacit collusion is difficult to detect. In the United States, antitrust laws prohibit collusion and conspiracies to restrain trade.

What happens if the current price is greater than P_c, perhaps because the market has not yet adjusted fully to a recent reduction in resource prices that lowered production costs? As a result, price is above per-unit cost, and the firms are making economic profit. However, any *individual firm* that reduces its price slightly, by 1 or 2 percent, for example, will gain numerous customers if the other firms maintain the higher price. The price-cutting firm will attract some new buyers to the market, but more importantly, it will also lure many buyers away from rival firms charging higher prices. Thus, if the rival sellers act independently, each will have a strong incentive to reduce price in order to increase sales and gain a large

Exhibit 11-5 Price and Output in an Oligopoly

If oligopolists were to act independently and compete with one another, price cutting would drive price down to P_c. In contrast, perfect cooperation among firms would lead to a higher price of P_m and a smaller output (Q_m rather than Q_c). The shaded area shows profit if firms collude. Demand here is the market demand.

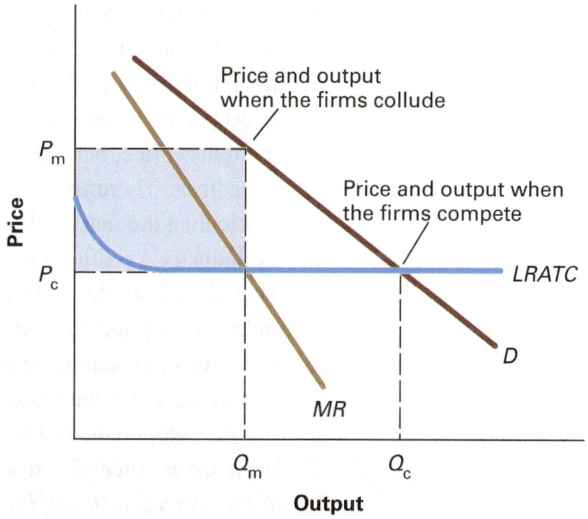

share of the total market. Price will be driven down to P_c, and the economic profit will be eliminated.

However, oligopolists don't always compete with one another. They have a strong incentive to collude—to raise prices and restrict output in order to maximize their joint profits. The collusion may be either formal or informal. Formal collusion might even involve the formation of a **cartel**, like the Organization of the Petroleum Exporting Countries (OPEC). Under federal antitrust laws, both formal and informal collusive agreements to restrict output and raise prices are illegal in the United States. This is not true around the world. In Canada, for example, there is even a formal cartel for the maple syrup industry, the Federation of Quebec Maple Syrup Producers (PPAQ). Quebec produces 72 percent of global syrup production, and this organization restricts the joint output of the syrup producers to increase prices. Now let's examine what happens when oligopolists follow this course.

Cartel
An organization of sellers designed to coordinate supply decisions so that the joint profits of the members will be maximized. A cartel will seek to create a monopoly in the market.

Exhibit 11-5 shows the marginal revenue curve that would accompany the market demand *D* for the product. Under perfect cooperation, the oligopolists would refuse to produce units for which marginal revenue to the group was less than marginal cost. Thus, they would restrict joint output to Q_m, where $MR = MC$. The market price would rise to P_m. With collusion, substantial joint profits (the shaded area of Exhibit 11-5) can be attained. If the collusion were perfect, the outcome would be identical to the one that would occur under monopoly.

Real-world outcomes are likely to be between the two polar case extremes of price competition and perfect collusion. Oligopolists generally recognize their interdependence and try to avoid vigorous price competition because they know it will drive down the price to the level of per-unit costs. But there are also obstacles to collusion, which is why prices in oligopolistic industries are unlikely to rise to the monopoly level. ***As a result, oligopoly prices are typically above per-unit cost but below those a monopolist would charge.***

11-4a The Incentive to Collude . . . and to Cheat

Rival oligopolists can profit as a group by colluding to restrict output and raise price. To achieve the higher price, however, they must reduce total market output. Returning to Exhibit 11-5, from a competitive outcome of Q_c and P_c, output must be restricted toward the monopoly level of Q_m to achieve a higher price near P_m. This raises a point of conflict: None of the oligopolists want to reduce their output independently, especially at a higher price! Although the firms have an incentive to collude in order to achieve higher prices, each of them also has an incentive to cheat on the agreement by producing and selling more units than would maximize profit for the industry as a whole.

Exhibit 11-6 explains why this is the case. An undetected price cut by a single firm will have a larger percentage impact on its sales than a similar price cut would have on total industry sales. For example, if all firms lowered price by 10 percent total industry sales might only rise by 10 percent, but if one firm lowers price by 10 percent its sales might rise by 30 percent. Both price cuts attract additional customers who normally wouldn't buy at the higher price, but a price cut by one firm also attracts current customers away from the other firms. Therefore, the demand facing each *individual firm* will be considerably more elastic than the market demand curve. As Exhibit 11-6 shows, the price P_i that maximizes the industry's profits will be higher than the price P_F that is best for a single oligopolist when the others stay with the higher price. If a firm can use secret rebates or other ways to undercut the price set by the collusive agreement while the other sellers maintain the higher price, it can expand its sales (beyond the level agreed upon by the cartel). This will more than make up for the reduction in per-unit profit margin from the price cut.

In oligopolistic industries, there are two conflicting tendencies. ***An oligopolistic firm has a strong incentive to cooperate with its rivals so that joint profit can be maximized. But it also has a strong incentive to cheat—to expand output secretly in order to increase its profit. Oligopolistic agreements, therefore, tend to be unstable.***

Exhibit 11-6 Gaining from Cheating

The industry demand (D_i) and marginal revenue (MR_i) curves show that the joint profits of oligopolists would be maximized at Q_i, where $MR_i = MC$. Price P_i would be best for the industry as a whole (a). However, as panel (b) shows, the demand curve (d_F) facing each firm (under the assumption that no other firms cheat) will be much more elastic than D_i. Given the greater elasticity of its demand curve, an individual firm will have an incentive to cut its price to P_F and expand output to q_F, where $MR_F = MC$. In other words, an individual oligopolist can gain by secretly cutting its price and cheating on the collusive agreement–until the other firms find out and react by cutting their price.

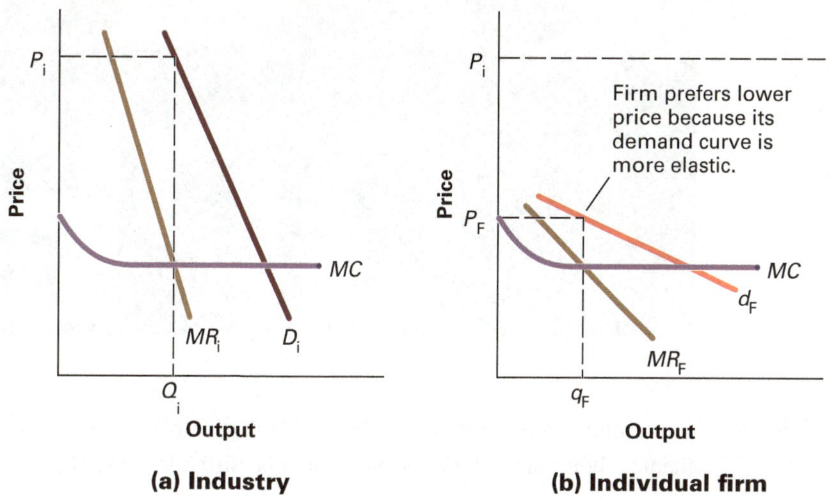

11-4b Obstacles to Collusion

There are certain situations in which it is more difficult for oligopolists to collude. Five major obstacles limit collusive behavior.

1. As the number of firms in an oligopolistic market increases, the likelihood of effective collusion declines. Other things being constant, an increase in the number of firms in an industry will make it more difficult for the oligopolists to communicate, negotiate, and enforce agreements among themselves. Opinions about the best collusive price arrangement are likely to differ because marginal costs, unused plant capacity, and estimates of market demand elasticity will often differ among the firms. As the number of firms expands, conflict arising from these and other sources will increase and make it more difficult to maintain collusive agreements.

2. When it is difficult to detect and eliminate price cuts, collusion is less attractive. Unless firms have a way of policing the pricing and output activities of rivals, effective collusion will be unlikely as firms will cheat on the agreement. The history of the oil cartel OPEC highlights this point. Cheating by members on production and sales quota agreements is not easy to monitor by the others, and it has been a persistent problem for the cartel.

Some forms of price cutting are difficult for the rival firms to identify. For example, a firm might freely provide better credit terms, faster delivery, and other related services that improve the package offered to the buyer. In an industry supplying differentiated products, oligopolists can hold money prices constant and still use improvements in quality and style to provide consumers with more value. "Price cuts" like this cannot be easily and quickly duplicated by rivals. As a result, collusive agreements on price are largely ineffective when quality and style are important competitive weapons. The bottom line is this: When cheating

Bloomberg/Getty Images

Collusive agreements among oligopolists and cartels like OPEC are difficult to maintain because any individual cartel member would be better off if it could cheat on the agreement and charge a slightly lower price, so long as other members do not.

(price cutting) is profitable and difficult for rivals to detect and police, collusive agreements—both formal and informal—will be difficult to maintain.

3. Low entry barriers are an obstacle to collusion. Without barriers to entry oligopolists will be unable to sustain long-run economic profits because the profits will attract new competitors into the market. High prices will also make it more attractive for potential rivals to develop substitutes, which will reduce the demand for the product provided by the oligopolists. Of course, these factors will not work instantaneously, but over time they will reduce the ability to charge abnormally high prices and earn economic profits.

Again, the experience of OPEC illustrates this point. When OPEC attempts to cut production and push up world oil prices, the non-OPEC producers develop new oil fields and expand their output from existing sources. The higher prices also encourage energy conservation and greater use of alternative energy sources, such as coal, natural gas, and nuclear energy, and make it more profitable for firms across many other industries to introduce substitutes like more fuel-efficient, hybrid-electric cars. These innovations from rival sellers who can enter and compete with OPEC for customers cause the demand for oil to decrease and make it difficult for OPEC to collude successfully.

4. Unstable demand conditions are an obstacle to collusion. Honest differences of opinion among oligopolists about what is best for the industry always exist, but unstable demand increases the likelihood of conflict. One firm might want to expand because it anticipates a sharp increase in future demand, whereas a more pessimistic rival may want to hold the line on existing industrial capacity. The larger the differences in expectations about future demand, the greater the potential for conflict among oligopolistic firms. When demand is more stable, successful collusion will be more likely.

5. Vigorous antitrust action increases the cost of collusion. Under existing antitrust laws in many nations, collusive behavior is prohibited by law. Secretive illegal agreements do, of course, happen. Simple informal cooperation might be conducted without having explicit discussions or collusive agreements. However, unlike formal (legal) collusive agreements, these informal agreements are not easily enforceable. Thus, vigorous antitrust action can discourage firms from making illegal agreements. As the threat of getting caught increases, participants will be less likely to attempt collusive behavior.

11-4c Uncertainty and Oligopoly

Uncertainty and imprecision characterize the theory of oligopoly. We know that firms will gain if they successfully restrict output and raise prices. However, collusion is fraught with conflicts and difficulties. In some industries, these difficulties are so great that the **market power** of the oligopolists is relatively small. In other industries, oligopolistic cooperation, although not perfect, can raise prices significantly, indicating a higher degree of market power. The use of **game theory** to analyze the costs and benefits of collusive behavior under varying degrees of cooperation and conflict has become an important part of economics. (Refer to the accompanying Applications in Economics feature on this topic.) Although this developing field of economics does not yield precise predictions on oligopoly pricing and output, it does suggest the conditions that make it more likely that an oligopolist will be kept in check by competitive pressures.

Market power
The ability of a firm that is not a pure monopolist to earn persistently large profits, indicating that it has some monopoly power. Because the firm has few (or weak) competitors, it has a degree of freedom from vigorous competition.

Game theory
A tool used to analyze the strategic choices made by competitors in a conflict situation, like the decisions made by firms in an oligopoly.

Applications in Economics

Oligopolistic Decision-Making, Game Theory, and the Prisoner's Dilemma

In an oligopoly, a few firms compete in the same market, and the actions of each influence the demand faced by the others. One firm can gain customers at the expense of the others by cutting its price or increasing its advertising. The firms that fail to follow suit will lose customers. But if the other firms react competitively by doing the same, then all the firms lose. Thus, each firm finds itself on the horns of a dilemma–something like the classic "prisoner's dilemma."

Economists have increasingly used game theory like the prisoner's dilemma to analyze strategic choices made by competitors, particularly those in an oligopoly. To understand the prisoner's dilemma, consider the following hypothetical case. Asha and Bob are taken prisoner and hauled into the local police station to be questioned separately. They are suspected of being the two individuals who robbed a local merchant, and each is told that if they make the job of the police easier by confessing immediately, they will get only a six-month sentence. But each is also told that if they say nothing while the other confesses, then the one who did not confess immediately will get a 12-month sentence. If neither confesses, both will be held for three months while the investigation continues. Asha and Bob will not be allowed to communicate with each other. Will they confess?

To analyze such a situation, the game theorist begins by laying out the alternative outcomes and showing how they are related to choices made by the players of the game, as we do in **Exhibit 11-7**. For each person individually, in this version of the dilemma, the box reveals that the best choice depends on what the other does. If Asha confesses, then Bob can save six months of jail time by also confessing. The same holds for Asha, if she thinks Bob will confess. But if neither confesses, both serve only three months in jail. The proper strategy for each prisoner depends heavily on their estimate of the likelihood that the other will confess. The problem becomes more complex if we consider prisoners who face a series of such decisions over time and each prisoner learns what the other has done before making their next choice.

Firms in an oligopoly must make decisions somewhat like those of the prisoners: Should a firm cut its price in order to attract more customers–luring some of them away from its competitors–or should it keep its price high and risk losing customers to competitors who cut *their* prices? If all firms keep the price high, then as a group they will reap more profit.

If all of them cut prices, then as a group they will reap less profit. But the firm that fails to cut price when the others do will lose many customers. The decision about whether or not to advertise has similar characteristics.

For example, consider the pricing policies or advertising strategies of large automakers, like Ford, Toyota, and General Motors. Suppose the profit rate of each would be 15 percent if all the major automobile producers raised their prices by a similar amount. In contrast, each would earn a profit rate of only

Exhibit 11-7 The Prisoner's Dilemma

Asha and Bob must each decide, without communicating with each other, whether to confess. Asha knows that if Bob does not confess, then she can either confess and spend six months in jail, or not confess and spend three months. But if Bob does confess, then Asha's failure to confess will cost her an additional six months in jail. Bob is in a similar situation, facing the same options under the same assumptions about whether Asha confesses. Each person has an incentive to confess if they think the other one will, but an incentive not to confess if they think the other will also remain silent.

Bob's Choice	**Asha's Choice:** Confess	**Asha's Choice:** Not Confess
Confess	6 months each	Asha: 12 months Bob: 6 months
Not Confess	Asha: 6 months Bob: 12 months	3 months each

10 percent if intense competition led to lower prices. Industry profits are highest when all firms decide to charge high prices. However, if one automaker cuts prices, it will be able to steal customers away from its rivals and increase its profit rate to 20 percent. Thus, if the firm thinks its rivals will continue to charge the higher prices, it will be tempted to cut its price. If the other firms follow a similar course, however, the strategy will backfire and the profit rate of all the firms in the industry will be less than the level it would have achieved had they all charged the higher prices.

Although our simplified analysis highlights the interdependence among the firms and the importance of probability estimates concerning the strategy of rivals, the real world is much more complex. The choices of the rival firms will be repeated over and over again, although often in modified forms. A prior strategy will be modified in light of previous reactions on the part of rivals. How attractive a strategy will be depends on its likelihood of being detected by rivals and the speed with which they will respond. In addition, the strategies of oligopolistic firms will be influenced by market conditions and the threat of foreign competition–factors that change with the passage of time. Additional assumptions are necessary to account for these and other complex factors.

Economists have used game theory extensively to show how results change when the "rules of the game" change for the firms in an oligopolistic market, as well as for auction-bidding markets and other business decision-making situations. When the rules of the game are carefully defined and enforced, as they are in economic experiments held in laboratories, game theory has yielded interesting and important testable conclusions. Successful collusion, for example, is more likely to occur if the parties face the game repeatedly together. But in open markets in the real world, empirical work using game theory has been less successful. The use of models is always difficult when the problem to be solved is complex and when human expectations about the changing strategic choices of other human beings must be taken into account. There is no question, however, that game theory can be useful for scholars and business practitioners alike, by helping them frame the issues involved in strategic decision-making.[1]

[1]For a further explanation of game theory and the prisoner's dilemma, refer to Avinash Dixit and Barry Nalebuff, "Game Theory," in *The Concise Encyclopedia of Economics*, ed. David R. Henderson (Indianapolis, IN: Liberty Fund, Inc., 2002), https://www.econlib.org/library/Enc/GameTheory.html.

11-5 Market Power and Profit–The Early Bird Catches the Worm

Our analysis of both monopoly and oligopoly indicates that because entry barriers into these markets are often high, firms can sometimes earn economic profits over lengthy periods of time. Does that mean that buying stock in one of these companies is a better investment? The answer is no because the price of a share of stock in such a corporation would long ago have risen to reflect the firm's expected future profitability. Many of the present stockholders paid high prices for their stock because they expected these firms to continue to be highly profitable. In other words, these shareholders paid for any above-normal economic profits generated by the firm's market power at the time they purchased their ownership shares.

11-6 Defects of Markets with High Entry Barriers

From Adam Smith's time to the present, economists have generally considered monopoly to be a problem. The attitude toward markets with few sellers and high entry barriers has been only slightly more tolerant. Generally, economists offer three major criticisms. We will outline each of them.

1. When entry barriers are high and there are few, if any, alternative suppliers, the discipline of market forces is weakened. In contrast, when alternatives are present, consumers are in a position to direct the behavior of suppliers. If you do not like the food at a local restaurant, you eat elsewhere. If you think prices are high and the selection poor at a particular grocery store, you go to a different one. But consider your alternatives if you do not like the local electric company's service. You can voice a complaint to the company or your legislative representative, but the only exit option might be to convert your home entirely to solar power, an imperfect substitute with disadvantages. When consumers do not have good exit options, they must either take what the seller offers or do without. Consequently, their ability to keep sellers in check is greatly reduced.

2. Reduced competition results in allocative inefficiency. The formal condition for allocative efficiency requires that all units are produced that are valued more highly than what it costs to produce them. When barriers to entry are low, profit-seeking producers of each good expand their output until its price is driven down to the level of per-unit costs. Because price equals cost, all units of the good that consumers value higher than the cost of production will be produced and sold. With high barriers to entry, however, price may exceed per-unit costs, even over the long run. Therefore some units might not be produced, even though consumers value them more than their costs. These are the units valued by consumers more than cost, but less than the higher monopoly price.

3. Government grants of monopoly power will encourage rent seeking; resources will be wasted by firms attempting to secure and maintain grants of market protection. Special favors granted by the government will lead to costly activities for those who seek such favors. As we noted in Chapter 6, economists refer to such activities as rent seeking. When licenses or other entry barriers erected by the government enhance the profitability and provide protection from the rigors of market competition, people will expend scarce resources to secure and maintain these political favors. From an efficiency standpoint, these rent-seeking costs related to getting and keeping monopoly power add to the welfare losses resulting from the allocative inefficiencies we previously mentioned.

Suppose the government issues a license providing a single seller the exclusive right to sell liquor in a specific market. If this grant of monopoly power permits the licensee to earn monopoly profit, potential suppliers will compete, each trying to convince government officials that it should be the one firm granted the license. The potential monopolists will lobby government officials, make political contributions, hire representatives to do consulting studies, and undertake other actions designed to obtain the monopoly grant. Each firm may be willing to spend up to the present value of the future expected monopoly profits trying to obtain the monopoly license. With several potential suppliers, the total rent-seeking expenditures of all firms combined may even exceed the economic profit expected from the monopoly enterprise.

The resources devoted to rent seeking have an opportunity cost (for example, the company could have instead used the money to provide better service to customers), and thus are wasteful from a societal point of view. Therefore, the total losses to society from monopolies created through government favors can far exceed the losses caused by allocative inefficiency.

11-7 Policy Alternatives When Entry Barriers Are High

What government policies might be used to counteract the problems that result from high barriers to entry? Economists suggest four policy options:

1. Control the structure of the industry to ensure the presence of rival firms.
2. Reduce artificial barriers that limit competition.
3. Regulate the price and output of firms in the market.
4. Supply the market with goods produced by a government firm.

Each of these policies has been used to either reduce entry barriers or counteract their negative results. We will briefly consider each of them and analyze both their potential and limitations as tools that can be used to improve the efficiency of resource use.

11-7a Antitrust Policy and Controlling the Structure of an Industry

The major problems associated with high barriers to entry and monopoly power are not present when rival sellers are present and compete. The United States, to a greater degree than most Western countries, has adopted antitrust laws designed to prevent monopoly and promote competition. Antitrust legislation began in 1890 with the passage of the Sherman Antitrust Act. Additional legislation, including the Clayton Act and the Federal Trade Commission Act of 1914, has buttressed policy in this area.

Antitrust laws give the U.S. Department of Justice the power to prosecute firms engaging in collusive behavior or other actions designed to create a monopoly or cartel. They also give the government the power to break up an existing monopoly and prevent mergers that significantly reduce competition. The Federal Trade Commission (FTC) is allowed to bring charges under the Sherman Act. Private firms can also bring suits charging antitrust violations by a rival under the Sherman and Clayton acts and collect up to three times any actual damages caused by the rival firm. Each year, far more cases are brought by private firms against their competitors than by the two federal agencies. Rival firms can also ask the two agencies to bring antitrust cases against successful competitors who may have, or threaten to gain, monopoly power.

Economists do not fully agree on the usefulness of antitrust action to increase the number of rival firms in an industry. Those who support such policies believe that only by preserving numerous competitors in a market can we be confident that monopoly has been controlled. Opponents point to the danger of protecting high-cost firms at the expense of both consumers and the more aggressive and successful firm(s) in the market. Protection of less efficient firms from successful competitors, they say, is all too common in the actual practice of antitrust policy.

There is one situation in which the application of antitrust action would clearly be inappropriate. When substantial economies of scale are present, unit cost will be minimized only if the entire industry output is produced by a single firm, a case known as **natural monopoly**. Here, breaking up the one large firm in order to increase the number of rivals in the industry would lead to higher per-unit costs. Because of their higher costs, the prices charged by the smaller firms might even exceed those of the lower-cost natural monopoly. Therefore, using antitrust laws to expand the number of firms is not an attractive option when economies of scale in an industry produce a natural monopoly.

Natural monopoly
A market situation in which the average costs of production continually decline with increased output. In a natural monopoly, the average costs of production will be lowest when a single, large firm produces the entire output demanded by the marketplace.

11-7b Reduce Artificial Barriers to Trade

When government-imposed restrictions are the source of the monopoly power, the appropriate policy action is obvious: Remove the government restraints. But this is easier said than done. The restraints are generally in place because of the political influence of special-interest groups—the producers currently in the industry—who have a vested interest in restricting competition and keeping prices high. The politicians who supply these restrictions get political support from current producers in return, and removing them would be a costly political move. Thus, political considerations often make it difficult to remove government-imposed barriers to entry, such as licensing restrictions and tariff and quota restrictions on imported goods.

The interest groups behind government-imposed barriers to entry are highly concentrated and generally well organized politically. In contrast, the consumers who would benefit from more competitive markets are poorly organized, and the costs imposed on them by the restraints are nearly always thinly spread among them. As we discussed in Chapter 6, the political process often works to the advantage of the concentrated interests. As a result, even when lower barriers are needed to increase the competitiveness of an industry, political factors often prevent them.

11-7c Regulate the Price

Can government regulation improve the allocative efficiency of a monopoly or an oligopoly? **Exhibit 11-8** illustrates why ideal government price regulation, in the case of a monopolist, could theoretically improve resource allocation. The firm illustrated here is a natural monopoly. Its *LRATC* falls over the entire relevant range of output. Antitrust action dividing the firm into several smaller rivals will not help consumers because the unit costs of the smaller firms will be higher than if the output were produced by the monopolist. The profit-maximizing monopolist will set price at P_0 and produce output Q_0, where $MR = MC$. Consumers, however, would value additional units of output beyond Q_0 more than the cost of producing them, violating the conditions for allocative efficiency. Let's consider the potential of two regulatory options and also analyze some of their real-world limitations.

Average cost pricing If a regulatory agency forces the firm in Exhibit 11-8 to reduce the price to P_1, at which point the *LRATC* curve intersects the market (and firm) demand curve, then the firm will expand output to Q_1. Because it cannot charge a price above P_1, the firm cannot increase its revenues by selling a smaller output at a higher price. Once the price ceiling is instituted, the firm can increase its revenues by P_1, and by only P_1, for each unit it sells. The regulated firm's *MR* is constant at P_1 for all units sold until output is increased to Q_1. Because the firm's *MC* is less than P_1 (and therefore less than *MR*), the profit-maximizing regulated firm shown here will expand output from Q_0 to Q_1. The benefits from the consumption of these units (ABQ_1Q_0) clearly exceed their costs (CEQ_1Q_0). Social welfare has improved as a result of the regulatory action (we will ignore the impact on the distribution of income). At this output level, revenues are sufficient to cover costs. The firm is making zero economic profit (or "normal" accounting profit).

Marginal cost pricing Even at the Q_1 output level, marginal cost is still less than price. Additional welfare gains could be achieved if output were increased to Q_2. However, if a

Exhibit 11-8 Regulating a Monopolist

If unregulated, a profit-maximizing monopolist with the costs indicated here will produce Q_0 units and charge P_0. If a regulatory agency forced the monopolist to reduce price to P_1, then the monopolist would expand output to Q_1. Ideally, we would like output to be expanded to Q_2, where $P = MC$, but regulatory agencies usually do not attempt to keep prices as low as P_2. Can you explain why?

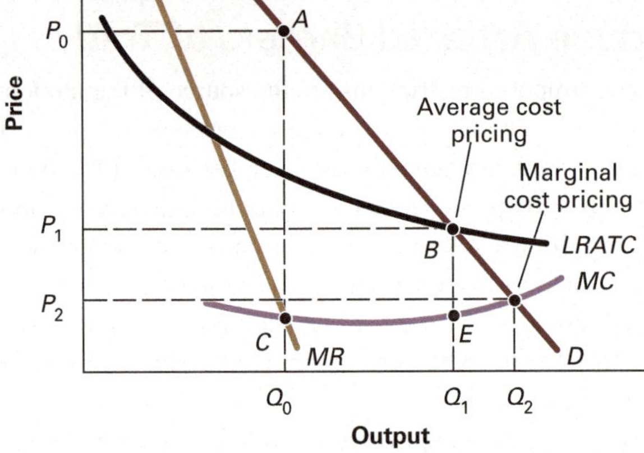

regulatory agency forced the monopolist to reduce the price to P_2 (so the price would equal the marginal cost at the output level Q_2), economic losses would result. Even a monopolist, unless it is subsidized, wouldn't produce the product at P_2 or any price below P_1. But how large should a subsidy be? No one has the knowledge to set this subsidy, partly because prices, technologies, and the value of output change daily. Also, who has the incentive to fight the pressures on both sides for higher (or lower) subsidies? Marginal cost pricing is seldom practical.

11-7d Problems with Regulation

Although regulating a monopoly might seem like a way to improve the efficiency of markets, both economic analysis and the history of regulation suggest that it has serious short-comings. In practice, three factors tend to reduce the effectiveness of regulation and the probability that regulators will act on behalf of all citizens to control monopolies. Let's look at each of these factors.

1. Lack of information. When we discussed ideal regulation, we assumed that we knew what the firm's *ATC, MC,* and demand curves looked like. In reality, of course, regulators do not. Even the firms themselves will have difficulty knowing their costs, and especially their demand curves, with any precision. Furthermore, both supply and demand will vary over time and by location. The market for electricity is an excellent example. Because electricity cannot be stored for later use, the highly variable supply-and-demand conditions in that market cause the opportunity cost of power to change dramatically from one day, or even one hour, to the next. There is simply no way to have government-determined prices that are flexible and correct enough to avoid causing major shortages and surpluses of the good through time. For example, sharply changing cost conditions for California utilities coupled with inflexible, regulated retail power rates often have historically combined to produce widespread power outages.

Because it is virtually impossible to estimate demand and marginal costs, regulatory agencies usually gauge profits (or the rate of return) to determine whether the regulated price is too high or too low. The regulatory agency seeks to impose a "fair" or "normal" rate of return on the firm. If the firm is making economic profits (that is, an abnormally high rate of return), the regulated price must be higher than P_1 in Exhibit 11-8, and therefore it should be reduced. Alternatively, if the firm is incurring losses (less than the fair, or normal, rate of return), this indicates that the regulated price is less than P_1 and that the firm should be permitted to charge a higher price.

The actual existence of profits, though, is not easily identifiable. Accounting profit, or the rate of return, is not the same as economic profit, which includes opportunity cost. Also, regulated firms have a strong incentive to adopt reporting techniques and accounting methods that conceal profits. Because of this, a regulatory agency will find it difficult or impossible to identify and impose a price consistent with allocative efficiency.

2. Cost shifting. Regulation changes incentives, so it can affect costs. If demand is sufficient, the owners of the regulated firm can expect the long-run rate of profit to be essentially fixed, regardless of whether efficient management reduces costs or inefficient management allows costs to increase. If costs decrease, the "fair return" rule imposed by the regulatory agency will force a price reduction; if costs increase, the "fair return" rule will allow a price increase. Compared to the managers of unregulated firms, managers of a regulated monopoly have more freedom to pursue personal objectives and less incentive to seek lower costs. Predictably, they will often fly first class, entertain lavishly at company expense, grant unwarranted wage increases, and so on. Production inefficiency and higher costs will result, but consumers are in a weak position to shift away from the good supplied by the monopolist.

3. Special-interest influence. The difficulties of government regulation discussed so far are practical limitations a regulatory agency confronts. Unfortunately, the political element of government regulation exacerbates the problem. Regulated firms have a strong incentive to see that "friendly," "reasonable" people serve as regulators, and they will invest political and economic resources toward this end. Just as rent-seeking activities designed to gain monopoly privileges in the first place can be expected, so, too, can activities to influence regulators' decisions. Few consumers will invest the time and resources required to understand regulatory policy and make the political contributions needed to counteract the influence peddling. Over time, regulatory commissions are therefore likely to reflect the views and interests of the business and labor interests they regulate.

In summary, regulation not only has the potential to improve resource allocation in markets with few competitors, but it also generates adverse side effects. Both economic reasoning and decades of experience indicate that regulation is not a magic cure. Real-world cases of regulation, such as in electricity markets, provide evidence consistent with the idea that there is no single best solution.

11-7e Supply Market with Government Production

Government-operated firms—like the U.S. Postal Service and many local public utilities—present an alternative to both private monopoly and regulation. Here, too, however, economic thinking and experience indicate that these firms will fail to counteract fully the problems that stem from high barriers to entry. The same perverse managerial incentives that regulated firms experience—incentives to ignore efficiency and pursue personal or professional objectives at the firm's expense—also tend to plague government-operated firms. In addition, the rational ignorance effect comes into play here. Individual voters have little incentive to acquire information about the operation of government firms because, unlike the case of a personal investment, the individual's choices will not decide which investment will be purchased with the voter's money. Predictably, the "owners" of a government-operated firm (voters) will be uninformed about how well the firm is run, how it might be run better, or if another firm has a better plan. This is especially true when there are no direct competitors against which the firm's performance might be compared.

The operation of enterprises by the government does not create an environment that rewards managers or investors for efficient management and reductions in cost. Unlike in the private sector, no small group of investors can increase their wealth by taking over the firm and improving its management. Even more than with monopoly or oligopoly in the private sector, customers of the socialized monopoly cannot easily switch their business to other sellers. Voter-taxpayers who do not even consume the product often have to pay taxes to support its provision. When the government operates a business, there is typically less investor scrutiny, less reward for efficiency, and less penalty for inefficiency or the production of inferior goods. Higher costs and lower-valued outputs are predictable results.

Government ownership, like unregulated monopoly and government regulation, is a less-than-ideal solution. Even those who denounce private sector monopoly seldom point to a government-operated monopoly as an example of how an industry should be run.

11-7f Pulling It Together

The policy alternatives available when high barriers to entry are present are less than satisfying. Most are just not very attractive. Economies of scale often make antitrust actions impractical. When larger firms have lower per-unit costs, restructuring the industry to increase the number of firms will be both costly and difficult to maintain. Furthermore, antitrust policy opens the door for firms to use it against successful rivals that have simply given consumers a better deal and captured a large part of the market in the process. Policy actions to stop or to punish such progress are counterproductive for customers and for economic efficiency. Lifting government restrictions such as licensing requirements, quotas, and tariffs that limit competition is perhaps the surest way to improve the performance of markets with few suppliers. But the nature of the political process, particularly its tendency to cater to the views of well-organized interest groups at the expense of the unorganized majority of consumers/voters, often undermines the feasibility of this option. In some cases, innovative entrepreneurs can find ways around these restrictions, as has been the case with ride-sharing services such as Uber. The politically protected industries fight back hard, however, and in some cases, ride-sharing has been banned or severely restricted.

Price regulation is also a less-than-ideal solution. Regulators do not possess the information necessary to impose an efficient outcome, and as part of the political process, they will be susceptible to manipulation by special interests. When firms are operated by the government, political objectives will be pursued at the expense of consumer interests and economic efficiency. Thus, government operation of firms also has its problems. In short, when economies of scale lead to a tendency toward monopoly, there is no ideal solution.

11-8 Dynamic Competition in the Digital Age

How competitive are markets today? As George Stigler points out in the second of his chapter-opening quotations, "Competition is a tough weed, not a delicate flower." The competitiveness of markets is complex and difficult to measure directly. Firms in markets that appear to be unrelated often compete with one another. For example, sellers of swimming pools compete with airlines, hotels, casinos, and automobile rental companies for the vacation and leisure time expenditures of consumers.

Most economists believe that, propelled by substantial reductions in transportation and communication costs, the competitiveness of the U.S. economy increased throughout the second half of the twentieth century. The trend during the first few decades of the twenty-first century, however, is subject to more debate.[3] Measures of industrial concentration at the national level have increased in most sectors since around 1997, corresponding roughly to the start of the digital age. The share of sales of the four (or fewer) largest firms has increased in many industries, including personal computers, airline travel, auto rentals, package delivery, cell phones, cable television, home improvement and hardware, and home washing machines and clothes dryers. Both mean and median revenues for publicly held corporations, which were on the decline in real terms, have trended upward since the mid to late 1990s. There is also evidence of larger markups and increased profitability among large firms. In addition, large Internet companies such as Google (Alphabet), Amazon, Facebook (Meta), and X (formerly Twitter) now dominate their respective online segments of the marketplace and social media, and this has caused increased concerns about privacy and growing demands for government antitrust actions.

Despite the growing number of industries seemingly dominated by a few large firms, however, there is substantial evidence that the economy is actually more competitive than it was prior to the digital age. Let us consider some of these factors in more detail.

First, there is the growth of the gig economy and the rise of **platform businesses**—firms that create synergies between crowdsourced resources that aren't necessarily owned or controlled by the firm. Uber and Airbnb are examples of platform businesses. Rather than owning taxicabs or hotel properties, these business firms instead provide an infrastructure for a large number of decentralized entrepreneurial individuals to offer rides or rooms to others. They create value by lowering transaction costs, facilitating exchanges, and helping to provide a framework within which a spontaneous order of buyers and sellers can operate. Similarly, Amazon is a marketplace where many individual sellers offer their products in competition with one another within the platform. YouTube, Instagram, TikTok, Facebook (Meta), and X (formerly Twitter) are platforms that allow others to create content to share. Apple's app store is also based on a crowdsourced platform business model in which it is easy for individuals to create content and start competing against other similar sellers. Although each of these market segments is dominated by a large firm, numerous competitors are operating within the platform.

Platform businesses
A firm that provides the environment for the creation of synergies among decentralized crowdsourced resources that aren't necessarily owned or controlled by the firm.

All of these businesses operate in environments where their products or services become more valuable the more people use them—a characteristic known as a **network effect**. A social media site with only several hundred people on it would not be as desirable to join as one with millions; an online property rental platform with only a few dozen rooms in a handful of cities wouldn't generate many customers; and an online marketplace with only a few sellers and products would not be a very attractive place to shop. When network effects are important, the benefit to consumers is greatest when only a single or a few large networks dominate a market. In these markets, the type of competition we tend to witness is one of rivalry and replacement among large firms. Companies such as America Online, Yahoo!, and MySpace once dominated the marketplace and have been replaced by other large firms such as Instagram, Facebook (Meta), and X (formerly Twitter). Because these markets are contestable—that is, the cost of entry is low—there are many potential rivals that are always seeking to become the next dominant firm and replace the ones currently at the top. The existing dominant firms live under the constant threat of being replaced. In order to keep their dominant position, they must continually satisfy consumers. This constant competitive threat means these large firms do not behave the same as monopolies that are protected from competition by barriers to entry. Rather than restricting output and raising prices, they innovate, expand, and cut prices to defend their dominant positions.

Network effect
When the value of a product or service to each consumer increases as the number of users expands. This is also known as a network externality.

[3]Refer to Tim Sablik, "Are Markets Too Concentrated?" *Econ Focus* (Federal Reserve Bank of Richmond, First Quarter 2018): 10–13; Esteban Rossi-Hansberg, Pierre-Daniel Sarte, and Nicholas Trachter, "Diverging Trends in National and Local Concentration," National Bureau of Economic Research *Macroeconomics Annual*, 2020, forthcoming; and W. Michael Cox and Richard Alm, "Big Business: Disruptive Technologies, Market Structure and Competition in the 21st Century," *O'Neil Center for Global Markets and Freedom 2018–19 Annual Report* (SMU Cox School of Business, 2019).

Second, there have been significant improvements in technology, communications, and transportation that have lowered transaction and monitoring costs and weakened the forces that lead to diseconomies of scale. These factors have led to larger firm sizes being relatively the most cost effective (and price competitive) and a growing number of large firm mergers, such as AT&T acquiring DirecTV and Time Warner. The ability to implement standardized business practices and coordinate and monitor multiple and distant locations has improved, while at the same time, it has become faster and cheaper to buy and sell goods and services across greater distances. Quite the opposite of what one would expect if these markets dominated by large firms were becoming less competitive, we are seeing firms in more concentrated markets having a larger number of new patents, showing that innovation in these industries is rising at the same time firm size is expanding and concentration increasing.

Third, the digital age has changed marketing, advertising, and information costs in ways that make it easier to reach a larger customer base more rapidly and cost effectively. Many online businesses and apps provide their services free to customers because they are able to rely on advertising for their revenue. For example, Instagram provides a free social networking platform. Google provides "free services" such as Internet search, Gmail, and cloud storage space to expand its user base. Instead of restricting output and raising prices as monopolists would do, these online platform firms seek to expand output to increase the value of their advertising space. Because most of their costs are fixed and there is a very low marginal cost of having additional individuals download or use the app or website, their business model is one of growing as big as possible to exploit the falling average cost per user and rising advertising revenue.

The costs of searching for information have fallen dramatically, as have the costs of reaching new consumers. An endorsement from a famous influencer or a favorable review from a reputable expert can now generate millions of new customers in a short period of time for a new innovative company or great new product. Online advertisements can now be targeted toward large but specific customer groups likely to purchase a product based on their past interests and behaviors. Google has made it easy for customers to find even rare or distant products or businesses that meet their desires. Digital purchasing means even a small company can take dozens of orders per second without the constraints imposed by the need for human staffing. The time it takes for new innovations to penetrate the market and gain large market share has fallen dramatically over the past few decades. Although it took almost 50 years for products like electricity, the automobile, and air conditioning to reach a market share of 67 percent, the digital camera and smartphone both did it in less than a decade. Again, these patterns of dynamic change are indicative of stronger, rather than weaker, competitive forces.

In the modern digital economy, the degree of competition is not measured well by simple measures of industrial concentration, especially ones at the national level. In fact, while measures of concentration at the national level are rising, in these same industries, when concentration is measured at the local level, the opposite is true—concentration is falling. The typical consumer in the United States now has more choices and a greater selection than in the past when viewed from a local or individual perspective. Improvements in technology and transportation have led to efficiency improvements that have allowed what were once regional or local sellers to become nationwide or even global retailers.

Technological change itself is also a powerful force for competitive markets. Innovation and nonprice competition on product quality, design, convenience, and other factors are used constantly by firms seeking greater market share and profitability. For a firm, innovation is the key to (temporary) profits. Successful innovation can give the innovating firm some degree of relief from competition while other firms struggle to catch up. Technical improvements, like newer and better computers or ways to make and sell them, cheaper and better inventory control methods, robotics and artificial intelligence, and innovative cell phones, have all made fortunes for the firms developing the information technology behind them.

But the advantage is generally temporary. As long as the market is contestable—that is, there are low barriers to new firm entry—new rival firms will eventually rise to displace existing firms, even big ones. While this has always been true, with Netflix replacing Blockbuster, Apple displacing Microsoft, and Walmart replacing Kmart and Sears, this dynamic process of large-firm replacement is becoming an even more important factor with rising economies of scale and the network effects associated with platform businesses in the digital age. Over time, consumers are the big winners, as this dynamic process provides them with more options and innovative new products at attractive prices.

Key Points

- The four major sources of barriers to entry are economies of scale, government licensing, patents, and control of an essential resource.
- A monopoly is present when there is a single seller of a well-defined product for which there are no good substitutes and the entry barriers into the market are high. Although there are only a few markets in which the entire output is supplied by a single seller, the monopoly model also helps us better understand the operation of markets dominated by a small number of firms.
- Like other price searchers, a profit-maximizing monopolist will lower the price and expand its output as long as marginal revenue exceeds marginal cost. At the maximum-profit output, *MR* will equal *MC*. The monopolist will charge the price on its demand curve consistent with that output.
- If a monopolist is earning a profit, high barriers to entry will shield the firm from direct competition, thereby enabling it to earn long-run economic profits. But sometimes demand and cost conditions will be such that even a monopolist will be unable to earn economic profit.
- An oligopolistic market is characterized by (1) a small number of rival firms, (2) interdependence among the sellers, (3) substantial economies of scale, and (4) high entry barriers into the market.
- There is no general theory for the determination of a unique price and output in an oligopolistic market. If rival oligopolists acted totally independently of their competitors, they would drive the price down to the per-unit cost of production. Alternatively, if they colluded perfectly, the price would rise to the level a monopolist would charge. The actual outcome under oligopoly will generally fall between these two extremes.
- Oligopolists have a strong incentive to collude and raise their prices. However, each firm will be able to gain if it (alone) can cut its price (or improve the quality of its product) because the demand curve confronted by the firm is more elastic than the industry demand curve. This introduces a conflict that makes it difficult to maintain collusive agreements, even where no law prohibits them.
- Oligopolistic firms are less likely to collude successfully against the interests of consumers if (1) there are more rival firms in the market, (2) it is costly to prohibit competitors from offering secret price cuts (or quality improvements) to customers, (3) entry barriers are low, (4) market demand conditions tend to be unstable, and/or (5) the threat of antitrust action is present.
- Economists criticize high barriers to market entry because (1) the ability of consumers to discipline producers is weakened, (2) the unregulated monopolist or oligopoly group can often gain by restricting output and raising price, and (3) legal barriers to entry encourage firms to engage in wasteful rent-seeking activities.
- When entry barriers are high and competition among rival firms weak, the major policy alternatives are (1) antitrust action designed to maintain or increase the number of firms in the industry, (2) relaxation of regulations that limit entry and trade, (3) price regulation, and (4) provision of output by government firms. When feasible, option (2) is the most attractive alternative. Under most circumstances, all the other options have shortcomings.
- Despite the growing number of industries seemingly dominated by a few large firms, there is reason to believe that the economy is actually more competitive than it was before the digital age. The rise of the gig economy and platform businesses, increased gains from network effects, improvements in technology that weakened the forces leading to diseconomies of scale, and digital tools that reduce search costs all expand consumer options and increase the competitiveness of markets.

Critical Analysis Questions

1. "Barriers to entry are crucial to the existence of long-run profits, but they cannot guarantee the existence of profits." Evaluate.
2. What are the major reasons why economists have been so critical of monopoly and high entry barriers into markets?
3. *Do monopolists charge the highest prices for which they can sell their products? Do they maximize their average profit per sale? Are monopolistic firms always profitable? Why or why not?
4. Compare the price and output policy of a purely competitive industry with the policy that would be established by a profit-maximizing monopolist or cartel. Who benefits and who is hurt? Construct the appropriate graphs to illustrate your answer.
5. Does economic theory indicate that an ideal regulatory agency that forces a monopolist to charge a price equal to either marginal or average total cost will improve economic efficiency? Explain. Does economic theory suggest that a regulatory agency will in fact regulate in a manner consistent with economic efficiency? What are some of the factors that complicate the regulatory function?
6. What is a natural monopoly? When a natural monopoly is present, will antitrust policy be a good way to improve allocative efficiency? Why or why not?
7. How will high entry barriers into a market influence
   a. the long-run profitability of the firms,
   b. the cost efficiency of the firms in the industry,
   c. the likelihood that some inefficient (high-cost) firms will survive, and
   d. the incentive of entrepreneurs to develop substitutes for the product supplied by the firms? Are competitive pressures present in markets with high barriers to entry? Discuss.
8. *Why is oligopolistic collusion more difficult when there is product variation than when the products of all firms are identical?
9. Historically, in many cities, taxi fares were often way above the market equilibrium rate, due to government licensing restrictions. In essence, these taxi cartels used government laws to earn excess profits by erecting barriers to entry. However, modern ride-sharing services such as Uber have found innovative ways to bypass these government restrictions, and protests by the taxi industry have been frequent. In some cases, governments responded by banning Uber. Compare and contrast resource allocation and market outcomes under the restricted license system and a competitive system. In which case will it be easier (and cheaper) for customers to get a ride? Do you think governments should ban Uber to increase the profits of taxi drivers? Why or why not?
10. What are the factors that increase the likelihood that oligopolists will be able to restrict output and raise price? What are the factors that will reduce their ability to do so? How can game theory help us understand the decisions made by oligopolists?
11. *Historically, the real costs of transporting both goods and people have declined substantially. What impact do lower transportation costs have on the market power of individual producers? Do you think the U.S. economy is more or less competitive today than it was 100 years ago? Explain.
12. *"My uncle just bought 1,000 shares of Apple, one of the largest and most profitable companies in the United States. Given Apple's high profit rate, he will make a bundle from this purchase." Evaluate this statement. Is it necessarily true? Explain.
13. Gouge-em Cable Company is the only cable television and Internet service company licensed to operate in Backwater County. Most of its costs are access fees and maintenance expenses. These fixed costs total $6,400,000 monthly. The marginal cost of adding another subscriber to its system is constant at $20 per month. Gouge-em's demand curve can be determined from the data in the accompanying table.

Subscription Price	Number of Subscribers (per Month)
$250	20,000
200	40,000
150	60,000
100	80,000
50	100,000
10	150,000

   a. What price will Gouge-em charge for its services? What are its profits at this price?
   b. Now suppose the Backwater County Public Utility Commission has the data and believes that subscription rates in the county are too expensive and that Gouge-em's profits are unfairly high. What regulated price will it set so that Gouge-em makes only a normal rate of return on its investment?
14. Have the Internet and the rise of platform businesses increased or decreased the competitiveness of markets? How has the size of firms been impacted

by the growing importance of network effects and the reduction in transaction and monitoring costs associated with improvements in technology, communications, and transportation?

15. Suppose that you produce and sell children's tables in a local market. Past experience enables you to estimate your demand and marginal cost schedules. This information is presented in the accompanying table.

a. Fill in the missing revenue and cost schedules.

b. Assuming you are currently charging $55 per table set, what should you do if you want to maximize profits?

c. Given your demand and cost estimates, what price should you charge if you want to maximize your weekly profit? What output should you produce? What is your maximum weekly profit?

Price	Quantity Demanded (per Week)	Marginal Cost	Total Revenue	Marginal Revenue	Fixed Cost	Total Cost
$60	1	$50	—	—	$40	—
55	2	20	—	—	—	—
50	3	24	—	—	—	—
45	4	29	—	—	—	—
40	5	35	—	—	—	—
35	6	45	—	—	—	—

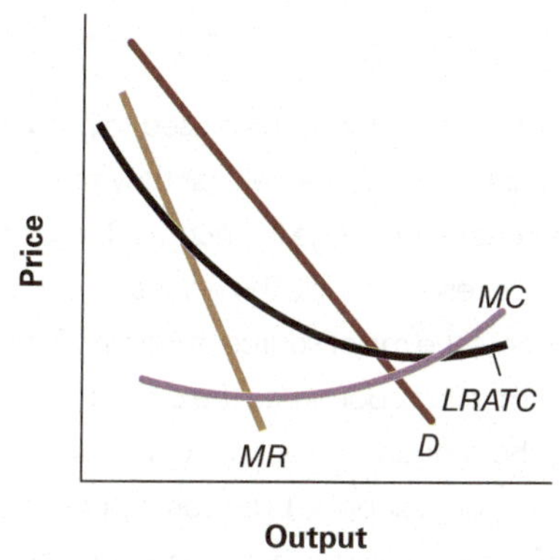

16. The accompanying diagram shows demand and long-run cost conditions in an industry.

a. Explain why the industry is likely to be monopolized.

b. Indicate the price that a profit-maximizing monopolist would charge and label it *P*.

c. Indicate the monopolist's output level and label it *Q*.

d. Indicate the maximum profits of the monopolist.

e. Will the profits attract competitors to the industry? Why or why not? Explain.

*Asterisk denotes questions for which answers are given in Appendix B.

Chapter 12 The Supply of and Demand for Productive Resources

> It is . . . necessary to attach price tags to the various factors of production . . . in order to guide those who have the day-to-day decisions to make as to what is plentiful and what is scarce.
>
> –James Meade[1]

Recent chapters have focused on product markets, markets in which consumers purchase goods and services supplied by business firms. Our analysis now shifts to **resource markets**, markets in which firms hire productive resources like machines and workers and use them to produce goods and services. (*Note*: Because resources are often referred to as *factors or inputs*, these markets are also known as *factor markets* or *input markets*.)

As in product markets, the forces of supply and demand combine to determine prices in resource markets. The buyers and sellers in resource markets are just the reverse of what they are in product markets. In resource markets, business firms are the purchasers; they demand resources used to produce goods and services. Households are the sellers; they (and firms they own) supply resources in exchange for income. The income from supplying productive resources, like the wages received from the sale of labor services, is the major source of income for most of us. Prices in resource markets coordinate the choices of buyers and sellers and bring the amount of each resource demanded into harmony with the amount supplied. Resource prices also help to channel factors of production into the areas where they are most productive. This enables us to have higher incomes and a larger supply of consumer goods than would otherwise be the case.

Learning Objectives

12.1 Indicate the two broad categories of resources.

12.2 Identify the buyers and sellers in resource markets and explain how they differ from product markets.

12.3 Define an investment in human capital and indicate what motivates individuals to improve their skills and supply resources.

12.4 Explain why the demand for a resource is considered a derived demand.

12.5 Indicate the major factors that will change the demand for a resource.

12.6 Calculate the marginal revenue product for the usage of a resource and use this information to decide how much of a resource to employ.

12.7 Explain why the ratio of price to marginal productivity for each resource is consistent across resources when the firm is minimizing the cost of producing a product.

12.8 Explain why the supply of a resource will be more elastic in the long run than in the short run.

12.9 Indicate how changes in the supply and demand for a resource affect the equilibrium price and quantity employed.

[1] James E. Meade was a longtime professor of economics at Cambridge University.

12-1 Resource Markets and Human and Nonhuman Resources

As the circular flow diagram of **Exhibit 12-1** illustrates, there is a close relationship between product and resource markets. Households earn income by selling factors of production—for example, the services of their labor and capital—to business firms. Their offers to sell form the supply curve in resource markets (bottom loop). The income that households get from the sale of resources gives them the buying power they need to purchase goods and services in product markets. These expenditures by households generate revenue and motivate firms to produce goods and services (top loop). In turn, firms demand resources because they contribute to the production of goods and services that can be sold in product markets.

Resource markets
Markets in which business firms demand factors of production (for example, labor, capital, and natural resources) from household suppliers. The resources are then used to produce goods and services. These markets are sometimes called factor markets or input markets.

Broadly speaking, there are two different types of productive inputs, nonhuman and human. **Nonhuman resources** can be further broken down into physical capital, land, and natural resources. *Physical capital* consists of human-made resources, like tools, machines, and buildings that are used to produce other things.

Nonhuman resources
The durable, nonhuman inputs used to produce both current and future output. Machines, buildings, land, and raw materials are examples. Investment can increase the supply of nonhuman resources. Economists often use the term *physical capital* when referring to nonhuman resources.

Investment involves the use of resources in a manner that will increase future production capacity. The use of resources to produce machines, upgrade the quality of land, or discover natural resources provide examples of investments in nonhuman resources. Of course, investments involve a cost because the resources used to expand future production capacity could have been used to produce consumption goods directly. Why take the roundabout path? Investment and the indirect method often expand total output. The investment will be attractive if the value of the future output exceeds the cost of the reduction in current output.

Exhibit 12-1 The Market for Resources

Until now, we have focused on product markets, in which households demand goods and services that are supplied by firms (upper loop). We now turn to resource markets, in which firms demand factors of production–human capital (like the skills and knowledge of workers) and physical capital (like machines, buildings, and land). Factors of production are supplied by households in exchange for income (bottom loop). In resource markets, firms are buyers and households are sellers–just the reverse of the case for product markets.

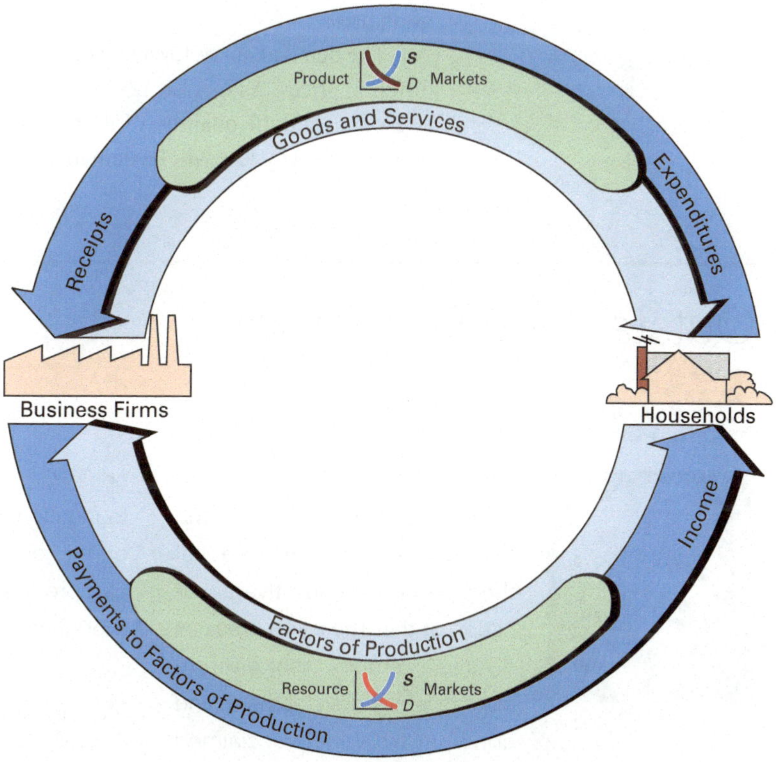

Human resources
The abilities, skills, and health of human beings that contribute to the production of both current and future output. Investment in training and education can increase the supply of human resources.

Investment in human capital
Expenditures on training, education, skill development, and health designed to increase human capital and people's productivity.

Human resources consist of the skills and knowledge of workers. Investments in education, training, health, and experience can enhance the skills, abilities, and ingenuity of individuals and thereby increase their productivity. Economists refer to activities like these as **investment in human capital**. Like physical capital, human capital also depreciates—people's skills, for example, can decline with age or lack of use. Education and training will add to the stock of human capital, whereas depreciation detracts from it.

Decisions to invest in human capital are no different than other investment decisions we make. Consider your decision about going to college. As you know, an investment in a college education requires you to sacrifice some current earnings as well as pay for direct expenses, like tuition and books. However, you are making the investment anyway because you expect it to lead to a better job and other benefits later. A rational person will attend college only if the expected future benefits outweigh the current costs.

In competitive markets, the price of resources, like the price of products, is determined by supply and demand. We will begin our analysis of resource markets by focusing on the demand for resources, both human and nonhuman.

12-2 The Demand for Resources

Derived demand
The demand for a resource; it stems from the demand for the final good the resource helps produce.

Profit-seeking producers employ laborers, machines, raw materials, and other resources because they help produce goods and services. The demand for a resource exists because there is a demand for goods that the resource helps to produce. ***The demand for each resource is thus a derived demand; it is derived from the demand of consumers for products.***

For example, the demand for inputs like carpenters, plumbers, lumber, and glass windows is derived from the demand of consumers for houses and other consumer products these resources help to make. Most resources contribute to the production of numerous goods. For example, glass is used to produce windows, lightbulbs, and mirrors, among other things. The total demand for a resource is the sum of the derived demands for each of its uses.

The demand curve for a resource shows the amount of the resource that will be used at different prices. As **Exhibit 12-2** shows, there is an inverse relationship between the price of a resource and the quantity of it demanded. As the price of a resource increases, there are two reasons why less will be demanded: (1) Producers will turn to substitute resources, and

Outstanding Economist

Gary Becker (1930-2014)

Phil McCarten/Reuters

This 1992 Nobel Prize recipient is best known for his role in the development of human capital theory and his innovative application of that theory to areas as diverse as employment discrimination, family development, and crime. In his widely acclaimed book *Human Capital*,* Becker developed the theoretical foundation for human investment decisions in education, on-the-job training, migration, and health. Becker was a past president of the American Economic Association and a longtime professor at the University of Chicago.

*Gary Becker, Human Capital (New York: Columbia University Press, 1964).

Exhibit 12-2 The Demand Curve for a Resource

As the price of a resource increases, producers that use the resource intensely will (1) turn to substitute resources and (2) face higher costs, which will lead to higher product prices and lower output. At the lower rate of output, producers will use less of the resource that increased in price. Both of these factors contribute to the inverse relationship between the price and amount demanded of a resource.

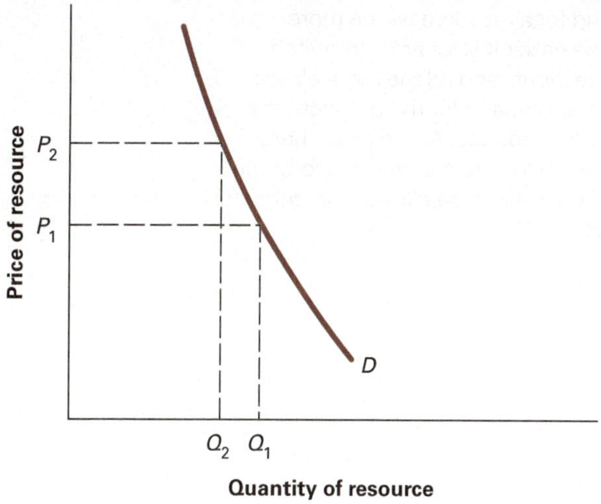

(2) consumers will buy less of goods that become more expensive as the result of higher resource costs. Let us examine each of these factors.

12-2a Substitution in Production

Firms use the combination of resources that minimizes costs. When the price of one resource goes up, firms switch to other lower-cost substitute resources. If the price of oak lumber increases, furniture manufacturers will begin to use other types of wood (like maple) or metals and plastics more intensely. Sometimes, producers will alter the style and dimensions of a product, or even relocate the business, in order to use less of a more expensive resource. The degree to which firms will be able to cut back on a more expensive resource will depend on the availability of substitute resources. ***Other things constant, the demand for a resource will be more elastic the more (and better) substitute resources are available for it.***

12-2b Substitution in Consumption

An increase in the price of a resource will lead to higher costs of production and thus higher prices for the products it helps to produce. Faced with these higher product prices, *consumers* will turn to substitute products and cut back on their purchases of the now more expensive products. In turn, fewer resources will be required to produce the smaller amount of the product demanded by consumers at the now higher price (including less of the resource that rose in price).

Other things constant, the more elastic the demand for a product is, the more elastic the demand for the resources used to make it. This relationship stems from the derived nature of resource demand. An increase in the price of a product for which consumer demand is highly elastic will cause a sharp fall in the sales of the good. As a result, there will be a relatively sharp fall in the demand for the resources used to produce it.

12-2c How Time Changes the Demand for Resources

The elasticity of resource demand is also influenced by time. It takes time for both producers and consumers to make the adjustments described above after a resource price has changed. Producers may have to alter their plant and equipment, while consumers also need time to identify and utilize other substitutes. Thus, the demand for a resource generally becomes more elastic with the passage of time.

Exhibit 12-3 Time and the Demand Elasticity of Resources

The demand for a resource will be more elastic (1) the easier it is for firms to switch to substitute inputs and (2) the more elastic the consumer demand for the products the resource helps produce. As the graph here shows, demand for a resource in the long run (D_{lr}) is nearly always more elastic than demand in the short run (D_{sr}).

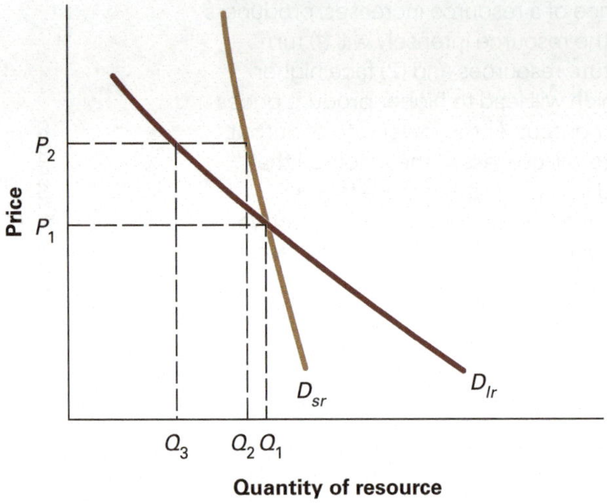

Exhibit 12-3 shows how time affects the elasticity of resource demand. The slope of the long-run demand curve (D_{lr}) is less steep, showing it is more elastic, than the slope of the short-run demand curve (D_{sr}). An increase in price from P_1 to P_2 will lead to only a small reduction in the quantity of the resource used (from Q_1 to Q_2) in the short run. Given more time, however, the increase in price to P_2 causes a much larger reduction in the quantity demanded (to Q_3).

12-2d Shifts in the Demand for a Resource

Like the demand curve for a product, the entire demand curve for a resource may shift. There are three major reasons why.

1. A change in the demand for a product will cause a similar change in the demand for the resources used to produce it. Because the demand for a resource is a derived demand, an increase in the demand for a consumer good simultaneously increases the demand for resources needed to make it. For example, the demand for personal computers and other computerized equipment has increased substantially over the past couple of decades. In turn, this stronger demand for the equipment generated an increase in demand for computer chips required for its production. Of course, a reduction in the demand for a product will have the opposite impact. Lower demand for the product will lead to a reduction in demand for the resources required for its production.

2. Changes in the productivity of a resource will alter demand—the higher the productivity of a resource, the greater will be the demand for it. As the productivity of a resource increases, so does its value to potential users. Improvements in the quality of a resource—in the case of workers, their skill levels—will increase the productivity of the resource and therefore the demand for it. For example, as workers gain valuable new knowledge and/or upgrade their skills, they enhance their productivity and essentially move into a different skill category—one in which demand is greater.

The productivity of a resource will also depend on the amount of other resources used with it in the production process. The quantity and quality of the equipment with which employees work will significantly affect their productivity. Technological advances in robotics and computing have substantially increased the productivity of a wide range of occupations, including journalists, book authors, autoworkers, coal miners, and forensic

The demand for resources is a derived demand. A more complex tax code would increase the demand for (and thus the wages of) accountants, whereas a simpler tax code would have the opposite impact.

scientists. The link between technological advances and worker productivity helps explain why improvements in technology generally do not simply displace workers and thereby exert a large negative impact on employment, even in the occupations most directly affected. Of course, when firms substitute new technology for labor services, the demand for labor will fall. However, the new technology both makes labor more productive and lowers the cost of production and prices for consumers, both of which increase the demand for labor. These positive impacts of technology on the employment of labor will partially, and sometimes more than completely, offset any negative effects.

The productivity–demand link sheds light on why wage rates in the United States, Canada, Western Europe, and Japan are higher than in most other areas of the world. Given the skill level of workers, the technology, and the capital equipment with which they work, individuals in these countries produce more goods and services per hour of labor than workers in most other countries. In turn, the demand for their labor (relative to supply) is greater because of their high productivity. Essentially, the workers' greater productivity leads to their higher wage rates.

3. A change in the price of a related resource will affect the demand for the original resource. A rise in the price of a resource will cause the demand for substitute resources to expand. For example, when the price of lumber increases, the demand for bricks will increase as homebuilders switch to building more brick homes and fewer wood homes. Conversely, an increase in the price of a resource that is a *complement* to a given resource will decrease the demand for the given resource. For example, higher lumber prices will tend to lower the demand for nails.

12-3 Marginal Productivity and the Firm's Hiring Decision

How does a producer decide whether to employ additional units of a resource? As with other decisions, the marginal benefit relative to the marginal cost provides the answer. In resource markets, firms are mostly price takers, which means they can hire as many units of the resource

CaroleGomez/Getty Images

Christina Richards/Shutterstock.com

Compared to a person working with a shovel, a worker using a backhoe can dig the trenches for water or sewer lines more rapidly. The productivity of workers increases when they are working with more and better equipment.

as they wish without affecting the market price of the resource. Thus, the marginal cost of hiring one more worker is simply the worker's wage, while the marginal cost of purchasing a machine is its price. These represent the increase in the firm's costs from employing one more unit of each resource. But what about the marginal benefit of the resource to the firm? It is measured by the increase in the firm's revenue from employing one more unit of the resource. This is called the resource's **marginal revenue product (*MRP*)**. A profit-maximizing firm will only hire an additional unit of the resource if it generates more revenue for the firm than the cost of employing it. If the marginal revenue product of employing an additional unit of a resource is less than the cost, the firm will not employ it.

Marginal revenue product (*MRP*)
The change in the total revenue of a firm that results from the employment of one additional unit of a resource. The marginal revenue product of an input is equal to its marginal product multiplied by the marginal revenue of the good or service produced.

Suppose a retail store was considering hiring a security guard for $25 per hour to help reduce shoplifting. If the security guard could prevent $20 worth of shoplifting per hour, should the profit-maximizing firm hire the guard? Because the marginal cost of employing the security guard (the wage of $25) is higher than the guard's marginal revenue product (the $20 reduction in shoplifting per hour), the wise decision is for the firm not to hire the security guard. Hiring the guard will lower the firm's profit by $5 per hour. The guard should be employed only if the reduction in shoplifting exceeds the guard's wage cost. In most situations, the direct impact of hiring an additional resource on a firm's revenue is not as clear, so let's examine the firm's decision and how marginal revenue product is determined.

12-3a Using a Variable Resource with a Fixed Resource

When an additional unit of the resource is used relative to a fixed amount of other resources, the firm's output will increase by an amount equal to the resource's **marginal product (*MP*)**. Because this is measured in units of physical output, it is sometimes referred to as marginal physical product. How much additional revenue can the firm derive from the employment of the resource? Recall that **marginal revenue (*MR*)** is the increase in the firm's revenue that results from the sale of each additional unit of output. Thus, a resource's marginal revenue product is equal to the marginal product of the resource multiplied by the marginal revenue of the good or service produced. ***Because of the law of diminishing returns, the marginal product of a resource will fall as employment of the resource expands. As a result, the marginal revenue product of a resource will also decline as its employment expands.***

Marginal product (*MP*)
The change in total output that results from the employment of one additional unit of a resource.

Marginal revenue (*MR*)
The change in a firm's total revenue that results from the production and sale of one additional unit of output.

The relationship between the marginal revenue a firm gets from selling an additional unit of output and the price for which it is sold is different for *price-taker* firms than for *price searchers*, however. Because a price-taker firm sells all units produced at the same price, the price taker's marginal revenue will be equal to the market price of the product. The price searcher, however, must reduce the price of all units in order to expand the number of units sold. Consequently, the price searcher's marginal revenue will be less than the sales price of the units. The marginal product of a resource multiplied by the selling price of the product is called the resource's **value marginal product (*VMP*)**. ***For a price-taker firm, the* MRP *of a resource is equal to its* VMP *because price and marginal revenue are equal. For a price-searcher firm, however, the* MRP *of a resource will be lower than its* VMP *because marginal revenue is less than price.***

Value marginal product (*VMP*)
The marginal product of a resource multiplied by the selling price of the product it helps produce. For a price-taker firm, marginal revenue product (*MRP*) will be equal to the value marginal product (*VMP*).

Using these measures, **Exhibit 12-4** illustrates how a firm decides how much of a resource to employ. Compute-Accounting, Inc., uses computer equipment and data entry operators to supply clients with monthly accounting statements. The firm is a price taker: It sells its service in a competitive market for $200 per statement. Given the fixed quantity of computer equipment owned by Compute-Accounting, column 2 shows how much total output (quantity of accounting statements) the firm can produce with different numbers of data entry operators. One data entry operator can process five statements per week. When two operators are employed, nine statements can be completed. Column 2 indicates how total output is expected to change as additional data entry operators are employed. Column 3 presents the marginal product schedule for data entry operators. Column 6, the *MRP* schedule, shows how the employment of each additional operator affects total revenue. Both the marginal product and the *MRP* of workers decline as additional operators are employed due to the law of diminishing returns.

Because Compute-Accounting is a price taker, the marginal revenue product and the value marginal product of labor are equal. Thus, the marginal revenue product of labor (column 6) can be calculated by multiplying the marginal product (column 3) times the sales price of an accounting statement (column 4).

How does Compute-Accounting decide how many operators to employ? It analyzes the benefits relative to the costs. As additional operators are employed, the output of processed statements (column 2) will increase, which will expand total revenue (column 5). Employing additional operators, though, will also add to production costs because the operators must be paid. Applying the profit-maximization rule, Compute-Accounting will hire additional

Exhibit 12-4 The Short-Run Demand Schedule of a Firm

Compute-Accounting, Inc., uses computer technology and data entry operators to provide accounting services in a competitive market. For each accounting statement processed, the firm receives a $200 fee (column 4). Given the firm's current fixed capital, column 2 shows how total output changes as additional data entry operators are hired. The marginal revenue product (MRP) schedule (column 6) indicates how hiring an additional operator affects the total revenue of the firm. Because a profit-maximizing firm will hire an additional employee if, and only if, the employee adds more to revenues than to costs, the marginal revenue product curve is the firm's short-run demand curve for the resource (refer to Exhibit 12-5).

Units of Variable Factor (Data Entry Operators) (1)	Total Output (Accounting Statements Processed per Week) (2)	Marginal Product (Change in Column 2 Divided by Change in Column 1) (3)	Sales Price per Statement (4)	Total Revenue (2) × (4) (5)	MRP (3) × (4) (6)
0	0.0	—	$200	$0	—
1	5.0	5.0	200	1,000	1,000
2	9.0	4.0	200	1,800	800
3	12.0	3.0	200	2,400	600
4	14.0	2.0	200	2,800	400
5	15.5	1.5	200	3,100	300
6	16.5	1.0	200	3,300	200
7	17.0	0.5	200	3,400	100

operators as long as their employment adds more to revenues than to costs. This will be the case as long as the *MRP* (column 6) of the data entry operators exceeds their wage rate. At a weekly wage of $1,000, Compute-Accounting would hire only one operator. If the weekly wage dropped to $800, two operators would be hired. At still lower wage rates, additional operators would be hired.

Profit-maximizing firms, both price takers and price searchers, will expand their employment of each variable resource until the* MRP *of the resource (the firm's additional revenue generated by the resource) is just equal to the price of the resource (the firm's marginal cost of employing the resource).

12-3b *MRP* and the Firm's Demand Curve for a Resource

Using the data in Exhibit 12-4, we can construct Compute-Accounting's demand curve for data entry operators. Recall that the height of a demand curve shows the maximum price (in this case, the wage) the buyer (the firm) would be willing to pay for the unit. Because the marginal revenue product of the first data entry operator is $1,000, the firm would be willing to hire this worker only up to a maximum price of $1,000. Because of this relationship, as **Exhibit 12-5** shows, a firm's short-run demand curve for a resource is precisely the *MRP* curve for the resource.[2] Using this demand curve yields the identical solutions as the table. Underlying the downward-sloping demand curve is the law of diminishing returns causing *MP*, and thus *MRP*, to fall as more workers are hired.

The location of the firm's *MRP* curve depends on (1) the price of the product, (2) the productivity of the resource, and (3) the amount of other resources with which the resource is working. Changes in any one of these three factors will cause the *MRP* curve to shift. For example, if Compute-Accounting purchased additional computer equipment making it

Exhibit 12-5 The Firm's Demand Curve for a Resource

The firm's demand curve for a resource will reflect the marginal revenue product (MRP) of the resource. In the short run, it will slope downward because the marginal product of the resource will fall as more of it is used with a fixed amount of other resources. The location of the MRP curve will depend on (1) the price of the product, (2) the productivity of the resource, and (3) the quantity of other factors working with the resource.

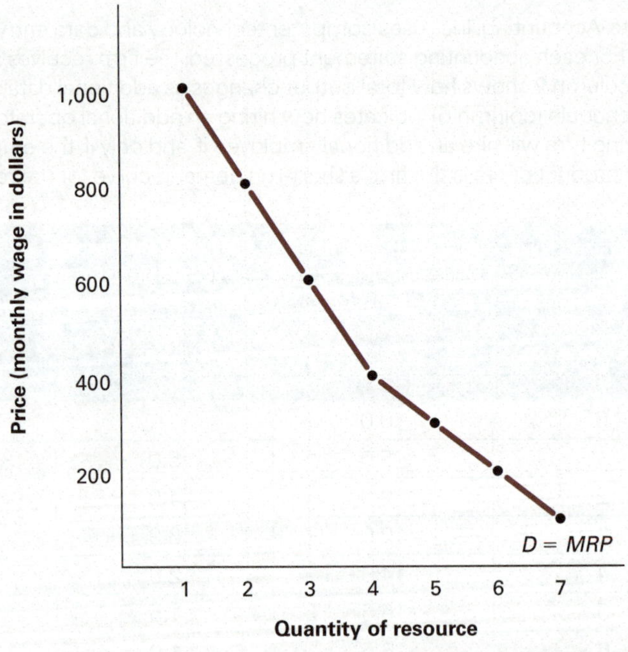

[2]Strictly speaking, this is true only for a variable resource that is employed with a fixed amount of another factor.

possible for the operators to complete more statements each week, the *MRP* curve for labor would increase (shift outward). This increase in the quantity of the other resources working with labor would increase labor's productivity.

12-3c Multiple Resources and How Much to Use of Each

So far, we have analyzed the firm's hiring decision assuming that it used one variable resource (labor) and one fixed resource. Production, though, usually involves the use of many resources. How should these resources be combined to produce the product? We can answer this question by considering either the conditions for profit maximization or the conditions for cost minimization.

12-3d Maximizing Profits When Multiple Resources Are Used

The same decision-making considerations apply when the firm employs several factors of production. The profit-maximizing firm will expand its use of a resource as long as the *MRP* of the resource exceeds its employment cost. If we assume that resources are perfectly divisible, the profit-maximizing decision rule implies that, in equilibrium, the *MRP* of each resource will be equal to the price of the resource. Therefore, the following conditions will exist for the profit-maximizing firm:

MRP of skilled labor = Price (wage rate) of skilled labor
MRP of unskilled labor = Price (wage rate) of unskilled labor
MRP of machine A = Price (explicit or implicit rental price) of machine A and so on, for all other factors

12-3e Cost Minimization When Multiple Resources Are Used

To maximize its profits, the firm must produce the profit-maximizing output at the least possible cost. If the firm is minimizing costs, the marginal dollar expenditure for each resource will have the same impact on output as an additional dollar expenditure on other resources used to produce the product. Factors of production will be employed such that the marginal product *per last dollar spent* on each factor is the same for all factors.

To understand why, consider a situation in which a \$100 expenditure on labor caused output to rise by ten units, whereas an additional \$100 expenditure on machines generated only a five-unit expansion in output. In this case, the firm could employ \$100 less in machines, spend the \$100 on labor instead, and produce five more units of output for the same total cost. By substituting labor for machines, it will reduce its *per-unit* cost.

If the marginal dollar spent on one resource increases output by a larger amount than a dollar expenditure on other resources, substituting the one with the high marginal product per dollar for the low one will always reduce costs. Substitution will continue to reduce unit costs (and increase profit) until the marginal product per dollar expenditure on each resource is equalized. This will occur because as additional units of a resource are hired, their marginal product will fall. Thus, the proportional relationship between the price of each resource and its marginal product will eventually be achieved.

***Therefore, the following condition exists when per unit costs are minimized*:**

$$\frac{\textit{MP}\textbf{ of skilled labor}}{\textbf{Price of skilled labor}} = \frac{\textit{MP}\textbf{ of unskilled labor}}{\textbf{Price of unskilled labor}} = \frac{\textit{MP}\textbf{ of machine A}}{\textbf{Price (rental value) of machine A}}$$

This relationship explains why workers with different skill levels earn different wages. If skilled workers are twice as productive as unskilled workers, their wage rates will tend to be twice those of unskilled workers. For example, suppose that a construction firm hiring workers to hang doors is choosing among skilled and unskilled workers. If skilled door hangers can complete four doors per hour, while unskilled workers can hang only two doors per hour, a cost-minimizing firm would hire only skilled workers—as long as their wages are less than twice the wages of unskilled workers. In contrast, only unskilled workers would be hired if the wages of skilled workers are more than twice that of unskilled workers. Because of competition, wages across skill categories will tend to mirror productivity differences.

It is important to note that low wages do not necessarily mean low cost. In other words, it is not always cheaper to hire the lowest-wage workers. It is not just wages, but rather wages *relative to productivity* that matter. If the wages of skilled workers are twice those of unskilled workers, it will still be cheaper to hire additional skilled workers if their marginal productivity (output per hour) is more than twice that of the unskilled workers.

Do employers in the real world really think in terms of equating the marginal product/price ratio (*MP/P*) for each factor of production? Probably not. Their thought process is likely going to be something more like this: "Can we reduce costs by using more of one resource and less of another?" However, regardless of how managers think about the problem, when a firm maximizes its profits and minimizes its costs, its marginal product/price ratio will be equal for all factors of production. The outcome will be *the same as if* the firm followed the cost-minimization, decision-making rule presented here.

Summing up, resources will only be employed if they generate enough revenue to cover the cost of their employment. (Review the Applications in Economics feature, "Why Do Star Athletes in the WNBA Make So Much Less Than Their Counterparts in the NBA?") Resources that are more productive will be able to command higher prices (or wage rates) because they generate more revenue for the firm. The marginal-productivity theory underlies the demand for resources. Of course, resource prices will also be influenced by supply. We now turn to that topic.

Applications in Economics

Why Do Star Athletes in the WNBA Make So Much Less than Their Counterparts in the NBA?

Steph Curry, two-time MVP and superstar of the Golden State Warriors of the National Basketball Association (NBA), earned $48 million in 2023. In contrast, the highest-paid player in the Women's National Basketball Association (WNBA) in 2023 was the Seattle Storm superstar Jewell Loyd, with a salary of $228,094.

Reacting to salary differentials like these, Skylar Diggins-Smith, the star point guard of the Dallas Wings of the WNBA, told a reporter that she wanted to be paid like a man.[1] As Diggins-Smith argues, WNBA players work just as hard and just as long as NBA players. Some even play during the off-season in Europe to earn extra money. Star WNBA players earn less than even bench players in the NBA. Where is the fairness in this?

Why are players in the NBA paid so much more than those in the WNBA? Marginal revenue product provides the answer. Compensation is not about effort; it is about revenue generated.

Players in the NBA earn a lot more than those in the WNBA because they generate a lot more revenue for their employers. The average attendance for NBA games in 2022-2023 was about 17,000, more than 11,000 greater than the

Rocky Widner/National Basketball Association/Getty Images

Gary Dineen/NBAE/Getty Images

average for WNBA games. In addition, there are 30 teams in the NBA, and each team plays 82 games during the regular season. In contrast, there are only 12 teams in the WNBA, and each team plays only 36 regular season games. The NBA television contract revenue for 2023 was $2.6 billion, more than 60 times the $42 million TV contract of the WNBA. While the precise figures are difficult to obtain, the revenue per team in the NBA is approximately 60 times the revenue for WNBA teams.[2]

Revenues generated impact earnings, independent of gender. Major League Baseball players make a lot more than top-notch softball players. Players in the National Football League are compensated far more handsomely than professional volleyball players. High-level professional golfers do much better than professional bowlers. Why? Again, marginal revenue product provides the answer. Professional athletes who generate more revenue from paying customers and television viewers will command higher salaries. This is true regardless of gender or sport.

Should the WNBA teams start paying their players as much as those in the NBA? They might like to, but they cannot do so and still survive. The revenues generated by the WNBA teams are insufficient to permit them to pay their players salaries similar to those of NBA players. Employers in both sports and more typical businesses cannot, at least not for long, pay employees more than their marginal revenue product.

[1]Anna Peele, "Skylar Diggins-Smith Wants to Be Paid Like a Man and Isn't Afraid to Say It," *Wealthsimple*, August 21, 2018, at https://www.wealthsimple.com/en-ca/magazine/skylar-diggins-smith.

[2]Richard Janvrin, "NBA vs WMNA: Revenue, Salaries, Viewership, Attendance, and Ratings," *WSN*, March 7, 2023, at https://www.wsn.com/nba/nba-vs-wnba/.

12-4 The Supply of Resources

Just as benefits and costs direct the choices of employers, so too will they guide the actions of resource suppliers. Resource owners will supply their services to an employer only if they perceive that the benefits of doing so exceed their costs (the value of the other things they could do with their time or resources). Because of this, employers must offer resource owners at least as good a deal as they can get elsewhere. For example, if an employer does not offer a potential employee pay, benefits, and working conditions as good as, or better than, others, the employer will be unable to hire that worker.

Resource owners will supply their services to those who offer them the best employment alternative. Other things constant, as the price of a specific resource increases, the incentive of potential suppliers to provide the resource increases.

Exhibit 12-6 The Supply of a Resource

As the price of a resource increases, individuals have a greater incentive to supply it. Therefore, a direct relationship will exist between the price of a resource and the quantity supplied.

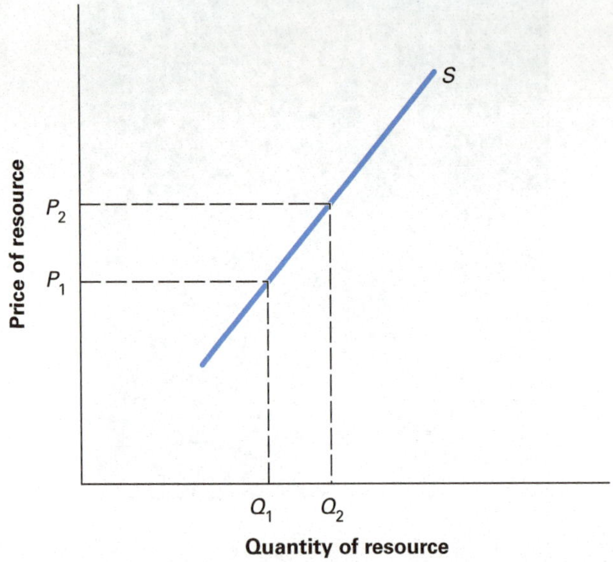

An increase in the price of a resource will lure resource suppliers into the market. A decrease will cause them to shift into other activities. Therefore, as **Exhibit 12-6** illustrates, the supply curve for a specific resource will slope upward to the right.[3]

12-4a Short-Run Versus Long-Run Resource Supply

Like demand, supply in resource markets can be different in the short run than in the long run. If the wage rate for certified public accountants (CPAs) rose, for example, we would expect more workers supplying their services as CPAs. But where do these additional CPAs come from? In the short run, the additional supply must come from those who are already qualified as CPAs but are currently doing other things. The higher wages might induce some college accounting professors and some stay-at-home spouses with accounting credentials to move into employment as CPAs. In the short run, however, there isn't enough time to alter the availability of a resource through investment in human and physical capital. In contrast, in the long run, resource suppliers have time to adjust their investment choices in response to a change in resource prices. With time, the higher wages and easier employment opportunities for CPAs will cause more students to major in accounting and other people to pursue the coursework needed to become a CPA. Higher resource prices will increase the quantity supplied in both the short run and the long run, but the response will be greater in the long run. Therefore, as **Exhibit 12-7** shows, the long-run supply of a resource will be more elastic than the short-run supply.

12-4b Short-Run Supply

Resource mobility
The ease with which factors of production are able to move among alternative uses. Resources that can easily be transferred to a different use or location are said to be highly mobile. Resources with few alternative uses are immobile.

The short-run supply response to a change in price is determined by how easily the resource can be transferred from one use to another—that is, **resource mobility**. The supply of resources with high mobility will be relatively elastic even in the short run. Conversely,

[3]Although the supply for nonhuman resources will always slope upward, the supply of labor at very high wage rates can become backward bending. As wages rise, individuals will substitute toward more work, but simultaneously the higher income will cause them to desire more leisure. At very high wage rates, the income effect might dominate, causing a negative relationship between wage rates and quantity of labor supplied in this range. For example, at a wage of $10,000 per hour, many individuals would probably supply fewer hours of work than at $500 per hour!

Exhibit 12-7 Time and the Elasticity of Supply for Resources

If the wage rate for CPAs rises, for example, to P_2, we would expect more workers to supply CPA services. Because it takes time to be trained as a CPA, though, the quantity of CPA services supplied in the short run (S_{sr}) won't increase by much–just to Q_2. The supply of CPA services is therefore relatively inelastic in the short run. In the long run, though, it is more elastic and the quantity supplied increases to Q_3.

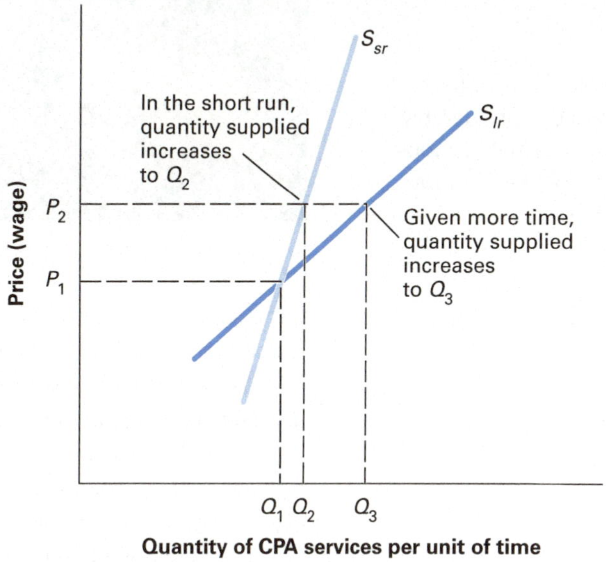

resources that have few alternative uses (or are not easily transferable) are said to be immobile. The short-run supply of immobile resources will be highly inelastic.

Consider the mobility of labor. Within a skill category (for example, plumber, store manager, accountant, or secretary), labor will be highly mobile within the same geographic area. Movements between geographic areas and from one skill category to another are more costly to accomplish, though. Labor will thus be less mobile for movements of this variety. In addition, because it is easier for a highly skilled person to perform effectively in a lower-skill position than vice versa, short-run mobility will tend to decline as the skill level of the occupation rises. Thus, the short-run supply curve in high-skill occupations like architect, mechanical engineer, and medical surgeon is usually quite inelastic.

What about the mobility of land? Land is highly mobile among uses when location doesn't matter. For example, the same land can often be used to raise corn, wheat, soybeans, or oats. As a result, the supply of land allocated to the production of each of these commodities will be highly responsive to changes in their relative prices. Undeveloped land on the outskirts of cities is particularly mobile among uses. It can be used for agriculture, but it can also quickly be subdivided and used for a housing development or a shopping center. Because land is totally immobile physically, you might think its supply is unresponsive to changes in price when it comes to how desirable it is (or isn't) due to its location. You can't move it to make it more desirable and get a better price, obviously. You can, however, expand its usable space by constructing multiple-story buildings, for instance. As the demand for a given location increases, higher and higher multilevel construction will be justified. This is why tall buildings are generally located in city centers, for example—because the demand for space is highest in these locations.

12-4c Long-Run Supply

In the long run, the supply of resources can change substantially. Machines wear out, human skills depreciate, and even the fertility of land declines with use and erosion. These factors reduce the supply of resources. In contrast, investment can replace and expand the supply of productive resources, including machines, buildings, and durable assets. Correspondingly, investments in training and education can develop and improve the skills of future labor

The supply curve for truck drivers will be considerably more elastic than the supply curve for doctors. Can you explain why?

JAC77/Shutterstock.com

Monkey Business Images/Shutterstock.com

force participants. Thus, the supply of both physical and human resources in the long run is determined primarily by investment and depreciation.

As the price of a resource increases, more and more people will make the investments necessary to supply it. This will be true for human as well as physical resources. For example, higher salaries for engineers stimulate engineering degree enrollments. According to a study by Jaewoo Ryoo and Sherwin Rosen, a 1 percent increase in starting engineering salaries causes enrollment in engineering degree programs to rise by 2.5 percent to 4.5 percent.[4]

The long run, of course, is not a specified length of time. Investment can increase the availability of some resources fairly quickly. For example, it does not take very long to train additional truck drivers. However, it takes a long time to train physicians, dentists, lawyers, and pharmacists. Higher earnings in these occupations may have only a small impact on their current availability. Additional investment will flow into these areas, but it will typically be several years before there is a substantial increase in the quantity supplied.

12-5 Supply, Demand, and Resource Prices

In a market economy, resource prices will be determined by the forces of supply and demand and will bring the choices of buyers and sellers into line with each other. **Exhibit 12-8** illustrates how the forces of supply and demand push the market wage rates of engineers toward equilibrium, where quantity demanded and quantity supplied are equal. Equilibrium is achieved when the price (wage rate) for engineering services is *P*. Given the market conditions illustrated by Exhibit 12-8, an excess supply is present if the price of engineering services exceeds *P*. Some engineers will be unable to find jobs at the above-equilibrium wage. This excess supply of engineers will cause the wage rate for engineers to fall. This will cause some of the engineers to look for jobs in other fields, and quantity supplied will fall, pushing the market toward equilibrium. In contrast, if the resource price is less than *P*, excess demand is present. Employers are unable to hire the amount of engineering services they want at a below-equilibrium resource price. Rather than doing without the resource, employers will attempt to hire engineers away from other firms by bidding the price up to *P* and thereby eliminating the excess demand.

How will a resource market adjust to an unexpected change in market conditions? Suppose there is a sharp increase in the demand for houses, apartments, and office buildings. The increase in demand for these products will also increase the demand for resources required for their construction. Thus, the demand for resources like steel, lumber, brick, and the labor services of carpenters, architects, and construction engineers will increase.

[4]Jaewoo Ryoo and Sherwin Rosen, "The Engineering Labor Market," *Journal of Political Economy* 112, no. S1 (February 2004): S110-S140.

Exhibit 12-8 Equilibrium in a Resource Market

The market demand for a resource, such as engineering services, is a downward-sloping curve, reflecting the declining *MRP* of the resource. The market supply curve slopes upward because higher resource prices (wage rates) will motivate people to supply more of the resource. Market price will move toward equilibrium (*P*), where the quantity demanded and the quantity supplied are in balance.

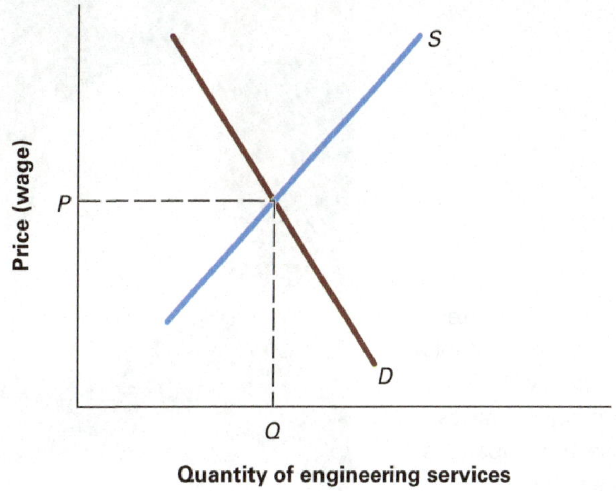

Exhibit 12-9 shows the increase in demand for new houses and buildings (panel a) and the accompanying increase in demand for construction engineers. The market demand for the services of construction engineers increases from D_1 to D_2 (panel b), and initially there is a sharp rise in their wages (price increases from P_1 to P_2). The higher wages will motivate additional people to get the education and training necessary to become construction

Exhibit 12-9 Adjusting to Dynamic Change

An increase in the demand for housing and commercial buildings (panel a) will lead to an increase in demand for the services of construction engineers (panel b) and other resources used in the construction industry. Initially, the increase in the resource price will be substantial, jumping from P_1 to P_2 (point *a* versus point *b* in the graph). The increase will be particularly sharp if the supply of the resource is highly inelastic in the short run. The higher resource price will attract additional human capital investment, and, with time, the resource supply curve will become more elastic, which will moderate the price (or wage) increase to P_3 (point *c*).

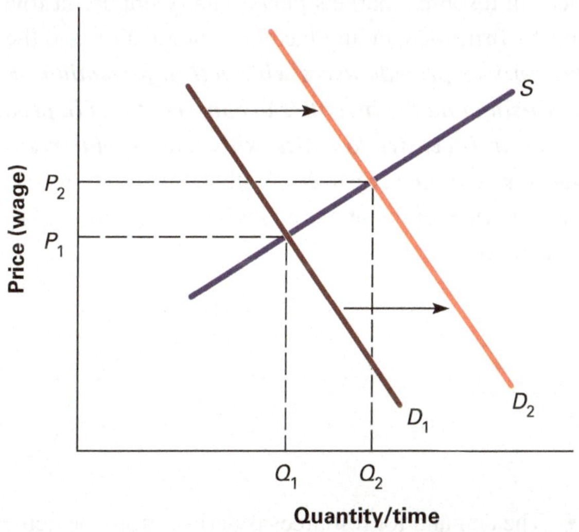

(a) Product market—new houses and commercial buildings

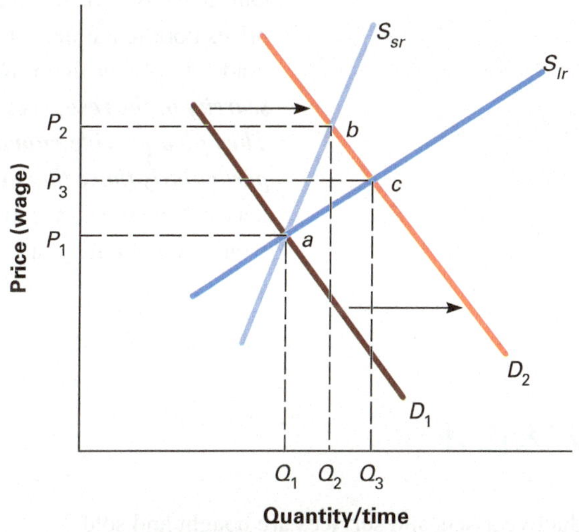

(b) Resource market—services of construction engineers

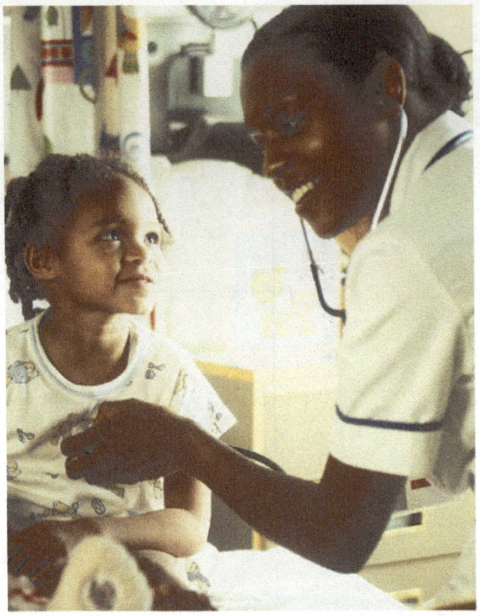

Flying Colours Ltd/Getty Images

wavebreakmedia/Shutterstock.com

Workers in occupations like nursing that require substantial skill and education will generally earn higher wages than will those in occupations requiring little training or experience.

engineers. Over time, the entry of the newly trained construction engineers will increase the elasticity of the resource supply curve. As these new construction engineers eventually enter the occupation, the supply curve will become more elastic (S_{lr} rather than S_{sr}), which will place downward pressure on wages in the occupation (the move from *b* to *c*). Therefore, as panel (b) of Exhibit 12-9 illustrates, the long-run price increase (to P_3) will be less than the short-run increase (to P_2).

The market adjustment to an unexpected reduction in demand for a resource is the same. The price falls farther in the short run than in the long run. At the lower price, some resource suppliers will use their talents in other areas, and the incentive for potential new suppliers to offer the resource will be less. With time, the quantity of the resource supplied will decline, moderating the reduction in its price. Those with the poorest alternatives (that is, lowest opportunity cost) will continue to provide the resource at the lower prices. Those with better alternatives will look for other opportunities.

12-5a The Coordinating Function of Resource Prices

Our analysis indicates that prices in resource markets play a vitally important role. These prices coordinate the actions of the firms demanding factors of production and the households supplying them. ***Resource prices provide users with both information about the scarcity of the resources they're using and the incentive to conserve them in production. They also provide suppliers with an incentive to learn skills and provide resources—particularly those that are intensely demanded by users.*** Without the use of resource markets and the price incentives they provide, efficient use and wise conservation of resources would be extremely difficult to achieve.

Key Points

- Productive assets and services are bought and sold in resource markets. There are two broad classes of productive resources: (1) nonhuman capital and (2) human capital.
- The demand for resources is derived from the demand for products that the resources help produce. The quantity of a resource demanded is inversely related to its price because of substitutions made by both producers and consumers.

- The demand curve for a resource, like the demand for a product, can shift. The major factors that increase the demand for a resource are (1) an increase in demand for products that use the resource, (2) an increase in the productivity of the resource, and (3) an increase in the price of substitute resources.
- Profit-maximizing firms will hire additional units of a resource up to the point at which the marginal revenue product (MRP) of the resource equals its price. With multiple inputs, firms will expand their use of each until the marginal product divided by the price (*MP/P*) is equal across all inputs. When real-world decision-makers minimize per-unit costs, the outcome will be as if they had followed these mathematical procedures, even though they may not consciously do so.
- The amount of a resource supplied will be directly related to its price. The supply of a resource will be more elastic in the long run than in the short run. In the long run, investment can increase the supply of both physical and human resources.
- The prices of resources are determined by supply and demand. Changes in the market prices of resources will influence the decisions of both users and suppliers. Higher resource prices give users a greater incentive to turn to substitutes and suppliers a greater incentive to provide more of the resource.
- Resource prices coordinate the actions of resource owners and business firms demanding their services. Changes in resource prices in response to changing market conditions are essential for the efficient allocation of resources in a dynamic world.

Critical Analysis Questions

1. "The demand for resources is a derived demand." What is meant by that statement? Why is the employment of a resource inversely related to its price?
2. How does a firm decide whether or not to employ an additional unit of a resource? What determines the combination of skilled and unskilled workers employed by a firm?
3. *Use the information in Exhibit 12-4 of this chapter to answer the following:
   a. How many employees (operators) would Compute-Accounting hire at a weekly wage of $250 if it were attempting to maximize profits?
   b. What would the firm's maximum profit be if its fixed costs were $1,500 per week?
   c. Suppose there were a decline in demand for accounting services, reducing the market price per monthly statement to $150. At this demand level, how many employees would Compute-Accounting hire at $250 per week in the short run? Would Compute-Accounting be able to stay in business at the lower market price? Explain.
4. *Are productivity gains the major source of higher wages? If so, how does one account for the rising real wages of barbers, who, by and large, have used the same techniques for a half-century? (*Hint*: Do not forget opportunity cost and supply.)
5. Are the following statements both correct? Are they inconsistent with each other? Explain.
   a. "Firms will hire a resource only if they can make money by doing so."
   b. "In a market economy, each resource will tend to be paid according to its marginal product. Highly productive resources will command high prices, whereas less productive resources will command lower prices."
6. *Many school districts pay teachers on the basis of their highest degree earned and number of years of service (seniority). They often find it quite easy to fill the slots for English and history teachers, but very difficult to find the required number of math and science teachers. Can you explain why?
7. Suppose that you were the manager of a large retail store that was currently experiencing a shoplifting problem. Every hour, approximately $15 worth of merchandise was being stolen from your store. Suppose that a security guard would completely eliminate the shoplifting in your store. If you were interested in maximizing your profits, should you hire a security guard if the wage rate of security guards was $20 per hour? Why or why not? What does this imply about the relationship between average shoplifting per hour in the economy and the wage rates of security guards?
8. *A dressmaker uses labor and capital (sewing machines) to produce dresses in a competitive market. Suppose the last unit of labor hired cost $1,000 per month and increased output by 100 dresses. The last unit of capital hired (rented) cost $500 per month and increased output by 80 dresses. Is the dressmaker minimizing costs? If not, what changes need to be made?
9. A firm is considering moving from the United States to Mexico. The firm pays its U.S. workers $30 per hour. Current U.S. workers have a marginal product of 40, whereas the Mexican workers have a marginal product of ten. How low would the Mexican wage

have to be for the firm to reduce its wage cost per unit of output by moving to Mexico?

10. "The earnings of engineers, doctors, and lawyers are high because lots of education is necessary to practice in these fields." Evaluate this statement.

11. Other things constant, what impact will a highly elastic demand for a product have on the elasticity of demand for the resources used to produce the product? Explain.

12. *The following chart provides information on a firm that hires labor competitively and sells its product in a competitive market.

Units of Labor	Total Output	Marginal Product	Product Price	Total Revenue	MRP
1	14	—	$5	—	—
2	26	—	$5	—	—
3	37	—	$5	—	—
4	46	—	$5	—	—
5	53	—	$5	—	—
6	58	—	$5	—	—

a. Fill in the missing columns.

b. How many units of labor would be employed if the market wage rate were $40? Why?

c. What would happen to employment if the wage rate rose to $50? Explain.

13. Leisure Times, Inc., employs skilled workers and capital to install hot tubs. The capital includes the tools and equipment workers use to construct and install the tubs. The installation services are sold in a competitive market for $1,200 per hot tub. Leisure Times is able to hire workers for $2,200 per month, including the cost of wages, fringe benefits, and employment taxes. As additional workers are hired, the increase in the number of hot tubs installed is indicated in the table.

Number of Workers Employed	Number of Hot Tubs Installed (per Month)
1	5
2	12
3	18
4	23
5	27
6	30
7	32
8	33
9	34

a. Indicate the marginal product and MRP schedules of the workers.

b. What quantity of workers should Leisure Times employ to maximize its profit?

c. If a construction boom pushes the wages of skilled workers up to $2,500 per month, how many workers would Leisure Times employ to maximize its profit?

d. Suppose that strong demand for hot tubs pushes the price of installation services up to $1,500 per month. How would this affect employment of the skilled workers if the wage rate of the workers remained at $2,500 per month?

14. A recent flyer on a university campus stated that consumers should boycott sugar due to the low wages earned by laborers on sugarcane farms in Florida. Using the notion of derived demand, what impact would a boycott on sugar have on the wages of the farm laborers in the short run? In the long run?

15. Why are players in the National Basketball Association (NBA) paid so much more than those in the Women's National Basketball Association (WNBA)? Is this fair? Why or why not?

*Asterisk denotes questions for which answers are given in Appendix B.

Chapter 13 Earnings, Productivity, and the Job Market

> How can I be overpaid? The boss wouldn't pay me that amount if I wasn't worth it.
>
> –Jackie Gleason[1]

The earnings of U.S. workers are among the highest in the world. However, they vary widely. An unskilled laborer may earn $15 per hour, or even less. Lawyers and physicians often earn $300 per hour, or more. Dentists and even economists might receive $250 per hour. This chapter will provide insight on why earnings vary and their change through time.

Learning Objectives

13.1 Describe the sources of wage differences.

13.2 Explain how unfavorable working conditions will impact wages.

13.3 Analyze why earnings differ according to race and gender.

13.4 Explain how employment discrimination affects workers and employers, and why competitive forces reduce the profitability of firms that discriminate.

13.5 Explain the link between productivity and earnings, and how it explains wage differences over time and across countries.

13.6 Analyze the impact of robotics and other forms of automation on employment and worker productivity.

[1]This statement was made in response to a question about the amount he was being paid for the popular television show *The Honeymooners*, which ran during the 1950s and 1960s.

13-1 Why Do Earnings Differ?

The earnings of individuals in the same occupation or with the same amount of education often differ substantially. So do the earnings of people in the same family. For example, one researcher found that the average annual earnings differential between brothers was $49,774, compared with $54,220 for men paired randomly.[2] The earnings of people with the same intelligence, level of training, or amount of experience also typically differ.

Several factors combine to determine a person's earning power. Some seem to be the result of good or bad luck. Others are clearly the result of conscious decisions people make. In the previous chapter, we analyzed how the market forces of supply and demand operate to determine resource prices. Wages are a resource price, and therefore the supply and demand model can be used to examine earnings differentials among workers.

For simplicity, we have proceeded as if employees earned only money payments. In reality, most workers receive a compensation package that includes **fringe benefits** as well as money wages. The fringe benefit component typically includes medical insurance, life insurance, pension benefits, and paid vacation days. When we use the terms *wages* and *earnings* in the following discussions, we are referring to the total compensation package that includes both wages and fringe benefits.

Fringe benefits
Benefits other than normal money wages that are supplied to employees in exchange for their labor services. Higher fringe benefits come at the expense of lower money wages.

Real earnings
Earnings adjusted for differences in the general level of prices across time periods or geographic areas. When real earnings are equal, the same bundle of goods and services can be purchased with the earnings.

The **real earnings** of all employees in a competitive market economy would be equal if (1) all individuals were identical in preferences, skills, and background; (2) all jobs were equally attractive; and (3) workers were perfectly mobile among jobs. Given these conditions, if higher real wages existed in an area of the economy, the supply of workers in that area would expand until the wage differential was eliminated. Similarly, low wages in an area would cause workers to exit until wages there returned to normal. Of course, that's not the way things work in the real world. We all know that earnings differences are a fact of life. There are three reasons for this, and we'll discuss each one.

13-1a Earnings Differentials due to Nonidentical Workers

Workers differ in several important respects that affect both the supply of and demand for their services. In turn, these factors affect their wage rates. Let's consider these differences.

1. Worker skill level. The demand for employees who are highly productive is greater than the demand for those who are less productive. People who can operate a machine more skillfully, hit a baseball more consistently, or sell life insurance policies with greater regularity are more valuable to employers. Compared with their less skillful counterparts, these employees contribute more to the firm's revenue. Put another way, the marginal revenue product (*MRP*) of the more productive employees is higher than the *MRP* of less productive ones. In competitive labor markets, workers earn a wage equal to their marginal revenue product. As a result, the labor services of more productive workers will command higher wages in the marketplace.

Worker productivity is the result of a combination of factors, including native ability, parental training, hard work, and investment in human capital. The link between higher productivity and higher earnings motivates people to invest in themselves in order to upgrade their knowledge and skills. If additional worker productivity didn't lead to higher earnings, people would have little incentive to incur the costs of skill development, including paying to go to college or acquire additional training.

Exhibit 13-1 shows the demand, supply, and wage rates for skilled versus unskilled workers. The productivity of skilled workers exceeds that of unskilled workers, and so does

[2]Christopher Jencks, *Inequality* (New York: Basic Books, 1972), 220. The salary figures are in 2023 dollars.

Exhibit 13-1 Demand, Supply, and Wage Rates for Skilled and Unskilled Workers

The productivity–and therefore marginal product (*MP*)–of skilled workers is greater than that of unskilled workers. As a result, as panel (a) illustrates, the demand for skilled workers (D_s) will exceed the demand for unskilled workers (D_u). Education and training generally enhance skills. Because upgrading one's skills through investments in human capital is costly, the supply of skilled workers (S_s) is smaller than the supply of unskilled workers at any given wage (panel b). As panel (c) illustrates, the wages of skilled workers are high relative to those of unskilled workers due to the strong demand and small supply of skilled workers relative to unskilled workers. (*Note:* The quantity of skilled labor employed may be far smaller, far larger, or, by accident, equal to the quantity of unskilled labor hired.)

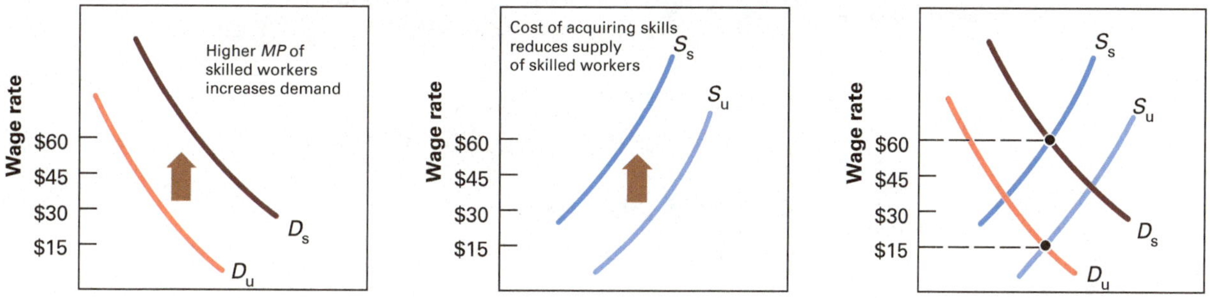

(a) Demand for skilled and unskilled labor

(b) Supply of skilled and unskilled labor

(c) Wages of skilled and unskilled labor

the demand for them. The vertical distance between the demand curve for skilled workers (D_s) and the demand curve for unskilled workers (D_u), shown in panel (a), reflects the higher marginal product (*MP*) of skilled workers. Because human capital investments (education, training, and so on) are costly, the supply of skilled workers (S_s) will be smaller than the supply of unskilled workers (S_u). This is shown in panel (b). The vertical distance between the two supply curves is the wage differential employers will need to pay skilled workers for the costs they incurred to acquire their skills.

Wages are determined by demand relative to supply (panel c). Because the demand for skilled workers is large whereas their supply is small, the equilibrium wage of skilled workers will be high ($60 per hour). In contrast, because the supply of unskilled workers is large relative to the demand, their wage rates will be substantially lower ($15 per hour).

The skills that one person gains from a year of education, vocational school, or on-the-job training might be better or worse than those of someone else. Therefore, we should not expect a rigid relationship to exist between years of education (or training) and skill level. On average, however, there is a strong positive relationship between investment in education and earnings.

Exhibit 13-2 presents annual earnings data according to educational level for year-round, full-time workers in 2022. Notice that the earnings of both men and women increased consistently with additional schooling. High school graduates earned about one-third more than their counterparts with less than a high school education. Male college graduates working full-time, year-round earned $111,700, compared with $59,590 for men with only a high school education. In the case of women, college graduates earned $79,210, compared with $45,650 for those who only graduated from high school. The earnings of both men and women continued to increase as they earned master's and doctoral/professional degrees.

In addition to education, a person's intelligence, native ability, and motivation also affect their productivity and earnings. Research shows, however, that much of the extra income earned by high-wage earners is, in fact, the result of the knowledge and skills they acquired by making an investment in additional education. Studies also show that on-the-job

Exhibit 13-2 Education and Earnings

The accompanying graph presents data for the mean annual earnings of year-round, full-time workers based on their gender and education. Note that the earnings of both men and women increased with additional education. Even though the data are for full-time workers, the earnings of women were approximately 75 percent those of men with similar education.

Source: http://www.census.gov/

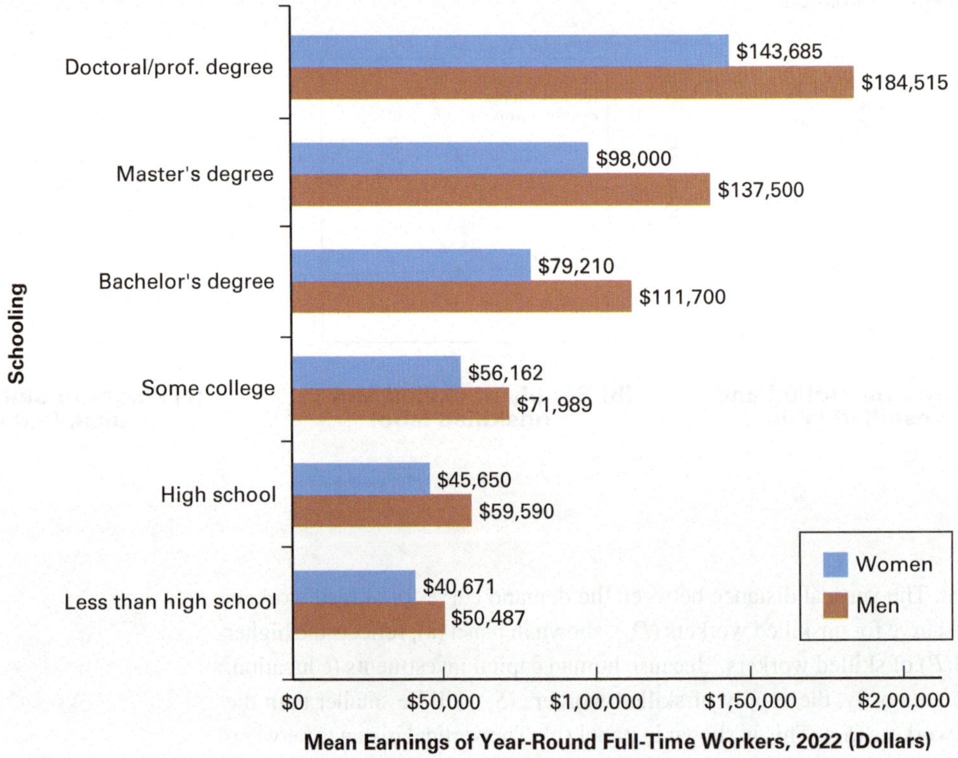

training and experience enhance the earnings of workers. However, some of the higher earnings of well-educated workers may merely reflect signaling. (Refer to the accompanying Applications in Economics feature, "A College Degree as a Job Market Signal.")

An investment in human capital and development of specialized skills can protect high-wage workers from the competition of others willing to offer their services at a lower price. Few people could develop the specialized skills of Taylor Swift, LeBron James, or Scarlett Johansson. Similarly, the supply of heart surgeons, trial lawyers, engineers, business entrepreneurs, and many other specialized workers is limited in occupations in which specific skills, knowledge, and human capital investments contribute to job performance.

What about the large salaries received by CEOs of major corporations? Decisions made by CEOs can have a huge financial impact on their companies' profitability. Because of this, a good CEO can be particularly valuable when a company is in trouble, is facing new competitors, or is confronting a changing technological or regulatory environment. A CEO who turns losses into profits is worth millions to the stockholders of a major corporation.

The annual earnings of star athletes, entertainers, and television personalities often run into the millions of dollars. What is the marginal revenue product of a superstar entertainer like Scarlett Johansson? How many more people will go see a movie starring Johansson rather than another actress less known or less talented? If an additional 2 million or 3 million people spend $10 to attend a movie, this will generate $20 million or $30 million of additional revenue. It is easily understandable how hiring a "box office" star will generate a lot

Applications in Economics

A College Degree as a Job Market Signal: Why You Should Take More Math

"Why should I take this difficult course?" "When will I ever use this?" Students often complain about taking courses not directly related to their future career. This complaint often reflects an incomplete understanding of exactly why college graduates do better in the job market than those without a college degree. A college degree increases a person's earnings because of both human capital (knowledge that will directly increase job productivity) and signaling ("signals" to employers about a person's attitude and motivational characteristics), as well as their general analytical skills.

Suppose that an employer is looking for an employee who is a very good analytical problem solver. Without a way to observe this ability directly, the employer will likely look for indicators that signal this attribute. For example, even if a job doesn't directly require calculus, people with a good calculus grade are likely to possess better problem-solving skills than those with a poor grade (or those who dodged the subject). Thus, employers may favor job applicants with good calculus grades, even if calculus isn't directly used on the job.

In other words, even if a college degree added nothing to the knowledge or skills required to do a particular job, it could still help employers identify people with abilities and attitudes that are difficult to observe. Similarly, students who are admitted to and graduate from elite universities like Harvard and Yale are likely to have superior abilities relative to those attending lower-ranked schools. Because of this signaling device, even mediocre graduates from top universities often have better entry-level job market prospects than do students from lesser-known schools. The signaling function also explains why students who choose majors considered "hard" (like mathematics, economics, or finance) generally do better in the job market than those choosing "easy" majors (like physical education, marketing, or social work).

"When will I ever use this stuff?" "When will a good grade in challenging courses like math and economics matter?" The answer to these questions is "Soon!" They will matter most when you're searching for a job at the beginning stages of your career–when it's still difficult for employers to judge your true abilities.

more money for a movie company. In turn, competitive labor markets will ensure that big stars get paid their marginal revenue product.

Economic studies have found that the marginal revenue product of many sports and entertainment superstars is pretty much in line with their salaries.[3] However, there may be another factor at work here. The earnings in some markets resemble tournaments. In tournaments, only the top-ranked person receives the big payoff, whereas those who finish second receive much less. This type of compensation is called **tournament pay**.[4] This name refers to reward systems structured like golf tournaments, in which a slight difference in productivity (perhaps one or two shots) is associated with a difference in pay of several hundred thousand dollars.

Tournament pay
A form of compensation in which the top performer (or performers) receives much higher rewards than do other competitors, even if the others perform at only a slightly lower level.

The tournament pay environment creates a strong incentive for potential superstars to expend considerable effort to become a top performer. As a result, many people spend long hours developing skills that will increase their chances of becoming a "star" in athletics, entertainment, professions, and business. The tournament system also encourages those who are unwilling to make such sacrifices to follow another path. Is this good or bad? Economics does not answer that question; it merely explains how these markets work.

---

[3]Paul M. Sommers and Noel Quinton, "Pay and Performance in Major League Baseball: The Case of the First Family of Free Agents," *Journal of Human Resources* (Summer 1982): 426–35.

[4]Edward Lazear and Sherwin Rosen, "Rank Order Tournaments as an Optimum Labor Contract," *Journal of Political Economy* 89 (October 1981): 841–64; and Jed DeVaro, "Internal Promotion Competitions in Firms," *RAND Journal of Economics*, Autumn 2006, pp. 521–42.

Jon Kopaloff/WireImage/Getty Images

What is the marginal revenue product of entertainment stars like Scarlett Johansson? Do the earnings of star entertainers, athletes, and even business executives reflect the tournament pay nature of markets in these areas?

Employment discrimination
Unequal treatment of people on the basis of their race, gender, religion, or other attributes, restricting their employment and earnings opportunities compared with others of similar productivity. Employment discrimination may stem from the prejudices of employers, customers, fellow employees, or all three.

2. Worker preferences. An important source of earnings differentials that is sometimes overlooked is worker preferences. People have different objectives in life. Some want to make a great deal of money. Many are willing to work two jobs or very long hours, undergo agonizing training and many years of education, or sacrifice social and family life to make money. Others might be "workaholics" because they enjoy their jobs. Still others might be satisfied with just enough money to get by, preferring to spend more time with their family, coaching little leaguers, watching television, on vacation, with a hobby, or at the local tavern.

Economics doesn't dictate that one set of worker preferences is more desirable than another any more than it suggests that people should eat more spinach and less pastrami. It does, however, show that worker preferences in the areas of money, work, and skill development will contribute to differences in earnings. Other things being constant, people who are more highly motivated by monetary objectives will be more likely to do the things necessary to command higher wage rates.

3. Race and gender. Discrimination on the basis of race, gender, or other attributes such as religion or disability may also contribute to earnings differences among people. **Employment discrimination** can directly limit earnings opportunities. Employment discrimination occurs when some employees are treated differently from similarly productive employees because of a characteristic such as ethnicity or gender. Of course, the earnings of, say, women or Black workers, may also differ from those of White men for reasons other than employment discrimination. For example, discrimination that preceded their employment, such as difficulty in obtaining high-quality education or specialized training, can limit the opportunities of racial groups and women to acquire the human capital that would enhance their productivity and earnings. Other factors, like the limited opportunities that can result from growing up in a low-income or a single-parent family, can also influence skill development and educational achievement. In a later section in this chapter, we will analyze the impact of employment discrimination in more detail.

4. Worker Attitudes. In addition to one's skill level, attitudes also influence productivity. Consider the following set of attitudes: honesty, dependability, persistence, reliability, creativity, desire to learn and improve, and ability to work with others.[5] These attitudes will impact the productivity of employees. To a large degree, production within the firm is a team effort. Therefore, ability to work with others and enhance the productivity of other team members is a valuable attribute.

Some of the attitudes that influence productivity positively are difficult to identify and measure. They are often overlooked, sometimes even by economists. Their importance may vary across firms and industries. Nonetheless, they influence productivity, and employers will search for and reward employees with personal attitudes that increase the total output generated by the team.

13-1b Earnings Differentials due to Nonidentical Jobs

When people evaluate employment alternatives, they consider working conditions as well as wage rates. Is a job dangerous? Does it offer the opportunity to acquire the experience and training that will enhance future earnings? Is the work strenuous and nerve wracking?

[5]The importance of attitudes as a source of productivity is closely related to what psychologists call emotional intelligence (EQ). Many psychologists now believe that EQ is more important than IQ as a determinant of personal success. Refer to "What Is Emotional Intelligence (EQ)?" by Michael Akers & Grover Porter at https://psychcentral.com/lib/what-is-emotional-intelligence-eq.

Entrepreneurs Who Have Changed Our Lives

Oprah Winfrey

Theo Wargo/Getty Images Entertainment/Getty Images

When you generate a lot of revenue, employers (both actual and potential) will pay you a lot. The career of Oprah Winfrey illustrates this point. Winfrey changed television by winning an international audience through candid and heartfelt discussion. She has inspired millions of people, especially women, to advance emotionally and intellectually. She is also an astute executive, a billionaire, a successful entrepreneur, and a one-person conglomerate.

Winfrey overcame personal difficulties to achieve her success. Her parents never married, and her childhood was spent traveling among temporary homes with family members in Mississippi, Nashville, and Milwaukee. She attended Tennessee State University in Nashville but left early to take a job at a local radio station and later became a TV news reporter in Baltimore.

As a reporter, she didn't really enjoy her work, and, she wrote, her bosses didn't seem to like her. "They told me I was the wrong color, the wrong size, and that I showed too much emotion." But in 1978, she was "demoted" to an afternoon talk show, and everything changed. In her first on-air interview (with Tom Carvel, founder of the ice cream company Carvel), she felt the excitement of personal communication that she had been missing. "That day, my 'job' ended and my calling began."

In 1984, she became a talk show host in Chicago, and her program was soon the top talk show in the country. It aired until 2011 and remains among the most successful day-time talk shows in television history.

Always inspirational, Winfrey decided in the mid-1990s that her show, which was often about dysfunctional relationships, was too negative. She began to make it more upbeat and also began to develop "lifestyle" products that were attractive and uplifting. As a child, Winfrey loved to read, so she formed Oprah's Book Club, which created many bestsellers. She launched her own magazine, *O, the Oprah Magazine*, which has now been rebranded as *Oprah Daily*. She was a co-founder of the Oxygen Network, a cable television network, and in 2011, she launched a network called OWN. She has her own company, Harpo, Inc. (that's Oprah spelled backward). Few entrepreneurs have changed more lives than Oprah has.

Sources: Sarah Berger, "Oprah Winfrey: This Is the Moment My 'Job Ended' and My 'Calling Began,'" *Make It*, CNBC, April 1, 2019, at https://www.cnbc.com/2019/04/01/how-oprah-winfrey-found-her-calling.html.

Wikipedia, "Oprah Winfrey Show," at https://en.wikipedia.org/wiki/The_Oprah_Winfrey_Show and "Oprah Winfrey Network," at https://en.wikipedia.org/wiki/Oprah_Winfrey_Network.

Are the working hours, job location, and means of transportation convenient? These factors are what economists call **nonpecuniary job characteristics**. People will accept jobs with undesirable working conditions if the wages are high enough, compared to potential job alternatives with better working conditions. Because the higher wages, in essence, compensate workers for the unpleasant nonpecuniary attributes of a job, economists refer to wage differences stemming from this source as **compensating wage differentials**.

Nonpecuniary job characteristics Working conditions, prestige, variety, location, employee freedom and responsibilities, and other nonwage characteristics of a job that influence how employees evaluate the job.

Compensating wage differentials Wage differences that compensate workers for risk, unpleasant working conditions, and other undesirable nonpecuniary aspects of a job.

Examples abound of higher wages that compensate various workers for less-attractive working conditions. Because of the dangers involved, aerial window washers (those who hang from windows 20 stories up) earn higher wages than other window washers. Sales jobs involving a great deal of out-of-town travel typically pay more than similar jobs that aren't so inconvenient. Because the jobs are both physically demanding and sometimes dangerous, the wages of coal miners and oil rig workers are generally higher than those in other occupations available to low-skilled workers. Compensating factors even influence the earnings of economists. When economists work for colleges or universities, they generally enjoy a more independent and intellectually stimulating work environment than when they are employed in the business sector. Unsurprisingly, the earnings of academic economists are typically lower than those of business economists. However, it is important to remember that the academic economists with the lower earnings have chosen this job over business-sector employment. Thus, the lower earnings do not imply that they are worse off.

13-1c Earnings Differentials due to the Immobility of Labor

It is costly to move to a new location or train for a new occupation in order to get a job. As a result, labor, like other resources, isn't perfectly mobile. Some wage differentials therefore result because wages have not yet adjusted fully to changes in market conditions.

For example, as we've learned, when strong demand leads to wage increases, more and more people will train for the occupation in high demand. Eventually, supply will increase and moderate the wage increases. But this process will take time. Just the opposite will happen when demand falls. When the demand for workers in a given occupation or skill category falls, wages are likely to fall sharply in the short run. With time, some workers will move into other occupations, which eventually moderates the reduction in wages. But this will also take time. Some of the wage differences reflect the fact that this adjustment process doesn't happen instantly.

Institutional barriers can also limit the mobility of labor. Because minimum wages raise the cost to employers of hiring workers, they may reduce the ability of low-skilled workers to obtain employment in certain sectors of the economy. Labor unions often promote policies designed to increase the demand for union labor and reduce the labor supply in unionized job categories. Their actions, though, often limit the ability of nonunionized workers (and firms) to enter and compete in the unionized sectors of the economy. To the extent that unions are successful, they hamper the mobility of nonunionized workers and create higher wages for those who are unionized.

Licensing requirements limit the mobility of labor into many occupations. Because of the importance of licensing, we will address this topic in detail.

How does occupational licensing influence labor markets? In the United States, occupational licensing generally occurs at the state level. To obtain a license to offer services in many occupations, an individual must pay fees ranging from modest to exorbitant, take training courses for 6 to 12 months, and pass examinations.

In 1952, less than 5 percent of Americans worked in jobs that required a license. Today, the figure is nearly 30 percent, six times the level of the early 1950s. In the mid-1980s, 800 occupations were licensed in at least one state; now, according to the Council on Licensure, Enforcement and Regulation, more than 1,100 occupations are licensed.

The supporters of licensing argue that it is necessary to protect consumers from shoddy and potentially unsafe services. But licenses are required in numerous occupations that have little to do with public safety or protection of the consumer.[6] For example, one or more states require a person to be licensed to work in the following occupations: interior designer, makeup artist, florist, hair braider, shampoo specialist, dietician, private detective, athletic trainer, tour guide, hearing-aid fitter, funeral attendant, casket seller, and even a ferret breeder and a palm reader. The pressure for licensing seldom originates from consumer groups. Instead, it usually arises from those already in the occupation.

[6]Refer to the Department of Treasury, Office of Economic Policy, *Occupational Licensing: A Framework for Policy-makers*, 2015; Maury Gittleman, Mark A. Klee, and Morris M. Kleiner, "Analyzing the Labor Market Outcomes of Occupational Licensing," *Industrial Relations*, January 2018, pp. 57–100; Janna E. Johnson and Morris M. Kleiner, "Is Occupational Licensing a Barrier to Interstate Migration?" *American Economic Journal: Economic Policy*, August 2020, pp. 347–73; and Morris M. Kleiner and Evan J. Soltas, "A Welfare Analysis of Occupational Licensing in U.S. States," *Review of Economic Studies*, October 2023, pp. 2481–2516.

This is not surprising to economists because the current suppliers are the primary beneficiaries of licensing.

Licensing, particularly when it mandates lengthy formal training and levies expensive fees, reduces supply and drives up the price of the goods and services provided by the licensed practitioners. Those currently in the occupation gain at the expense of consumers and unlicensed potential producers. Research indicates that having a license raises hourly wages by about 11 percent, about the same as the effect of labor unions on the earnings of their members. The restrictiveness of licensing varies considerably across states. The five states where licensed occupations constitute the largest share of the workforce are Iowa, Nevada, Washington, Florida, and Kentucky. At the other end of the spectrum, the five states with the least restrictive licensing requirements are South Carolina, Rhode Island, New Hampshire, Indiana, and Kansas.[7]

Individuals can often acquire the skills necessary for high-level performance in many licensed occupations by acquiring on-the-job experience and working with others skilled in the trade. The licensing requirements prohibit persons developing their skills via these methods from entry into the occupation. The employment opportunities of the unlicensed producers are diminished, and potential gains from trade are lost.

Certification provides an attractive alternative to licensing. With certification, the government could require suppliers to provide information about their education, training, and other qualifications to consumers, without prohibiting anyone from working in their chosen field. In essence, certification makes information about the suppliers' qualifications readily available to consumers, without restricting their choices. Further, it would make it possible for practitioners to develop and demonstrate their competence while still providing consumers the information they need to make informed choices.

13-1d Sources of Wage Differentials: A Summary

As the accompanying Thumbnail Sketch shows, wage differentials stem from many sources, which can be categorized in three main ways: differences in workers, differences in jobs, and immobility of resources. Many of the wage differentials in these categories play an important allocative role, compensating people for (1) human capital investments that increase their productivity or (2) unfavorable working conditions. Other wage differentials reflect, at least partially, locational preferences or the desires of individuals for higher money income rather than nonmonetary benefits. Still other differentials, like those related to discrimination and occupational restrictions, are unrelated to worker productivity or preferences and do not promote efficient production.

We have focused on why real earnings will differ. In addition to the factors contributing to differences in real earnings, nominal earnings will also vary because of cost of living differences. In a large, geographically diverse country like the United States, the cost of living varies substantially across cities, regions, and communities. In cities like New York and San Francisco, the level of prices can be 50 percent or even 100 percent higher than in other parts of the country. Put another way, the quantity of goods and services that can be purchased with $50,000 of earnings is substantially less in New York City than in rural Georgia or Kansas. Therefore, differences in nominal wages will also reflect cost-of-living differences among geographic locations.

[7]Morris M. Kleiner and Evgeny Vorotnikov, "Analyzing Occupational Licensing among the States," *Journal of Regulatory Economics*, June 2017, pp. 132–158. Note: This section was adapted from James Gwartney, Richard Stroup, Dwight Lee, Tawni Ferrarini, and Joseph Calhoun, *Common Sense Economics: What Everyone Should Know about Wealth and Prosperity* (New York: St. Martin's Press, 2016).

Thumbnail Sketch

What Are the Sources of Earnings Differentials?

Differences in Workers

1. Specialized skills that reflect native ability, parental training, and investment in human capital (education)
2. Worker preferences (the trade-off that workers are willing to make between money earnings and other factors)
3. Discrimination on the basis of race, gender, religion, or other attributes.
4. Worker attitudes (attitudes that influence productivity)

Differences in Jobs

1. Location of job
2. Working conditions (such as job safety and comfort in the workplace)
3. Opportunity for training and skill-enhancing work experience

Immobility of Resources

1. Temporary disequilibrium resulting from market changes
2. Institutional restrictions (for example, occupational licensing and union-imposed restraints)

13-2 The Economics of Employment Discrimination

How does employment discrimination affect the job opportunities available to groups that are discriminated against? Do employers gain from discrimination? Economics sheds light on both these questions. There are two ways in which labor market discrimination can occur: wage rates and employment exclusion.

Exhibit 13-3 illustrates the impact of wage discrimination. When a favored group of workers is preferred to an unfavored group of workers, the demand for the latter group declines and, as a result, their wages will be lower. Essentially, there are two labor markets—one market for the favored group and another for the group against which the discrimination is directed. The demand for the favored group, such as White workers, is higher, but the less expensive labor of minority workers is a substitute productive resource. Both White and minority employees are employed, but the White workers are paid a higher wage rate.

Exclusionary practices are another form of employment discrimination. Either in response to outside pressure or because of their own views, employers might primarily hire White men for certain types of jobs. When racial minorities or women are excluded from a large number of occupations, they are crowded into a smaller number of remaining jobs and occupations. If entry restraints prevent people from becoming supervisors, plumbers, electricians, and airline pilots, they will be pushed elsewhere. As a result, the supply of labor in the unrestricted occupations increases, causing wage rates in these occupations to fall. In turn, the exclusionary practices reduce supply and push wages up in occupations and industries dominated by White men.

Discrimination is costly to employers when they merely reflect their own prejudices. ***If employers can hire equally productive employees of color (or women) at a lower wage than White men, then the profit motive gives them a strong incentive to do so. Hiring the higher-wage White men when similar employees of color are available will increase the costs of firms that discriminate.*** Employers who hire employees regardless of their race or gender will have lower costs and higher profits than rival firms that try to fill positions with (mostly) White men. Thus, competitive forces tend to reduce the profitability of firms that discriminate.

Discriminatory hiring practices can stem from factors other than employer prejudice, however. If either the firm's employees or its customers have a preference for or against various groups, this may lead to discriminatory hiring, even if the employer is totally unbiased.

Exhibit 13-3 The Impact of Direct Wage Discrimination

If there is employment discrimination against racial minorities or women, then the demand for their services will decline, and their wage rate will fall from W_w to W_m.

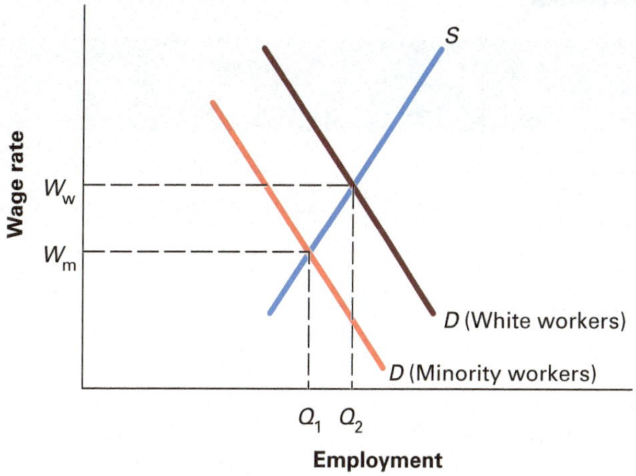

When discrimination is customer based, a worker from a favored group will be able to bring in more revenue for the firm. For example, historically, baseball cards of Black players sold for a lower price than those of White players. Similarly, Chinese restaurants that hire all (or almost all) Chinese servers are likely to do better than if the ethnic and racial composition of their employees mirrors that of the labor force.

13-2a How Much Impact Does Employment Discrimination Have on Earnings?

If we want to isolate the impact of employment discrimination, we must (1) identify groups of employees who have similar education, experience, and other productivityrelated factors and (2) then determine if such similarly qualified groups of employees who differ only by race, gender, or some other specific characteristic are treated differently.

How do the earnings of minority workers compare with those of similarly productive White workers? **Exhibit 13-4** presents the actual wages of various minority groups relative to White workers and the "productivity-adjusted" minority/White wage ratio. The adjusted ratio is an estimate of how the wages of minority workers would compare with those of White workers if the two groups had the same productivity characteristics (schooling, work experience, marital status, regional location, and union and industry status). During 2021–2023, the actual wages of Black men were 76 percent of the wages of White men. When the workforce characteristics of Black men were taken into account, however, the adjusted hourly earnings of Black men rose to 84 percent of the earnings of White men. This implies that productivity-related factors accounted for approximately two-fifths of the wage differential between the two groups. A 16 percent differential, which may well be the result of employment discrimination, remained after adjustment for the productivity characteristics.[8]

[8]The figures presented in Exhibit 4 do not control for the lower average quality of schooling received by Blacks. Other researchers using more refined data have found that productivity factors account for a larger share of the earnings differential between White and Black workers. For evidence on this point, refer to Donal O'Neill, Olive Sweetman, and Dirk Van de Gaer, "The Impact of Cognitive Skills on the Distribution of the Black–White Wage Gap," *Labour Economics*, June 2006, pp. 343–56; and Sergio Urzua, "Racial Labor Market Gaps: The Role of Abilities and Schooling Choices," *Journal of Human Resources*, Fall 2008, pp. 919–71. For a detailed explanation of how the adjusted ratios of Exhibit 4 were derived and information on the significance of productivity factors and employment discrimination on the basis of gender, refer to David A. Macpherson and Barry T. Hirsch, "Wages and Gender Composition: Why Do Women's Jobs Pay Less?," *Journal of Labor Economics* (July 1995); and John T. Addison, Orgul D. Ozturk, Si Wang, "The Occupational Feminization of Wages," *Industrial and Labor Relations Review* (January 2018): 208–241. Also review Carolyn M. Sloane, Erik G. Hurst, and Dan A. Black., "College Majors, Occupations, and the Gender Wage Gap." *Journal of Economic Perspectives*, Fall 2021, pp. 223–48.

Exhibit 13-4 The Actual and Productivity-Adjusted Wages of Minority Groups Compared to White Workers: 2021-2023

	Men		Women	
	Actual	Adjusted	Actual	Adjusted
White	100	100	100	100
African American	75	84	85	90
American Indian	81	95	87	98
Asian American	116	99	113	100
Mexican American	71	90	77	92
Other Hispanic	78	90	84	92

Source: These data were supplied by David Macpherson. They were derived from the 2021–2023 *Current Population Surveys*. The three-year time period was used to increase the sample size for the various groups. The data were adjusted for years of schooling, work experience, part-time status, citizenship status, region, industry, sector of employment, union status, and marital status.

Mexican Americans and Asian Americans constitute two other large minority groups in the United States. Even though the actual wages of Mexican American men were only 71 percent of the wages of White men, their "adjusted" earnings were 90 percent of those for White workers. Thus, the productivity-related factors accounted for two-thirds of the earnings difference between White and Mexican American men. This figure was not adjusted for the ability to speak English. Adjustment for this factor would almost certainly further narrow the differential. Interestingly, adjustment for productivity factors reduces the wages of Asian Americans relative to White workers. The *Current Population Survey* data reveals that Americans typically have more education and tend to live in large cities where nominal earnings and the cost of living are higher. As a result, the "adjusted" earnings of Asian Americans are lower than their actual earnings figures.

Turning to the data for women, the productivity-adjusted wage rates of minority women relative to White women are between 90 percent and 100 percent for each of the groups included in Exhibit 13-4. This implies that employment discrimination on the basis of race adds between 0 percent and 10 percent to earnings differentials that may reflect discrimination on the basis of gender. For an analysis of earnings differences according to gender, refer to the special topic entitled "Earnings Differences Between Men and Women" in the final section of this book.

13-3 How Do Unions Influence Wages?

A labor union is an organization of employees, usually working in either the same occupation or same industry, who have consented to joint bargaining with employers about their wages, working conditions, grievance procedures, and other elements of employment. The union–management bargaining process often leaves people with the impression that wages are established primarily by the talents of those sitting at the bargaining table. It might appear that market forces play a relatively minor role. However, as both union and management are well aware, market forces provide the setting in which the bargaining is conducted. They often tip the balance of power one way or the other.

High wages increase the firm's costs. When union employers face stiff competition from nonunion producers or foreign competitors, they will be less able to pass along higher wage costs to their customers. Competition in the product market thus limits the bargaining power of a union. Changing market conditions also affect the balance of power between unions and management. When the demand for a product is strong, the demand for labor will be high, and the firm will be much more willing to consent to a significant wage increase. When demand is weak, however, the product inventory level of the firm (or industry) is more likely to be high. Under these circumstances, wage increases will be more difficult to obtain because the firm will be much less vulnerable to a **strike** on the part of the union. (*Note:* When we speak of wage rates, we are referring to the total compensation package, including both fringe benefits and money wages.)

Strike
An action of unionized employees in which they (1) discontinue working for the employer and (2) take steps to prevent other potential workers from offering their services to the employer.

A union can use three basic strategies to increase the wages of its members: supply restrictions, bargaining power, and increased demand for union labor. We will examine each of these in turn.

13-3a Supply Restrictions

If a union can successfully reduce the supply of competitive labor, higher wage rates will automatically result. Licensing requirements, long apprenticeship programs, immigration barriers, high initiation fees, refusal to admit new members to the union, and prohibition of nonunion workers from holding jobs are all practices that unions have used to limit the supply of labor to various occupations and jobs. Craft unions, in particular, have been able to restrict the supply of workers in various occupations and boost the wages of their members.

Panel (a) of **Exhibit 13-5** illustrates the effect of supply restrictions on wage rates. Successful exclusionary tactics will reduce the supply, shifting the supply curve to the left from S_0 to S_1. Facing the supply curve S_1, employers will consent to the wage rate W_1. Compared to a free-entry market equilibrium, the wage rate has increased from W_0 to W_1, but employment has declined from E_0 to E_1. At the higher wage rate, W_1, an excess supply of labor, *AB*,

Exhibit 13-5 Supply Restrictions, Bargaining Power, and Wage Rates

The impact of higher wages obtained by restricting supply is very similar to that obtained through bargaining power. As illustrated in panel (a), when union policies reduce the supply of one type of labor, higher wages result. Similarly, when bargaining power is used in order to obtain higher wages (W_1) (panel b), employment declines and an excess supply of labor results.

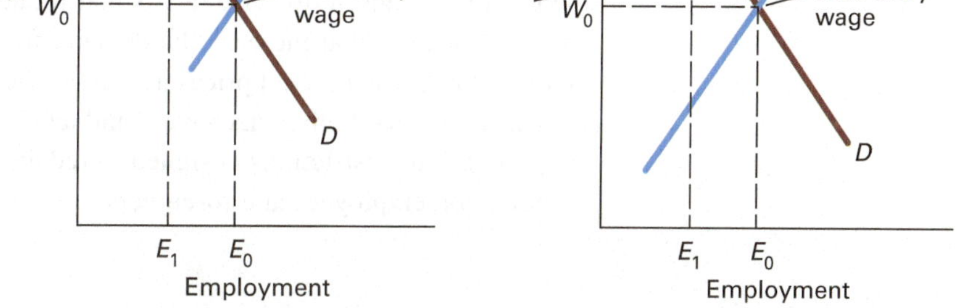

(a) Supply restriction **(b) Bargaining power**

will result. The restrictive practices will prevent this excess supply from undercutting the above-equilibrium wage rate. Because of the exclusionary practices, the union will be able to obtain higher wages for E_1 employees. Other employees willing to accept work even at wage rate W_0 will be forced into other areas of employment.

13-3b Bargaining Power

Must unions restrict entry? Why can't they simply use their bargaining power, enhanced by the threat of a strike, to raise wages? If they have enough economic power, this will be possible. A strike by even a small percentage of vital employees can sometimes halt the flow of production. For example, a work stoppage by airline pilots can force major airlines to cancel their flights. Because the pilots perform an essential function, an airline cannot operate without their services, even though they constitute only 10 percent of all airline employees.

If the union is able to obtain an above-free-entry wage rate, the effect on employment will be similar to a reduction in supply. As panel (b) of Exhibit 4 illustrates, employers will hire fewer workers at the higher wage rate obtained through bargaining power. Employment will decline below the free-entry level (from E_0 to E_1) as a result of the rise in wages. An excess supply of labor, *AB*, will exist, at least temporarily. More employees will seek the high-wage union jobs than employers will choose to hire. Nonwage methods of rationing jobs will become more important.

13-3c Increased Demand

Unions can attempt to increase the demand for union labor by appealing to consumers to buy only union-produced goods. Union-sponsored promotional campaigns instructing consumers to "look for the union label" or "buy American" are generally designed to increase the demand for union-made products.

Most people, however, are primarily interested in getting the most for their consumer dollar. Thus, the demand for union labor is usually determined primarily by factors outside the union's direct control, such as the availability of substitute inputs and the demand for the product. Unions, though, can sometimes use their political power to increase the demand for their services. They may be able to induce legislators to pass laws that reduce competition from nonunion and/or foreign workers. In some areas, required inspections on construction projects will be undertaken only if the electrical or plumbing services have been performed by "licensed" (mostly union) craft workers. Unions are often supportive of import restrictions designed to increase the demand for products that they produce. The steelworkers union, which represents both aluminum and steel workers, has successfully lobbied for higher tariffs restricting the entry of foreign-produced aluminum and steel into the U.S. market. Garment workers have used their political muscle to raise tariffs and reduce import quotas for clothing produced abroad. Practices that increase the demand for goods and services produced by union labor will increase product prices as well as the wages of unionized workers. Thus, it is not surprising that both management and labor of unionized firms often join together to support various restrictions designed to reduce the competitiveness of goods produced by nonunion employees and foreigners.

13-4 The Wages of Union and Nonunion Employees

The precise effect of unions on the wages of their members is not easy to determine. To isolate the union effect, one must eliminate differences in other factors. Comparisons must be made between union and nonunion workers who have similar productivity (skills) and who are working in similar jobs.

Exhibit 13-6 provides estimates of the union–nonunion wage differential for private-sector workers, adjusted for productivity characteristics.[6] Private-sector union workers received a 27 percent premium compared with similar nonunion workers during the 1983–1984 period. Since the mid-1980s, the private-sector union premium has been shrinking. By 2022–2023, the premium had fallen to 15 percent.

Our theory indicates that some unions will be much stronger than others—that is, better able to achieve higher wages for their members. In some occupations, the size of the union–nonunion differential will be well above the average, whereas in other occupations, unions will have little effect on wages. Strong unions, such as those of electricians, plumbers, tool and die makers, metal craft workers, truckers (before deregulation), and commercial airline pilots, are able to raise the wages of their members substantially more than the average for all unions. Economists have found that the earnings of unionized merchant seamen, postal workers, and rail, auto, and steelworkers, for example, exceed the wages of similarly skilled nonunion workers by 25 percent or more.

Unionization appears to have had the least effect on the earnings of cotton/textile, footwear, furniture, hosiery, clothing, and retail sales workers. In these areas, the power of the union has been considerably limited by the existence of a substantial number of nonunion firms. The demands of union workers in these industries are moderated by the fear that unionized employers will be at a competitive disadvantage relative to nonunion employers in the industry.

Exhibit 13-6 The Wage Premium of Private-Sector Union Workers, 1983-2023

The wages of union workers in the private sector fell relative to similar nonunion workers in the past three decades. In 2022-2023, 2013-2014 (XX percent), the estimated union-nonunion differential was 15 percent for private sector workers, down from 27 percent during 1983-1984.

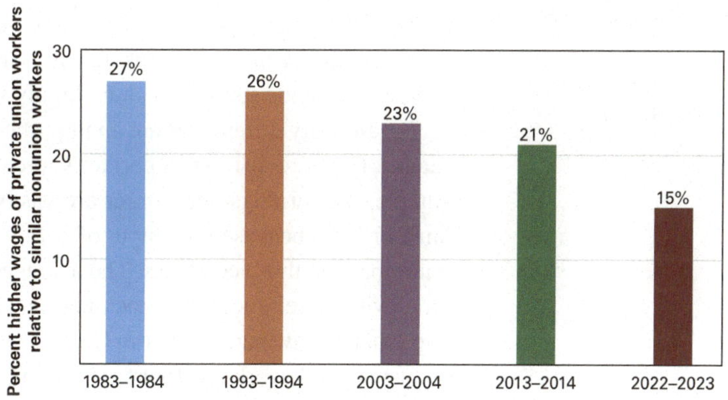

Source: Author calculations from the Current Population Survey.

[6]Author calculations from the Current Population Survey. The union wage premium for all wage and salary workers is slightly smaller than for private-sector workers only. The premium for all workers (private sector and public sector) was the following: 1983–1984 (21 percent), 1993–1994 (22 percent), 2003–2004 (19 percent), 2013–2014 (17 percent), and 2022–2023 (11 percent).

Outstanding Economist

Claudia Goldin (1946-)

In 2023, Claudia Goldin won the Nobel Prize in Economics for her contributions to economic history and labor economics. She was the third woman to win the award and the first to do it solo. She was the first woman to earn a tenured professorship in Harvard's economics department and has served as president of the American Economic Association. Her research has helped advance our understanding of women's labor market outcomes, such as women's participation in the workforce and reasons for the gender pay gap. She has examined a wide variety of other issues, including family work-life balance, women's surnames after marriage, and the impact of the contraceptive pill on women's careers. Her book *Career & Family: Women's Century-Long Journey toward Equity* (Princeton University Press, 2021) discusses the historical challenges women have faced in the labor market, including the negative effects of the COVID-19 pandemic on women's advancement.

Keys to Economic Prosperity

Productivity and Earnings

In a market economy, productivity and earnings are closely linked. High productivity is the source of high earnings. To earn a large income, one must provide others with goods and services they value highly.

13-5 The Link Between Productivity and Earnings

In a competitive market setting, productivity—that is, output per worker—and earnings are closely linked. When workers are more productive, the demand for their services will be higher, and therefore they will be able to command higher wages. ***High productivity provides the underlying source of high wages. When the output per hour of workers is high, the real wages of the workers will also be high.***

In turn, the link between productivity and earnings provides individuals with a strong incentive to develop their talents and utilize their resources in ways that are helpful to others. As the value of the services provided to others increases, so too will the amount others are willing to pay for those services. If you want to earn a lot of money, you had better figure out how to provide services that are highly valued by others.

Productivity differences are an important source of differences in earnings among individuals. They are also an important source of earnings differences across countries. For example, the earnings per worker are vastly greater in the United States than they are in China or India because the output of U.S. workers is much greater than the output of their counterparts in those countries. The average worker in the United States is better educated, works with more productive machines, and benefits from more efficient economic organization than the average worker in China or India. Thus, the value of the output produced by the average U.S. worker is four to eight times that produced by the average worker in China or India. American workers earn more because they produce more. If they did not produce more, they would not be able to earn more.

Productivity differences also affect earnings across time. Today, American workers are substantially more productive than they were 50 years ago.[10] The output of goods and services per hour of U.S. workers in 2023 was about 2.5 times the level of the early 1970s. Similarly, average real earnings (total compensation) per hour in 2019 were 1.6 times those

[10]For more on productivity growth, refer to Kevin J. Stiroh, "What Drives Productivity Growth?," *Economic Policy Review* (Federal Reserve Bank of New York) (March 2001): 37–59.

Chad Ehlers/Alamy Stock Photo

Robots and other labor-saving equipment can improve productivity. But profit-maximizing firms will adopt them only when they reduce costs. Cost-effective automation releases labor and other resources so that they can be used to expand production in other areas. In turn, the higher worker productivity and expansion in production makes higher income levels and living standards possible.

of 50 years ago. Earnings rose because productivity increased. If productivity had not increased, the increase in earnings would not have been possible.

Increased physical capital, improvements in the skill level of the labor force, and advances in technology drive productivity and earnings growth. For several decades, both the educational level of American workers and the capital equipment per worker have steadily increased. Technological advances have also enhanced productivity and contributed to the growth of output and income. Some people argue that technology and **automation** adversely affect workers. In fact, just the opposite is true. ***Once you recognize that higher output is the source of higher earnings, the gains from capital formation and improvements in technology are apparent: Better machines and technological improvements make larger outputs possible. In turn, more productive workers will have higher earnings.***

Automation
A production technique that reduces the amount of labor required to produce a good or service. It is beneficial to adopt the new labor-saving technology only if it reduces the cost of production.

Equipment and technology can improve productivity. But profit-maximizing firms will invest in new equipment and advanced technology only when they reduce costs. Cost-effective investments enhance output. In turn, the increased output per worker makes higher income levels and living standards possible.

13-5a Robots, Productivity, and the Future of Employment

As robots and technological advancements perform a wider range of productive activities, some fear that machines will replace people and the future employment opportunities of humans will be bleak. Is this view correct? As you contemplate the answer to this question, consider the following three points.

First, robots will be substituted for a human employee only if doing so reduces the cost of producing a good or service. Robots are not free. It is costly to produce robots and other labor-saving machines capable of performing various productive tasks. They will be adopted if, and only if, they reduce costs. The power shovel has largely replaced human ditch diggers because it is a lower-cost method of digging ditches. Similarly, household appliances such as automatic washers and dryers have replaced household employees because the machines are cheaper.

Second, when robots reduce costs, they will increase productivity and release humans to perform other tasks. In turn, the higher productivity and expansion in output will enhance our income levels, living standards, and quality of life.

Applications in Economics

Artificial Intelligence and Labor

How will artificial intelligence (AI) affect the workforce? Will the United States need more highly skilled technicians, possibly with PhDs, or will such people lose their jobs to AI? Or will both happen?

Although it began with research in the 1950s and 1960s, AI started its meteoric rise around 2010. Since then, AI has been using large data networks driven by algorithms (that is, very specific step-by-step instructions) for a myriad of purposes. You benefit from AI if you use Google's search engine, Amazon's Alexa, or Apple's Siri. For example, Alexa searches through a gigantic database to find the specific song you want—and plays it. The interactive maps in your smartphone use AI, as do chatbots, facial recognition programs, banks' monitoring of credit scores, cancer research, and many other activities.

In 2022, the company Open AI came out with ChatGPT, which represents an even higher level of intelligence called generative AI. Instead of just searching through vast amounts of information, generative AI can use the data to create written texts, images, videos, and more. The databases are constantly growing, and the algorithms are increasingly complex. In some cases, AI software can create algorithms on its own.

By the time you read these pages, it's likely that more remarkable events will have unfolded. By the time you read these pages, more amazing things will probably have happened.

AI is ranked as a pivotal historic milestone like the steam engine, railroads, and the automobile. With those inventions, everyone knew they were important but couldn't predict how they would change the world. So, it is with AI.

AI is expanding because it can dramatically increase productivity in many fields. But will it reduce the number of workers, as robots have started reducing the number of manufacturing workers?[1] Writers and editors are being replaced by generative AI programs. Fewer code writers are needed because AI is able to write the code.

In 2019, a group of authors headed by Morgan Frank reviewed many studies predicting the impact of AI on jobs. One study estimated that "47% of current U.S. employment is at high risk of computerization," but "another study, using a different methodology, concluded that a less alarming 9% of employment is at risk."[2]

Those studies may already need to be updated. "Uncertainty is our only certainty when it comes to AI and the future of work," wrote Brent Orrell and David Veldran in early 2024.[3]

As a student, how should you prepare for such an uncertain future? According to Orrell and Veldran, the key is building two types of skill. One entails technical knowledge, so you will be in a position to understand and work with AI. But the other kind is equally significant—social or "noncognitive" skills. This includes "resiliency, communication, integrity, initiative, adaptability, and flexibility."[4] Whatever you do in life, they say, these "noncognitive" or social skills will be increasingly important as you move up the corporate ladder or follow your entrepreneurial adventure.

In sum, they advise:

"Students and workers with strong quantitative and technical skills should seek to improve in nontechnical domains, while those with strong nontechnical skills should bolster their knowledge of and abilities in math, science, and technology to create a balanced education and training 'portfolio.'"[5]

[1] Daron Acemoglu and Pascual Restrepo, "Robots and Jobs: Evidence from U.S. Labor Markets," *Journal of Political Economy* 128, no. 6 (2020).

[2] Morgan R. Frank, David Autor, James E. Bessen, Erik Brynjolfsson, Manuel Cebrian, David J. Deming, Maryann Feldman, Matthew Groh, José Lobo, Esteban Moro, Dashun Wang, Hyejin Youn, and Iyad Rahwan, "Toward Understanding the Impact of Artificial Intelligence on Labor," *Proceedings of the National Academy of Sciences* 116, no. 14 (April 2, 2019): 6531-9.

[3] Brent Orrell and David Veldran, "The Age of Uncertainty—and Opportunity: Work in the Age of AI," American Enterprise Institute, February 2024, 15.

[4] Orrell and Veldran, 13.

[5] Orrell and Veldran, 13.

Third, robots will make it possible for humans to focus on work that is more enjoyable and more rewarding. Robots can perform tasks that are monotonous, onerous, physically demanding, or dangerous, releasing humans to focus their efforts elsewhere. Some will choose to work fewer hours, but others will focus on discoveries that will improve human life, such as finding a cure for cancer or heart disease. Still others will focus on providing goods with entertainment value, such as performing arts, sporting events, and video games. Because robots will eliminate much of the onerous work, more and more people will be able to do things they really love to do. Moreover, when people are doing what they love, their creativity will result in some amazing achievements, at least by current standards. Thus, the future of work will be more exciting and rewarding. Many may not even think of it as work.[11]

Of course, technological advances can diminish the earnings of individual people or groups. Computer technology has reduced job opportunities for secretaries and clerks. Voice recognition technology has lowered the demand for telephone operators. In the future, self-driving vehicles may reduce the demand for taxi and truck drivers, and online courses and videotaped lectures may even reduce the job opportunities of many college professors. It is understandable why groups directly affected in this manner often fear and oppose automation.

Focusing on the loss of specific jobs, however, is misleading. Clearly, running out of jobs is not a problem. Jobs represent obstacles—tasks that must be accomplished to loosen the bonds of scarcity. As long as our ability to produce goods and services falls short of our consumption desires, there will be jobs. A society running out of jobs would be in an enviable position: It would be nearing the impossible goal—victory over scarcity!

13-5b Productivity and Compensation: Measurement Problems

What has been happening to the growth of productivity, and how has this influenced the wages of workers? **Exhibit 13-7**, left panel, presents the official Bureau of Labor Statistics data for the average growth rate of productivity per hour and real hourly compensation for 1948–1973, 1974–1999, and 2000–2023. Economic analysis indicates that the growth of productivity and real hourly compensation tend to move together. Historically, this has generally been the case. This was true during 1948–1973, when productivity and real compensation both grew at an annual rate of approximately 3 percent. However, during 1974–1999, productivity growth averaged 1.8 percent annually but real compensation rose at an annual rate of only 1.0 percent. An even larger gap between the growth of productivity and compensation was present during 2000–2023 as productivity increased by 1.9 percent annually, compared to an annual growth rate of just 0.8 percent for real compensation. Thus, the official data indicate that real hourly compensation has been lagging behind the growth of productivity, and the gap has been widening.

How can the increasing gap since the mid-1970s be explained? A major source of the widening gap in the official statistics is that real hourly compensation and productivity are calculated using two different measures of inflation. Hourly compensation is converted into real terms using the consumer price index, which is based on a bundle of goods purchased by a typical consumer. Productivity is computed using the implicit price deflator, which is based on all output. The former tends to overstate price increases relative to the latter, and this overstatement can be large over lengthy time periods.

To examine the impact of the use of the differing price indexes, the growth rates were recalculated using the implicit price deflator to adjust real compensation as well as productivity. These figures are presented in Exhibit 13-7 (right panel). During 1948–1973, the average productivity growth rate was 3.2 percent compared to a 3.0 average growth rate for real compensation. During 1974–1999, the annual growth rates of productivity and real compensation were 1.8 percent and 1.7 percent, respectively. Finally, during 2000–2023, the average annual productivity growth was 1.9 percent compared to 1.3 percent for annual real compensation growth. As the right panel indicates, once the same price index is used to calculate the productivity and real compensation measures, the two series move together in tandem, particularly before 2000.

---

[11]Refer to John Tamny, "Robots Will Not Put Us Out of Work; They'll Cause Us to Fall in Love with It," *Cayman Financial Review*, pp. 54–55.

Exhibit 13-7 Productivity and Employee Compensation in the United States, 1948-2023

As shown in the left panel, worker productivity has been increasing at a faster rate than real compensation per hour in the official statistics. The consumer price index is used to derive real compensation, and the implicit price deflator is used to calculate productivity. The right panel shows that the gap between productivity and compensation is significantly smaller when both productivity and compensation are converted into real terms using the implicit price deflator.

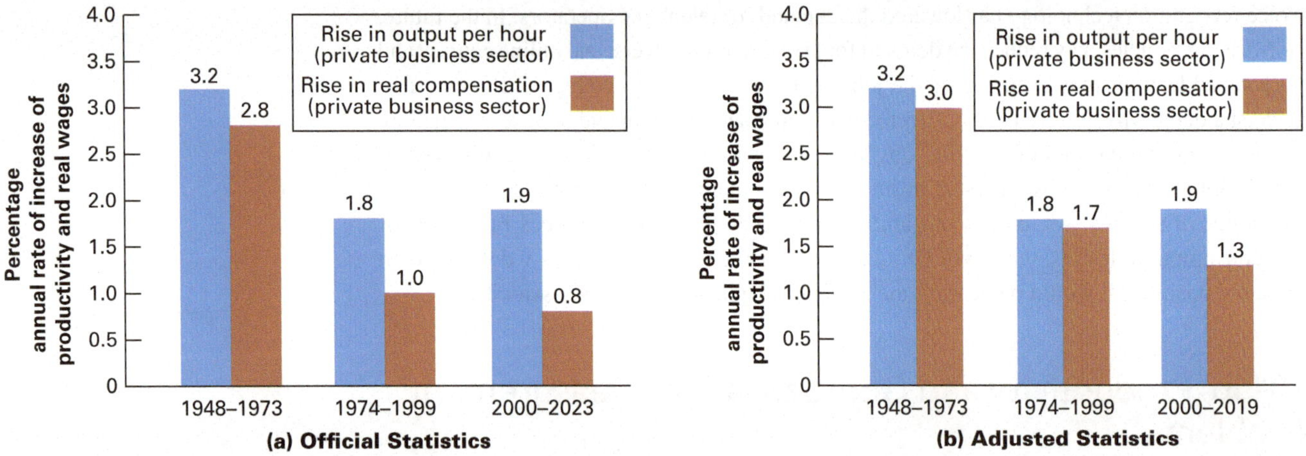

Source: Bureau of Labor Statistics, http://www.bls.gov/.

What about the remaining gap between growth of productivity and real compensation since 2000? Improvements in non-pecuniary job attributes such as reductions in physical demands and risk of injury accompanying the work may help explain part of the gap. In addition, research indicates that three additional factors are at work during this recent period. First, part of the gap is an artifact of the method used to impute labor income for self-employed individuals.[12] That is, self-employed workers have more labor income and less capital income than is indicated in the official statistics. Second, offshoring of the labor-intensive portion of production causes the productivity of domestic workers to be overstated. Third, both advancement and dissemination of technology may be exerting a greater impact on the growth of productivity in recent years than was the case in the past. Certainly, high-tech products like 3D printing, artificial intelligence (AI), Google, Uber, Facebook, and X (formerly Twitter) have expanded rapidly and increase the quality of life of people around the world. Because products like these reflect technological improvements and they generally save labor and time, they increase productivity more than employee compensation. Once these factors are accounted for, even the gap between the growth of productivity and real compensation for 2000–2023 is quite small.[13]

The precise calculation of productivity and compensation is complex in the era of rapid innovations in information technology and globalization. Although these challenges generate measurement issues, they also add an interesting dimension to the field of labor economics.

[12]Michael W. L. Elsby, Bart Hobijn, and Aysegül Sahin, "The Decline of the U.S. Labor Share," *Brookings Papers on Economic Activity*, Fall 2013, pp. 1–61.

[13]For more evidence on the role of differing price indexes and the speed of technological change in the gap between productivity and real compensation growth rates in official statistics, refer to Susan Fleck, John Glaser, and Shawn Sprague, "The Compensation-Productivity Gap: A Visual Essay," *Monthly Labor Review*, January 2011, pp. 57–91; and David Autor, David Dorn, Lawrence F. Katz, Christina Patterson, and John Van Reenen, "Concentrating on the Fall of the Labor Share," *American Economic Review*, May 2017, pp. 180–185.

Key Points

- The real earnings of individuals would be equal if (1) all individuals were identical in skills, preferences, attitudes, and background; (2) all jobs were equally attractive; and (3) workers were perfectly mobile among jobs. Earnings differences among individuals result from the absence of these conditions.
- Wage differences play an important allocative role. They generally compensate people for (1) investments in education and training that enhance productivity and the development of highly specialized skills and (2) unfavorable working conditions and/or job locations. Wage differences can also result from differences in workers' preferences, employment discrimination, and institutional factors that restrict worker mobility.
- Employment discrimination reduces the wages of people being discriminated against by either lowering the demand for their services or restricting their entry into various job categories. Productivity differences also contribute to earnings differentials between groups. Research indicates that the earnings of Black and Mexican American men are, respectively, approximately 85 percent and 91 percent those of White men of similar productivity.
- A union can use three basic methods to increase the wages of its members: (1) restrict the supply of competitive inputs, including nonunion workers; (2) apply bargaining power enforced by a strike or threat of one; and (3) increase the demand for the labor service of union members.
- Studies suggest that the wage premium of private-sector union members relative to similar nonunion workers has fallen during the last four decades. In the period 2022–2023, private-sector union workers earned about 15 percent more, on average, than similar nonunion workers.
- Productivity is the ultimate source of high wages and earnings. Workers in the United States (and other high-income industrial countries) earn high wages because their output per hour is high as the result of (1) greater worker knowledge and skills (human capital) and (2) the use of modern machinery (physical capital).
- Robotics and other labor-saving methods of production will be adopted only if they reduce costs. Although automation might reduce employment in a specific industry, it also releases resources that can be employed in other areas. Improved technology permits us to achieve larger output and income levels than would otherwise be possible.
- Economic theory indicates that productivity and earnings growth will move together. Official statistics indicate that since the mid-1970s, productivity has grown more rapidly than real hourly compensation. However, when the same price index is used to adjust both through time, the gap in the growth rates between the two is largely eliminated.

Critical Analysis Questions

1. Why do some people earn higher wages than others? Why are wages in some occupations higher than in others? How do wage differentials influence the allocation of resources? Explain.
2. *Why are real wages in the United States higher than in other countries? Is the labor force itself responsible for the higher wages of American workers? Explain.
3. Indicate the major sources of earnings differences between (a) a lawyer and a minister; (b) an accountant and an elementary school teacher; (c) a business executive and a social worker; (d) a country lawyer and a Wall Street lawyer; (e) an experienced, skilled craftsperson and a 20-year-old high school dropout; and (f) an upper-story and a ground-floor window washer?
4. **a.** If minority employees are discriminated against, how will this affect their earnings? Use supply and demand analysis to explain your answer.

   b. If the average earnings differ between two groups of employees (for example, White workers and Black workers), does this mean that the group with the lower earnings is experiencing employment discrimination? Why or why not?
5. Why are workers with higher productivity able to earn higher wages? How does the linkage between productivity and earnings affect the incentive of individuals to improve their skill levels? What impact will this have on earnings through time? Can a person achieve high earnings without high productivity? Why or why not? Discuss.
6. *"Jobs are the key to economic progress. Unless we create more jobs, our standard of living will fall." Is this statement true or false? Explain.
7. "If Diaz has a skill that is highly valued, she will be able to achieve high market earnings. In contrast, Chen may work just as hard or even harder and still earn only a low income."

   a. Does hard work necessarily lead to a high income?

   b. Why are the incomes of some workers high and others low?

c. Do you think the market system of wage determination is fair? Why or why not?

d. Can you think of a more equitable system? If so, explain why it is more equitable.

8. People who have invested heavily in human capital (for example, lawyers, doctors, and even college professors) generally have higher wages, but they also generally work more hours than other workers. Can you explain why?

9. *"If individuals had identical abilities and opportunities, earnings would be equal." Is this statement true or false?

10. Other things being constant, how will the following influence the hourly earnings of employees? Explain your answer.

   a. The employee must work the midnight to 8:00 a.m. shift.

   b. The job involves split shifts (work three hours, off two hours, work three additional hours, and so on).

   c. The employer provides low-cost child care services on the premises.

   d. The job is widely viewed as prestigious.

   e. The job requires employees to move often from city to city.

   f. The job requires substantial amounts of out-of-town travel.

11. *Consider two occupations (A and B) in which people have the same skills and abilities. When employed, workers in the two occupations work the same number of hours per day. In occupation A, employment is stable throughout the year, whereas employment in B is characterized by seasonal layoffs. In which occupation will the hourly wage rate be highest? Why? In which occupation will the annual wage be highest? Why?

12. Is automation bad for the economy? Do we need to fear that robots will take the jobs of people, and drive wages downward? Would we be better off if there was less technological change?

13. If an individual is motivated primarily by the desire to make money, will they have an incentive to be helpful to others? Will they have an incentive to develop skills that others value highly? Why or why not?

14. What does the relationship between additional years of schooling and earnings reflect? Could it merely reflect that years of schooling are a signaling mechanism? Discuss. If this is the case, what are the implications with regard to the payoff from additional investment in education?

15. Do competitive markets encourage employment discrimination? Why or why not?

16. Assume that the primary objective of a union is to raise the wages of its members.

   a. Discuss the conditions that will help the union achieve this objective.

   b. Why might a union be unable to meet its goal?

17. Evaluate the following statements.

   a. "An increase in the price of steel will be passed along to consumers in the form of higher prices for automobiles, homes, appliances, and other products made with steel." Do you agree or disagree?

   b. "An increase in the price of craft union labor will be passed along to consumers in the form of higher prices of homes, repair and installation services, appliances, and other products that require craft union labor." Do you agree or disagree?

   c. Are the interests of labor unions in conflict primarily with the interests of union employers? Explain.

*Asterisk denotes questions for which answers are given in Appendix B.

Chapter 14 Investment, the Capital Market, and the Wealth of Nations

> To produce capital, people must forgo the opportunity to produce goods for current consumption. People can choose whether to spend their time picking apples or planting apple trees. In the first case there are more apples today; in the second, more apples tomorrow.
>
> –Steven Landsburg[1]

As we noted in the previous chapter, there is a close relationship between productivity and earnings. In turn, productivity is influenced by investment choices. Consider choices about whether to construct an apartment building, purchase a new computer, or go to law school. The returns derived from investments like these are usually spread over years or even decades. Some costs, such as maintenance expenses, can also be incurred over time. When the benefits and costs are spread across lengthy periods of time, comparison is complex. This chapter will address this issue and related topics.

Learning Objectives

14.1 Indicate why people invest and how the decision is influenced by a positive rate of time preference.

14.2 Compare and contrast savings and investment.

14.3 Differentiate between the money (nominal) interest rate and the real interest rate.

14.4 Explain why lenders are willing to loan funds and investors are willing to pay interest to get loanable funds.

14.5 Explain why the interest rate is vitally important when evaluating costs and revenues across time periods.

14.6 Indicate how the present value of future income and cost and asset values are calculated.

14.7 Explain how profitable and unprofitable investments influence the wealth of nations.

14.8 Explain why an efficiently operating capital market is vitally important for the growth and prosperity of a nation.

[1]Steven E. Landsburg, *Price Theory and Applications* (Fort Worth: Dryden Press, 1992), 581.

14-1 Why People Invest

Capital
Resources that enhance our ability to produce output in the future.

Investment
The purchase, construction, or development of capital resources, including both nonhuman capital and human capital. Investments increase the supply of capital.

Saving
Current income that is not spent on consumption goods. Saving makes it possible for resources to be devoted to investments (like the making of tractors or other equipment used in production).

Capital is a term used by economists to describe long-lasting resources that are valued because they can help us produce goods and services in the future. As we previously discussed, there are two broad categories of capital: (1) *physical capital* (buildings, machines, tools, and natural resources) and (2) *human capital* (the knowledge and skills of people). **Investment** is the purchase, construction, or development of a capital resource. Thus, investment expands the availability of capital resources.

Saving is income not spent on current consumption. Investment and saving are closely linked. In fact, the two words describe different aspects of the capital formation process. ***Saving refers to the nonconsumption of income, while investment refers to the use of the unconsumed income to produce a capital resource.*** Sometimes saving and investment are conducted by the same person, like when a farmer saves current income (refrains from spending it on consumption goods) in order to purchase a new tractor (an investment good).

It is important to recognize that saving is required for investment. Someone must save—refrain from consumption—in order to provide the resources for investment. When investors finance a project with their own funds, they are also saving (refraining from current consumption). Investors, however, do not always use their own funds to finance investments. Sometimes they will borrow funds from others. When this is the case, it is the lender rather than the investor who is doing the saving.

Consumption is the goal of economic activity. Why would anyone want to delay consumption in order to undertake an investment? Sometimes more consumption goods can be produced by first using resources to produce capital resources and then using these resources to produce the desired consumer goods. Using capital to produce consumption goods makes sense, but only if it allows us to produce more consumption goods than we otherwise could.

For example, suppose that Robinson Crusoe can catch fish by either (1) combining his labor with natural resources (direct production) or (2) constructing a net and eventually combining his labor with this capital resource (indirect production). Let's assume that Crusoe can catch two fish per day by hand-fishing, but three fish per day if he constructs and uses a net that will last for 310 days. Now suppose it will take Crusoe 55 days to build the net. The opportunity cost of constructing the net will be 110 fish (two fish per day not caught for each of the 55 days he spends building the net). As the accompanying chart shows, if Crusoe invests in the capital resource (the net), his output during the next year (including the 55 days required to build the net) would be 930 fish (three per day for 310 days). Alternatively, hand-fishing during the year would lead to an output of only 730 fish (two fish per day for 365 days).

	Number of Fish Caught	
	Without Net	With Net
Per day	2	3
Annually	730	930

In other words, Crusoe's investment will enhance his net productivity by 200 fish annually. In the short term, however, investing in the net will require a sacrifice. During the 55 days it takes to construct the net, Crusoe's production of consumption goods will decline.

Positive rate of time preference
The desire of consumers for goods now rather than in the future.

How can Crusoe or any other investor know if the value of the larger future output is worth the short-term cost? Most of us have a preference for goods now rather than later. For example, if you are typical, you would prefer a sleek new sports car now rather than the same car ten years from now. On average, individuals possess a **positive rate of time preference**. That is, other things being the same, people subjectively value goods obtained sooner more highly than goods obtained later.

When only Crusoe is involved, the attractiveness of the investment in the fishing net depends on his rate of time preference. If he places a high value on a couple of fish per day during the next 55 days, as indeed he may if he is on the verge of starvation, the cost of the investment may well exceed the value of the larger future output. If Crusoe could find someone who would loan him fish while he built the net, however, he could consume the borrowed fish now while building the net and pay later with the extra fish made possible by the net. If such a loan is available, the attractiveness of the investment (building the net instead of hand-fishing now) will be influenced by the price of borrowing fish. Is the cost of borrowing fish in order to maintain his consumption while he constructs the net worth the extra cost? To answer this question, Crusoe must consider the cost of paying for earlier availability—he must consider, in effect, the interest rate.

14-2 Interest Rates

The interest rate links the future to the present. It allows individuals to evaluate the value today—the present value—of future income and costs. In essence, it is the market price of earlier availability. From the viewpoint of a potential borrower, the interest rate is the premium that must be paid in order to acquire goods sooner and pay later. From the lender's viewpoint, it is a reward for waiting—a payment for supplying others with current purchasing power in terms of greater purchasing power in the future.

In a modern economy, people often borrow funds to finance current investments and consumption. Because of this, the interest rate is often defined as the price of loanable funds. But we should remember that it is the earlier availability of goods and services purchased, not the money itself, that is desired by the borrower.

14-2a How Interest Rates Are Determined

Interest rates are determined by the demand for and supply of loanable funds. Investors demand funds in order to finance capital assets they believe will increase output and generate profit. Simultaneously, consumers demand loanable funds because they have a positive rate of time preference: They prefer earlier availability.

The demand of investors for loanable funds stems from the productivity of capital. Investors are willing to borrow in order to finance the use of capital in production because they expect that expanding future output will provide them with more than enough resources to repay the amount borrowed—the principal—and interest on the loan. Our example of Robinson Crusoe illustrates this point. Remember, Crusoe could increase his output by 200 fish this year if he could take off 55 days from hand-fishing in order to build a net. But doing so would reduce Crusoe's fish production by 2 fish per day while he was constructing the net. Suppose a fishing crew from a neighboring island visited Crusoe and offered to lend him 110 fish so he could undertake the capital investment project (building the net). If Crusoe could borrow the 110 fish (the principal) in exchange for, say, 165 fish one year later (110 fish to repay the principal and 55 as interest on the loan), the investment project would be highly profitable. Crusoe could repay the funds borrowed, plus the 50 percent interest rate, and still have 145 additional fish (the 200 additional fish caught minus the 55 fish paid in interest).

Investors can gain by borrowing funds to undertake investment projects only when the capital assets they purchase permit them to expand output (or reduce costs) by enough to make the interest payments and still have more output than they would have without the investment.

As **Exhibit 14-1** illustrates, the interest rate brings the choices of investors and consumers wanting to borrow funds into harmony with the choices of lenders willing to supply funds. Higher interest rates make it more costly for investors to undertake capital spending

Exhibit 14-1 Determining the Interest Rate

The demand for loanable funds stems from the consumer's desire for earlier availability and the productivity of capital. As the interest rate rises, current goods become more expensive in comparison with future goods. Therefore, borrowers will demand a smaller quantity of loanable funds. In contrast, higher interest rates will stimulate lenders to supply additional funds to the market.

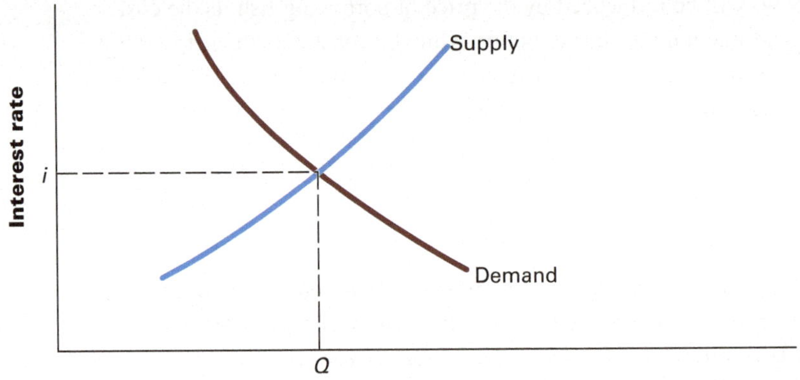

projects and for consumers to buy now rather than later. Both investors and consumers will therefore curtail their borrowing as the interest rate rises. Investors will borrow less because some investment projects that would be profitable at a low interest rate will be unprofitable at higher rates. Some consumers will reduce their current consumption rather than pay the high interest premium when the interest rate increases. Therefore, the amount of funds demanded by borrowers is inversely related to the interest rate.

The interest rate also rewards people (lenders) willing to reduce their current consumption in order to provide loanable funds to others. If some people are going to borrow in order to undertake an investment project (or consume more than their current income), others must curtail their current consumption by an equal amount. In essence, the interest rate provides lenders with the incentive to reduce their current consumption so that borrowers can either invest or consume beyond their present income. Higher interest rates give people willing to save (willing to supply loanable funds) the ability to purchase more goods in the future in exchange for sacrificing current consumption. Even though people have a positive rate of time preference, they will give up current consumption to supply funds to the loanable funds market if the price is right. Higher interest rates will induce people to save more. Therefore, as the interest rate rises, the quantity of funds supplied to the loanable funds market will increase.

As Exhibit 14-1 illustrates, the interest rate will bring the quantity of funds demanded into balance with the quantity supplied. ***At the equilibrium interest rate, the quantity of funds borrowers demand for investment and consumption will just equal the quantity of funds lenders save,*** so the interest rate brings the choices of borrowers and lenders into harmony.

Money (nominal) rate of interest
The rate of interest in monetary terms that borrowers pay for borrowed funds. During periods when borrowers and lenders expect inflation, the money rate of interest exceeds the real rate of interest.

14-2b The Money Rate Versus the Real Rate of Interest

We have emphasized that the interest rate is a premium paid by borrowers for earlier availability and a reward received by lenders for delaying consumption of *goods and services*. However, during a period of inflation—a general increase in prices—the nominal interest rate, or **money rate of interest**, is a misleading indicator of really how much borrowers are paying and lenders are receiving. Inflation reduces the purchasing power of money. Rising prices mean that when the borrower repays the loan principal in the future, the money received by the lender will not be able to purchase as many goods and services as when the funds were initially loaned.

When inflation is common, lenders will recognize they are being repaid with dollars of less purchasing power. Unless they are compensated for the anticipated inflation by an upward adjustment in the interest rate, they will supply fewer funds to the loanable funds market. At the same time, when borrowers anticipate inflation, they will want to purchase goods and services now before they become even more expensive in the future. Thus, they are willing to pay an **inflationary premium**, an additional amount of interest that reflects the expected rate of future price increases. For example, if borrowers and lenders were willing to agree on a 4 percent interest rate when both anticipated price stability, they would have the same incentive to agree to a 9 percent interest rate when both anticipated a 5 percent rate of inflation.

Therefore, when people anticipate inflation, the money interest rate will rise and it will overstate the "true" cost of borrowing and the yield from lending. This true cost is the **real rate of interest**, which is equal to the money rate of interest minus the inflationary premium. It reflects the real burden to borrowers and the payoff to lenders in terms of their being able to buy goods and services.

Our analysis indicates that high rates of inflation will lead to a high money rate of interest. The real world is consistent with this view. Money interest rates rose to historical highs in the United States as inflation soared to double-digit rates during the 1970s. Inflation rates have been much lower since the mid-1980s and, so too, have nominal interest rates. Cross-country comparisons also illustrate the link between inflation and high interest rates. The world's lowest money interest rates are found in nations such as Germany, Switzerland, and Japan, all with low rates of inflation. In contrast, the highest money interest rates have been present in Russia, Venezuela, Zimbabwe, and other countries with high rates of inflation.

Inflationary premium
A component of the money interest rate that reflects compensation to the lender for the expected decrease, due to inflation, in the purchasing power of the principal and interest during the course of the loan. It is determined by the expected rate of future inflation.

Real rate of interest
The money rate of interest minus the expected rate of inflation. The real rate of interest indicates the interest premium in terms of real goods and services that one must pay for earlier availability.

14-2c Interest Rates and Risk

So far, we've assumed there is only a single interest rate present in the loanable funds market. In the real world, of course, there are many interest rates. They include the mortgage rate, the prime interest rate (the rate charged to business firms with strong credit ratings), the consumer loan rate, and the credit card rate, to name but a few.

Interest rates in the loanable funds market will differ mainly because of differences in the risks associated with the loans. It is riskier, for example, to loan money to an unemployed worker than to a well-established business with substantial assets. Similarly, unsecured credit card loans are riskier than loans secured with an asset such as a house or a plot of land. Moreover, as recent experience vividly illustrates, a mortgage loan for the purchase of a house is far riskier when the down payment of the borrower is small. The risk also increases with the duration of the loan. The longer the time period of the loan, the more likely it is that the borrower's ability to repay the loan will deteriorate or market conditions change in a highly unfavorable manner.

As **Exhibit 14-2** shows, the money rate of interest on a loan has three components. The pure-interest component is the real price one must pay for earlier availability. The inflationary-premium component reflects the expectation that the loan will be repaid with dollars of less purchasing power as the result of inflation. The risk-premium component reflects the probability of default—the risk imposed on the lender by the possibility that the borrower may be unable to repay the loan.

14-3 The Present Value of Future Income and Costs

If you deposited $100 today in a savings account earning 6 percent interest, you would have $106 one year from now. To put it another way, to have $106 one year from now requires that you invest $100 today. ***The interest rate allows us to make this conversion***

Exhibit 14-2 The Three Components of Money Interest

The money interest rate reflects three components: pure interest, inflationary premium, and risk premium. When decision-makers expect a high rate of inflation while the loan is outstanding, the inflationary premium will be substantial. Similarly, the risk premium will be large when the probability of default by the borrower is high.

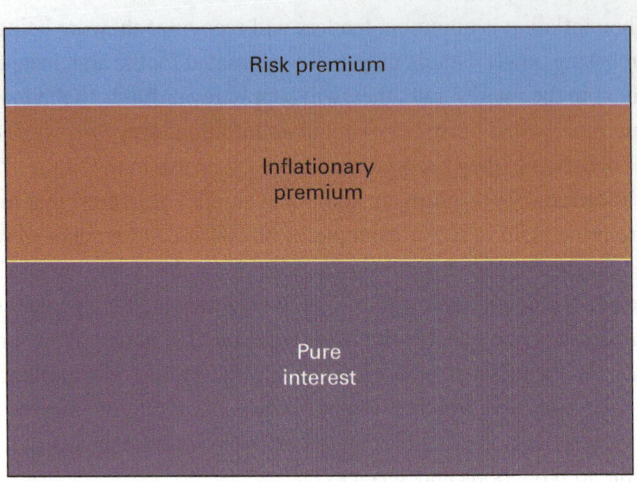

from present to future dollars. The interest rate connects the value of dollars (and capital assets) today with the value of dollars (expected income and receipts) in the future. It is used to "discount" the value of a dollar received in the future so that its present worth can be determined today.

Present value (PV)
The current worth of future income after it is discounted to reflect the fact that revenues in the future are valued less highly than revenues now.

The **present value (PV)** of a payment received one year from now can be expressed as follows:

$$PV = \frac{\text{Receipt One Year from Now}}{1 + \text{Interest Rate}}$$

If the interest rate is 6 percent, the current value of $100 to be received one year from now is

$$PV = \frac{100}{1.06} = \$94.34$$

If you put $94.34 in a savings account yielding 6 percent interest, during the year the account would earn $5.66 interest (6 percent of $94.34) and grow to $100 one year from now. Thus, the present value of $100 to be received a year from now is $94.34.

Discounting
The procedure used to calculate the present value of future income, which is inversely related to both the interest rate and the amount of time that passes before the funds are received.

Economists use the term **discounting** to describe this procedure of reducing the value of a dollar to be received in the future to its present worth. Clearly, the value of a dollar in the future is inversely related to the interest rate. For example, if the interest rate is 10 percent, the present value of $100 received one year from now would be only $90.91 ($100 divided by 1.10). At still higher interest rates, the present value of $100 a year from now would be even lower.

The present value of $100 received two years from now is

$$PV = \frac{100}{(1 + \text{Interest Rate})^2}$$

If the interest rate is 6 percent, $100 received two years from now would be equal to $89 today ($100 divided by 1.06^2). In other words, $89 invested today would yield $100 two years from now.

The present-value procedure can be used to determine the current value of any future income (or cost) stream. If R represents receipts received at the end of various years in the future (indicated by the subscripts) and i represents the interest rate, the present value of the future income stream is

$$PV = \frac{R_1}{(1+i)} + \frac{R_2}{(1+i)^2} + \cdots + \frac{R_n}{(1+i)^n}$$

Exhibit 14-3 The Present Value of $100 to Be Received in the Future

The columns indicate the present value of $100 to be received a designated number of years in the future at different discount (interest) rates. For example, at a discount rate of 2 percent, the present value of $100 to be received five years from now is $90.57. Note that the present value of the $100 declines as either the interest rate or the number of years in the future increases.

	Present Value of $100 to be Received a Designated Number of Years in the Future at Alternative Discount Rates					
Years in the Future	2 Percent	4 Percent	6 Percent	8 Percent	12 Percent	20 Percent
1	98.04	96.15	94.34	92.59	89.29	83.33
2	96.12	92.46	89.00	85.73	79.72	69.44
3	94.23	88.90	83.96	79.38	71.18	57.87
4	92.39	85.48	79.21	73.50	63.55	48.23
5	90.57	82.19	74.73	68.06	56.74	40.19
6	88.80	79.03	70.50	63.02	50.66	33.49
7	87.06	75.99	66.51	58.35	45.23	27.08
8	85.35	73.07	62.74	54.03	40.39	23.26
9	83.68	70.26	59.19	50.02	36.06	19.38
10	82.03	67.56	55.84	46.32	32.20	16.15
15	74.30	55.53	41.73	31.52	18.27	6.49
20	67.30	45.64	31.18	21.45	10.37	2.61
30	55.21	30.83	17.41	9.94	3.34	0.42
50	37.15	14.07	5.43	2.13	0.35	0.01

Exhibit 14-3 shows the present value of $100 received at various times in the future at several different discount rates. The chart clearly illustrates two points. First, the present value of income received in the future declines with the interest rate. The present value of the $100 received one year from now, when discounted at a 4 percent interest rate, is $96.15, compared with $98.04 when a 2 percent discount rate is used. Second, the present value of the $100 also declines as the date of its receipt is set farther into the future. If the discount rate is 6 percent, the present value of $100 received one year from now is $94.34, compared with $89 if the $100 is received two years from now. If the $100 is received five years from now, its current worth is only $74.73. ***So the present value of a future dollar payment is inversely related both to the interest rate and to how far in the future the payment will be received.***

To understand in a more personal way the importance of interest and the value of saving, consider what you could gain by saving just $1,000 per year ($83.33 per month) for ten years in a tax-free individual retirement account. If you begin at age 25 and continue only until age 35 (putting nothing into the account after that), and the account returns 8 percent annually, it will be worth $168,627 when you reach age 65. In contrast, if you wait until age 35 and then save $1,000 per year for 30 years (not ten years of savings as before) with the same 8 percent annual return, by age 65 your account will be worth only $125,228. Ten years of saving, starting with age 25, yields far more than 30 years of saving at the same amount each year but waiting until age 35 to start. Which savings plan is more attractive to you?

14-4 Present Value, Profitability, and Investment

Investment involves an up-front cost of acquiring a machine, skill, or other asset expected to generate additional output and revenue in the future. How can an investor know if the expected future revenues will be sufficient to cover the costs? The discounting procedure helps provide the answer. It permits the investor to place both the costs and the expected future revenues of an investment project into present-value terms. If the present value of the revenue derived from the investment exceeds the present value of the cost, it makes sense to undertake the investment. If the revenues and costs of such an investment turn out as expected, the investor will earn a profit, and the project will create wealth.

In contrast, if the cost of the project exceeds the discounted value of the future receipts, losses will be incurred. The losses reflect that the project diminished the value of the resources. Investments like these are counterproductive.

Let's pencil in the figures for a hypothetical investment option and determine whether it is a good investment. Suppose a truck rental firm is contemplating the purchase of a new $100,000 truck. Past experience indicates that after figuring in the truck's operational and maintenance expenses, the firm can rent it out for a net revenue of $30,000 annually (received at the end of each year). The firm will be able to do this every year for four years—the expected life of the vehicle.[2] Because the firm can borrow and lend funds at an interest rate of 8 percent, we will discount the future expected income at an 8 percent rate. **Exhibit 14-4** illustrates the calculation. Column 4 shows how much $30,000, available at year-end for each of the next four years, is worth today. In total, the present value of the expected rental receipts is $99,360—less than the purchase price of the truck. Therefore, the project should not be undertaken.

If the interest rate in our example had been 6 percent, the results would have been different. The present value of the future rental income would have been $103,950.[3] It pays to purchase a capital good whenever the present value of the income generated by it exceeds its purchase price. At the lower interest rate, the investment project would have been productive (and profitable).

14-4a Expected Future Earnings, the Interest Rate, and Asset Values

The present value of the expected revenue from a project minus the cost of an investment will tell us whether the project should be undertaken. Once *an investment project has been completed*, its market value will be directly linked to the present value of the expected future net earnings from the asset. If the present value of the expected net earnings rises (or falls), so too will the value of the asset.

---

[2]For the sake of simplicity, we assume that the truck has no scrap value at the end of four years.

[3]The derivation of this figure is shown in the following tabulation:

Year	Expected Future Income (Dollars)	Discounted Value per Dollar (6% rate)	Present Value of Income (Dollars)
1	30,000	0.943	28,290
2	30,000	0.890	26,700
3	30,000	0.840	25,200
4	30,000	0.792	23,760
Total			103,950

Exhibit 14-4 The Discounted Present Value of $100,000 of Truck Rental for Four Years (Interest Rate = 8 Percent)

Year (1)	Expected Future Income Received at Year-End (2)	Discounted Value per Dollar (8 Percent Rate) (3)	Present Value of Income (4)
1	$30,000	$0.926	$27,780
2	30,000	0.857	25,710
3	30,000	0.794	23,820
4	30,000	0.735	22,050
Total			$99,360

The value of an asset is equal to the present value of the expected net revenues that can be earned by the asset. If the asset is expected to generate a constant annual net income each year in the future, its value would be equal to

$$\textbf{Asset Value} = \frac{\textbf{Annual Net Income from the Asset}}{\textbf{Interest Rate}}$$

What is the market value of a tract of land if it is expected to generate $1,000 of net rental income each year indefinitely into the future? If the market interest rate is 10 percent, investors would be willing to pay $10,000 for the land ($1,000 divided by 0.10). When purchased at this price, the land would provide an investor with the 10 percent market rate of return. Similarly, if an asset generates $2,500 of net earnings annually and the market interest rate is 10 percent, the asset would be worth $25,000 ($2,500 divided by 0.10). There is a direct relationship between the expected future earnings generated by an asset and the asset's market value. ***As the present value of the future earnings of an asset increases, so too does the market value of the asset.***

The interest rate will also influence the market value of assets. Higher interest rates will reduce the present value of the future income and therefore the market value of the asset generating the income stream. This inverse relationship between the interest rate and asset prices highlights the linkage between interest rates and stock prices. Owners of corporate stock have a property right to the future earnings generated by the business firm. When interest rates rise, the discounted value of the future earnings will fall, causing stock prices to decline. On the other hand, when interest rates decline, the discounted value of the future earnings will increase, causing stock prices to rise. Thus, investors in corporate stock have a strong incentive to keep a close eye on interest rates. Refer to the special topic in the final section of this book titled "The Stock Market: Its Function, Performance, and Potential as an Investment Opportunity" for additional details on the stock market.

14-4b Asset Prices, Business Investment, and Efficiency

The direct link between expected future earnings and the price of an asset provides asset owners with a strong incentive to make sure the assets are being used wisely. Some entrepreneurial investors are particularly good at (1) identifying a business that is poorly operated, (2) purchasing the business at a depressed price, (3) improving the operational efficiency of the firm, and then (4) reselling the business at a handsome profit. Suppose that a poorly run business currently has net earnings of $1 million per year. What is the market value of the business? If the firm is expected to continue earning $1 million per year, the market value of the firm would be $10 million if the interest rate is 10 percent.

Suppose that an alert entrepreneur buys the business for $10 million and improves the operational efficiency of the firm. As the result of these changes, the annual net earnings of the firm increase to $2 million per year. Now how much is the firm worth? If the $2 million annual earnings are expected to continue into the future, the net present value of the firm would rise to $20 million. Thus, the entrepreneur would be able to sell the firm for a very substantial profit.

As this example illustrates, business managers and asset owners have a strong incentive to use the resources under their control efficiently. If they fail to do so, the value of the assets will decline, and the business will be vulnerable to a takeover by those capable of using the resources more efficiently and thereby improving the firm's profitability.

In modern market economies, investment choices are often made by corporate officers, under the scrutiny of corporate boards of directors. Nevertheless, individual investors (buyers and sellers of stock) influence that process through the stock market. Stock market investors who believe that a corporation is currently making decisions likely to increase its future profits will buy more of the corporation's stock, driving up its price. Similarly, stockholders who believe that the corporation's current investment decisions will reduce future profits have an incentive to "bail out" by selling their stock holdings, reducing the market value of the stock. Either way, the price of a corporation's shares gives corporate officers fast feedback on what investors think of their decisions.

Often corporate officers own stock themselves and the value of their pay package generally depends on the stock price. Also, the members of the corporate board (which hires and fires the officers) are typically large shareholders. Thus, the corporate officers have a strong incentive to act on the feedback from the stock market. The choices of consumers of the firm's products are the ultimate judge of its future profitability. However, the choices of investors and their fund managers provide early information today about the expected future success of business ventures.

14-5 Investing in Human Capital

Investments in human capital (like the decision to go to college, for example) are the same as other investment decisions. Just like physical capital, discounting can also help us gauge whether or not to make a human capital investment.

Exhibit 14-5 shows the human capital decision confronting Juanita, an 18-year-old high school graduate thinking about pursuing a bachelor's degree in business administration. Just as an investment in a truck involves a cost in order to generate a future income, so does a degree in business administration. If Juanita does not go to college, she will be able to begin work immediately, starting at annual earnings of E_1. But if she goes to college, she will incur direct costs (C_d) in the form of tuition, books, transportation, and related expenses. She will also bear the opportunity cost (C_0) of lower earnings while she's in college. However, studying business will expand Juanita's knowledge and skills, and enable her to earn more money later (refer to the areas in the exhibit labeled "Earnings with college" versus "Earnings without college"). Will the higher future income be worth the cost? To answer this question, Juanita must project the additional income she would earn by getting a business degree, discount each year's additional income, and compare the total with the discounted value of the cost of getting the degree—including the opportunity cost of the earnings she forgoes while attending college. If the discounted present value of Juanita's additional future income exceeds the discounted present value of the cost, acquiring the degree is a worthwhile investment. Of course, other nonmonetary considerations might also affect Juanita's decision, but the return on the investment is an important factor. For additional information about investment in a college education, review accompanying Applications in Economics feature, "Does It Pay to Go to an Elite University?"

Exhibit 14-5 Investing in Human Capital

Juanita, an 18-year-old who has just finished high school, is trying to decide whether or not to go to college and get a business degree. If Juanita goes to college and majors in business administration, she will incur the direct cost (C_d) of the college education–tuition, books, transportation, and so on–plus the opportunity cost (C_0) of earnings she forgoes while in college. However, with a business degree, she can expect to earn an additional amount of income (*B*) during her career. If the discounted present value of the additional future earnings exceeds the discounted value of the direct and indirect costs of a college education, the business degree will be a profitable investment for Juanita.

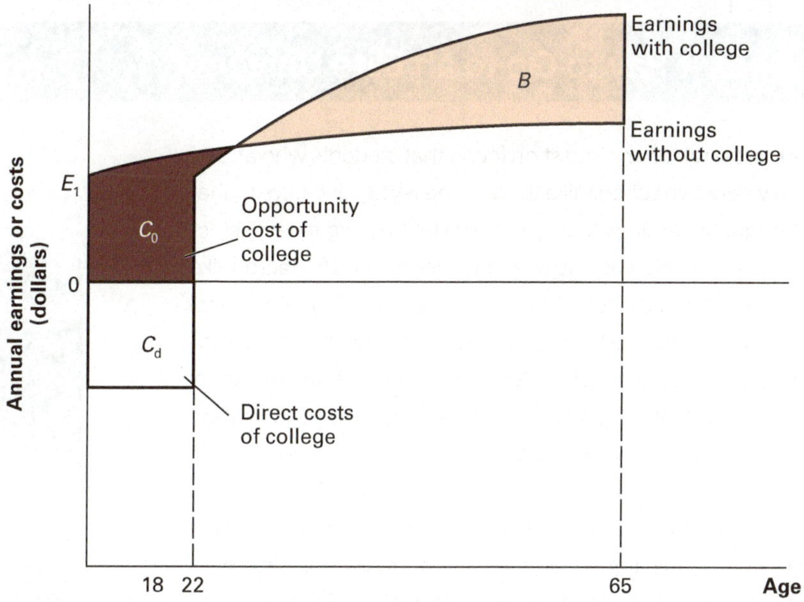

14-6 Uncertainty, Entrepreneurship, and Profit

Firms and individual investors can sometimes earn persistent economic profits—returns in excess of the opportunity cost of funds—if they can restrict entry into various industries and occupations. Economic profits, however, can also be earned in competitive markets with no entry restrictions. ***In competitive markets, there are two sources of economic profit: uncertainty and entrepreneurship.***

First, let's talk about how uncertainty enables people to earn an economic profit. Investment opportunities put people in a position to earn a handsome return, but they also expose them to additional uncertainty. We live in a world of uncertainty, imperfect information, and dynamic change. Unanticipated changes create winners and losers. If people didn't care about the uncertainty related to different investment projects, they wouldn't demand higher returns for higher risk projects. Most people, though, dislike uncertainty; they would prefer to know they'll collect $1,000 rather than take a 50–50 chance of collecting either nothing or $2,000. To accept the uncertainty accompanying riskier investments, they will demand a premium—an economic profit. For example, compared to government bonds, the returns on stocks are considerably more uncertain. This uncertainty of return is one reason why stocks have historically yielded a higher average return than bonds.

Entrepreneurship is a second source of economic profit. As we previously discussed, at any given time, there are an infinite number of potential investment projects from which to choose. Investing in some of them will increase the value of resources and lead to handsome returns. Successful entrepreneurship involves the identification of previously unnoticed profit opportunities (see the boxed feature, "Entrepreneurs Who Have Changed Our Lives: Berry Gordy," for an example). To finance their investments, would-be entrepreneurs usually have to use their own money and the money of co-venturers, in addition to whatever they can borrow. Entrepreneurs with successful track records will find it easier to get capital for

Applications in Economics

Does It Pay to Go to an Elite University?

Early research on this question found that students who attend highly selective schools like those of the Ivy League have higher subsequent earnings than similar students going to less selective colleges. This was true even after accounting for factors like the students' SAT score, the average SAT score of the school attended, race, gender, high school GPA, income of parents, and student athlete status. But there remained one question: Did the students attending the more selective schools earn more because they received a better education or because they were more ambitious and highly motivated?

A study by economists Stacy Dale and Alan Krueger sheds light on this question.[1] In addition to controlling for the typical set of student characteristics, Dale and Krueger were able to make earnings comparisons between students (1) who were accepted by a more selective college but decided to attend a less selective one and (2) those who actually attended a more selective college. This technique enabled them to account more fully for the potential impact of motivation and ambition on earnings. Further, the earnings data used by Dale and Krueger were from actual Social Security records rather than the less accurate self-reported earnings.

Dale and Krueger found that students attending a more selective college such as Yale University did not earn more than similar students attending a less selective school such as Penn State University. However, students from historically marginalized communities and students with poorly educated parents were exceptions. The latter groups did have higher earnings if they attended a more selective school. This is consistent with the view that going to more selective schools provides these groups with important contacts and connections that they would not otherwise be able to obtain.

Sandra Baker/Alamy Stock Photo

The Dale and Krueger study also reports two other intriguing results. First, earnings were higher for those who applied to more selective schools. This suggests that ambition and a willingness to work hard are more important determinants of earnings than the selectivity of the school one actually attends. Second, students who attended schools with higher tuition did not earn more income than similar students who attended less expensive schools. Thus, students may want to think twice before attending an expensive school, particularly if they are borrowing money to do so.

[1]Stacy Dale and Alan B. Krueger. "Estimating the Return to College Selectivity over the Career Using Administrative Earning Data," *Journal of Human Resources*, Spring 2014, pp. 323-358. For evidence that attending a selective college does not increase the earnings of men but it does so for women if hours worked are not accounted for, see Suqin Ge, Elliott Isaac, and Amalia Miller, "Elite Schools and Opting In: Effects of College Selectivity on Career and Family Outcomes," *Journal of Labor Economics*, April 2022, pp. S383-S427.

their investment projects. Thus, over time, capital markets will allocate more control over investment dollars to those entrepreneurs with the most successful investment records.

The great Harvard economist Joseph Schumpeter believed that entrepreneurial discovery of new, improved ways of doing things drove economic progress and improved living standards. As Schumpeter put it, "The fundamental impulse that sets the capitalist engine in motion comes from the new consumer's goods, the new methods of production or transportation, and new markets, and the new forms of industrial organization that capitalist enterprise creates."[4]

[4]Joseph A. Schumpeter, *Capitalism, Socialism, and Democracy* (New York: Harper Torchbooks, 1950), 83.

My Good Images/Shutterstock.com

Phil Barker/Future Publishing/Getty Images

AP Images/Vladimir Astapkovich

Oleksiy Mark/Shutterstock.com

Bogdandimages/Shutterstock.com

PixieMe/Shutterstock.com

The introduction of new products often makes older ones obsolete. Examples abound: The personal computer replaced the typewriter, digital cameras replaced film models, and smartphones are replacing landline telephones. Joseph Schumpeter referred to this process of dynamic change as “creative destruction.” How does creative destruction influence the living standards of people like you?

Schumpeter is correct: Entrepreneurial discovery directed by profit and loss and the accompanying innovative actions are a central force for human progress. Think about how the entrepreneurial innovations of the past 40 years have altered our lives. The personal computer, cellular phone, laser surgery, digital photography, GPS technology, and numerous other new products have either been developed or vastly improved during the past 40 years. Consider the impact of just one innovation: the smartphone. In 1990, a cellular phone was the size of a brick and could perform only a tiny fraction of the functions of today’s smartphones. Moreover, it cost approximately $3,000 and less than 2 percent of Americans owned one. Today, Americans own more than 225 million smartphones, and globally, the number of users is approaching 2.5 billion. The smartphone provides ordinary people with benefits, including free or low-cost access to literature greater than the world’s most extensive library, instant news from around the world, information far greater than the best encyclopedia set, and past and present movies and music well beyond what anyone could have dreamed of only a few decades ago. Without economic freedom and the direction of the capital market, the positive impact of entrepreneurial activities would be stifled and human progress slowed.

Entrepreneurs Who Have Changed Our Lives

Berry Gordy, Jr.

Berry Gordy, Jr., is the entrepreneur behind the famous Motown record label that played a major role in helping to racially integrate popular music in the 1960s and 1970s. Gordy's "Motown Sound"–a unique blend of pop music and rhythm and blues, with strains of soul and gospel–remains a major influence on today's popular music. More than any other music genre of the period, Motown appealed to a broad range of Americans. Motown stars included Diana Ross and the Supremes, Smokey Robinson and the Miracles, Mary Wells, Stevie Wonder, Marvin Gaye, and the Jackson 5–to name only a few.

Gordy named his record label in honor of his hometown Detroit, which is often called the "Motor Town." Gordy's path to becoming a successful entrepreneur was filled with many twists and turns. He started as a boxer but was drafted by the U.S. Army to serve in the Korean War. After returning home, Gordy opened a jazz record store but had insufficient sales to continue. He then worked at Ford Motor Company, where he began writing songs in his head while working on the assembly line. Gordy eventually met rhythm-and-blues singer Jackie Wilson, who turned several of the songs Gordy had co-written into hit records. In 1959, Gordy started a music production studio with the financial help of his parents, which he renamed the Motown Record Corporation in 1960.

Gordy had a unique ability to discover new talent and to meld musical styles in a way that would forever change popular music. Gordy recognized a profit opportunity that others had overlooked. His early successes, with two top hits in his first two years ("Shop Around" by the Miracles and "Please Mr. Postman" by the Marvelettes), helped build his reputation and garner the additional resources he needed to grow his record label into a major force in the music industry. With his rising success, talented singers were eager to work with him, and radio stations were eager to play Gordy's Motown music. His selection of innovative songwriters, and strong control over singers and their music, soon earned him major success–more than 100 Top Ten hit songs within a decade. Gordy eventually moved his company to Los Angeles, where he diversified into also producing motion picture films. Gordy was inducted into the Rock and Roll Hall of Fame in 1988 and will always be recognized as an entrepreneur who forever changed popular music.

Sources:

Gerald Early, "Motown," *Encyclopedia Britannica*, January 17, 2024, at https://www.britannica.com/topic/Motown.

"Berry Gordy," *The HistoryMakers*, November 12, 2012, at https://www.thehistorymakers.org/biography/berry-gordy.

"Gordy, Berry Jr." *Encyclopedia of Detroit*, Detroit Historical Society, n.d., at https://detroithistorical.org/learn/encyclopedia-of-detroit/gordy-berry-jr.

Mark Edward Nero, "The History of Motown and Its Distinctive Sound," *Liveabout Dotcom*, March 2, 2019, at https://www.liveabout.com/what-is-the-motown-sound-2850870

14-6a Returns to Physical and Human Capital

Income reflects the returns from both human and physical capital. The earnings of employees and self-employed workers are mostly returns to human capital, while interest, corporate profits, and rental income are primarily returns to physical capital.[5] **Exhibit 14-6** presents data on these measures of human and physical capital earnings as a share of national income for the United States since 1950. Prior to 2008, the earnings share of human capital was approximately 80 percent of national income while the share of physical capital summed to around 20 percent. Moreover, these income shares fluctuated within a relatively narrow range. During the last decade, however, the share going to physical capital rose to 22 percent, while the share allocated to human capital shrank to only 78 percent.

[5]As used here, rent is income derived by owners who lease (rent) assets like buildings and equipment to another party for a period of time.

Outstanding Economist

Joseph Schumpeter (1883-1950)

©Bettmann/CORBIS

Born in Austria, Joseph Schumpeter was a longtime professor of economics at Harvard University. Generally recognized as one of the top five economists of the twentieth century, Schumpeter is perhaps best known for his views on entrepreneurship and the future of capitalism. He believed that the discovery and introduction of new and better products and organizational methods were constantly making the old ways of doing things obsolete. He referred to this process as "creative destruction" and argued that it was the primary fuel of economic progress.

Exhibit 14-6 The Income Shares of Human and Physical Capital, 1950-2023

The shares of national income derived from human capital (employee compensation and self-employment income) and physical capital (interest, corporate profits, and rents) are shown here. Between 1950 and 2008, approximately 80 percent of national income was earned by the owners of human capital, while the share of physical capital owners summed to around 20 percent. During the past decade, the share going to physical capital rose to approximately 22 percent, while the share of human capital fell to 78 percent.

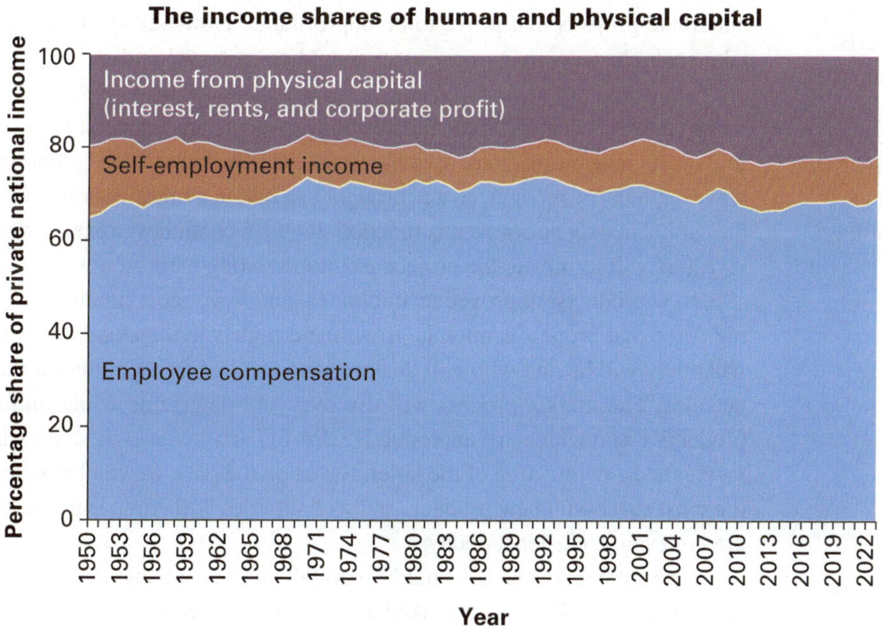

Note: Private national income is the sum of employee compensation, self-employment income, interest, rents, and corporate profits.

Source: http://www.bea.gov/.

What accounts for the increase in the share of income going to capital in recent years? Corporate profits reflect the return to both (1) investments in physical capital such as the firm's plant and equipment and (2) entrepreneurship, innovation, and technological improvements. There is some evidence that the latter has increased in recent decades. Measured as a share of national income, corporate profits rose from 9.8 percent during 1999–2003 to 14.2 percent during 2019–2023, even though business investment in plant and equipment fell 0.7 percent during the period. There is also evidence that entrepreneurship and technological advancements (and their more rapid dissemination) are exerting a greater impact on our lives today compared to the past. Prior to 2000, established companies with large physical assets such as auto manufacturers and oil refineries dominated the list of ten companies with the largest market value. This is no longer the case. Apple, Microsoft, Alphabet (Google), Amazon, Meta (Facebook), and Nvidia, which derive a substantial share of their revenues from the advanced technology embodied in their products and services, were six of the seven top firms with the highest market value in mid-2024. The increased movement into and out of the S&P 500 largest firms also indicates that dynamic change is now more rapid. During 1965–1980, the average company lifespan in the S&P 500 ranged between 24 and 35 years. Since 2000, that lifespan has declined to between 15 and 25 years.[6] If entrepreneurship, innovation, and technological improvements are now more important than in the past, this may account for the recent increase in the share of income going to capital.

14-7 Why Is the Capital Market So Important?

Keys to Economic Prosperity

Innovation and the Capital Market

If the potential gains from innovative ideas and human ingenuity are going to be fully realized, it must be relatively easy for individuals to try their innovative and potentially ingenious ideas, but difficult to continue if the idea is a bad one.

If a nation is going to reach its full potential, it must have a mechanism that will attract savings and channel them into the investments that are most likely to create wealth. In a market economy, the capital market performs this function. Private investors, such as small business owners, corporate stockholders, and venture capitalists, place their own funds at risk in the capital market. Investors will sometimes make mistakes; sometimes they will undertake projects that prove to be unprofitable. However, if investors were unwilling to take such chances, many new ideas would go untested and many worthwhile, but risky, projects would not be undertaken.

In a world of uncertainty, mistaken investments are a necessary price that must be paid for fruitful innovations in new technologies and products. Such counterproductive projects, however, must be recognized and brought to a halt in a timely manner. In a market economy, the capital market performs this function. If a firm continues to experience losses, eventually investors will terminate the project and stop wasting their money.

New products, improved technologies, and lower-cost production methods are a driving force that propels economic growth and higher living standards. But we do not know what they will be and who will discover and implement them during the next two or three decades. The market process will discover and determine which innovative actions are productive and which are unproductive. Profits and losses will lead to an expansion of the former and a contraction of the latter. Based on the past, we can be pretty sure that many of the most successful new products and technologies will come from start-up businesses that are not even in existence today.

Measured on the basis of market capitalization, Alphabet (Google), Amazon, and Meta (Facebook), and Nvidia all ranked among the ten largest companies in the United States in early 2024. Interestingly, all three were founded after 1990 and went public in 1997 or later. None of them were ranked higher than 303rd on the Fortune 500 in 1995. Thus, in a relatively short time span these companies grew from midgets to giants. As they did so, they were a powerful driving force for economic growth. This linkage between innovation and growth highlights why it is vitally important that entrepreneurs are both able to try out their new ideas but are forced to shut them down if they do not generate revenues sufficient to cover cost.

[6]S. Patrick Viguerie, Ned Calder, and Brian Hindo, "2021 Corporate Longevity Forecast," Innosight Executive Briefing, May 2021.

Dmitry Kalinovsky/Shutterstock.com

The capital market will channel the savings of individuals into the finance of investment goods like trucks and earth-moving equipment. Does it make any difference whether these investment projects are profitable? Why or why not?

Given the pace of change and the diversity of entrepreneurial talent, the knowledge required for sound decision-making about the allocation of capital is far beyond the scope of any single leader, industrial planning committee, or government agency. Without a private capital market, there is no mechanism that can be counted on to consistently channel investment funds into wealth-creating projects.

When investment funds are allocated by the government, rather than by the market, an entirely different set of factors comes into play. Political influence rather than market returns will decide which projects will be undertaken. Businesses will use contributions, lobbying, and other resources to curry favor with key political officials. In turn, the politicians will use subsidies, tax breaks, trade restrictions, and "bailouts" to help those most willing to provide them with political support. Clearly, this system of cronyism will encourage rent-seeking and favor large firms with more lobbying clout at the expense of new start-up businesses. It will protect inefficient firms and slow the innovation and discovery process.

Profits and losses direct investors toward productive projects and away from those that are counterproductive. The political process does not have anything similar to profit and loss that can be counted on to direct funds toward wealth creation. As a result, inefficient allocation of capital is a predictable outcome.

The experiences of Eastern Europe and the former Soviet Union illustrate this point. For four decades (1950–1990), the investment rates in these countries were among the highest in the world. Central planners allocated approximately one-third of the national output into capital investment. Even these high rates of investment, however, did little to improve living standards because political rather than economic considerations determined which projects would be funded. Resources were often wasted on impractical projects and high visibility ("prestige") investments favored by important political leaders. Misdirection of investment and failure to keep up with dynamic change eventually led to the collapse of these systems.

Historically, the government of the United States has played a minor role in the allocation of capital. But this has changed in recent years. Beginning in the latter half of the 1990s, federal regulations and subsidies played a major role in directing capital toward the housing industry. Regulations imposed on the banking industry and the policies of two large government-sponsored corporations, Fannie Mae and Freddie Mac, expanded the availability of credit and promoted mortgage loans with little or no down payment. The policies were designed to increase the affordability of housing and promote home ownership among those with low and moderate incomes. These policies played a central role in the creation of a housing boom, followed by a bust and the 2008 financial crisis. (*Note:* For a detailed analysis of this issue, refer to Special Topic 6: The Great Recession of 2008–2009: Causes and Response.)

Further, the government has become much more involved in the allocation of capital in other ways. During the last decade, borrowing to finance the large federal deficits has consumed a sizeable share of the loanable funds market. In the energy area, the government has used mandates and subsidies to favor high-cost energy sources such as ethanol, wind, and solar, while regulations have reduced the supply of lower-cost petroleum and natural gas. During the 2008–2009 financial crisis, the government provided emergency loans to several companies, including large banks, the American Insurance Group, General Motors, and Chrysler. Since 2018, the Trump and Biden administrations used trade policy to favor some businesses and punish others. Tariffs were imposed on washing machines and solar panels and later on steel and aluminum. When the politicians favor some businesses at the expense of others, investors will have less incentive to evaluate risks and act prudently, and they will have more incentive to cater to political officials willing to provide them with favoritism. When political allocation replaces markets, the capital market will be undermined, and economic inefficiency, cronyism, and political corruption will increase.

Has the nature of the capital market in the United States been permanently altered? Will political considerations and centralized government decision-making play a much larger role in future allocation of capital? At this point, it is too early to know the answer to these questions. But one thing is for sure: How they are answered will exert a dramatic impact on America's future.

Key Points

- We can often produce more consumption goods by first using our resources to produce physical and human capital resources and then using these capital resources to produce the desired consumption goods. Because resources used to produce capital goods will be unavailable for the direct production of consumption goods, saving is necessary for investment.
- The interest rate is the price of earlier availability. It is the premium that borrowers must pay to lenders to acquire goods now rather than later.
- The demand for loanable funds reflects the productivity of capital resources and the positive rate of time preference. The market interest rate will bring the quantity of funds demanded by borrowers into balance with the quantity supplied by lenders.
- During inflationary times, the money rate of interest incorporates an inflationary premium reflecting the expected future increase in the price level. When inflation is expected, the money rate of interest exceeds the real rate of interest.
- The money rate of interest on a specific loan reflects three basic factors—the pure interest rate, an inflationary premium, and a risk premium that is directly related to the probability of default by the borrower.
- The interest rate allows individuals to put a current value on future revenues and costs. The discounting procedure can be used to calculate the present value of an expected net income stream from a potential investment project. If the present value of the expected revenues exceeds the present value of the expected costs—and if things turn out as anticipated—the project will be profitable.
- The present value of expected future net earnings will determine the market value of existing assets. An increase in the expected future earnings of an asset will increase its market value.
- Economic profit plays a central role in allocating capital and determining which investment projects will be undertaken. In a competitive environment,

economic profit reflects uncertainty and entrepreneurship—the ability to recognize and undertake profitable projects that have gone unnoticed by others.

- To grow and prosper, a nation must have a mechanism that will attract savings and channel them into investments that create wealth. The capital market performs this function in a market economy.

Critical Analysis Questions

1. *How would the following changes influence the rate of interest in the United States?
   - a. an increase in the share of the population in age groups with a high saving rate
   - b. an increase in government borrowing to finance budget deficits
   - c. an increase in domestic inflation
   - d. increased uncertainty about a nuclear war
   - e. improved investment opportunities in Europe
2. What is capital investment? Why do business firms often use machinery and other capital assets to produce goods and services?
3. How are human and physical capital investment decisions similar? How do they differ? What determines the profitability of a physical capital investment? Do human capital investors make profits? If so, what is the source of the profit? Explain.
4. *A lender made the following statement to a borrower: "You are borrowing $1,000, which is to be repaid in twelve monthly installments of $100 each. Your total interest charge is $200, which means your interest rate is 20 percent." Is the effective interest rate on the loan really 20 percent? Explain.
5. In a market economy, investors have a strong incentive to undertake profitable investments. What makes an investment profitable? Do profitable investments create wealth? Why or why not? Do all investments create wealth? Discuss.
6. *Over long periods of time, the rate of return of an average investment in the stock market has exceeded the return on high-quality bonds. Is the higher return on stocks surprising? Why or why not?
7. How has the discovery of new products impacted the living standards of Americans during the past 40 years? Can you think of products that you use and enjoy that were not even available 40 years ago?
8. *If the money rate of interest on a low-risk government bond is 10 percent and the inflation rate for the last several years has been steady at 4 percent, what is the estimated real rate of interest?
9. Suppose you are contemplating the purchase of a commercial lawn mower at a cost of $10,000. The expected lifetime of the machine is three years. You can lease the asset to a local business for $4,000 annually (payable at the end of each year) for three years. The lessee is responsible for the upkeep and maintenance of the machine during the three-year period. If you can borrow (and lend) money at an interest rate of 8 percent, will the investment be a profitable undertaking? Is the project profitable at an interest rate of 12 percent? Provide calculations in support of your answer.
10. *Alicia's philosophy of life is summed up by the proverb "A penny saved is a penny earned." She plans and saves for the future. In contrast, Mike's view is "Life is uncertain; eat dessert first." Mike wants as much as possible now.
    - a. Who has the highest rate of time preference?
    - b. Do people like Alicia benefit from the presence of people like Mike?
    - c. Do people like Mike benefit from the presence of people like Alicia? Explain.
11. *Some countries with very low incomes per capita are unable to save very much. Are people in these countries helped or hurt by people in high-income countries with much higher rates of saving?
12. *According to a news item, the owner of a lottery ticket paying $3 million over twenty years is offering to sell the ticket for $1.2 million cash now. "Who knows?" the ticket owner explained. "We might not even be here in 20 years, and I do not want to leave it to the dinosaurs."
    - a. If the ticket pays $150,000 per year at the end of each year for the next twenty years, what is the present value of the ticket when the appropriate rate for discounting the future income is thought to be 10 percent?
    - b. If the discount rate is in the 10 percent range, is the sale price of $1.2 million reasonable?
    - c. Can you think of any disadvantages of buying the lottery earnings rather than a bond?
13. Suppose you are moving into a new apartment you expect to rent for five years. The owner of the apartment offers to provide you with a used refrigerator for free and promises to maintain and repair the refrigerator during the next five years. You also have the option of buying a new energy-efficient refrigerator (with a five-year free maintenance agreement) for $700. The new refrigerator will reduce

your electric bill by $150 per year and will have a market value of $200 after five years. If necessary, you can borrow money from the bank at an 8 percent rate of interest. Which option should you choose?

14. *Suppose that you are considering whether to enroll in a summer computer-training program that costs $2,500. If you take the program, you will have to give up $1,500 of earnings from your summer job. You figure that the program will increase your earnings by $500 per year for each of the next ten years. Beyond that, it is not expected to affect your earnings. If you take the program, you will have to borrow the funds at an 8 percent rate of interest. From a strictly monetary viewpoint, should you enroll in the program?

15. "In a world of uncertainty, it is important that entrepreneurs be able to introduce new products and try out innovative ideas. But it is also important that unproductive projects be brought to a halt." Evaluate this statement.

16. *Will political officials be more likely to channel funds into wealth-creating projects than private investors and entrepreneurs? Why or why not? Discuss.

17. The interest rates charged on outstanding credit card balances are generally higher than the interest rate that banks charge customers with a good credit rating. Why do you think the credit card rate is so high? Should the government impose an interest rate ceiling of, say, 10 percent? If it did, who would be hurt and who would be helped? Discuss.

*Asterisk denotes questions for which answers appear in Appendix B.

Chapter

15 Income Inequality and Poverty

> All animals are equal, but some animals are more equal than others.
>
> –George Orwell[1]

Differences in resource prices and the productivity of individuals will cause incomes to vary. Of course, economic inequality is present in all societies. Neither politics nor central planning will eliminate it. Nonetheless, most of us are troubled by the extremes of inequality–the extravagant luxury of some and the grinding poverty of others.

Learning Objectives

15.1 Indicate the magnitude of income inequality in the United States and how it has changed in recent decades.

15.2 Explain how age, education, family size, marital status, number of earners in the family, and time worked impact incomes and the degree of income inequality.

15.3 Explain what is meant by income mobility and how it differs from income inequality.

15.4 Explain how the poverty rate is measured.

15.5 Indicate the size of the poverty rate in the United States and how it has changed during the past six decades.

15.6 Analyze whether or not the government should try to reduce income inequality and evaluate the effectiveness of government action in this area.

[1]George Orwell, *Animal Farm* (New York: Harcourt and Brace Company, 1946), 112.

15-1 How Much Income Inequality Exists in the United States?

Money income is only one component of economic well-being. Factors such as leisure, noncash-transfer benefits, the nonmonetary advantages and disadvantages of a job, and the expected stability of future income also affect people's economic welfare. Money income is quite important, however, because it makes it possible to buy market goods and services. It is also easy to measure and is therefore widely used as a yardstick of economic well-being and degree of inequality.

Exhibit 15-1 presents data on money income in the United States. First, the left panel shows the share of *before-tax* annual money income by quintile—that is, by each fifth of the total population of families—ranked from the lowest to the highest. If there were total income equality, each quintile (20 percent) of families would generate 20 percent of the aggregate income. Given the differences in education, skills, ability, work effort, age, family

Exhibit 15-1 Changes in Share of Money Income by Quintile

Source: http://www.census.gov and Congressional Budget Office, *The Distribution of Household Income, 2020*, November 2023. The data for the left panel are for family income, and the data for the right panel are for household income. The income after taxes and transfers for 2020 is the latest available. The before-tax income in the right panel includes market income. The after-tax and transfer income is market income plus cash and in-kind transfers less federal personal income, payroll, corporate income, and excise taxes.

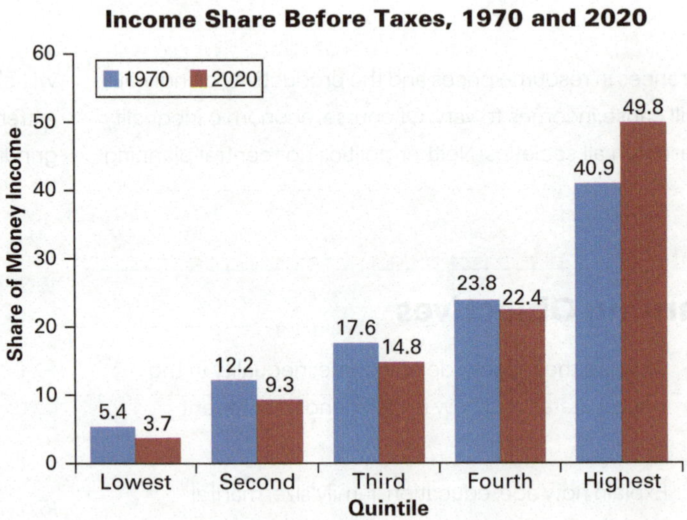

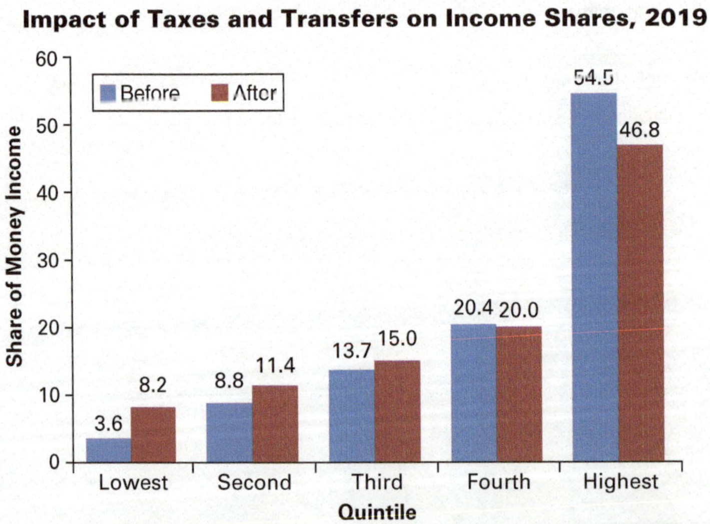

size, and other factors among families, clearly we would not expect this to be the case. Some families will be able to generate more income than others. It is, however, informative to examine the shares of income by quintile.

During the last four decades, the share of income earned by the top quintile has steadily risen, whereas that earned by the bottom group has fallen.[2] In 1970, the top quintile earned 40.9 percent of the aggregate money income, while the share earned by the lowest quintile was 5.4 percent. By 2022, the share of before-tax money income of the top group had risen to 49.8 percent, whereas that earned by the bottom 20 percent of families had fallen to 3.7 percent. Thus, in 2022, the top quintile of families earned approximately 13 times as much before-tax money income as the bottom quintile of families.

The right panel of Exhibit 15-1 presents data on household income by quintile. There are two major differences between the data of the left and right panels. First, the data for the right panel are for households rather than families. In addition to families, households include individuals living by themselves and unrelated people living together. Second, the right panel includes income shares after taxes and transfers. Under a system of progressive taxation, such as that of the United States, taxes take a larger share of income as one's earnings increase. In-kind government transfers are targeted at those with lower incomes. As a result, we would expect after-tax and transfer incomes to be more equal than before-tax and transfer incomes. This is indeed the case. The after-tax and transfer income share of the bottom quintile was 8.2 percent of the total in 2020 (compared with 3.6 percent before taxes and transfers). The after-tax and transfer income share of the top quintile was 46.8 percent of the total (compared with 54.5 percent before taxes and transfers). The income of the top quintile before taxes and transfers was 15.1 times that of the bottom quintile, but the ratio declines to 5.7 after taxes. (*Note:* 2020 household income is used because neither family income nor more recent after-tax income is available.)

A market economy does not have a central distributing agency that carves up the economic pie and allocates slices to various individuals. Rather, each individual produces their own slice of the pie. If one person's income grows, it does not mean that another's must shrink. The distribution of income is actually a result of many individual efforts and decisions. We now turn to the consideration of the factors that underlie the distribution of income in the United States.

15-1a The Factors Affecting Income Distribution

How meaningful are the data of Exhibit 15-1? If all families (and households) were similar except with regard to the amount of income they earned, the use of annual income data as an index of inequality would be quite reasonable. However, the fact is that the aggregate data lump together (1) small and large families, (2) prime-age earners and elderly retirees, (3) multi-earner families and families without any current earners, and (4) husband-wife families and single-parent families.

Consider just one factor: the impact of age and the pattern of lifetime income. Typically, the annual income of young people is low, particularly if they are going to school or are getting training. Many people under 25 years of age studying to be lawyers, doctors, engineers, and economists will have low annual incomes during this phase of their lives. But this does not mean that they are poor—at least not in the usual sense. After completing their formal education and acquiring work experience, these people move into their prime working years. At this point, their annual incomes are generally quite high, particularly in families in which both spouses are employed outside the home. Remember, however, that this is also a time when families are purchasing homes and providing for their children, which is costly.

[2]A reduction in the share of income earned by the bottom quintile income group does not imply that their income level fell. It merely indicates that their income did not grow as rapidly as that of other groups, particularly the top quintile. The inflation-adjusted income of the bottom quintile of earners has increased in recent decades.

Exhibit 15-2 Differing Characteristics of High- and Low-Income Families, 2022

	Bottom 20 Percent of Income Recipients	Top 20 Percent of Income Recipients
Education of Householder		
Percent with less than high school	19	2
Percent with college degree or more	16	77
Age of Householder (Percent Distribution)		
Under 35	27	13
35–64	52	81
65 and older	23	11
Family Status		
Married-couple family (percentage of total)	51	94
Single-parent family (percentage of total)	49	6
Persons per Family	3.3	3.7
Earners per Family	0.9	2.3
Percent of married-couple families in which wife works full time	13	69
Percent of Total Work Hours Supplied by Group	8	27

Source: http://www.census.gov and author calculations from the March 2023 *Current Population Survey*.

Consequently, the economic well-being of these people as measured by their earnings may well be overstated. In other words, although these people are earning more at this stage in their lives, they also have more responsibilities. Finally, people reach the retirement phase, characterized by less work, more leisure, and smaller family sizes. Even families that are quite well off tend to experience incomes well below average during the retirement phase. ***Given the life cycle of income, lumping together families of different ages (phases of their life-cycle earnings) results in substantial inequality in the annual income figures. This would be so even if the incomes of families over a lifetime were approximately equal.***

Exhibit 15-2 highlights major differences between high- and low-income families that underlie the distributional data of Exhibit 15-1. The typical high-income family (top 20 percent) is headed by a well-educated person in the prime working-age phase of life. Their income is supplemented by the earnings of other family members, particularly working spouses. In contrast, people with little education, nonworking retirees, younger workers (under age 35), and single-parent families are substantially overrepresented among low-income families (the bottom 20 percent of income recipients). In 2022, 19 percent of the householders in the lowest income quintile failed to complete high school, compared with only 2 percent for the highest income quintile. Although only 16 percent of the household heads in the bottom quintile completed college, 77 percent of the householders in the top group did so. Eighty-one percent of the high-income families had household heads in the prime working-age category (ages 35–64), compared with only 52 percent of the low-income families. Only one parent was present in 49 percent of the low-income families, whereas 94 percent of the high-income group were dual-parent families. High-income families are also larger than low-income families, which might surprise you. In 2022, there were 3.7 people per family in the top income quintile, compared to only 3.3 people per family in the bottom quintile.

Applications in Economics

The Increasing Leisure Time of Americans

In the United States, people spend approximately 54 hours per week commuting to and from a job and performing work activities either in the marketplace or at home. The rest of their time is available for leisure activities.

Leisure time is a valuable commodity. It is the time that you are not working at a job or at home performing tasks such as washing clothes and cutting the grass. Your leisure time is the time that you have simply to do things that you enjoy. It includes activities like watching TV, playing video games, visiting friends, going to bars, and attending sporting events.

Like an increase in market income, an increase in leisure makes us better off. How has the leisure time of Americans changed in recent decades? After adjusting for demographic changes, Timo Boppart and L. Rachel Ngai find that leisure rose, between 1965 and 2013, on average by 4.5 hours per week.[1] This increase in leisure time is roughly equal to six extra weeks of vacation from work. Recent evidence from the American Time Use Survey indicates that there has been a further slight increase in the leisure time of both men and women in the past decade.

The increase in leisure has not been evenly spread out across education groups. In 1965, the amount of leisure was quite similar across various levels of education for both men and women. However, this situation has changed significantly during the last five decades. The average hours of leisure rose by 8.2 hours for individuals with less than a high school degree but by only 0.7 hours for those with a college degree or more. Given their higher hourly earnings, the opportunity cost of leisure time is greater for those with more education. Thus, it is not surprising that individuals with more education had smaller increases in leisure time than those with less schooling.

Interestingly, the increase in leisure inequality across education groups is the mirror image of the change in market income inequality. In recent decades, the market earnings of those with more education have increased more rapidly than have those with less schooling. However, just the opposite has been the case for the increase in leisure time. Thus, the increase in time worked (and reduction in leisure) has contributed to the growing income gap between college graduates and those with only a high school education that has been observed in recent decades.

[1]Timo Boppart and L. Rachel Ngai, "Rising Inequality and Trends in Leisure," *Journal of Economic Growth* 26 (March 2021): 153-185.

Moreover, there was a striking difference between low- and high-income families in the percentage of hours each group worked. No doubt, much of this difference reflected factors like family size, the age of the wage earners, whether both spouses worked, and whether two spouses were present in the home. In high-income families, the average number of workers per family was 2.3, compared with 0.9 for low-income families. Among married-couple families, a wife working full time was present only 13 percent of the time in low-income families, compared with 69 percent of the time in high-income families. As we would expect, couples who decide not to have the wife work full-time pay for this choice by falling down the income distribution ladder.

In terms of their work effort, the top 20 percent of income recipients contributed 27 percent of the total number of hours worked in the economy, whereas the bottom 20 percent contributed only 8 percent of the total work time. In other words, high-income families worked 3.4 times as many hours as low-income families. As we noted earlier, they also earned approximately 13 times as much before-tax income. Clearly, differences in the amount of time worked were a major factor contributing to the income inequality of Exhibit 15-1. Less work time generally means more time for leisure. Refer to Application in Economics: "The Increasing Leisure Time of Americans" for information on recent changes in this factor.

In summary, Exhibit 15-2 sheds a great deal of light on the distributional data presented in Exhibit 15-1. ***Those with high incomes are far more likely to be well-educated, dual-parent families with both parents working outside the home in their prime earning years. In contrast, those with low incomes are often single-parent families headed by a poorly educated adult who is either youthful or elderly.*** The household heads of those families with little income are often either out of the labor force or working only part-time. Given these factors, it is not surprising that the top 20 percent of recipients have substantially higher incomes, both before and after taxes, than the bottom quintile.

15-1b Why Has Income Inequality Increased?

Exhibit 15-1 indicates that there has been an increase in income inequality in the United States during the last couple of decades. Why has the gap between rich and poor been growing? Research in this area shows that at least four factors have contributed to the rise in income inequality.

1. The increasing proportion of single-parent and dual-earner families. The nature of the family and the allocation of work responsibilities within the family have changed dramatically in recent decades. In 2023, about one-third (34 percent) of all families with children were headed by a single parent, triple the figure of the mid-1960s. At the same time, the labor force participation rate of married women increased from 40 percent in 1970 to 59 percent in 2023.

As a result, today we have more single-parent families and more dual-earner families. Both of these changes tend to promote income inequality. Consider two hypothetical families, the Smiths and the Browns. In 1970, both were middle-income families with two children and one parent working earning $80,000 (in 2025 dollars). Now consider their 2025 counterparts. The Smiths of 2025 are divorced, and one of them, probably Mrs. Smith, is trying to work part-time and take care of the two children. The probability is very high that the single-parent Smith family of 2025 will be in the low-income rather than the middle-income category. The Smith family may well be in the bottom quintile of the income distribution. In contrast, the Browns of 2025 both work outside the home, and each earns $80,000 annually. Given their dual incomes, the Browns are now a high-income rather than a middle-income family. Along with many other dual-income families (refer to Exhibit 15-2), the Browns' 2025 family income will probably place them in the top quintile of income recipients.

Even if there were no changes in earnings between skilled and less-skilled workers, the recent changes within the family would increase the income inequality among families and households. Today, more single-parent families like the Smiths fall into the low-income quintile, whereas more dual-earner families like the Browns fall into the high-income quintile. The gap between the earnings of these two groups has therefore increased the overall income inequality in the United States.

2. Earnings differentials between skilled and less-skilled workers. In 1970, workers with little education who were willing to work hard, often in a hot and sweaty environment, received high wages. This is less true today. In 1974, the annual earnings of men who graduated from college were only 27 percent higher than the earnings of male high school graduates—hardly a huge payoff for the time and cost of a college degree. Since 1974, however, things have changed dramatically. By the mid-1980s, the earnings premium of male college graduates relative to male high school grads rose to the 50–60 percent range, approximately twice the premium of 1974. By 2023, the income premium of male college graduates relative to high school graduates rose to 87 percent. Similarly, during the last four decades, the earnings of women college graduates have increased sharply relative to women with only a high school education.

Why have the earnings of people with more education (and skill) risen relative to those with less education (and skill)? As the Applications in Economics feature indicates, the time worked of those with more education has increased relative to those with less schooling. This enhances the earnings of the former relative to the latter. Structural factors have also contributed. Deregulation of the transportation industry and the declining power of unions may have reduced the number of high-wage, blue-collar jobs available to workers with little education. International competition has also played a role because, increasingly, American workers must compete in a global economy. Furthermore, innovations and cost reductions in both communications and transportation have made it easier for firms to hire workers in different locations. Firms producing goods that require substantial amounts of less-skilled labor can easily move to places like Korea, Taiwan, and Mexico, where less-skilled labor is cheaper. In contrast, the United States is more attractive than most other countries to firms requiring substantial amounts of high-skilled, well-educated workers. Globalization has, therefore, reduced the demand for American workers with few skills and little education but increased the demand for high-skilled workers with college degrees. This has made for a wider earnings gap among workers in high-income countries like the United States. However, it is worth noting that this process enhances income levels in low-income countries and thereby reduces *worldwide* income inequality.

3. The increasing number of markets characterized by a few people at the top with very high earnings. As we discussed in the chapter on wage differentials, the market compensation of star entertainers and athletes, the most talented professionals, and top business executives is often like that of winner-take-all tournaments. At any point in time, a few people at the top have huge earnings, whereas most others in these areas have modest or even low incomes. As transportation and communication costs have declined, markets have increasingly become national and even global, rather than local. This not only increases the incomes of a few people at the top, but it also increases the degree of income inequality.

4. Sharply lower marginal tax rates than in the 1970s. Prior to 1981, high-income Americans confronted top marginal tax rates of up to 70 percent. High marginal tax rates encourage high-income earners to structure their business affairs and invest in ways that shelter much of their income from the Internal Revenue Service. Since the mid-1980s, the top marginal federal income tax has remained below 40 percent. The lower marginal tax rates compared to years prior to 1980 have encouraged those with unique skills to both increase their work effort and reduce their incentive to engage in tax shelter activities. As a result, the income of the rich becomes more observable. In turn, money income statistics such as those of Exhibit 15-1 will register an increase in income inequality.

Outstanding Economist

Deirdre McCloskey (1942-)

Gage Skidmore/Creative Commons

Deirdre McCloskey is best known for her work on human achievement and economic history, including a trilogy that started with her book *The Bourgeois Virtues: Ethics for an Age of Commerce*. She is also renowned for her work on economic methodology and exposing the widespread misuse of tests of statistical significance in economic research. She has been a vocal critic of research on the relationship between capital and income inequality, highlighting how the failure to account for government failure and public choice theory result in erroneous conclusions. Born male, she details her transition from male to female and the difficult challenges she faced in her personal and professional life in her book *Crossing: A Memoir* (University of Chicago Press, 1999).

15-2 Household Expenditures and Economic Inequality

Many economists argue that household expenditures are a more accurate indicator of economic well-being than annual income. While the annual income figures will reflect temporary fluctuations, annual spending will be more reflective of long-term economic status. If your income or earnings prospects in the future are good, you're likely to spend more than your current income. On the other hand, if your future income is expected to be lower, you are likely to save more, resulting in expenditures that are less than your current income. Compared to annual income figures, current expenditures are more indicative of long-term or permanent economic status.

What do expenditures reveal about the degree of inequality in the United States? The 90/10 expenditure ratio, which is the expenditures of families (including single individuals) at the 90th percentile divided by those of families at the 10th percentile, provides a measure of expenditure inequality. A rise in the 90/10 ratio signifies an increase in inequality, while a decline is indicative of a reduction in inequality.

The expenditure statistics indicate that the degree of inequality is significantly smaller than the corresponding figure for annual after-tax income. **Exhibit 15-3** presents the 90/10 ratio of after-tax income and expenditures for 1984 to 2017.[3] In 2017, the 90/10 ratio was 3.7 for family expenditures, while the 90/10 ratio for after-tax income was 6.9, or nearly twice as much. This indicates that the degree of inequality of long-term or permanent income is less than the parallel figure for after-tax annual income. Moreover, between 1984 and 2017, the 90/10 ratio of family expenditures rose by only 8 percent, while the 90/10 ratio of after-tax income rose by 20 percent. This suggests that the increase in inequality as measured by the annual income data is partially a reflection of dynamic change, temporary fluctuations in annual income, and measurement issues rather than a real increase in economic inequality.

Exhibit 15-3 90/10 Ratio of After-Tax Income and Expenditures, 1984-2017

The 90/10 ratios for after-tax income and for expenditures for 1984-2017 are shown here. The degree of inequality of the expenditure ratio is substantially less than that of the after-tax income ratio. Moreover, the increase in inequality during the period was smaller for the measure using the expenditure ratio.

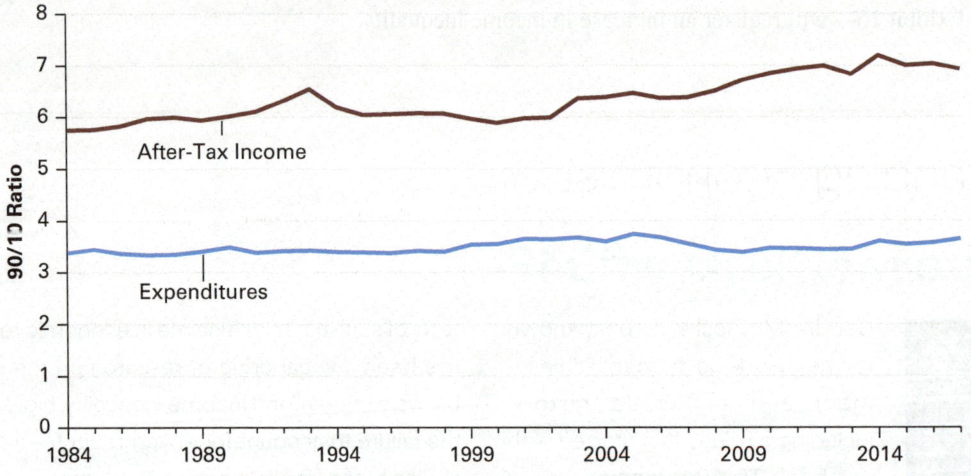

Source: Bruce Meyer and James Sullivan, "Consumption and Income Inequality in the U.S. since the 1960s," *Journal of Political Economy* 131 (February 2023): 247–284. The expenditures figures are based on "well-measured" spending.

[3]Bruce Meyer and James Sullivan, "Consumption and Income Inequality in the U.S. Since the 1960s," *Journal of Political Economy* 131 (February 2023): 247–284.

15-3 Income Mobility and Inequality in Economic Status

Statistics on the distribution of annual income do not reflect **income mobility**—movements up and down the income ladder. Therefore, they may be misleading. Consider two countries with identical distributions of annual income. In both cases, the annual income of the top quintile of income recipients is ten times greater than the bottom quintile. Now, suppose that in the first country—we will refer to it as Static—the same people are at the top of the income distribution year after year. Similarly, the low-income people of Static remain low-income year after year. Static is characterized by an absence of income mobility. In contrast, earners in the second country, which we will call Dynamic, are constantly changing places. Indeed, during every five-year period, each family spends one year in the upper-income quintile, one year in each of the three middle-income quintiles, and one year in the bottom-income quintile. In Dynamic, no one is rich for more than one year (out of each five), and no one is poor for more than a year. Obviously, the nature of economic inequality in Static is vastly different from that in Dynamic. You would not know it, though, by looking at their identical annual income distributions.

Income mobility
Movement of individuals and families either up or down income-distribution rankings when comparisons are made at two different points in time. When substantial income mobility is present, a person's current position in the rankings will not be a very good indicator of what their position will be a few years in the future.

The contrast between Static and Dynamic highlights an important point: Income mobility is an important facet of economic inequality. Until recently, detailed data on income mobility were sparse. This is now beginning to change.[4] **Exhibit 15-4** presents data on the mobility of individual income between 2005 and 2019 in the United States of those aged 25–50 in 2005. The data compare the relative income positions of the *same individuals* at two different points in time. Based on an individual's 2005 income, each individual was placed into income quintiles ranked from highest to lowest. Later, the 2019 real-income level of the *same individuals* was used once again to group the income of each by quintiles.

The first row of Exhibit 15-4 shows the relative income position in 2019 of people in the top quintile of income recipients in 2005. Approximately one-half (53 percent) of those

Exhibit 15-4 Income Mobility-Income Ranking, 2005 and 2019

	Percent Distribution by Income Status of Individuals in 2019				
Percent Distribution by Income Status of Individual in 2005	Highest Quintile	Next-Highest Quintile	Middle Quintile	Next-Lowest Quintile	Lowest Quintile
Highest quintile	52.6	21.3	11.3	7.4	7.4
Next-highest quintile	24.5	30.8	21.5	13.6	9.7
Middle quintile	11.9	24.9	27.5	21.2	14.5
Next-lowest quintile	6.0	14.9	25.1	30.0	23.9
Lowest quintile	3.8	7.4	14.6	28.5	45.8

Source: U.S. Census Bureau, Mobility, Opportunity, and Volatility Statistics (MOVS), https://www.census.gov/library/visualizations/interactive/movs.html. Data include individuals aged 25 to 50 in 2005 and 39 to 64 in 2019.

[4]For a review of the literature on income mobility, refer to Isabel V. Sawhill and Daniel P. McMurrer, *Income Mobility in the United States* (Washington, DC: Urban Institute, 1996); and Gary S. Fields and Efe A. Ok, "The Measurement of Income Mobility: An Introduction to the Literature" in *Handbook of Income Inequality Measurement*, ed. Jacques Silber (Boston: Kluwer Academic, 1999). For recent research on income mobility, refer to Pew Charitable Trust's Economic Mobility Project: http://www.economicmobility.org.

Generational Mobility: There is a positive correlation between the earnings of fathers and sons. If a father has lifetime earnings 20 percent above the average of his generation, a son can expect to earn about 10 percent more. If a grandfather had earnings 20 percent above the average, his grandson can expect to have earnings about 5 percent above the average.

with incomes in the top quintile in 2005 were able to maintain this lofty position 14 years later. Slightly less than one-half (47 percent) of the top income group in 2005 had fallen to a lower-income quintile by 2019. However, only about 15 percent of the high-income individuals fell to one of the bottom two quintiles of the 2019 income distribution. This suggests that once individuals are able to achieve high-income status, they rarely fall back to a very low level of income.

The bottom row of Exhibit 15-4 tracks the experience of those in the lowest income quintile in 2005. Nearly one-half (45.8 percent) of the individuals in the lowest income quintile remained there in 2019. About one-quarter (25.8 percent) moved up to one of the top three income quintiles in 2019. Among those in the next-to-lowest income quintile in 2005, nearly half (46.1 percent) had moved up to one of the three higher-income groupings by 2019.

The income mobility data reveal something concealed by the annual figures: There is considerable movement up and down the economic ladder. Relative income positions often change over time. A sizable portion of those with a high relative income during one year subsequently find themselves in a lower-income position. At the same time, many of those with low relative incomes during a given year move up to higher-income quintiles in subsequent years. What about intergenerational income mobility? Individuals whose parents' income was in the bottom or top quintile are more likely to remain there as adults. Forty percent of children who started in the highest income quintile remained in the top quintile as an adult.[5] Likewise, 43 percent of children who initially were in the bottom quintile stayed there. Those who started in the middle quintile, however, were almost evenly distributed across the quintiles as adults.

[5]See Economic Mobility Project, The Pew Charitable Trusts, "Pursuing the American Dream: Economic Mobility Across Generations," July 2012. For additional information about intergenerational income mobility, refer to Sandra E. Black and Paul J. Devereux, "Recent Developments in Intergenerational Mobility," in *Handbook of Labor Economics, Volume 4B*, eds., Orley Ashenfelter and David Card (Amsterdam: Elsevier, 2011), pp. 1487–541.

15-4 Poverty in the United States

In an affluent country like the United States, income inequality and poverty are related issues. Poverty could be defined in strictly relative terms—the bottom one-fifth of all income recipients, for example. However, this definition would not be very helpful because it would mean that the poverty rate would never change, as 20 percent of the population would always be classified as poor.

The official definition of poverty in the United States was developed by the Social Security Administration in 1964. Because survey data indicated that families with three or more members generally spent about one-third of their income on food, the poverty rate income threshold was set at three times the cost of an economical, nutritionally adequate food plan. In 1964, this resulted in a **poverty threshold income level** for a family of four of approximately $3,000. The poverty income threshold varies with family size and composition, and it is adjusted annually for changes in the general level of prices. Thus, measured in real dollars, the threshold is a measure of absolute income level. In 2024, the poverty income threshold for a family of four was $31,200. The official poverty rate is the number of people or families living in households with a money income below the poverty threshold as a percentage of the total. In the calculation of income, only money income is counted. Various types of in-kind income such as food, medical care, and housing supplements are excluded. A survey of about 60,000 households representing the population of the United States is used to derive the poverty rate for each year.

Poverty threshold income level
The level of money income below which a family is considered to be poor. It differs according to family characteristics (e.g., number of family members) and is adjusted when consumer prices change.

How large is the poverty rate and how has it changed through time? **Exhibit 15-5** presents data on both the number of poor families and the poverty rate for 1959, 1976, 2011, and 2022. In 2022, 7.4 million families, 8.8 percent of the total, were classified as poor. There has been a substantial change in the composition of the poverty population during the last several decades. In 1959, elderly people and the working poor formed the core of the poverty population. Twenty-two percent of the poor families were headed by an elderly person in 1959 versus only 17.6 percent in 2022. In 1959, 70 percent of the heads of poor families worked at least part of the year, but in 2022, only 40 percent of them worked during the year.

In recent decades, the proportion of families headed by women in the United States has increased, whereas the proportion of husband–wife families has declined. Because the poverty rate of families headed by women is several times higher than the rate for husband–wife families (23.0 percent compared with 5.0 percent in 2022), an increase in family instability tends to push the poverty rate upward. It also tends to increase the number of households headed by women among poor families. In 2022, 47 percent of the poor families were headed by a woman, compared with only 23 percent in 1959.

Rather than calculating the poverty rate of families, one could measure the poverty rate of individuals. The poverty rate of individuals is, in fact, somewhat higher than the poverty rate of families. In 2022, 11.5 percent of people in the United States were classified as poor, compared with 8.8 percent for families. The poverty rate of Black individuals in 2022 was 17.1 percent, compared with 10.5 percent for White individuals. Nonetheless, more than two-thirds of the people in poverty were White. Perhaps the most tragic consequence of poverty is its impact on children. Moreover, the poverty rate among children has been increasing. In 2022, 15.0 percent of the children in the United States lived in poverty, slightly down from 16 percent in 1976.

15-4a Transfer Payments and the Poverty Rate

In the mid-1960s, it was widely believed that an increase in income transfers directed toward the low-income people would substantially reduce, if not eliminate, the incidence of poverty. The 1964 *Economic Report of the President* argued that poverty could be virtually eliminated if the federal government increased its expenditures on transfer programs by approximately 2 percent of aggregate income. Following the declaration of the "War on Poverty" by President

Exhibit 15-5 The Changing Composition of the Poor and Poverty Rates, Selected Groups: 1959, 1976, 2011, and 2022

	1959	1976	2011	2022
Number of Poor Families (in millions)	8.3	5.3	9.5	7.4
Percent of Poor Families Headed by a:				
Female	23	48	52	46.8
Black person	26	30	26	21.4
Elderly person (age 65 and over)	22	14	7	17.6
Person who worked at least some part of the year	70	55	44	40.3
Poverty Rate				
All families	18.5	10.1	11.8	8.8
Married-couple families	15.8	7.2	6.2	5.0
Female-headed families	42.6	32.5	31.2	23.0
All individuals	22.4	11.7	15.0	11.5
White person	18.1	9.1	12.8	10.5
Black person	55.1	31.1	27.6	17.1
Children (under age 18)	27.3	16.0	21.9	15.0

Note: Person who worked at least part of the year

Source: U.S. Department of Commerce, *Characteristics of the Population below the Poverty Level: 1982*, Table 5; and http://www.census.gov/.

Means-tested income transfers
Transfers that are limited to people or families with an income below a certain cutoff point. Eligibility is thus dependent upon low-income status.

Lyndon Johnson's administration, transfer expenditures increased rapidly. Measured in 1982–1984 dollars, **means-tested income transfers**—those limited to people with incomes below a certain cutoff point—tripled, expanding from $24 billion in 1965 to $70 billion in 1975. After 1975, transfer expenditures continued to expand, but the rate of increase was slower.

Did the expansion in government income transfers reduce the poverty rate as the 1964 *Economic Report of the President* anticipated? **Exhibit 15-6** shows the official poverty rate from 1947 through 2022. Interestingly, the poverty rate declined substantially during the period prior to the War on Poverty. It fell from 32 percent in 1947 to 13.9 percent in 1965. The downward trend continued for a few more years, reaching 10 percent in 1968. However, shortly after the War on Poverty was initiated, the downward trend in the poverty rate came to a halt. Since 1968, the official poverty rate has fluctuated within a range generally between 9 percent and 12 percent. In 2022, it was 9 percent—one percentage point lower than in 1968.

Exhibit 15-6 also presents the poverty rate for 1995–2022 adjusted for taxes, in-kind transfer benefits, and health insurance benefits provided by employers. The tax adjustments include both the taxes paid and tax credits received, such as those for the earned income and child tax credits. The adjusted poverty rate was between 7 percent and 8 percent throughout most of 1995–2022. On average, the adjusted rate was 3 percentage points lower than the official rate. In 2022, the adjusted poverty rate was 5.3 percent, over four percentage points lower than the official rate in 1970. This modest progress against poverty during the past half century is startling when you consider that real income per person in the United States has more than doubled during this period.

15-4b Why Haven't Anti-Poverty Programs Been More Effective?

The anti-poverty transfers generate three unintended secondary effects that slow progress against poverty. **First, income-linked transfers reduce the incentive of low-income individuals to earn, develop their skills, move up the job ladder, and escape poverty.** When

Exhibit 15-6 The Poverty Rate, 1947-2022

The official poverty rate of families fell sharply during the 1950s and 1960s, but it has been relatively stable in the 9 percent to 12 percent range since 1968. The poverty rate adjusted for taxes, in-kind transfer benefits, and employer-provided health insurance is also shown for 1995-2022. This adjusted poverty rate is generally about 3 percentage points lower than the official rate.

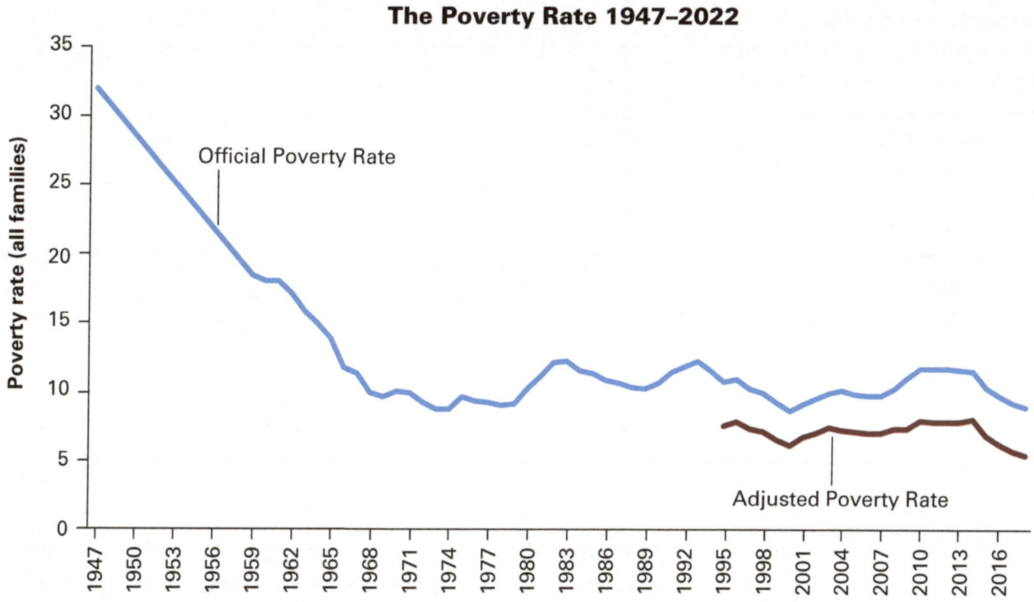

Source: U.S. Department of Commerce, Characteristics of the Population Below the Poverty Level: 1982, table 5; and http://www.census.gov/. The adjusted poverty rate data for families is unavailable prior to 1995 and after 2014. The adjusted poverty rate starting in 2015 is equal to official rate minus the 2014 difference between the official poverty rate and the adjusted poverty rate.

the size of transfers is linked to income, larger transfers tend to increase the implicit marginal tax rate imposed on low-income people. The implicit marginal tax rate is the amount of additional (marginal) earnings that must be paid explicitly in taxes or—in the case of low-income individuals—implicitly in the form of lower-income supplements. The marginal tax rate determines the fraction of an additional dollar earned that an individual is permitted to keep, so it is an important determinant of the incentive to earn. Participants in the food supplement program, for example, have their food stamp benefits reduced by $30 for every $100 of income they earn. Consequently, every $100 of additional income leads to only a $70 increase in well-being (spendable net income) after the reduction in food stamp benefits is taken into account. There are more than 75 means-tested government programs. When a person qualifies for several programs like food stamps, Medicaid, and housing benefits, the problem is compounded, and the combined implicit marginal tax rate can exceed 50, 60, or even 70 percent. Because high implicit marginal tax rates reduce the incentive of poor families to work and earn, transfers often merely replace income that otherwise would have been earned. When this is the case, they add little or nothing to the *net* income of low-income people.

Exhibit 15-7 provides evidence on the high implicit marginal tax rates confronted by those with low incomes. This exhibit presents the Congressional Budget Office estimates of the 2016 implicit marginal tax rates faced by a single-parent family with one child as their earnings increase up to $70,000. As earnings increase from $10,000 to $20,000, the family faces an implicit marginal tax rate of 63 percent. In the $20,000 to $30,000 range, the implicit marginal rate is 72 percent, and in the $30,000 to $40,000 range, the marginal rate is even higher, 77 percent. Thus, if family earnings increased from $30,000 to $40,000, the family gets to keep

Exhibit 15-7 Implicit Marginal Tax Rate on Earnings: Single-Parent Family with One Child

Here we show the Congressional Budget Office figures for the 2016 implicit marginal tax rate confronted by a single-parent family with one child as earnings increase up to $70,000. The implicit marginal tax rate reflects both the additional taxes paid and loss of benefits as earnings increase. Between $20,000 and $30,000, the implicit marginal tax rate is 72 percent. For earnings between $30,000 and $40,000, the implicit rate was even higher, 77 percent. Thus, in this range, the family gets to keep only 23 percent of an additional $10,000 of earnings. These high implicit marginal tax rates make it more difficult for families below and near the poverty level to move up the job ladder and escape poverty.

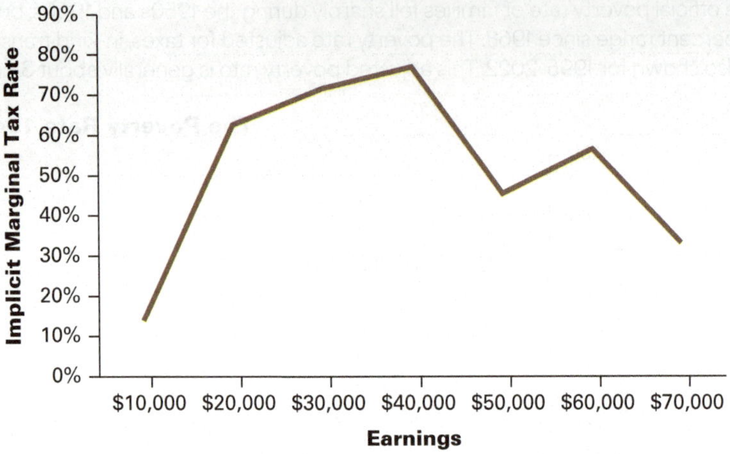

Source: Congressional Budget Office, *Effective Marginal Tax Rates for Low- and Moderate-Income Workers in 2016*, November 2015. The implicit marginal tax rates are derived for $10,000 incremental increases in earnings.

only 23 percent of the additional $10,000 of earnings. The implicit marginal rates are also presented for earnings levels up to $70,000. Note that the highest marginal rates are present in the $10,000 to $40,000 range, precisely the income intervals where families are struggling to deal with or escape from poverty. The numbers would be somewhat different for families of different size and structure, but the pattern would be the same: families at or near the poverty rate confront exceedingly high implicit marginal tax rates.

Second, transfer programs that significantly reduce the hardship of poverty also reduce the opportunity cost of choices that often lead to poverty. This factor is sometimes called the **Samaritan's dilemma**. To the extent that antipoverty programs reduce the negative effects of, for example, births by unmarried mothers, abandonment of children by fathers, dependency on drugs or alcohol, or dropping out of school, they inadvertently encourage people to make choices that result in these conditions. Of course, this is not the intent of the transfers, but nonetheless it is one of their side effects. In the short run, these secondary effects are probably not very important. Over the longer term, however, their negative consequences can be substantial.

Samaritan's dilemma
The dilemma that occurs when assisting low-income citizens with transfers reduces the opportunity cost of choices that lead to poverty. Providing income transfers to low-income individuals and discouraging behavior that leads to poverty are conflicting goals.

Implicit marginal tax rate
The amount of additional (marginal) earnings that must be paid explicitly in taxes or implicitly in the form of reduced income supplements. The marginal tax rate establishes the fraction of an additional dollar earned that an individual is permitted to keep, so it is an important determinant of the incentive to work and earn.

Third, government antipoverty transfers crowd out private charitable efforts. When people perceive that the government is providing for low-income individuals, action by families, churches, and civic organizations becomes less urgent. When taxes are levied and the government does more, predictably private individuals and groups do less. Further, private givers are more likely to see the real nature of the problem, be more sensitive to the lifestyles of recipients, and focus their giving on those making a good effort to help themselves. As a result, private charitable efforts will tend to be more effective than those of the government, and therefore, the problem worsens as the private efforts are crowded out.

Given the structure of incentives and secondary effects of the anti-poverty transfers, the slow progress against poverty is not surprising. Economics is insightful, but it does not always bring good news.

15-4c Estimating the Costs of Redistribution

The U.S. government has numerous income-transfer programs, including many that are unrelated to helping low-income people. In 2023, income-transfer and subsidy programs intended to help various groups purchase food, housing, and health care summed to

18 percent of aggregate income.[6] As we discussed in Chapter 6, politicians will often be able to gain by proposing programs that provide concentrated benefits to readily identifiable groups (for example, farmers, senior citizens, or unemployed workers) while imposing a small personal cost on disparate groups like taxpayers and consumers in general. Because of this, the presence and size of transfer programs are not surprising.

Income transfers are also costly in terms of the economy's overall output level. The higher marginal tax rates needed to finance transfers and subsidies mean that taxpayers get to keep less of what they earn. Furthermore, recipients often qualify for larger transfers if their income is lower, which causes them to earn even less. Thus, transfer programs typically weaken the incentive of both taxpayer-donors and the subsidy recipients to work and earn. As a result, the cost of the transfers will be greater than the amount of income transferred. A study by economists Sam Allgood and Arthur Snow sought to measure the loss of output due to the lower supply of labor associated with higher marginal tax rates accompanying income transfers.[7] Allgood and Snow estimated that it costs between $1.26 and $3.22 in terms of lost output for every additional dollar redistributed from the top 60 percent of income recipients to the bottom 40 percent.

Helping transfer recipients achieve long-term well-being is also more difficult than it first appears. Competition for the transfers and subsidies will often erode much of the recipient's gain.

15-4d Why Transfers Often Fail to Improve the Well-Being of Their Recipients

To non-economists, income transfers look like an easy way to help targeted beneficiaries. However, economic analysis indicates that it is far more difficult than it initially appears to transfer income to a group of recipients in a manner that will do much to improve their well-being. As is often the case in economics, the unintended secondary effects explain why this is true.

Governments must establish criteria to determine who should get the transfers, subsidies, and other political favors and who should not. Without these criteria, benefit programs would exhaust their budgets. Typically, governments require potential recipients to do something, own something, buy something, or be something in order to qualify for the transfer. However, as people take the steps necessary to qualify, they erode much of the benefit.

Consider the case in which the recipients have to do something (for example, fill out forms, take an exam, submit a detailed proposal, lobby government officials, endure delays, or contribute to selected political campaigns) in order to obtain the transfer. These actions are costly and will reduce the recipient's net gain. In some cases, almost all of the gain may be eroded. Perhaps a simple example will help illustrate this important point. Suppose the U.S. government decided to give away a $100 bill between 9 a.m. and 5 p.m. each weekday to anyone willing to show up at one of six teller windows at the U.S. Department of Treasury. Certainly, a line would emerge. How much time would people be willing to wait in the line? A person whose time was worth $10 per hour would be willing to spend up to 10 hours waiting in line for the $100. But it might take longer than 10 hours if there were enough other people, whose time was worth less, say $5 or $7 per hour. And everyone would find that the waiting consumed much of the value of the $100 transfer. If the government's objective is to make the recipients $100 richer, it will fail. In fact, some of those waiting in line for the $100 bill will gain very little. For example, if the wait were 10 hours, the net

---

[6]http://www.bea.gov.

[7]See Sam Allgood and Arthur Snow, "The Marginal Cost of Raising Tax Revenue and Redistributing Income," *Journal of Political Economy* (December 1998). This study builds on earlier work by Edgar K. Browning and William Johnson, "The Trade-Off between Equality and Efficiency," *Journal of Political Economy* (April 1984), and Charles L. Ballard, "The Marginal Efficiency Cost of Redistribution," *American Economic Review* (December 1988).

benefit of a person with an opportunity cost of $9.90 per hour would be only $1. So it is with real-world transfers. When you consider the cost of what has to be done for someone to qualify for the transfer, the net gain of the recipient is often small.

In other cases, the government will require recipients to own something (for example, land with an acreage allotment to grow cotton, a license to operate a taxicab, or a permit to sell in a restricted market) in order to qualify for a transfer or subsidy. Recipients will gain when programs like this are initiated or unexpectedly expanded. But once programs of this type are established, people will bid up the price of the asset needed to acquire the subsidy. The higher price of the asset, such as the taxicab license or the land with a cotton allotment, will capture the value of the expected future subsidy. Once this happens, the rate of return in the business or occupation (for example, farming or operating a taxicab) will be driven down to the normal level. The current recipients don't benefit from the subsidy program continuing at the expected benefit level. Essentially, they paid for the expected benefit of the subsidy when they purchased the asset needed to get it.

However, even though they don't benefit, current recipients will fight to keep the program going if it is threatened. Repealing (or reducing) the subsidies will be harmful because it will reduce the value of the asset they currently hold. This explains why eliminating farm subsidies, for example, is difficult even though the subsidies do not make farming more profitable for the current operators. Economist Gordon Tullock refers to this as the *transitional gains trap*, because once programs like these get started, they will be difficult to eliminate even though current recipients aren't benefiting from them.[8]

Sometimes, recipients are required to purchase a good or service in order to qualify for a subsidy. For example, the Medicare and Medicaid programs subsidize health care purchases made by senior citizens and low-income people. Several states provide educational subsidies for college tuition or the purchase of textbooks. As we discussed in Chapter 4, subsidizing the purchase of a good will increase its demand and lead to higher prices. As a result, some of the benefits of such subsidies will accrue to the suppliers rather than the purchasers. Again, the subsidized recipients will not gain as much as it might appear.

Consider the impact of the subsidies (grants and low-cost loans) to college students. These programs were designed to make college more affordable. But the subsidies increase the demand for college, which pushes the prices of tuition and other college-related purchases upward. A recent study by the Federal Reserve Bank of New York estimates that about 65 percent of the increases in transfers to students is passed through in the form of higher costs of going to college.[9] It is no coincidence that as the grant and loan aid programs for college students have increased substantially during the past two decades, so too has college tuition. Furthermore, the subsidy programs have contributed to an increase in the supply of college students entering the job market, which places downward pressure on their earnings. When the secondary effects on both tuition costs and employment opportunities are taken into consideration, it is clear that the net benefits to college students are substantially less than the transfers.

Finally, sometimes the government requires that recipients be something in order to qualify for the subsidy. Programs of this type are often intended to help protect people against the adverse effects of certain events such as unemployment or catastrophic storms. Unfortunately, the programs also encourage choices that increase the adverse effects of such events. For example, consider the impact of subsidized insurance premiums for those living in hurricane-prone areas. These subsidies reduce the owners' personal cost if their property is damaged by a hurricane. But the lower personal costs also encourage people to build in hurricane-prone areas. As more of them do so, the overall cost of damage from

[8]See Gordon Tullock, "The Transitional Gains Trap," *Bell Journal of Economics* 6 (Autumn 1975): 671–78.

[9]See David O. Lucca, Taylor Nadauld, and Karen Shen, "Credit Supply and the Rise in College Tuition: Evidence from the Expansion in Federal Student Aid Programs." *Federal Reserve Bank of New York Staff Reports*, no. 733. July 2015. http://www.newyorkfed.org/research/staff_reports/sr733.pdf.

hurricanes increases. The secondary effects of unemployment insurance are much the same. The benefits paid to the unemployed will reduce the opportunity cost of continuing a job search while unemployed. As a result, periods of unemployment will be longer and the rate of unemployment higher than would have otherwise been the case.

The ability of transfers to improve the well-being of a designated group is far more limited than is generally recognized. Transfer programs alter incentives and generate unintended consequences that erode some, if not most, of the benefits derived by the recipients. Thus, the net gains of the intended beneficiaries are less, and often substantially less, than the transfers received.

15-5 Income Inequality: Some Concluding Thoughts

Is there too much inequality in the United States? Should transfer programs be expanded or contracted? These are normative questions that positive economics cannot definitively answer. Economics can help identify and quantify the cost (in terms of lost output) and the expected effectiveness of alternative programs, but it can't make a judgment about whether that cost or amount is good or bad. Many people, including a good number of economists, would like to see income inequality reduced. This is a stated objective of many government programs. The progressive income tax system, the **earned income tax credit** (a tax credit that provides supplementary payments to workers with low incomes), and means-tested programs like food stamps, Medicaid, and housing subsidies provide examples.

Earned income tax credit
A feature of the personal income tax system that provides supplementary payments to workers with low incomes.

However, the political process is multidimensional. It represents a diverse set of forces, including powerful special-interest groups. Therefore, it should not be surprising that real-world transfers are often designed to benefit specific interest groups, including those with relatively high incomes. Social Security, the largest income-transfer program, redirects income toward the elderly, today a group with above-average levels of both income and wealth. Agriculture subsidies constitute another large transfer program; the bulk of these benefits go to large farmers with incomes well above the average. Another sizable share of government transfers is allocated to business interests, including many that are large and highly profitable. Thus, several government programs transfer income from those with modest incomes to those with incomes well above the average, thereby increasing income inequality.

Further, it is important to recognize that income in a market economy is not like manna from heaven. It is something people produce and earn by providing others with goods and services they are willing to pay for. The allocation of income reflects the choices of individuals with differing preferences, talents, educational levels, entrepreneurial skills, rates of saving, and so on. Wage differentials, profits, losses, and interest rates coordinate the choices of these vastly different individuals and bring them into harmony with one another. Income inequality is a natural outgrowth of this process. Indeed, policies that modify the process can generate perverse, counterproductive incentives.

When thinking about the distribution of income and role of transfers, some people argue that the process—the system, in other words—that generates the outcomes is more important than the actual result. Do all people in the economy have an opportunity to acquire education and training? Are people from all segments of society free to compete in business and labor markets? Do incomes reflect their choices, voluntary exchanges, and productive efforts? These questions are about opportunity, economic freedom, and how income is acquired. Many people believe that these things, rather than the income-distribution patterns that result from them, are the key elements of economic fairness.

Perhaps the following example will illustrate the difference between the process and pattern view. Suppose a million people purchase a $10 lottery ticket, and the proceeds are used to finance a $10 million jackpot for one person. This activity will clearly increase income inequality. But is it unfair? Those who adhere to the process view would stress that the outcome merely reflects the voluntary choices of participants who were well aware of the rules of the game prior to their purchasing a ticket. According to this view, it is the process rather than the outcome that is the primary determinant of fairness.

Economics provides insight into both the allocative role and sources of differences in income. It also indicates that it will be costly, in terms of lost output, to redistribute income through taxes and transfers. Of course, this does not reveal whether there is too much inequality or whether the government should play a larger or smaller role in the allocation of income. It does, however, enable us to address these normative issues in a more thoughtful way.

Key Points

- In 2022, the bottom 20 percent of families earned 3.7 percent of aggregate income; the top 20 percent of families earned approximately thirteen times that amount (49.8 percent). After taxes and transfers are taken into account, the top quintile of households earn 5.7 times the income of the bottom quintile.
- A substantial percentage of the inequality in annual income reflects differences in age, education, family size, marital status, number of earners in the family, and time worked. Young inexperienced workers, students, single-parent families, and retirees are overrepresented among those with low current incomes. Married couples, college graduates, prime-age earners, and families with multiple market workers are overrepresented among the high-income recipients.
- Income inequality has risen during the last four decades. The following four factors contributed to this increase: (1) an increase in the proportion of both single-parent and dual-earner families, (2) an increase in earnings differentials on the basis of skill and education, (3) more "winner-take-all" markets, and (4) increases in the reported income of those in the top tax brackets due to lower marginal tax rates.
- The tracking of household income over time indicates that there is considerable movement of individuals both up and down the income spectrum. The data on the distribution of income at a particular point in time can be misleading because they do not reflect this movement up and down the income ladder.
- One in 11 American families were officially classified as poor in 2022. Those living in poverty were generally younger, less educated, less likely to be working, and more likely to be living in families headed by a woman than those who were not poor.
- During the last several decades, income transfers—including means-tested transfers—have expanded rapidly both in real dollars and as a share of personal income. As a weapon against poverty, transfers have been relatively ineffective. Even though per capita income more than doubled between 1970 and 2018, there was little reduction in the overall poverty rate during this period.
- Means-tested income transfers will (1) confront low-income recipients with high implicit marginal tax rates and thereby reduce their incentive to earn, (2) encourage behavior that increases the risk of poverty, and (3) crowd out private antipoverty charitable activities.
- Transfer recipients are generally required to meet certain criteria in order to receive the transfers. Meeting these criteria generally results in costs that erode some of the benefits of the recipients. Thus, the net benefits of the recipients are generally less, and often substantially less, than the transfers.
- Positive economics cannot determine how much inequality should be present. The nature of the income-generating process as well as the pattern of income distribution are relevant to the issue of fairness.

Critical Analysis Questions

1. Do you think the current distribution of income in the United States is too unequal? Why or why not? What criteria do you think should be used to judge the fairness of the distribution of income? Is the final outcome more important than the process that generates the income?

2. *Is annual money income a good measure of economic status? Is a family with an $80,000 annual income able to purchase twice the quantity of goods and services as a family with $40,000 of annual income? Is the standard of living of the $80,000 family twice as high as that of the $40,000 family? Discuss.
3. What is income mobility? If there is substantial income mobility in a society, how does this influence the importance of income distribution data?
4. *Consider a table such as Exhibit 15-4 in which the family income of parents is grouped by quintiles down the first column, and that of their offspring is grouped by quintiles across the other columns. If there were no intergenerational mobility in this country, what pattern of numbers would appear in the table? If the nation had attained complete equality of opportunity, what pattern of numbers would emerge? Explain.
5. Do individuals have a property right to income they acquire from market transactions? Is it a proper function of government to tax some people in order to provide benefits to others? Why or why not? Discuss.
6. *Because income transfers to low-income individuals typically increase the implicit marginal tax rate they confront, does a $1,000 transfer payment necessarily increase the income of poor recipients by $1,000? Why or why not?
7. *Sue is a single parent with two children. She is considering a part-time job that pays $1,600 per month. She is currently drawing monthly cash benefits of $600, food stamp benefits of $200, and Medicaid benefits valued at $160. If she accepts the job, she will be liable for employment taxes of $112 per month and lose all transfer benefits. What is Sue's implicit marginal tax rate for this job?
8. What groups are overrepresented among those with relatively low incomes? Do low-income individuals in the United States generally stay low-income? Why or why not?
9. Some people argue that taxes exert little effect on people's incentive to earn income. Suppose you were required to pay a tax rate of 50 percent on all money income you earn while in school. Would this affect your employment? How might you minimize the personal effects of this tax?
10. Large income transfers are targeted toward the elderly, farmers, and the unemployed, regardless of their economic condition. Why do you think this is so? Do you think there would be less income inequality if the government levied higher taxes in order to make larger income transfers? Why or why not?
11. The outcome of a state lottery game is certainly a very unequal distribution of the prize income. Some players are made very rich, whereas others lose their money. Using this example, discuss whether the fairness of the process or the fairness of the outcome is more important, and how they differ.
12. What has happened to the size of transfer payments directed toward those with low incomes in recent decades? How do means-tested transfers impact the implicit marginal tax rate of those with low incomes? Why is this important?
13. As income transfer programs accompanying the War on Poverty increased beginning in the latter half of the 1960s, what happened to the poverty rate? Does economics indicate that this was surprising? Why or why not?
14. Suppose points are taken away from all students who earn A's and redistributed to those students who earn F's. As a result, the A students end up with B's and the F students end up with D's. How would this redistribution affect the incentive of students to study and learn?
15. Suppose one family has annual income of $100,000 whereas another has only $20,000. Is this outcome fair? What is your initial reaction? Compare and contrast your views depending on the following:
    a. The family with the higher income has two persons working full-time, while the lower-income family derives its income from Social Security.
    b. The family with the higher income is headed by a person who completed a college degree, whereas the other family is headed by someone who dropped out of high school.
    c. The family with the higher income derived most of its income from the farm subsidy program.
    d. The family with the higher income received it as an inheritance from parents who just died.
16. Why is it far more difficult to help a targeted group with transfer programs than it would initially appear? Do college students gain an amount equal to the expenditures on grants and low-interest loans provided to college students? Why or why not?
17. Would other Americans be better off if there were fewer rich people? In a market economy, if someone makes lots of money, what impact does this have on others?

*Asterisk denotes questions for which answers are given in Appendix B.

Part 4

International Economics

The world is becoming a global village.

The volume of international trade has grown dramatically in recent decades. Although the same general principles apply to both domestic and international trade, the latter also involves the exchange of one currency for another. Thus, this part will analyze the impact of both international trade and the operation of the foreign exchange market.

Chapter

16 Gaining from International Trade

The evidence is overwhelmingly persuasive that the massive increase in world competition—a consequence of broadening trade flows—has fostered markedly higher standards of living for almost all countries who have participated in cross-border trade. I include most especially the United States.

—Alan Greenspan[1]

We live in a shrinking world. Spurred by substantial cost reductions in transportation and communications, the volume of international trade has grown rapidly in recent decades. The breakfast of many Americans includes bananas from Honduras, coffee from Brazil, or hot chocolate made from Nigerian cocoa beans. Many Americans listen to music on iPhones assembled in China, fuel their automobiles with gasoline refined from crude oil from Mexico or Canada, and watch television on a set produced in South Korea. Similarly, many Americans work for companies that sell a substantial number of their products to foreigners. Why do people engage in international trade? The expectation of gain provides the answer. If both parties did not expect to gain, they would not agree to the exchange.

Learning Objectives

16.1 Indicate how the international trade sector of the United States has changed in recent decades.

16.2 Explain the reasons why a nation can gain from international trade.

16.3 Analyze the impact of imports and exports within the supply and demand model for a good.

16.4 Identify the different types of trade restrictions.

16.5 Explain how tariffs or quotas on a good will impact price and output, differentiating between domestic and world output and prices.

16.6 Indicate the reasons why a nation may impose trade restrictions, and why they are often attractive to political decision-makers even if they exert an adverse impact on the overall economy.

16.7 Compare the economic performance of economies with open trade policies to those that are more closed to international trade.

16.8 Identify the errors in logic within the popular fallacies that trade restrictions increase employment and result in lower wages.

16.9 Identify the major international organizations and trade agreements, and their impacts on tariff levels and the level of international trade.

[1]Alan Greenspan, speech before the Alliance for the Commonwealth Conference on International Business (Boston, Massachusetts, June 2, 1999).

16-1 The Trade Sector of the United States

As **Exhibit 16-1** illustrates, the size of the trade sector of the United States has grown rapidly during the last several decades. In 1960, total exports of goods and services accounted for 5.0 percent of the U.S. economy, whereas imports summed to 4.2 percent. By 1980, both exports and imports were approximately 10 percent of the economy. In 2023, exports accounted for 11.1 percent of total output, while imports summed to 14.0 percent. Thus, U.S. international trade (exports + imports) in goods and services has risen by 25 percent as a share of the economy since 1980 and almost tripled since 1960.

Who are the major trading partners of Americans? **Exhibit 16-2** shows the share of U.S. trade (exports + imports) with each of its ten leading trading partners. These ten countries account for approximately two-thirds of the total volume of U.S. trade. China, Canada, Germany, and Mexico are the four largest trading partners of Americans. Almost half of all U.S. trade is with these four countries. The United States also conducts a substantial volume of trade with Asian nations, particularly Japan, South Korea, Taiwan, Vietnam, and India.

What are the leading imports and exports of the United States? Capital goods like automobiles, computers, semiconductors, telecommunications equipment, and industrial machines are bought and sold in worldwide markets. The United States both imports and exports substantial quantities of these goods. Civilian aircraft, electrical equipment, chemicals, and plastics are also among the leading products the United States exports. Crude oil, textiles, toys, sporting goods, and pharmaceuticals are major products it imports.

Clearly, the impact of international trade differs across industries. The majority of the television sets, diamonds, shoes, DVD players, and motorcycles consumed in the United States are imported. In contrast, a large proportion of the aircraft, power-generating equipment, scientific instruments, construction equipment, and fertilizers produced in the United States are exported to foreigners.

Exhibit 16-1 The Growth of the Trade Sector in the United States: 1960-2023

During the past several decades, international trade has persistently risen as a share of GDP. Imports of goods and services as a share of GDP rose from 4 percent in 1960 to 10 percent in 1980 and 14 percent in 2023. Similarly, exports increased from 5 percent of GDP in 1960 to 10 percent in 1980 and 11 percent in 2023.

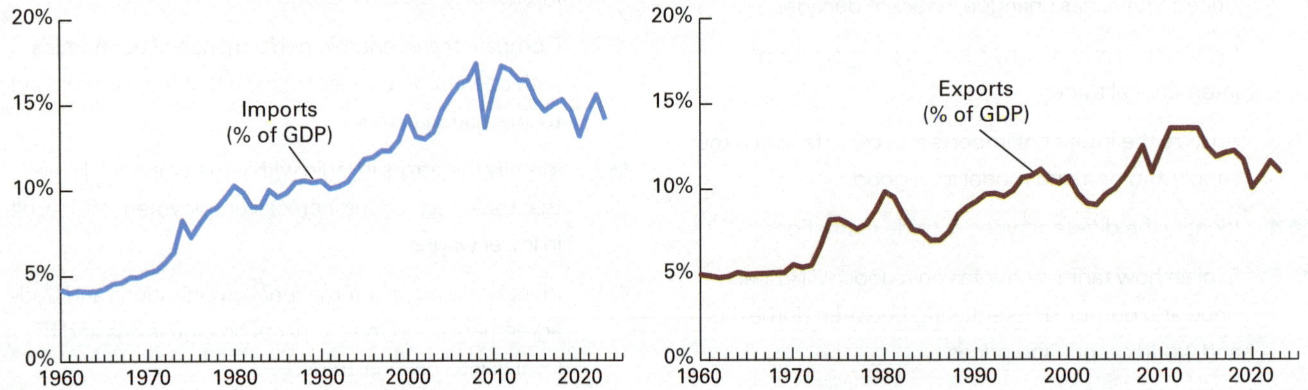

(a) Imports as a share of GDP **(b) Exports as a share of GDP**

Source: http://www.economagic.com. The figures are based on data for imports, exports, and GDP.

Exhibit 16-2 The 2023 Leading Trading Partners of the United States

China, Canada, Mexico, and Germany are the leading trading partners of the United States. Almost one-half of all U.S. trade involves imports from or exports to these four countries.

Source: http://www.census.gov.

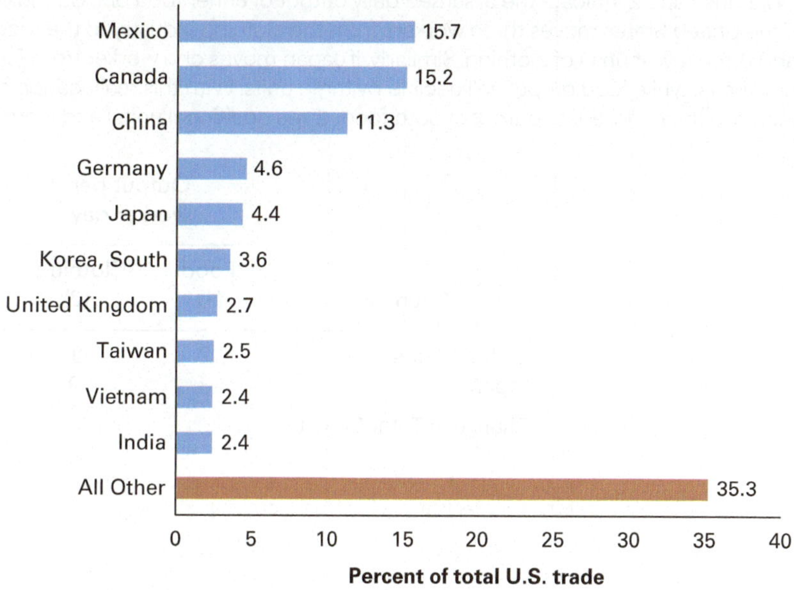

16-2 Gains from Specialization and Trade

Like domestic trade, international trade promotes growth and prosperity. The law of **comparative advantage** explains why a group of individuals, regions, or nations can gain from specialization and exchange. International trade leads to mutual gains because it allows residents of different countries to (1) specialize in the production of those things they do best and (2) import goods foreign producers are willing to supply at a lower cost than domestic producers. Resources and labor-force skills differ substantially across countries, and these differences influence costs. A good that is quite costly to produce in one country might be produced at a lower cost in another. For example, the warm, moist climates of Brazil, Colombia, and Guatemala make it more economical to produce coffee. Countries with temperate climates and an abundance of fertile land, such as Canada and Australia, are able to produce products such as wheat, feed grains, and beef at a low cost. In contrast, land is scarce in Japan, a nation with a highly skilled labor force. The Japanese, therefore, specialize in manufacturing, using their comparative advantage to produce cameras, automobiles, and electronic products for export. With international trade, the residents of different countries can gain by specializing in the production of goods they can produce economically. They can then sell those goods in the world market and use the proceeds to import other goods that are expensive to produce domestically.

Comparative advantage
The ability to produce a good at a lower opportunity cost than others can produce it. Relative costs determine comparative advantage.

Because the law of comparative advantage is often misunderstood, we will take the time to illustrate the principle in some detail. To keep things simple, let's consider a case involving only two countries, the United States and Japan, and two products, food and clothing. Furthermore, let's assume that labor is the only resource used to produce these products. In addition, because we want to illustrate that gains from trade are nearly always possible, we are going to assume that Japan has an **absolute advantage**—that the Japanese workers are more efficient than the Americans—at producing both food and clothing. **Exhibit 16-3** illustrates this situation. Perhaps due to their prior experience or higher skill levels, Japanese workers can produce three units of food per day, compared with only two

Absolute advantage
A situation in which a nation, as the result of its previous experience and/or natural endowments, can produce more of a good (with the same amount of resources) than another nation can.

Exhibit 16-3 Gains from Specialization and Trade

Columns 1 and 2 indicate the assumed daily output of either food or clothing of each worker in the United States and Japan. If the United States moves three workers from the clothing industry to the food industry, it can produce six more units of food and three fewer units of clothing. Similarly, if Japan moves one worker from food to clothing, clothing output will increase by nine units, while food output will decline by three units. With this reallocation of labor, the United States and Japan are able to increase their aggregate output of both food (three additional units) and clothing (six additional units).

	Output per worker day		Potential change in output[a]	
Country	Food (1)	Clothing (2)	Food (3)	Clothing (4)
United States	2	1	+6	−3
Japan	3	9	−3	+9
Change in Total Output			+3	+6

[a]Change in output if the United States shifts three workers from the clothing to the food industry and if Japan shifts one worker from the food to the clothing industry.

units per day for U.S. workers. Similarly, Japanese workers are able to produce nine units of clothing per day, compared with one unit of clothing per day for U.S. workers.

Can two countries gain from trade if one of them can produce both goods with fewer resources? The answer is "Yes." As long as the *relative* production costs of the two goods differ between Japan and the United States, gains from trade will be possible. Consider what would happen if the United States shifted three workers from the clothing industry to the food industry. This reallocation of labor would allow the United States to expand its food output by six units (two units per worker), while clothing output would decline by three units (one unit per worker). Suppose Japan reallocates labor in the opposite direction. When Japan moves one worker from the food industry to the clothing industry, Japanese clothing production expands by nine units, while food output declines by three units. The exhibit shows that this reallocation of labor *within* the two countries has increased their joint output by three units of food and six units of clothing.

The source of this increase in output is straightforward: Aggregate output expands because the reallocation of labor permits each country to specialize more fully in the production of the goods it can produce at a *relatively* low cost. Our old friend, the opportunity-cost concept, reveals the low-cost producer of each good. If Japanese workers produce one additional unit of food, they sacrifice the production of three units of clothing. Therefore, in Japan the opportunity cost of one unit of food is three units of clothing. Conversely, one unit of food in the United States can be produced at an opportunity cost of only a half-unit of clothing. American workers are therefore the low-opportunity-cost producers of food, even though they cannot produce as much food per day as the Japanese workers. Simultaneously, Japan is the low-opportunity-cost producer of clothing. The opportunity cost of producing a unit of clothing in Japan is only a third of a unit of food, compared with two units of food in the United States. The reallocation of labor illustrated in Exhibit 16-3 expanded joint output because it moved resources in both countries toward areas where they had a comparative advantage.

To reiterate: As long as the relative costs of producing the two goods differ in the two countries, gains from specialization and trade will be possible. Both countries will find it cheaper to trade for goods they can produce only at a high opportunity cost. For example, both countries will gain if the United States trades food to Japan for clothing at a trading ratio greater than one unit of food to one half-unit of clothing (the U.S. opportunity cost of food) but less than one unit of food to three units of clothing (the Japanese opportunity cost of food). Any trading ratio between these two extremes will permit the United States to acquire clothing more cheaply than it could be produced within the country and simultaneously permit Japan to acquire food more cheaply than it could be produced domestically.

16-2a How Trade Expands Consumption Possibilities

Because trade permits nations to expand their joint output, it also allows each nation to expand its consumption possibilities. The production possibilities concept can be used to illustrate this point. Suppose that there were 200 million workers in the United States and 50 million in Japan. Given these figures and the productivity of workers indicated in Exhibit 16-3, **Exhibit 16-4** presents the production possibilities curves for the two countries. If the United States used all of its 200 million workers in the food industry, it could produce 400 million units of food per day—two units per worker—and zero units of clothing (*N*). Alternatively, if the United States used all its workers to produce clothing, daily output would be 200 million units of clothing and no food (*M*). Intermediate output combinations along the production possibilities line (*MN*) between these two extreme points also could be achievable. For example, the United States could produce 150 million units of clothing and 100 million units of food (US_1).

Panel (b) of Exhibit 16-4 illustrates the production possibilities of the 50 million Japanese workers. Japan could produce 450 million units of clothing and no food (*R*), 150 million units of food and no clothing (*S*), or various intermediate combinations, like 225 million units of clothing and 75 million units of food (J_1). The slope of the production possibilities constraint reflects the opportunity cost of food relative to clothing. Because Japan is the high-opportunity-cost producer of food, its production possibilities constraint is steeper than the constraint for the United States.

In the absence of trade, the consumption of each country is constrained by its own production possibilities. Trade, however, expands the consumption possibilities of both. As we previously said, both countries can gain from specialization if the United States

Exhibit 16-4 The Production Possibilities of the United States and Japan Before Specialization and Trade

Here, we illustrate the daily production possibilities of a U.S. labor force with 200 million workers and a Japanese labor force with 50 million workers, given the cost of producing food and clothing presented in Exhibit 16-3. In the absence of trade, consumption possibilities will be restricted to points such as US_1 in the United States and J_1 in Japan along the production possibilities curve of each country.

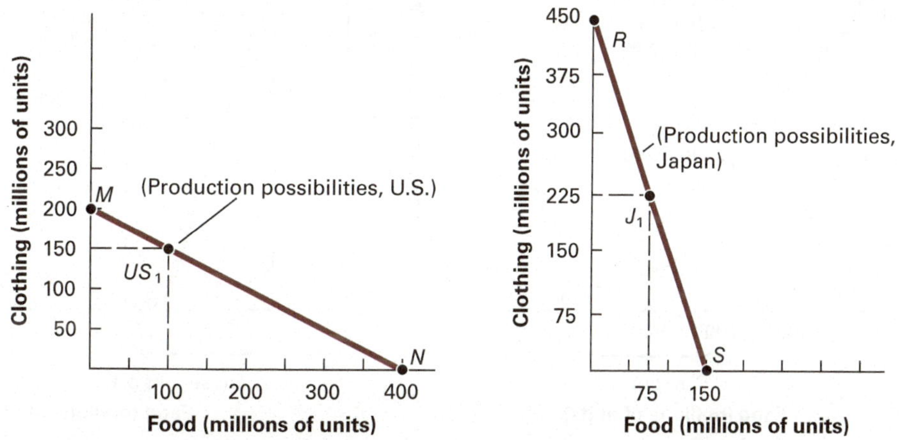

(a) United States **(b) Japan**

trades food to Japan at a price greater than one unit of food equals one half-unit of clothing but less than one unit of food equals three units of clothing. Suppose that they agree on an intermediate price of one unit of food equals one unit of clothing. As panel (a) of **Exhibit 16-5** shows, when the United States specializes in the production of food (where it has a comparative advantage) and trades food for clothing (at the price ratio where one unit of food equals one unit of clothing), it can consume along the line *ON*. If the United States insisted on self-sufficiency, it would be restricted to consumption possibilities like US_1 (100 million units of food and 150 million units of clothing) along its production possibilities constraint of *MN*. With trade, however, the United States can achieve a combination like US_2 (200 million units of food and 200 million units of clothing) along the line *ON*. Trade permits the United States to expand its consumption of both goods.

Simultaneously, Japan is able to expand its consumption of both goods when it is able to trade clothing for food at the one-to-one price ratio. As panel (b) of Exhibit 16-5 illustrates, Japan can specialize in the production of clothing and consume along the constraint *RT* when it can trade one unit of clothing for one unit of food. Without trade, consumption in Japan would be limited to points like J_1 (75 million units of food and 225 million units of clothing) along the line *RS*. With trade, however, it is able to consume combinations like J_2 (200 million units of food and 250 million units of clothing) along the constraint *RT*.

Look what happens when Japan specializes in clothing and the United States specializes in food. Japan can produce 450 million units of clothing, export 200 million to the United States (for 200 million units of food), and still have 250 million units of clothing remaining for domestic consumption. Simultaneously, the United States can produce 400 million units of food, export 200 million to Japan (for 200 million units of clothing), and still have 200 million units of food left for domestic consumption.

Exhibit 16-5 Consumption Possibilities with Trade

The consumption possibilities of a country can be expanded with specialization and trade. If the United States can trade one unit of clothing for one unit of food, it can specialize in the production of food and consume along the *ON* line (rather than its original production possibilities constraint, *MN*). Similarly, when Japan is able to trade one unit of clothing for one unit of food, it can specialize in the production of clothing and consume any combination along the line *RT*. For example, with specialization and trade, the United States can increase its consumption from US_1 to US_2, gaining 50 million units of clothing and 100 million units of food. Simultaneously, Japan can increase consumption from J_1 to J_2, a gain of 125 million units of food and 25 million units of clothing.

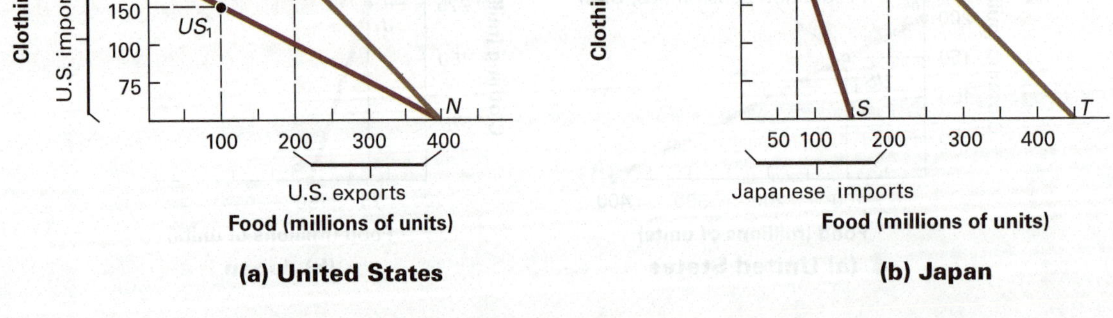

(a) United States **(b) Japan**

The implications of the law of comparative advantage are clear: Trade between nations will lead to an expansion in total output and mutual gain for each trading partner when each country specializes in the production of goods it can produce at a relatively low cost and uses the proceeds to buy goods that it could produce only at a high cost.

16-2b Some Real-World Considerations

To keep things simple, we ignored the potential importance of transportation costs, which, of course, reduce the potential gains from trade. Sometimes transportation and other transaction costs, both real and artificially imposed, exceed the potential for mutual gain. In this case, exchange does not occur.

We also assumed that the cost of producing each good was constant in each country. This is seldom the case. Beyond some level of production, the opportunity cost of producing a good will often increase as a country produces more and more of it. Rising marginal costs as the output of a good expands will limit the degree to which a country will specialize in the production of a good. This situation would be depicted by a production possibilities curve that was convex, or bowed out from the origin. In a case like this, there will still be gains from trade, but generally such a situation won't lead to one country completely specializing in the production of the good.

Keys to Economic Prosperity

International Trade

When people are permitted to engage freely in international trade, they are able to achieve higher income levels and living standards than would otherwise be possible.

Like trade within a country, trade between people living in different nations is mutually beneficial. As we just explained, the trading partners will be able to produce a larger joint output and consume a larger, more diverse bundle of goods when they each specialize in areas where they have a comparative advantage. Open markets also lead to gains from other sources. We will briefly discuss three of them.

1. More gains from large-scale production. International trade makes it possible for both domestic producers and consumers to derive larger gains from the lower per-unit costs that often accompany large-scale production, marketing, and distribution activities. When economies of scale are important in an industry, successful domestic firms will be able to produce larger outputs and achieve lower unit costs than they would if they were unable to sell their products internationally. This is particularly important for firms located in small countries. For example, textile manufacturers in Malaysia, Taiwan, and South Korea would face much higher per-unit costs if they could not sell abroad because the domestic markets of these countries are too small to support large-scale production. There simply aren't enough buyers. However, if the firms can access the world market, where there are many more buyers, they can operate on a large scale and compete quite effectively.

Domestic consumers also benefit because international trade often makes it possible for them to acquire goods at lower prices from large-scale producers in other countries. The aircraft industry vividly illustrates this point. Given the huge design and engineering costs it takes to produce a single jet, no firm would be able to produce them economically if it weren't able to sell them abroad. Because of international trade, however, consumers around the world are able to purchase planes economically from large-scale producers like Boeing, which is based in the United States.

International trade generates gains from specialization, economies of scale, and more competitive markets. As a result, trading partners are able to achieve higher living standards.

2. Gains from more competitive markets. International trade promotes competition and encourages production efficiency and innovation. Competition from abroad keeps domestic producers on their toes and gives them a strong incentive to improve the quality of their products.

International trade also allows technologies and innovative ideas developed in one country to be disseminated to others. In many cases, local entrepreneurs will emulate production procedures and products that have been successful in other places and even further improve or adapt them for local markets. Dynamic competition of this type is an important source of growth and prosperity, particularly for less-developed countries (LDCs).

3. More pressure to adopt sound institutions. Not only do firms in open economies face more intense competition, so, too, do their governments. The gains from trade and the prosperity that results from free trade motivate political officials to establish sound institutions and adopt constructive policies. If they do not, both labor and capital will move toward more favorable environments. For example, neither domestic nor foreign investors will want to put their funds in countries characterized by hostile business conditions, monetary instability, legal uncertainty, high taxes, and inferior public services. When labor and capital are free to move elsewhere, implementing government policies that penalize success and undermine productive activities becomes more costly. This aspect of free trade is generally overlooked, but it may well be one of its most beneficial attributes.[2]

16-3 Supply, Demand, and International Trade

Like other things, international trade can be analyzed within the supply and demand framework. An analysis of supply and demand in international markets can show us how trade influences prices and output in domestic markets.

Consider the market for a good that U.S. producers are able to supply at a low cost. Using soybeans as an example, **Exhibit 16-6** illustrates the relationship between the domestic and world markets. The price of soybeans is determined by the forces of supply and demand in the world market. In an open economy, domestic producers are free to sell and domestic consumers are free to buy the product at the world market price (P_w). At this price, U.S. producers will supply Q_p, and U.S. consumers will purchase Q_c. Reflecting their low cost (comparative advantage), U.S. soybean producers will export $Q_p - Q_c$ units at the world market price.

Let's compare this open-economy outcome with the outcome that would occur in the absence of trade. If U.S. producers were not allowed to export soybeans, the domestic price would be determined by the domestic supply (S_d) and demand (D_d) only. A lower "no-trade" price (P_n) would emerge.

Who are the winners and losers as the result of free trade in soybeans? Clearly, soybean producers gain. Free trade allows domestic producers to sell a larger quantity (Q_p rather than Q_n). As a result, the net revenues of soybean producers will rise by P_wbcP_n. In contrast, domestic consumers of soybeans will have to pay a higher price under free trade. Soybean consumers will lose (1) because they have to pay P_w rather than P_n for the Q_c units they purchase and (2) because they lose the consumer surplus on the $Q_n - Q_c$ units now purchased at the higher price. Thus, free trade imposes a net cost of P_wacP_n on consumers. As you can see in Exhibit 16-6, however, the gains of soybean producers outweigh the losses to the consumers by the triangle *abc*. In other words, free trade leads to a net welfare gain.

This exporting example makes it seem like free trade benefits producers relative to consumers, but this ignores the secondary effects: If foreigners do not sell goods to Americans, they will not have the purchasing power necessary to purchase goods from Americans. U.S. imports—the purchase of goods from low-cost foreign producers—provide foreigners with the dollar purchasing power necessary to buy U.S. exports. In turn, the lower prices in the

[2]For evidence that trade openness helps improve the institutional quality of a country, see International Monetary Fund, "Building Institutions," *IMF World Economic Outlook* (September 2005).

Exhibit 16-6 Producer Benefits from Exports

The price of soybeans and other internationally traded commodities is determined by the forces of supply and demand in the world market (b). If U.S. soybean producers are prohibited from selling to foreigners, the domestic price will be P_n (a). Free trade permits the U.S. soybean producers to sell Q_p units at the higher world price (P_w). The quantity $Q_p - Q_c$ is the amount U.S. producers export. Compared with the no-trade situation, the producers' gain from the higher price (P_wbcP_n) exceeds the cost imposed on domestic consumers (P_wacP_n) by the triangle abc.

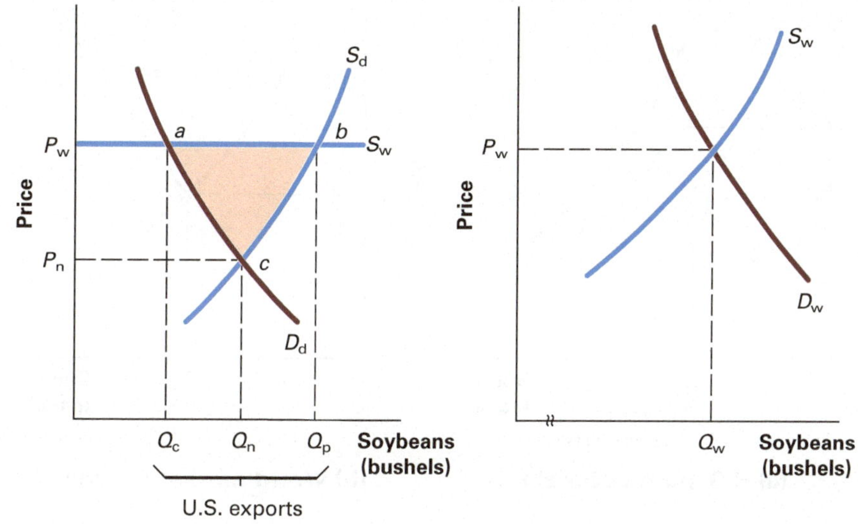

(a) U.S. market for soybeans **(b) World market for soybeans**

import-competitive markets will benefit the U.S. consumers, who appeared at first glance to be harmed by the higher prices (compared with the no-trade situation) in export markets.

Using shoes as an example, **Exhibit 16-7** illustrates the situation when the United States is a net importer. In the absence of trade, the price of shoes in the domestic market would be P_n, the intersection of the domestic supply and demand curves. However, the world price of shoes is P_w. In an open economy, many U.S. consumers would take advantage of the low shoe prices available from foreign producers. At the lower world price, U.S. consumers would purchase Q_c units of shoes, importing $Q_c - Q_p$ from foreign producers.

Compared with the no-trade situation, free trade in shoes results in lower prices and greater domestic consumption. The lower prices lead to a net consumer gain of P_nabP_w. Domestic producers lose P_nacP_w in the form of lower sales prices and reductions in output. However, the net gain of the shoe consumers exceeds the net loss of producers by *abc*.

International competition will direct resources toward producers who have a comparative advantage. If domestic producers have a comparative advantage in the production of a good—if they are a low opportunity cost producer, they will be able to compete effectively in the world market and profit from the export of goods to foreigners. In turn, the exports will generate the purchasing power necessary to buy goods that foreigners can supply more economically.

16-4 The Economics of Trade Restrictions

Despite the benefits provided by free trade, almost all nations have erected trade barriers. Tariffs, quotas, and exchange rate controls are the most commonly used trade-restricting devices. Let's consider how various types of trade restrictions affect the economy.

Exhibit 16-7 Consumer Benefits from Imports

In the absence of trade, the domestic price of shoes would be P_n. Because many foreign producers have a comparative advantage in the production of shoes, international trade leads to lower prices. At the world price P_w, U.S. consumers will demand Q_c units, of which $Q_c - Q_p$ are imported. Compared with the no-trade situation, consumers gain P_nabP_w, while domestic producers lose P_nacP_w. A net gain of *abc* results.

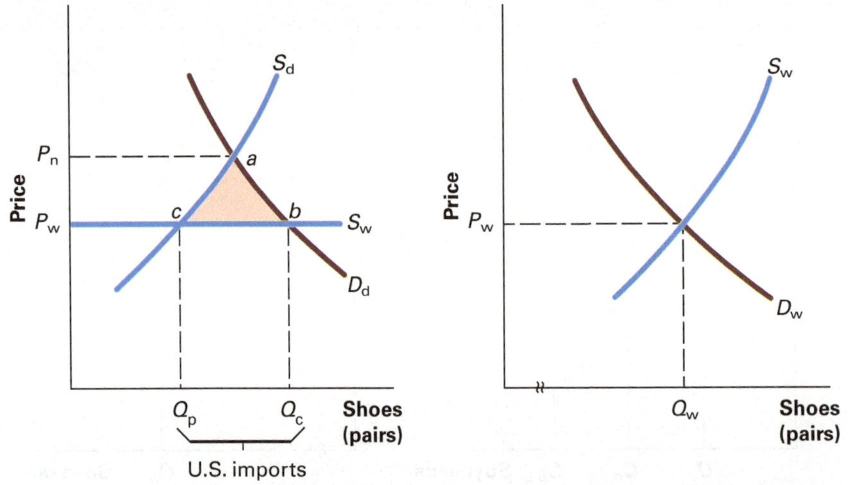

(a) U.S. market for shoes **(b) World market for shoes**

16-4a The Economics of Tariffs

Tariff
A tax levied on goods imported into a country.

A **tariff** is a tax on imports from foreign countries. As **Exhibit 16-8** shows, average tariff rates of between 30 percent and 50 percent of product value were often levied on products imported to the United States prior to 1945. The notorious Smoot-Hawley Tariff Act of 1930 pushed the average tariff rate upward to 60 percent. Many economists believe that this legislation contributed significantly to the length and severity of the Great Depression. During the past 90 years, however, tariff rates in the United States have declined substantially. In 2020, the average tariff rate on imported goods was 8.8 percent. Since 2017, tariff rates have been increasing as a result of the Trump administration raising tariffs.

Exhibit 16-9 shows the impact of a tariff on automobiles. In the absence of a tariff, the world market price of P_w would prevail in the domestic market. At that price, U.S. consumers purchase Q_1 units. Domestic producers supply Q_{d1}, while foreigners supply $Q_1 - Q_{d1}$ units to the U.S. market. When the United States levies a tariff, *t*, on automobiles, Americans can no longer buy cars at the world price. U.S. consumers now have to pay $P_w + t$ to purchase an automobile from foreigners. At that price, domestic consumers demand Q_2 units (Q_{d2} supplied by domestic producers and $Q_2 - Q_{d2}$ supplied by foreigners). The tariff results in a higher domestic price and lower level of domestic consumption.

The tariff benefits domestic producers and the government at the expense of consumers. Because domestic producers don't have to pay the tariff, they will expand their output in response to the higher (protected) market price. In effect, the tariff acts as a subsidy to domestic producers. Domestic producers gain the area *S* (Exhibit 16-9) in the form of additional net revenues. The tariff raises revenues equal to the area *T* for the government. The areas *U* and *V* represent costs imposed on consumers that do not benefit the government. Simply put, *U* and *V* represent *deadweight losses*: consumer surpluses that could have been gained if the tariff hadn't been imposed.

As a result of the tariff, resources that could have been used to produce other U.S. goods more efficiently (compared with producing them abroad) are diverted to automobile

Exhibit 16-8 How High Are U.S. Tariffs?

Tariff rates in the United States spiked up sharply in the early 1930s, then declined during the period from 1935 to 1950. After rising slightly during the late 1950s, they have trended downward from 1960 to 2017. They have trended upward since then. In 2020, the average tariff rate on merchandise imports was 8.8 percent.

Source: https://www.usitc.gov/documents/dataweb/ave_table_1891_2018.pdf. The average tariff rate is for those goods for which tariffs are imposed.

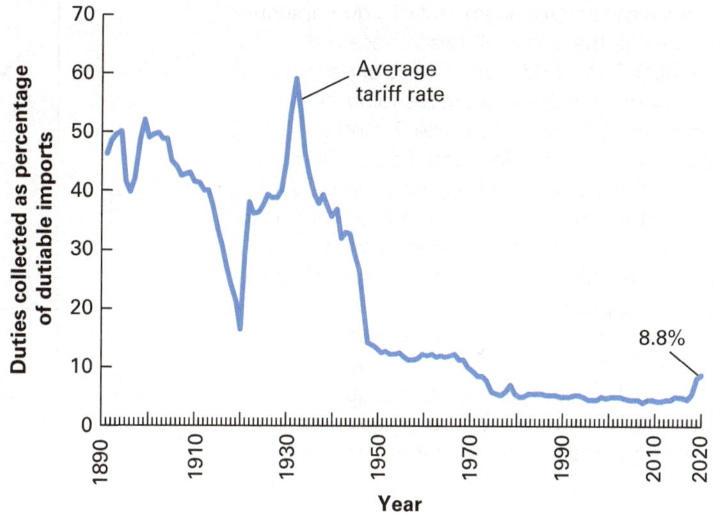

Exhibit 16-9 The Impact of a Tariff

Here, we illustrate the impact of a tariff on automobiles. In the absence of the tariff, the world price of automobiles is P_w. U.S. consumers purchase Q_1 units (Q_{d1} from domestic producers plus $Q_1 - Q_{d1}$ from foreign producers). The tariff makes it more costly for Americans to purchase automobiles from foreigners. Imports decline, and the domestic price increases. Higher prices reduce consumer surplus by the areas $S + U + T + V$. Producers gain the area *S*, and the tariff generates *T* tax revenues for the government. The areas *U* and *V* are deadweight losses.

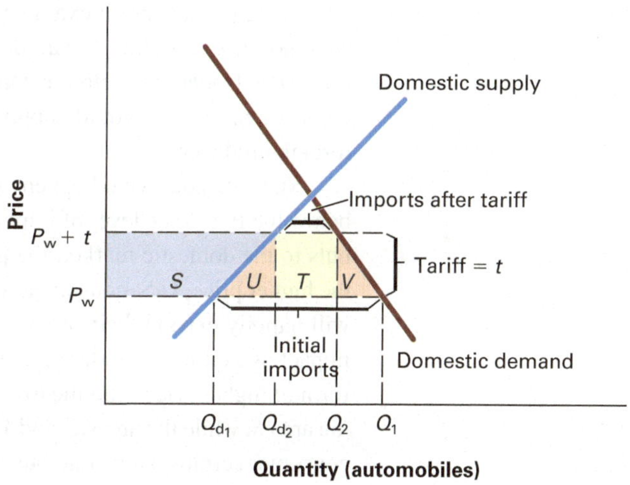

production. Ultimately, we end up producing fewer products in areas where we have a comparative advantage and more products in areas where we are a high-cost producer. Because of this, potential gains from specialization and trade will go unrealized. In addition, most nations, including the United States, impose higher tariffs on some goods than others. This encourages producers in specific industries to lobby for higher tariffs on goods they produce. This diverts resources away from production and toward plunder, which also reduces the overall size of the economic pie.

16-4b The Economics of Quotas

An **import quota**, like a tariff, is designed to restrict foreign goods and protect domestic industries from foreign competition. A quota places a ceiling on the amount of a product that can be imported during a given period (typically a year). The United States imposes

Import quota
A specific limit or maximum quantity (or value) of a good permitted to be imported into a country during a given period.

Exhibit 16-10 The Impact of a Quota

Here, we illustrate the impact of a quota, such as the one the United States imposes on peanuts. The world market price of peanuts is P_w. If there were no trade restraints, the domestic price would also be P_w, and the domestic consumption would be Q_1. Domestic producers would supply Q_{d1} units, while $Q_1 - Q_{d1}$ would be imported. A quota limiting imports to $Q_2 - Q_{d2}$ would push up the domestic price to P_2. At the higher price, the amount supplied by domestic producers increases to Q_{d2}. Consumers lose the sum of the area $S + U + T + V$, while domestic producers gain the area S. In contrast with tariffs, quotas generate no revenue for the government. The area T goes to foreign producers, who are granted permission to sell in the U.S. market.

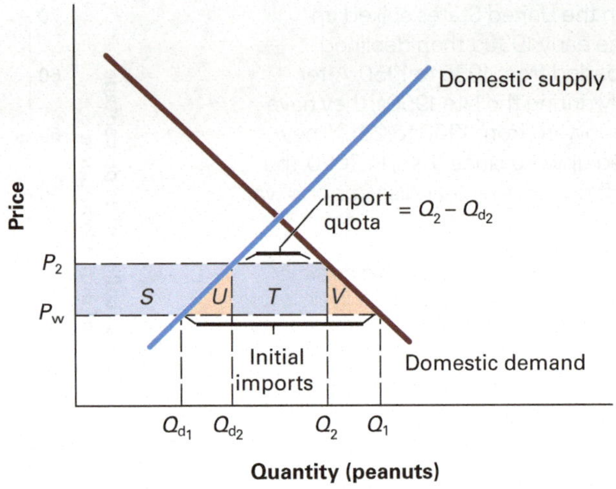

quotas on several products, including brooms, shoes, sugar, dairy products, and peanuts. For example, since 1953, the United States has imposed an annual peanut quota that in 2018 limited imports to 116.6 million pounds, about one-third of a pound per American.

Using peanuts as an example, **Exhibit 16-10** illustrates the impact of a quota. If there were no trade restraints, the domestic price of peanuts would be equal to the world market price (P_w). Under those circumstances, Americans would purchase Q_1 units. At the price P_w, domestic producers would supply Q_{d1}, and the amount $Q_1 - Q_{d1}$ would be imported from foreign producers.

Now consider what happens when a quota limits imports to $Q_2 - Q_{d2}$, a quantity well below the free-trade level of imports. Because the quota reduces the foreign supply of peanuts to the domestic market, the price of the quota-protected product increases (to P_2). At the higher price, U.S. consumers will reduce their purchases to Q_2, and domestic producers will happily expand their production to Q_{d2}. With regard to the welfare of consumers, the impact of a quota is similar to that of a tariff. Consumers lose the area $S + U + T + V$ in the form of higher prices and the loss of consumer surplus. Similarly, domestic producers gain the area S, while the areas U and V represent deadweight losses in the form of reductions in consumer surplus, gains that buyers would have derived in the absence of the quota.

While the adverse impact of a quota on consumer welfare is similar to that of a tariff, there is a big difference with regard to the area T. Under a tariff, the U.S. government would collect revenues equal to T, representing the tariff rate multiplied by the number of units imported. With a quota, however, these revenues will go to foreign producers, who are granted licenses (quotas) to sell various amounts in the U.S. market. Clearly, this right to sell at a premium price (because the domestic price exceeds the world market price) is extremely valuable. Thus, foreign producers will compete for the permits. They will hire lobbyists, make political contributions, and engage in other rent-seeking activities in an effort to secure the right to sell at a premium price in the U.S. market.

In many ways, quotas are more harmful than tariffs. With a quota, foreign producers are prohibited from selling additional units regardless of how much lower their costs are relative to those of domestic producers. In contrast to a tariff, a quota brings in no revenue for the government. Whereas a tariff transfers revenue from U.S. consumers to the Treasury, quotas transfer these revenues to foreign producers. Rewarding domestic producers with higher prices and foreign producers with valuable import permits will create *two* interest groups with a strong incentive to lobby for a quota. As a result, lifting the quota will often be more difficult than lowering a tariff would be.

In addition to tariffs and quotas, governments sometimes use regulations and political pressure to restrain foreign competition. For example, the United States prohibits foreign airlines from competing in the domestic air travel market. Japanese regulations make it illegal for domestic automobile dealers to sell both foreign and domestically produced vehicles; this makes it more difficult for foreign manufacturers to establish the dealer networks they need to penetrate the Japanese market effectively. Like tariffs and quotas, regulatory barriers such as these reduce the supply to domestic markets and the gains from potential trades. Overall output is reduced, and domestic producers benefit at the expense of domestic consumers.

16-4c Exchange Rate Controls as a Trade Restriction

Some countries fix the exchange rate value of their currency above the market rate and impose restrictions on exchange rate transactions.[3] At the official (artificially high) exchange rate, the country's export goods will be extremely expensive to foreigners. As a result, foreigners will purchase goods elsewhere, and the country's exports will be small. In turn, the low level of exports will make it extremely difficult for domestic residents to obtain the foreign currency they need to purchase imports. Exchange rate controls both reduce the volume of trade and lead to underground-market currency exchanges. Indeed, a large underground-market premium indicates that the country's exchange rate policy is substantially limiting the ability of its citizens to trade with foreigners. While exchange rate controls have declined in popularity, they are still an important trade barrier in countries such as Algeria, Argentina, and Venezuela.

16-5 Why Do Nations Adopt Trade Restrictions?

As social philosopher Henry George noted over a century ago, trade restraints act like blockades. Why would political officials want to erect blockades against their own people? As we consider this question, we will take a look at three arguments often raised by the proponents of trade restrictions: the national-defense, infant-industry, and antidumping arguments. Finally, we will look at the politics of trade restrictions and analyze how the nature of the restraints influences their political popularity.

16-5a The National-Defense Argument

According to the national-defense argument, certain industries—aircraft, petroleum, and weapons, for example—are vital to a nation's defense. Therefore, these industries and their inputs should be protected from foreign competitors so that a domestic supply of necessary materials would be available in case of an international conflict. Would we want to be entirely dependent upon Arabian or Russian petroleum? Would complete dependence on French aircraft be wise? Many Americans would answer "no," even if it meant imposing trade restrictions that would lead to higher prices on products they buy.

Although the national-defense argument has some validity, it is often abused. Relatively few industries are truly vital to our national defense. If a resource is important for national

Protective tariffs are as much applications of force as are blockading squadrons, and their objective is the same—to prevent trade. The difference between the two is that blockading squadrons are a means whereby nations seek to prevent their enemies from trading; protective tariffs are a means whereby nations attempt to prevent their own people from trading.

—Henry George[4]

[3]The most common exchange rate restriction is that individuals are required to obtain approval from the government before they engage in transactions involving foreign currency.

[4]Henry George, *Protection or Free Trade* (Washington, DC: U.S. Government Printing Office, 1886), 37.

defense, often it would make more sense to stockpile the resource during peacetime rather than follow protectionist policies to preserve a domestic industry. Furthermore, fostering an economy robust enough to produce the mass quantity of goods necessary to sustain a war effort in the first place is, itself, part of a strong defense.

16-5b The Infant-Industry Argument

Infant-industry advocates believe that new domestic industries should be protected from foreign competition for a period of time so that they will have a chance to develop. As the new industry matures, it will be able to stand on its own feet and compete effectively with foreign producers, at which time the protection can be removed.

The infant-industry argument has a long and often notorious history. Alexander Hamilton used it to argue for the protection of early U.S. manufacturing. The major problem with the argument is that the protection, once granted, will be difficult to remove. For example, a century ago, this argument was used to gain tariff protection for the newly emerging steel industry in the United States. Over time, the steel industry developed and became very powerful, both politically and economically. Despite its maturity, the tariffs remained. To this day, legislation continues to provide the steel industry with various protections that limit competition from abroad.

16-5c The Antidumping Argument

Dumping
Selling a good in a foreign country at a lower price than what it cost to produce, or at a lower price than it's sold for in the domestic market.

Dumping involves the sale of goods by a foreign firm at a price below cost or below the price charged in the firm's home-base market. Dumping is illegal and if a domestic industry is harmed, current law provides relief in the form of antidumping duties (tariffs imposed against violators). Proponents of the antidumping argument argue that foreign producers will temporarily cut prices, drive domestic firms out of the market, and then use their monopoly position to gouge consumers. However, there is reason to question the effectiveness of this strategy. After all, the high prices would soon attract competitors, including other foreign suppliers.

Antidumping cases nearly always involve considerable ambiguity. The prices charged in the home market generally vary, and the production costs of the firms charged with dumping are not directly observable. This makes it difficult to tell whether a dumping violation has really occurred. Furthermore, aggressive price competition is an integral part of the competitive process. When demand is weak and inventories are large, firms will often temporarily slash prices below per unit production cost in order to reduce excessively large inventories. Domestic firms are permitted to engage in this practice, and consumers benefit from it. Why shouldn't foreign firms be allowed to do the same?

One thing is for sure: Antidumping legislation gives politicians another way to channel highly visible benefits to powerful business and labor interests—another open invitation for rent seeking. The dumping charges are adjudicated by political officials in the International Trade Commission and the Department of Commerce. Consequently, it's naive to believe that political considerations won't be an important element underlying the charges that are levied and how they are resolved. Unsurprisingly, the number of claimants bringing charges of dumping has increased substantially over the past few decades.

16-5d Special Interests and the Politics of Trade Restrictions

Regardless of the arguments made by the proponents of trade restrictions, their political attractiveness is primarily the result of their special interest nature. Murray Weidenbaum, former chairman of the President's Council of Economic Advisors, put it this way: "Protectionism is a politician's delight because it delivers visible benefits to the protected parties while imposing the costs as a hidden tax on the public."[5] As we discussed in Chapter 6, special interest issues are often a source of economic inefficiency.

The politics of trade restrictions are straightforward and play out over and over again. Well-organized business and labor interests gain substantially from restrictions that limit competition from abroad. Because their personal gain is large, they will feel strongly about the issue and provide politicians with various forms of political support based on their positions on trade restrictions. Most important, the special-interest groups will be an attractive source of political contributions. When it comes to consumers, however, even if the total cost of the restrictions is quite large, it will be spread thinly among them; most consumers will be unaware that they are paying slightly higher prices for various goods because of the restrictions.

As you can see, courting special-interest groups helps politicians solicit campaign contributions and generate votes on the one hand. On the other hand, little political gain can be derived from poorly organized and largely uninformed consumers. Given this incentive structure, the adoption of trade restrictions is not surprising.

The U.S. tariff code itself is a reflection of the politics of trade restrictions. It is both lengthy (the schedule fills more than 3,000 pages) and highly complex. This makes it difficult for even a well-educated citizen to figure out how it works. High tariffs are imposed on some products (for example, apparel, tobacco, light trucks, brooms, Japanese leather products, and footwear), whereas low tariffs are imposed on others. Highly restrictive quotas limit the import of a few commodities, most notably agricultural products. Even though this complex system of targeted trade restrictions is costly to administer, it is no accident. It reflects the rent seeking of special-interest groups and the political contributions and other side payments the system generates for politicians.

Proponents of trade restrictions usually frame the issue as a conflict between American and foreign producers. But this is a misrepresentation designed to mislead. The real conflict is between American producers and American consumers. Why do Americans buy from foreigners? The answer is because they are getting more for their money. The trade restrictions help producers in the protected sectors but harm consumers, who now must pay higher prices and confront more limited options. Do we want our government to harm one group of Americans to favor another? Moreover, when a government becomes heavily involved in favoring some at the expense of others, how will this impact rent seeking, cronyism, and even corruption? In addition to their economic impact, trade barriers also influence the operation of the political process.

16-6 Do More Open Economies Perform Better?

Economic theory indicates that trade openness will improve the performance of an economy. Is this true? To address this question, a measure of trade openness—the freedom of individuals to engage in voluntary exchange across national boundaries—is needed. The international exchange area of the *Economic Freedom of the World* data provides information on the trade openness of 123 countries for 2000–2021. To achieve a high rating on the zero-to-ten scale (with ten representing more trade openness) on this measure, a country had to maintain low tariff rates, maintain a freely convertible currency (no exchange rate controls), and refrain from imposing quotas and other regulations that restrict its residents from trading with foreigners.[6]

[5]Murray L. Weidenbaum, personal correspondence with the authors. Weidenbaum was a former chairman of the President's Council of Economic Advisers and former director of the Center for the Study of American Business of Washington University.

[6]The measure of trade openness used here follows the methodology developed by Charles Skipton, *The Measurement of Trade Openness* (PhD diss., Florida State University, 2003).

Exhibit 16-11 Trade Openness, Income, and Growth

	Average Trade Openness Score 2000-2021 (0 to 10 Scale)	GDP Per Capita (2021 Dollars)	Average Annual Rate (2000-2021)
Ten Most Open Economies			
Hong Kong SAR, China	9.57	$65,885	2.4%
Singapore	9.48	$1,31,864	3.2%
Ireland	9.13	$1,14,121	3.7%
New Zealand	9.10	$48,194	1.4%
Netherlands	9.06	$67,693	0.9%
Estonia	8.96	$44,652	3.7%
United Kingdom	8.86	$52,842	0.8%
Denmark	8.86	$69,879	0.9%
France	8.85	$53,835	0.6%
Belgium	8.83	$62,123	0.9%
Average	**9.07**	**$71,109**	**1.9%**
Ten Least Open Economies			
Syrian Arab Republic	5.05	$2,915	−2.5%
Ethiopia	5.04	$2,628	5.7%
Central African Republic	4.89	$1,057	−0.9%
Algeria	4.84	$14,691	1.1%
Burundi	4.42	$864	−0.8%
Iran, Islamic Rep.	4.34	$15,042	1.5%
Zimbabwe	3.93	$3,276	−1.2%
Myanmar	3.66	$5,139	6.6%
Libya	3.66	$18,172	−0.5%
Sudan	3.55	$3,420	−0.4%
Average	**4.34**	**$6,720**	**0.9%**

Source: Derived from *Economic Freedom of the World* 2013 Dataset and World Bank, *World Development Indicators*. The purchasing power parity method was used to convert the per capita GDP figures into 2021 international dollars.

Exhibit 16-11 shows the countries with the ten highest and ten lowest trade openness ratings. The ratings reflect the average degree of openness for the entire 2000–2021 period. This is important because the gains from increased openness can only be realized over time. Expanding the openness of trade is a long-term growth strategy, not a short-term "quick fix." Hong Kong, Singapore, Ireland, New Zealand, and the Netherlands headed the list of the ten most open economies during 2000–2021. At the other end of the spectrum, the trade openness measure indicates Sudan, Libya, Myanmar, and Zimbabwe were the least open economies during the period. Note that all of the ten most open economies have openness ratings of 8.83 or above, whereas the ratings of the ten least open economies are all 5.05 or lower.

As Exhibit 16-11 shows, the 2021 average GDP per person of $71,109 for the ten most open economies was ten times the $6,720 figure for the ten least open economies. Moreover, the more open economies also grew more rapidly. During 2000–2021, real GDP per person in the ten most open economies expanded at an annual rate of 1.9 percent, compared with

0.9 percent in the ten least open economies. Of course, the data of Exhibit 16-11 do not take into account other cross-country differences that theory indicates will influence growth. However, more detailed statistical analysis indicates that even after the differences in other factors such as legal system, geography, climate, inflation, and initial income level are taken into account, trade openness continues to have a strong positive impact on both per capita GDP and growth rates.[7]

16-7 Trade Barriers and Popular Trade Fallacies

Fallacies abound in the area of international trade. Why? Failure to consider the secondary effects of international trade is part of the answer. Key elements of international trade are closely linked; you cannot change one element without changing the other. For example, you cannot reduce imports without simultaneously reducing the demand for exports. The political incentive structure is also a contributing factor. As business, labor, and political leaders seek to gain from trade restrictions, they will often use half-truths and wrong-headed ideas to achieve their political objectives. Two of the most popular trade fallacies involve the effects of imports on employment and the impact of trade with low-wage countries. Let's take a closer look at both.

16-7a Trade Fallacy 1: Trade Restrictions That Limit Imports Save Jobs and Expand Employment

Like most fallacies, this one has just enough truth to give it some credibility. When tariffs, quotas, and other trade barriers limit imports, they are likely to foster employment in the industries shielded from competition. But this is only half of the story: Simultaneously, jobs in other domestic sectors will be destroyed. Here's how: When trade barriers reduce the amount of goods Americans buy from foreigners, sales to foreigners will also fall. This is because our imports provide foreigners with the dollars they need to buy our exports. Because foreigners cut back on the items they would normally buy from us, other U.S. sectors will suffer job losses because they're selling less.

In addition, the trade barriers will mean higher prices for domestic consumers. Because the domestic consumers are spending more on the "protected goods," they will have less to spend on other things. This, too, will reduce domestic employment.

Furthermore, when trade restrictions are imposed on a resource domestic producers use as an input, they will increase the cost of domestic firms, reduce their sales, and make it more difficult for them to compete in international markets. The 2018 steel and aluminum tariff increases imposed by the Trump administration and continued under the Biden administration under a seldom used 1962 national security law illustrate this point. These tariffs increased the costs of a Missouri nail manufacturer and resulted in a 50 percent decline in sales. An Indiana cookware manufacturer experienced a similar reduction in sales as the result of the higher steel and aluminum prices. Similarly, import quotas that pushed the domestic price of sugar to approximately twice the world level have led to employment reductions in the domestic candy manufacturing industry. Several large candy makers relocated abroad so that they could buy sugar at the lower world price. Again, the jobs lost in U.S. industries using sugar were an offset to any employment gains of the domestic sugar producers.

---

[7]For additional information on the relationship between international trade and economic growth, see Jeffrey A. Frankel and David Romer, "Does Trade Cause Growth?" *American Economic Review* (June 1999): 379–99; and Jeffrey D. Sachs and Andrew Warner, "Economic Reform and the Process of Global Integration," *Brookings Papers on Economic Activity*, no. 1 (1995): 1–95.

Applications in Economics

A Bizarre Tale of Differential Tariffs

The United States imposes a tariff of 2.5 percent on passenger vehicles, but 25 percent on light trucks for the transport of goods. As a result, sometimes importers modify the vehicle so that it will qualify for the lower tariff rate. For example, Subaru added carpeting, two seats, and seat belts to the bed of its small two-seat pickup, the Brat, turning it into a passenger vehicle so that it qualified for the lower tariff rate. Upon taking delivery, many owners simply removed the extra seats.

Car Collection/Alamy Stock Photo

The Ford Transit Connect, which was produced in Turkey, provides another example of importers making modifications to avoid the higher tariff rates imposed on light trucks. All Transit Connects were imported with rear windows and rear seats with seat belts, making them passenger vehicles. Once they cleared U.S. customs, however, Ford ripped out and recycled the windows, seats, and rear seat belts and blocked the rear windows with solid panels. Doing this transformed them into light trucks. Actions such as these result in waste and inefficiency over and above those highlighted by the economic analysis of tariffs. Furthermore, they reduce the competitiveness in the market for light trucks.[6]

Source: This application is based on Michael Hammock, "Bizarre Tales of Tariffs," http://www.econlib.org/library/Columns/y2016/Hammock-tariffs.html.

Sometimes the results of trade restrictions are ironic and almost comical. When the Trump administration imposed tariffs of 20 percent and up on washing machines in January of 2018, the American manufacturer Whirlpool applauded the action. But five months later when the administration imposed tariffs on steel and aluminum, Whirlpool charged that the actions were unfair. While the tariffs on washing machines increased the demand for their product, the steel and aluminum tariffs increased their cost, partially if not entirely eliminating their gains from the initial trade restrictions.

Once the secondary "jobs lost" as the result of the restrictions are considered, on balance, there is no reason to expect that the trade barriers will either create or destroy jobs. Instead, they will reshuffle them. More Americans will be employed producing things we do poorly and fewer will be employed producing things we do well. As a result, our overall income level will be lower than it would have been otherwise.

16-7b Trade Fallacy 2: Free Trade with Low-Wage Countries Like Mexico and China Will Reduce the Wages of Americans

Many Americans believe that without trade restrictions, their wages will fall to the wage levels of workers in poor countries. How can Americans compete with workers in countries like Mexico and China who are willing to work for $1 or less per hour? This fallacy stems from a misunderstanding of both the source of high wages and the law of comparative advantage. Workers in the United States generally are well educated, possess high skill levels, and work with large amounts of capital equipment. These factors contribute to their high productivity, which is the source of their high wages. Similarly, in countries like Mexico and China, wages are low precisely because productivity is low. Workers are generally less skilled in these countries, and there is less capital equipment to make them more productive.

The key thing to remember, though, is that gains from trade emanate from comparative advantage, not absolute advantage (see Exhibits 16-3, 16-4, and 16-5). The United States cannot produce *everything* more cheaply than Mexico or China merely because U.S. employees are more productive and work with more capital. Neither can Mexico and China produce *everything* more cheaply merely because their wage rates are low compared with the United Sates.

As long as there are differences between countries when it comes to their comparative advantages, gains from trade will be possible, no matter what the wages of the employees in the two countries are. Trade reflects relative advantage, not wage levels. We can illustrate this point using trade between individuals. No one argues that trade between doctors and lawn service workers, for example, will cause the wages of doctors to fall. Because of their different skills and costs of providing alternative goods, both high-wage doctors and low-wage lawn-care workers can gain from trade. The same is also true for trade between rich and poor nations.

If foreigners have a comparative advantage and can sell us a product for less than we ourselves can produce it, we can gain by buying it. This will give us more resources to invest in and produce other things. Perhaps an extreme example will illustrate this point. Suppose a foreign producer is willing to supply us automobiles free of charge (perhaps because its employees were willing to work for nothing). Would it make sense to impose tariffs or quotas to keep the automobiles from coming into the country? Of course not. Resources that were previously used to produce automobiles would then be freed up to produce other goods, and the real income and availability of goods would expand. It makes no more sense to erect trade barriers to keep out cheap foreign goods than it would to keep out the free autos.

16-8 Institutions and the Changing Nature of Global Trade

Since World War II, liberalized trade policies and lower transportation and communication costs have propelled the growth of international trade. The growth of trade has also resulted in a changing institutional environment. In the aftermath of World War II, the major industrial nations of the world established the **General Agreement on Tariffs and Trade (GATT)**. For almost five decades, GATT played a central role in reducing tariffs and relaxing quotas. The average tariff rates of GATT members fell from approximately 40 percent in 1947 to about 3.0 percent in 2010, for example.

Following 1993, GATT was given a new name: the **World Trade Organization (WTO)**. This organization of 164 countries is now responsible for monitoring and enforcing the trade agreements developed through GATT. The WTO gives member nations a forum for development of trade rules and the settlement of disputes among members.

Many countries have also entered into special trade agreements, particularly with regional neighbors. The 1994 North American Free Trade Agreement (NAFTA) established by the United States, Canada, and Mexico is an example. As a result of NAFTA, the tariffs of most goods moving among the three countries have been eliminated. As **Exhibit 16-12** shows, U.S. trade with both Mexico and Canada grew rapidly following the adoption of NAFTA. Measured as a share of GDP, trade with Mexico jumped from 1.2 percent in 1990

General Agreement on Tariffs and Trade (GATT)
An organization formed after World War II to set the rules for the conduct of international trade and reduce trade barriers among nations.

World Trade Organization (WTO)
The new name given to GATT in 1994; the WTO is currently responsible for monitoring and enforcing multilateral trade agreements among its 164 member countries.

to 3.3 percent in 2023. During the same period, trade with Canada remained at 3.4 percent of GDP.

However, this growth of trade, particularly with Mexico, has not been without controversy. Even though growth of both output and employment in the United States was strong following the NAFTA agreement, many nonetheless argued that American firms and employee groups were disadvantaged by the agreement. In 2018, the Trump administration renegotiated a new treaty, called the United States–Mexico–Canada Agreement. Most of the provisions of the original NAFTA agreement were left intact. The modifications were mixed: some reduced trade barriers while others increased them. The major modifications will affect the auto and dairy industries. The domestic content requirements for automobiles were tightened. In order to avoid a 2.5 percent tariff on autos produced in one of the three countries, but sold in another, the North American content requirement was increased from 62 percent to 75 percent as a share of auto value. Moreover, by 2020, 30 percent (increasing to 40 percent by 2023) of auto production must be done by workers earning an average wage of at least $16 per hour. The agreement also eased Canadian restrictions on imports of American dairy products. These changes are expected to increase the cost of automobiles by at least $500 per vehicle and expand the potential U.S. share of the Canadian dairy market to 3.5 percent. On balance, the changes will exert little, if any, positive impact on the total trade among the three countries.

Since the end of World War II, the United States and most other high-income countries have been leaders among those pursuing and promoting more liberal trade policies. In contrast, India, China, and most of the less-developed economies of Africa and Latin America imposed sizable trade restraints that they were reluctant to relax. However, this pattern has changed during the past three decades. Observing the success of open economies like Hong Kong and Singapore, many less-developed countries (LDCs) unilaterally reduced many of their trade restrictions. On average, the tariff rates of LDCs are now less than half their levels of the early 1980s. Recognizing that trade is an important source of higher income levels, many leaders of LDCs are now among the leading advocates of trade liberalization. By contrast, the United States, Japan, and the European Union nations have agricultural price support and subsidy programs that are difficult to maintain in a free trade environment.

Exhibit 16-12 U.S. Trade with Canada and Mexico 1980-2023

Measured as a share of GDP, U.S. trade with both Canada and Mexico has increased following the passage of NAFTA.

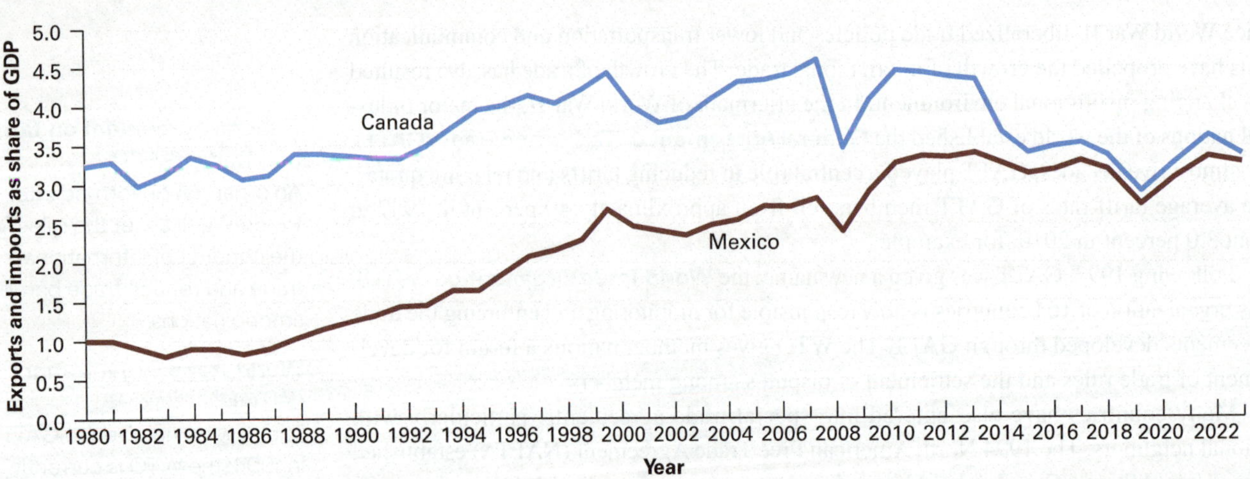

Source: Statistical Abstract of the United States (various years) and http://www.bea.gov.

These programs are now major stumbling blocks that reduce support for trade liberalization. Furthermore, protectionist proponents—particularly those in high-income countries like the United States—have successfully lobbied to impose labor and environmental regulations that block trade liberalization.

In the 2020s, political forces seeking to restrain international trade have strengthened worldwide. In 2024, the Biden administration, to protect U.S. industries, sharply increased tariffs on various Chinese goods. For example, it quadrupled the tariffs on electric vehicles to 102.5 percent. It also increased the tariffs on electric vehicle batteries from 7.5 percent to 25 percent and on photovoltaic cells used to make solar panels from 25 percent to 50 percent. At the same time, the internet and other technological changes continue to reduce transport and communications costs and thereby encourage the movement of goods, ideas, and people across national boundaries. This combination of forces is sure to enliven the debate on trade issues in the years immediately ahead.

Key Points

- The volume of international trade has grown rapidly in recent decades. In the United States, international trade (imports plus exports) summed to 2025 percent of GDP in 2023, compared with 20 percent in 1980 and 9 percent in 1960.
- Comparative advantage rather than absolute advantage is the source of gains from trade. As long as relative production costs of goods differ, trading partners will be able to gain from trade. Specialization and trade make it possible for trading partners to produce a larger joint output and expand their consumption possibilities.
- Imports increase the domestic supply and lead to lower prices for consumers. Exports reduce the domestic supply and push prices upward, but this means the exporters can sell their products at higher prices. The net effect of international trade is an expansion in total output and higher income levels for both trading partners.
- Import restrictions, such as tariffs and quotas, reduce the supply of foreign goods to domestic markets. This results in higher prices. Essentially, the restrictions are a subsidy to producers (and workers) in protected industries at the expense of (1) consumers and (2) producers (and workers) in export industries. Jobs protected by import restrictions are offset by jobs destroyed in export-related industries.
- Trade restrictions generally provide concentrated benefits to the producers in industries they're designed to protect. The costs are spread thinly among consumers in the form of higher prices. Even though the impact of trade restrictions on the economy as a whole is harmful, they generate benefits for interest groups that politicians can then tap for campaign contributions and other side payments.
- Persistently open economies have grown more rapidly and have achieved higher per capita income levels than economies more closed to international trade.

Critical Analysis Questions

1. Why do American households and businesses buy things from foreigners? What are the characteristics of the items we buy from foreigners? What are the characteristics of the things we sell to foreigners?
2. *"Trade restrictions limiting the sale of cheap foreign goods in the United States are necessary to protect the prosperity of Americans." Evaluate this statement made by an American political leader.
3. Suppose as the result of the Civil War that the United States had been divided into two countries and that, through the years, high trade barriers had grown up between the two. How might the standard of living in the "divided" United States have been affected? Explain.
4. *Can both of the following statements be true? Why or why not?
   a. "Tariffs and import quotas promote economic inefficiency and reduce the real income of a nation. Economic analysis suggests that nations can gain by eliminating trade restrictions."

b. "Economic analysis suggests that there is good reason to expect that trade restrictions will exist in the real world."

5. "Imports destroy jobs; exports create them. The average American is hurt by imports and helped by exports." Do you agree or disagree with this statement? Explain.

6. *"An increased scarcity of a product benefits producers and harms consumers. In effect, tariffs and other trade restrictions increase the domestic scarcity of products by reducing the supply from abroad. Such policies benefit domestic producers of the restricted product at the expense of domestic consumers." Evaluate this statement.

7. In 2024, the Biden administration imposed a 25 percent tariff on Chinese electric vehicle batteries. What is the expected impact on employment in the U.S. electric vehicle industry? (*Hint:* Think about how higher electric battery prices will impact the cost of producing electric vehicles.)

8. "Getting more Americans to realize that it pays to make things in the United States is the heart of the competitiveness issue." (This is a quote from an American business magazine.)

a. Would Americans be better off if more of them paid higher prices in order to "buy American" rather than purchase from foreigners? Would U.S. employment be higher? Explain.

b. Would Californians be better off if they bought goods produced only in California? Would the employment in California be higher? Explain.

9. How do tariffs and quotas differ? Can you think of any reason why foreign producers might prefer a quota rather than a tariff? Explain your answer.

10. *It is often alleged that Japanese producers receive subsidies from their government permitting them to sell their products at a low price in the U.S. market. Do you think we should erect trade barriers to keep out cheap Japanese goods if the source of their low price is a government subsidy? Why or why not?

11. The European Union has virtually eliminated trade restrictions among its members, and most members now use a common currency. What impact have these changes had on European economies?

12. *Does international trade cost Americans jobs? Does interstate trade cost your state jobs? What is the major effect of international and interstate trade?

13. "The United States is suffering from an excess of imports. Cheap foreign products are driving American firms out of business and leaving the U.S. economy in shambles." Evaluate this view.

14. The United States uses an import quota to maintain the domestic price of sugar well above the world price. Analyze the impact of the quota. Use supply and demand analysis to illustrate your answer. To whom do the gains and losses of this policy accrue? How does the quota affect the efficiency of resource allocation in the United States? Why do you think Congress is supportive of this policy?

15. As U.S. trade with low-wage countries like Mexico increases, will wages in the United States be pushed down? Why or why not? Are low-wage workers in the United States hurt when there is more trade with Mexico? Discuss.

16. *"Tariffs not only reduce the volume of imports, they also reduce the volume of exports." Is this statement true or false? Explain your answer.

17. "Physical obstacles like bad roads and stormy weather increase transaction costs and thereby reduce the volume of trade. Tariffs, quotas, exchange rate controls, and other human-made trade restrictions have similar effects." Evaluate this statement. Is it true? Why or why not?

*Asterisk denotes questions for which answers are given in Appendix B.

Part 5

Applying the Basics: Special Topics in Economics

Economics Is About How the Real World Works.

Economics has a lot to say about current issues and real-world events. How are government spending, taxes, and borrowing affecting the future prosperity of Americans? Are stocks a good investment for a young person? What caused the Great Recession of 2008-2009, and the Great Depression of the 1930s, and what are the important lessons we need to learn from these crises? What might be done to improve the quality of health care? Why do the earnings of men and women differ? This section focuses on these topics and several other current issues.

Special Topic 1

Government Spending and Taxation

> I'm proud to be paying taxes in the United States. The only thing is—I could be just as proud for half the money.
> —Comedian Arthur Godfrey

In Chapters 5 and 6, we analyzed the economic role of government and the operation of the political process. We learned that whereas the political process and markets are alternative ways of organizing the economy, a sound legal system, secure property rights, and stable monetary regime are vitally important for the efficient operation of markets. We also noted that there may be advantages of using government to provide certain classes of goods that are difficult to supply efficiently through markets. However, as public-choice analysis indicates, the political process is not a corrective device. Even democratic representative government will often lead to the adoption of counterproductive programs. This feature will examine government in the United States and will provide additional details with regard to its spending, taxing, and borrowing.

Learning Objectives

Upon completing this special topic, you will be able to:

ST01.1 Describe how per capita government spending and the composition of government spending have changed during the past century in the United States.

ST01.2 Indicate the share of taxes paid by the rich and how this share has changed in recent decades.

ST01.3 Indicate how government spending as a share of GDP of the United States compares with that of other countries.

ST01.4 Explain the relationship between the size of government and economic growth.

ST01.5 Explain why it is going to be difficult to control the growth of government expenditures in the years immediately ahead.

ST01-1 Government Expenditures

As we noted in Chapter 6, total government spending (federal, state, and local) sums to approximately 37 percent of the U.S. economy. The size of government has grown substantially over the past century. Measured as a share of GDP, total government spending rose from less than 10 percent in 1930 to roughly 46 percent in 2020 during the COVID-19 pandemic and associated economic recession.

Approximately three-fifths of the spending by government now takes place at the federal level. Federal expenditures on just four things—(1) income transfers (including Social Security and other income-security programs), (2) health care, (3) national defense, and (4) net interest on the national debt—accounted for 84 percent of federal spending in 2023. (Refer to Chapter 6, Exhibit 2.) This means that expenditures on everything else—the federal courts, national parks, highways, education, job training, agriculture, energy, natural resources, federal law enforcement, and numerous other programs—were less than 16 percent of the federal budget. Major spending categories at the state and local level include education, public welfare and health, transportation and highways, utilities, and law enforcement.

ST01-1a Federal Spending per Person

Article 1, Section 8, of the U.S. Constitution outlined a limited set of functions that the federal government was authorized to perform. These included the authority to raise up an army and navy, establish a system of weights and measures, issue patents and copyrights, operate the post office, and regulate the value of money that it issued. Beyond this, the federal government was not authorized to do much else. The founders of the United States were skeptical of governmental powers, and they sought to limit those powers, particularly those at the federal level.

During the first 125 years of the United States, the constitutional limitations worked pretty much as planned; the economic role of the federal government was quite limited, and its expenditures were modest. In the nineteenth century, except during times of war, most government expenditures were undertaken at the state and local level. The federal government spent funds on national defense and transportation (roads and canals) but not much else.

Exhibit ST01-1 presents data on real federal spending per person (measured in terms of the purchasing power of the dollar in 2020). Just before the Civil War, real federal expenditures were $65 per person, not much different than the $50 figure of 1800. Federal spending per person rose sharply during the Civil War, but it soon receded and remained in a range between $125 and $225 throughout the 1870–1916 period. Thus, before World War I, federal expenditures per person were low and the growth of government was modest.

Beginning with the World War I spending of 1917, however, the situation changed dramatically. Federal spending remained well above the prewar levels during the 1920s and rose rapidly during the 1930s. It soared during World War II, and after receding at the end of the war, federal spending continued to grow rapidly throughout the 1950–1990 period. After a brief reduction during the 1990s, per capita real federal spending began to trend upward again, with a spike after the 2008 recession, and another spike associated with the COVID-19 pandemic when federal spending soared to $19,768 per person. Whereas per capita federal spending fell by 4.6 percent during the 1990s, it increased by 77 percent during 2000–2024. In 2024, it amounted to $16,885, roughly 120 times the $142 figure of 1916. The additional government expenditures came with a cost. On average, Americans pay more inflation-adjusted federal taxes in one week today than they would have paid during the entire year in 1916. The rising interest payments on the national debt and unfunded obligations of the Social Security program will push this even higher in the next decade.

Exhibit ST01-1 Real Federal Expenditure per Capita: 1792-2024

Real federal spending per person (measured in 2020 dollars) was generally less than $75 before the Civil War, and it ranged from $125 to $225 throughout the 1870-1916 period. However, beginning with the spending buildup for World War I in 1917, real federal spending per person soared, reaching $16,885 in 2024–roughly 120 times the level of 1916.

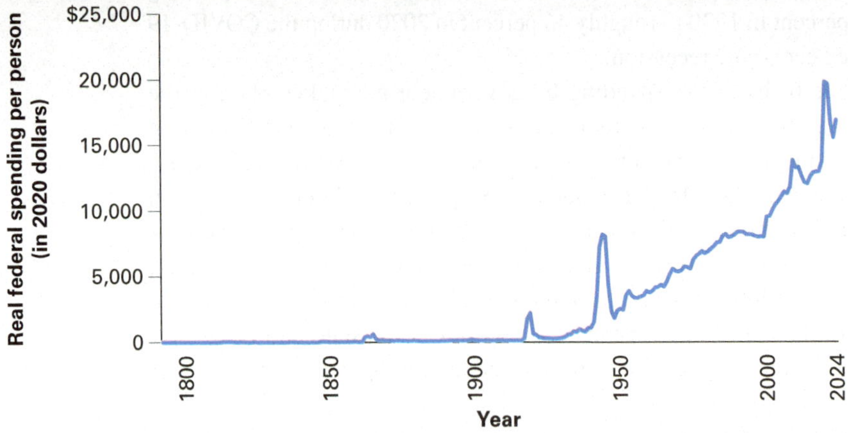

Source: U.S. Census Bureau, *Historical Statistics of the United States* (Washington, DC: U.S. Dept. of Commerce, U.S. Bureau of the Census, 1975); *Economic Report of the President* (Washington, DC: U.S. Government Printing Office, 2024); and Bureau of Labor Statistics.

ST01-1b The Changing Composition of Federal Spending

Not only has federal spending grown rapidly, but there has also been a dramatic shift in the composition of that spending. Since 1960, spending on defense has fallen as both a share of the budget and a share of the economy, whereas expenditures on health care, transfer payments, and subsidies have soared.

As **Exhibit ST01-2** illustrates, defense expenditures constituted more than half (52.2 percent) of federal spending in 1960. By 2024, defense spending was only 13.1 percent of the federal budget. Government expenditures on income transfers (including Social Security and other transfer programs) and health care (primarily Medicare and Medicaid) have soared during the past half century. As **Exhibit ST01-2** shows, income transfers and health care expenditures rose from 21.5 percent of the federal budget in 1960 to 65.8 percent in 2024.

Thus, there has been a dramatic change in the composition of federal spending during the last five decades. In contrast with earlier times, national defense is no longer the primary focus of the federal government. In essence, the federal government has become an entity that taxes working-age Americans in order to provide income transfers and health care benefits primarily for senior citizens. Furthermore, spending on the elderly will continue to increase as more baby boomers move into the retirement phase of life during the next two decades.

ST01-2 Taxes and the Finance of Government

Government expenditures must be financed through taxes, user charges, or borrowing.[1] Borrowing is simply another name for future taxes that will have to be levied to pay the interest on the borrowed funds. Thus, it affects the timing but not the level of taxes. In the

[1]In addition to user charges, taxes, and borrowing, the operations of government might be financed by printing money. But this is also a type of tax (it is sometimes called an "inflation tax") on those who hold money balances.

Exhibit ST01-2 The Changing Composition of Federal Spending

In 2024, national defense expenditures accounted for 13.1 percent of the federal budget, down from 52.2 percent in 1960. In contrast, spending on income transfers and health care rose from 21.5 percent of the federal budget in 1960 to 65.8 percent in 2024.

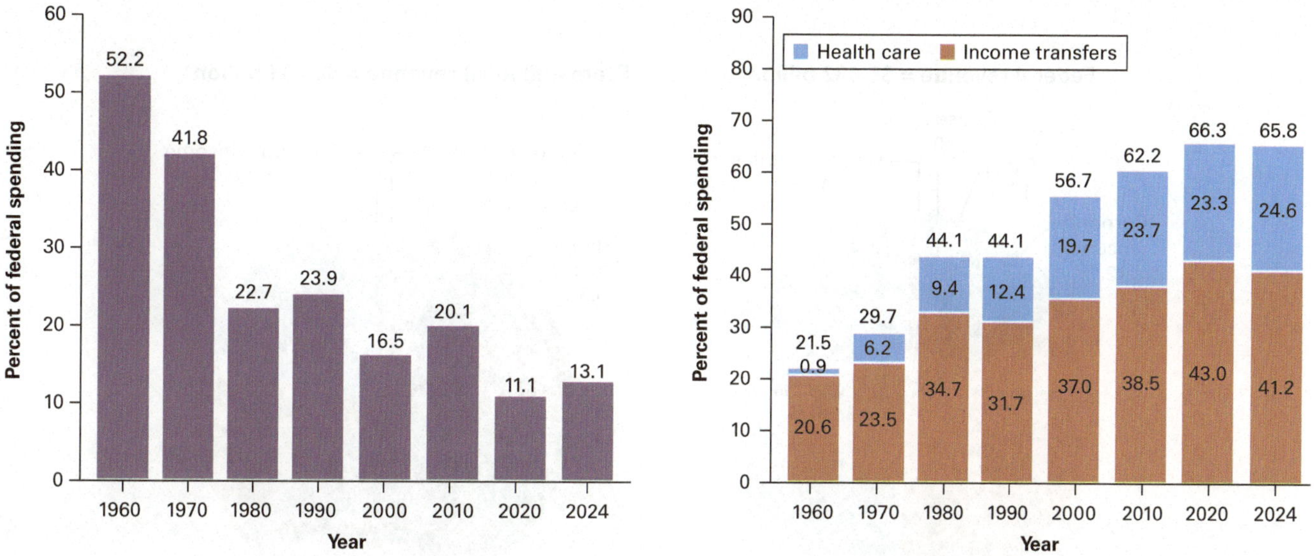

(a) Defense expenditures **(b) Health & income transfer expenditures**

Source: *Economic Report of the President* (Washington, DC: U.S. Government Printing Office, 2024).

United States, taxes are by far the largest source of government revenue. The power to tax sets governments apart from private businesses. Of course, a private business can put whatever price tag it wishes on its products, but no private business can force you to buy its goods. With its power to tax, a government can force citizens to pay, whether or not they receive something of value in return. As government expenditures have increased, so, too, have taxes. Taxes now take approximately one-third of the income generated by Americans.

ST01-2a Types of Taxes

Exhibit ST01-3 indicates the major revenue sources for the federal (panel a) and state and local (panel b) levels of government. At the federal level, the personal income tax accounts for more than 49 percent of all revenue. Although income from all sources is covered by the income tax, only earnings derived from wages and salaries are subject to the payroll tax. Payroll taxes on the earnings of employees and self-employed workers finance the Social Security and Medicare programs. The payroll tax accounts for about 34 percent of federal revenue. The remaining sources of revenue, including the corporate income tax, excise taxes, and customs duties, account for a little less than 17 percent of federal revenue.

Both sales and income taxes are important sources of revenue for state governments. A sales tax is levied by 45 of the 50 states (Alaska, Delaware, Montana, New Hampshire, and Oregon are the exceptions). State and local governments derive 12 percent of their revenue from this source. Personal income taxes on wage and salary income are imposed by 41 states (Alaska, Florida, Nevada, New Hampshire, South Dakota, Tennessee, Texas,

Exhibit ST01-3 Sources of Government Revenue

The major sources of government revenue are shown here. Almost half of federal revenues are derived from the personal income tax. The share of federal revenue derived from the payroll tax is only slightly less. The major revenue sources of state and local governments are sales and excise taxes, personal income taxes, user charges, insurance trust (including employee retirement, unemployment compensation, and workers' compensation), grants from the federal government, and property taxes.

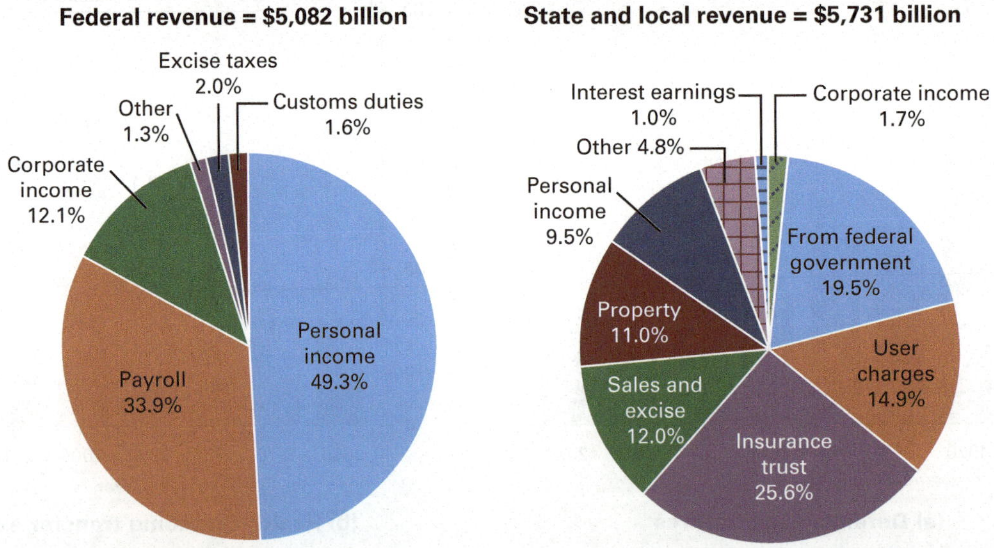

(a) Federal government, 2024 **(b) State and local governments, 2021**

Source: *Economic Report of the President* (Washington, DC: Government Printing Office, 2024) and U.S. Census Bureau, *State and Local Government Finances*, 2021.

Washington, and Wyoming are the exceptions), and they provide approximately 9.5 percent of state and local government revenue.[2] Property taxes (levied mostly at the local level), insurance trust revenue (including employee retirement contributions, workers' compensation, and unemployment compensation), grants from the federal government, and user charges (prices for government services) also provide substantial revenues for state and local governments.

ST01-3 Taxes and the Cost of Government

There are no free lunches. Regardless of how they are financed, activities undertaken by the government are costly. When governments purchase resources and other goods and services to provide missiles, education, highways, health care, and other goods, the resources used by the government will be unavailable to produce goods and services in the private sector. As a result, private-sector output will be lower. This reduction in private-sector output is an opportunity cost of government. Furthermore, this cost will be present whether government activities are financed by taxes or borrowing.

[2]New Hampshire and Tennessee have limited income taxes; they only tax income derived from dividend and interest (so wage and salary income is not subject to the personal income tax).

Moreover, a tax dollar extracted from an individual or a business ends up costing the private economy much more than just one dollar. There are two main reasons why this is the case. ***First, the collection of taxes is costly.*** The administration, enforcement, and compliance of tax legislation require a sizable volume of resources, including the labor services of many highly skilled experts. The IRS itself employs more than 80,000 people. In addition, an army of bookkeepers, tax accountants, and lawyers is involved in the collection process. Each year individuals and businesses spend more than 9 billion hours (the equivalent of 4.5 million full-time year-round workers) keeping records, filling out forms, and learning the tax rules and other elements of the tax-compliance process.[3] The estimated compliance costs imposed on individuals and businesses by the IRS amount to over $400 billion annually. In total, the resources involved amount to between 3 percent and 4 percent of national income (or 12 to 15 percent of the revenues collected). If these resources were not tied up with the tax-collection process, they could be employed producing goods and services for consumption.

Second, taxes impose an additional burden on the economy because they eliminate some productive exchanges (and cause people to undertake some counterproductive activities). As we noted in Chapter 4, economists refer to this as an *excess burden* (or *deadweight loss*) because it imposes a burden over and above the tax revenue transferred to the government. It results because taxes distort incentives. When buyers pay more and sellers receive less due to the payment of a tax, trade and the production of output become less attractive and decline. Individuals will spend less time on productive (but taxed) market activities and more time on tax avoidance and untaxed activities such as leisure. Research indicates that these deadweight losses add between 9 percent and 16 percent to the cost of taxation.[4] This means that $1 in taxes paid to the government imposes a cost of somewhere between $1.20 and $1.30 on the economy. Thus, the cost of a $100 million government program financed with taxes is really somewhere between $120 million and $130 million. As a result, the government's supply of goods and services generally costs the economy a good bit more than either the size of the tax bill or the level of government spending implies.

When considering the cost of taxation, it is also important to recognize that all taxes are paid by people. Politicians often speak of imposing taxes on "business" as if part of the tax burden could be transferred from individuals to a nonperson (business). This is not the case. Business taxes, like all other taxes, are paid by individuals. A corporation or business firm might write the check to the government, but it merely collects the money from someone else—from its customers in the form of higher prices, its employees in the form of lower wages, or its stockholders in the form of lower dividends—and transfers the money to the government.

ST01-4 How Has the Structure of the Personal Income Tax Changed?

The personal income tax is the largest single source of revenue for the federal government. The rate structure of the income tax is progressive; taxpayers with larger incomes face higher tax rates. During the past half century, the structure of the rates has been modified several times. In the early 1960s, there were 24 marginal tax brackets ranging from a low of 20 percent to a high of 91 percent. The Kennedy–Johnson tax cut reduced the lowest marginal rate to 14 percent and the top rate to 70 percent. The rate reductions during the Reagan years cut the top marginal rate initially to 50 percent in 1981 and later to approximately 30 percent during the period 1986–1988. During the 1990s, the top rate was increased to

[3]Scott A. Hodge, "The Compliance Costs of IRS Regulations," Tax Foundation Fiscal Fact No. 512 (June 2016).

[4]The classic article on this topic is Edgar K. Browning, "The Marginal Cost of Public Funds," *Journal of Political Economy* 84, no. 2 (April 1976): 283–98.

39.6 percent, but the tax reductions during the administration of George W. Bush rolled back the top rate to 35 percent. The top rate was increased back to 39.6 percent in 2013, but was then reduced to 37 percent beginning in 2018 as part of the Tax Cuts and Jobs Act (TCJA) of 2017, which is set to expire on December 31, 2025, if it is not renewed.

Thus, since the late 1980s, Americans with the highest incomes have paid sharply lower top marginal tax rates—rates in the 30 to 40 percent range, compared to top rates of 91 percent in the early 1960s and 70 percent before 1981. These reductions in the top rate make it tempting to jump to the conclusion that high-income Americans are now getting a free ride—that they now shoulder a smaller share of the personal income tax burden than in the past. But such a conclusion would be fallacious.

Exhibit ST01-4 presents the Internal Revenue Service data on the share of the personal income tax paid by various classes of high-income taxpayers, as well as those in the bottom half of the income distribution, for the years 1963, 1980, 1990, 2010, 2017, and 2021. These data show that the share of the personal income tax paid by high-income Americans has increased substantially since 1963, and the increase has been particularly sharp since 1980. For example, the top 1 percent of earners paid 45.8 percent of the personal income tax in 2021, up from 38.5 percent in 2017, 25.1 percent in 1990, and 19.1 percent in 1980. The top 10 percent of income recipients paid 75.8 percent of the personal income tax in 2021, compared to 49.3 percent in 1980 and 47 percent in 1963. At the same time, the share of the personal income tax paid by the bottom half of the income recipients has fallen from 10.4 percent of the total in 1963 to 7.1 percent in 1980 and 2.3 percent in 2021.

What is going on here? How can one explain the fact that high-income Americans are now paying more of the personal income tax even though their rates are now sharply lower than those in effect before 1981? Two major factors provide the answer. First, when marginal rates are cut by a similar percentage, the "incentive effects" are much greater in the top tax brackets. For example, when the top rate was cut from 91 percent to 70 percent during the Kennedy–Johnson years, high-income taxpayers in this bracket got to keep $30 out of every $100 of additional earnings after the tax cut, compared to only $9 before the rates were reduced. Thus, their incentive to earn additional income increased by a whopping 233 percent (30 minus 9, divided by 9)! Conversely, the rate reduction in the lowest

Exhibit ST01-4 Share of Federal Income Taxes Paid by Various Groups, 1963-2021

Even though marginal tax rates have been reduced substantially during the past three decades, upper-income Americans pay a much larger share of the federal income tax today than was previously the case. In 2021, the richest 1 percent of Americans paid 45.8 percent of the federal income tax, up from 37.4 percent in 2010 and 19.1 percent in 1980. The 5 percent of Americans with the highest incomes paid almost two-thirds of all personal income tax revenue, whereas the entire bottom half of the income distribution (the bottom 50 percent) paid only 2.3 percent of the total.

	Share of Total Federal Personal Income Tax Paid					
INCOME GROUP	**1963**	**1980**	**1990**	**2010**	**2017**	**2021**
Top 1%	18.3%	19.1%	25.1%	37.4%	38.5%	45.8%
Top 5%	35.6%	36.8%	43.6%	59.0%	59.1%	65.6%
Top 10%	47.0%	49.3%	55.4%	70.6%	70.1%	75.8%
Top 25%	68.8%	73.0%	77.0%	87.1%	86.1%	89.2%
Top 50%	89.6%	93.0%	94.2%	97.6%	96.9%	97.7%
Bottom 50%	10.4%	7.1%	5.8%	2.4%	3.1%	2.3%

Source: Internal Revenue Service (also available online from the Tax Foundation).

tax bracket from 20 percent to 14 percent meant that the low-income taxpayers in this bracket now got to keep $86 of each additional hundred dollars that they earned compared to $80 before the tax cut. Their incentive to earn increased by a modest 7.5 percent (86 minus 80, divided by 80). Because the rate reductions increased the incentive to earn by much larger amounts in the top tax (and therefore highest-income) brackets, the income base on which high-income Americans were taxed expanded substantially as their rates were reduced. As a result, the tax revenues collected from them declined only modestly. In the very highest brackets, the rate reductions actually increased the revenues collected from high-income Americans. (Refer to the Laffer curve analysis of Chapter 4.) In contrast, the incentive effects were much weaker in the lower tax brackets, and, as a result, rate reductions led to approximately proportional reductions in revenues collected from low- and middle-income taxpayers. This combination of incentive effects shifts the share of taxes paid toward those with higher incomes, the pattern observed in Exhibit ST01-4.

Second, both the standard deduction and personal exemption have been increased substantially during the last couple of decades. This means that Americans are now able to earn more income before they face any tax liability. In 2021, for example, 43 percent of those filing an income tax return either had zero tax liability or actually received funds from the IRS as the result of the **Earned Income Tax Credit**. This change in the structure of the personal income tax explains why people in the bottom half of income now pay such a small percentage of the personal income tax: 2.3 percent in 2021 compared to 10.4 percent in 1963.[5]

Earned Income Tax Credit
A provision of the tax code that provides a credit or rebate to people with low earnings (income from work activities). The credit is eventually phased out if the recipient's earnings increase.

ST01-5 Income Levels and Overall Tax Payments

In addition to the personal income tax, the federal government also derives sizable revenues from payroll, corporate income, and excise taxes. How is the overall burden of federal taxes allocated among the various income groups? **Exhibit ST01-5** presents Congressional Budget Office estimates for the average amount of federal taxes paid in 2019 according to income. On average, the top quintile (20 percent) of earners are estimated to pay 24.3 percent of their income in federal taxes. The average federal tax rate for the quintile with the next-highest level of income falls to 16.7 percent, and the average tax rate continues to fall as income declines. The average tax rate of the bottom quintile is 0.6 percent, less than one-fortieth the average rate for the top quintile of earners. Clearly, the federal tax system is highly progressive, meaning that it takes a larger share of the income of those with higher incomes than from those with lower income levels.

ST01-6 Size of Government: A Cross-Country Comparison

There is substantial variation in the size of government across countries. As **Exhibit ST01-6** illustrates, the relative size of government in most other high-income industrial countries is greater than that of the United States. In 2022, government spending summed to more than 50 percent of the economies of France, Italy, Austria, Belgium, and Greece, with Germany,

[5]The data of Exhibit ST01-4 consider only the tax liability of taxpayers. They do not reflect the payments from IRS to taxpayers as the result of the Earned Income Tax Credit, which was established in the mid-1980s. If these payments to taxpayers were taken into consideration, the net taxes paid by the bottom half of income recipients would have been less than 1 percent. Thus, the data of Exhibit ST01-4 actually understate the reduction in the net share of taxes paid by the bottom half of income recipients during the last two decades.

Exhibit ST01-5 Total Federal Taxes as a Share of Income, 2019

Federal taxes are highly progressive. In 2019, federal taxes took 24.3 percent of the income generated by the top quintile (20 percent) of earners, compared to 13 percent from the middle-income quintile and 0.6 percent from the lowest quintile of earners.

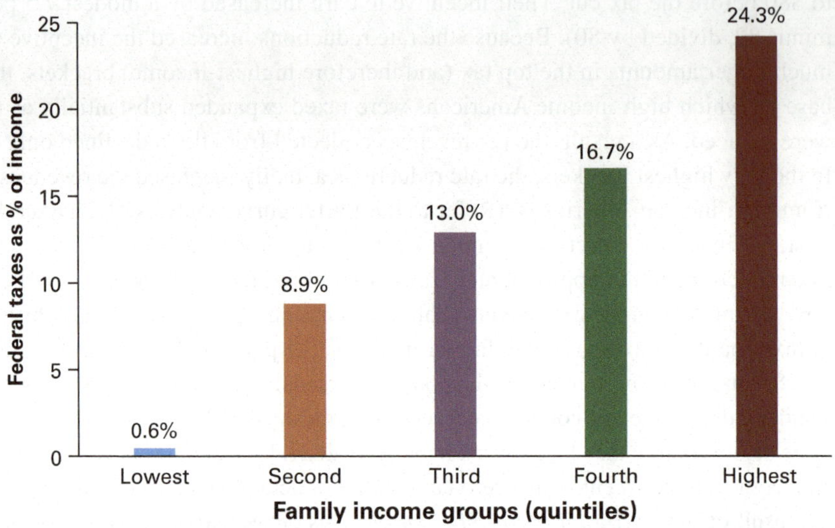

Source: Congressional Budget Office, The Distribution of Household Income and Federal Taxes 2019 (https://www.cbo.gov/publication/58353). Total federal taxes include income, payroll, corporate income, and excise taxes.

Spain, Sweden, and the United Kingdom not far behind. Government spending as a share of the economy in Norway, Australia, and South Korea was similar to that of the United States, about 37 percent. Interestingly, the size of government was substantially smaller in Singapore, Thailand, and Hong Kong—three Asian nations that have achieved rapid growth and substantial increases in living standards during the last four decades. However, the size of government has been growing in Hong Kong now that mainland China has taken control of the island, and it will be interesting to find out if this trend continues into the future.

ST01-7 How Does the Size of Government Affect Economic Growth?

Throughout this text, we have analyzed how governments influence the efficiency of resource use and the growth of income. It is clear that a legal environment that protects people and their property and provides for the impartial enforcement of contracts is vitally important. So, too, is a monetary and regulatory environment that provides the foundation for the smooth operation of markets. As we discussed in Chapter 5, there are also a few goods—economists call them *public goods*—that may be difficult to provide through markets. National defense, roads, and flood-control projects provide examples. Because they generate joint benefits and it is difficult to limit their availability to paying customers, sometimes they can be provided more efficiently through government. But public goods are rare, and the market can often devise reasonably efficient methods of dealing with them without any government involvement. If resources are going to be allocated efficiently, government spending on provision of public goods will generally be only a small share of the economy.

As governments expand beyond these core functions, however, the beneficial effects wane and eventually become negative as government moves into areas ill-suited for political action and in which the political process works poorly. Thus, expansion of government activities beyond a certain point will eventually exert a negative impact on the economy.

Exhibit ST01-6 The Size of Governments–An International Comparison, 2022

The size of governments varies substantially across countries. In France, government spending sums to almost 58 percent of the economy, compared to 37 percent in the United States and roughly 25 percent or less in Hong Kong, Thailand, Ireland, and Singapore.

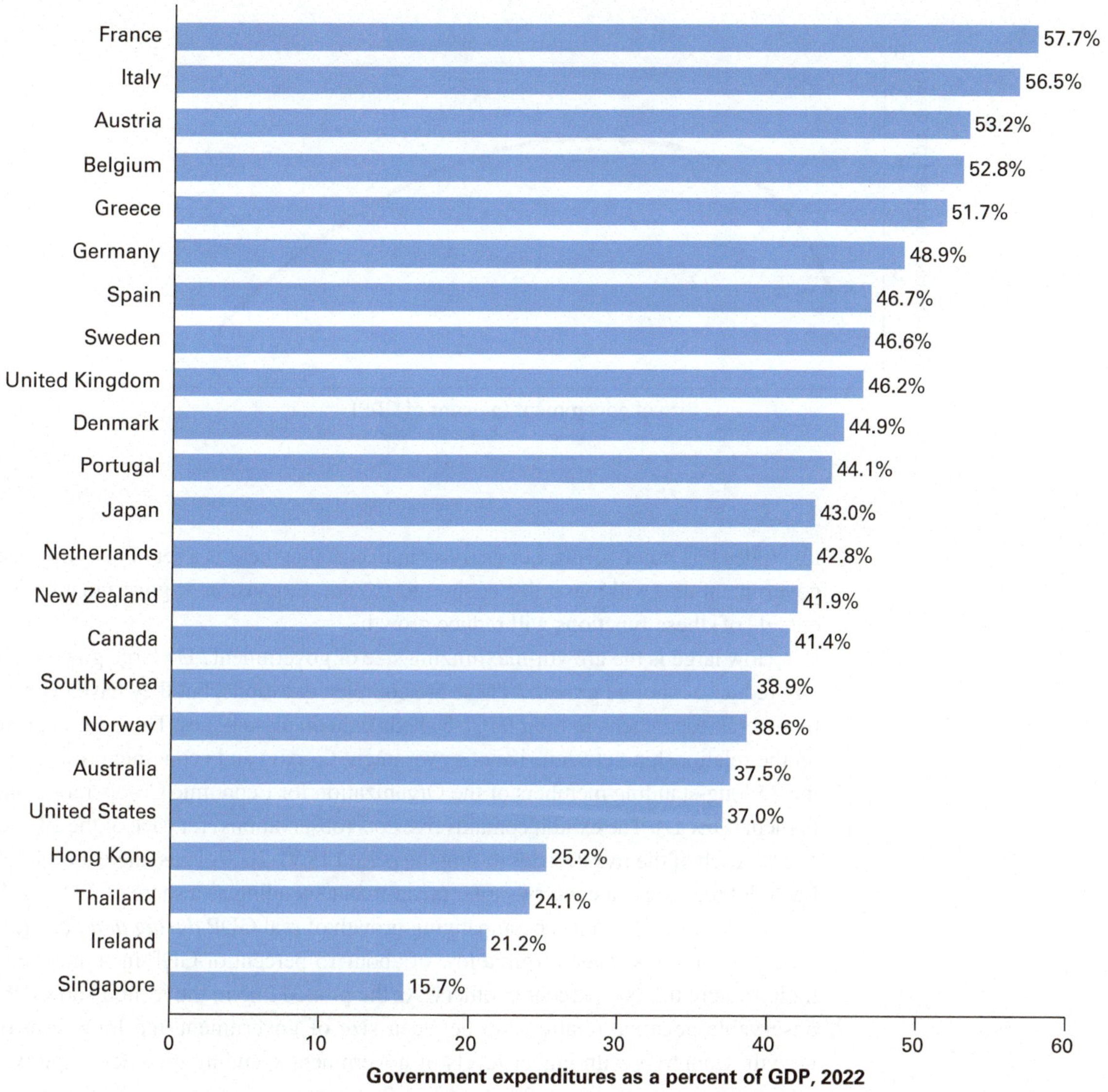

Source: International Monetary Fund, World Economic Outlook Database, Government Finance Statistics series GF2 (2022).

Exhibit ST01-7 illustrates the implications with regard to the expected relationship between the size of government and economic growth, *assuming that governments undertake activities based on their rate of return.* As the size of government, measured on the horizontal axis, expands from zero (complete anarchy), initially the growth rate of the economy—measured on the vertical axis—increases. The *A* to *B* range of the curve illustrates this situation. As government continues to grow as a share of the economy, expenditures are channeled into less-productive (and later counterproductive) activities, causing the rate of economic growth to diminish and eventually to decline. The range of the curve beyond *B*

Exhibit ST01-7 Economic Growth Curve and Government Size

If a government undertakes activities in the order of their productivity, its expenditures will promote economic growth (the growth rate will move from *A* to *B*). Additional expenditures, however, will eventually reduce growth (the growth rate will move along the curve to the right of *B*).

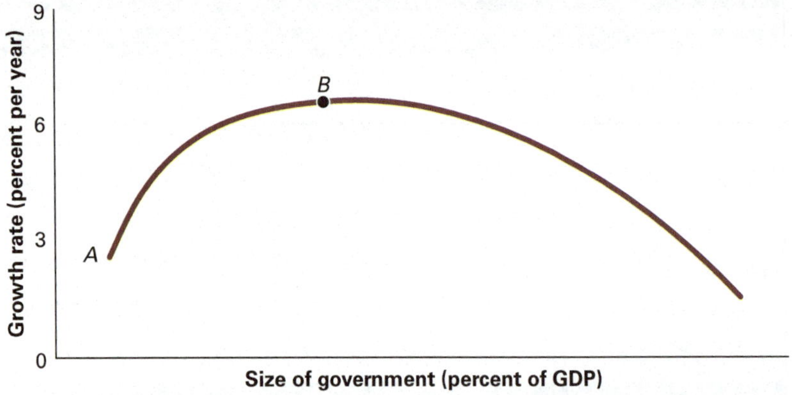

illustrates this point.[6] Thus, our analysis indicates that there is a set of activities and size of government that will maximize economic growth. Expansion of government beyond (and outside of) these functions will reduce growth.

How large is the growth-maximizing size of government? Do large governments actually reduce economic growth? These are complex questions, but they have been addressed by several researchers. **Exhibit ST01-8** sheds light on these issues. This exhibit presents data on the relationship between size of government (*x*-axis) and economic growth (*y*-axis) for the 23 long-standing members of the Organization for Economic Co-operation and Development (OECD). The exhibit contains five dots (observations) for each of the 23 countries—one for each of the five decades during the period 1960–2009. Thus, there are 115 total dots. Each dot represents a country's total government spending as a share of GDP *at the beginning of the decade* and its accompanying growth of real GDP *during that decade*. Government expenditures ranged from a low of about 15 percent of GDP in some countries to a high of more than 60 percent in others. As the plotted line in the exhibit shows, there is an observable negative relationship between size of government and long-term real GDP growth. Countries with higher levels of government spending grew less rapidly. The line drawn through the points of **Exhibit ST01-9** indicate that a 10-percentage-point increase in government expenditures as a share of GDP leads to approximately a 1-percentage-point reduction in economic growth.[7]

Time series data for specific countries have also been used to investigate the link between size of government and growth. Edgar Peden estimates that for the United States, the "maximum productivity growth occurs when government expenditures represent about 20% of GDP." Gerald Scully estimates that the growth-maximizing size of government (combined federal, state, and local) is between 21.5 percent and 22.9 percent of the

[6]In the real world, governments may not undertake activities based on their rate of return and comparative advantage. Many governments that are small relative to the size of the economy fail to focus on the core activities that are likely to enhance economic growth. Thus, one would expect that the relationship between size of government and economic growth will be a loose one.

[7]For additional information on the relationship between size of government and growth, refer to James Gwartney, Robert Lawson, and Randall Holcombe, "The Scope of Government and the Wealth of Nations," *The Cato Journal* (Fall 1998): 163–90.

Exhibit ST01-8 Government Spending and Economic Growth Among the 23 OECD Countries

Here we show the relationship between size of government and the growth of real GDP for the 23 longtime OECD members during each decade from 1960 to 2009. The data indicate that a 10 percent increase in government expenditures as a share of GDP reduces the annual rate of growth by approximately 1 percent. The data also imply that the size of government in these countries is beyond the range that maximizes economic growth.

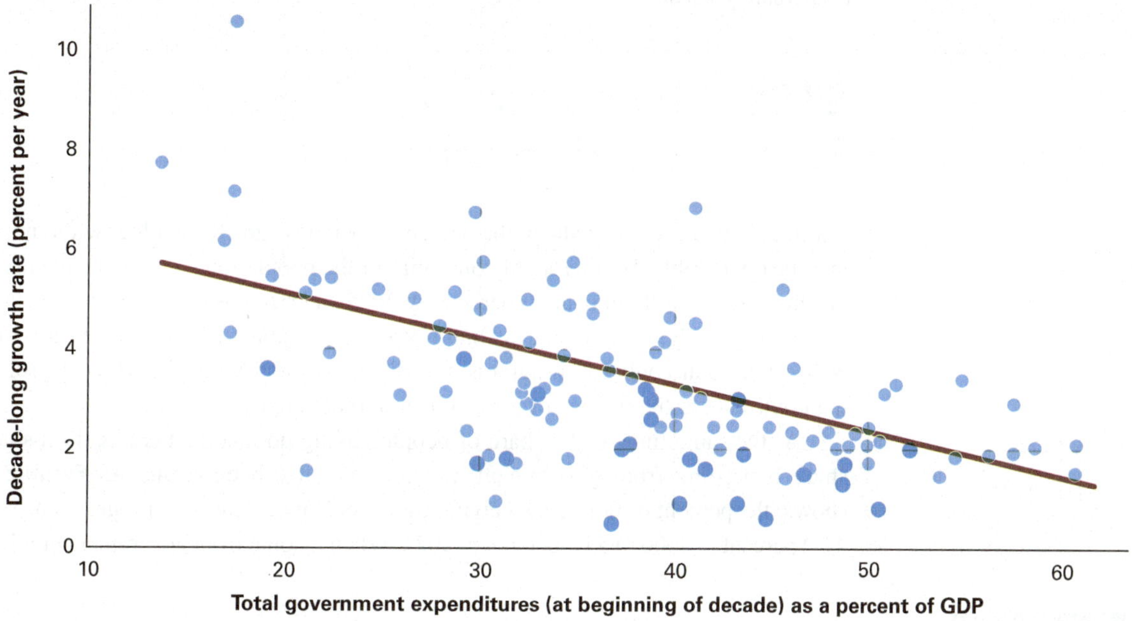

Source: OECD, OECD *Economic Outlook* (various issues), and the World Bank, *World Development Indicators* (various issues).

Exhibit ST01-9 Share of Population 18 and Older Without a Personal Income Tax Liability, 2000-2021

The percent of the population age 18 and older without a personal income tax liability is shown here. In 2000, the share with no income tax liability was about one-third of the adult population. This rose to 41.1 percent in 2005. In 2021, 43.1 percent of Americans did not have an income tax liability.

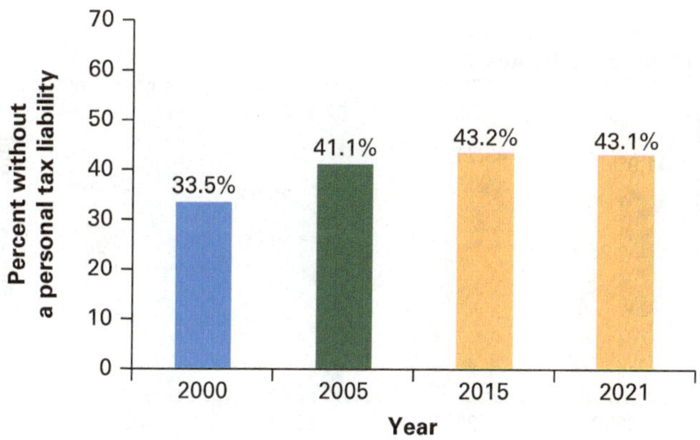

Source: Internal Revenue Service and U.S. Census Bureau. The number of persons without an income tax liability was derived by summing (1) the joint returns without a tax liability times two and (2) the number of individual returns without a tax liability. This figure was then divided by the population age 18 and older to derive the percentage of the 18 and older population without a tax liability.

economy. Although the methodology of these studies differs, they do have one thing in common: They indicate that in the ranges observed, high levels of government spending tend to reduce economic growth.[8] They also indicate that the size and scope of most governments around the world are larger than the size that would maximize the income growth of their citizens. Moreover, the estimates imply that the recent expansion in the size of the government sector in the United States is likely to reduce the growth of income in the years immediately ahead.

ST01-8 Expenditures, Taxes, Debt Finance, and Democracy

Exhibit ST01-9 presents data on the percent of persons age 18 and older without a personal income tax liability. While roughly one-third of the population paid no income tax in 2000, this had risen sharply to over 40 percent by 2005 and remains high at 43.1 percent in 2021. While many without an income tax liability are responsible for payroll taxes, the payroll tax is directed toward only two programs: Social Security and Medicare. Thus, payroll taxes do not contribute to the finance of government in other areas.

At the same time as the share of people paying no income tax has risen sharply, the share benefiting from government transfers has also been rising. As **Exhibit ST01-10** shows, the percent of families receiving transfers from at least one program has risen from 41.9 percent in 2000 to 55.6 percent in 2022. When income from government employment is

Exhibit ST01-10 Share of Families Deriving Income from Government

More than half of American families derive income from transfer programs. The percent of families receiving transfers from at least one program rose from 41.9 percent in 2000 to 55.6 percent in 2022. When income from government employment is also included, 64.9 percent of American families now derive income from the government, up from 54.5 percent in 2000. When only families with individuals younger than age 62 are included, the percentage receiving transfers is somewhat lower, but the pattern over the past two decades is the same.

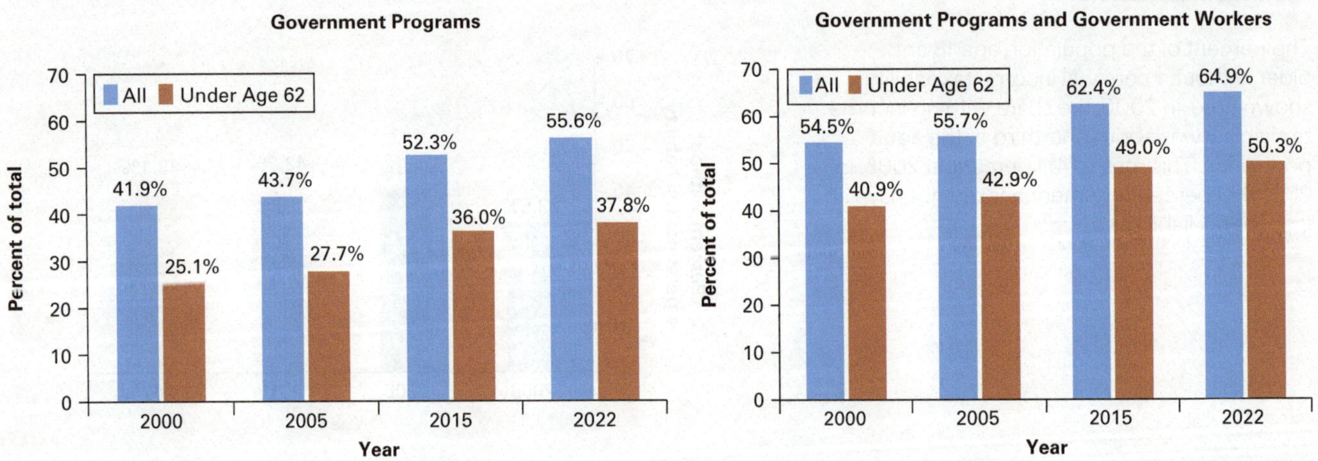

Source: These figures were derived from the Current Population Survey data. The following income transfers were included: Medicare, Medicaid, food stamps, unemployment compensation, school lunch program, Social Security, and welfare.

[8]Refer to Edgar Peden, "Productivity in the United States and Its Relationship to Government Activity: An Analysis of 57 Years, 1929–1986," *Public Choice* 69 (1991): 153–73; and Gerald Scully, *What Is the Optimal Size of Government in the United States?* (Dallas, TX: National Center for Policy Analysis, 1994).

included, 64.9 percent of families derived income from either transfer programs or government employment in 2022. If the people employed by businesses with government contracts and those receiving subsidies (for example, housing subsidies, the producers of ethanol, sugar and several other agricultural products, and wind and solar energy) were also included, the share of Americans heavily dependent on government would be even larger.

One might think that the large share of Americans receiving transfers is driven by the Medicare and Social Security retirement programs. In order to shed light on this issue, the share receiving transfers for families with only individuals younger than the age of 62 was derived. The pattern for this group was essentially the same as for all families. The percent of the younger family group that were recipients of transfer payments rose from 25.1 percent in 2000 to 37.8 percent in 2022. When government employees are included, just over half of the families with individuals younger than 62 derived income from the government.

What are the implications of these patterns of tax payments and government spending? People who are not paying taxes have little reason to resist increases in government spending because they are not paying for them. In fact, they have every incentive to pressure politicians for more government services and transfers because someone else will be covering their cost. Similarly, people who are dependent on government spending for a sizable share of their income will be more supportive of government spending than those who derive their income from private-sector activities.

Debt financing is also related to the observed pattern of taxing and spending. Borrowing makes it possible for politicians to provide voters with current benefits without having to impose a parallel visible cost in the form of higher taxes. This enables elected officials to increase the number of people dependent on government spending without having to increase current taxes.

To a large degree, the modern democratic political process has become a game in which politicians seek to use the fiscal powers of government to assemble a political majority. Is this a dangerous trend that may undermine democracy and lead to fiscal collapse? Eighteenth-century Scottish philosopher Alexander Tytler warned of this possibility:

> A democracy cannot exist as a permanent form of government. It can only exist until the voters discover that they can vote themselves largesse from the public treasury. From that moment on, the majority always votes for the candidates promising the most benefits from the public treasury with the result that a democracy always collapses over loose fiscal policy.[9]

Is Tytler correct? Are the spending, taxing, and debt financing policies of the United States going to cause a dangerous fiscal crisis? We do not know the answer to this question, but there are troubling signs. Government spending as a share of GDP has increased substantially since 2000. Large budget deficits, even during good times, have pushed the federal debt to more than 100 percent of GDP. The huge expansion in federal debt has resulted in a national debt as a share of the economy that is now well above the level at the conclusion of World War II. Further, the retirement of the baby-boom generation and shortfall of revenues for Social Security and Medicare will continue to push the federal deficit upward in the decade immediately ahead. Rising interest rates have led to a sharp increase in the size of the interest payments on the national debt. Other countries, Greece most recently, have been caught in a debt trap. Actions could be taken to avoid a future crisis, but special interest politics and the myopic nature of the political process make them politically unpopular. We are in the midst of an interesting, though unattractive, experiment in political economy as the United States and other Western democracies face troubled fiscal waters in the years immediately ahead.

---

[9]Some attribute this statement to Lord Thomas Macaulay. The author cannot be verified with certainty. For additional information on this topic, refer to Loren Collins, "The Truth About Tytler" at www.lorencollins.net/tytler.html.

Key Points

- During the first 125 years of U.S. history, federal expenditures per person were small and grew at a relatively slow rate. But the size and nature of government has changed dramatically during the past 100 years. Today, the real (adjusted for inflation) spending per person of the federal government is roughly 120 times the level of 1916.
- During the last six decades, the composition of federal spending has shifted away from national defense and toward spending on income transfers and health care.
- As the size of government has grown, taxes have increased. Taxes impose a burden on the economy over and above the revenue transferred to the government because of (1) the administration and compliance costs and (2) the deadweight losses that accompany taxation.
- Overall, the federal tax system of the United States is highly progressive. Taxes as a percentage of income are approximately 40 times greater for the top quintile (20 percent) of families than for the bottom quintile.
- The size of government of the United States is smaller than that of the major Western European countries but is larger than for a number of high-growth Asian economies.
- When governments focus on the core activities of providing (1) a legal and enforcement structure that protects people and their property from aggression by others and (2) a limited set of public goods, they promote economic growth. However, when governments grow beyond this size, expanding into activities for which they are ill-suited, they deter growth.
- More than half of American families derive benefits from various transfer programs, while the share of the population paying federal income tax has declined substantially during the past two decades. The Social Security and Medicare programs are now running large deficits as the huge baby-boom generation moves into the retirement phase of life. Large budget deficits have already pushed the debt-to-GDP ratio to levels even higher than at the conclusion of World War II, and rising interest rates are causing a sharp increase in the interest payments on the national debt. Special interest politics and the shortsighted nature of political decision-making make it difficult to control government spending and debt and to take the steps needed to avoid a fiscal crisis.

Critical Analysis Questions

1. *How do taxes influence the efficiency of resource use? How much does it cost for the government to raise an additional dollar (or $1 billion) of tax revenue?
2. During the past six decades, there has been a shift in the composition of the federal budget toward more spending on income transfers and health care and a smaller share for national defense. Does economics indicate that this change will help Americans achieve higher living standards? Discuss.
3. Because the structure of the personal income tax is progressive, a larger share of income is taxed at higher rates as real income increases. Therefore, economic growth automatically results in higher taxes unless offsetting legislative action is taken. Do you think this is an attractive feature of the current tax system? Why or why not?
4. Compared with the situation before 1981, the marginal tax rates imposed on individuals and families with high incomes are now lower. What was the top marginal personal income tax rate in 1980? What is the top rate now? What has happened to the share of the income taxes paid by those with high incomes as a result of their lower tax rates? Are you in favor of or opposed to the lower marginal rates? Why?
5. *As the result of changes during the last two decades, the bottom half of income recipients now pay little or no personal income tax. Rather than paying taxes, many of them now receive payments back from the IRS as the result of the Earned Income Tax Credit and Child Tax Credit programs. Do you think the increase in the number of people who pay no taxes will affect the efficiency of the political process? Why or why not?
6. How have the size and functions of government changed during the last two centuries? Did the framers of the U.S. Constitution seek to limit the size of the federal government? If so, how?
7. Can democracy survive if a majority of citizens pay little or nothing in taxes while benefiting directly from a higher level of government spending? Why or why not? Discuss.

*Asterisk denotes questions for which answers are given in Appendix B.

Special Topic 2 The Stock Market: Its Function, Performance, and Potential as an Investment Opportunity

> Though the stock market functions as a voting machine in the short run, it acts as a weighing machine in the long run.
>
> –Ben Graham[1]

The market for corporate shares is called the *stock market*. The stock market makes it possible for investors, including small investors, to share in the profits (and the risks) of large businesses. About one-half of all households now own stock, either directly or indirectly through shares in an equity mutual fund. In recent years, changes in stock prices have often been front-page news. This feature will focus on the economic functions of the stock market and analyze its potential as an investment tool through which people can build their wealth.

Learning Objectives

- **ST02.1** Differentiate between a stock and a bond.
- **ST02.2** Identify the central economic functions performed by the stock market.
- **ST02.3** Explain the random walk theory and its implications in forecasting the future direction of a stock price or the overall stock market.
- **ST02.4** Explain why regular investments into a diverse bundle of stocks over a long period of time are likely to yield an attractive return with minimal risk.

[1]As quoted by Warren Buffett in Carol Loomis, "Warren Buffett on the Stock Market," *Fortune* (December 10, 2001), 80-87.

ST02-1 The Difference Between Stocks and Bonds

Stocks
Ownership shares of a corporation. Corporations raise funds by issuing stock ownership shares, which entitle the owners to a proportional share of the firm's profits. The stock owners are not liable for the debts of the corporation beyond their initial investment. However, there is no assurance that the owners will receive either their initial investment or any return in the future.

Bonds
A promise to repay the principal (amount borrowed) plus interest at a specified time in the future. Organizations such as corporations and governments issue bonds as a method of borrowing from bondholders.

The two most common financial assets are stocks and bonds. Let's make sure you understand the nature of these two instruments. **Stocks** represent ownership of corporate businesses. Stock owners are entitled to the fraction of the firm's future revenues represented by their ownership shares. If the business generates attractive future revenues, the stockholders will gain. The gains of stockholders typically come in the form of either dividends (regular payments to owners) or appreciation in the value of the stock. But there is no assurance the business will be successful and earn income in the future. If unsuccessful, the value of the firm's stock will decline. Although the stockholders are not liable for the debts of the corporation, they may lose all of the funds used to purchase the stock. (Note: Equity is another term for stock.)

Bonds provide businesses, governments, and other organizations with a convenient way to borrow money. These organizations acquire funds from bond purchasers in exchange for the promise (and legal obligation) to pay interest and repay the entire principal (amount borrowed) at specified times in the future. In contrast with ownership of stock shares, owners of bonds can count on the principal and interest to be repaid as long as the organization issuing the bond is solvent.

ST02-2 The Economic Functions of the Stock Market

The stock market performs several important functions in a modern economy. Let's consider three of the most important.

1. The stock market provides investors, including those who are not interested in participating directly in the operation of the firm, with an opportunity to own a fractional share of the firm's future profits. As a firm earns profits, its shareholders may gain as the result of both dividend payments and increases in the market value of the stock. Ownership of stock is risky. There is no guarantee that any firm will be profitable in the future. But the shareholders' potential losses are limited to the amount of their initial investment. Beyond this point, shareholders are not responsible for the debts of the corporations that they own.

2. New stock issues are often an excellent way for firms to obtain funds for growth and product development. Essentially, there are three ways for a firm to obtain additional financing. It can use retained earnings (profits earned but not paid out to stockholders), it can borrow money, or it can sell stock. When borrowing, the firm promises to repay the lender a specific amount, including principal and interest. Conversely, new stock issues provide the firm with additional financing, and the owner of the stock acquires an ownership right to a fraction of the future revenues generated by the firm.

Primary market
The market in which financial institutions aid in the sale of new securities.

Secondary markets
The market in which financial institutions aid in the buying and selling of existing securities.

Newly issued stocks are sold to the public through specialized firms. A firm that issues new stock sells it in the **primary market**. When news reports tell us about how stock prices are changing, they are referring to **secondary markets**, in which previously issued stocks are traded. Secondary markets make it easy to buy and sell listed stock. This is important to the primary market. The initial buyers want to know that their stock will be easy to sell later. Entry is more attractive when exit will be easy. This will help the corporation issuing new stock to sell it for a higher price.

A stock exchange is a secondary market. It is a place where stockbrokers come to arrange trades for buyers and sellers. The largest and best-known stock market is the New York Stock Exchange, in which 8,000 stock and exchange-traded funds are traded. There are other such markets in the United States, as well as in London, Tokyo, Hong Kong, and other trading centers around the world.

3. Stock prices provide information about the quality of business decisions. Changing stock prices reward good decisions and penalize bad ones. It pays for a stockholder, especially a large one, to be alert to whether the firm's decisions are good or bad. Those who spot a corporation's problems early can sell part or all of their stock in that firm before others notice and lower the price by selling their own stock. Similarly, those who first notice decisions that will be profitable can gain by increasing their holdings of the stock. Stockholder alertness benefits the corporation, too. The firm's board of directors can utilize the price changes resulting from investor vigilance to reward good management decisions. They often do so by tying the compensation of the top corporate officers to stock performance. How? Rather than paying these officers entirely in the form of salaries, a board of directors can integrate **stock options** into the compensation package of top executives. On the one hand, when good decisions drive the stock price up, the executives' options will be very valuable. On the other hand, if bad decisions cause the stock price to fall, then the options will have little or no value.

Stock options
The option to buy a specified number of shares of the firm's stock at a designated price. The designated price is generally set so that the options will be quite valuable if the firm's shares increase in price but of little value if their price falls. Thus, when used to compensate top managers, stock options provide a strong incentive to follow policies that will increase the value of the firm.

ST02-3 Stock Market Performance: The Historical Record

Investors in American stocks have done exceedingly well. Furthermore, this has been true over a lengthy period of time. During the last two centuries, after adjustment for inflation, corporate stocks have yielded an average real return of approximately 7 percent per year, compared with a real return of about 3 percent for bonds. The historic returns derived from savings accounts and money market mutual funds are even lower. A 7 percent real return may not sound particularly good, but when it is compounded, it means that the real value of your investment will double every ten years. In contrast, it will take 23 years to double your money at a 3 percent interest return.[2]

The Standard and Poor's 500 Index (S&P 500) is one measure of the performance of the broad stock market. This index factors in the value of dividends as if they were reinvested in the market. Thus, it provides a measure of the rate of return received by investors in the form of both dividends and changes in share prices. **Exhibit ST02-1** presents data on the real rate of return earned by stockholders each year since 1950 as measured by the changes in the S&P 500 during the year. The compound annual nominal rate of return of the S&P 500 was 10.8 percent during the 74-year period. Even after adjustment for inflation, the real compound annual return was 7.2 percent over this lengthy time period. The returns during the 1980s and 1990s were even higher, but the returns since 2000 have been lower than the historic average. During 2008 alone investors experienced a negative 37 percent return.

Exhibit ST02-1 highlights one of the risks that accompanies the ownership of stock: The returns and therefore the value of the stock can be quite volatile. The broad stock market, as measured by the S&P 500, provided double-digit returns during 46 of the 74 years between 1950 and 2023, but the returns were negative during 16 of those years. Stock market investors can never be sure what return they will earn or what the value of their stock holdings will be at a specified time in the future.

---

[2]You can approximate the number of years it will take to double your funds at alternative interest rates by simply dividing the yield into 70. This is sometimes referred to as the *rule of 70*.

Exhibit ST02-1 Annual Return for Stocks, 1950-2023

During the past 74 years, the broad S&P 500 Index indicates that stock investors earned a 10.8 percent compound annual rate of return. Double-digit returns were earned in 46 of the 74 years, whereas returns were negative during only 16 of the years.

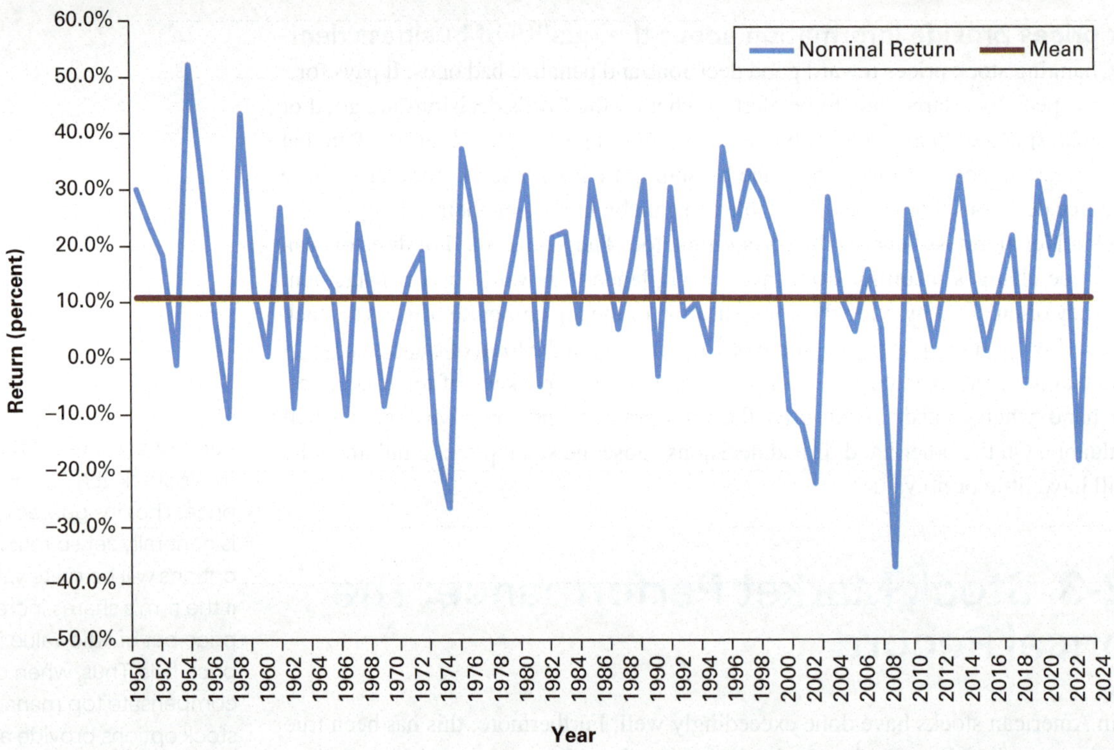

Source: Global Financial Data, http://www.globalfindata.com; and Standard & Poor's, www.standardandpoors.com.

But this volatility is a big reason that stocks yield a significantly higher return than savings accounts, money market certificates, and corporate or government bonds, all of which guarantee you a given nominal return in the future. Because most people value the additional certainty in the yields that bonds and savings accounts provide over stocks, the average return on stocks has to be higher to attract investors away from financial assets with more predictable returns.

As large reductions in stock prices like those of 2008 illustrate, stocks are risky. However, historically stock prices have rebounded and yielded attractive returns when held over a lengthy time frame. Even if one would have started a regular monthly investment program at just about the worst possible time in the history of the U.S. stock market—just before the crash of 1929 and the Great Depression of the 1930s in which the value of stocks declined by almost 90 percent—one would still have earned a better return within four years than a person who had invested in U.S. Treasury bills and would have ended up with a 13 percent nominal return (or an 11 percent real return) over the next 30 years.

ST02-4 The Interest Rate, the Value of Future Income, and Stock Prices

The present value of the firm's expected future net earnings (profit) underlies today's price of a firm's stock. What those future profits are worth to an investor today depends on three things: (1) the expected size of future net earnings, (2) when these earnings will be achieved, and (3) how much the investor discounts the future income. The last depends on the interest rate. As we noted in an earlier chapter, the present-value procedure can be used to determine the current value of any future income (or cost) stream. If *D* represents dividends (and gains from a higher stock price) earned in various years in the future (indicated by the subscripts) and *i* represents the discount or interest rate, the present value of the future income stream is:

$$PV = \frac{D_1}{(1+i)} + \frac{D_2}{(1+i)^2} + \cdots + \frac{D_3}{(1+i)^3}$$

For a specific annual income stream in perpetuity, the present value is simply equal to *R*/*i*, where *R* is the annual revenue stream and *i* is the interest rate. Thus, for example, when the interest rate is 12.5 percent, the discounted value of $10 of future income to be received each year in perpetuity is $80 ($10 divided by 0.125), eight times the stream of earnings. But when the interest rate is 5 percent, the discounted value of this same income stream is $200 ($10 divided by 0.05), or 20 times the stream of earnings. Therefore, if the $10 represented the expected future income stream from a share of stock, the present value of the income stream would be higher when the interest rate was lower. Other things being constant, lower interest rates will increase the value of future income and thereby increase the market value of stocks.

As the present value formula indicates, an increase in future net earnings that the asset is expected to generate will increase the current market value of the asset. On the other hand, higher interest rates will reduce the present value of the future income and therefore reduce the market value of the asset generating the income stream. Lower interest rates will exert the opposite impact. Thus, the market value of an asset will be directly related to the expected future net income stream generated by the asset and inversely related to the interest rate.

Exhibit ST02-2 presents data for the nominal interest rates on ten-year U.S. Treasury bonds since 1900. Note that nominal interest rates were particularly high in the late 1970s and early 1980s. On the other hand, interest rates were low—less than 4 percent during 1900–1911, 1925–1958, and 2008–2022. In fact, the nominal interest rate has been less than 3 percent throughout 2012–2022. Starting in 2022, the nominal interest rate started to rise, reaching over 4 percent in early 2024.

How can you determine whether stock prices are high or low? The present value formula indicates that the price of a stock (or group of stocks) will depend on both the interest rate and the expected future earnings of the stock. The price/earnings ratio for a stock provides some information, but the ratio of price to current earnings is often a misleading indicator because of the fluctuations in corporate earnings over the business cycle. Corporate earnings generally fall sharply during a recession, and this will push the price/earnings ratio upward, making it look like stocks are really expensive. In turn, corporate earnings generally increase substantially during an economic boom. This will reduce the price/earnings ratio, making it appear that stocks are cheap. Because of the fluctuations in corporate earnings over the business cycle, the current price/earnings ratio is often misleading. In many cases, it provides investors with precisely the wrong signal. Therefore, instead of focusing on the current price/earnings ratio, it makes sense to focus on the relationship between the stock price and earnings over a more lengthy time frame such as a decade.

This is precisely what Robert Shiller, the 2013 Nobel Prize winner, has done. Shiller's methodology averages the inflation-adjusted earnings figures over a ten-year period to minimize the distortions resulting from both business cycle and inflation effects. **Exhibit ST02-3** presents Shiller's cyclically adjusted price/earnings (CAPE) ratio for the S&P 500 for 1900–2023. This ratio is a weighted average of the current stock price divided by the ten-year average of earnings adjusted for inflation of the 500 stocks in the index. Other things constant, when this ratio is high, it indicates that stocks are relatively expensive. In contrast, when the ratio is low, it signals that stocks are relatively cheap.

As Exhibit ST02-3 shows, the cyclically adjusted price/earnings ratio indicated that stock prices were exceedingly high in the late 1920s, late 1960s, and late 1990s. Interestingly,

Exhibit ST02-2 Long-Term Government Bond Rate, 1900-2023

The nominal interest rate on the ten-year Treasury bond is shown here. Note the rate rose gradually during the two decades following World War II and increased still more rapidly during the 1970s and early 1980s. Since the early 1980s, it has trended downward and declined to less than 3 percent during 2012-2022. What is the expected impact of the recent low-interest rates on stock prices? Is the data of Exhibit 1 for 2012-2022 consistent with this view?

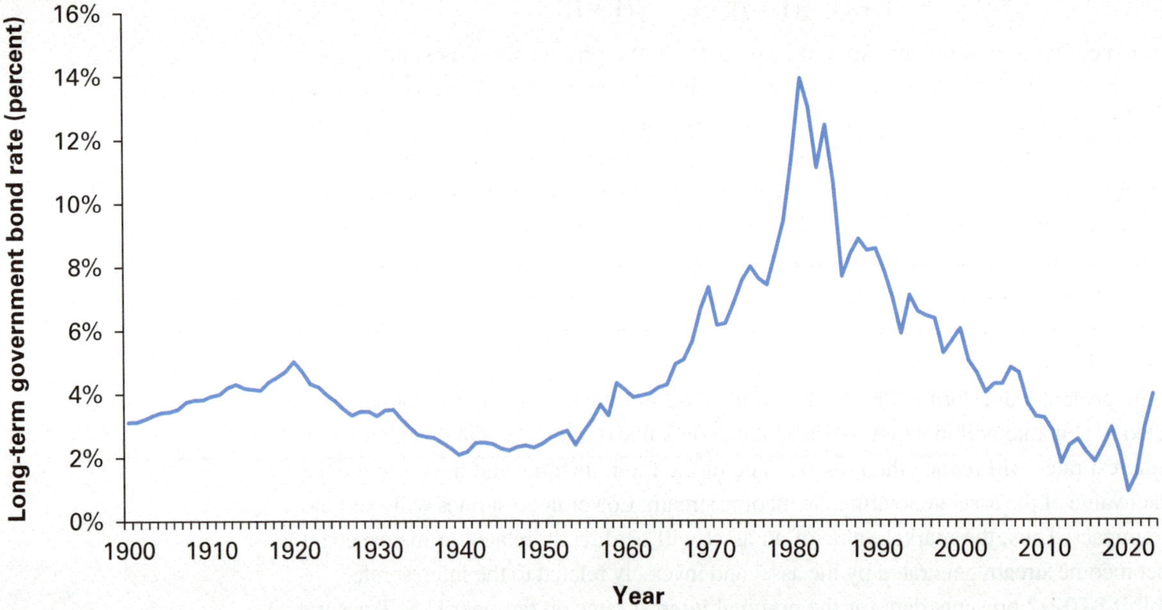

Source: http://www.econ.yale.edu/~shiller/data.htm. The interest rate is the ten-year Treasury bond rate starting in 1953. Before 1953, it is the government bond yield from Sidney Homer and Richard Sylla, *A History of Interest Rates*, 4th Edition (Hoboken, NJ: Wiley, 2005)

each of these time intervals was followed by an extended period of declining stock values and poor stock market performance. In contrast, the CAPE ratio indicated that stocks were relatively cheap during 1918–1923, 1932, 1942–1944, and 1978–1984. Each of these periods was followed by a substantial move upward in stock prices.

ST02-5 The Random Walk Theory of the Stock Market

Random walk theory
The theory that current stock prices already reflect known information about the future. Therefore, the future movement of stock prices will be determined by surprise occurrences. This will cause them to change in a random fashion.

Most economists adhere to the **random walk theory** of stock prices. According to this theory, current stock prices already reflect all available information that is known or can be predicted with any degree of accuracy, including information about the future state of corporate earnings, interest rates, the health of the economy, and other factors that influence stock prices. In other words, current stock prices will already reflect the best information currently available. In the future, the direction of stock prices will be driven by surprise occurrences—things that differ from what people are currently anticipating. By their very nature, these factors are unpredictable. If they were predictable, they would already be reflected in current stock prices.

The random walk theory applies to the price of a specific stock as well as to the market as a whole. The prices of specific stocks will reflect their future earnings prospects. The stock prices of firms with attractive future profit potential will be high relative to their

Exhibit ST02-3 Cyclically Adjusted Price/Earnings Ratio, 1900-2023

The cyclically adjusted price/earnings (CAPE) for the S&P 500 is shown here. This ratio is the stock price divided by the ten-year average of earnings adjusted for inflation. It is an indicator of whether stock prices are high or low. Note that, the ratio signaled that stock prices were exceedingly high in the late 1920s, late 1960s, and the late 1990s. Each of these periods was followed by poor stock market performance. Similarly, the CAPE ratio indicated that stocks were relatively cheap during 1918-1923, 1932, 1942-1944, and 1978-1984. Each of these periods was followed by a substantial upward move in stock prices.

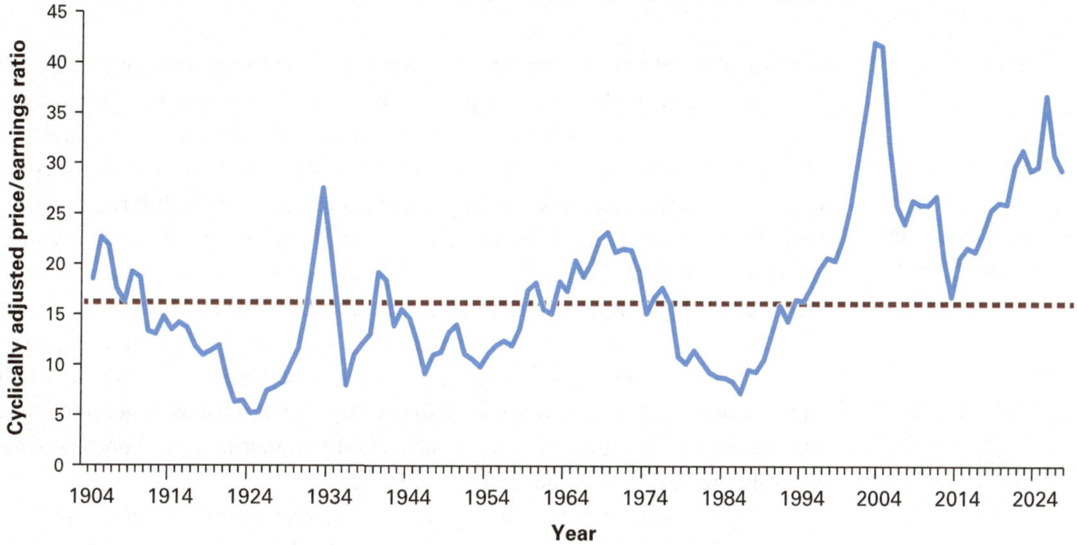

Source: http://www.econ.yale.edu/~shiller/data.htm.

current earnings. Consequently, their current prices will already reflect their attractive future earnings prospects. The opposite will be true for firms with poor future prospects. Although numerous factors affect the future price of any specific stock, changes in the current price will be driven by changes that differ from current expectations. Thus, because the future prices of both specific stocks and the market as a whole are driven by unexpected and unpredictable factors, no one can consistently forecast their future path with any degree of accuracy.

As Exhibit ST02-3 shows, the cyclically adjusted price/earnings ratio for the S&P 500 has been above 29 since mid-year 2017. Compared to historic levels, the CAPE ratio was exceedingly high in early 2024. Does this mean that stock prices will soon plunge to substantially lower levels? Some analysts fear that this will be the case, and the high CAPE ratio provides reason for caution. But, do not forget that low interest rates will result in higher asset prices, including the prices of stocks. During the past decade, the share of population in high-income developed countries age 50 to 75 years has increased relative to the share under age 50. Because the expanding age grouping tends to be savers and the contracting group borrowers, these changes are increasing the supply of loanable funds relative to the demand, thereby placing downward pressure on interest rates.[3] This demographic factor is expected to continue for at least another decade. If interest rates drop in the future, stock prices (and the CAPE ratio) may remain high relative to their expected earnings in the future. However, demographics are not the only factor influencing interest rates. If nominal interest rates are high in the future, stock prices are likely to fall from their

[3]For a detailed analysis of the impact of demographic changes on interest rates, refer to Michael A. Walker, "Why Are Interest Rates So Low? A Framework for Modeling Current Global Financial Developments," Fraser Institute Report, February 2016, https://www.fraserinstitute.org/sites/default/files/why-are-interest-rates-so-low.pdf.

lofty 2024 levels. But no one can be certain about the future direction of interest rates. Therefore, as the random walk theory indicates, no one will be able to forecast the future direction of stock prices with any degree of certainty.

ST02-6 How the Ordinary Investor Can Beat the Experts

Portfolio
All the stocks, bonds, or other securities held by an individual or corporation for investment purposes.

Equity mutual funds
A corporation that pools the funds of investors, including small investors, and uses them to purchase a bundle of stocks.

Historically, ordinary Americans have often refrained from investing in the stock market because of the volatility of stock prices. The value of any specific stock can rise or fall by a huge amount within a relatively short time period. But the risk accompanying these movements can be reduced by holding a diverse **portfolio**, a collection of stocks characterized by relatively small holdings of a large number of companies in different markets and industries. **Equity mutual funds** make this possible. They provide the ordinary investor with a low-cost method of owning a diverse bundle of stocks. An equity mutual fund is a corporation that buys and holds shares of stock in many firms. This diversification puts the law of large numbers to work for you. Whereas some of the investments in a diversified portfolio will do poorly, others will do extremely well. The performance of the latter will offset that of the former, and the rate of return will converge toward the average. Remember, the average real return of equities has been substantially higher than for bonds, savings accounts, and other readily accessible methods of saving.

A second source of risk facing the stock market investor is the possibility that nearly all stocks in the market can rise or fall together when expectations about the entire economy change. This has happened on several occasions. For example, on October 19, 1987, the stocks listed in the Dow Jones Industrial Average lost more than 22 percent of their value in just one trading day. The high-tech stocks listed on the NASDAQ exchange lost about 70 percent of their value during 2000 and 2001; and most recently the S&P 500 lost about 57 percent of its value between October 2007 and March 2009. However, the risks accompanying such short-term movements can be substantially reduced if an investor either continually adds to or holds a diverse portfolio of stocks over a lengthy period of time, say, 30 or 35 years.

Exhibit ST02-4 illustrates this point. This exhibit shows the highest and lowest real returns (the returns adjusted for inflation) earned from stock market investments for periods of varying lengths between the years 1871 and 2023. The exhibit assumes that the investor paid a fixed amount annually into a mutual fund that mirrored the S&P 500, a basket of stocks thought to represent the market as a whole. Clearly, huge swings are possible when stocks are held for only a short time period. During the 1871–2023 period, the single-year returns of the S&P 500 ranged from 47.2 percent to −40.8 percent. Even over a five-year period, the compound annual returns ranged from 29.8 percent to −16.7 percent. Note that the "best returns" and "worst returns" converged as the length of the investment period increased. When a 35-year period was considered, the compound annual return for the best 35 years between 1871 and 2023 was 9.5 percent, compared with 2.7 percent for the worst 35 years.[4] Thus, the annual real return of stocks during the worst-case scenario was about the same as the real return for bonds. Furthermore, the annual real rate of return from the stock investments during the period was 7 percent—more than twice the comparable rate for bonds.

The bottom line is this: When held over a lengthy period, a diverse portfolio of stocks has yielded a high rate of return, and the variation in that return has been low. Thus, for the

[4]Based on Liqun Liu, Andrew J. Rettenmaier, and Zijun Wang, "Social Security and Market Risk" (Working Paper Number 244, National Center for Policy Analysis, Washington, DC, July 2001). Data updated through 2023.

Exhibit ST02-4 The Risk of Holding Stocks Is Lower When Held for a Lengthy Time Period

This exhibit shows the best and the worst annualized real performance for each investment period from 1871 to 2023. It shows that there is less risk of a low or negative return when an investment in a portfolio of stocks (S&P 500) is held for a longer period of time.

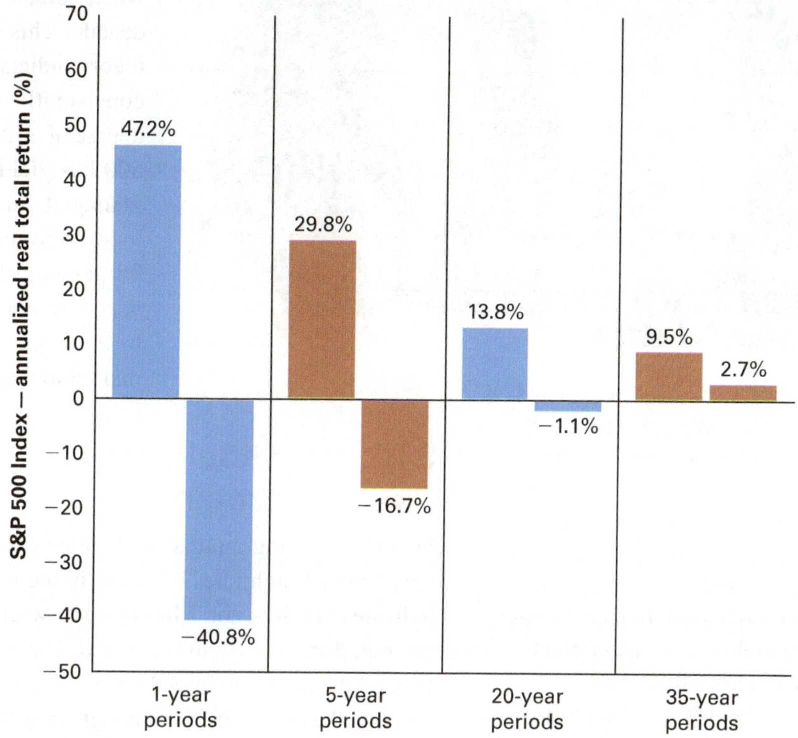

Source: Liqun Liu, Andrew J. Rettenmaier, and Zijun Wang, "Social Security and Market Risk," National Center for Policy Analysis Working Paper Number 244 (July 2001). The returns are based on the assumption that an individual invests a fixed amount for each year in the investment period. Data updated through 2023.

long-term investor, such as a person saving for their retirement years, a diverse portfolio of stocks is not particularly risky.

ST02-7 The Advantages of Indexed Mutual Funds

When purchasing a mutual fund, the investor can choose either a managed or an indexed fund. A **managed equity mutual fund** is one in which an "expert," generally supported by a research staff, tries to pick and choose the stock holdings of the fund in a manner that will maximize its rate of return. In contrast, an **indexed equity mutual fund** merely holds stocks in the same proportion as they exist in a broad stock market index like the S&P 500 or the Dow Jones Industrials.

In the case of indexed funds, neither comprehensive research nor extensive stock trading is needed because the fund merely seeks to mirror the index and earn the rate of return of the broad market that it represents. Thus, because they do not spend much on either research or stock trading, the operating costs of indexed funds are substantially lower than they are for managed funds. Therefore, they are able to charge lower fees, which means that a larger share of the investor's money flows directly into the purchase of stock.

Managed equity mutual fund
An equity mutual fund that has a portfolio manager who decides what stocks will be held in the fund and when they will be bought or sold. A research staff generally provides support for the fund manager.

Indexed equity mutual fund
An equity mutual fund that holds a portfolio of stocks that matches their share (or weight) in a broad stock market index such as the S&P 500. The overhead of these funds is usually quite low because their expenses on stock trading and research are low.

fizkes/iStock/Getty Images

Are stocks riskier than bonds? If held for only a short time—five years, for example—stocks are riskier. However, when held over lengthy periods, such as 20 or 30 years, historically the rate of return on stocks has been both higher and less variable than that of bonds. What does this imply for people in their twenties and thirties who are saving for their retirement? Where should they put their funds?

The average rate of return yielded by a broad indexed fund beats the return of almost all managed mutual funds when comparisons are made over periods of time such as a decade. This is not surprising because, as the random walk theory indicates, not even the experts will be able to forecast consistently the future direction of stock prices with any degree of accuracy. Over the typical ten-year period, the S&P 500 has yielded a higher return than 85 percent of actively managed funds. And over 20-year periods, mutual funds indexed to the S&P 500 have generally outperformed about 98 percent of actively managed funds.[5] Thus, the odds are very low, about 1 in 50, that you or anyone else will be able to select an actively managed fund that will do better than the market average *over the long run*.

ST02-7a Should You Invest in a Fund Because of Its Past Performance?

People marketing mutual funds often encourage customers to invest in mutual funds that have yielded high rates of return in the past. This sounds like a good strategy, but history indicates that it is not. Mutual funds with outstanding records over a 5- or 10-year period often perform poorly in the future. The top 20 managed equity funds of the 1990s outperformed the S&P 500 by 3.9 percent per year over the course of the decade. But if investors entering the market in 2000 thought they would beat the market by choosing the "hot" funds of the 1990s, they would have been disappointed. The top 20 funds of the 1990s underperformed the S&P 500 by 1.3 percent per year during the 2000s.

Why is past performance such an unreliable indicator? Two factors provide insight on the answer to this question. First, some of the mutual funds with above-average returns during a period were merely lucky. After all, if you flip a coin 100 times, you will not always get 50 heads and 50 tails. Sometimes, the coin will come up heads maybe 60 times out of 100. But this does not mean you can expect 60 heads during the next sequence of 100. So it is with stock market mutual funds. Given that there are a large number of funds, some of them will have above-average performance for a time period. But this does not mean that the above-average performance can be expected in the future.

Second, a strategy that works well in one environment, inflationary conditions, for example, is often disastrous when conditions change. For example, mutual funds with substantial holdings of gold-mining companies did exceedingly well during the inflationary 1970s. But their performance was disastrous during the 1980s and 1990s as the inflation was brought under control. Similarly, some mutual funds that performed well during the bull market of the 1990s were among the worst performers during the bear market that began in 2000.

What is the most important takeaway from this analysis? Virtually none of the experts are able to "beat the market average" consistently over lengthy time periods and changing market conditions. Regular contributions into an indexed equity mutual fund will provide you with attractive returns on long-term investments because broad market indexes such as the S&P 500 will outperform the "expert" stock pickers in the long run. This is valuable information, and you are unlikely to hear it from brokerage firms and other experts trying to sell their services to you. But knowing this will make you a smarter investor.

[5]Refer to Jeremy J. Siegel, *Stocks for the Long Run*, 3rd ed. (New York: McGraw-Hill, 2002), 342-43.

Key Points

- The stock market makes it possible for investors without either specialized business skills or the time to become involved in the operation of a business firm to share in the risks and opportunities that accompany the ownership of corporate businesses.
- During the last two centuries, after adjustment for inflation, corporate stocks have yielded a real return of approximately 7 percent per year, compared with a real return of about 3 percent for bonds and even lower yields for savings accounts and money market mutual funds.
- The present value of an asset such as shares of a stock will reflect the expected future stream of income generated by the asset discounted by the interest rate. As interest rates decline, this discounted value will rise. This explains why stock prices (a) are highly sensitive to a change in the interest rate and (b) generally move in the opposite direction of the interest rate change.
- Most economists adhere to the random walk theory of stock prices. According to this theory, current stock prices already reflect all information about factors influencing stock prices that is known or can be forecast with any degree of accuracy. Thus, the future direction of stock prices will be driven by surprise occurrences, and, as a result, no one will be able to forecast future stock prices with any degree of accuracy.
- Buying and selling individual stocks without specialized knowledge for a quick profit is very risky. But regular investment into a diverse portfolio of unrelated stocks over a lengthy period of time greatly reduces the risk of stock ownership.
- An equity mutual fund that is tied to a broad stock market index like the S&P 500 provides an attractive method for long-term investors to obtain relatively high yields with minimal risk. Indexed mutual funds have substantially lower operating costs than managed funds because they engage in less trading and have no need for either a market expert or research staff.

Critical Analysis Questions

1. *A friend just inherited $50,000. She informs you of her investment plans and asks for your advice. "I want to put it into the stock market and use it for my retirement in 30 years. What do you think is the best plan that will provide high returns at a relatively low risk?" What answer would you give? Explain.
2. Suppose that more expansionary monetary policy leads to inflation and higher nominal interest rates. How is this likely to affect the value of stocks? Explain.
3. *Alphabet (Google) stock rose from $5 at year-end 2004 to $151 per share at year-end 2023. Google has made sizable profits but never paid a dividend. Why were people willing to pay such a high price knowing that they might not get dividends for many years?
4. If an investment adviser gives you some hot new stock tip, is it likely to be a "sure thing"? Why or why not? If you have a stockbroker and purchase the stocks promoted by the broker, are you likely to earn a high return on your stock investments? Why or why not?
5. *Nominal interest rates were historically low during 2010–2020, and they trended slightly downward. What impact did the low and declining interest rates have on stock prices during this period? Why?
6. What is an indexed equity mutual fund? What is a managed equity mutual fund? How will the administrative costs of the two differ?
7. What is the random walk theory of stock prices? What does it indicate about the ability of "experts" to forecast accurately the future direction of stock prices?
8. Are stocks a risky investment? How can one reduce the risk accompanying stock market investments?

*Asterisk denotes questions for which answers are given in Appendix B.

Special Topic 3

Keynes and Hayek: Contrasting Views on Sound Economics and the Role of Government

> We've been going back and forth for a century
> [Keynes] I want to steer markets,
> [Hayek] I want them set free
>
> —Chorus from Keynes-Hayek video[1]

John Maynard Keynes and Friedrich August Hayek are two of the most important economists of the twentieth century. Moreover, their scholarly work represents sharply contrasting theories and ideas about the central issues of our day, including economic instability, central planning, and the operation of the political process. The debate between Keynes and Hayek provides a vivid example of how scholarly writings have consequences.

Learning Objectives

ST03.1 Explain why the views of John Maynard Keynes and Friedrich Hayek are often compared and contrasted.

ST03.2 Describe the views of Keynes and Hayek with regard to the primary cause of economic instability and what might be done to reduce it.

ST03.3 Describe the views of Keynes and Hayek regarding the ability of government intervention to improve the efficiency of markets.

[1]From the video "Fear the Boom and Bust: Keynes versus Hayek" available at www.youtube.com/watch?v=d0nERTFo-Sk.

ST03-1 Keynes and Hayek: Two Great Economists

Even though their views are in many ways polar opposites, Keynes and Hayek both command respect among professional economists. Keynes is widely regarded as the most influential economist of the twentieth century. Hayek was the recipient of the 1974 Nobel Prize in Economics. Interestingly, Keynes and Hayek were contemporaries at Cambridge University and the London School of Economics in the early 1940s. During World War II, they even spent a night together on the roof of the chapel of King's College, Cambridge watching for German bombers.

Keynes's *General Theory* provided a reasonable explanation of what went wrong during the Great Depression and what could be done to prevent such an event from occurring in the future. His ideas inspired a generation of economists that transformed macroeconomic analysis. Hayek was born in Vienna in 1899, and he was a rising star in the 1930s. The London School of Economics lured him from Austria, at least partly to counter the influence of Keynes and the reputation he brought to rival Cambridge University. In his 1944 book *The Road to Serfdom*, Hayek argued that the growth of government was endangering freedom and leading to tyranny in the Western democracies, just as it had done in both Nazi Germany and the Soviet Union.

Keynes and Hayek were polar opposites not only in their economic views but also in their personality characteristics. Keynes was outgoing and dominant. Some charged that he was arrogant, but all recognized that his skills as a persuader were supreme. In contrast, Hayek was quiet and unassuming. While Keynes reveled in policy-making, Hayek was content to remain outside policy circles. Keynes was optimistic, and his message was well suited for the "We're fixing it" mentality of politicians. On the other hand, Hayek's message was not one political officials like: Policy-makers have messed things up, and it will take time for the market to correct their errors.

A popular PBS video series, *Commanding Heights* (Episode One: "The Battle of Ideas"), used the contrasting views of these two economists to illustrate how major trends in economic thinking impacted global economic events during the twentieth century.[2] Following in this tradition, this special topic will use the ideas of Keynes and Hayek to explain and contrast their viewpoints and the alternative theories they represent. Most economists recognize the validity of many of the arguments presented by both sides. Hence, most are eclectic; their views are a mixture of these two polar views.[3]

An entertaining pair of rap videos, "Fear the Boom and Bust: Keynes versus Hayek" and "Fight of the Century: Keynes vs. Hayek Round Two," available on YouTube, contrast the views of these two famous economists.

Photo of Keynes and Hayek

ST03-2 Keynes, Hayek, and Great Debates in Economics

The contrasting views of Keynes and Hayek can be generalized to help illustrate the most important debates in economics. Much of the disagreement can be attributed to differing views of the effectiveness of markets versus the political process in coordinating economic activity.

[2]The PBS series was based on the book by Daniel Yergin and Joseph Stanislaw, *The Commanding Heights: The Battle Between Government and the Marketplace That Is Remaking the Modern World* (New York: Simon & Schuster, 1998).
[3]There is some evidence that just prior to his heart attack and untimely death in 1946, Keynes developed a genuine appreciation for the views of Hayek. After reading the *Road to Serfdom*, Keynes wrote the following to Hayek in a personal letter about the book: "Orally and philosophically I find myself in agreement with virtually the whole of it, and not only in agreement with it, but in a deeply moved agreement."

ST03-2a What Is the Cause and Cure for the Business Cycle?

The underlying causes of the business cycle and potential effectiveness of policy responses have been focal points of debate among economists for at least a century. The perspectives of Keynes and Hayek represent alternative viewpoints on this issue.

The Keynesian viewpoint argues that capitalist market economies are inherently unstable. Private investment in particular is fickle and prone to extreme fluctuations driven by changes in business optimism, or what Keynes referred to as "animal spirits." Moreover, the booms and busts will tend to feed on themselves, and therefore, a market economy will swing back and forth between a boom that will lead to inflation and a bust that will generate high rates of unemployment that may persist for long periods of time.

But there is good news in the Keynesian theory. Government can use fiscal and monetary policy to control aggregate demand and thereby promote economic stability. During a recession, government spending should be increased to offset the weak private investment, taxes should be reduced to stimulate consumption, budget deficits should be used to finance these activities, and monetary policy should keep interest rates low. With large multiplier effects, debt-financed government spending can have large impacts on aggregate spending, helping to cure the recessions. Keynesians focus on policies that promote consumption (both private and government) over those that encourage savings. In Keynesian models, spending is the key component driving the economy. In fact, Keynesians refer to "the paradox of thrift" in which if individuals increase their savings, the economy will be harmed because the saving will drain funds away from consumption spending. Keynesians view government spending as more stimulating than tax cuts precisely because individuals will save part of a tax cut, and therefore, the entire amount of the tax cut will not flow into consumption.

In contrast, the Hayekian viewpoint argues that booms and busts are caused by perverse government policy and that the economy would be considerably more stable if political decision-makers followed stable policies and refrained from activist interventions. Several schools of thought in macroeconomics share this view but differ with regard to the explanation. The monetarists, for example, would point to the improper timing of changes in monetary policy, whereas the Austrians (including Hayek) would blame excessive credit expansion by the Fed that pushes interest rates to artificially low levels. At the abnormally low interest rates, businesses are induced to undertake investments that will later prove to be both unprofitable and unsustainable. In the wake of the financial crisis of 2008–2009, the Austrian theory of the business cycle attracted renewed interest because it provided a plausible explanation of what actually occurred, particularly in the housing market.

The core of the Austrian view is that the market interest rate is one of the most important prices in the economy and when the central bank manipulates this rate, it distorts the signals sent to borrowers and lenders. In the Austrian view, the interest rate is a key determinant of the time structure of capital and the length of the production process. When interest rates are low, the time structure of production lengthens as longer-term investments become more profitable. On the other hand, when interest rates are high, the time structure of production shortens as the higher interest rates make longer-term investments less attractive. Undertaking a five-year process of building a new factory, for example, might be profitable at a lower interest rate but not a higher one.

Normally, changes in the market interest rate correspond to changes in the time preferences of consumers. When households cut back on current consumption and save more for their retirement, for example, they are sending a signal to producers that they want fewer goods today in exchange for more goods in the future. The increase in saving (the supply of loanable funds) will result in lower real interest rates. In turn, the lower interest rates will provide entrepreneurs with the incentive to undertake longer-term investments that will expand the supply of consumer goods in the future.

Hayekians believe savings is a key source of growth. Saving provides the necessary funds for bank loans and the funding of business investment for machinery and equipment that increase productivity. When individuals save, this doesn't harm the economy by reducing consumption, it helps the economy by expanding investment, and this investment enhances our ability to produce in the future, leading to economic growth.

Summarizing, Keynesians believe that the economy is inherently unstable and that government should play an active role in offsetting swings in private spending and aggregate demand. In contrast, Hayekians believe that the primary source of economic instability is government intervention and that a more hands-off policy would result in more stability, investment, and long-term growth.

ST03-2b Should an Economy be Directed By Government Planning or Decentralized Individual Planning and the Invisible Hand of Market Prices?

The Keynesian view holds that government intervention is needed not only to keep the macroeconomy on track but also to correct market failures and ensure an equitable distribution of income. Relying on information derived from economists and other experts, Keynesians believe that policy-makers will be able to selectively intervene in ways that will improve market outcomes. In Keynesian models, government is often portrayed as a benevolent social planner that can step in whenever market outcomes are less than ideal and implement an idealized correction.

Keynesian economists are more likely to view potential market failures such as externalities, information problems, public goods, and lack of competition as widespread and damaging to the overall economy. As a result, they are also more likely to favor increased government regulations on the behavior of individuals and businesses as well as controls on prices and wages (including minimum wages). In addition, they view markets and prices as more rigid and not rapidly adjusting to equilibrium.

In contrast, Hayekians argue that government planners do not have sufficient information to direct the economy and their efforts to do so will do more damage than good. According to the Hayekian view, decentralized decision-making, directed by market prices, will be a more reliable method of directing resources into productive projects and away from ones that are counterproductive. Instead of centralized planning, individuals should be left free to make their own plans, relying on information and incentives communicated by market prices, competitive forces, and the profit and loss system. Hayekians believe that a spontaneous order will emerge from the market process and that this order will result in more economic freedom and economic progress. The contrast is not between having planning and not having planning; instead, the contrast is between having a centralized government make plans for everyone versus allowing individuals to make their own plans over the resources they control.

Moreover, dynamic competition provides decision-makers with a strong incentive to discover better ways of doing things, improve technologies, and institute practical innovations that will improve our lives. In this view, the information necessary to guide the economy is not known to anyone in total, but instead is generated through the process of decentralized market interaction. According to Hayekians, the proper role of government is simply to provide the rule of law, enforce contracts, and protect property rights, leaving the rest to market forces.

Put simply, Keynesians believe that markets suffer from widespread problems that result in inefficient allocation of resources and undesirable outcomes and that interventions by government planners will generally improve the situation. On the other hand, Hayekians believe that the invisible hand of markets will be more likely to direct individuals and businesses toward productive actions and that political decision-makers have neither the incentive nor information to direct resources reliably toward productive projects and away from unproductive projects.

ST03-2c Can Democratic Decision-Making Be Counted On to Allocate Resources Efficiently?

As we discussed in Chapter 6, public-choice analysis provides insights on the operation of the political process. It indicates that the incentives confronted by voters, interest groups, politicians, and bureaucrats will sometimes conflict with sound policy and the efficient allocation of resources. Even when decisions are made democratically, the political process will often favor well-organized interest groups and shortsighted policies that generate highly visible gains at the expense of costs that are less visible. Predictably, some inefficient use of resources will arise from these forces. Put another way, there is "government failure" as well as "market failure."

The Keynesian perspective seldom addresses this issue directly. Instead, it is assumed that the job of the economists is to figure out the ideal or optimal solutions, and once these are developed, political decision-makers can be expected to adopt them. Moreover, many Keynesians charge that analysis of how the political process works is outside the scope of economics and therefore that those who address this issue are not really addressing economic issues. Keynes himself had great confidence in his ability to convince policy-makers to adopt his advice. Within the Keynesian framework, it is essentially assumed that political decision-makers will implement policies in a proper manner.

The Hayekian perspective argues that the structure of incentives and institutions exert a major impact on how government works. The government failures described within public-choice theory will be a major problem or barrier to implementing good policy. Thus, it is vitally important to adopt institutions and constitutional rules that bring personal self-interest of policy-makers into harmony with growth and prosperity.

The father of economics, Adam Smith, held a similar view. Smith stated,

> The man of system is apt to be very wise in his own conceit. He seems to imagine that he can arrange the different members of a great society with as much ease as the hand arranges the different pieces upon a chess-board; he does not consider that the pieces upon the chess-board have not another principle of motion besides that which the hand impresses upon them; but that, in the great chess-board of human society, every single piece has a principle of motion of its own, although different from that which the legislature might choose to impress upon it. If those two principles coincide and act in the same direction, the game of human society will go on easily and harmoniously, and is very likely to be happy and successful. If they are opposite or different, the game will go on miserably, and the society must be at all times in the highest degree of disorder.[4]

Whereas some economists view the government as a corrective device that can be counted on to fix problems within the market, others view the potential failures of government to be larger than the potential failures of the market. Public policies are determined by a complex interaction of special-interest groups, voters, elected officials, and government employees who react to the personal incentives they face. The individuals involved in the process of collective decision-making react to incentives in their personal behavior as workers and consumers, and their actions within the political realm are governed by these same incentives. In other words, there is no reason to assume that voters or elected officials behave any differently in their motivations when they step into political roles.

When voters are uninformed about the political process, powerful interest groups will be able to get government policies enacted that favor them at the expense of the general

[4]Adam Smith, *The Theory of Moral Sentiments*, Glasgow Edition of Oxford University Press (Indianapolis: Liberty Fund, Inc., [1790] 1976): 233–34. Also available at www.econlib.org/library/Smith/smMS6.html#VI.II.42).]

public. The government failures discussed in Chapter 6, including the special-interest effect, the shortsightedness effect, and the lack of incentives for efficiency within government budgets, create a situation in which one cannot automatically assume government intervention will improve even a problematic area within the market.

Thus, an area of continued debate in economics regards the relative effectiveness of the political process in allocating resources. This debate takes on two dimensions: disagreements about the degree to which markets are efficient and need correction and disagreements about the degree to which government actions are efficient at solving these potential shortcomings.

Keynes and Hayek represent two of the most important strands of economic thinking. Although it is somewhat of an oversimplification to consider it simply a debate of Keynes versus Hayek, it is a general framework for understanding the two main sides of the larger debates within economic theory. In reality, there are many different schools of thought, each with its own explanations for the relative effectiveness of market outcomes and government interventions that generally reflect some elements of both sides. As a student in economics, it is useful to understand both of these perspectives and their underlying foundations.

Key Points

- John Maynard Keynes and Friedrich Hayek are giants in the economics profession. Their theories and ideas represent contrasting views on several of the central issues of economics.
- Although there are many different schools of thought in economics, they can be grouped roughly into (1) those that view market outcomes as often problematic and government interventions as effective and (2) those that alternatively view market outcomes as generally efficient and government interventions as suffering from various shortcomings.
- Keynes believed that market economies were inherently unstable and government intervention in the form of fiscal and monetary stimulus could be used effectively to promote economic stability. Hayek believed that economic instability was primarily the result of malinvestment generated by monetary and credit expansion and that government stimulus would slow market adjustments and the recovery process.
- Keynesians stress the role of aggregate demand and spending in the macroeconomy and view savings as a leakage detrimental to the economy. In contrast, Hayekians have a more favorable view of the role of savings in providing the funds necessary for investment and growth in productivity and output.
- Keynesians believe that government intervention can generally improve market outcomes. Hayekians believe that policy-makers simply do not have the information or incentives to plan the economy effectively and that their efforts to do so would be far less efficient than allocation through markets.
- Keynesians believe that the job of the economist is to develop policies that will reduce economic instability and correct market failures. Keynesian analysis largely ignores how economic incentives influence the operation of the political process. Hayekians recognize that the political incentive structure often caters to well-organized interest groups and results in the adoption of shortsighted policies. Thus, they stress the importance of legal and political institutions that will provide both market participants and political decision-makers with incentives to engage in productive rather than counterproductive actions.

Critical Analysis Questions

1. *According to Keynes, when the economy is in a recession, increased government spending can bring the economy back to full employment. This spending could be on conducting a war with the military or on financing public works projects. Hayekians would alternatively argue that building and dropping bombs only destroys valuable resources. Why would a Keynesian view a war as stimulating?

2. Is savings harmful or beneficial to the economy? Contrast the views of Keynes and Hayek on this issue.
3. Without government intervention, would the economy fluctuate more or less over the business cycle? Contrast the views of Keynes and Hayek on this issue. Be sure to address both the inherent stability of the market economy and the impact of government interventions to steer the economy.
4. Can markets generally be counted on to achieve desirable outcomes and adjust quickly and appropriately to changes, or are they rigid and subject to frequent problems that need correction? Discuss the potential problems with the market and how government intervention could potentially solve these problems.
5. Can government intervention generally be counted on to act more like a benevolent social planner, fixing problems with the best interest of citizens as the goal, or will government tend to cater toward special-interest groups at the expense of the general public? Discuss the potential problems with the incentives faced by those involved in collective decision-making.

*Asterisk denotes questions for which answers are given in Appendix B.

Special Topic 4

The Great Recession of 2008-2009: Causes and Response

> U.S. housing policies are the root cause of the current financial crisis. Other players–"greedy" investment bankers; foolish investors; imprudent bankers; incompetent rating agencies; irresponsible housing speculators; shortsighted homeowners; and predatory mortgage brokers, lenders, and borrowers–all played a part, but they were only following the economic incentives that government policy laid out for them.
>
> –Peter J. Wallison[1]

The headlines of 2008 were dominated by falling housing prices, rising default and foreclosure rates, failure of large investment banks, and huge bailouts arranged by both the Federal Reserve and the U.S. Treasury. The Great Recession of 2008-2009 substantially reduced the wealth of most Americans and generated widespread concern about the future of the U.S. economy. This crisis is one of the most important macroeconomic events in American history. This special topic will examine what happened, why things went wrong, and the lessons that need to be learned from the experience.

Learning Objectives

ST04.1 Explain why housing prices soared during 2002-2005 and then fell in the following years.

ST04.2 Analyze the major factors that caused the Great Recession of 2008-2009.

ST04.3 Indicate how the Great Recession changed the structure of the U.S. economy.

[1]Peter J. Wallison, "Cause and Effect: Government Policies and the Financial Crisis," AEI Financial ServicesOutlook, www.aei.org/publication29015.

ST04-1 Key Events Leading Up to the Great Recession

Mortgage default rate
The percentage of home mortgages on which the borrower is late by 90 days or more with the payments on the loan or it is in the foreclosure process. This rate is sometimes referred to as the serious delinquency rate.

Foreclosure rate
The percentage of home mortgages on which the lender has started the process of taking ownership of the property because the borrower has failed to make the monthly payments.

The housing boom and bust during the first seven years of the twenty-first century are central to understanding the economic events of 2008. As **Exhibit ST04-1** shows, housing prices were relatively stable during the 1990s, but they began to increase rapidly toward the end of the decade. By 2002, housing prices were booming. Between January 2002 and mid-year 2006, housing prices increased by a whopping 87 percent. This translates to an annual growth rate of approximately 13 percent. But the housing boom began to wane in 2006. Housing prices leveled off, and by the end of 2006, they were falling. The boom had turned to a bust, and the housing price decline continued throughout 2007 and 2008. By year-end 2008, housing prices were approximately 30 percent below their 2006 peak.

Exhibit ST04-2 panel (a) presents data on the **mortgage default rate** from 1979 through 2008. (*Note:* The default rate is also known as the serious delinquency rate.) As these figures illustrate, the default rate fluctuated, within a narrow range, around 2 percent prior to 2006. It increased only slightly during the recessions of 1982, 1990, and 2001.

However, even though the economy was relatively strong and unemployment low, the default rate began to increase sharply during the second half of 2006. By the fourth quarter of 2007, it had already risen to 3.6 percent, up from 2 percent in the second quarter of 2006. The increase continued and the default rate reached 5.2 percent in 2008.

As Exhibit ST04-2 panel (b) illustrates, the pattern of the housing **foreclosure rate** was similar. It fluctuated between 0.2 and 0.5 during 1978–2005. The recessions of 1980, 1982, 1990, and 2001 exerted little impact on the foreclosure rate. However, like the mortgage default rate, the foreclosure rate started to increase during the second half of 2006, and it tripled over the next two years.

During 2008, housing prices were falling, default rates were increasing, and the confidence of both consumers and investors was deteriorating. These conditions were reinforced

Exhibit ST04-1 Annual Change in the Price of Existing Houses, 1987-2008

Housing prices increased slowly during the 1990s, but they began rising more rapidly toward the end of the decade. Between January 2002 and mid-year 2006, housing prices increased by a whopping 87 percent. But the boom turned to a bust during the second half of 2006, and the housing price decline continued throughout 2007-2008.

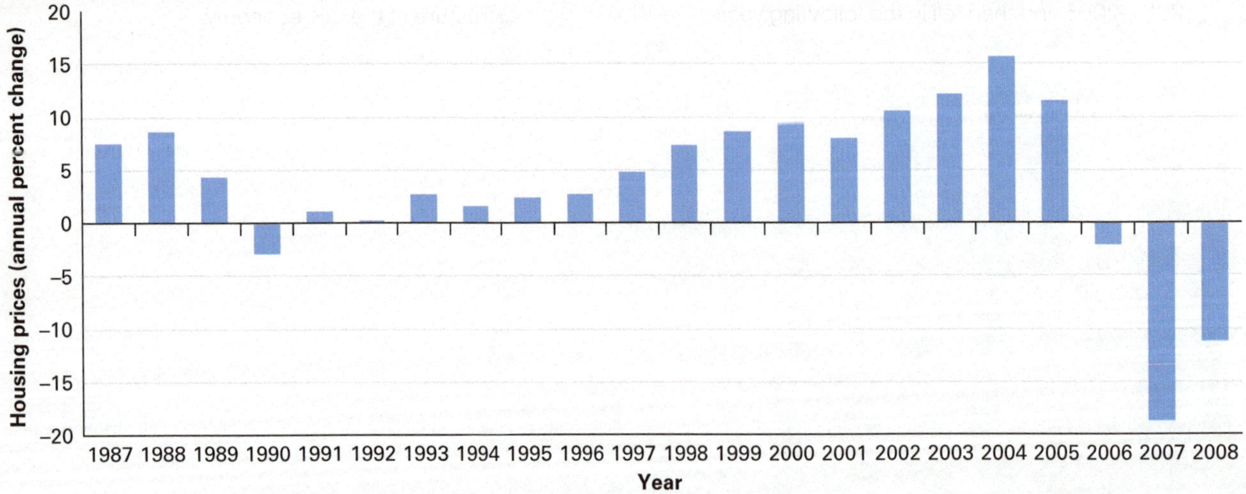

Source: www.standardpoors.com, S&P Case-Schiller Housing Price Index.

Exhibit ST04-2 Mortgage Default and Housing Foreclosure Rates, 1979-2008

As panel (a) shows, the mortgage default rate fluctuated within a narrow range around 2 percent for more than two decades before 2006. It increased only slightly during the recessions of 1980, 1982, 1990, and 2001 but started to increase in the second half of 2006 and soared to more than 5 percent in 2008. As panel (b) shows, the foreclosure rate followed a similar pattern. It ranged between 0.2 and 0.5 percent before 2006, before soaring to 1.2 percent in 2008.

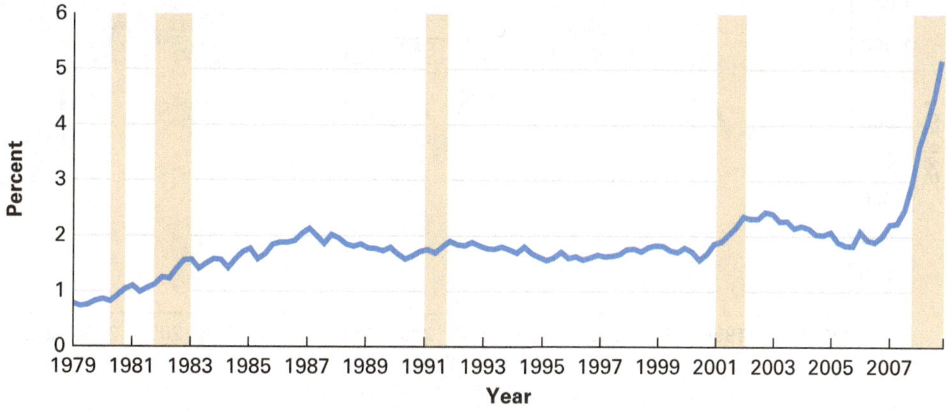

(a) Mortgage default rate

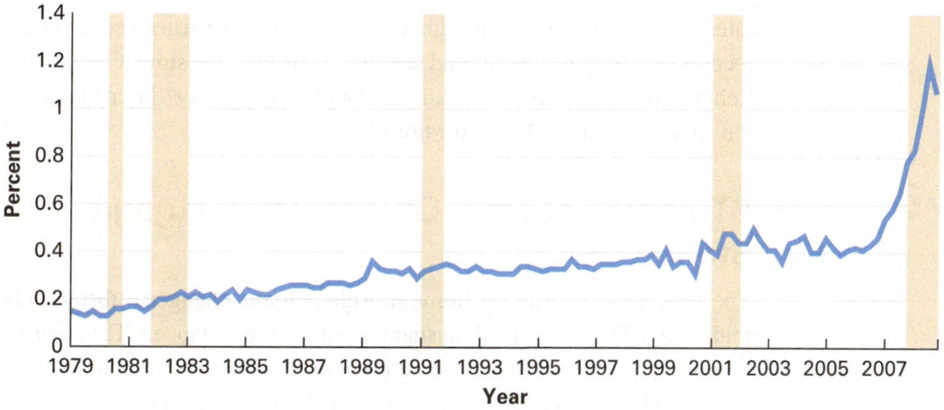

(b) Housing foreclosure rate

Source: http://mbaa.org, National Delinquency Survey.

by sharply rising prices of crude oil, which pushed gasoline prices to more than $4 per gallon during the first half of the year. Against this background, the stock market took a huge tumble. As **Exhibit ST04-3** shows, the S&P 500 index of stock prices fell by 55 percent between October 2007 and March 2009. This collapse eroded the wealth and endangered the retirement savings of many Americans.

ST04-2 What Caused the Great Recession?

Why did housing prices rise rapidly, then level off, and eventually collapse? Why did the mortgage default and housing foreclosure rates increase rapidly well before the start of the recession, which did not begin until December 2007? Why were the default and foreclosure

Exhibit ST04-3 Changes in Stock Prices, 1996-2009

Stock prices as measured by the Standard & Poor's 500 are shown here. Note how stock prices fell by approximately 55 percent between October 2007 and March 2009. This collapse eroded the wealth and endangered the retirement savings of many Americans.

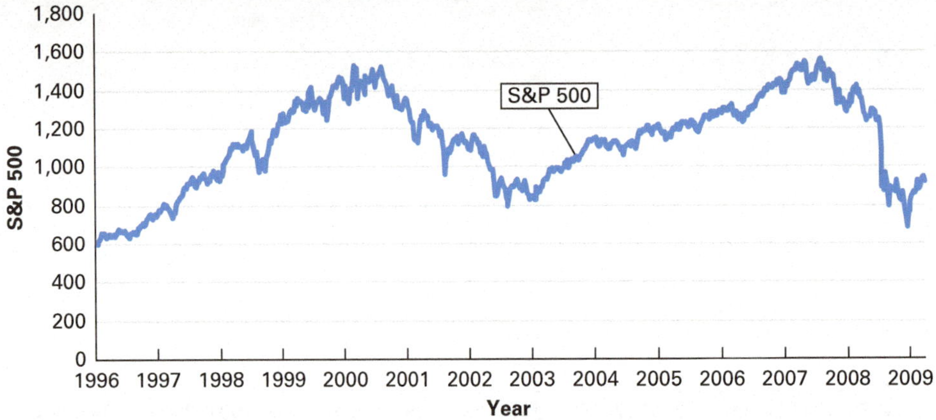

Source: www.standardpoors.com.

rates during 2007 so much higher than the rates of earlier years, including those of prior recessions? Why did large, and seemingly strong, investment banks like Bear Stearns and Lehman Brothers run into financial troubles so quickly? Four factors combine to provide the answers to all of these questions.[2]

ST04-2a Factor 1: Change in Mortgage Lending Standards

The lending standards for home mortgage loans changed substantially beginning in the mid-1990s. The looser lending standards did not just happen. They were the result of federal policy designed to promote home ownership among households with incomes below the median. Home ownership is a worthy goal, but it was not pursued directly through transparent budget allocations and subsidies to homebuyers. Instead, the federal government imposed a complex set of regulations and regulatory mandates that forced various lending institutions to extend more loans to low- and moderate-income households. To meet these mandates, lenders had to lower their standards. By the early years of the twenty-first century, it was possible to borrow more (relative to your income) and purchase a house or condo with a lower down payment than was the case a decade earlier.

The Federal National Mortgage Association and Federal Home Loan Mortgage Corporation, commonly known as Fannie Mae and Freddie Mac, played a central role in this relaxation of mortgage lending standards. These two entities were created by Congress to help provide liquidity in secondary mortgage markets. Fannie Mae, established by the federal government in 1938, was spun off as a *government-sponsored enterprise* (GSE) in 1968. Freddie Mac was created in 1970 as another GSE to provide competition for Fannie Mae.

---

[2]For additional details on the Great Recession, refer to Thomas Sowell, *The Housing Boom and Bust* (New York: Basic Books, 2009); Stan J. Liebowitz, "Anatomy of a Train Wreck: Causes of the Mortgage Meltdown," in *Housing America: Building Out of a Crisis*, ed. Randall G. Holcombe and Benjamin Powell (New Brunswick, NJ: Transaction Publishers, 2009); Peter J. Wallison, "Cause and Effect: Government Policies and the Financial Crisis," *Critical Review: A Journal of Politics and Society*, Issue 2-3 2009, pp. 365–376; and Fernando Ferreira and Joseph Gyourko, "A New Look at the U.S. Foreclosure Crisis: Panel Data Evidence of Prime and Subprime Borrowers from 1997 to 2012," NBER Working Paper 21261, August 2015.

Fannie Mae and Freddie Mac were privately owned (for-profit) businesses, but because of their federal sponsorship, it was widely perceived that the government would back their bonds if they ever ran into financial trouble. As a result, Fannie and Freddie were able to borrow funds at 50 to 75 **basis points** cheaper than private lenders. This gave them a competitive advantage, and they were highly profitable for many years. However, the GSE structure also meant that they were asked to serve two masters: their stockholders, who were interested in profitability; and Congress and federal regulators, who predictably were more interested in political objectives.

Basis points
One one-hundredth of a percentage point. Thus, 100 basis points are equivalent to one percentage point.

As a result of their GSE structure, Fannie Mae and Freddie Mac were highly political. The top management of Fannie and Freddie provided key congressional leaders with large political contributions and often hired away congressional staffers into high-paying jobs lobbying their former bosses. Between the 2000 and 2008 election cycles, high-level managers and other employees of Fannie Mae and Freddie Mac contributed more than $14.6 million to the campaign funds of dozens of senators and representatives, most of whom were on congressional committees important for the protection of their privileged status.

The lobbying activities of Fannie Mae and Freddie Mac were legendary. Between 1998 and 2008, Fannie spent $79.5 million and Freddie spent $94.9 million on congressional lobbying, placing them among the biggest spenders on these activities. They also set up "partnership offices" in the districts and states of important legislators, often hiring the relatives of these lawmakers to staff these local offices.[3] The politicians, for their part, and the regulators who answered to them fashioned rules that made very high profits possible for the GSEs, at least in the short run. Although it was a relationship that reflected political favoritism (some would say corruption), members of Congress, particularly those involved in banking regulation, were highly supportive of the arrangement.

Fannie Mae and Freddie Mac did not originate mortgages. Instead, they purchased the mortgages originated by banks, mortgage brokers, and other lenders. Propelled by their cheaper access to funds, Fannie Mae and Freddie Mac grew rapidly during the 1990s. As **Exhibit ST04-4** shows, the share of all mortgages held by Fannie Mae and Freddie Mac jumped from 25 percent in 1990 to 45 percent in 2001. Their share fluctuated around 40 percent during 2001–2008. Their dominance of the **secondary mortgage market** was even greater. During the decade prior to their insolvency and takeover by the federal government during the summer of 2008, Fannie Mae and Freddie Mac purchased about 90 percent of the mortgages sold in the secondary market. Because of this dominance, their lending practices permitted them to exert a huge impact on the standards accepted by mortgage originators.

Secondary mortgage market
A market in which mortgages originated by a lender are sold to another financial institution. In recent years, the major buyers in this market have been Fannie Mae, Freddie Mac, and large investment banks.

Responding to earlier congressional legislation, the Department of Housing and Urban Development (HUD) imposed regulations designed to make housing more affordable. The HUD mandates, adopted in 1995, required Fannie Mae and Freddie Mac to extend a larger share of their loans to low- and moderate-income households. For example, under the HUD mandates, 40 percent of new loans financed by Fannie Mae and Freddie Mac in 1996 had to go to borrowers with incomes below the median. This mandated share was steadily increased to 50 percent in 2000 and 56 percent in 2008. Similar increases were mandated for borrowers with incomes of less than 60 percent of the median. Moreover, in 1999, HUD guidelines required Fannie Mae and Freddie Mac to accept smaller down payments and permitted them to extend larger loans relative to income.

[3]For additional details, refer to Peter J. Wallison and Charles W. Calomiris, "The Destruction of Fannie Mae and Freddie Mac," American Enterprise Institute, online (posted Tuesday, September 30, 2008). Also refer to Common Cause, "Ask Yourself Why . . . They Didn't See This Coming" (September 24, 2008), available at http://www.commoncause.org/research-reports/National_092408_Education_Fund_Report_Lending_Industry_in_the_Financial_Crisis.pdf; and Center for Responsive Politics, "Lobbying: Top Spenders" (2008), available at www.opensecrets.org/lobby/top.php?indexType=s.

Exhibit ST04-4 The Share of Total Outstanding Mortgages Held by Fannie Mae and Freddie Mac, 1990-2008

Fannie Mae and Freddie Mac dominated the mortgage market for many years. Because of their government sponsorship, they were able to obtain funds cheaper than private firms. They held 45 percent of all mortgages in 2001, up from 25 percent in 1990. During 2001-2008, their share fluctuated around 40 percent. Their dominance of the secondary market, where loans are purchased from originators, is even greater. In July 2008, they were declared insolvent and taken over by the U.S. Treasury.

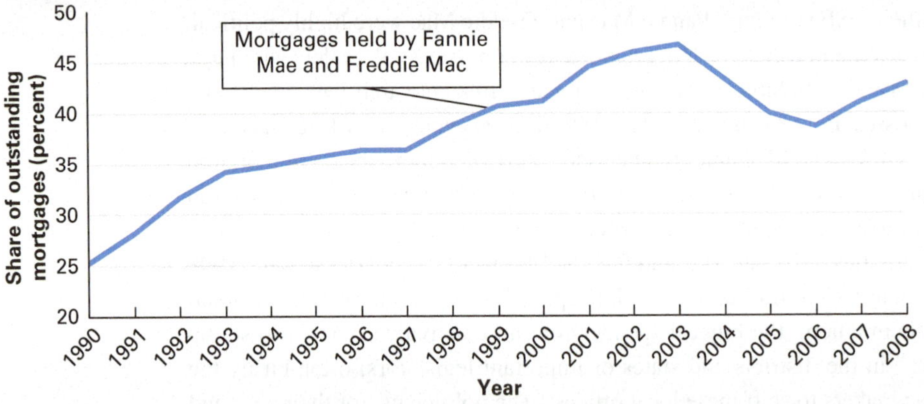

Source: Office of Federal Housing Enterprise Oversight, www.ofheo.gov.

The policies of Fannie Mae and Freddie Mac exerted an enormous impact on the actions of banks and other mortgage lenders. Recognizing that riskier loans could be passed on to Fannie and Freddie, mortgage originators had less incentive to scrutinize the creditworthiness of borrowers and more incentive to reduce the required down payment, in order to sell more mortgages. After all, when the mortgages were soon sold to Fannie or Freddie, the risk was transferred to them also. The bottom line: Required down payments were reduced and the accepted credit standards lowered.

Subprime loans
A loan made to a borrower with blemished credit or one who provides only limited documentation of income, employment history, and other indicators of creditworthiness.

FICO score
A credit score measuring a borrower's likely ability to repay a loan. A person's FICO score will range between 300 and 850. A score of 700 or more indicates that the borrower's credit standing is good. FICO is an acronym for the Fair Isaac Corporation, the creators of the FICO score.

Alt-A loans
Loans extended with little documentation or verification of the borrowers' income, employment, and other indicators of their ability to repay. Because of this poor documentation, these loans are risky.

As the HUD regulations tightened, the share of loans that were **subprime loans** steadily increased. **Exhibit ST04-5** illustrates this point. Measured as a share of mortgages originated during the year, subprime mortgages rose from 4.5 percent in 1994 to 13.2 percent in 2000 and 20 percent in 2005 and 2006. (*Note:* Bank examiners consider a loan to be subprime if the borrower's **FICO score** is less than 660.) When the **Alt-A loans**, those extended without full documentation, were added to the subprime, a third of the mortgages extended in 2005–2006 were to borrowers with either poor or highly questionable credit records.

As the mortgages extended to those with weak credit soared, so too did the number with little or no down payment. **Exhibit ST04-6** shows both the number of loans issued by Fannie Mae and Freddie Mac and the share extended to borrowers with 5 percent or less down payment. Note how the number of new loans financed by the government sponsored corporations increased from less than one hundred thousand in the late 1990s to more than six hundred thousand in 2007. At the same time, the share of mortgages to borrowers making a down payment of 5 percent or less rose from 4 percent in 1998 to 12 percent in 2003 and 23 percent in 2007. Thus, Fannie Mae and Freddie Mac were flooding the market with low-down-payment loans extended to borrowers with weak credit. Meanwhile, conventional loans for which borrowers were required to make at least a 20 percent down payment fell from two-thirds of the total in the early 1990s to only one-third in 2005–2006.

The shift from conventional loans to "creative finance" and "flexible standards," as the regulators called the new criteria, is highly important because the default and foreclosure rates for subprime loans ranges from seven to ten times the rate for conventional loans to

Exhibit ST04-5 Subprime and Alt-A Mortgages as a Share of the Total, 1994-2007

Both subprime and Alt-A mortgages reflect loans to borrowers with a weak credit history. Note how the share of loans to borrowers in these two categories jumped from roughly 10 percent in 2001-2003 to 33 percent in 2005-2006.

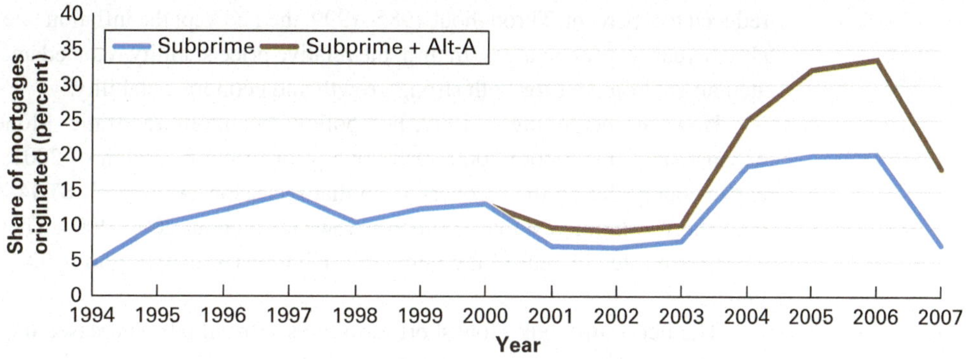

Source: The data for 1994–2000 are from Edward M. Gramlich, Financial Services Roundtable Annual Housing Policy Meeting, Chicago, Illinois (21 May 2004), www.federalreserve.gov/boarddocs/speeches/2004/20040521/default.htm. The data for 2001–2007 are from the Joint Center for Housing Studies of Harvard University, The State of the Nation's Housing 2008, www.jchs.harvard.edu/son/index.htm.

Exhibit ST04-6 Growth of Low-Down-Payment Loans Extended by Fannie Mae and Freddie Mac

Following the 1999 HUD guidelines encouraging Fannie Mae and Freddie Mac to extend more low-down-payment loans, the GSEs both increased the number of their mortgages (left frame) and the share extended with a down payment of 5 percent or less. As the right frame shows, the share of these low-down-payment mortgages extended by Fannie Mae and Freddie Mac increased from 4 percent in 1998 to 12 percent in 2003 and 23 percent in 2007.

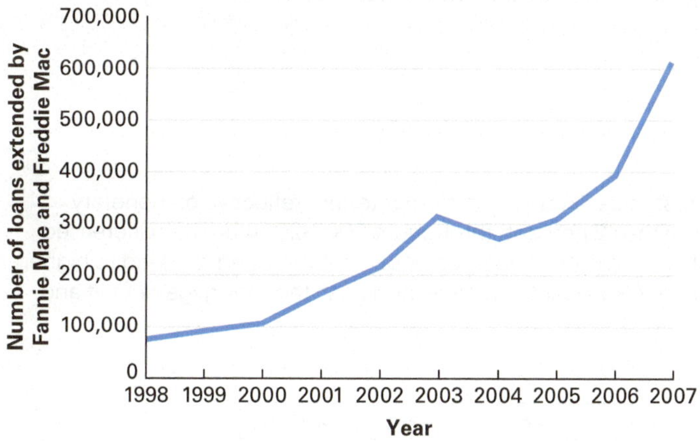

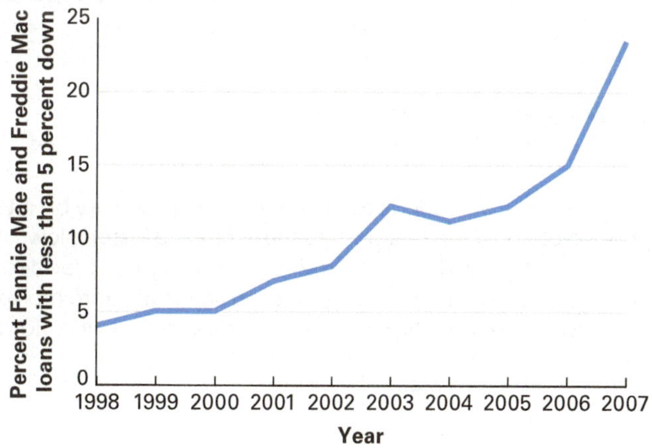

Sources: Russell Robert's, *Gambling With Other Peoples Money*, Mercatus Center, http://mercatus.org/publications/gambling-other-peoples-money.

prime borrowers. This differential is even greater in the case of mortgages with little or no down payment. Initially, this easy credit policy increased demand and pushed housing prices upward. But, the policy was not sustainable, and it was predictable where it would lead. Eventually, the growing share of low-down-payment loans extended to those with weak credit would result in substantially higher default and foreclosure rates. This is precisely what happened.

ST04-2b Factor 2: Prolonged Low Interest Rate Policy of the Fed During 2002-2004

Following the high and variable inflation rates of the 1970s, Federal Reserve policy focused on keeping the inflation rate low and stable. By the mid-1980s, the inflation rate had been reduced to 3 percent. Throughout 1985–1999, the Fed kept the inflation rate low and avoided abrupt year-to-year changes. In turn, the relative price stability reduced uncertainty and created an environment for both strong growth and economic stability.

However, beginning in 1999, Fed policy became more erratic. Monetary policy was expansionary just before 2000, restrictive prior to the recession of 2001, and then highly expansionary during the recovery from that recession. As **Exhibit ST04-7** shows, the Fed kept short-term interest rates at historic lows throughout 2002–2004. These extremely low short-term rates increased the demand for interest-sensitive goods like automobiles and housing.

The Fed's artificially low short-term rates substantially increased the attractiveness of **adjustable rate mortgages (ARMs)** to both borrowers and lenders. As **Exhibit ST04-8** shows, adjustable rate mortgages jumped from 10 percent of the total outstanding mortgages in 2000 to 21 percent in 2005. The low initial interest rates on adjustable rate mortgages made it possible for homebuyers to afford the monthly payments for larger, more expensive homes. This easy credit provided fuel for the housing boom. But the low rates and ARM loans also meant that as short-term interest rates increased from their historic low levels, home buyers would face a higher monthly payment two or three years in the future. Unsurprisingly, this is precisely what happened.

Adjustable rate mortgages (ARMs)
A home loan in which the interest rate, and thus the monthly payment, is tied to a short-term rate like the one-year Treasury bill rate. Typically, the mortgage interest rate will be two or three percentage points above the related short-term rate. It will be reset at various time intervals (e.g., annually), and thus the interest rate and monthly payment will vary over the life of the loan.

By 2005, the expansionary monetary policy of 2002–2004 was clearly placing upward pressure on the general level of prices. The Fed responded with a shift to a more restrictive monetary policy, which pushed interest rates upward (refer to Exhibit ST04-7). Many who purchased houses with little or no down payment and adjustable rate loans when interest rates were low during 2002–2004 faced substantially higher monthly payments as interest rates rose and the monthly payments on their ARM loans were reset during 2006 and 2007. These owners had virtually no equity in their homes. Therefore, when housing prices leveled

Exhibit ST04-7 Fed Policy and Short-Term Interest Rates, 1995-2009

Here we show the federal funds and one-year Treasury bill interest rates. These short-term rates are reflective of monetary policy. Note how the Fed pushed these rates to historic lows (less than 2 percent) throughout 2002-2004 but then increased them substantially during 2005-2006. The low rates provided fuel for the housing price boom, but the rising rates led to higher interest rates and monthly payments on adjustable rate mortgage (ARM) loans, which helped push the mortgage default and foreclosure rates upward beginning in the second half of 2006.

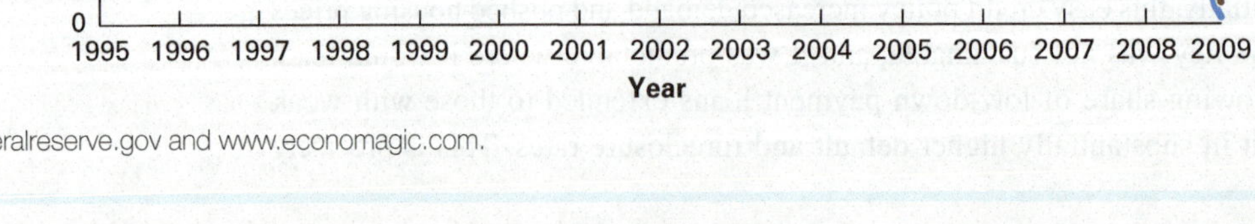

Sources: www.federalreserve.gov and www.economagic.com.

Exhibit ST04-8 Adjustable Rate Mortgages (ARMs) as a Share of Total Outstanding Mortgages, 1990-2008

The interest rate and monthly payment on ARMs are tied to a short-term interest rate (e.g., the one-year Treasury bill rate). The Fed's low-interest rate policy of 2002-2004 increased the attractiveness of ARMs. Note how ARM loans increased as a share of total mortgages from 10 percent in 2000 to 21 percent in 2005.

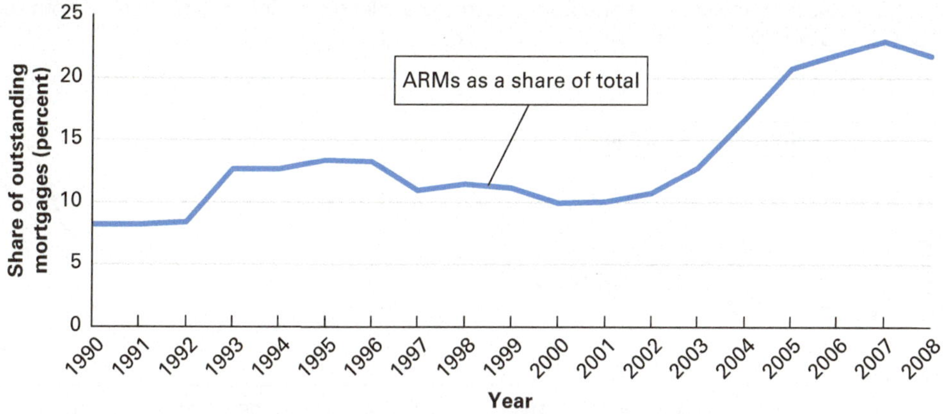

Source: Office of Federal Housing Enterprise Oversight, www.ofheo.gov.

off and began to decline during the second half of 2006, the default and foreclosure rates on these loans began to rise almost immediately (refer to Exhibits ST04-1 and ST04-2). Some owners with little or no initial equity simply walked away as their outstanding loan exceeded the value of their house.

Essentially, the small down payment and ARMs combination made it possible for homebuyers to gamble with someone else's money. If housing prices rose, buyers could reap a sizable capital gain without risking much of their own investment capital. Based on the rising housing prices of 2000–2005, many of these homebuyers expected to sell the house for a profit and move on in a couple of years. There were even television programs and investment seminars pushing this strategy as the route to riches.

Exhibit ST04-9 shows the foreclosure rates for fixed interest rate and ARM loans for both subprime and prime loans. Compared to their prime borrower counterparts, the foreclosure rate for subprime borrowers was approximately ten times higher for fixed rate mortgages and seven times higher for adjustable rate mortgages. These huge differentials explain why the increasing share of loans to subprime borrowers substantially increased the default and foreclosure rates.

As Exhibit ST04-9 shows, there was no upward trend in the foreclosure rate on fixed interest rate loans for either prime or subprime borrowers during 2000–2008. On the other hand, the foreclosure rate on ARMs soared for both prime and subprime loans during 2006–2008. In fact, the percentage increase in foreclosures on ARM loans was higher for prime than subprime borrowers. This is highly revealing. It illustrates that both prime and subprime borrowers played the low-down-payment, mortgage casino game.

The loan default problem is often referred to as the *subprime mortgage crisis*. This is true, but it is only part of the story. It was also an ARM loan crisis. Fed policy encouraging ARM loans, the increasing proportion of these loans as a share of the total, and their higher default and foreclosure rates also contributed substantially, first to the housing boom and then to the bust. The combination of the mortgage lending regulations and the Fed's artificially low interest rate policies encouraged decision-makers to borrow more money and make unwise and inefficient investments.

Exhibit ST04-9 The Foreclosure Rate of Fixed and Adjustable Rate Mortgages for Subprime and Prime Borrowers, 1998-2008

The foreclosure rates on fixed and adjustable interest rate mortgages are shown here for both subprime (panel a) and prime (panel b) borrowers. Note how the foreclosure rate was generally seven to ten times higher for subprime loans than for those to prime borrowers. As housing prices leveled off and declined in 2006-2008, the foreclosure rate on fixed interest rate mortgages did not change much. In contrast, the foreclosure rate for ARM loans soared beginning in the second half of 2006, and this was true for ARM loans to both subprime and prime borrowers. Clearly, the increasing share of both subprime and ARM loans during 2000-2005 contributed to the boom and bust of the housing market.

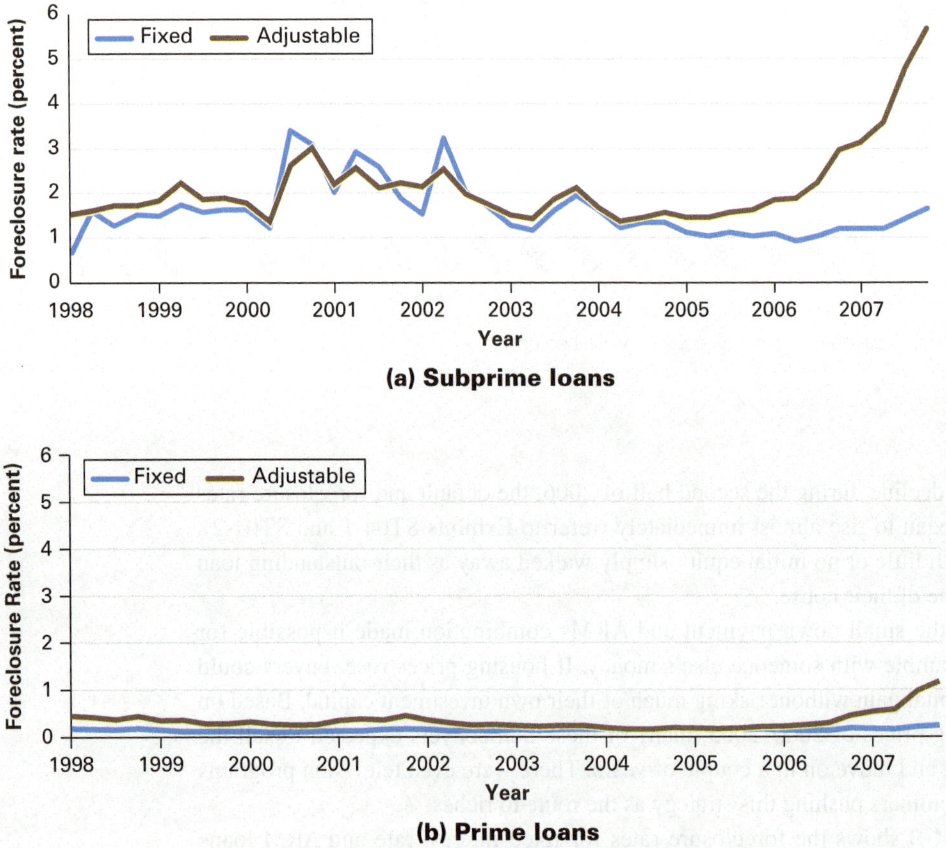

Source: Stan J. Liebowitz, "Anatomy of a Train Wreck: Causes of the Mortgage Meltdown," Ch. 13 in Randall G. Holcombe and Benjamin Powell, eds, *Housing America: Building Out of a Crisis* (New Brunswick, NJ: Transaction Publishers, 2009). We would like to thank Professor Liebowitz for making this data available to us.

Investment banks
An institution that acts as an underwriter for securities issued by other corporations or lenders. Unlike traditional banks, investment banks do not accept deposits from, or provide loans to, individuals.

Leverage ratio
The ratio of loans and other investments to the firm's capital assets.

ST04-2c Factor 3: The Increased Debt-to-Capital Ratio of Investment Banks

A rule change adopted by the Securities and Exchange Commission (SEC) in April 2004 made it possible for **investment banks** to increase the leverage of their investment capital, which eventually led to their collapse. A firm's **leverage ratio** is simply the ratio of its investment holdings (including loans) relative to its capital. Thus, if a firm had investment funds that were 12 times the size of its equity capital, its leverage ratio would be 12 to 1. Prior to the SEC rule change, this was approximately the leverage ratio of both investment and commercial banks.

Essentially, the SEC applied regulations known as Basel I to investment banking. These regulations, which have been adopted by most of the industrial countries, require banks to maintain at least 8 percent capital against assets like loans to commercial businesses. This implies a leverage ratio of approximately 12 to 1. However, the Basil regulations provide more favorable treatment of residential loans. The capital requirement for residential mortgage loans is only 4 percent, which implies a 25 to 1 leverage ratio. Even more important, the capital requirement for low-risk securities is still lower at 1.6 percent. This means that the permissible leverage ratio for low-risk securities could be as high as 60 to 1.

Key investment banking leaders, including Henry Paulson, who was CEO of Goldman Sachs at the time, urged the SEC to apply the higher leverage ratio to investment banks. Ironically, Paulson later became Secretary of the Treasury and was in charge of the federal "bailout" of the banks that got into trouble because of the excessive leveraging of their capital.

Following the rule change, large investment banks, like Lehman Brothers, Goldman Sachs, and Bear Stearns, expanded their mortgage financing activities. They bundled large holdings of mortgages together and issued securities for their finance. Because of the diversity of the mortgage portfolio, investment in the underlying securities was thought to involve minimal risk. If the **security-rating** firms provided the **mortgage-backed securities** with a AAA rating, then the investment banks could leverage them up to 60 to 1 against their capital.

Security-rating
A rating indicating the risk of default of the security. A rating of AAA indicates that the risk of default is low.

Mortgage-backed securities
Securities issued for the financing of large pools of mortgages. The promised returns to the security holders are derived from the mortgage interest payments.

The mortgage-backed securities, financed with short-term leveraged lending, were highly lucrative. The large number of mortgages packaged together provided lenders with diversity and protection against abnormally high default rates in specific regions and loan categories. But it did not shield them from an overall increase in mortgage default rates. As default rates increased sharply in 2006 and 2007, it became apparent that the mortgage-backed securities were far more risky than had been previously thought. When the risk of these mortgages became more apparent, the value of the mortgage-backed securities plummeted because it was difficult to know their true value. As the value of the mortgage-backed securities collapsed, the highly leveraged investment banks faced massive short-term debt obligations with little reserves on which to draw. This is why the investment banks collapsed so quickly. In fact, when the Fed financed the acquisition of Bear Stearns by JPMorgan Chase, the leverage ratio of Bear Stearns was an astounding 33 to 1, about two and a half times the historical level associated with prudent banking practices.

Why didn't key Wall Street decision-makers notice the looming danger? No doubt, they were influenced by the low and relatively stable default rates over the past several decades (refer to Exhibit ST04-2). Even during serious recessions like those of 1974–1975 and 1982–1983, the mortgage default rates were only a little more than 2 percent, less than half the rates of 2008. But one would still have thought that analysts at investment companies and security-rating firms would have warned that the low historical rates were for periods when down payments were larger, borrowing was more restricted relative to income, and fewer loans were made to subprime borrowers. A few analysts did provide warnings, but their views were ignored by high-level superiors.

However, the incentive structure also helps explain why highly intelligent people failed to refer to the oncoming danger. The bonuses of most Wall Street executives are closely tied to short-term profitability, and the mortgage-backed securities were highly profitable when housing prices were rising and interest rates were low. If a personal bonus of a million dollars or more is at stake this year, one is likely to be far less sensitive to the long-term dangers.

The incentive structure accompanying the regulation and rating of securities also played an important role. Only three firms—Moody's, Standard & Poor's, and Fitch—are legally authorized to rate securities. These rating agencies are paid by the firm requesting the rating. A Triple-A rating was exceedingly important. It made higher leveraging possible, but, even more important, the Triple-A rating made it possible to sell the mortgage-backed securities to institutional investors, retirement plans, and investors around the world looking for relatively safe investments. The rating agencies were paid attractive fees for their ratings, and Triple-A approval would mean more business for the rating agencies as well as the investment banks. Clearly, this incentive structure is not one that encourages careful scrutiny and hard-nosed evaluation of the quality of the underlying mortgage bundle. Paradoxically, the shortsighted and counterproductive incentive structures that characterize some of Wall Street's best-known firms contributed to their collapse.

ST04-2d Factor 4: High Debt/Income Ratio of Households

During 1985–2007, household debt grew to unprecedented levels. As **Exhibit ST04-10** shows, household debt as a share of disposable (after-tax) income ranged from 40 percent to 65 percent during 1953–1984. However, since the mid-1980s, the debt-to-income ratio of households climbed at an alarming rate. It reached 135 percent in 2007, more than twice the level of the mid-1980s. Unsurprisingly, more debt means that a larger share of household income is required just to meet the interest payments.

Interest payments on home mortgages and home equity loans are tax deductible, but household interest on other forms of debt is not. This incentive structure encourages households to concentrate their debt into loans against their housing. But a large debt against one's housing will mean that housing will be the hardest hit by unexpected events that force major adjustments. This is precisely what occurred in 2006–2008. The rising interest rates and mere leveling off of housing prices soon led to an increase in mortgage defaults and foreclosures, because households were heavily indebted and a huge share of that indebtedness was in the form of mortgages against their housing. As the economy weakened, of course, this situation quickly worsened. Thus, the high level of household indebtedness also contributed to the Great Recession.

ST04-3 The Great Recession, Perverse Incentives, and Potential Reforms

The combination of the HUD regulations, low-down-payment requirements, and the Fed's low interest policy of 2002–2004 resulted in the rapid growth of both subprime and ARM loans during the first five years of this century. As is often the case with policy changes,

Exhibit ST04-10 Household-Debt-to-Disposable-Personal-Income Ratio, 1953-2008

Between 1953 and 1984, household debt as a share of disposable (after-tax) income ranged from 40 percent to 65 percent. However, the household debt-to-income ratio rose steadily throughout 1985-2007. By 2007, it soared to 135 percent, more than twice the level of the mid-1980s.

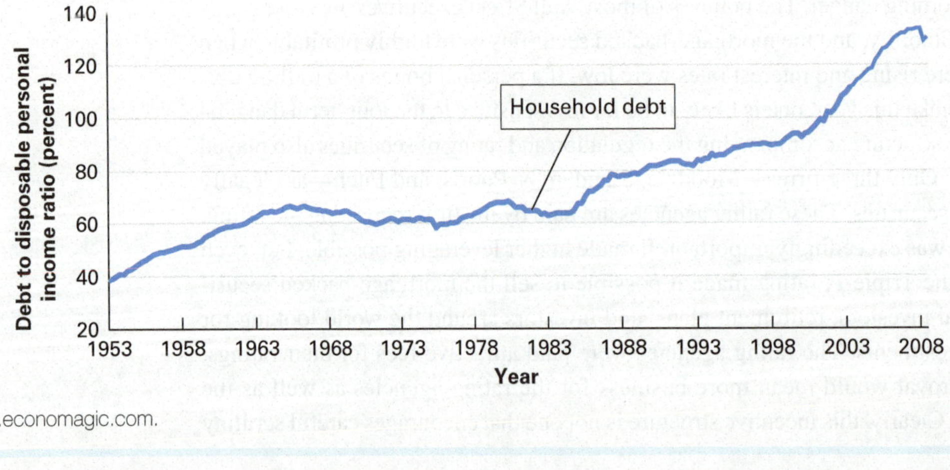

Source: http://www.economagic.com.

the initial effects were positive—strong demand for housing, rising housing prices, and a construction boom. But the long-term effects were disastrous. The increasing share of subprime loans began to push default rates upward. Similarly, the low short-term interest rates that made adjustable rate mortgages attractive during 2004 soon reversed and led to higher monthly payments as the interest rates on ARM loans were reset in the years immediately ahead. As these two factors converged in the latter half of 2006, they generated falling housing prices and soaring mortgage default and foreclosure rates. The housing and lending crisis soon spread to other sectors and economies around the world. Moreover, the Triple-A rated mortgage-backed securities were marketed throughout the world, and, as their value plunged with rising default rates, turmoil was created in global financial markets.

It is important to note that both the mortgage default and foreclosure rates soared well before the recession began in December 2007. This illustrates that the housing crisis was not caused by the recession. Instead, it was the other way around.

Policies that generated perverse incentives and undermined sound lending practices were a central cause of the Great Recession of 2008–2009. Has action been taken to alter the structure of incentives that plague the mortgage loan market? To a large degree, the mortgage loan market has been nationalized. Fannie Mae and Freddie Mac were declared insolvent and taken over by the federal government in 2008. The federal government now dominates the mortgage market. When the mortgage loans of the Federal Housing Administration are added to those of Fannie Mae and Freddie Mac, 90 percent of the new mortgages for housing are currently financed by the federal government. The operating policies of Fannie Mae and Freddie Mac are largely unchanged. Both continue to accept mortgages from borrowers with little or no down payment. Moreover, because of their federal ownership, both continue to have access to funds at 50 to 75 basis points below the funds available to private firms in the lending market.

Further, the tax deductibility of mortgage interest payments continues to encourage Americans to overinvest in housing and concentrate their indebtedness in mortgage loans. High-income recipients are the primary beneficiaries of the deductibility. Even though this policy helped to fuel the housing boom, no action has been taken in this area.

A decade later, most of the perverse incentives that generated the Great Recession remain in place. Constructive reforms would focus on getting the incentives right. Consider the following questions. Would the mortgage market work better if loan originators were held responsible for defaults on loans they originated, even if they sold them to another party? Does it make sense to encourage the purchase of housing with little or no down payment? Does it make sense to encourage people to concentrate their indebtedness in the form of a mortgage loan against their housing, as current tax policy does? Although the precise action is debatable, the Great Recession suggests that review of current policies that generate counterproductive incentives would be wise.

Key Points

- After soaring during the previous five years, housing prices began to decline during the second half of 2006, and mortgage defaults and housing foreclosures started to increase. As the housing bust spread to other sectors, stock prices plunged, major investment banks experienced financial troubles, unemployment increased sharply, and by 2008 the economy was in a severe recession.
- Fannie Mae and Freddie Mac grew rapidly during the 1990s. Their government sponsorship made it possible for them to obtain funds cheaper than private rivals. Because of their dominance of the secondary market, in which mortgages are purchased from originators, their lending standards exerted a huge impact on the mortgage market.

- Beginning in the mid-1990s, mandates imposed on Fannie Mae and Freddie Mac, along with regulations imposed on banks, forced lenders to reduce their lending standards, extend more mortgages to subprime borrowers, and reduce down payment requirements. The share of mortgages extended to subprime borrowers (including Alt-A loans) rose from 10 percent in 2001–2003 to 33 percent in 2005–2006. Correspondingly, the share of low-down-payment loans extended by Fannie Mae and Freddie Mac soared from 4 percent in 1998 to 23 percent in 2007. These changes were highly important because the default and foreclosure rates on subprime and low-down-payment loans are several times higher than for conventional loans to prime borrowers.
- The historically low interest rate policies of the Fed during 2002–2004 increased the demand for housing and the attractiveness of adjustable rate mortgages. This provided fuel for the soaring housing prices. ARM loans increased from 10 percent of total mortgages in 2000 to 21 percent in 2005. Fed policy pushed interest rates up in 2005–2006 and ARM loans were reset, pushing monthly payments higher. As a result, the default and foreclosure rates on these loans soared for prime as well as subprime borrowers.
- As a result of regulations adopted in April 2004, investment banks were allowed to leverage their capital by as much as 60 to 1 when financing mortgages with Triple-A rated securities. The rating agencies provided the Triple-A ratings, and the mortgage-backed securities were sold around the world. As the mortgage default rates rose in 2007–2008, Fannie Mae, Freddie Mac, and the major investment banks holding large quantities of these securities quickly fell into financial troubles, and several collapsed.
- The ratio of household debt to personal income increased steadily during 1985–2007, reaching a historic high at the end of that period.
- Low-down-payment requirements, the growth of subprime and ARM loans, the Fed's easy credit policy, highly leveraged mortgage-backed securities, and heavy borrowing by households fueled the run-up in housing prices. With time, however, this was a disastrous combination that provided the ingredients for the Great Recession.

Critical Analysis Questions

1. What were the major causes of the Great Recession of 2008–2009?
2. Why did housing prices rise rapidly during 2002–2005? Why did the mortgage default rate increase so sharply during 2006 and 2007 even before the 2008–2009 recession began?
3. *If owners have little or no equity in their houses, how will this influence the likelihood that they will default on their mortgage? Why?
4. What happened to the credit standards (e.g., minimum down payment, mortgage loan relative to the value of the house, and creditworthiness of the borrower) between 1995 and 2005? Why did the credit standards change? How did this influence the 2002–2005 housing price bubble and later the default and foreclosure rates?
5. *When mortgage originators sell mortgages to Fannie Mae, Freddie Mac, and investment banks the originators have no additional liability for possible default by the borrower. How will this arrangement influence the incentive of the originators to scrutinize the creditworthiness of the borrower? Would the incentive structure be different if the originator planned to hold the mortgage until it was paid off? Why or why not?
6. Some charge that the crisis of 2008 was caused by the "greed" of Wall Street firms and other bankers. Do you agree with this view? Do you think there was more greed on Wall Street in the first five years of this century than during the 1980s and 1990s? Why or why not?

*Asterisk denotes questions for which answers are given in Appendix B.

Special Topic 5

Lessons from the Great Depression

> We now know, as a few knew then, that the depression was not produced by a failure of private enterprise, but rather by a failure of government in an area in which the government had from the first been assigned responsibility.
>
> –Milton and Rose Friedman[1]

The Great Depression is perhaps the most catastrophic economic event in American history. It is also one of the most misunderstood. Misconceptions abound with regard to what actually happened. The Great Depression is a tragic story about economic illiteracy and the adverse impact of unsound policies. People who do not learn from the lessons of history are prone to repeat them. If we want to avoid similar experiences in the future, it is vitally important that we understand the factors underlying the tragic events of this era.

Learning Objectives

ST05.1 Analyze the impact of the October 1929 stock market crash on the Great Depression.

ST05.2 Indicate the major policy changes that caused the Great Depression to be so long and severe.

ST05.3 Consider whether the New Deal policies ended the Great Depression.

ST05.4 Analyze whether the Great Depression reflects a failure of markets or a failure of government.

[1]Milton and Rose Friedman, *Free to Choose* (New York: Harcourt Brace Jovanovich, 1980), 71.

ST05-1 The Economic Record of the Great Depression

Exhibit ST05-1 presents data on the change in real GDP and the rate of unemployment during 1929–1940. As panel (a) illustrates, real GDP fell by 8.6 percent in 1930, 6.5 percent in 1931, and a whopping 13.1 percent in 1932. By 1933, real GDP was nearly a third less than that in 1929. There was a temporary rebound during 1934–1936, but growth slowed in 1937, and real GDP fell once again in 1938. In 1939, a full decade after the disastrous downturn started, the real GDP per capita of the United States was about the same as it had been in 1929.

While output was declining during the depression era, unemployment was soaring. As Exhibit ST05-1 panel (b) shows, the rate of unemployment rose from 3.2 percent in 1929

Exhibit ST05-1 Real GDP and the Rate of Unemployment, 1929-1940

The change in real GDP (panel a) and rate of unemployment (panel b) figures during the Great Depression are shown here. These data illustrate both the severity and length of the economic contraction. For four successive years (1930-1933), real output fell. Unemployment soared to nearly one-quarter of the work-force in 1932 and 1933. Although real output expanded and the rate of unemployment declined during 1934-1937, the economy again fell into the depths of a depression in 1938. In 1939, a decade after the economic plunge started, 17.2 percent of the labor force was still unemployed and real GDP was virtually unchanged from the level of 1929.

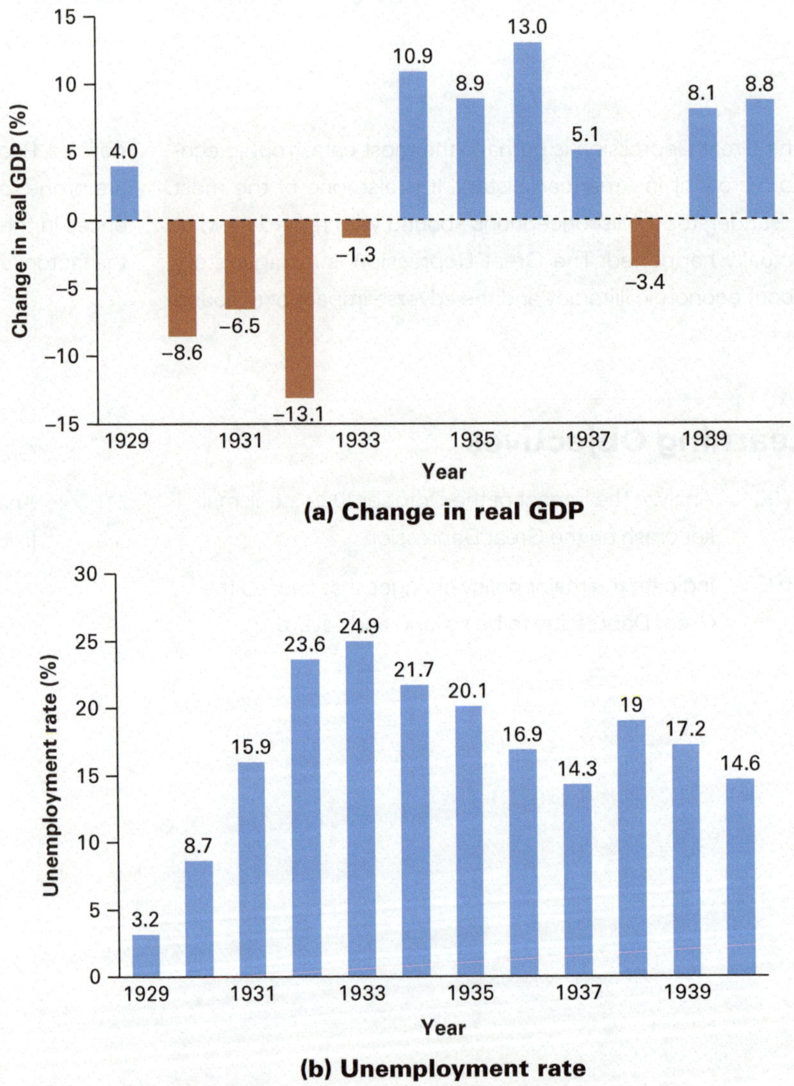

Sources: Real GDP growth rates are from www.bea.gov. The unemployment data are from the Bureau of Labor Statistics (BLS) at www.bls.gov.

to 8.7 percent in 1930 and 15.9 percent in 1931. During 1932 and 1933, the unemployment rate soared to nearly one-quarter of the labor force. Even though real GDP grew substantially during 1934 and 1935, the unemployment rate remained above 20 percent during both of those years. After declining to 14.3 percent in 1937, the rate of unemployment rose to 19.0 percent during the downturn of 1938, and it was still 17.2 percent in 1939, a full decade after the catastrophic era began. The unemployment rate was 14 percent or more throughout the ten years from 1931 through 1940. By way of comparison, the unemployment rate has averaged less than 6 percent during the past quarter of a century, and it has never reached 11 percent during the 80 years from 1940 through 2019. Moreover, the statistics conceal the hardship and suffering accompanying the economic disaster. It was an era of farm foreclosures, bank failures, soup kitchens, unemployment lines, and even a sharply declining birthrate. America would never quite be the same after the 1930s.

ST05-2 Was the Great Depression Caused by the 1929 Stock Market Crash?

The prices of stock shares rose sharply during the 1920s. But this is not surprising because the 1920s was a remarkable decade of innovation, technological advancement, and economic growth. The production of automobiles increased more than tenfold during the 1920s. Households with electricity, telephones, and indoor plumbing spread rapidly throughout the economy. The first regularly scheduled radio programs were broadcast in the early 1920s, providing an amazing new vehicle for mass communication. Air conditioning received a boost from its use in "movie houses," as theaters were called at the time. There is good reason why the decade was known as the "Roaring Twenties." Perhaps more than any other era, the lives of ordinary Americans were transformed during the 1920s. To a large degree, the stock market was merely registering the remarkable growth and development of the decade.[2]

Generations of students have been told that the Great Depression was caused by the stock market crash of October 1929. Is this really true? Let's review the figures. As **Exhibit ST05-2** panel (a) shows, the Dow Jones Industrial Average opened in 1929 at 300, rose to a high of 381 on September 3, 1929, but gradually receded to 327 on Tuesday, October 22. A major sell-off started the following day, and the Dow began to plunge. By October 29, which is known as Black Tuesday, the Dow closed at 230. Thus, in exactly one week, the stock market lost nearly one-third of its value. A couple of weeks later on November 13, the Dow fell to an even lower level, closing at 199.

However, it is interesting to see what happened during the next five months. From mid-November 1929 through mid-April 1930, the Dow Jones Industrial Average increased every month, and by mid-April the index had risen to 294, regaining virtually all of the losses experienced during the late October crash. This raises an interesting question: If the October crash caused the Great Depression, how can one explain that the stock market had regained most of those losses by April 1930?

The Great Depression was a prolonged period of falling incomes, high unemployment, and difficult living conditions. The decline in output and high unemployment were the most severe in American history. Why was the economy so weak for so long?

INTERFOTO/Alamy Stock Photo

[2]Popular writers often argue that speculators drove the stock market to unsustainable highs in the late 1920s, but this view is an exaggeration. The price/earnings ratio for the Dow was 19 just before the crash. This places it at the upper range of normal but not at an unprecedented high. On October 9, 1929, *The Wall Street Journal* reported that railroad stocks were selling at 11.9 times earnings, which would place their P/E ratio toward the lower range of normal. RCA was the hot "high-tech" company of the era, and it earned \$6.15 per share in 1927 and \$15.98 per share in 1928. It traded at a high in 1928 of \$420. This would imply a P/E ratio of 26, not unreasonable for a growth stock with outstanding prospects for future earnings.

But from mid-April throughout the rest of 1930, stock prices moved steadily downward and closed the year at 165. Apparently something happened during May–June 1930, which caused the stock market to head downward. We will return to this issue in a moment. **Exhibit ST05-2** panel (b) presents data for the Dow Jones Industrials for 1931–1940. The index continued to fall in 1931–1932 and rebounded strongly in 1933 but then fluctuated between 100 and 200 for the remainder of the decade. Note the Dow stood at 131 at year-end 1940, even lower than the closing figure for 1930.

Exhibit ST05-2 The Stock Market (Dow Jones Industrial Average), 1928-1940

The figures for the Dow Jones Industrial Average (DJIA) are shown here. Clearly, stock prices plunged in September-October 1929, but note how they recovered during the five months from mid-November 1929 through mid-April of 1930. However, this recovery reversed as the Smoot-Hawley tariff bill was debated, passed, and eventually signed into law on June 17, 1930. As panel (b) shows, the Dow continued to fall throughout 1931 and 1932 and never reached 200 throughout the remainder of the decade.

Sources: www.finance.yahoo.com and www.analyzeindices.com.

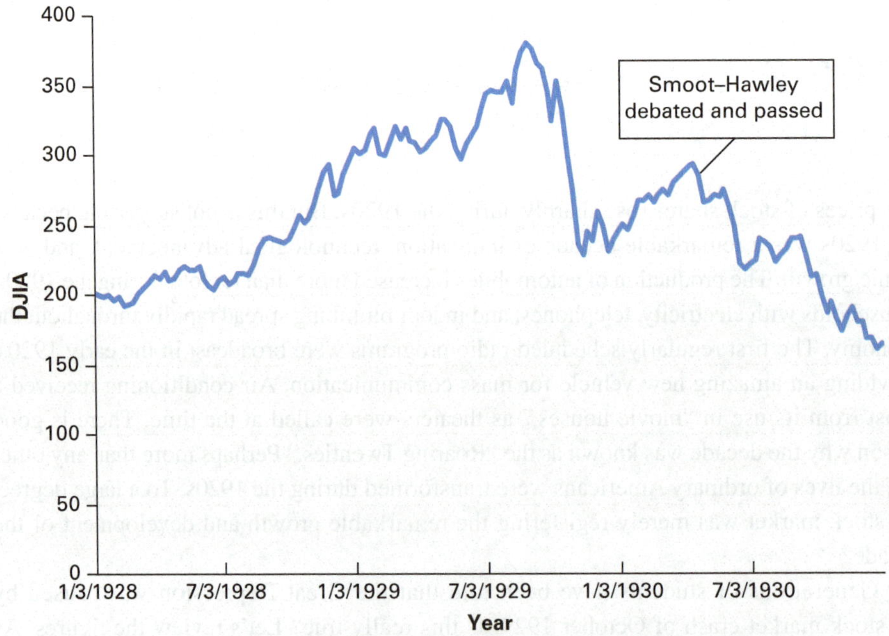

(a) Stock prices: 1928 to 1930

(b) Stock prices: 1931 to 1940

There have been several downturns in stock prices of the magnitude experienced during 1929, both before and after the Great Depression, and none of them resulted in anything like the prolonged unemployment and lengthy contraction of the 1930s. For example, the stock market price declines immediately before and during the recessions of 1973–1975 and 1982–1983 were as large as those of the 1929 crash, approximately 50 percent. But both of these recessions were over in about 18 months. Moreover, in 1987, the Dow Industrials fell from 2,640 on October 2 to 1,740 on October 19, a decline of 34 percent. Whereas the collapse of stock prices in 1987 was similar to the October 1929 crash, that is where the similarity ends. The 1987 crash did not lead to economic disaster. In fact, it was not even followed by a recession.

Of course, the 1929 decline in stock prices reduced wealth and thereby contributed to the reduction in aggregate demand and real output. But stock prices have fallen by 50 percent or more during other recessions, and the economy nonetheless moved toward a recovery within a year or two at the most. Thus, although the decline in stock prices may well have triggered the initial economic decline, the length and severity of the Great Depression were the result of other factors. We will now consider this issue in more detail.

ST05-3 Why Was the Great Depression So Lengthy and Severe?

The length and severity of the Great Depression were the result of bad policies. There were four major policy mistakes that caused the initial downturn to worsen and the depressed conditions to continue on and on. Let's review each of them.

1. A sharp reduction in the supply of money during 1930-1933 and again in 1937-1938 reduced aggregate demand and real output. The supply of money expanded slowly but steadily throughout the 1920s. From 1921 through 1929, the money stock increased at an annual rate of 2.7 percent, approximately the economy's long-term real rate of growth. There was even a slight downward trend in the general level of prices during the decade.

In spite of this price stability, the Fed increased the discount rate, the rate it charges banks for short-term loans, four times between January 1928 and August 1929. During this 20-month period, the discount rate was pushed from 3.5 percent to 6 percent. After the October stock market crash, the Fed aggressively sold government bonds, which drained reserves from the banking system and reduced the money supply. As **Exhibit ST05-3** panel (a) shows, the money supply fell by 3.9 percent during 1930, by 15.3 percent in 1931, and by 8.9 percent in 1932. During 1930–1932, numerous banks failed, confidence in the banking system dissipated, and bank runs became commonplace. The Fed was established in 1913 to act as a lender of last resort for banks. The Fed could have engaged in large-scale purchases of government bonds, which would have provided banks with additional reserves, minimized bank runs, and restored confidence in the banking system. Instead, the Fed permitted the money supply to collapse and even failed to fulfill its assigned role as the lender of last resort. The quantity of money at year-end 1933 was 33 percent less than that in 1929.

Predictably, this huge monetary contraction placed downward pressure on prices. As Exhibit ST05-3 panel (b) illustrates, the general level of prices fell by 2.3 percent in 1930, 9.0 percent in 1931, and 9.9 percent in 1932.

Economic activity takes place over time. The deflation during 1929–1933 meant that many people who bought businesses and farms in the late 1920s were unable to pay for them as the prices of their output fell during the 1930s. In essence, the monetary contraction caused unexpected changes in economic conditions. As a result, many people who

Exhibit ST05-3 The M1 Money Supply and the Change in the General Level of Prices, 1925-1940

Note how the M1 money supply fell sharply during 1930-1933, rose during 1934-1937 but dipped again in 1938 (panel a). The general level of prices followed the same pattern (panel b). The sharp reduction in the supply of money and deflation during 1930-1933 changed the terms of loans, investments, and other economic activities that take place across time periods. This was a major factor underlying the initial plunge into the Great Depression. Further, the monetary contraction of 1938 stifled the recovery and contributed to still another downturn.

Sources: Change in the money supply is from December to December. The data are from Milton Friedman and Anna J. Schwartz, *A Monetary History of the United States, 1867–1960* (Princeton, NJ: Princeton University Press, 1963); for CPI data: www.bls.gov.

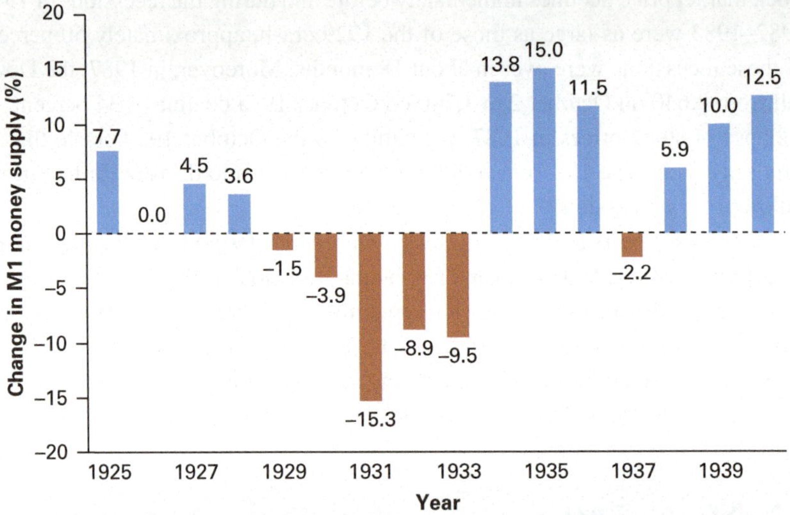

(a) Change in money supply (M1)

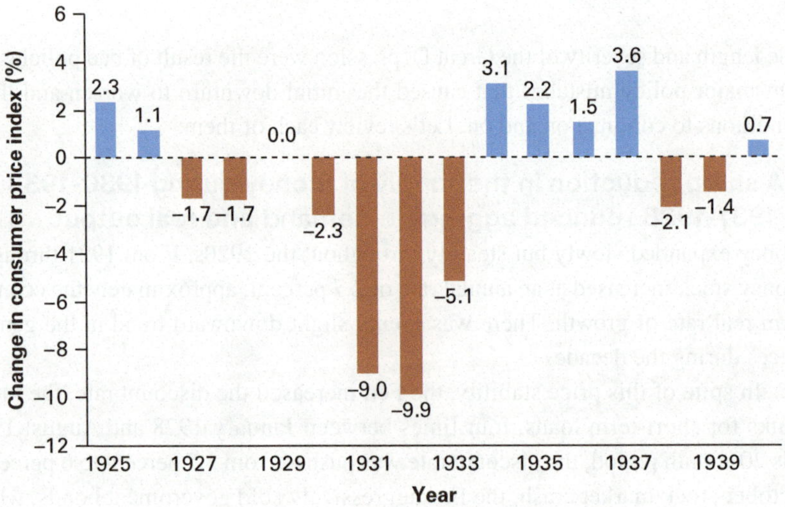

(b) Change in CPI

undertook investments and borrowed funds suffered losses and were unable to fulfill their contracts. As the gains from trade dissipated and aggregate demand plunged, so, too, did output and employment. By 1933, real GDP was 29 percent lower than the 1929 level, and the unemployment rate had soared to nearly 25 percent.

During 1934–1937, the Fed reversed itself and expanded the supply of money. The monetary expansion halted the deflation, and the general level of prices increased. So, too, did the level of economic activity. Real GDP expanded and the unemployment rate fell during 1934–1937. But the Fed doubled the reserve requirements between August 1936 and May 1937, leading to another decline in the money supply and the general level of prices. This caused the economy to falter again and pushed the unemployment rate to almost 20 percent in 1938.

Sound monetary policy is about price stability—following a monetary policy that keeps the inflation rate low and steady. The Federal Reserve totally failed the American people during the 1930s. The severe monetary contraction led to near-double-digit deflation. This was followed by a shift to monetary expansion, which generated inflation, but the Fed soon shifted again toward contraction, which caused still more deflation. Essentially, the monetary instability of the 1930s generated uncertainty and undermined the exchange process.[3]

Senator Reed Smoot and Congressman Willis Hawley (shown here) spearheaded legislation passed in June 1930 that increased tariff rates by an average of more than 50 percent. They thought their bill would "save jobs" and promote prosperity. Instead, it did the opposite, as other nations retaliated with higher tariffs on American products and world trade fell substantially.

2. The Smoot-Hawley trade bill of 1930 increased tariffs and led to a huge reduction in the volume of international trade. Signed into law on June 17, 1930, the Smoot–Hawley trade bill increased tariffs by more than 50 percent on approximately 3,200 imported products. Many of these tariff increases were in dollars per unit, so the subsequent deflation pushed them still higher relative to the price of the product.

Like their protectionist counterparts today, President Herbert Hoover, Senator Reed Smoot, and Congressman Willis Hawley argued that the trade restrictions would "save jobs." As Congressman Hawley put it, "I want to see American workers employed producing American goods for American consumption."[4] The proponents of the Smoot–Hawley legislation also believed the higher tariffs would bring in additional revenue for the federal government.

More than 100 years before the Great Depression, Adam Smith and David Ricardo explained how nations gained when they specialized in the production of goods they could supply at a low cost while trading for those they could produce only at a high cost. Trade makes it possible for both trading partners to generate a larger output and achieve a higher living standard. Moreover, a nation cannot reduce its imports without simultaneously reducing its exports. If foreign firms sell less to Americans, then they will earn fewer of the dollars needed to buy from Americans. Thus, a reduction in imports will also lead to a reduction in exports. Jobs created in import-competing industries will be offset by jobs lost in exporting industries. There will be no net expansion in employment. The view that import restrictions will generate a net creation of jobs is fallacious.

Having read both Smith and Ricardo, the economists of 1930 were well aware of the benefits derived from international trade and the harm generated by trade restrictions. More than a thousand of them signed an open letter to President Hoover warning of the harmful effects of Smoot–Hawley and pleading with him not to sign the legislation. He rejected their pleas, but history confirmed the validity of their warnings.

The higher tariffs did not generate additional revenue, and they certainly did not save jobs. The import restrictions harmed foreign suppliers, and predictably they retaliated. Sixty countries responded with higher tariffs on American products. By 1932, the volume of U.S. trade had fallen to less than half its earlier level. As a result, the federal government actually derived less revenue at the higher tariff rates. Tariff revenues fell from $602 million in 1929 to $328 million in 1932. Similarly, output and employment declined, and the unemployment rate soared. The unemployment rate was 7.8 percent when Smoot–Hawley was passed, but it ballooned to 23.6 percent of the labor force just two years later. Moreover, the "trade war" helped spread the recessionary conditions throughout the world.

There was substantial opposition to the Smoot–Hawley bill, and the Senate vote was close (44–42). Last-minute changes in the rate schedules were made in order to gain the

---

[3]For a comprehensive analysis of monetary policy during the Great Depression, refer to the chapter on the Great Contraction in Milton Friedman and Anna Schwartz, *A Monetary History of the United States, 1867–1960* (New York: National Bureau of Economic Research, 1963; ninth paperback printing by Princeton University Press, 1993): 411–15.

[4]Frank Whitson Fetter, "Congressional Tariff Theory," *American Economic Review* 23, no. 3 (September 1933): 413–27.

final votes needed for passage. Some businesses, seeking to gain advantage at the expense of consumers and foreign rivals, lobbied hard for the legislation. But, like the economists, other business leaders recognized that trade restrictions would harm rather than help the economy.

As we previously discussed, stock prices had increased for five straight months following the November 1929 lows, and by mid-April of 1930, the Dow Jones Industrials had returned to the level just before the October 1929 crash (refer to Exhibit ST05-2). But as the Smoot–Hawley bill moved through Congress and its prospects for passage improved, stock prices moved steadily downward. In fact, the reduction in stock prices following the debate and passage of Smoot–Hawley was even greater than that of the 1929 October crash. By year-end 1930, recovery was nowhere in sight, and the Dow Jones Industrial index had fallen to 165, down from 294 in mid-April.

The combination of highly restrictive monetary policy and the Smoot–Hawley trade restrictions was enough to push the economy over the cliff, but Congress and the president were not through.

3. A large tax increase in the midst of a severe recession made a bad situation worse. Before the Keynesian revolution, the dominant view was that the federal budget should be balanced. Reflecting the ongoing economic downturn, the federal budget ran a deficit in 1931, and an even larger deficit was shaping up for 1932. Assisted by the newly elected Democratic majority in the House of Representatives, the Republican Hoover Administration passed the largest peacetime tax rate increase in the history of the United States. As **Exhibit ST05-4** indicates, the lowest marginal tax rate on personal income was raised from 1.5 percent to 4 percent in 1932. At the top of the income scale, the highest marginal tax rate was raised from 25 percent to 63 percent. Essentially, personal income tax rates were increased at all levels by approximately 150 percent in one year! This huge tax increase reduced both the after-tax income of households and the incentive to earn and invest.

Fiscal policy analysis indicates that a tax increase of this magnitude in the midst of a severe downturn will be disastrous. Review of Exhibit ST05-1 shows that this was indeed the

Exhibit ST05-4 Marginal Income Tax Rates, 1925–1940

The lowest and highest marginal tax rates imposed on personal income are shown here for the period before, and during, the Great Depression. Note how the top marginal rate was increased from 25 percent in 1931 to 63 percent in 1932. Real GDP fell by 13.3 percent in 1932, and the unemployment rate soared to nearly a quarter of the labor force (refer to Exhibit ST05-1). In 1936, the top rate was pushed still higher to 79 percent.

Sources: The Tax Foundation, www.taxfoundation.org; and the IRS at www.irs.gov.

case. In 1932, real output fell by 13 percent, the largest single-year decline during the Great Depression era. Unemployment rose from 15.9 percent in 1931 to 23.6 percent in 1932.

In 1936, the Roosevelt administration increased taxes again, pushing the top marginal rate to 79 percent. Thus, during the latter half of the 1930s, high earners were permitted to keep only 21 cents of each additional dollar they earned. Moreover, the 1936 tax legislation also imposed a special tax on the retained earnings of corporations, a major source of funds for business investment. These 1936 tax increases further reduced both income levels and the incentive to earn and invest, prolonging the Great Depression and increasing its severity.

Franklin D. Roosevelt Library, courtesy of the National Archives and Records Administration

The Agricultural Adjustment Act of 1933 sought to increase the prices of farm products by reducing their supply. Under this act, 6 million baby pigs were slaughtered in 1933. Did this help bring the Great Depression to an end?

4. Price controls, anticompetitive policies, and constant structural changes during the Roosevelt administration generated uncertainty and undermined the normal recovery process. President Roosevelt was elected in 1932, and many history books still credit his New Deal policies with bringing the Great Depression to an end. Numerous policy changes were instituted during the Roosevelt years, and some of them were helpful. In 1933, President Roosevelt revalued the price of gold from $20 per ounce to $35 per ounce, and this contributed to the expansion in the money supply during the years immediately following. The Roosevelt administration also passed the Federal Deposit Insurance program, which provided depositors with protection against bank failures and reduced the occurrence of "bank runs."

However, it is equally clear that many of the major initiatives of the Roosevelt administration were counterproductive and prolonged the Great Depression. Roosevelt perceived that falling prices were a problem, but he failed to recognize that this was because of the monetary contraction. Instead, he tried to keep product prices high by reducing their supply. Under the Agricultural Adjustment Act (AAA) passed in 1933, farmers were paid to plow under portions of their cotton, corn, wheat, and other crops. Potato farmers were paid to spray their potatoes with dye so that they would be unfit for human consumption. Healthy cattle, sheep, and pigs were slaughtered and buried in mass graves in order to keep them off the market. In 1933 alone, 6 million baby pigs were killed under the Roosevelt agricultural policy. The Supreme Court declared the AAA unconstitutional in 1936, but not before it had kept millions of dollars of agricultural products from American consumers.

The National Industrial Recovery Act (NIRA) was another New Deal effort to keep prices high. Under this legislation passed in June 1933, more than 500 industries ranging from automobiles and steel to dog food and dry cleaners were organized into **cartels**. Business representatives from each industry were invited to Washington to work with NIRA officials to set production quotas, prices, wages, working hours, distribution methods, and other mandates for their industry. Once approved by a majority of the firms, the regulations were legally binding, and they applied to all businesses in the industry, regardless of whether they approved or participated in development of the regulations. Firms that did not comply were fined, and, in some cases, owners were even thrown in jail. A tax was levied on all firms in these industries in order to cover the administrative cost of the act. Before the NIRA, collusive behavior of this type would have been prosecuted as a violation of antitrust laws, but with the NIRA, the government itself provided the organizational structure for the cartels and prosecuted firms that dared to reduce prices or failed to comply with other regulations. Clearly, the NIRA reduced competition, promoted monopoly pricing, and undermined the market process.

Cartels
An organization of sellers designed to coordinate supply and price decisions so that the joint profits of the members will be maximized. A cartel will seek to create a monopoly in the market for its product.

Exhibit ST05-5 tracks industrial output before, and during, the NIRA's existence. Interestingly, a recovery had started during the first half of 1933. Industrial output increased sharply, and factory employment expanded by 25 percent during the four months before the NIRA took effect. But as the act was implemented in July 1933, industrial output began to decline precipitously. By the end of 1933, output had fallen by more than 25 percent from

Exhibit ST05-5 The NIRA and Industrial Production, 1932-1936

The change in industrial production before and following the passage of the National Industrial Recovery Act (NIRA) is shown here. Note how industrial output increased sharply during April-July 1933. However, when the implementation of the NIRA began in July, industrial output fell by more than 25 percent over the next six months. It never reached the June 1933 level again until after the act was declared unconstitutional in May 1935.

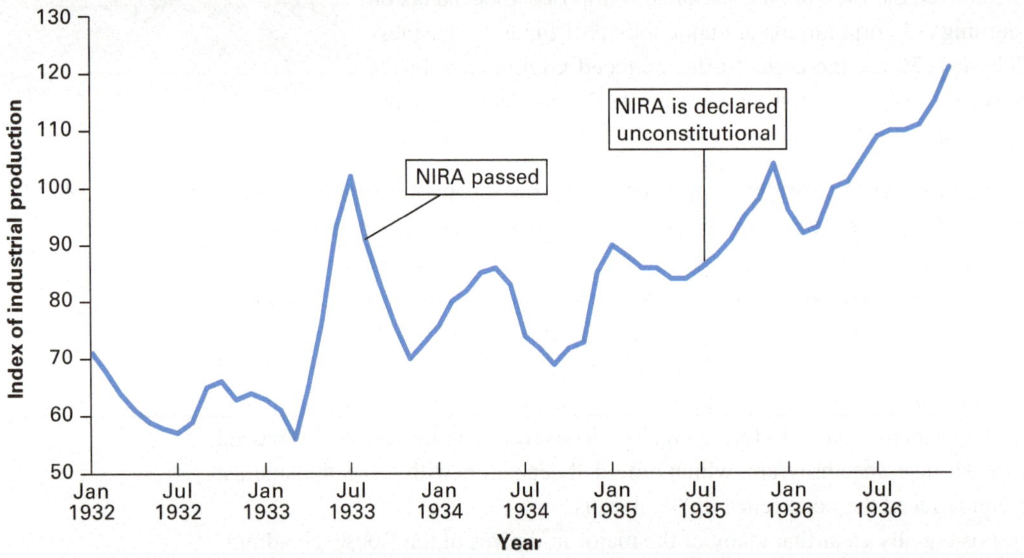

Source: Historical Statistics of the United States. The base period (equal to 100) was the average of the monthly figures during 1923–1925.

its mid-summer high. There were some ups and downs during the next year, but industrial output never returned to its pre-NIRA level until after the Supreme Court in a 9–0 vote declared the act unconstitutional in May 1935.[5]

The AAA and NIRA were just part of the persistent policy changes during the Roosevelt years. The Wagner Act took labor law out of the courts and assigned it to a new regulatory commission, the National Labor Relations Board. Pro-union appointments to this new board dramatically changed collective bargaining and led to a sharp increase in unionization. The Works Progress Administration (WPA) and Civilian Conservation Corps (CCC) vastly expanded government employment. The Davis–Bacon Act required government contractors to employ higher wage union workers, which, in effect, reduced the employment opportunities of minorities and those with fewer skills. Unprecedented high marginal tax rates, establishment of a minimum wage, pay-as-you-go Social Security, and several other programs changed the structure of the U.S. economy.

This persistent introduction of massive new programs and regulations created what Robert Higgs calls "regime uncertainty," the situation in which people are reluctant to undertake business ventures and investments because the government is constantly changing the "rules."[6] Against this background, business planning was undermined and private investment came to a virtual standstill. Roosevelt's close friend and Treasury Secretary Henry Morgenthau tried to get the president to make a public statement to reassure investors and the business community. He was unsuccessful. Lammont duPont highlighted the uncertainty generated by the constant whirlwind of New Deal policy changes when he stated,

[5]For additional details on the impact of the NRA, refer to Chapter 4 of the book by historian Burton Folsom, *New Deal or Raw Deal* (New York: Simon & Schuster, 2008).

[6]Robert Higgs, "Regime Uncertainty: Why the Great Depression Lasted So Long and Why Prosperity Resumed After the War," *The Independent Review* 1, no. 4 (Spring 1997).

> Uncertainty rules the tax situation, the labor situation, the monetary situation, and practically every legal condition under which industry must operate. Are taxes to go higher, lower or stay where they are? We don't know. Is labor to be union or non-union? Are we to have inflation or deflation, more government spending or less? Are new restrictions to be placed on capital, new limits on profits? It is impossible to even guess at the answers.[7]

Did the New Deal policies bring the Great Depression to an end?[8] Through the years, many students have been taught that this was the case. It is difficult to understand how anyone could objectively review the data and accept this proposition. Before the Great Depression, recessions lasted only one or two years, three years at the most, and recovery pushed income to new highs. The Great Depression was different. In 1933, the monetary contraction was reversed, and there was evidence of a private-sector recovery. But the NIRA, AAA, and 1936 tax increases dampened productive activity, and the second monetary contraction pushed the economy into another recession within the depression. In 1938, per capita real GDP of the United States was still below the level of 1929, and the rate of unemployment was 19 percent. In 1939, seven years after the beginning of the New Deal, 17 percent of the labor force was still unemployed. The Great Depression was eventually diminished by the increase in demand for military goods of the English and Russians and our own military buildup before World War II.[9]

ST05-4 Fiscal Policy During the Great Depression

What happened to fiscal policy during the Great Depression? This was, of course, before the Keynesian revolution, and the view that the government should balance its budget, except perhaps during wartime, was widely accepted. **Exhibit ST05-6** panel (a) presents the data for government spending as a share of GDP. The size of the government was much smaller as a share of the economy during this era. Total government spending (federal, state, and local) increased from 8 percent of GDP in 1929 to 16 percent in 1933. To a large degree, however, this increase reflected the maintenance of nominal government expenditures during a period of deflation and declining GDP. After 1933, total government spending as a share of GDP remained in the 15 percent to 16 percent range for the rest of the decade, except during 1937, when the ratio fell to 13 percent.

Exhibit ST05-6 panel (b) provides the figures for the federal deficit. The budget was in surplus during both 1929 and 1930. After that, the deficit was generally around 2 percent of GDP, except during 1934 and 1936, and in 1937 when a small surplus was present. Measured

---

[7]Quoted in Herman E. Krooss, *Executive Opinion: What Business Leaders Said and Thought on Economic Issues, 1920s–1960s* (Garden City, NY: Doubleday and Co., 1970), 200.

[8]For additional details on the Great Depression, refer to Gene Smiley, *Rethinking the Great Depression* (Ivan R. Dee, Chicago, IL 2002); Robert J. Samuelson, "Great Depression," in *The Fortune Encyclopedia of Economics*, ed., David R. Henderson (New York: Warner Books, 1993), available online at www.econlib.org; Burton Folsom, *New Deal or Raw Deal?* (New York: Simon & Schuster, 2008); and Amity Shlaes, *The Forgotten Man: A New History of the Great Depression* (New York: HarperCollins Publishers, 2007).

[9]Many argue that the spending increases and large budget deficits of World War II provided sufficient demand stimulus to direct the economy back to full employment and solid growth. Robert Higgs challenges this view. Higgs notes that with 12 million young Americans drafted during the war, this would obviously reduce the unemployment rate to a low level. However, the growth of real GDP is more debatable because almost half of measured output was government spending, and it was added to GDP at cost. Moreover, the income of households was overstated because many goods they would have purchased were unavailable as a result of the price controls. The sharp decline in GDP following the war and the lifting of price controls also imply that the growth of GDP during the war was overstated. Thus, Higgs does not believe that real recovery from the Great Depression occurred until 1946. Refer to Robert Higgs, *Depression, War, and Cold War: Studies in Political Economy* (New York: Oxford University Press, 2006).

Exhibit ST05-6 Government Expenditures and Federal Budget Deficits as a Share of GDP, 1929–1940

Measured as a share of the economy, government spending increased during the 1930s, and the federal government generally ran a budget deficit. However, given the depth of the economic decline, the deficits were too small to provide much fiscal stimulus during this era.

Source: www.bea.gov.

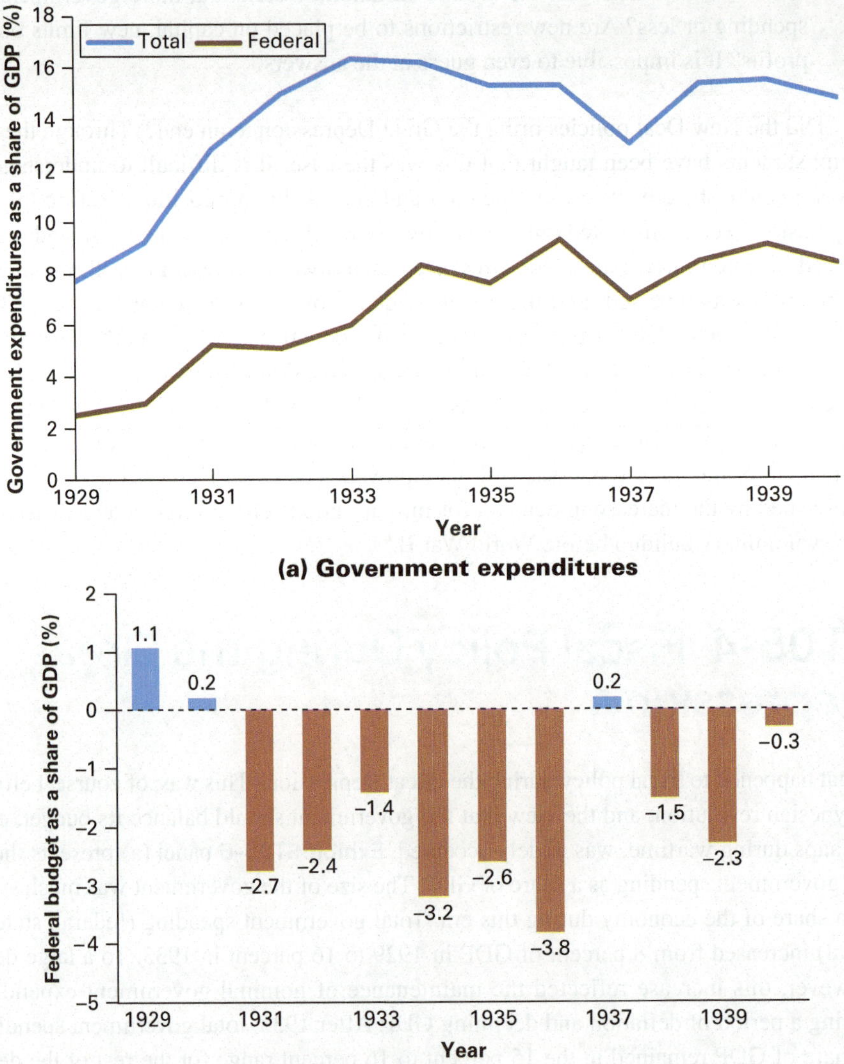

(a) Government expenditures

(b) Budget deficit (–) or surplus (+)

as a share of the economy, the increases in government spending and federal deficits during the 1930s were relatively small. Thus, there is little reason to believe that fiscal policy exerted much impact on the economy. Certainly, there is no reason to believe that spending increases and budget deficits were a significant source of fiscal stimulus during the era.

ST05-5 Lessons from the Great Depression

The Great Depression provides several lessons that can help us avoid severe downturns in the future. First, the Great Depression clearly indicates that a prolonged period of monetary contraction will undermine time-dimension economic activity and exert disastrous effects on the economy. We seemed to have learned this lesson well. As the severity of the 2008 downturn increased, the Fed injected abundant reserves into the banking system and shifted to a more expansionary monetary policy. However, it is also true that Fed policy during 2002–2006 contributed to the housing boom and bust and, thereby, the Great Recession. Monetary and price stability is crucially important for the smooth operation of markets. The Great Depression, along with experience since that era, vividly illustrates this point.

Second, the Great Depression illustrates the fallacy of the "trade restrictions will promote domestic industry" argument. Policies that reduce imports will simultaneously reduce exports. Foreign firms will not have the dollars to purchase as much from us if they sell less to us. Trade restrictions will not save jobs. Instead, they will shift employment from sectors in which we are a low-cost producer to those in which we are a high-cost producer. The results are fewer gains from trade, a smaller output, and lower income levels. Both economic theory and the experience of the Smoot–Hawley trade restrictions are consistent with this view.

Third, raising taxes in the midst of a severe recession is a bad idea. Pushing taxes to exceedingly high rates is a recipe for disaster. All of the major macroeconomic theories—Keynesian, new classical, and supply side—indicate that tax increases will be counterproductive during a severe downturn. The experience with the tax increases during the Great Depression reinforces these views.

Fourth, the political incentive structure during a severe downturn is likely to encourage politicians to "do something." Even bad policies are likely to be popular, at least for a while. A better strategy would be the oath of the medical profession, "do no harm." The constant policy changes under both Hoover and Roosevelt created uncertainty and froze private-sector investment and business activity. Everyone waited to see what the next new policy regime would be; and, as they did so, the depressed conditions were prolonged.

The experience of the 1930s highlights the importance of economic literacy. The decade-long catastrophic decline did not have to happen. It was the result of wrong-headed policies based on the economic illiteracy of both voters and policy-makers.

Finally, as we noted in Chapter 1, good intentions are no substitute for sound policy. The Great Depression provides a vivid illustration of this point. There is every reason to believe that Presidents Hoover and Roosevelt, Senator Smoot, Congressman Hawley, other members of Congress, and the monetary policy-makers of the 1930s had good intentions. But, it is equally clear that their actions tragically turned what would have been a normal business cycle downturn into a decade of hardship and suffering. The good intentions of political decision-makers do not protect the general citizenry from the adverse consequences of unsound policies. This was true during the Great Depression, and it is still true today. If we do not learn from the adverse experiences of history, we are likely to repeat them.

Key Points

- The Great Depression was a severe economic plunge that resulted in unemployment rates of nearly 25 percent during 1932–1933 and rates of more than 14 percent for an entire decade. It was the longest, most severe period of depressed economic conditions in American history.
- Contrary to a popular view, the Great Depression was not caused by the 1929 stock market crash. We have had similar reductions in stock prices to those of 1929, both before and after the Great Depression, without experiencing prolonged depressed conditions like those of the 1930s.
- There were four major reasons why the Great Depression was long and severe:
  1. Monetary instability: The money supply contracted by 33 percent between 1929 and 1933, and it took another tumble during 1937–1938.

2. Smoot–Hawley trade bill: This 1930 legislation increased tariffs by more than 50 percent and led to a sharp reduction in world trade.
3. 1932 tax increase: This huge tax increase reduced demand and undermined the incentive to invest and produce.
4. Structural policy changes: Persistent major changes, particularly during the Roosevelt years, generated uncertainty and undermined investment and business planning.

- The budget deficits and increases in government spending were relatively small and failed to exert much impact on total demand and the level of economic activity during the 1930s.
- The Great Depression highlights the importance of monetary stability, free trade, avoidance of high tax rates, and avoidance of price controls, entry restraints, and persistent policy changes that generate uncertainty and undermine the security of property rights. Perhaps most important, the Great Depression vividly illustrates that good intentions are not a substitute for sound economic policy.

Critical Analysis Questions

1. "The Great Depression was caused by the 1929 stock market crash. The 1929 collapse of stock prices was the most severe in U.S. history, and therefore it is not surprising that it caused a prolonged period of economic hardship." Evaluate this statement.
2. Do the length and severity of the Great Depression reflect a defect in the operation of markets? Do they reflect a failure of government policy? Discuss.
3. "Franklin Roosevelt was one of our greatest presidents because it was his New Deal policies that brought the Great Depression to an end." Evaluate this statement.
4. Was the Great Depression the result of the inherent instability of a market economy, as John Maynard Keynes argued? Alternatively, was it the result of counterproductive government policy, as Milton Friedman argued? Cite evidence supportive of your view.
5. *"I'm for international trade, but not when it takes jobs from Americans. If the American worker can produce the product, Americans should not buy it from foreign firms." Do you agree with this statement? Why or why not?
6. What are the most important lessons Americans should learn from the Great Depression? Do you think we have learned them? Why or why not?

*Asterisk denotes questions for which answers are given in Appendix B.

Special Topic 6

The Economics of Health Care

> Americans increasingly have been driven to pay for their health care through third party insurers and to purchase that insurance, when possible, from their employers. This, in turn, has led to rising health care costs while making it harder for Americans without employer-provided insurance to obtain coverage.
>
> –Michael Tanner[1]

Some categories of health care spending have substantial public good components. For example, this is true for expenditures on pure research and activities that reduce, and in some cases eliminate, the incidence of communicable diseases. In these cases, health care spending can generate spillover benefits for the general populace, and it would be difficult, if not impossible, to exclude nonpaying consumers from the receipt of these benefits. As we discussed in Chapter 5, under these conditions, government action might lead to an improvement in the allocation of resources. The National Institutes of Health and the Centers for Disease Control and Prevention provide examples of government organizations that justify their funding primarily on the basis of the public-good nature of their services. However, the vast majority of health care spending, including that of the government, involves private goods, goods for which the benefits accrue primarily to the consumer. This feature will focus on the provision of these personal consumption health care services.

Learning Objectives

ST06.1 Indicate how much Americans spend on health care.

ST06.2 Analyze why health care prices and expenditures have risen rapidly in recent decades.

ST06.3 Consider whether fundamental reform is needed in the health care industry.

ST06.4 Identify policies that would improve the delivery of health care services.

[1]Michael Tanner, "What's Wrong with the Current System," in *Empowering Health Care Consumers Through Tax Reform*, Grace-Marie Arnett, ed. (Ann Arbor: University of Michigan Press, 1999).

ST06-1 Expenditures and the Structure of the Health Care Industry

There is considerable dissatisfaction with the operation of the health care industry in the United States. This is certainly understandable. Both the expenditures on and prices of health care have soared in recent decades. **Exhibit ST06-1** presents the expenditure figures as a share of GDP. Health care spending, including both private and government, jumped from 5 percent of GDP in 1960 to 8.9 percent in 2022 and 17.3 percent in 2022.

Goods and services may be produced by either private or government-operated firms. Correspondingly, they may be paid for by the consumer directly or by the taxpayer or some other third party.

Health care in many countries, including Canada and most of the high-income countries of Europe, is a socialized industry.[2] In these countries, hospitals are operated by the government, and their services are financed through taxes. Physicians, nurses, and other health care workers are government employees. Of course, socialization does not eliminate scarcity, costs, and the need to ration the available supply. Resources must be attracted to the health care industry, and this will involve a cost. No country is able to provide as much health care, free of charge, as its citizens would like. Therefore, when price plays a secondary role, nonprice factors will have to be used to ration health care services. Thus, in these countries, political rules, waiting lists for various treatments, and the absence (or highly restricted availability) of services such as MRIs that involve expensive equipment are used to allocate health care resources.

In the United States, there is widespread use of both private and government-operated enterprises in the health care industry. Whereas the services of doctors are generally

Exhibit ST06-1 Health Care Expenditures as a Share of GDP, 1960-2022

Total expenditures (including both private- and government-financed) on health care as a share of GDP have persistently increased during the last five decades. In 2022, the United States spent 17.3 percent of its GDP on health care, up from 8.9 percent in 1980 and 5 percent in 1960.

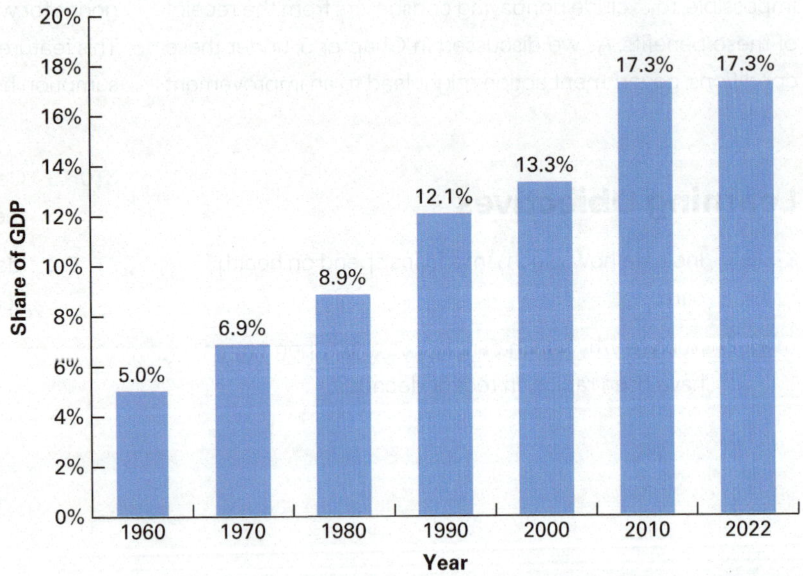

Source: http://www.cms.hhs.gov.

[2]For a cross-national comparison of spending on health care, review Uwe E. Reinhardt, "Health Care for Aging Baby Boomers: Lessons from Abroad," *Journal of Economic Perspectives* (Spring 2000): 71–83.

supplied privately, hospitals are often operated by the government, particularly local governments. Many communities, however, also have privately operated hospitals. Some of the privately operated hospitals are for-profit businesses, whereas others are operated by charitable institutions. In contrast with other U.S. industries, most health care spending (87 percent) is paid for by a third party, either the taxpayer or a private insurance company.

The Medicare and Medicaid programs have covered the bulk of the health care cost of the elderly and the poor since their establishment in the mid-1960s. Medicare's hospitalization program (Part A) uses a 2.9 percent payroll tax (3.8 percent on all income above $200,000) to finance virtually all of the cost of hospitalization incurred by persons aged 65 and older. Medicare's Part B Supplementary Medical Insurance covers outpatient medical services, and Part D subsidizes the purchase of prescription drug insurance. The latter two programs are financed 75 percent by general revenues and 25 percent by beneficiary premiums. The Medicaid program provides low-income families with access to health care either free or at a nominal cost. It is a combination federal–state program financed from general revenues. The federal government covers 60 percent of the Medicaid costs, whereas states cover the other 40 percent and have some discretion regarding the structure and coverage of the program.

Exhibit ST06-2 presents data for real expenditures (measured in 2022 dollars) on the Medicare and Medicaid programs. From the very beginning, spending on the programs rose rapidly. By 1970, combined spending on the two summed to $98 billion. Real expenditures on the Medicare program doubled between 1970 and 1980, nearly doubled between 1980 and 1990, and doubled again between 1990 and 2014. In 2022, the total expenditures on Medicare summed to $944 billion. Spending on Medicaid has also increased rapidly. In 2022, government spending on Medicaid ($806 billion) was more than three times the level

Exhibit ST06-2 Real Expenditures on Medicare and Medicaid (Measured in 2022 Dollars)

Expenditures on both Medicare and Medicaid have soared in recent decades. Adjusted for inflation, the 2022 expenditures on Medicare are more than three times the level of 1990 and 16 times the figure for 1970. The real Medicaid expenditures also increased rapidly.

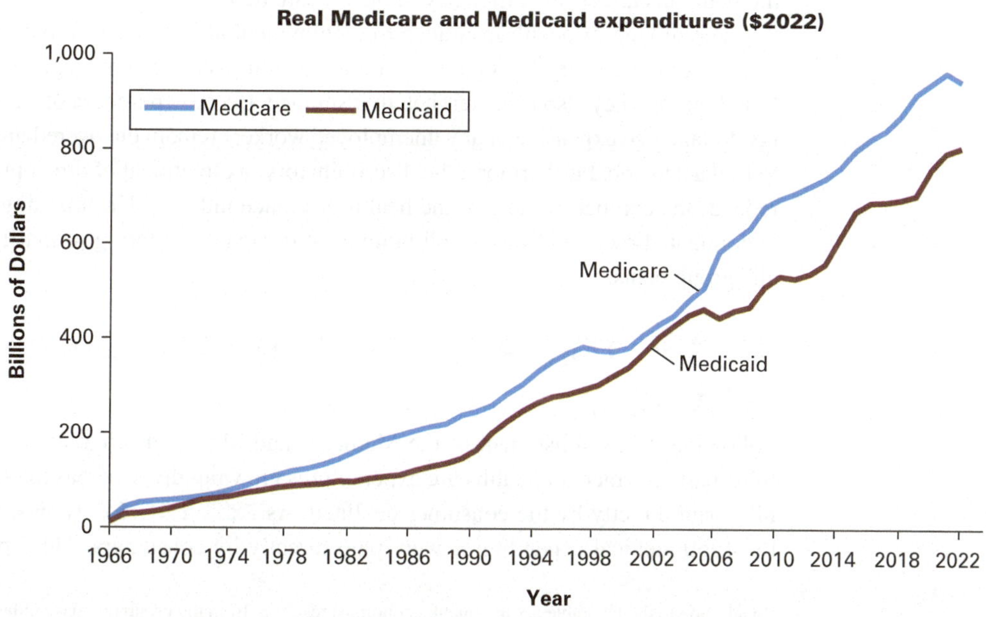

Source: http://www.cms.hhs.gov and http://www.bls.gov.

of 1990 and 16 times the figure for 1970. As Exhibit ST06-2 shows, spending on Medicaid is now 85 percent that of Medicare.

ST06-1a Discrimination Against the Direct Purchase of Health Insurance

Health insurance is also an integral part of the health care industry in the United States. About two-thirds of nonelderly adults have health insurance through group plans offered by their employers. Employee compensation in the form of health insurance is not subject to taxation. This makes group health insurance programs provided through one's employer particularly attractive.[3] Interestingly, this favorable tax treatment of employer-provided health insurance is a historical relic dating back to the wage and price controls of World War II. Because health insurance benefits were not counted as wages, employers were able to use them as a means to increase compensation and attract additional workers while still complying with the wage controls imposed during the war.

In contrast with health insurance purchased through one's employer, both personal medical bills and the direct purchase of insurance by an individual or family must be paid for with after-tax dollars. When employees are provided with additional income rather than health insurance benefits, the income is subject to both payroll and personal income taxes. This makes the direct purchase of health insurance far more costly than purchase through an employer. For example, a lower-middle-income family confronting a 12 percent federal income tax and the 15.3 percent payroll tax would have to earn approximately $14,000 of additional income in order to purchase a $10,000 health insurance policy. A family in the 32 percent federal tax bracket would have to earn approximately $19,000 more in order to purchase the policy. When state and local income and payroll taxes are present, these figures are still higher.

This discriminatory tax treatment encourages employees to demand and employers to provide low-deductible, small-copayment health insurance policies. In essence, health care expenses covered in this manner are tax deductible, whereas those paid for out of pocket or through the direct purchase of health insurance are not.[4] As a result of this distortion, more health care bills are paid for by third-party insurers and fewer are covered directly by the health care consumer or through high-deductible insurance plans. As we will discover in a moment, this affects the efficiency of health care delivery.

The linking of health insurance to employment also reduces employee mobility and increases the number of people without any health insurance coverage. When employees lose their job, they also lose their health insurance. Because purchase of a policy with after-tax dollars is so expensive, many unemployed workers remain uncovered until they are able to find a new job. Furthermore, the discriminatory tax treatment of direct purchase policies reduces the competitiveness of the health insurance industry. Unsurprisingly, the industry is dominated by a relatively small number of companies offering primarily "one size fits all" group plans.

ST06-1b Third-Party Payments and Health Care Inflation

Following the establishment of the Medicare and Medicaid programs in the mid-1960s, third-party payment of health care expenditures grew rapidly, whereas the share of medical bills paid directly by the consumer declined. As **Exhibit ST06-3** shows, 55.7 percent of the 1960 medical expenditures were paid directly by consumers. Third parties financed

[3]In addition to the favorable tax treatment, economies resulting from the group purchase of health insurance may also make employer-provided plans more attractive.

[4]Out-of-pocket health care expenses can only be deducted if the taxpayer files an itemized return. Even in this case, only health care expenses in excess of 10 percent of the taxpayer's adjusted gross income are deductible.

Exhibit ST06-3 Distribution of Payments for Health Care Expenditures, 1960 and 2022

In 1960, out-of-pocket medical care expenditures of consumers accounted for 55 percent of the total, while private insurance and government programs paid 45 percent of the medical bills. By 2022, the out-of-pocket payments had fallen to only 13 percent of expenditures, while those covered by a third party had risen to 47 percent of the total. Economic theory indicates that growth of third-party payments will reduce the incentive to economize and lead to both higher prices and expenditure levels.

Source: http://www.cms.hhs.gov. Here, medical care payments are defined as personal health-care expenditures.

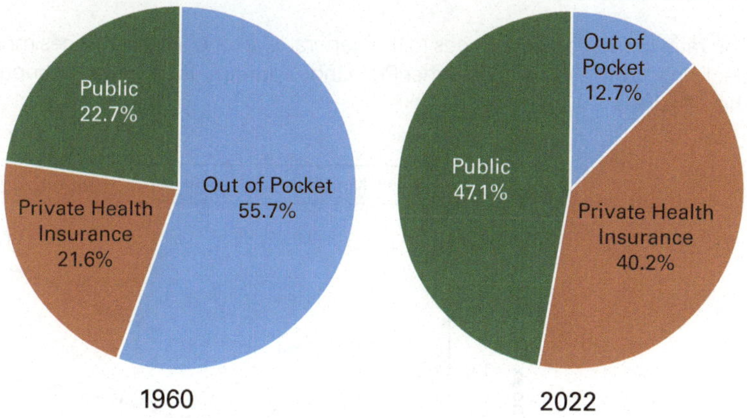

only 44.3 percent of the 1960 total. Through the years, the share paid out of pocket has declined, whereas that financed by third parties has risen. By 2022, third-party payments accounted for 87 percent of the medical care purchases, 47.1 percent by the government, and 40.2 percent by private insurers. Only 13 percent of the medical bills in 2022 were paid for directly by consumers.

Economic theory indicates that the growth of subsidies to health care consumers and the accompanying expansion in third-party payments will push prices upward. There are two reasons why this will be the case. First, subsidies like those provided by Medicare and Medicaid will increase the demand for medical care. In turn, the stronger demand will lead to higher prices. As we discussed in Chapter 4, when the supply of a good or service is highly inelastic, suppliers will be the primary beneficiaries even if the subsidies are directed toward consumers. This is the case in the health care industry: The supply of most medical services is highly inelastic. As a result, the primary impact of the subsidies will be higher prices and increased returns for health care providers.

Second, the growth of third-party payments weakens the incentive of consumers to economize and shop for low-cost services and the incentive for producers to provide the goods at a low price. In a normal market, consumers will shop around and patronize those suppliers that provide the most value per dollar of expenditure. In turn, this shopping by consumers provides suppliers with a strong incentive to control their costs and offer their services at attractive prices. But when someone else is paying all or most of the bill, the incentive to economize is eroded. Rather than search for value relative to cost, consumers will attempt to purchase from the "best available" supplier, pretty much regardless of price.

Perhaps the following example will help explain why the substitution of third-party payments for out-of-pocket spending will lead to higher prices. Suppose that the government, insurance companies, or some other third party was willing to pay 90 percent of the bill of customers purchasing hair-styling services. Think how the behavior of both potential consumers and suppliers in the hair-styling business would be altered. Because someone else is paying most of the bill, many consumers will now get their hair styled more often, search for the very best stylists even if they are quite expensive, and patronize those providing extra services (for example, shoulder massages, pleasant surroundings, and valet parking). The strong demand will make it possible for hair stylists to raise their prices, and many will begin providing the "extras" designed to convince consumers that their services

Exhibit ST06-4 Ratio of Health Care Price Indexes Relative to the Consumer Price Index. 1960-2023

The ratio of medical care prices to the general level of consumer prices more than doubled between 1965 and 2023. After declining relative to the Consumer Price Index during 1960-1980, prescription drug prices have increased far more rapidly than the CPI since 1980.

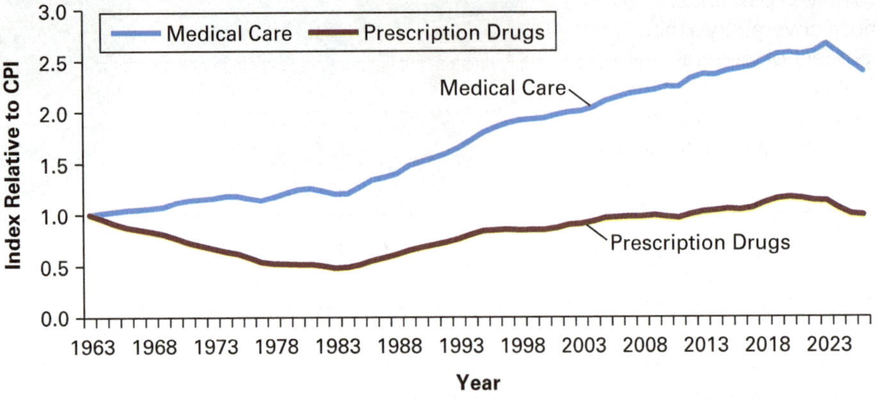

Source: www.bls.gov.

are the best. All of these adjustments will drive the price of hair-styling services upward and cause the third-party expenditures to soar.

Summarizing, economic theory indicates that higher subsidies and increased third-party payments will increase demand for the service, reduce the incentive to economize, and lead to rising prices and expenditures. Moreover, when the supply of the service is highly inelastic, the producers will be the primary beneficiaries of the subsidies.

The evidence is supportive of this view. **Exhibit ST06-4** shows the ratio of the medical care price index to the overall consumer price index. If the prices of medical services increase more than the prices of other consumer purchases, this ratio will rise. Note that this has been the case year after year. Since the passage of the Medicare and Medicaid programs in 1965, the prices of medical services have more than doubled relative to the general consumer price index. Thus, during this lengthy time span, on average, the prices of health care services rose at more than twice the rate of other consumer items. In fact, the increase in medical prices relative to the general index of consumer prices has accelerated since 1980. More-over, the prices of prescription drugs, which rose less than the consumer price index during the 1960s and 1970s, have increased more rapidly than the CPI in recent decades. There is some evidence that health care inflation is slowing. Between 2020 and 2023, both medical care and prescription drug prices have risen more slowly than the general level of consumer prices. It is uncertain whether this trend will continue in the future given the aging of the population.

As prices and expenditures soar, third-party payees, including both insurance companies and the government, will try to control the growth of their expenditures. They may limit the amount paid for various services, require consumers to patronize only certain providers, make it more difficult to obtain permission for costly procedures, impose delays, and the like. This is essentially the route taken by the "managed-care movement" of the 1990s. Regulatory controls of this type, however, are difficult to implement successfully because they often conflict with the interest of both consumers and health care providers. As the experience with managed care illustrates, this path will tend to result in unhappy consumers and decisions that, with the benefit of hindsight, were clearly inappropriate and in some cases life-threatening. Controlling costs through rules and regulations imposed by a third party is an imperfect substitute for competition and the choices of consumers spending their own money.

Exhibit ST06-5 Growth in the U.S. Population Age 70 and Over, 2000-2040

Between 2000 and 2010, the number of people age 70 and over increased by 2.4 million. Since 2010, however, the population 70 and over has grown far more rapidly. This rapid growth increases both the demand for health care and the Medicare expenditures because the medical expenses of people in this age category are exceedingly high

Source: www.census.gov.

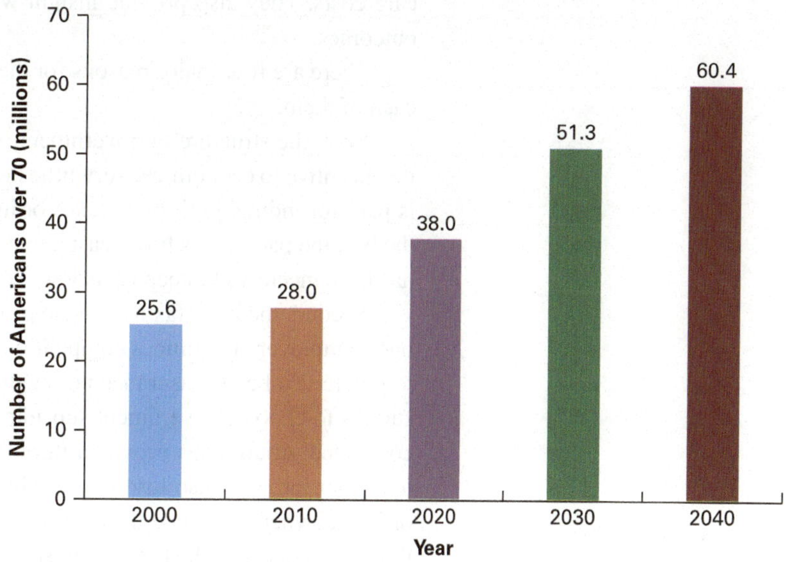

ST06-1c The Growth of the Elderly Population and the Health Care Sector

As **Exhibit ST06-5** illustrates, the number of Americans aged 70 and older expanded by 2.4 million between 2000 and 2010. But the growth of the population in this age category will soar as the baby boomers (the generation born after World War II) reach age 70 in large numbers. This is now happening. By 2030, the population aged 70 and over will rise to 51.3 million, an increase of 23.3 million (83 percent) since 2010.

This huge increase in elderly Americans has enormous implications for the health care industry. Because health care expenses are much higher for people in their 70s than in their 60s and younger, this growth of Americans aged 70 and older will increase the demand for both medical services and the share of those services financed by third parties. This will push both health care prices and expenditures upward. It will also cause spending on Medicare and other health care programs to soar and necessitate higher taxes for their finance.

The Medicare Trustees estimate that Medicare's unfunded promises—projected spending beyond revenues anticipated at current tax rates—are $53 trillion.[5] That figure is more than the official national debt and more than two times the unfunded liability of the Social Security system. Even more important, it is nearly one and a half times the size of the U.S. economy.

ST06-2 What Accounts for the Poor Performance of the Health Care Industry?

Some charge that market forces have failed in health care and therefore government must intervene. However, past government intervention has generated problems. Past interventions have resulted in perverse incentives that encourage people to engage in actions that

[5]Refer to *2023 Annual Report of the Boards of Trustees of the Federal Hospital Insurance and Federal Supplementary Medical Insurance Trust Fund*, www.cmhs.hhs.gov.

impose costs on others and use resources inefficiently. Understanding these incentives clarifies the forces underlying both the poor performance of the industry and the rising health care costs. They also provide insight with regard to effective action that would improve outcomes.

There are four major reasons for the poor performance of this sector. We will consider each of them.

First, the structure of government programs relies on third-party payments that erode the incentive to economize. Very little health care is purchased directly by consumers. Most is paid for indirectly through taxes or insurance premiums. When someone else is paying the bill, the patient has little reason to conserve on the use of the resource and the provider has little incentive to keep costs low.

Second, the huge tax advantage provided for the purchase of health insurance through one's employer undermines competition and makes it very costly for individuals or families to purchase a health insurance policy that fits their preferences. Rather than allowing consumers to choose, government subsidies and regulations push them into standardized and controlled group plans provided through employers. Moreover, under this system, if you lose your job, you also lose your health insurance. People do not generally buy auto, life, or homeowner insurance through their employer. Why do so many buy health insurance this way? Answer: The tax system subsidizes them to do so and punishes them with higher personal costs if they do not.

Third, state regulations that force insurers operating in the state to cover numerous items such as in vitro fertilization, drug rehabilitation, marriage counseling, acupuncture, and massage therapy also drive up costs and make it still more difficult for consumers to purchase a policy that fits their preferences. Interestingly, the political pressure for this coverage almost always comes from special interest producer associations wanting taxpayers to subsidize the purchase of their services.

Fourth, regulations prevent consumers from purchasing a health insurance plan offered in another state. Thus, if you would like to purchase insurance that would provide you with inexpensive basic coverage at a low cost, but you happen to live in a state that has adopted many of the expensive mandates, you are out of luck. Essentially, the government has organized the health insurance business into separate cartels that operate in each of the 50 states. You can buy almost everything ranging from groceries and automobiles to life and auto insurance from providers in other states, but not health insurance.

The poor performance and dissatisfaction with the health care sector led to the passage of the Patient Protection and Affordable Care Act in 2010. This legislation required everyone to purchase an approved health care insurance plan and imposed a tax penalty if they did not. This portion of the act was later repealed. Several other provisions were also either repealed or substantially modified. However, two major elements of the Affordable Care Act remain. First, the act requires insurers to cover children of policyholders up to age 26 and prohibits them from charging higher rates or rejecting anyone because of an existing health condition (for example, cancer, diabetes, or heart disease). Second, the legislation established exchanges for the purchase of health care insurance. The exchanges are operated by states or by the federal government. Four alternative plans ranging from low to high coverage are offered through the exchanges. Insurance providers bid on the premiums they are willing to charge for each of the alternative plans. The purchase of health care insurance through the exchanges is subsidized for those earning up to 400 percent of the poverty income threshold, an annual income of about \$125,000 in the case of a family of four.[6] Those with incomes less than 134 percent of the poverty level are covered by Medicaid. In spite of the Affordable Care Act and the later modifications, widespread dissatisfaction with the health care sector remains.

[6]The 400 percent of the poverty income threshold was eliminated for 2021–2025.

ST06-3 Empowering Consumers and Increasing Competitiveness

The health care system of the United States is heavily regulated, politically directed, and sometimes internally contradictory as the result of numerous "political fixes" over several decades. While most doctors operate privately, their fees (prices) and method of delivery are largely set by either the government or private insurers. The federal government now sets more than 7,000 reimbursement rates for various medical procedures. The power of consumers is severely limited because they pay only a small share of the cost of their health care services. Without consumer choice, you cannot expect the system to reflect the preferences of consumers. In addition, the structure of the health care sector stifles competition, innovation, and the use of modern technology. How can consumers be empowered and competitiveness enhanced? Numerous policy changes would be helpful, but the following five alternatives are particularly important.

1. Equalize the tax treatment of out-of-pocket medical expenses and the direct purchase of health insurance with that of health insurance purchased through an employer. One way to achieve this objective would be to provide all taxpayers with a 30 percent refundable tax credit, a tax saving similar to that of employer-provided plans, for expenditures on the direct purchase of medical insurance and out-of-pocket payment of medical bills. This would make it cheaper for people without access to employer-provided insurance to purchase coverage and pay medical bills directly.

2. Allow the residents of each state to purchase health care from out-of-state providers. This would break up the government-protected cartels now operating in each state and make the health insurance industry more competitive. It would also expand the options available to consumers and make it easier for them to purchase a plan more consistent with their personal preferences.

3. Encourage health savings accounts (HSAs) and the direct payment of medical bills from the accounts. In recent years, **health savings accounts** have been treated more favorably, but they are still treated less favorably than insurance purchased through one's employer. Individuals have a property right to the funds in their HSA, and their ownership is not dependent upon their employment. Funds can be drawn from these accounts for the direct payment of medical bills not covered by the high-deductible policies. Balances in the accounts can earn interest tax-free and be rolled over from year to year. Accumulated balances can either be used in retirement or passed on to heirs. HSAs reduce the incidence of third-party payments, and with time, as more health care consumers shop for value, medical suppliers will become more cost-sensitive. These accounts have grown substantially in recent years. In 2018, HSAs covered about 30 million individuals.

Health savings accounts
Special savings accounts that individuals and families can use for the payment of medical bills and the purchase of a catastrophic (high-deductible) health insurance plan.

4. Encourage the purchase of catastrophic health insurance and discourage the purchase of policies with first-dollar coverage and small copayments. HSAs are designed to be used with a high-deductible, modest copayment insurance plan that can be purchased at an economical price. Insurance works well when it compensates people for losses resulting from unpredictable events outside of their control that seldom occur, but when they do, they impose large losses on the unfortunate parties. Under these circumstances, the premiums of those experiencing little or no damage can be used to compensate those experiencing large losses. Large medical expenses such as those resulting from a severe injury or a catastrophic illness like diabetes or cancer generally fall into this category. It makes sense to promote the purchase of health insurance providing protection against large medical bills from sources like these. High-deductible policies—for example, one that covers most medical expenses in excess of $1,200 per year—are relatively cheap.

In contrast, insurance works poorly when the "losses" are widespread among the insurees and when the actions of those insured influence the size of the benefits they derive. Under these circumstances, many insurees will do less to avoid actions that increase the likelihood of events that trigger compensation; and, as a result, insurance premiums will be costly relative to the benefits. Many health care costs, including those resulting from routine illnesses (for example, colds and flu, common childhood diseases, minor injuries, and the like), fall into this category. In varying degrees, almost everyone can expect to experience such medical problems, and there are several alternative ways of dealing with them, some of which are far less costly than others. Predictably, insurance will work poorly for medical costs of this type. Furthermore, policies requiring only a small copayment for routine medical expenses promote the third-party payment system that reduces economizing behavior. Thus, it makes no sense for public policy to promote such schemes.

5. Place more emphasis on the supply side of the health care market. Each year, the government spends several hundred billion dollars subsidizing demand and helping people purchase medical services. Very little is spent encouraging additional supply. However, without additional supply, demand subsidies merely lead to higher prices and a reallocation of health care services among consumers. Thus, the primary beneficiaries of the demand-side subsidies are the health care suppliers, who receive the higher prices for their services. Supply-side programs would focus more on the training of health care providers. For example, they might provide more aid for the growth and development of medical schools. Aid to low-income students qualified to attend medical and nursing schools might also be expanded. In contrast with demand subsidies, programs that expand the supply of medical personnel would make it easier to control future costs.

ST06-4 Concluding Thoughts

Health care costs so much because consumers directly pay for so little of it. When consumers spend their own money, they will choose wisely, and their choices will provide suppliers with a strong incentive to control costs and offer quality service. While the proposals outlined here will not solve all of the health care problems, economic analysis suggests they are a major move in the right direction.

Key Points

- Spending on health care has soared in recent decades. Measured as a share of the economy, total health care spending has risen from 5 percent in 1960 to 8.9 percent in 1980 and 17.3 percent in 2022.
- Following the enactment of Medicare and Medicaid in the mid-1960s, the direct expenditures of health care consumers gradually declined and those of third-party payers expanded. The out-of-pocket spending of consumers accounted for only 13 percent of health care spending in 2022, down from 56 percent in 1960.
- The growth of subsidies to health care consumers and greater reliance on third-party payments of recent

decades (1) increased the demand for medical services and (2) reduced the incentive of both health care consumers and providers to economize. Both of these factors have contributed to the health care inflation and soaring expenditures of recent decades.

- As the baby-boom generation grows older, the number of people aged 70 and older will increase sharply in the years ahead. Under the current Medicare program, this will increase the demand for health care services and the share of medical payments financed by a third party. Unless reform is undertaken, this will mean both more health care inflation and substantially higher taxes to finance Medicare.
- Reforms that (1) place more emphasis on direct (rather than third-party) payment of medical bills, (2) increase competition in the health insurance industry, (3) encourage catastrophic insurance protection (but not low-deductible, low-copayment plans), and (4) expand the supply of health care would help empower consumers and increase the competitiveness of the health care sector.

Critical Analysis Questions

1. How does the substitution of third-party payments by insurance companies and the government for the out-of-pocket purchase of health care by consumers influence the demand and price of medical services? Explain.
2. *When an employer provides health insurance benefits as part of the compensation package, does this represent a gift by employers to their employees? Do employees earn these benefits? Why or why not? Justify your response.
3. Do individuals have a right to free health care? Do they have a right to force others to provide them with free health care? Discuss.
4. *How did the Medicare and Medicaid programs influence the cost of medical services purchased by Americans who were neither poor nor elderly? Explain.
5. Consider the five reform proposals suggested by the authors in this special topic. Indicate why you believe each is either a good or a bad idea. Explain your answers.
6. *Do personal choices influence health care expenditures? If health care is paid for by others or if everyone is charged the same premium for health care, how will this influence the incentive to make healthy lifestyle choices?
7. Suppose the government established a new program that would use revenues from a payroll tax to finance 85 percent of the maintenance and repair cost of automobiles incurred by those who are employed. How would this legislation influence (a) the prices of auto repair and maintenance services, (b) total spending on these services, and (c) the cost of this program in the years immediately ahead? Do you think this program should be adopted? Why or why not?
8. *The government now requires insurers to provide insurance to persons with preexisting adverse health conditions. How does this influence the incentive to purchase insurance when you are healthy?

*Asterisk denotes questions for which answers are given in Appendix B.

Special Topic 7

Earnings Differences Between Men and Women

We have shown that the gender pay gap in the United States fell dramatically from 1980 to 1989, with slower convergence continuing through 2010.

—Francine D. Blau and Lawrence M. Kahn[1]

Sixty years ago, the typical American woman spent most of her time at home caring for her children, preparing food, and doing laundry, cleaning, and other chores for her family. Only one in three married women worked outside the household in 1960. Today, the situation is dramatically different. Most women, including those who are married, work outside the home. This special topic analyzes earnings differences of men and women and the changing economic role of women.

Learning Objectives

ST07.1 Analyze why the earnings of women are lower than those of men.

ST07.2 Identify how the labor market experience of women has changed in recent decades.

ST07.3 Analyze how the educational choices and career goals of women have changed in recent decades and consider how these changes will affect their future earnings.

[1]Francine D. Blau and Lawrence M. Kahn, "The Gender Wage Gap: Extent, Trends, and Explanations," *Journal of Economic Literature* (September 2017): 852.

ST07-1 Employment Discrimination and the Earnings of Women

During the last several decades, there has been a huge shift in the household versus market work choices of women. As **Exhibit ST07-1** shows, the labor force participation rate of women rose from 37.6 percent in 1960 to 58.1 percent in 2022. Married women accounted for most of the increase.

Exhibit ST07-1 also shows that the female–male (F–M) median earnings ratio for full-time, year-round workers was approximately 60 percent during 1960 to 1980. In other words, women earned only about 60 percent of what men did. Since the early 1980s, though, the earnings of women have steadily increased relative to men. Nevertheless, in 2022, women working full-time, year-round still earned only 84.0 percent as much as their male counterparts. However, among those employed full time, women worked about 3 percent fewer hours than men. The median hourly earnings of women working full time were 86 percent of those of full-time male workers in 2021–2022.

Why are the earnings of women so low compared with those of men? Most people blame employment discrimination. Evidence appears to support this view. Key worker characteristics such as age, years of schooling, marital status, location, and language are similar between men and women. So these factors are not the source of the earnings difference according to gender. Women were also crowded into a few low-paying jobs, occupational

Exhibit ST07-1 Labor Force Experience of Women, 1960-2022

Between 1960 and 2022, the labor force participation of women rose from 37.6 to 58.1 percent. However, the female/male earnings ratio for full-time workers fluctuated around 60 percent during the period 1960-1980, before climbing throughout the 1980s and 1990s. By 2022, this ratio had risen to 84.0 percent. The hourly earnings of women working full-time were 86 percent those of men in 2021-2022.

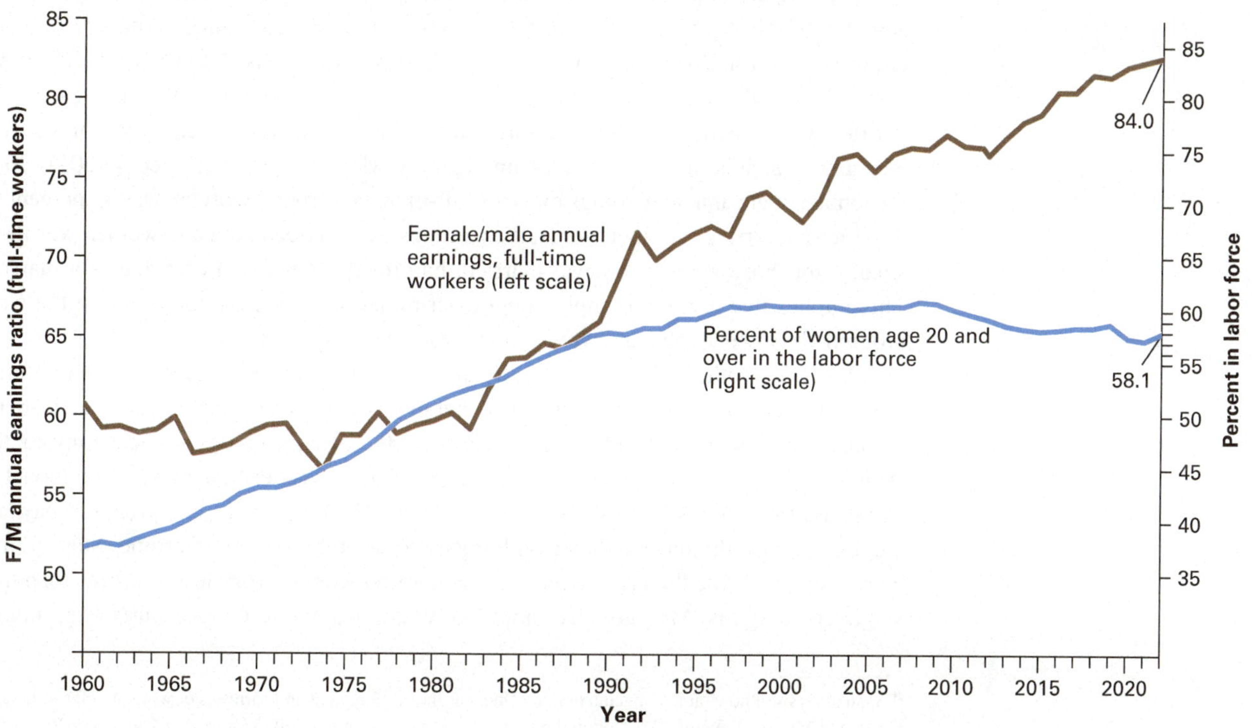

data show. As recently as 1990, about half of all women were employed in just four occupations: clerical workers, teachers, nurses, and food service workers.

Still, attributing all or most of the pay differences between men and women to employment discrimination is an argument that's less than airtight. The very size of the difference makes the argument suspect. If an employer could really hire women who were willing and able to do the same work as men for 15 percent less, the profit motive would give them a strong incentive to do so. Surely employers (both men and women) who don't consider themselves to be "sexist" would jump at the chance to cut their wage cost so dramatically. Of course, as more and more employers substituted women for men workers, the F–M earnings gap would close.

ST07-2 Marital Status, Earnings, Work Environment, and the Gender Pay Gap

It is helpful to think about the gender pay gap in a historical light. Before 1980, married men typically pursued paid employment aggressively because they were expected to be the family's primary breadwinners. Because they shouldered most of the responsibility for "bringing home the bacon," they were more likely to (1) participate continuously in the labor force; (2) relocate if necessary to get a higher paying job; and (3) accept jobs with long working hours, uncertain schedules, and out-of-town travel.

In contrast, married women, who were traditionally more responsible for running the households and rearing children, sought part-time work and jobs with more flexible hours.[2] Further, they expected to drop out of the labor force or switch jobs from time to time in order to care for young children, to follow their husband to a new job location, or when their families' financial needs became less burdensome. Because they expected changes in their work status, many women sought job skills valued by a large number of employers at many locations and offering a variety of hours. Viewed from this perspective, the historical concentration of women in occupations like nursing, teaching, and clerical positions is not surprising.

How important are gender differences when it comes to specialization within the family and pay differences today? **Exhibit ST07-2** shows the median annual earnings of women relative to men in 2021–2022 according to their marital status. Clearly, married women earn substantially less than do married men. Even when working full time, year-round, married women earn only 78 percent as much as men. However, the earnings gap between men and women is substantially less among those who have never married. In 2021–2022, the female–male annual earnings ratio for full-time, year-round workers was 92 percent for those never married. In other words, the earnings gap between men and women was much smaller for those who were never married than for those married or previously married. This implies that although employment discrimination may well contribute to the wage differences between men and women, other factors also play a role.

Analysis of other differences in the employment situation of men and women reinforces this point. There is considerable evidence that men, particularly married men, place greater emphasis than women on monetary earnings. Men often give up compensating factors such as superior working conditions and more leisure in order to achieve more monetary compensation. This is observable in several areas. Overtime generates premium pay, and employees typically have a choice with regard to whether to work overtime. Married men work more overtime than single men, while married women work less overtime than their single counterparts. Men are also more likely than women to choose shifts (e.g., nights)

[2]For an analysis of how family specialization influences the employment and earnings of women, refer to James P. Smith and Michael P. Ward, "Women in the Labor Market and in the Family," *Journal of Economic Perspectives* (Winter 1989): 9–23.

Exhibit ST07-2 Female-Male Earnings According to Marital Status, 2021-2022

The earnings of women relative to men vary substantially with marital status and time worked. For those working fulltime, year-round, the female-male earnings ratio was only 78 percent for married women with spouse present, but it was 92 percent for those never married. This suggests that differences in specialization within the husband-wife family contribute substantially to earnings differentials according to gender.

Source: Author calculations from March 2022 and March 2023 *Current Population Surveys*. Those individuals with a non-binary gender classification are not included in the data.

with higher pay rates. Differences according to gender in commute times and working conditions also indicate that men place more emphasis on monetary earnings. On average, the commute time to work of men is 33 hours per year greater than women. Men are heavily overrepresented in dangerous jobs such as logger, coal miner, and oil rig operator. Men are also overrepresented in jobs with less desirable environmental working conditions (e.g., hot or cold outdoor jobs versus air-conditioned indoor employment). Of course, compensating higher pay rates are required to attract workers to jobs with unfavorable nonpecuniary factors. Thus, some of the higher earnings of men merely reflect that, on average, men are more likely than women to make choices that generate more earnings even though the employment situation is less desirable.

A recent study by Harvard economists Valentin Bolotnyy and Natalia Emanuel provides additional evidence that differences in the preferences of male and female employees contribute to gender pay differences.[3] The study examined data from the Massachusetts Bay Transportation Authority because this firm is a union shop that provides little discretion for discriminatory actions. Hourly wages are uniform. Rigid rules establish employment options. Promotion is on the basis of seniority. Male and female workers of the same seniority have the same options for scheduling, routes, vacation, and overtime. Under these conditions, even a sexist manager would have little opportunity to discriminate.

Nonetheless, female train and bus drivers earned about 11 percent less than their male colleagues. Bolotnyy and Emanuel found that the choices of employees impacted earnings according to gender. Male train and bus drivers worked about 83 percent more overtime than their female colleagues and were twice as likely to accept an overtime shift—which pays time-and-a-half—on short notice. Female workers were more likely to take less desirable routes if it meant working fewer nights, weekends, and holidays. Fathers were more likely than childless

[3]Valentin Bolotnyy and Natalia Emanuel, "Why Do Women Earn Less than Men? Evidence from Bus and Train Operators," *Journal of Labor Economics*, April 2022, pp. 283–323.

men to want the extra cash from overtime, and mothers were more likely to want time off than childless women. Opportunity to choose among employment options improves the status of employees, but it is also a contributing factor to earnings differences according to gender.

It is tempting to highlight discrimination as the source of earnings differences between men and women. However, economics indicates that gender pay differences reflect a complex set of factors, including marital status, presence of children, specialization within the family, and trade-offs between monetary earnings and working conditions. Further, the attachment to the labor force and career objectives of women are changing. Let's examine this factor.

ST07-3 The Changing Career Objectives of Women

Although the career objectives of men and women have differed substantially in the past, those differences have narrowed in recent years. In 1968, a national survey of women 14 to 24 years of age found that only 27 percent expected to be working at age 35. In contrast, a similar survey of young women in 1979 found that 72 percent expected to be working at that age.[4] These figures show that there was a dramatic increase during the 1970s in the number of young women preparing for a career and sustained labor force participation. Although this upward trend may have slowed, it has almost certainly continued during the last four decades.

As the percentage of women planning for a career rose, their educational choices also changed dramatically. In the early 1970s, women were much less likely than men to study and prepare for engineering, medicine, law, and similar high-paying fields traditionally dominated by men. But, as **Exhibit ST07-3** shows, the percentage of women earning degrees in these fields and others, such as business, veterinary medicine, dentistry, architecture, and pharmacy, increased dramatically in the 1970s and 1980s. By the 1990s, parity was achieved in several of these areas. Increasingly, women, like men, are planning for careers in diverse areas, including high-paying professions.

Exhibit ST07-3 Women as a Percentage of People Earning Selected Professional Degrees, 1970-1971, 1987-1988, and 2020-2021

Field of Study	1970-1971	1987-1988	2020-2021
Engineering	0.8	15.3	23.0
Dentistry	1.2	26.1	51.6
Optometry	2.4	34.3	65.8
Law	7.3	40.4	53.2
Veterinary Medicine	7.8	50.0	81.3
Medicine	9.2	33.0	50.5
Business	9.1	46.7	46.7
Architecture	12.0	38.7	49.4
Pharmacy	25.2	59.7	63.6

Source: Commission of Professionals in Science and Technology, *Professional Women and Minorities* (Washington, D.C.: CPST, 1987); and U.S. Department of Education, *Digest of Education Statistics*, 1990 and 2022 (Washington, D.C.: U.S. Government Printing Office).

[4]Refer to Chapter 7 of the *Economic Report of the President* (1987). The numbers presented here are from Table 7–3 of the report.

Exhibit ST07-4 Women as a Percentage of People Graduating from College, 1961-2024

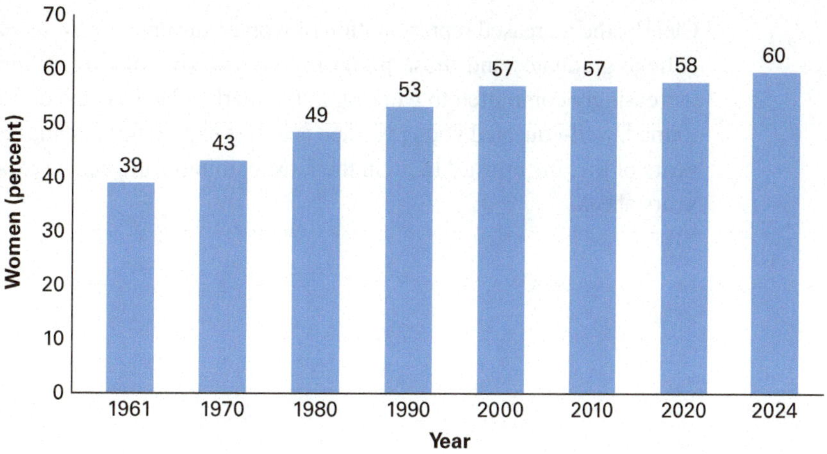

Source: U.S. Department of Education, *Digest of Education Statistics*, 2022 (Washington, D.C.: U.S. Government Printing Office, 2024), table 318.10. The data are for people graduating with a four-year degree.

The gender composition of new college graduates also suggests that women are increasingly planning for a career in the marketplace. During the last five decades, the percentage of women as a share of new college graduates has increased dramatically. As **Exhibit ST07-4** shows, only 39 percent of those completing an undergraduate degree in 1961 were women. By 1980, that figure had risen to 49 percent, and by 2024, it had jumped to 60 percent.

GaudiLab/Shutterstock.com

During the 1970s, an increasing proportion of women began to plan for full-time, long-term labor force participation. Reflecting this commitment, the career and educational choices of women shifted toward higher-paying professions (refer to **Exhibit ST07-3**). As this happened, the earnings of women began to increase steadily relative to men (refer to **Exhibit ST07-1**).

The fact that men are now a minority among those currently graduating from college is not particularly surprising. Jobs in fields like construction and heavy manufacturing offer attractive earnings opportunities, but they are also generally physically demanding and require employees to work either outdoors or in a less than ideal environment. Given their greater physical strength and perhaps less aversion to onerous outdoor working conditions, men are more likely than women to find these physically demanding jobs attractive. As a result, the opportunity cost of going to college is higher for young men than for young women. Thus, a smaller percentage of men pursue a college degree.

It is interesting to think about women's career choices in light of societal changes in the United States during the past six decades. In 1962, equal-pay legislation was passed requiring employers to pay equal wage rates to men and women doing the same jobs. In 1964, civil rights legislation was passed prohibiting employers from discriminating on the basis of both gender and race. Nonetheless, in the 1960s and 1970s, there was little change in the earnings of women relative to men. However, as the career objectives of women—perhaps pushed along by earlier legislative actions—began to change during the 1970s, the educational choices of men and women started to become more similar (refer to **Exhibit ST07-3**).[5] Soon thereafter, the earnings of women began to rise relative to men (refer to **Exhibit ST07-1**).

[5]For additional details on recent changes in the male/female earnings gap, refer to Francine D. Blau and Lawrence M. Kahn, "The Gender Wage Gap: Extent, Trends, and Explanations," *Journal of Economic Literature*, September 2017, p. 789–865.

ST07-4 Implications for the Future

Clearly, the increased representation of women during the past several decades among both college graduates and those preparing themselves for careers indicates that women are increasingly committed to working in the marketplace. As the current generation of highly trained, well-educated young women acquires experience and moves into the prime earning years of life, the upward trend in the F–M earnings ratio can be expected to continue in the years ahead.

Key Points

- The annual median earnings of women working full time are nearly 82 percent of those of men. Among full-time workers, the F–M earnings ratio is 77 percent for those married with spouse present but 90 percent for people who never married.
- In addition to employment discrimination, differences in specialization within the family, compensating wage factors, educational choices, and career goals contribute to the earnings differences between men and women.
- As the educational and career choices of women have become more like those of men, the earnings of women have risen relative to those of men. This trend is likely to continue in the future as more and more women prepare for and acquire experience in high-paying business and professional fields that have traditionally been dominated by men.

Critical Analysis Questions

1. Is employment discrimination the major cause of earnings differences between men and women? Carefully justify your answer.
2. *Between 1960 and 1990, the labor force participation rate of married women approximately doubled. What impact did this influx of married workers into the labor force have on (a) the average years of work experience of women relative to men, (b) the mean hours of work time of women relative to men, and (c) the female–male earnings ratio?
3. Physical strength is important in some jobs. Do you think differences in physical strength between men and women contribute to earnings differences according to gender? Why or why not? Do they also influence the share of men relative to women who will pursue a college education? Explain.
4. *In 2022, the median earnings of single men working full-time, year-round were only about 65 percent of their married counterparts. Does this indicate that employment discrimination existed against single men and in favor of married men?
5. Compared to women, men are overrepresented in occupations like coal mining and construction, in which working conditions are more dangerous. For example, in the United States in 2022, 5,041 men were killed on the job compared to 445 women. How will the more dangerous working conditions of men influence their earnings relative to women? Explain.
6. The representation of men is greater than women in engineering, mathematics, and economics, while the representation of women is greater than men in nursing, communications, and education? Are these differences the result of discrimination? Why or why not?
7. How have the educational choices of women changed during the past 60 years? Why have they changed?

*Asterisk denotes questions for which answers are given in Appendix B

Special Topic 8

The Question of Resource Exhaustion

> The massive scale of the global drilling sector, combined with its technological prowess, gives us every reason to believe that we will have cheap, abundant, reliable supplies of oil and gas for many years to come.
>
> –Robert Bryce[1]

For centuries, many social commentators have argued that the world is about to run out of various natural resources. Economic growth and the technological advances that help to fuel it have accelerated the use of many natural resources. Population growth has also added to the rate of resource use. Nonetheless, as the quote from Robert Bryce indicates, future depletion of natural resources is unlikely to be a problem, at least in the case of oil and natural gas. This feature examines the economic forces affecting the availability of natural resources and explains why the numerous forecasts of resource exhaustion throughout history have been wrong.

Learning Objectives

ST08.1 Consider why there have been repeated forecasts that the world will run out of key resources and why these forecasts have been consistently wrong.

ST08.2 Differentiate between proved reserves and the total future supply of a resource.

ST08.3 Describe how the prices of most key resources have changed over the past few decades and the implications for their future availability.

[1]Robert Bryce, "New Technology For Old Fuels: Innovation in Oil and Natural Gas Production Assures Future Supplies," Energy Policy & the Environment Report No. 12 (New York: Manhattan Institute, April 2013), http://www.manhattan-institute.org/html/eper_12.htm#.UWnReBnlV1g.

ST08-1 Forecasts of Resource Exhaustion

In 2005, Lee Raymond, CEO of Exxon, the largest energy company in the world, said publicly, "Gas production has peaked in North America." He added that the only reason he might be wrong is if "there's some huge find that nobody has any idea where it would be."[2] But in fact, the United States has almost doubled its natural gas production since Raymond made that statement, and the United States has become the largest producer in the world. The increase did not come from finding a major new field, as Raymond thought it might, but rather from technological improvements. Something similar happened with oil. As recently as 2011, scientists worried about "peak oil," the possibility that soon the world would reach its top production of oil and then start on a decline.[3] But oil production also has gone up dramatically in recent years, both around the world and in the United States.

In sixteenth-century England, fear arose that the supply of wood—widely used as a source of energy—would soon disappear. Higher wood prices, however, encouraged conservation and led to the development of coal. The wood crisis soon dissipated.

In the middle of the nineteenth century, fear arose that the United States was about to run out of whale oil, at that time the primary fuel for artificial lighting. As the demand for whale oil increased, many predicted that all the whales would soon be gone and that Americans would face long nights without light. Whale-oil prices rose sharply from $0.23 per gallon in 1820 to $1.42 per gallon in 1850. The higher prices motivated consumers and entrepreneurs to seek alternatives, which included distilled vegetable oils, lard oil, and coal gas. By the early 1850s, coal oil (kerosene) had won out. A little later, petroleum replaced coal as the primary resource used to produce kerosene. As for whale oil, by 1896 its price had fallen to $0.40 per gallon, and even at that price few people used it.

As people switched to petroleum, dire predictions about its future exhaustion arose almost immediately. In 1914, the Bureau of Mines reported that the total U.S. supply of oil was 6 million barrels, an amount well below that which the United States now produces each year. In 1926, the Federal Oil Conservation Board announced that oil would be depleted in the United States within seven years. The Interior Department predicted in 1939 that petroleum supplies in this nation would run out within 20 years. And in 1949, the Secretary of the Interior proclaimed that the end of oil supplies was near.[4]

Perhaps the most stunning prediction of disaster came in 1972 with the publication of *The Limits to Growth*.[5] This book made projections of resource depletion based on large computer models and received widespread publicity in the *New York Times* and major national magazines. As statistician and environmentalist BjØrn Lomborg explained in 2013, the 1972 book had tapped into the grim pessimism of the day—the anxiety surrounding the Vietnam War, the stagnating economy, mounting concerns about pollution, and what seemed to be out-of-control population growth. "The genius of *The Limits to Growth*," he wrote, "was to fuse these worries with fears of running out of stuff. We were doomed, because too many people were consuming too much." The authors of *The Limits to Growth* predicted that prior to 2013 "the world would run out of aluminum, copper, gold, lead, mercury, molybdenum, natural gas, oil, silver, tin, tungsten, and zinc."[6] Of course, this didn't happen.

---

[2]Reuters, Exxon CEO Says, "America Gas Production Has Peaked," June 21, 2005, http://www.reuters.com/article/Utilities/idUSN2163310420050621.

[3]Richard A. Kerr, "Peak Oil Production May Already Be Here," *Science*, March 25, 2011, p. 1510.

[4]Predictions are cited from Wallace Kaufman, *No Turning Back* (New York: Basic Books, 1994), 24; and from Charles Maurice and Charles Smithson, *The Doomsday Myth, 10,000 Years of Economic Crises* (Stanford, CA: Hoover Institution Press, 1987), 12.

[5]Donella H. Meadows, Dennis L. Meadows, and William W. Behrens, *The Limits to Growth* (New York: Universe Books, 1972).

[6]BjØrn Lomborg, "The Limits of Panic," Project Syndicate, June 17, 2013, http://www.project-syndicate.org/commentary/economic-growth-and-its-critics-by-bj-rn-lomborg.

ST08-2 Why Have the Forecasts of Resource Crises Been Wrong?

Technology has revolutionized the production of both oil and gas. The buzzword in energy production is "fracking," an innovative extraction method developed in Texas in the 1990s. Based on techniques that have been used for decades, fracking facilitates the extraction of a much larger share of oil from existing pools than was previously possible. "The dramatic increase in oil and gas resources is the result of a century of improvements to older technologies such as drill rigs and drill bits, along with better seismic tools, advances in materials science, better robots, more capable submarines, and, of course, cheaper computing power," writes Robert Bryce in a paper on energy industry innovations.[7] The development of technology and its application to the extraction of mineral resources crucially depends on economic forces—specifically, incentives.

The incentives generated by markets provide the means for the expansion of supply, and thus they explain why the forecasts of resource supply crisis have always been wrong when markets are allowed to work. Think about what happens when a resource becomes less available. This might happen because of either a reduction in supply or an increase in demand. In either case, the price of the resource will rise. In turn, the higher price will cause (1) users of the resource to cut back on their usage, (2) suppliers to figure out how to supply more of it or perhaps to recycle, and (3) both users and potential suppliers to search for substitutes. Each of these factors will tend to increase future supply relative to demand. The larger the initial increase in the price of a resource, the greater the incentive to cut back on usage, expand the future supply, and develop substitutes.

These adjustments will keep usage rates of the resource pretty much in line with the expected future supply. With time, they can often bring relief in the form of a lower future price. The key point is this: Although the price of a resource may increase sharply during some periods, the structure of incentives accompanying the price increase makes depletion highly unlikely and provides the seeds for future reversal.

As an analysis of the resource crisis forecasts indicates, these forces work again and again. Think about the actions producers, resource users, and consumers will take when oil prices go up. The higher prices will provide petroleum producers with a stronger incentive to search for and find new fields. They will also provide producers with an incentive to use technology to extract a larger share of the oil from existing fields. Up to 70 percent of the oil

When the price of gasoline increases substantially, many consumers will turn to hybrid or electric cars like the Toyota Prius or Tesla Model 3.

Grzegorz Czapski/Shutterstock.com

Aleksei Potov/Shutterstock.com

[7]Robert Bryce, "New Technology for Old Fuels: Innovation in Oil and Natural Gas Production Assures Future Supplies," Energy Policy & the Environment Report No. 12 (New York: Manhattan Institute, April 2013), www.manhattan-institute.org/html/eper_12.htm#.UWnReBnlV1g.

can now be extracted from highly productive wells that in prior decades would have yielded much less. When sustained price increases are large enough, generating expectations they will be sufficient to cover the higher-cost production methods, it becomes economical to produce petroleum products from exceedingly abundant, but less-rich petroleum resources. These include oil shale and tar sands, and, indeed, such production has already begun.

On the demand side, higher oil prices also provide users with a strong incentive to reduce their consumption of petroleum. Electric power-generating firms will search for and some will shift to alternatives like coal and nuclear power. Manufacturers of plastics and other products that use petroleum as a resource will face higher costs; they, too, will seek to shift to substitute resources and cut back on their future use of petroleum. For their part, consumers will use less of the oil-intensive products and adjust their behavior accordingly, purchasing more fuel-efficient cars and trucks, commuting less, and finding other ways to economize on oil-intensive products.

These adjustments and many more on both the supply and the demand sides of the crude oil market will tend to reduce demand over time, increase supply, and thus moderate price increases. This has happened for oil and other resources many times, and these constructive pressures will continue to do so whenever resource availabilities change and market forces are permitted to work.

ST08-3 Proved Reserves and Running Out of Resources

Proved reserves
Specific mineral deposits that have been shown by scientific examination and cost calculation to be extractable and deliverable to the market for use, with current technology and expected market conditions.

Geologists use the term **proved reserves** to mean the specific mineral deposits that have been shown by scientific examination and cost calculation to be extractable and deliverable to the market for use at a cost that users can pay, using known technologies under expected market conditions. Proved reserves have often been used by doomsday forecasters to calculate the future time when we will run out of a resource. But this is a misapplication of the concept. Proved reserves are quite different from the total quantity of a resource in the ground. Put simply, proved reserves are the verified quantity that can be extracted, given investors' expectations of developing technologies and expected prices.

We have examined how improvements in technology and higher future prices can increase proved reserves. **Exhibit ST08-1** shows the proved reserves for several minerals.

Exhibit ST08-1 World Reserves and Cumulative Production of Selected Minerals, 1950 to 2019 (Millions of Metric Tons)

For most mineral resources, existing proved reserves are constantly being used up but are being amply replaced by the "proving" of new reserves from existing resources in the ground.

Mineral	Reserves 1950	Production 1950-2000	Reserves 2000	Reserves 2024
Tin	6	11	10	4.3
Copper	100	339	340	1,000
Iron Ore	19,000	37,583	140,000	190,000
Lead	40	150	64	95
Zinc	70	266	190	220

Source: Sue Anne Batey Blackman and William J. Baumol, "Natural Resources," in *The Concise Encyclopedia of Economics*, 2nd ed., ed. David R. Henderson (Indianapolis: Liberty Fund), available online at http://econlib.org/library/Enc/NaturalResources.html; and Department of the Interior, USGS, Mineral Commodity Surveys (2024), http://minerals.usgs.gov/minerals/pubs/mcs/.

While existing reserves are constantly being used up, in most cases they are amply replaced with the "proving" of new reserves in the ground. For example, in 1950, there were 100 million metric tons of known copper ore reserves in the world. Over the next 50 years, 339 million tons of copper ore reserves were mined and used. Yet, in 2000, the reserves stood at 340 million tons, and by 2024, the reserves had reached 1,000 million tons. Additional reserves had been discovered and technology had advanced, so that the existing known reserves were larger in 2000 than 50 years earlier, even after 50 years of steady depletion, and are even greater today after another quarter-century. The other minerals listed show similar trends, except for tin. In 1950, the world had 6 million tons of tin ore reserves. Fifty years later, after 11 million tons of production, reserves had grown to 10 million. Since then, however, reserves have declined substantially, to 4.3 million tons. Why? Not because we are running out of tin. We know there is no long-term shortage because the price of tin, which has fluctuated over the past six decades, shows no consistent upward trend. Given the cost of finding and proving reserves, it has not been worthwhile for suppliers to expand reserves, particularly because tin consumption has been declining (by 10 percent over the past 5 years in the United States alone). And, since world production of tin is around 290,000 tons per year, even known existing reserves could supply that production for at least 15 more years.

It is important to note that in shorter time periods, it is not uncommon for known world reserves of a natural resource to fall. World tin reserves fell from 10 million tons in 2000 to less than 5 million tons in 2019, while reserves of the other four minerals in **Exhibit ST08-1** all rose. The forces described earlier do not guarantee that resource prices must fall, but as we will examine in the following in more detail, when those forces have been allowed to operate, the results have tended to make natural resources more available to us, even as their physical abundance in nature declines.

For producers, proved reserves are like an inventory of products to a manufacturer. They are the quantity that can be available quickly for sale. Just as it is costly for a manufacturer to hold more inventory, it is costly for a firm to discover and sufficiently research a mineral deposit to qualify it as proved reserves. Producers who buy or develop proved reserves do not want to pay for them farther in advance than needed, just as any manufacturer wants to have products available in stock but not too far ahead of the time they can be sold.

As with inventories, it is costly to develop and hold proved reserves for lengthy time periods. If it takes two years, say, for a producer of iron ore to replace its iron ore reserves, then a four-year supply of those reserves might be a desired amount to have available. Just as inventories are a poor indicator of the total future supply of a good, proved reserves are a poor indicator of the total future supply of a mineral resource. Proved reserves will always be a small fraction of what they could be simply because proving and holding them are costly.

ST08-4 Are Resources Becoming Less Abundant?

If the supply of a resource decreases relative to demand, its price will rise. If a resource is increasing in supply relative to demand and is becoming less costly to supply, its price will fall. Therefore, resource price trends provide information about how the availability of various resources is changing.

What have resource prices been telling us? During the past century and more, the real price of most mineral resources fell. A classic study by Harold Barnett and Chandler Morse illustrates this point.[8] Using data from 1870 to 1963, Barnett and Morse found that the real

[8]Harold Barnett and Chandler Morse, *Scarcity and Growth: The Economics of Natural Resource Availability* (Baltimore: The Johns Hopkins University Press for Resources for the Future, 1963). Also refer to Julian L. Simon, *The State of Humanity* (Cambridge, MA: Blackwell Publishers, 1995), Part III, Natural Resources.

Exhibit ST08-2 Real Crude Oil and Natural Gas Prices, 1968 to 2024 (in 2024 Dollars)

The real prices of crude oil and natural gas show a similar pattern over the past fifty years. They rose in the 1970s, fell in the 1980s and 1990s, then rose sharply again. More recently, they have slid dramatically (starting around 2009 for natural gas and 2013 for crude oil). Technological innovations, especially fracking, have greatly expanded production from existing oil and gas fields without requiring new "finds."

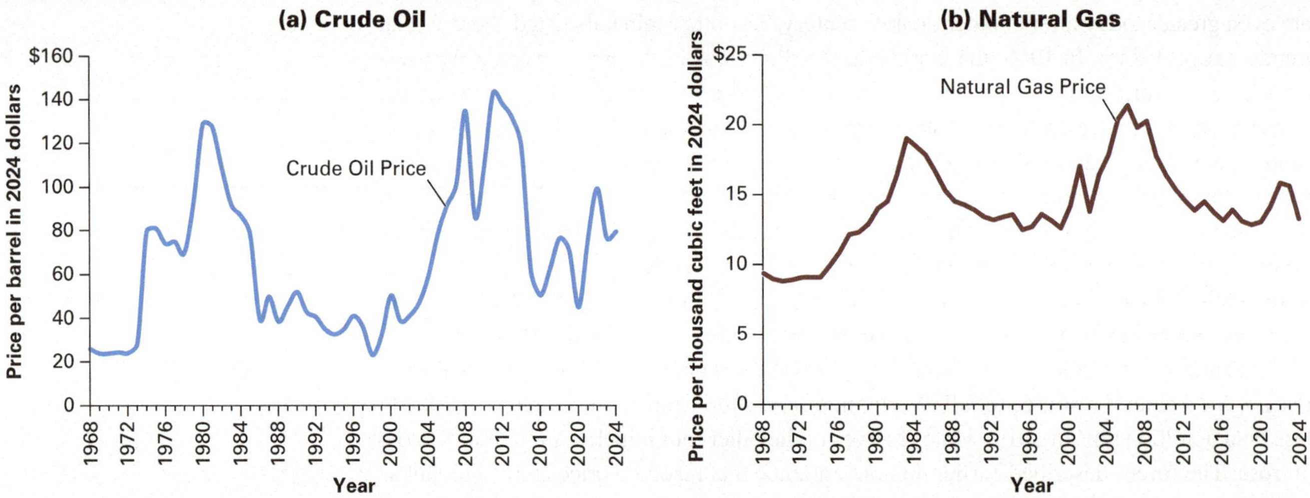

Source: Energy Information Administration, Short-Term Energy Outlook, May 2024, https://www.eia.gov/forecasts/steo/realprices/.

price of resources declined during that long period. A later study by William Baumol and Sue Anne Batey Blackman buttresses this view. They cite a composite mineral price index, corrected for inflation and published by the U.S. Geological Survey, showing a decline in the price index from 185 in 1905 to 100 in 2000. Thus, the real price of minerals fell, on average, by 46 percent in 95 years, even as the use of those minerals had greatly expanded.[9]

As **Exhibit ST08-2** panel (a) shows, the real price of crude oil was flat from 1968 to 1973 (it had actually trended downward before that), but it rose sharply during the 1970s, before falling again during most of the 1980s and 1990s. Then crude oil prices began to rise. Measured in 2024 dollars, the price of oil rose from $23.18 per barrel in 1998 to $142.83 in 2011 and then started a massive slide to $50.50 in 2016, before rising slightly to $79.51 in 2024. Today, media articles deplore the glut of oil that is causing some marginal exploration companies to shut down. The pattern of natural gas prices in panel (b) was similar to that of crude oil except that the recent slide started earlier. The price of natural gas plunged from $20.22 per thousand cubic feet in 2008 to $13.22 in 2024. Fracking provides the explanation. Fracking has facilitated a substantial increase in the production of natural gas.

Some environmentalists are concerned about possible pollution from this technique. While such problems are genuine, a 2011 report from MIT indicates they are also manageable.[10] As Robert Nelson explained in a column for *Forbes*, it is unlikely that fracking itself, usually thousands of feet beneath the surface, can affect land or usable water aquifers, which are almost always located much nearer the surface. However, after the shale is fractured, some of the water returns to the surface. This "flowback water" contains both natural

[9]Quoted by Sue Anne Batey Blackman and William J. Baumol, "Natural Resources," in *The Concise Encyclopedia of Economics*, 2nd ed., ed. David R. Henderson (Indianapolis: Liberty Fund, Inc., 2007), available online at http://econlib.org/library/Enc/NaturalResources.html.

[10]MIT Energy Initiative, The Future of Natural Gas. Cambridge, MA: Massachusetts Institute of Technology, June 2011, http://energy.mit.edu/wp-content/uploads/2011/06/MITEI-The-Future-of-Natural-Gas.pdf.

Applications In Economics

Is It Smart to Bet on Higher Resource Prices?

Rapid rises in prices of oil and other commodities in the 1970s led to widespread anxiety that the world was running out of major resources. In 1980, economist Julian Simon argued that this run-up was temporary and that, over time, prices were likely to fall. Simon offered a $1,000 bet that any raw materials selected in 1980 would be lower ten years later after adjustment was made for inflation. Environmentalist Paul Ehrlich took up the bet. He and his associates chose five metals (chrome, copper, nickel, tin, and tungsten), put $200 on each, and bet that the inflation-adjusted prices in 1990 would be higher.

Simon easily won the bet. During the decade, the real prices declined not only for the bundle but also for each of the five minerals chosen by Ehrlich. In 1990, Ehrlich wrote a check to Simon to pay off the bet. (The wager became famous after an article about it appeared in *The New York Times*.)

In 2005, a student and a professor at Michigan State University analyzed whether Simon would have won the bet had it extended over the entire twentieth century. Using U.S. Geological Survey price data for basic metals, they examined the change in prices from 1900 to 1999. "The person who took Simon's position would have won over the entire century," wrote David McClintick and Ross B. Emmett. "If someone invested $200 at 1900 metals' prices in each of these five metals, the inflation-adjusted value of the same bundle of metals in 1999 would have been 53 percent lower."[1] Of course, resource prices did not go down during every decade of the twentieth century, but they went down during most decades and for the century as a whole. Thus, history suggests that it is not too smart to bet on rising resource prices.

[1]David McClintick and Ross B. Emmett, "Betting on the Wealth of Nature," *PERC Reports* (September 2005), https://www.perc.org/wp-content/uploads/2018/01/sept05.pdf.

contaminants and the chemicals used in the fracturing. Writes Nelson: "The water must therefore be disposed of safely or—as is increasingly the case—be cleaned up and recycled for use in the next well."[11] Nelson points out that some environmental abuses have occurred, such as dumping this water into rivers and streams. "As a result of increasing regulation, however, and growing recognition within the gas industry that its future depends on public acceptance, the treatment of flowback water has improved greatly."

Resource prices fluctuate from month to month and year to year, but the trends have been mainly downward, often with the assistance of technical changes like fracking. For the bigger picture, refer to the box feature, "**Is It Smart to Bet on Higher Resource Prices?**"

ST08-5 Renewable Resources

To this point, we have focused on **nonrenewable resources**—those that are not created or renewed at a significant rate, and therefore they could potentially be used up over time. Our analysis, however, indicates that this is unlikely to be the case in a market setting. What about **renewable resources**, like timber, that can be continually replanted and replenished? Those resources, too, can become less abundant and more expensive in a market depending on (1) the ability of users to find substitutes and reduce the quantity demanded and, over time, the demand and (2) producers' ability to produce more output at the higher price and to find substitute products to bring to market for buyers.

Nonrenewable resources
Those that are not created or renewed naturally at a significant rate.

Renewable resources
Those that are renewed in nature, like water flows, or grown, like timber.

[11]Robert Nelson, "Ernest Moniz and Fracking Drive Environmentalists Off of the Rails," *Forbes*, March 26, 2013, http://www.forbes.com/sites/realspin/2013/03/26/ernest-moniz-and-fracking-drive-environmentalists-off-of-the-rails.

Forests are an example of a renewable resource for which there has been concern about future availability. Deforestation can lead to a loss of timber, wildlife habitat, watershed protection, and recreational services. Are concerns about serious deforestation justified? Rivers, lakes, and other sources of freshwater are other important renewable resources for which depletion is a serious concern. What can economic thinking and a careful examination of history tell us about these two concerns?

ST08-5a Are Forests Disappearing?

How serious are the loss of timber and the loss of wildlife habitat? Not all the world's forests are in well-functioning market economies (that is, economies with property rights, the rule of law, and minimal corruption). Where strong market economies do exist, however, the forces of supply and demand are protecting forests from significant decline.

Currently, the United States has about the same amount of land devoted to forest as it did in 1920—and far more timber is growing on it. A U.S. Forest Service study of the northern United States (20 states stretching from Maine to Minnesota) reported that during the 100 years between 1907 and 2007, forest land in that region increased by 28 percent. During the past 50 years, timber production from the region expanded by 138 percent (from 104 to 248 billion cubic feet).[12] Clearly, the United States is not running out of wood.

A study by two natural resource economists, Roger Sedjo and Marion Clawson, found that even Latin America is undergoing a major transition, with an increase in tree plantations, in which trees are being grown as crops.[13] These changes reflect the response to demand for wood and put less pressure on the existing tropical rainforest.

Technology is also increasing the productivity of land and helping to preserve forest. While fertilizers, pesticides, and other technologies—"high-tech" farming—can have some negative environmental effects, they also free up a great deal of land from use for farming. By raising productivity per acre, technology reduces the amount of land required to produce food and fiber.

When resource users and suppliers are free to innovate and respond to changes in prices and in technologies as market participants, and when property rights hold them accountable for the cost of what they use while allowing them personally to reap benefits from fruitful innovations, the result has been economic progress in increasing prosperity from one generation to the next. Each generation has less in the way of physical natural resources in Earth, but successive new resource discoveries and improved technology allow the old resource base to deliver more services for a smaller sacrifice because it is better used and with less waste.

ST08-5b Natural Resources When Markets Are Not Allowed to Function Fully: The Case of Water

When property rights to a natural resource are insecure or when regulations undermine the operation of markets, problems of waste and shortages are common. This is often the case with water. In the words of economist Terry L. Anderson, Earth "has more than enough water to meet human demands." But, he says, "Water is often found in the wrong place at the wrong time."[14] Water supply problems reflect the fact that in most situations, water markets are missing or are incomplete. Therefore, the smoothly functioning market that might bring more effective cooperation among users and suppliers, or buyers and sellers, seldom exists.

[12]Stephen R. Shifley et al., "Forests of the Northern United States," General Technical Report NRS-90 (Newtown Square, PA: U.S. Department of Agriculture, Forest Service, Northern Research Station, 2012).

[13]Refer to Roger A. Sedjo and Marion Clawson, "Global Forests Revisited," in *The State of Humanity*, ed. Julian Simon (Cambridge, MA: Blackwell Publishers, 1995).

[14]Terry L. Anderson, "Water Options for the Blue Planet," in *The True State of the Planet*, ed. Ronald Bailey (New York: Free Press, 1995), 275.

Throughout the world, the sources of water—lakes, rivers, and streams—are often kept under tight control by governments, preventing transferable ownership that would allow supply and demand to operate. This approach is defended on the grounds that water, which is necessary for life, needs to be treated differently. To establish a system of transferable property rights is complicated by the fact that changing a water use in one place on a stream can influence everyone downstream also. But it is also true that the difficulty of obtaining a property right to water provides a less certain water supply than market trades could make available.

In some places, people do own a right to water or at least the right to use some water from a lake or stream. In the arid western United States, for example, a person may own a right to divert a specific amount of water from a stream in order to irrigate crops. But state and federal laws may prevent that person from selling the right for use elsewhere or even changing its use in its current location. Other uses of the water may be far more valuable, but the owner cannot sell the water or the right to use it. Thus, the market mechanism that allocates copper and tin efficiently and prevents waste, shortages, or total depletion is very often missing in the case of water.

Government subsidies to current water uses and users may also distort the allocation of this key resource. Consider, for example, the federally funded Central Utah Project (CUP), which delivers water to farms from dams built on rivers. It illustrates the lack of complete and tradable property rights in water as well as the distortions caused by subsidies. According to the Department of the Interior, the annual cost of delivering CUP water is $161 per acre-foot (326,000 gallons), not counting the cost of building and maintaining the dam. But farmers pay less than $30 per acre-foot. Taxpayers cover the rest ($131 per acre-foot). The farmers have the politically awarded right to the water and the subsidy, but they cannot sell the right and other potential users cannot bid the water away from the farmers. Meanwhile, cities and other water users in the region face shortages and are making plans to increase their own water supplies by costly means. Water trading could help buyers and sellers to reap large mutual gains from trade, but the trades are not allowed.

Some water-short cities near the ocean or other saltwater bodies are considering desalination, which uses massive amounts of energy and special equipment to make saltwater into freshwater at a cost of up to $2,000 per acre-foot. Others are seeking permission (and federal subsidies) to build more dams dedicated to storing water for their own use. The economic and environmental costs of building more dams are very high, but water is quite valuable once a shortage develops.

Progress is possible, and in some cases when water became extremely valuable, decision-makers figured out a way to move it toward higher-valued uses. For example, when droughts occurred in California in 1991 and 2009, trading through the mechanism of "water banking" reduced the damage. The state of California bought water from farmers, who, in return for cash, fallowed their land or used water more efficiently. The water they saved was sold to drought-stricken farmers and municipalities. The water bank was not a genuine market, because the state of California set the price (it bought at $125 an acre-foot and sold at $175), but it shows the direction that could be taken to ease shortages and improve efficiency. If farmers in northern California were provided with a secure and transferable property right to the water for which they currently have access, they could sell their water rights to southern California municipalities. In turn, water would be moved away from low marginal value in agriculture toward higher marginal valued municipal uses, improving economic efficiency and making both parties better off.[15] Ironically, rather than strengthening and expanding water rights by making them tradable, the California legislature has been trying to strip these rights away in recent years—a move that would have significant negative secondary effects on the water problems faced in that state. While defining property rights and permitting markets to allocate resources is sometimes complicated, it can be done, and this is the path to better allocation of resources in this area.

---

[15]The source for these examples is Terry L. Anderson, Brandon Scarborough, and Lawrence R. Watson, *Tapping Water Markets, 2012* (New York: Routledge, 2012), 22, 71, 73–4.

Key Points

- Forecasts that the world will soon run out of key resources have been made for centuries. These forecasts have consistently been wrong.
- Resource prices fluctuate from month to month and year to year, but for long periods, the trends have been mainly downward. Refer to the Applications of Economics feature, "Is It Smart to Bet on Higher Resource Prices?"
- When resources are allocated by markets, decreased availability leads to higher prices. The higher prices will strengthen the incentive for (1) users to reduce their consumption, (2) suppliers to search for ways to expand future supply, and (3) both producers and users to search for substitutes. All of these adjustments will increase future supply relative to demand and make it highly unlikely that the resource will be depleted.
- Proved reserves are the verifiable quantity of a resource available at current prices and technology. They are not the total supply of the resource that will be available in the future. Proved reserves can be expanded with improvements in technology and increases in prices.
- The trend in the price of resources has been downward for at least a century, indicating that the relative availability of most resources has been increasing.
- When property rights are poorly defined or when regulations make a resource nontradable, waste will result because the resource will often be directed toward less valuable uses.

Critical Analysis Questions

1. If the world were about to run out of a highly valued resource, what would happen to its price? How would this affect the future supply of the resource relative to the quantity demanded?
2. *"If China and India continue their economic expansion, the world cannot provide enough raw materials without terrible shortages worldwide." Evaluate this statement.
3. In the industrial nations, have succeeding generations, each with a higher income than before, left the world resource-poor, with only low-grade mineral ores left, for example? Have they been "consuming the birthright" of future generations? Explain your answer.
4. Why have agricultural fields retreated and forests returned in many areas of the southeastern United States? With fewer acres farmed, will the nation continue to be able to provide food and fiber for itself? Explain.
5. *"Water is a necessity of life. It should not be bought and sold, or traded in markets!" Use the economic way of thinking to evaluate this statement.
6. How do plastic bag bans affect the demand for forest products? What does this do to the price of timber and how does it influence the value of keeping land in timber production versus selling it off for housing development?

*Asterisk denotes questions for which answers are given in Appendix B.

Special Topic 9

Difficult Environmental Cases and the Role of Government

A little richer is a lot safer.

–Aaron and Adam Wildavsky[1]

Private property rights can promote prosperity and cooperation and, at the same time, protect the environment, but do they protect the environment sufficiently? In recent years, people have increasingly turned to the government to achieve additional environmental improvements. Sometimes they turned to the government because property rights failed to hold polluters accountable for the costs they were imposing on others. In other instances, people with strong desires for various environmental amenities (for example, green spaces, hiking trails, and wilderness lands) want the government to force others to help pay for them. In this special topic, we examine the potential to achieve environmental goals through governmental control, as well as the problems that arise from government action in these areas.

Learning Objectives

ST09.1 Explain why markets may result in inefficient outcomes when property rights are not defined or when a large number of people are involved.

ST09.2 Identify the shortcomings of using government regulation to pursue environmental goals.

ST09.3 Analyze the economic costs and benefits of policies regarding global warming and climate change.

ST09.4 Explain how property rights and market-like mechanisms can be used to solve environmental problems.

[1]Aaron Wildavsky and Adam Wildavsky, "Risk and Safety," in *The Concise Encyclopedia of Economics*, 2nd ed., ed. David R. Henderson (Indianapolis, IN: Liberty Fund, Inc., 2007), http://econlib.org/library/Enc/RiskandSafety.html.

ST09-1 Government Regulation and the Environment

During the past 70 years, Americans became increasingly concerned about the pollution of air and water. The late 1960s brought some spectacular incidents—such as reports that the Cuyahoga River in Ohio was on fire and thousands of gallons of oil had escaped from a drilling rig off the coast of Santa Barbara, California. Senator Gaylord Nelson of Wisconsin decided to enlist public support for taking action on the environment, and he launched the first Earth Day—a teach-in, a protest against pollution, and a celebration of Earth—on April 22, 1970. An estimated 20 million people took part. Earth Day has been celebrated each year since.

Although there had been pollution in the past, it had only gradually become a major issue. Indeed, active smokestacks were often viewed favorably as a sign of job-creating factories. And court actions had usually kept severe pollution at bay by protecting property rights. For example, in 1903, ranchers in Montana sued Anaconda Smelting for destroying their grass and killing livestock with the smelter's emissions (that contained arsenic). The ranchers won, so the company had to compensate the ranchers for damages. Conflict continued, so in 1918 the company responded by building what was for many years the tallest smokestack in the world. By the time the plume from the stack reached the ground, it was so diluted that concentrations were far less harmful.[2]

In Wisconsin in the nineteenth century, paper companies routinely bought miles of downstream property to avoid polluting others. Their wastewater emissions, which were costly to control, could be diluted by water from tributary streams before reaching others' downstream properties. If they had not done so, the high initial concentrations could have subjected the companies to litigation. By owning the land located well below their production facility, the paper companies were imposing costs on themselves, not on others.[3]

Property rights, properly enforced, help optimize decisions to produce greater net social benefits from activities that also pollute. But it is difficult—if not impossible—to define, establish, and fully protect property rights when there are a large number of polluters or a large number of people harmed by the emissions, or both. Consider the air quality in a large city such as Los Angeles or Denver. Millions of people can be harmed when the pollutants are put into the air. Yet many of those affected people also contribute to the pollution as they drive their cars and operate industrial and commercial establishments. In such cases, high transaction costs make it hard to rely on the protection of rights (protection against damage to one's body or one's property) to clean up the air. Who, exactly, would sue whom? Under these circumstances, the Wisconsin rivers common-law solution would not be a practical option.

Such large-number problems grew during the last century, spawning the modern environmental movement—and with it, a push for federal legislation. Numerous environmental acts were passed, including the Clean Air Act of 1970 and the Clean Water Act of 1972, followed by many others.

Although government regulation is an alternative method of protecting the environment—and after Earth Day, the most readily adopted approach—the regulatory approach also has some deficiencies, which economists, sensitive to trade-offs, recognize. First, government regulation is often sought precisely because the harms are uncertain, and the source of the problem cannot be demonstrated in a court of law, so relief from the courts is difficult to obtain. But when the harms are uncertain and thus speculative, so too are the benefits of reducing them. The costs of reducing them, however, are real and often substantial.

---

[2]Gordon Morris Bakken, "Was There Arsenic in the Air?" *Montana the Magazine of Western History* 41, no. 3 (Summer, 1991): 30–41, and "Anaconda Smoke Stack Creates Unique Montana State Park," *Billings Gazette*, March 12, 2019.

[3]Peter Davis, "Theories of Water Pollution Litigation," *Wisconsin Law Review* 3 (1971): 738–816, at 777–80.

Second, by its very nature, regulation overrides or ignores the information and incentives provided by market signals. Accountability of regulators for the costs they impose is lacking, just as accountability for polluters is missing in the market sector when secure and tradable property rights are not in place. The tunnel vision of regulators, each assigned to oversee a small part of the economy, is not properly constrained by readily observable costs.

Third, regulation generates potential opportunities for powerful special interests, both for and against regulatory actions, to use their political power to pursue objectives that are quite different from the popularized environmental goals. The global warming issue illustrates both the potential gains from regulations and the problems they may generate. Let's examine this high-profile issue.

ST09-2 The Economics of Global Warming

The highly publicized issue of global warming, also called climate change, generates a legitimate reason for considering governmental intervention. But the global nature of the issue and the secondary effects of potential responses illustrate the problems that come with regulation.

Burning fuels such as coal, oil, and natural gas emits carbon dioxide. This emission causes no direct harm, unlike traditional pollutants such as particulates and sulfur dioxide. But long-term concern about its environmental impact has been growing since 1988, when James Hansen, then a scientist with the National Aeronautics and Space Administration, told a congressional panel that he was "99 percent confident" that the global warming signal had arrived.[4]

As the world has become warmer and more industrialized, more carbon dioxide has been building up in the atmosphere. Although carbon dioxide represents only a tiny part of the atmosphere, it contributes to the formation of an invisible blanket that traps some heat

Roy Johnson/Alamy Stock Photo

Coal-fired power generators put large amounts of visible steam and invisible carbon dioxide into the air. Carbon dioxide is a greenhouse gas that may be warming the Earth significantly.

[4]Quoted in Michael Weisskopf, "Scientist Says Greenhouse Effect Is Setting In," *Washington Post,* June 24, 1988, p. A04.

on Earth that would otherwise be radiated into space. In 2009, the U.S. Environmental Protection Agency (EPA) began regulating carbon dioxide as a pollutant and started to develop plans for controlling emissions of carbon dioxide from factories and power plants. The EPA's regulations have changed over time due to both changes in presidential administrations and decisions of the U.S. Supreme Court, but have generally tended to put increasing regulations and controls on emissions from coal-fired plants.

From an economic perspective, proper analysis of global warming and potential policy alternatives involves an examination of costs relative to benefits. Many believe that the costs of continuing the use of fossil fuels and the emission of carbon dioxide into the atmosphere are extremely high. Proponents of this view argue that increased carbon dioxide emissions will cause the Earth's temperatures to rise by 5 to 10 degrees centigrade by the end of this century, if not sooner. As a result, destructive weather events such as hurricanes, tornadoes, floods, and droughts will occur with increasing frequency. Deaths from climate-related diseases such as malaria and yellow fever will become more common. Hunger and malnutrition will soar due to the adverse weather effects. Perhaps most important, large segments of the glacier mountains of the Antarctic will melt, causing the sea level to rise. The glacier ice in the Antarctic often runs two or more miles in depth. This region contains 95 percent of the Earth's surface ice. If it melts in large quantities, the sea level will rise by a rather large amount, perhaps 10 to 15 feet, in a relatively short period of time, causing many coastal areas to flood and become uninhabitable. Clearly, the cost of these events would run into the tens of trillions of dollars and have devastating effects on people around the world.

Others argue that the models used to project the large temperature increases have persistently overstated the impact of carbon dioxide levels on global temperatures. Proponents of this view believe that the projected future emissions of carbon dioxide will result in temperature increases of only 1 to 3 degrees centigrade during the next 50 to 75 years. Temperature increases of this magnitude will result in minimal increases in destructive weather events, and the rise in sea level will be approximately 1 to 3 inches per decade, as has been the case for centuries. Moreover, there will be some benefits from a warmer climate. For example, a warmer climate will result in a longer frost-free growing season in Canada and the northern parts of the United States, enhancing agricultural output in these regions. Climate researcher Indur Goklany points out that since 1920, as carbon dioxide emissions increased with industrialization and Earth's temperature rose, deaths per million people from all extreme weather events (droughts, floods, temperature extremes, etc.) fell globally by 98 percent.[5] Further, people appear to have a preference for warmer climates. When they retire and have more freedom to live where they wish, many move to places like Florida and Arizona, seeking more warmth and less rigorous winters.

Why is the global warming issue so divisive? Wide variation in the expected costs and benefits provides at least part of the answer. Those who believe we are on a disastrous course that will result in massive destruction of both assets and lives of people cannot understand the failure of others to support their policies. In contrast, those who believe the threat is exaggerated cannot understand why anyone would want to spend trillions of dollars seeking to combat the cost of future events that, in their view, are highly unlikely. Still others believe harmful changes to the climate are occurring, but costly actions by the United States and other high-income countries are imprudent as long as China, India, and other developing countries continue to emit large volumes of carbon into the atmosphere.

The United States has reduced carbon dioxide emissions more than most countries. In 2021, U.S. emissions were 18 percent below those of 2005, according to the U.S. EPA.[6] That reduction was primarily the result of the substitution of natural gas for coal. As Jeffrey

[5]Indur M. Goklany, "Economic Development in Developing Countries: Advancing Human Well-Being and the Capacity to Adapt to Global Warming," in *Climate Coup* (Washington, DC: Cato Institute, 2011).

[6]U.S. Environmental Protection Agency, "Data Highlights: Inventory of U.S. Greenhouse Gas Emissions and Sinks: 1990-2021," https://www.epa.gov/ghgemissions/inventory-us-greenhouse-gas-emissions-and-sinks.

Frankel, an economist at the Harvard Kennedy School, notes, the production of natural gas by fracking has resulted in a surge in the supply of natural gas and sharply lower prices. In turn, the lower natural gas prices induced users to substitute it for coal. Compared to coal, natural gas emits substantially less carbon dioxide per unit of energy produced. Thus, this substitution resulted in a substantial decline in the carbon dioxide emissions of the United States. A combination of structural changes and increasing energy efficiency have resulted in U.S. total greenhouse gas emissions per dollar of real GDP declining by 53 percent since 1990 also according to the same U.S. EPA report.

The global nature of this issue is also a complicating factor. Even if the United States substantially reduced its carbon emissions, that would not exert much impact unless other large emitters also did so. Many developing countries are continuing to expand their carbon dioxide emissions. In 2021, China was the largest emitter at 10.7 gigatons, compared with the United States, which was next, with 4.6 gigatons, and India third at 2.3 gigatons.[7] Without an enforceable global agreement, even a rather significant reduction in carbon dioxide emissions by the United States and other high-income countries would be, to a large degree, offset by emission increases in China, India, and other developing countries.

Can political action be counted on to develop a sound response to global warming? Remember, political action is merely an alternative form of organization. Like markets, it has shortcomings, including special interest politics and rent-seeking. Predictably, interest groups will use global warming and other environmental concerns as a way of obtaining a competitive advantage relative to rivals. This is already observable. For example, producers of corn-based ethanol have used environmental arguments to lobby for subsidies and mandates, expanding the use of ethanol in the production of gasoline. Similarly, wind and solar producers have lobbied for subsidies and tax breaks and opposed fracking to gain an advantage relative to natural gas producers. Clearly, regulation and political allocation do not assure effective policy in this area.

Information about the benefits and costs of alternatives is essential for the development of sound policy. But this information is characterized by both uncertainty and imprecision. Consider the following set of questions. If highly restrictive regulations limiting carbon emissions were adopted, how much would they cost? What benefits would they generate? How will future changes in technology impact carbon emissions? How will future technological changes impact the cost of reducing global temperatures? Experts differ widely with regard to their answers to these questions. Given the uncertainties and imprecision in the measurement of both benefits and costs, and the potential impact of technology both now and in the future, proper policy in this area is far from obvious.

ST09-3 Mitigation Versus Adaptation Strategy

Until recently, the most talked-about approach was *mitigation*—reducing carbon emissions, primarily by government regulation, to keep global temperatures from rising as much as they would otherwise. Adaptation, making changes when and if actual problems begin to occur, provides an alternative approach. Climate change researcher Indur M. Goklany suggests that adaptation is the superior strategy. He examines four risk factors—hunger, malaria, water shortages, and coastal flooding—that might worsen if global temperatures increase significantly. He concludes that acting now to address these already serious problems, independent of global warming, would cost far less than trying to reduce temperature

[7]International Energy Agency, "IEA Greenhouse Gas Emissions from Energy Data Explorer," August 2, 2023, https://www.iea.org/data-and-statistics/data-tools/greenhouse-gas-emissions-from-energy-data-explorer.

increases, and the payoff in improved human lives would be achieved before any significant benefits from greenhouse gas reductions.[8]

Instead of forcing a smaller carbon footprint, which would significantly reduce national income, nations might be better off dealing with the uncertainties of global warming through growth and development. As Aaron and Adam Wildavsky implied in the quotation at the opening of this special topic, wealthier people can better handle all sorts of risks. A wealthier society provides better health care, makes more emergency transport and care facilities available, builds safer cars, and supplies more safety measures of all kinds. A more prosperous country is more resilient when faced with major threats, whether from a new disease, an earthquake, an asteroid striking Earth, or global warming. In fact, economist Donald Coursey estimated that a rise of 1 percent in a population's income produces a 2.5 percent increase in that group's willingness and ability to pay for environmental improvements.[9]

ST09-4 Market-Like Schemes: Reducing the Cost of Specific Regulations

Control of emissions is costly. Two major market-like approaches could potentially reduce the cost of controlling emissions related to global warming. We now turn to the consideration of each.

1. Cap-and-trade. Some emitters of carbon dioxide can cut back on their emissions at a much lower cost than others, and that fact suggests that an approach to reducing carbon emissions called "cap-and-trade" might be useful. Under "cap-and-trade," a pollution-control authority, such as the EPA in the United States, sets the total amount of emissions, in effect setting "caps" on emissions. Then it issues tradeable permits allowing each emitter a set amount of pollution.

Cap-and-trade gives each emitter an incentive to reduce or even eliminate its emissions. A company that can cheaply reduce emissions below its allowed level can sell emissions permits ("credits") to other companies that face higher costs. The total reduction in pollution will not change, but the overall costs of achieving it will generally be much lower. The result at that point is greater efficiency in attaining any specified overall emissions level.

The Clean Air Act Amendments of 1990 established what is perhaps the best-known "cap-and-trade" program in the United States. The act authorized the EPA to set up a nationwide system for trading sulfur dioxide emission reductions among power plants. The utilities that face the highest cost of emission control can purchase permits from those who can more easily control emissions. This program has lowered the long-run costs to electric utilities of meeting the legislated targets.

Cap-and-trade can play a useful role, at least with some pollutants, but difficulties remain. One is how to set the appropriate amount of pollution reduction. Or put another way, "How clean is clean enough?" And a second is how much should be spent to achieve it. Policy analysts familiar with the negotiations over the 1990 Act say that the chosen standard, a national reduction of 10 million tons of sulfur dioxide per year, was arbitrary, not backed by well-estimated, clearly relevant health and aesthetic standards. So even though the trades reduced the total cost of meeting the standard, the standard may have been unreasonably strict—or, for that matter, too lax.[10]

---

[8]Indur M. Goklany, "Relative Contributions of Global Warming to Various Climate Sensitive Risks, and Their Implications for Adaptation and Mitigation," *Energy & Environment* 14 (2003): 797–822.

[9]Donald Coursey, *The Demand for Environmental Quality* (St. Louis: John M. Olin School of Business, Washington University at St. Louis, December 1992).

[10]Robert W. Crandall, "Is There Progress in Environmental Policy?" *Contemporary Economic Policy* 12, no. 1 (1994): 80–83.

Setting the pollution levels at the ideal level, where the marginal costs of additional emissions reduction are equal to the marginal benefits, would require information that is unavailable to government officials. When enforceable property rights exist, however, and the emission permits are exchanged in workable markets, this information is generated through voluntary trades—by individuals who know their own costs of selling and by buyers judging the expected benefits of the purchase.

When courts decide who has the property rights in environmental matters—when, for example, a court decides that a factory must cut pollution to protect a nearby resident's property rights—trades are still possible. The resident might prefer a cash payment to be entirely free of pollution. But such negotiations are not allowed when the issue is decided by direct regulation of each emitter.

2. Pollution charges or taxes. Pollution charges or taxes can also be used to reduce emissions. In recent years, one version of a pollution tax that has gained momentum is the imposition of a carbon tax imposed on the carbon content of fuels such as coal, oil, and natural gas, or the carbon dioxide levels of emissions. Carbon taxes in one form or another have been implemented or are scheduled for implementation in several subnational jurisdictions and approximately two dozen countries, although others such as Australia have repealed their carbon taxes after implementation due to less-than-desirable results.

Most proposals call for the tax to be imposed at the point when these fuels are extracted or imported, and the tax rate to be increased gradually through time until emissions goals are reached. Proponents argue that a carbon tax will give consumers and producers a monetary incentive to reduce their use of carbon-based fuels, discover and invest in alternative energy sources, and thereby reduce carbon dioxide emissions in a manner that would replace the need for less-efficient, less-predictable, and more-cumbersome regulations. Many economists support the carbon tax as a method of dealing with global warming.[11] The revenue from a carbon tax could be rebated to citizens so that the policy is tax-neutral or could be spent to offset the economic damages to affected industries or lower-income consumers who would be adversely impacted by significantly higher energy prices, including electricity.

Opponents of a carbon tax generally point to several difficulties in designing and imposing a carbon tax. First, the tax may potentially result in large reductions in economic activity, growth, and income. These reductions will have secondary effects on health and well-being that could potentially offset any long-term gains from reduced carbon emissions. Second, a carbon tax imposed at the national or subnational level creates incentives for carbon-based production to relocate to other jurisdictions and reduces the competitiveness of domestic firms in export markets. However, a border adjustment tax designed to reflect the carbon emissions accompanying the production of the good could be imposed. Lastly, and perhaps most significantly, are the problems associated with the political implementation and administration of the tax. Given the nature of the political process and the influence of powerful interest groups that stand to gain from changes in the tax rate and its application, rent-seeking, political favoritism, and even corruption pose a danger to the effectiveness of this approach.

Ideally—to achieve efficiency—the amount of any pollution tax or emission charge must just equal the marginal costs imposed on those who are harmed by the emissions. But it is difficult or impossible to know this cost without property rights and market transactions to provide information, and even more difficult to achieve through the political decision-making process. There are no costless solutions to emissions problems.

The underlying case for the use of both cap-and-trade and a carbon tax to address global warming is similar. Markets fail to register the full adverse impact of carbon emissions

[11]By 2020, more than three thousand economists, including 27 Nobel Prize winners in economics, 15 former chairs of the Council of Economic Advisors, and four former chairs of the Federal Reserve, signed a letter supporting a revenue neutral carbon tax. Refer to https://clcouncil.org/economists-statement/.

on the environment and global temperatures. Both the purchase of permits in the case of cap-and-trade and the carbon tax seek to increase the relative cost of goods and services that emit carbon into the atmosphere. As the prices of goods with large carbon emissions increase relative to goods with smaller carbon emissions, people will reduce their consumption of the former relative to the latter. Of course, the emissions level or tax rate will still have to be set through the political decision-making process. Both uncertainties about the additional benefits relative to the cost of changes in emission levels and the political influence of various interest groups will affect the emissions level chosen. Thus, there is no assurance that either the emission level or tax will be set at the optimal level.

ST09-5 Property Rights as a Tool for Government Policy

When the government recognizes the power of private property rights, there is potential for successful government policy. Ocean fisheries are one example in which progress is being made.

ST09-5a Ocean Fisheries: A Lack of Property Rights Causes Overfishing

Overfishing in the oceans is a classic example of overexploitation of a resource that is not privately owned. This is typically called the "tragedy of the commons."[12] Without ownership of the fish or of fishing rights, each fisher has little to gain from holding back, because others will get most of the fish left in the water by any one fisher. To cope with this tragedy of the commons, governments try to institute regulations that protect the fish. Since the 1970s, the U.S. government has regulated fishing in coastal waters. Even so, at least a third of U.S. fisheries are overfished.

One reason is that the regulations encouraged a wasteful and dangerous "race to fish." To preserve the stock of fish, governments reduced the length of the fishing seasons (often to just a few days) and set limits on the kinds of gear that could be used. This sometimes meant that boats went out to sea in dangerous weather, took all the fish they could, even immature fish, and faced accidents and capsizing as their gear became entangled with other fishers' gear.

Property-rights strategies are increasingly used around the world instead of limits on season length. A prominent example is the adoption of individual transferable quotas (ITQs), which give fishers ownership of a portion of the annual allowable catch. For example, as economist Don Leal puts it in one case, "an individual who holds a 0.1-percent share in the South Atlantic wreckfish fishery is entitled to 7,400 pounds of wreckfish for the season if the total allowable catch is 7,400,000 pounds."[13] Regulators could be mistaken in setting the quota, of course. However, unlike the case of air pollution regulation, the fishery itself will give them rapid feedback. If the stock of fish falls, regulators can drop the total allowable catch to let the fishery recover. When they own ITQs, fishers support such limits to maintain the value of their fishing rights over time.

Environmental groups have begun to support these policies, called "rights-based" fishing. Amanda Leland of the Environmental Defense Fund was coauthor of a 2016 study predicting that fish populations around the world could double by 2050 if such approaches

[12]Garrett Hardin, "The Tragedy of the Commons," *The Concise Encyclopedia of Economics*, Library of Economics and Liberty, www.econlib.org/library/Enc/TragedyoftheCommons.html.

[13]Donald R. Leal, *Fencing the Fishery: A Primer on Ending the Race for Fish* (Bozeman, MT: Property and Environment Research Center, 2002), 8, https://www.perc.org/wp-content/uploads/2002/06/guide_fish.pdf.

were adopted. She told *National Geographic*, "I've spent my career working on fisheries issues and I did not expect such a dramatic finding."[14]

ST09-6 Government Ownership of Resources and Provision of Services

Much government intervention in environmental matters has to do with establishing regulations to control pollution. But the government also owns many natural resources and seeks to protect environmental quality through its parks, refuges, and other lands. It should come as no surprise that when the government owns resources, incentives change, and politics become more important. That is true even with management provided by highly qualified, well-intended professionals.

The National Park Service celebrated its 100th anniversary in 2016. Although there is much to praise about our national parks, the Park Service has managed to build up an $22.3 billion backlog of maintenance expenses. That is, it has deteriorating roads, sewer systems that leak, and time-worn buildings—and the cost of fixing them is about seven times its annual funding from Congress.

In 2020, Congress enacted a law that authorized automatic funding of up to $900 million per year to purchase more land for national parks. However, at the same time, it authorized up to $1.9 billion of automatic funding each year for the next five years to cover deferred maintenance. Both funds will come primarily from oil and gas leases. In addition, park fees are a source of maintenance funding. Park visitors pay only a small fraction of the cost of the services they receive—and for most of the Park Service's history, the fees went to the U.S. Treasury, not to the individual parks. But in 2004, Congress set higher fee schedules and allowed each park manager to keep 80 percent of the fees for use in the park. About half of those revenues are now used for maintenance.

Although the National Park Service and several other government agencies control a great deal of protected land, millions of acres of land are protected privately as well. One of the most recent initiatives to set land aside for wildlife is the American Prairie Reserve (APR), an ambitious nonprofit project. APR's plan is to create a reserve bigger than Yellowstone, Yosemite, and Grand Teton national parks combined, all of it open to the public while providing habitat for bison, badgers, bobcats, and more than 300 other wildlife species.[15]

Such land is available due in part to modern technology, which reduces the amount of land needed for farming. Matt Ridley highlights the dramatic impact of regeneration in Great Britain, which has "three times as much forest as it did 100 years ago." He recalls that in northern England in the 1970s, "otters had vanished, salmon were gone from the River Tyne because of pollution, and hawks and falcons had disappeared due to DDT." But today, "otters are thriving, salmon are back, and seabirds on the nearby Farne Islands have doubled in numbers." The improvement comes about through what Ridley calls "land sparing." Thanks to technology—from modern farming equipment to new crop varieties—less land is needed to produce food (and the same is true of fiber and fuel). That allows more and more land to return to a wild state.[16]

---

[14]Brian Clark Howard, "How Our Favorite Fish Could Recover in a Decade," *National Geographic*, March 28, 2016.

[15]Wendy Purnell, "American Prairie Reserve," *PERC Reports* 34, no 1 (Summer 2015), https://www.perc.org/2015/10/01/american-prairie-reserve/.

[16]Matt Ridley, "Ecology or Economics: Which Has Done More?" *PERC Reports* 31, no. 1 (Winter 2013): 22–27, https://www.perc.org/2013/02/07/ecology-or-economics-which-has-done-more-for-our-environmental-future/.

ST09-7 Conclusion

Government can provide protection from harms, as in regulation that reduces pollution, and it can produce goods and services, as in the provision of national parks. Government can indeed shift the cost of services from some citizens to others and can do the same with benefits from its programs. Moreover, in some cases, it can provide different services that are, on net, beneficial. There is little reason, however, to expect that political allocation will result in ideal outcomes. This is true in environmental matters as well as in other areas of citizen concern.

Key Points

- When it is difficult to assign and enforce private property rights, markets often result in outcomes that are inefficient. This is often the case when large numbers of people engage in actions that impose harm on others. Government regulation has some promise but also poses some problems of its own.
- Global warming could exert a sizable adverse impact on human welfare, but there is uncertainty about the costs and benefits derived from regulations that require reductions in emissions of carbon dioxide. These uncertainties increase the attractiveness of adaptation as an option to regulation.
- Market-like schemes such as cap-and-trade and a carbon tax have the potential to reduce carbon emissions more efficiently, although even these solutions are costly and imperfect. The emissions level or tax rate still must be set through the political decision-making process that is subject to the influence of various interest groups.
- Federal ownership of national parks, as with other lands, has brought undesirable outcomes along with benefits, but there is some progress in moving closer to market solutions that provide better information and incentives for federal managers.

Critical Analysis Questions

1. *The movie *The Perfect Storm* was set in a situation in which a very short fishing season forced the fishers to go to sea despite the dangerous conditions. Explain how a move to ITQs could solve that problem.
2. "The national parks belong to us all. No one should be charged money to enter." Evaluate this statement, using the economic way of thinking.
3. Explain how a carbon tax would work. What are the major advantages of a carbon tax? What are the major disadvantages?
4. *"Unlike a marketplace in which pollution is profitable, government control of resources and pollution can take into account the desires of all the people." Evaluate this statement, using economic thinking.
5. Explain the difference between mitigation and adaptation as strategic responses to global warming. What are some key factors that strengthen the case for adaptation?
6. Suppose you are highly concerned that carbon dioxide emissions are leading to global temperature increases that will result in severe future damages. Outline the key elements of an economically efficient strategy to combat this situation and the trade-offs involved.

*Asterisk denotes questions for which answers are given in Appendix B.

Appendix A

General Business and Economics Indicators for the United States

Section 1

Year	Personal Consumption Expenditures	Gross Private Domestic Investment	Govt Consumption and Gross Investment	Net Exports	Gross Domestic Product	REAL GDP: 2017 Prices	REAL GDP: Annual Real Rate	REAL GDP: Real GDP Per Capita
1970	646.7	170.0	252.6	3.9	1,073.3	5,316.4	0.2	25,922
1971	699.9	196.8	267.5	0.6	1,164.9	5,491.4	3.3	26,440
1972	768.2	228.1	286.2	−3.4	1,279.1	5,780.0	5.3	27,534
1973	849.6	266.9	304.8	4.1	1,425.4	6,106.4	5.6	28,812
1974	930.2	274.5	341.4	−0.8	1,545.2	6,073.4	−0.5	28,394
1975	1,030.5	257.3	381.1	16.0	1,684.9	6,060.9	−0.2	28,062
1976	1,147.7	323.2	404.2	−1.6	1,873.4	6,387.4	5.4	29,289
1977	1,274.0	396.6	434.3	−23.1	2,081.8	6,682.8	4.6	30,337
1978	1,422.3	478.4	476.3	−25.4	2,351.6	7,052.7	5.5	31,679
1979	1,585.4	539.7	524.8	−22.5	2,627.3	7,276.0	3.2	32,323
1980	1,750.7	530.1	589.6	−13.1	2,857.3	7,257.3	−0.3	31,869
1981	1,934.0	631.2	654.4	−12.5	3,207.0	7,441.5	2.5	32,353
1982	2,071.3	581.0	711.5	−20.0	3,343.8	7,307.3	−1.8	31,467
1983	2,281.6	637.5	766.6	−51.6	3,634.0	7,642.3	4.6	32,613
1984	2,492.3	820.1	827.9	−102.7	4,037.6	8,195.3	7.2	34,668
1985	2,712.8	829.7	910.5	−114.0	4,339.0	8,537.0	4.2	35,794
1986	2,886.3	849.1	976.1	−131.9	4,579.6	8,832.6	3.5	36,698
1987	3,076.3	892.2	1,031.5	−144.8	4,855.2	9,137.7	3.5	37,628
1988	3,330.0	937.0	1,078.9	−109.4	5,236.4	9,519.4	4.2	38,845
1989	3,576.8	999.7	1,151.9	−86.7	5,641.6	9,869.0	3.7	39,893
1990	3,809.0	993.4	1,238.6	−77.9	5,963.1	10,055.1	1.9	40,191
1991	3,943.4	944.3	1,299.0	−28.6	6,158.1	10,044.2	−0.1	39,618
1992	4,197.6	1,013.0	1,344.5	−34.7	6,520.3	10,398.0	3.5	40,472
1993	4,452.0	1,106.8	1,364.9	−65.2	6,858.6	10,684.2	2.8	41,048
1994	4,721.0	1,256.5	1,402.3	−92.5	7,287.2	11,114.6	4.0	42,188
1995	4,962.6	1,317.5	1,449.4	−89.8	7,639.7	11,413.0	2.7	42,811
1996	5,244.6	1,432.1	1,492.8	−96.4	8,073.1	11,843.6	3.8	43,912
1997	5,536.8	1,595.6	1,547.1	−102.0	8,577.6	12,370.3	4.4	45,319
1998	5,877.2	1,736.7	1,611.6	−162.7	9,062.8	12,924.9	4.5	46,803
1999	6,283.8	1,887.1	1,719.9	−259.6	9,631.2	13,543.8	4.8	48,487
2000	6,767.2	2,038.4	1,826.4	−381.1	10,251.0	14,096.0	4.1	49,915
2001	7,073.8	1,934.8	1,950.0	−376.7	10,581.9	14,230.7	1.0	49,893
2002	7,348.9	1,930.4	2,089.5	−439.7	10,929.1	14,472.7	1.7	50,260
2003	7,740.7	2,027.1	2,210.6	−522.0	11,456.5	14,877.3	2.8	51,191
2004	8,232.0	2,281.3	2,338.1	−634.1	12,217.2	15,449.8	3.8	52,682
2005	8,769.1	2,534.7	2,475.3	−739.9	13,039.2	15,988.0	3.5	54,015
2006	9,277.2	2,701.0	2,623.8	−786.5	13,815.6	16,433.1	2.8	54,994
2007	9,746.6	2,673.0	2,790.6	−735.9	14,474.2	16,762.4	2.0	55,561
2008	10,050.1	2,477.6	2,983.0	−740.9	14,769.9	16,781.5	0.1	55,104
2009	9,891.2	1,929.7	3,076.3	−419.2	14,478.1	16,349.1	−2.6	53,213
2010	10,260.3	2,165.5	3,155.6	−532.3	15,049.0	16,789.8	2.7	54,189
2011	10,698.9	2,332.6	3,147.9	−579.6	15,599.7	17,052.4	1.6	54,604
2012	11,047.4	2,621.8	3,136.5	−551.6	16,254.0	17,442.8	2.3	55,422
2013	11,388.2	2,838.3	3,132.6	−478.5	16,880.7	17,812.2	2.1	56,172
2014	11,874.5	3,074.0	3,168.6	−508.9	17,608.1	18,261.7	2.5	57,139
2015	12,297.4	3,288.5	3,233.4	−524.3	18,295.0	18,799.6	2.9	58,364
2016	12,726.8	3278.3	3303.0	−503.3	18,804.9	19141.7	1.8	58,968

Year	Personal Consumption Expenditures	Gross Private Domestic Investment	Govt Consumption and Gross Investment	Net Exports	Gross Domestic Product	Real GDP: 2017 Prices	Real GDP: Annual Real Rate	Real GDP: Real GDP Per Capita
2017	13,290.6	3467.7	3397.1	–543.3	19,612.1	19612.1	2.5	60,002
2018	13,934.4	3724.8	3590.4	–593.1	20,656.5	20193.9	3.0	61,418
2019	14,417.6	3892.4	3789.9	–578.5	21,521.4	20692.1	2.5	62,606
2020	14,206.2	3,748.4	3,994.8	–626.4	21,323.0	20,234.1	–2.2	60,983
2021	16,043.0	4,216.3	4,193.1	–858.2	23,594.0	21,407.7	5.8	64,410
2022	17,511.7	4,756.6	4,446.8	–971.1	25,744.1	21,822.0	1.9	65,420
2023	18,570.6	4,843.9	4,745.1	–798.7	27,360.9	22,376.9	2.5	66,755

Source: http://www.bea.gov

Section 2

Year	GDP Deflator: Index (2017 = 100)	GDP Deflator: Annual Percentage Change	Consumer Price Index: Index	Consumer Price Index: Percentage Change
1970	20.2	5.3	38.8	5.7
1971	21.2	5.1	40.5	4.4
1972	22.1	4.3	41.8	3.2
1973	23.3	5.5	44.4	6.2
1974	25.4	9.0	49.3	11.0
1975	27.8	9.3	53.8	9.1
1976	29.3	5.5	56.9	5.8
1977	31.1	6.2	60.6	6.5
1978	33.3	7.0	65.2	7.6
1979	36.1	8.3	72.6	11.3
1980	39.4	9.1	82.4	13.5
1981	43.1	9.4	90.9	10.3
1982	45.8	6.2	96.5	6.2
1983	47.5	3.9	99.6	3.2
1984	49.3	3.6	103.9	4.3
1985	50.8	3.2	107.6	3.6
1986	51.9	2.0	109.6	1.9
1987	53.1	2.5	113.6	3.6
1988	55.0	3.5	118.3	4.1
1989	57.2	3.9	124.0	4.8
1990	59.3	3.8	130.7	5.4
1991	61.3	3.4	136.2	4.2
1992	62.7	2.3	140.3	3.0
1993	64.2	2.4	144.5	3.0
1994	65.6	2.1	148.2	2.6
1995	66.9	2.1	152.4	2.8
1996	68.2	1.8	156.9	3.0
1997	69.3	1.7	160.5	2.3
1998	70.1	1.1	163.0	1.6
1999	71.1	1.4	166.6	2.2
2000	72.7	2.3	172.2	3.4
2001	74.4	2.3	177.1	2.8
2002	75.5	1.5	179.9	1.6
2003	77.0	2.0	184.0	2.3

Section 2 continued

	GDP Deflator		Consumer Price Index	
Year	Index (2017 = 100)	Annual Percentage Change	Index	Percentage Change
2004	79.1	2.7	188.9	2.7
2005	81.5	3.1	195.3	3.4
2006	84.1	3.1	201.6	3.2
2007	86.4	2.7	207.3	2.8
2008	88.0	1.9	215.3	3.8
2009	88.6	0.7	214.5	−0.4
2010	89.6	1.2	218.1	1.6
2011	91.5	2.1	224.9	3.2
2012	93.2	1.9	229.6	2.1
2013	94.8	1.7	233.0	1.5
2014	96.4	1.7	236.7	1.6
2015	97.3	0.9	237.0	0.1
2016	98.2	1.0	240.0	1.3
2017	100.0	1.8	245.1	2.1
2018	102.3	2.3	251.1	2.4
2019	104.0	1.7	255.7	1.8
2020	105.4	1.3	258.8	1.2
2021	110.2	4.6	271.0	4.7
2022	118.0	7.1	292.7	8.0
2023	122.3	3.6	304.7	4.1

Source: http://www.bea.gov and http://www.bls.gov

Section 3

					Unemployment Rates			
Year	Civilian Pop	Civilian Labor Force	Civilian Labor Force Participation	Civilian Employment/ Population	All	Age 16 to 19	Men Age 20+	Women Age 20+
1970	137.1	82.8	60.4	57.4	4.9	15.3	3.5	4.8
1971	140.2	84.4	60.2	56.6	5.9	16.9	4.4	5.7
1972	144.1	87.0	60.4	57.0	5.6	16.2	4.0	5.4
1973	147.1	89.4	60.8	57.8	4.9	14.5	3.3	4.9
1974	150.1	91.9	61.3	57.8	5.6	16.0	3.8	5.5
1975	153.2	93.8	61.2	56.1	8.5	19.9	6.8	8.0
1976	156.2	96.2	61.6	56.8	7.7	19.0	5.9	7.4
1977	159.0	99.0	62.3	57.9	7.1	17.8	5.2	7.0
1978	161.9	102.3	63.2	59.3	6.1	16.4	4.3	6.0
1979	164.9	105.0	63.7	59.9	5.8	16.1	4.2	5.7
1980	167.7	106.9	63.8	59.2	7.1	17.8	5.9	6.4
1981	170.1	108.7	63.9	59.0	7.6	19.6	6.3	6.8
1982	172.3	110.2	64.0	57.8	9.7	23.2	8.8	8.3
1983	174.2	111.6	64.0	57.9	9.6	22.4	8.9	8.1
1984	176.4	113.5	64.4	59.5	7.5	18.9	6.6	6.8
1985	178.2	115.5	64.8	60.1	7.2	18.6	6.2	6.6
1986	180.6	117.8	65.3	60.7	7.0	18.3	6.1	6.2
1987	182.8	119.9	65.6	61.5	6.2	16.9	5.4	5.4
1988	184.6	121.7	65.9	62.3	5.5	15.3	4.8	4.9
1989	186.4	123.9	66.5	63.0	5.3	15.0	4.5	4.7
1990	189.2	125.8	66.5	62.8	5.6	15.5	5.0	4.9

					Unemployment Rates			
Year	Civilian Pop	Civilian Labor Force	Civilian Labor Force Participation	Civilian Employment/ Population	All	Age 16 to 19	Men Age 20+	Women Age 20+
1991	190.9	126.3	66.2	61.7	6.8	18.7	6.4	5.7
1992	192.8	128.1	66.4	61.5	7.5	20.1	7.1	6.3
1993	194.8	129.2	66.3	61.7	6.9	19.0	6.4	5.9
1994	196.8	131.1	66.6	62.5	6.1	17.6	5.4	5.4
1995	198.6	132.3	66.6	62.9	5.6	17.3	4.8	4.9
1996	200.6	133.9	66.8	63.2	5.4	16.7	4.6	4.8
1997	203.1	136.3	67.1	63.8	4.9	16.0	4.2	4.4
1998	205.2	137.7	67.1	64.1	4.5	14.6	3.7	4.1
1999	207.8	139.4	67.1	64.3	4.2	13.9	3.5	3.8
2000	212.6	142.6	67.1	64.4	4.0	13.1	3.4	3.6
2001	215.1	143.7	66.8	63.7	4.7	14.7	4.2	4.1
2002	217.6	144.9	66.6	62.7	5.8	16.5	5.2	5.1
2003	221.2	146.5	66.2	62.3	6.0	17.5	5.4	5.1
2004	223.4	147.4	66.0	62.3	5.5	17.0	4.9	4.9
2005	226.1	149.3	66.0	62.7	5.1	16.6	4.5	4.6
2006	228.8	151.4	66.2	63.1	4.6	15.4	4.1	4.1
2007	231.9	153.1	66.0	63.0	4.6	15.7	4.1	4.0
2008	233.8	154.3	66.0	62.2	5.8	18.7	5.4	4.9
2009	235.8	154.1	65.4	59.3	9.3	24.8	9.6	7.5
2010	237.8	153.9	64.7	58.5	9.6	25.9	9.8	8.0
2011	239.6	153.6	64.1	58.4	8.9	24.4	8.7	7.9
2012	243.3	155.0	63.7	58.6	8.1	24.0	7.5	7.3
2013	245.7	155.4	63.2	58.6	7.4	22.9	7.0	6.5
2014	247.9	155.9	62.9	59.0	6.2	19.6	5.7	5.6
2015	250.8	157.1	62.7	59.3	5.3	16.9	4.9	4.8
2016	253.5	159.2	62.8	59.7	4.9	15.7	4.5	4.4
2017	255.1	160.3	62.9	60.1	4.4	14.0	4.0	4.0
2018	257.8	162.1	62.9	60.4	3.9	12.9	3.6	3.5
2019	259.2	163.5	63.1	60.8	3.7	12.7	3.4	3.3
2020	260.3	160.7	61.7	56.8	8.1	17.9	7.4	8.0
2021	261.4	161.2	61.7	58.4	5.3	11.7	5.2	5.0
2022	264.0	164.3	62.2	60.0	3.6	10.8	3.4	3.3
2023	266.9	167.1	62.6	60.3	3.6	11.2	3.5	3.2

Source: www.bls.gov

Section 4

				Federal Budget			National Debt†	
Year	M2	Annual Change	Interest Rate on AAA Bonds	Fiscal Year Outlays	Fiscal Year Receipts	Surplus/ Deficit	Billions of Dollars	Percent of GDP
1970	601.4	3.9	8.0	195.6	192.8	(2.8)	225.5	21.5%
1971	674.4	12.1	7.4	210.2	187.1	(23.0)	237.5	21.3%
1972	758.1	12.4	7.2	230.7	207.3	(23.4)	251.0	20.6%
1973	831.8	9.7	7.4	245.7	230.8	(14.9)	265.7	19.6%
1974	880.7	5.9	8.6	269.4	263.2	(6.1)	263.1	17.7%
1975	963.7	9.4	8.8	332.3	279.1	(53.2)	309.7	19.3%
1976	1,086.6	12.8	8.4	371.8	298.1	(73.7)	382.7	21.4%
1977	1,221.4	12.4	8.0	409.2	355.6	(53.7)	444.1	21.9%

Section 4 continued

				Federal Budget			National Debt†	
Year	M2	Annual Change	Interest Rate on AAA Bonds	Fiscal Year Outlays	Fiscal Year Receipts	Surplus/ Deficit	Billions of Dollars	Percent of GDP
1978	1,322.4	8.3	8.7	458.7	399.6	(59.2)	491.6	21.6%
1979	1,425.8	7.8	9.6	504.0	463.3	(40.7)	524.7	20.5%
1980	1,540.4	8.0	11.9	590.9	517.1	(73.8)	591.1	21.2%
1981	1,678.8	9.0	14.2	678.2	599.3	(79.0)	664.9	21.2%
1982	1,830.0	9.0	13.8	745.7	617.8	(128.0)	790.1	23.8%
1983	2,052.3	12.1	12.0	808.4	600.6	(207.8)	981.7	27.8%
1984	2,218.1	8.1	12.7	851.8	666.4	(185.4)	1,151.9	29.2%
1985	2,416.4	8.9	11.4	946.3	734.0	(212.3)	1,337.5	31.4%
1986	2,612.2	8.1	9.0	990.4	769.2	(221.2)	1,549.8	34.2%
1987	2,781.9	6.5	9.4	1,004.0	854.3	(149.7)	1,677.7	35.2%
1988	2,929.5	5.3	9.7	1,064.4	909.2	(155.2)	1,822.4	35.5%
1989	3,051.6	4.2	9.3	1,143.7	991.1	(152.6)	1,970.6	35.5%
1990	3,221.8	5.6	9.3	1,253.0	1,032.0	(221.0)	2,177.1	36.9%
1991	3,342.4	3.7	8.8	1,324.2	1,055.0	(269.2)	2,430.4	39.9%
1992	3,404.5	1.9	8.1	1,381.5	1,091.2	(290.3)	2,703.3	42.1%
1993	3,439.6	1.0	7.2	1,409.4	1,154.3	(255.1)	2,922.7	43.1%
1994	3,483.3	1.3	8.0	1,461.8	1,258.6	(203.2)	3,077.9	42.9%
1995	3,553.4	2.0	7.6	1,515.7	1,351.8	(164.0)	3,230.3	42.7%
1996	3,727.1	4.9	7.4	1,560.5	1,453.1	(107.4)	3,343.1	42.0%
1997	3,924.8	5.3	7.3	1,601.1	1,579.2	(21.9)	3,347.8	39.6%
1998	4,204.3	7.1	6.5	1,652.5	1,721.7	69.3	3,262.9	36.5%
1999	4,515.0	7.4	7.1	1,701.8	1,827.5	125.6	3,135.7	33.1%
2000	4,786.5	6.0	7.6	1,789.0	2,025.2	236.2	2,898.4	28.6%
2001	5,201.8	8.7	7.1	1,862.8	1,991.1	128.2	2,785.5	26.5%
2002	5,592.2	7.5	6.5	2,010.9	1,853.1	(157.8)	2,936.2	27.1%
2003	5,981.6	7.0	5.7	2,159.9	1,782.3	(377.6)	3,257.3	28.9%
2004	6,264.1	4.7	5.6	2,292.8	1,880.1	(412.7)	3,595.2	29.9%
2005	6,531.0	4.3	5.2	2,472.0	2,153.6	(318.3)	3,855.9	30.0%
2006	6,870.6	5.2	5.6	2,655.1	2,406.9	(248.2)	4,060.0	29.8%
2007	7,294.9	6.2	5.6	2,728.7	2,568.0	(160.7)	4,255.5	29.7%
2008	7,788.2	6.8	5.6	2,982.5	2,524.0	(458.6)	5,311.9	35.9%
2009	8,415.4	8.1	5.3	3,517.7	2,105.0	(1,412.7)	6,775.5	46.8%
2010	8,623.6	2.5	4.9	3,457.1	2,162.7	(1,294.4)	8,207.2	55.1%
2011	9,246.8	7.2	4.6	3,603.1	2,303.5	(1,299.6)	8,463.5	54.7%
2012	10,047.9	8.7	3.7	3,526.6	2,450.0	(1,076.6)	9,635.8	59.8%
2013	10,728.0	6.8	4.2	3,454.9	2,775.1	(679.8)	9,910.4	59.4%
2014	11,388.2	6.2	4.2	3,506.3	3,021.5	(484.8)	10,328.2	59.3%
2015	12,042.5	5.7	3.9	3,691.9	3,249.9	(442.0)	10,654.7	58.7%
2016	12,852.8	6.7	3.7	3,852.6	3,268.0	(584.7)	11,704.2	62.8%
2017	13,583.8	5.7	3.7	3,981.6	3,316.2	(665.5)	12,200.0	63.0%
2018	14,103.2	3.8	3.9	4,109.0	3,329.9	(779.1)	13,436.4	65.7%
2019	14,818.5	5.1	3.4	4,447.0	3,463.4	(983.6)	14,687.4	69.0%
2020	17,634.3	19.0	2.5	6,553.6	3,421.2	(3,132.5)	16,571.2	77.8%
2021	20,486.6	16.2	2.7	6,822.5	4,047.1	(2,775.4)	16,850.9	73.5%
2022	21,580.3	5.3	4.1	6,273.3	4,897.3	(1,375.9)	18,618.5	73.6%
2023	20,845.4	–3.4	4.8	6,134.7	4,440.9	(1,693.7)	21,282.7	78.9%

†National debt is debt held by private investors.

Source: fred.stlouisfed.org and www.whitehouse.gov/omb/

Section 5

	Size of Government as a Percent of GDP†				
Year	Expenditures	Revenues	Purchases	Nondefense	Transfer
1970	35.3	27.1	23.5	15.9	7.2
1971	35.5	26.4	23.0	15.9	7.9
1972	35.1	27.6	22.4	15.8	8.1
1973	34.2	27.7	21.4	15.4	8.1
1974	35.6	28.2	22.1	16.3	8.8
1975	37.6	26.6	22.6	17.0	10.2
1976	36.3	27.4	21.6	16.3	9.9
1977	35.2	27.7	20.9	15.8	9.4
1978	34.4	27.8	20.3	15.4	9.0
1979	34.2	28.0	20.0	15.2	9.0
1980	36.1	28.3	20.6	15.6	9.9
1981	36.3	28.9	20.4	15.3	9.9
1982	38.5	28.4	21.3	15.7	10.6
1983	38.5	27.8	21.1	15.5	10.5
1984	37.3	27.8	20.5	15.1	9.8
1985	37.8	28.3	21.0	15.6	9.7
1986	38.2	28.5	21.3	15.9	9.8
1987	37.9	29.2	21.2	15.9	9.6
1988	37.0	29.0	20.6	15.3	9.4
1989	36.9	29.1	20.4	15.3	9.6
1990	37.6	29.0	20.8	15.8	10.0
1991	38.4	28.9	21.1	16.0	10.2
1992	39.1	28.6	20.6	15.9	11.6
1993	38.4	28.7	19.9	15.5	11.8
1994	37.2	29.1	19.2	15.2	11.6
1995	37.2	29.4	19.0	15.1	11.6
1996	36.4	29.9	18.5	14.9	11.6
1997	35.3	30.2	18.0	14.6	11.2
1998	34.3	30.6	17.8	14.6	10.9
1999	33.7	30.6	17.9	14.7	10.6
2000	33.3	31.0	17.8	14.8	10.5
2001	34.4	29.9	18.4	15.4	11.1
2002	35.4	27.5	19.1	15.8	11.7
2003	35.7	26.8	19.3	15.7	11.8
2004	35.2	27.0	19.1	15.5	11.8
2005	35.2	28.5	19.0	15.3	11.7
2006	35.3	29.3	19.0	15.4	11.8
2007	35.9	29.3	19.3	15.6	12.1
2008	37.9	28.2	20.2	16.2	13.4
2009	40.9	25.7	21.2	17.0	15.0
2010	41.2	26.3	21.0	16.6	15.6
2011	40.2	26.6	20.2	15.9	15.2
2012	38.7	26.6	19.3	15.3	14.7
2013	37.5	28.8	18.6	14.9	14.5
2014	36.9	28.8	18.0	14.6	14.6
2015	36.6	29.0	17.7	14.5	14.8
2016	36.6	28.5	17.6	14.4	14.8
2017	36.2	29.2	17.3	14.3	14.7
2018	36.2	27.5	17.4	14.3	14.5

Section 5 continued

	Size of Government as a Percent of GDP†				
Year	Expenditures	Revenues	Purchases	Nondefense	Transfer
2019	36.8	27.4	17.6	14.5	14.7
2020	45.7	28.1	18.7	15.5	20.0
2021	43.1	29.2	17.8	14.8	19.7
2022	37.2	30.2	17.3	14.5	15.6
2023	37.3	27.2	17.3	14.5	15.0

†There are some differences across reporting agencies with regard to accounting procedures and the treatment of government enterprises. This results in some differences in statistical measures of the size of government.

Source: http://www.bea.gov

Section 6

	Share of Federal Income Tax Paid by Percentile				
Year	Top 1	Top 5	Top 10	Next 40	Bottom 50
1980	19.1	36.8	49.3	43.7	7.0
1981	17.6	35.1	48.0	44.6	7.5
1982	19.0	36.1	48.6	44.1	7.3
1983	20.3	37.3	49.7	43.1	7.2
1984	21.1	38.0	50.6	42.1	7.4
1985	21.8	38.8	51.5	41.4	7.2
1986	25.7	42.6	54.7	38.9	6.5
1987	24.8	43.3	55.6	38.3	6.1
1988	27.6	45.6	57.3	37.0	5.7
1989	25.2	43.9	55.8	38.4	5.8
1990	25.1	43.6	55.4	38.8	5.8
1991	24.8	43.4	55.8	38.7	5.5
1992	27.5	45.9	58.0	36.9	5.1
1993	29.0	47.4	59.2	36.0	4.8
1994	28.9	47.5	59.4	35.8	4.8
1995	30.3	48.9	60.7	34.6	4.6
1996	32.3	51.0	62.5	33.2	4.3
1997	33.2	51.9	63.2	32.5	4.3
1998	34.8	53.8	65.0	30.8	4.2
1999	36.2	55.5	66.5	29.5	4.0
2000	37.4	56.5	67.3	28.8	3.9
2001	33.2	52.2	63.7	31.4	4.9
2002	33.1	52.9	64.6	31.2	4.2
2003	33.7	53.5	64.9	31.0	4.1
2004	36.3	56.4	67.3	28.8	3.9
2005	38.8	58.9	69.5	27.0	3.6
2006	39.4	59.5	70.1	26.5	3.4
2007	39.8	59.9	70.4	26.2	3.4
2008	37.5	58.1	69.2	27.7	3.1
2009	36.3	58.2	69.9	27.7	2.5
2010	37.4	59.1	70.6	27.0	2.4
2011	35.1	56.5	68.3	28.9	2.9
2012	38.1	59.0	70.2	27.1	2.8
2013	37.8	58.6	69.8	27.4	2.8
2014	39.5	60.0	70.9	26.4	2.8

	Share of Federal Income Tax Paid by Percentile				
Year	Top 1	Top 5	Top 10	Next 40	Bottom 50
2015	39.0	59.6	70.6	26.6	2.8
2016	37.3	58.2	69.5	27.5	3.0
2017	38.5	59.1	70.1	26.8	3.1
2018	40.1	60.3	71.4	25.7	2.9
2019	38.8	59.4	70.8	26.1	3.1
2020	42.3	62.7	73.7	24.0	2.3
2021	45.8	65.6	75.8	21.9	2.3

Appendix B

Answers to Selected Critical Analysis Questions

Chapter 1: The Economic Approach

5. False. Intentions do not change the effect of the policy. If the policy runs counter to sound economics, it will lead to a counterproductive outcome even if that was not the intention of the policy. Bad policies are often advocated by people with good intentions.
8. Money has nothing to do with whether an individual is economizing. Any time a person chooses, in an attempt to achieve a goal, they are economizing.
9. Positive economics can help one better understand the likely effects of alternative policies. This will help one choose alternatives that are less likely to lead to disappointing results.
10. Association is not causation. It is likely that a large lead, near the end of the game, caused the third team to play more, rather than the third team causing the lead.
14. This is a question that highlights the importance of marginal analysis. In responding to the question, think about the following. After pollution has already been reduced substantially, how much will it cost to reduce it still more? If the quality of air and water were already high, how much gain would result from still less pollution?

Chapter 2: Some Tools of the Economist

2. Trade is based on the expectation of gain. Unless each of the parties expects to gain, the parties will not agree to the exchange. No, the gains of one trading partner are not at the expense of others. Trade is a positive sum activity. It moves goods from people who value them less to those who value them more. Trade also makes larger outputs possible as the result of gains from specialization and economies of scale. This, too, is a source of the mutual gains realized by the trading partners.
8. Yes. This question highlights the incentive of individuals to conserve for the future when they have private ownership rights. The market value of the land will increase in anticipation of the future harvest as the trees grow and the expected day of harvest grows closer. Thus, with transferable private property, the tree farmer will be able to capture the value added by his planting and holding the trees for a few years, even if the actual harvest does not take place until well after his death.
9. In general, it sanctions all forms of competition except for the use of violence (or the threat of violence), theft, or fraud.
12. Those who get tickets at the lower price gain, whereas those who are prevented from offering a higher price to ticket holders may not get a ticket even though both the prospective buyer and some ticket holders would have gained from the exchange at the higher price. Ticket holders may simply break the law or may sell at the regulated price only to buyers willing to provide them with other favors. Price controls, if they are effective, always reduce the gains from trade.
17. The opportunity cost of those individuals will rise, and they will likely consume less leisure.

Chapter 3: Supply, Demand, and the Market Process

1. Choices (a) and (b) would increase the demand for beef; (c) and (d) would affect primarily the supply of beef, rather than the demand; (e) leads to a change in quantity demanded, not a change in demand.
4. Prices reflect marginal value, not total value. The marginal value of a good is the maximum amount a consumer would be willing to pay for a specific unit. The height of the demand curve reflects the value that consumers place on each unit. The total value is the total benefit consumers derive from all units consumed. The area under the demand curve for the number of units consumed reflects the total value. Water provides an example of a good with high total value but low marginal value. With regard to the last question, are there more nurses or professional wrestlers?
8. Neither markets nor the political process leaves the determination of winners and losers to chance. Under market organization, business winners and losers are determined by the decentralized choices of millions of consumers who use their dollar votes to reward firms that provide preferred goods at a low cost and penalize others who fail to do so. Under political decision-making, the winners and losers are determined by political officials who use taxes, subsidies, regulations, and mandates to favor some businesses and penalize others.
10. **a.** Profitable production increases the value of resources owned by people and leads to mutual gain for resource suppliers, consumers, and entrepreneurs. **b.** Losses reduce the value of resources, which reduces the well-being of at least some people. There is no conflict.
12. The supply curve is constructed under the assumption that other things are held constant. A reduction in the supply of oranges such as would occur under adverse weather conditions would lead to both a higher price and smaller total quantity supplied. This is perfectly consistent with economic theory.

Chapter 4: Supply and Demand: Applications and Extensions

1. An increase in demand for housing will also increase the demand for the resources required for its production, including the services of carpenters, plumbers, and electricians. This will lead to higher wages and an increase in employment for people in these groups.

4. Agreement of both buyer and seller is required for an exchange. Price ceilings push prices below equilibrium and thereby reduce the quantity sellers are willing to offer. Price floors push prices above equilibrium and thereby reduce the quantity consumers wish to buy. Both decrease the actual quantity traded in the market.

6. **a.** Decreases; **b.** Increases; **c.** Decreases; **d.** Increases.

11. The deadweight loss is the loss of the potential gains of buyers and sellers emanating from trades that are squeezed out by the tax. It is an excess burden because even though the exchanges that are squeezed out by the tax impose a cost on buyers and sellers, they do not generate tax revenue (because the trades do not take place).

12. The employment level of low-skilled workers with large families would decline. Some would attempt to conceal the presence of their large family in order to get a job.

14. No. As the tax rate approaches the revenue maximum point, the higher rates substantially reduce the number of trades that take place. This is why the higher rates do not raise much additional revenue. As rates increase toward the revenue maximum point, the lost gains from trade are large and the additions to revenue are small. Thus, rates in this range are highly inefficient.

Chapter 5: Difficult Cases for the Market, and the Role of Government

1. When payment is not demanded for services, potential customers have a strong incentive to attempt a "free ride." However, when the number of nonpaying customers becomes such that the sales revenues of sellers are diminished (and in some cases eliminated), the sellers' incentive to supply the good is thereby reduced (or eliminated).

9. By reducing output below the efficient level, sellers of toasters would no longer produce or exchange some units of the good, despite the fact that the consumers value the marginal units more than it costs to produce them.

11. A public good reflects the characteristics of the good, not the sector in which it is provided. Elementary education is not a public good because it is relatively easy to exclude nonpaying customers and to establish a one-to-one link between payment for and receipt of the good.

Chapter 6: The Economics of Collective Decision-Making

4. The problem is not so much that the "wrong guys" won the last election as it is the incentive structure confronted by political decision-makers. Even if the "right people" were elected, they would be unlikely to improve the efficiency of government, at least not very much, given the strong incentive to support special-interest and shortsighted policies and the weak incentives for operational efficiency when decisions are made by the political process.

8. It is difficult for the voter to know what a candidate will do once elected, and the rationally ignorant voter is usually unwilling to spend the time and effort required to understand issues because the probability that any single vote will decide the issue is exceedingly small. Special-interest voters, in contrast, will know which candidate has promised them the most on their issue. Also, the candidate who is both competent and prepared to ignore special interests will have a hard time getting these facts to voters without financial support from special-interest groups. Each voter has an incentive to be a "free rider" on the "good government" issue. Interestingly, controlling government on behalf of society as a whole is a public good. As in the case of other public goods, there is a tendency for too little of it to be supplied.

10. No. The government is merely an alternative form of organization. Government organization does not permit us to escape either scarcity or competition. It merely affects the nature of the competition. Political competition (eg, voting, lobbying, political contributions, and politically determined budgets) replaces market competition. Neither is there any reason to believe that government organization modifies the importance of personal self-interest.

12. When the welfare of a special-interest group conflicts with that of a widely dispersed, unorganized majority, the legislative political process can reasonably be expected to work to the benefit of the special interest.

Chapter 7: Consumer Choice and Elasticity

2. If your opportunity cost of time is more than $15, it will make sense to take the plane. Thus, Kathy will take the bus and Rachel the plane.

3. It is likely that the income effect of e-cigarettes price changes is much larger for low-income users than for high-income users, perhaps because expenditures on e-cigarettes are a larger proportion of the household budget for those with lower incomes. Thus, the income effect will be larger for this group.

6. Both income and time constrain our ability to consume. Because, in a wealthier society, time becomes more binding and income less binding, time-saving actions will be more common in a wealthier society. As we engage in time-saving actions (fast food, automatic appliances, air travel, and so on) in order to shift the time restraint outward, our lives become more hectic.

10. The answer to the first question is "No." Even for things we like, we will experience diminishing returns. Eventually, the cost of additional units of pizza will exceed their benefits. And, in answer to the second question, perfection in any activity is generally not worth the cost. For example, reading every page of this text three, four, or five times may improve your grade, but it may not be worth it. One function of a text is to structure the material (highlighted points, layout of graphs, and so on) so that the reader will be able to learn quickly (at a lower cost).

11. Carole.

12. **a.** –0.33; inelastic **b.** –1.67 elastic.

Chapter 8: Costs and the Supply of Goods

5. True. If it could produce the output at a lower cost, its profit would be greater.

11. Because owners receive profits, profit maximization is in their interest. Managers, if they are not owners, have no property right to profit and therefore no direct interest in profit maximization. Because a solid record of profitability tends to increase the market value (salary) of corporate managers, they do have an indirect incentive to pursue profits. However, corporate managers may also be interested in gaining power, having nice offices, hiring friends, expanding sales, and other activities, which may conflict with profitability. Thus, owners need to provide incentives for managers to seek profits and to monitor the results.

12. **a.** The interest payments; **b.** The interest income forgone. The tax structure encourages debt rather than equity financing because the firm's tax liability is inversely related to its debt–equity ratio.

14. Check list. Did your marginal cost curve cross the *ATC* and *AVC* curves at their low points? Does the vertical distance between the *ATC* and *AVC* curves get smaller and smaller as output increases? If not, redraw the three curves correctly. Refer to Exhibit 6b.

17. $2,500: the $2,000 decline in market value during the year plus $500 of potential interest on funds that could be obtained if the machine were sold new. Costs associated with the decline in the value of the machine last year are sunk costs.

18. Because they believe they will be able to restructure the firm and provide better management so that the firm will have positive net earnings in the future. If the firm is purchased at a low enough price, this will allow the new owners to cover the opportunity cost of their investment and still earn an economic profit. Alternatively, they may expect to sell off the firm's assets, receiving more net revenue than the cost of purchasing the firm.

Chapter 9: Price Takers and the Competitive Process

2. The market price will decline because the profits will attract new firms (and capital investment) into the market and supply will increase, driving down the price until the profits are eliminated.

6. **a.** Decline; **b.** Increase; **c.** Decline; **d.** Decline.

9. Competition virtually forces firms to operate efficiently and produce goods and services that consumers value highly relative to cost. Firms that fail to do so will find it difficult to compete and eventually losses will drive them from the market.

11. **a.** The reduction in supply led to higher prices; **b.** Because demand is inelastic, the total revenue from sales increased; **c.** Overall, the profitability of farming increased, although some of the producers that were hardest hit by the drought experienced losses because of their sharp reduction in output.

15. **b.** Six or seven tons—$250 profit; **c.** seven or eight tons—$600 profit; **d.** five or six tons—$50 loss. Because the firm can cover its variable cost, it should stay in business if it believes that the low ($450) price is temporary.

Chapter 10: Price-Searcher Markets with Low Entry Barriers

3. The amount of variety is determined by the willingness of consumers to pay for variety relative to the cost of providing it. If consumers value variety highly and the added costs of producing different styles, designs, and sizes is low, there will be a lot of variety. Alternatively, if consumers desire similar products, or if variation can be produced only at a high cost, little variety will be present. Apparently, consumers place a substantial value (relative to cost) on variety in napkins but not in toothpicks.

8. In any of these cases, the answer is competition. To survive, a given type and size of firm must be able to produce at a low cost. Those firms with high per-unit cost will be driven from the market.

10. Building the new resort is more risky (and less attractive) because if the market analysis is incorrect, and demand is insufficient, it probably will be difficult to find other uses for the newly built resort. If the airline proves unprofitable, however, the capital (airplanes) should be extremely mobile. However, the resort would have one offsetting advantage: If demand were stronger than expected, and profits larger, it would take competitors longer to enter the market (build a new resort), and they would be more reluctant to make the more permanent investment.

12. In a competitive setting, only the big firms will survive if economies of scale are important. When economies of scale are unimportant, small firms will be able to compete effectively.

14. Competition provides the answer. If McDonald's fails to provide an attractively priced, tasty sandwich with a smile, people will turn to Burger King, Wendy's, Dairy Queen, and other rivals. If Walmart does not provide convenience and value, people will turn to Costco, Target, and other retailers. Similarly, as recent experience has shown, even a firm as large as General Motors will lose customers to Ford, Honda, Toyota, Tesla, Volkswagen, and other automobile manufacturers if it fails to please the customer as much as rival suppliers do.

Chapter 11: Price-Searcher Markets with High Entry Barriers

3. No; No; No.

8. Because use of product variation and quality improvements to obtain a larger share of the market will be more difficult to monitor and control than a simple price reduction.

11. Reductions in the cost of transportation generally increase competition because they force firms to compete with distant rivals and permit consumers to choose among a wider range of suppliers. As a result, the U.S. economy today is generally more competitive, in the rivalry sense, than it was hundred years ago.

12. The stock price, when the uncle bought the stock, no doubt reflected the well-known profits. The previous owners of the stock surely would not have sold it at a price that failed to reflect its high expected rate of future profit. Thus, there is no reason to believe that the stock purchase will earn a high rate of return for the uncle.

Chapter 12: The Supply of and Demand for Productive Resources

3. **a.** Five; **b.** $350; **c.** Four. The firm will operate in the short run, but it will go out of business in the long run unless the market prices rise.

4. Yes. General increases in the productivity of the labor force will cause a general increase in wages. The higher general wage rates will increase the opportunity cost of barbering and cause the supply of barbers to decline. The reduction in the supply of barbers will place upward pressure on the wages of barbers, even if technological change and worker productivity have changed little in barbering.

6. The job opportunities outside of teaching are more attractive for people with math and science training than for those with English and history degrees. Therefore, the same salary that attracts a substantial number of English and history teachers will be insufficient to attract the required number of math and science teachers.

8. No. The dressmaker needs to employ more capital and less labor because the marginal dollar expenditures on the former are currently increasing output by a larger amount than the latter.

12. **a.** MP 14; 12; 11; 9; 7; 5; 4. TR 70; 130; 185; 230; 265; 290; 310. MRP 70; 60; 55; 45; 35; 25; 20. **b.** 4; **c.** Employment would decline to 3.

Chapter 13: Earnings, Productivity, and the Job Market

2. U.S. workers are more productive. By investing in human capital, the laborers are somewhat responsible, but the superior tools and physical capital that are available to U.S. workers also contribute to their higher wages.

6. Although this statement, often made by politicians, sounds true, in fact, it is false. Output of goods and services valued by consumers, not jobs, is the key to economic progress and a high standard of living. Real income cannot be high unless real output is high. If job creation were the key to economic progress, it would be easy to create millions of jobs. For example, we could prohibit the use of farm machinery. Such a prohibition would create millions of jobs in agriculture. However, it would also reduce output and our standard of living.

9. False. Several additional factors, including differences in preferences (which would influence time worked, the trade-off between money wage and working conditions, and evaluation of alternative jobs), differences in jobs, and imperfect labor mobility, would result in variations in earnings.

11. Hourly wages will be highest in B because the higher wages will be necessary to compensate workers in B for the uncertainty and loss of income during layoffs. Annual earnings will be higher in A in order to compensate workers in A for the additional hours they will work during the year.

Chapter 14: Investment, the Capital Market, and the Wealth of Nations

1. (a) will reduce interest rates in the United States; all of the others will increase interest rates in the United States.
4. No. The average outstanding balance during the year is only about half of $1,000. Therefore, the $200 interest charge translates to almost a 40 percent annual rate of interest.
6. *Hints:* Which has been considered to be more risky—purchasing a bond or a stock? How does risk influence the expected rate of return?
8. 6 percent.
10. **a.** Mike; **b.** Yes, people who save a lot are able to get a higher interest rate on their savings as the result of people with a high rate of time preference; **c.** Yes, people who want to borrow money will be able to do so at a lower rate when there are more people (like Alicia) who want to save a lot.
11. They are helped. This question is a lot like prior questions involving Alicia and Mike. Potential gains from trade are present. If obstacles do not restrain trade, the low-income countries will be able to attract savings (from countries with a high saving rate) at a lower interest rate than would exist in the absence of trade. Similarly, people in the high-income countries will be able to earn a higher return than would otherwise be possible. Each can gain because of the existence of the other.
12. **a.** Approximately $1.277 million; **b.** Yes; **c.** The lottery earnings are less liquid. Because there is not a well-organized market transforming lottery earnings into present income, the transaction costs of finding a "buyer" (at a price equal to the present value of the earnings) for the lottery earnings "rights" may be higher than for the bond, if one wants to sell in the future.
14. No. The present value of the $500 annual additions to earnings during the next ten years is less than the cost of the schooling.
16. Consider the following when answering this question: Whose money is being invested by each of the two entities? If a private investment project goes bad, who is hurt? If a private project is successful, who reaps the gain? Answer the same two questions for political officials.

Chapter 15: Income Inequality and Poverty

2. Differences in family size, age of potential workers, nonmoney "income," taxes, and cost-of-living among areas reduce the effectiveness of annual money income as a measure of economic status. In general, high-income families are larger, are more likely to be headed by a prime-age worker, have less nonmoney income (including leisure), pay more taxes, and reside in higher-cost-of-living areas (particularly large cities). Thus, money income comparison between high- and low-income groups often overstates the economic status of the former relative to the latter.
4. If there were no intergenerational mobility, the diagonal numbers would all be 100 percent. If there were complete equality of opportunity and outcomes, the numbers in each column and row would be 20 percent.
6. No. The increase in marginal tax rates will reduce the incentive of low-income individuals to earn income. Therefore, their income will rise by $1,000 minus the reduction in their personal earnings due to the disincentive effects of the higher marginal tax rates.
7. 67 percent.

Chapter 16: Gaining from International Trade

2. Availability of goods and services, not jobs, is the source of economic prosperity. When a good can be purchased cheaper abroad than it can be produced at home, a nation can expand the quantity of goods and services available for consumption by specializing in the production of those goods for which it is a low-cost producer and trading them for the cheap (relative to domestic costs) foreign goods. Trade restrictions limiting the ability of Americans to purchase low-cost goods from foreign producers stifle this process and thereby reduce the living standard of Americans.
4. Statements (a) and (b) are not in conflict. Because trade restrictions are typically a special-interest issue, political entrepreneurs can often gain by supporting them even when they promote economic inefficiency.
6. True. The primary effect of trade restrictions is an increase in domestic scarcity. This has distributional

consequences, but it is clear that, as a whole, a nation will be harmed by the increased domestic scarcity that accompanies the trade restraints.

10. In thinking about this issue, consider the following points. Suppose that the Japanese were willing to give products such as automobiles, electronic goods, and clothing to us free of charge. Would we be worse off if we accepted the gifts? Should we try to keep the free goods out? What is the source of real income—jobs or goods and services? If the gifts make us better off, doesn't it follow that partial gifts would also make us better off?

12. Although trade reduces employment in import-competing industries, it expands employment in export industries. On balance, there is no reason to believe that trade either promotes or destroys jobs. The major effect of trade is to permit individuals, states, regions, and nations to generate a larger output by specializing in the things they do well and trading for those things that they would produce only at a high cost. A higher real income is the result.

16. True. If country A imposes a tariff, other countries will sell less to A and therefore acquire less purchasing power in terms of A's currency. Thus, they will have to reduce their purchases of A's export goods.

Special Topic 1: Government Spending and Taxation

1. Taxes reduce economic efficiency because they eliminate some exchanges and thereby reduce the gains from these transactions. Because of (a) the deadweight losses accompanying the elimination of exchanges and (b) the cost of collecting taxes, the costs of additional tax revenue will be greater than the revenue transferred to the government. Studies indicate that it costs between \$1.20 and \$1.30 for each dollar of tax revenue raised by the government.

5. As we discussed in Chapter 6, the political process works better when there is a close relationship between who pays for and who benefits from government programs. An increase in the number of people who pay no income taxes is likely to weaken this relationship. Whereas those with low incomes pay payroll taxes, the revenues from this tax are earmarked for the finance of the Social Security and Medicare programs. Thus, expansions in government are financed primarily by the personal income tax. In the future, exemption of large numbers of people from this tax is likely to make it more difficult to control the growth of government. If you do not have to help pay for more government spending, why would you oppose it?

Special Topic 2: The Stock Market: Its Function, Performance, and Potential as an Investment Opportunity

1. History shows that in the U.S. stock market, fairly high returns can be gained at a relatively low risk by people who hold a diverse portfolio of stocks in unrelated industries for a period of twenty years or more. An indexed equity mutual fund is an option that would allow a person to purchase a diverse portfolio while keeping commission costs low.

3. The expectation of high profits in the future drove up the price of the stock, despite the lack of a dividend payment in the early years of the firm. Investors are equally happy with high dividends or the equivalent in rising stock value due to the firm's retaining its profits for further investment.

5. The low and declining interest rates increase the present value of future income generated by stocks, which tends to push stock prices upward. The empirical evidence is consistent with this view. The S&P 500 rose from 1,115 at year end 2009 to 3,231 at year end 2019, an annual rate of increase of 11 percent.

Special Topic 3: Keynes and Hayek: Contrasting Views on Sound Economics and the Role of Government

1. Keynes is arguing that it does not matter much how the government spends stimulus funds. According to the Keynesian view, the key consideration is to spend the funds so they will generate income for those undertaking the project, and as those funds are spent, a multiple expansion in income and aggregate demand will result.

Special Topic 4: The Great Recession of 2008–2009: Causes and Response

3. The less equity the owner has in their house, the more likely their will default. This is particularly true in the United States because most home mortgages here are nonrecourse loans: The owner is not responsible for the debt beyond turning the property over to the lender in case of default. The lender has no legal claim on assets of the borrower beyond the asset that was mortgaged. Thus, when the value of a house falls below the outstanding loan, the borrower will often gain by simply abandoning the property. This is precisely what many have done in recent years.

5. The incentive to evaluate the borrower's creditworthiness carefully is reduced. If the mortgage originator had to keep the loan until it was repaid, there would be greater incentive for the lender to evaluate the creditworthiness of the borrower more diligently.

Special Topic 5: Lessons from the Great Depression

5. The statement reflects a failure to recognize the secondary effects of limiting imports. If we buy less from foreign producers, they will have fewer dollars that are required for the purchase of our exports. Therefore, a reduction in imports will also reduce exports and there is no reason to expect any net increase in employment. Instead, trade restraints lead to less output and lower incomes.

Special Topic 6: The Economics of Health Care

2. Health insurance benefits are a component of the employee's compensation package. Unless the employer values the services of the employee by an amount greater than or equal to the total cost of the employee's compensation, the worker will not be hired. Thus, like other components of the compensation package, health insurance benefits are earned by employees.
4. Medicare and Medicaid increased both total health care spending and the share of that spending paid by a third party. Both of these factors increased the demand for and prices of medical services, thereby making them more expensive for people who do not qualify for these programs.
6. Personal choices exert a major impact on health care expenditures. Individuals who smoke, consume alcohol, and eat excessively; fail to exercise and control their weight; use recreational drugs; and engage in other risky behavior will have higher health care costs. Under systems in which all are charged the same premium, the incentive to adopt a healthy lifestyle is reduced. Persons who make choices that promote good health are forced to subsidize those who do not. This perverse incentive structure also pushes health care costs upward.
8. The incentive to purchase insurance when you are healthy will be reduced.

Special Topic 7: Earnings Differences Between Men and Women

2. **a.** The average years of work experience of women relative to men would decline because many of the women entering the labor force would have little prior work experience; **b.** The average hours of work of women would also decline because many of the married women would be looking for part-time employment and hours that were complementary with their historic household responsibilities; **c.** The increased labor force participation of married women would cause the female–male earnings ratio to fall.
4. Not necessarily. Compared with married men, single men tend to be younger, have fewer dependents, be more likely to drop out of the labor force, and be less likely to receive earnings-enhancing assistance from another person. All these factors will reduce their earnings relative to married men.

Special Topic 8: The Question of Resource Exhaustion

2. When demand expands in resource markets, prices send signals and provide the incentives that will reduce future demand relative to supply. These forces will avoid lasting shortages.
5. If any resource, including water, is bought and sold, then market signals will automatically be provided to signal the desires of users to have, and the abilities of suppliers to supply, more. A market provides productive incentive to all concerned. Users conserve more when a market price rises, suppliers provide more, and there is greater incentive to develop and use substitutes for the higher priced resource. If markets are not used to allocate a resource, these benefits will be lost.

Special Topic 9: Difficult Environmental Cases and the Role of Government

1. The ITQ would allow fishers to fish at their own speed without fear of losing their quota to others.
4. In a market with strong property rights in place, a polluter would have to be concerned about harming others and being sued by them for damages. Without strong property rights in place, regulation might help. Or it might not. In any case, regulators need information available only in a market to judge how tightly to regulate if the regulator is seeking efficiency.

Glossary

A

Absolute advantage A situation in which a nation, as the result of its previous experience and/or natural endowments, can produce more of a good (with the same amount of resources) than another nation can.

Accounting profits The sales revenues minus the expenses of a firm over a designated time period, usually one year. Accounting profits typically make allowances for changes in the firm's inventories and depreciation of its assets. No allowance is made, however, for the opportunity cost of the equity capital of the firm's owners, or other implicit costs.

Adjustable rate mortgages (ARMs) A home loan in which the interest rate, and thus the monthly payment, is tied to a short-term rate like the one-year Treasury bill rate. Typically, the mortgage interest rate will be two or three percentage points above the related short-term rate. It will be reset at various time intervals (e.g., annually), and thus the interest rate and monthly payment will vary over the life of the loan.

Alt-A loans Loans extended with little documentation or verification of the borrowers' income, employment, and other indicators of their ability to repay. Because of this poor documentation, these loans are risky.

Automation A production technique that reduces the amount of labor required to produce a good or service. It is beneficial to adopt the new labor-saving technology only if it reduces the cost of production.

Average fixed cost Total fixed cost divided by the number of units produced. It always declines as output increases.

Average product The total product (output) divided by the number of units of the variable input required to produce that output level.

Average tax rate (ATR) Tax liability divided by taxable income. It is the percentage of income paid in taxes.

Average total cost Total cost divided by the number of units produced. It is sometimes called per-unit cost.

Average variable cost The total variable cost divided by the number of units produced.

B

Barriers to entry Obstacles that limit the freedom of potential rivals to enter and compete in an industry or market.

Basis points One one-hundredth of a percentage point. Thus, 100 basis points are equivalent to one percentage point.

Bonds A promise to repay the principal (amount borrowed) plus interest at a specified time in the future. Organizations such as corporations and governments issue bonds as a method of borrowing from bondholders.

C

Capital Human-made resources (such as tools, equipment, and structures) used to produce other goods and services. They enhance our ability to produce in the future.

Capitalism An economic system in which productive resources are owned privately and goods and resources are allocated through market prices.

Cartel An organization of sellers designed to coordinate supply decisions so that the joint profits of the members will be maximized. A cartel will seek to create a monopoly in the market.

Ceteris paribus A Latin term meaning "other things constant" that is used when the effect of one change is being described, recognizing that if other things changed, they also could affect the result. Economists often describe the effects of one change, knowing that in the real world, other things might change and also exert an effect.

Collective decision-making The use of the political process (voting, taxes, government spending, regulation, political bargaining, lobbying, and so on) to make decisions and allocate resources. In a democratic setting, the votes of citizens and their representatives will determine the actions undertaken.

Collusion Agreement among firms to avoid various competitive practices, particularly price reductions. It may involve either formal agreements or merely tacit recognition that competitive practices will be self-defeating in the long run. Tacit collusion is difficult to detect. In the United States, antitrust laws prohibit collusion and conspiracies to restrain trade.

Comparative advantage The ability to produce a good at a lower opportunity cost than others can produce it. Relative costs determine comparative advantage.

Compensating wage differentials Wage differences that compensate workers for risk, unpleasant working conditions, and other undesirable nonpecuniary aspects of a job.

Competition as a dynamic process Rivalry or competitiveness between or among parties (for example, producers or input suppliers) to deliver a better deal to buyers in terms of quality, price, and product information.

Competitive price-searcher markets A market in which the firms have a downward-sloping demand curve, and entry into and exit from the market are relatively easy.

Complements Products that are usually consumed jointly (for example, bread and butter, hot dogs and hot dog buns). A decrease in the price of one will cause an increase in demand for the other.

Constant returns to scale Unit costs that are constant as the scale of the firm is altered. Neither economies nor diseconomies of scale are present.

Constant-cost industry An industry for which factor prices and costs of production remain constant as market output is expanded. The long-run market supply curve is therefore horizontal in these industries.

Consumer surplus The difference between the maximum price consumers are willing to pay and the price they actually pay. It is the net gain derived by the buyers of the good.

Contestable markets A market in which the costs of entry and exit are low, so a firm risks little by entering. Efficient production and zero economic profits should prevail in a contestable market.

Corporations A business firm owned by shareholders who possess ownership rights to the firm's profits, but whose liability is limited to the amount of their investment in the firm.

Creative destruction The replacement of old products and production methods by innovative new ones that consumers judge to be superior. The process generates economic growth and higher living standards.

Crony capitalism A situation where the institutions of markets are maintained, but to a large degree the allocation of resources and the profit and loss of businesses are determined by political decision-making rather than consumer purchases and market forces. Many of the business firms will use contributions and other forms of political support to compete for government favors.

D

Deadweight loss The loss of gains from trade to buyers and sellers that occurs when a tax is imposed. The deadweight loss imposes a burden on both buyers and sellers over and above the actual payment of the tax.

Decreasing-cost industries An industry for which costs of production decline as the industry expands. The market supply is therefore inversely related to price. Such industries are atypical.

Derived demand The demand for a resource; it stems from the demand for the final good the resource helps produce.

Differentiated products Products distinguished from similar products by characteristics like quality, design, location, and method of promotion.

Discounting The procedure used to calculate the present value of future income, which is inversely related to both the interest rate and the amount of time that passes before the funds are received.

Diseconomies of scale Increases in the firm's per-unit costs associated with increases in firm size due to inefficiencies and monitoring problems.

Division of labor A method that breaks down the production of a product into a series of specific tasks, each performed by a different worker.

Dumping Selling a good in a foreign country at a lower price than what it cost to produce, or at a lower price than it's sold for in the domestic market.

E

Earned Income Tax Credit A provision of the tax code that provides a credit or rebate to people with low earnings (income from work activities). The credit is eventually phased out if the recipient's earnings increase.

Economic efficiency A situation in which all of the potential gains from trade have been realized. An action is efficient only if it creates more benefit than cost. With well-defined property rights and competition, market equilibrium is efficient.

Economic profit The difference between the firm's total revenues and its total costs, including both the explicit and implicit cost components.

Economic theory A set of definitions, postulates, and principles assembled in a manner that makes clear the "cause-and-effect" relationships.

Economies of scale Reductions in the firm's per–unit costs associated with the use of large plants to produce a large volume of output.

Economizing behavior Choosing the option that offers the greatest benefit at the least possible cost.

Employment discrimination Unequal treatment of people on the basis of their race, gender, religion, or other attributes, restricting their employment and earnings opportunities compared with others of similar productivity. Employment discrimination may stem from the prejudices of employers, customers, fellow employees, or all three.

Entrepreneur A person who decides what resources will be used, how they will be combined, and what goods and services they will be utilized to produce. Typically, entrepreneurs will undertake these activities within a business enterprise. A successful entrepreneur's actions will increase the value of resources and expand the size of the economic pie.

Equilibrium A state in which the conflicting forces of demand and supply are in balance. When a market is in equilibrium, the decisions of consumers and producers are brought into harmony with one another, and the quantity demanded will equal the quantity supplied.

Equity mutual funds A corporation that pools the funds of investors, including small investors, and uses them to purchase a bundle of stocks.

Excess burden of taxation Another term for deadweight loss. It reflects losses that occur when beneficial activities are forgone because they are taxed.

Explicit costs Payments by a firm to purchase the services of productive resources.

External benefit Spillover effects that generate benefits for nonconsenting parties.

External cost Spillover effects that reduce the well-being of nonconsenting parties.

Externalities Spillover effects of an activity that influence the well-being of nonconsenting parties.

F

Fallacy of composition Erroneous view that what is true for the individual (or the part) will also be true for the group (or the whole).

FICO score A credit score measuring a borrower's likely ability to repay a loan. A person's FICO score will range between 300 and 850. A score of 700 or more indicates that the borrower's credit standing is good. FICO is an acronym for the Fair Isaac Corporation, the creators of the FICO score.

Foreclosure rate The percentage of home mortgages on which the lender has started the process of taking ownership of the property because the borrower has failed to make the monthly payments.

Franchise A right or license granted to an individual to market a company's goods or services or use its brand name. The individual firms are independently owned but must meet certain conditions to continue to use the name.

Free riders People who receive the benefit of a good without paying for it. Because it is often virtually impossible to restrict the consumption of public goods to those who pay, these goods are subject to free-rider problems.

Fringe benefits Benefits other than normal money wages That are supplied to employees in exchange for their labor Services. Higher fringe benefits come at the expense of lower money wages.

G

Game theory A tool used to analyze the strategic choices made by competitors in a conflict situation, like the decisions made by firms in an oligopoly.

General Agreement on Tariffs and Trade (GATT) An organization formed after World War II to set the rules for the conduct of international trade and reduce trade barriers among nations.

Going out of business The sale of a firm's assets and its permanent exit from the market. By going out of business, a firm is able to avoid its fixed costs, which would continue during a shutdown.

Government failure A situation in which the structure of incentives is such that the political process, including democratic political decision-making, will encourage individuals to undertake actions that conflict with economic efficiency.

H

Health savings accounts Special savings accounts that individuals and families can use for the payment of medical bills and the purchase of a catastrophic (high-deductible) health insurance plan.

Human resources The abilities, skills, and health of human beings that contribute to the production of both current and future output. Investment in training and education can increase the supply of human resources.

I

Implicit costs The opportunity costs associated with a firm's use of resources that it owns. These costs do not involve a direct money payment. Examples include wage income and interest forgone by the owner of a firm who also provides labor services and equity capital to the firm.

Implicit marginal tax rate The amount of additional (marginal) earnings that must be paid explicitly in taxes or implicitly in the form of reduced income supplements. The marginal tax rate establishes the fraction of an additional dollar earned that an individual is permitted to keep, so it is an important determinant of the incentive to work and earn.

Import quota A specific limit or maximum quantity (or value) of a good permitted to be imported into a country during a given period.

Income effect That part of an increase (decrease) in Amount consumed that is the result of the consumer's real Income being expanded (contracted) by a reduction (rise) in The price of a good.

Income elasticity The percentage change in the quantity of a product demanded divided by the percentage change in consumer income that caused the change in quantity demanded. It measures the responsiveness of the demand for a good to a consumer's change in income.

Income mobility Movement of individuals and families either up or down income-distribution rankings when comparisons are made at two different points in time. When substantial income mobility is present, a person's current position in the rankings will not be a very good indicator of what their position will be a few years in the future.

Increasing-cost industry An industry for which costs of production rise as output is expanded. In these industries, even in the long run, higher market prices will be needed to induce firms to expand total output. As a result, the long-run market supply curve in these industries will slope upward to the right.

Indexed equity mutual fund An equity mutual fund that holds a portfolio of stocks that matches their share (or weight) in a broad stock market index such as the S&P 500. The overhead of these funds is usually quite low because their expenses on stock trading and research are low.

Inferior good A good that has a negative income elasticity, so that as consumer income rises, the demand for the good falls.

INFLATIONARY PREMIUM A component of the money interest rate that reflects compensation to the lender for the expected decrease, due to inflation, in the purchasing power of the principal and interest during the course of the loan. It is determined by the expected rate of future inflation..

Innovation The successful introduction and adoption of a new product or process; the economic application of inventions and marketing techniques.

Invention The creation of a new product or process, often facilitated by the knowledge of engineering and science.

Inventory investment Changes in the stock of unsold goods and raw materials held during a period.

Investment The purchase, construction, or development of capital resources, including both nonhuman capital and human capital. Investments increase the supply of capital.

Investment banks An institution that acts as an underwriter for securities issued by other corporations or lenders. Unlike traditional banks, investment banks do not accept deposits from, or provide loans to, individuals.

Investment in human capital Expenditures on training, education, skill development, and health designed to increase human capital and people's productivity.

Invisible hand principle The tendency of market prices to direct individuals pursuing their own interests to engage in activities promoting the economic well-being of society.

L

Laffer curve A curve illustrating the relationship between the tax rate and tax revenues. Tax revenues will be low at both very high and very low tax rates. When tax rates are quite high, lowering them can increase tax revenue.

Law of comparative advantage A principle that states that individuals, firms, regions, or nations can gain by specializing in the production of goods that they produce cheaply (at a low opportunity cost) and exchanging them for goods they cannot produce cheaply (at a high opportunity cost).

Law of demand A principle that states there is an inverse relationship between the price of a good and the quantity of it buyers are willing to purchase. As the price of a good increases, consumers will wish to purchase less of it. As the price decreases, consumers will wish to purchase more of it.

Law of diminishing marginal utility The basic economic principle that as the consumption of a product increases, the marginal utility derived from consuming more of it (per unit of time) will eventually decline.

Law of diminishing returns The postulate that as more and more units of a variable resource are combined with a fixed amount of other resources, using additional units of the variable resource will eventually increase output only at a decreasing rate. Once diminishing returns are reached, it will take successively larger amounts of the variable factor to expand output by one unit.

Law of supply A principle that states there is a direct relationship between the price of a good and the quantity of it producers are willing to supply. As the price of a good increases, producers will wish to supply more of it. As the price decreases, producers will wish to supply less.

Leverage ratio The ratio of loans and other investments to the firm's capital assets.

Licensing A requirement that one obtain permission from the government in order to perform certain business activities or work in various occupations.

Logrolling The exchange between politicians of political support on one issue for political support on another.

Long run (in production) A time period long enough to allow the firm to vary all of its factors of production.

Loss A deficit of sales revenue relative to the opportunity cost of production. Losses are a penalty imposed on those who produce goods even though they are valued less than the resources required for their production.

M

Macroeconomics The branch of economics that focuses on how human behavior affects outcomes in highly aggregated markets, such as the markets for labor or consumer products.

Managed equity mutual fund An equity mutual fund that has a portfolio manager who decides what stocks will be held in the fund and when they will be bought or sold. A research staff generally provides support for the fund manager.

Marginal Term used to describe the effects of a change in the current situation. For example, a producer's marginal cost is the cost of producing an additional unit of a product, given the producer's current facility and production rate.

Marginal benefit The maximum price a consumer will be willing to pay for an additional unit of a product. It is the dollar value of the consumer's marginal utility from the additional unit, and therefore it falls as consumption increases.

Marginal cost The change in total cost required to produce an additional unit of output.

Marginal product (*MP*) The change in total output that results from the employment of one additional unit of a resource.

Marginal propensity to consume (MPC) Additional current consumption divided by additional current disposable income.

MARGINAL REVENUE (*MR*) The change in a firm's total revenue that results from the production and sale of one additional unit of output.

Marginal revenue product (*MRP*) The change in the total revenue of a firm that results from the employment of one additional unit of a resource. The marginal revenue product of an input is equal to its marginal product multiplied by the marginal revenue of the good or service produced.

Marginal tax rate (MTR) The additional tax liability a person faces divided by his or her additional taxable income. It is the percentage of an extra dollar of income earned that must be paid in taxes. It is the marginal tax rate that is relevant in personal decision-making.

Marginal utility The additional utility, or satisfaction, derived from consuming an additional unit of a good.

Market An abstract concept encompassing the forces of demand and supply and the interaction of buyers and sellers with the potential for exchange to occur.

Market failure A situation in which the structure of incentives is such that markets will encourage individuals to undertake activities that are inconsistent with economic efficiency.

Market organization A method of organization in which private parties make their own plans and decisions with the guidance of unregulated market prices. The basic economic questions of consumption, production, and distribution are answered through these decentralized decisions.

Market power The ability of a firm that is not a pure monopolist to earn persistently large profits, indicating that it has some monopoly power. Because the firm has few (or weak) competitors, it has a degree of freedom from vigorous competition.

Means-tested income transfers Transfers that are limited to people or families with an income below a certain cutoff point. Eligibility is thus dependent upon low-income status.

Microeconomics The branch of economics that focuses On how human behavior affects the conduct of affairs within narrowly defined units, such as individual households or Business firms.

Middlemen People who buy and sell goods or services or arrange trades. A middleman reduces transaction costs.

Minimum wage Legislation requiring that workers be paid at least the stated minimum hourly rate of pay.

Money (nominal) rate of interest The rate of interest in monetary terms that borrowers pay for borrowed funds. During periods when borrowers and lenders expect inflation, the money rate of interest exceeds the real rate of interest.

Monopolistic competition A term often used by economists to describe markets characterized by a large number of sellers that supply differentiated products to a market with low barriers to entry. Essentially, it is an alternative term for a competitive price-searcher market.

Monopoly A market structure characterized by (1) a single seller of a well-defined product for which there are no good substitutes and (2) high barriers to the entry of any other firms into the market for that product.

Mortgage default rate The percentage of home mortgages on which the borrower is late by 90 days or more with the payments on the loan or it is in the foreclosure process. This rate is sometimes referred to as the serious delinquency rate.

Mortgage-backed securities Securities issued for the financing of large pools of mortgages. The promised returns to the security holders are derived from the mortgage interest payments.

N

Natural monopoly A market situation in which the average costs of production continually decline with increased output. In a natural monopoly, the average costs of production will be lowest when a single, large firm produces the entire output demanded by the marketplace.

Network effect When the value of a product or service to each consumer increases as the number of users expands. This is also known as a network externality.

Nonhuman resources The durable, nonhuman inputs used to produce both current and future output. Machines, buildings, land, and raw materials are examples. Investment can increase the supply of nonhuman resources. Economists often use the term *physical capital* when referring to nonhuman resources.

Nonpecuniary job characteristics Working conditions, prestige, variety, location, employee freedom and responsibilities, and other nonwage characteristics of a job that influence how employees evaluate the job.

Nonrenewable resources Those that are not created or renewed naturally at a significant rate.

Normal good A good that has a positive income elasticity, so that as consumer income rises, demand for the good rises, too.

Normal profit rate Zero economic profit, providing just the competitive rate of return on the capital (and labor) of owners. An above-normal profit will draw more entry into the market, whereas a below-normal profit will lead to an exit of investors and capital.

Normative economics Judgments about "what ought to be" in economic matters. Normative economic views cannot be proved false because they are based on value judgments.

O

Objective A fact based on observable phenomena that is not influenced by differences in personal opinion.

Oligopoly A market situation in which a small number of sellers constitutes the entire industry. It is competition among the few.

Opportunity cost The highest valued alternative that must be sacrificed as a result of choosing an option.

Opportunity cost of equity capital The rate of return that must be earned by investors to induce them to supply financial capital to the firm.

P

Partnership A business firm owned by two or more individuals who possess ownership rights to the firm's profits and are personally liable for the debts of the firm.

Platform businesses A firm that provides the environment for the creation of synergies among decentralized crowdsourced resources that aren't necessarily owned or controlled by the firm.

Pork-barrel legislation A package of spending projects bundled into a single bill. It is often used as a device to obtain funding for a group of projects intensely desired by regional or interest groups that would be unlikely to pass if voted on separately.

Portfolio All the stocks, bonds, or other securities held by an individual or corporation for investment purposes.

Positive economics The scientific study of "what is" among economic relationships.

Positive rate of time preference The desire of consumers for goods now rather than in the future.

Poverty threshold income level The level of money income below which a family is considered to be poor. It differs according to family characteristics (e.g., number of family members) and is adjusted when consumer prices change.

Present value (*PV*) The current worth of future income after it is discounted to reflect the fact that revenues in the future are valued less highly than revenues now.

Price ceiling A legally established maximum price sellers can charge for a good, service, or resource.

Price controls Government-mandated prices that are generally imposed in the form of maximum or minimum legal prices.

Price discrimination A practice whereby a seller charges different consumers different prices for the same product or service.

Price elasticity of demand The percentage change in the quantity of a product demanded divided by the percentage change in the price that caused the change in quantity. The price elasticity of demand indicates how responsive consumers are to a change in a product's price.

Price elasticity of supply The percentage change in quantity supplied divided by the percentage change in the price that caused the change in quantity supplied.

Price floor A legally established minimum price buyers must pay for a good, service, or resource.

Price searchers Firms that face a downward-sloping demand curve for their product. The amount the firm is able to sell is inversely related to the price it charges.

Price takers Sellers who must take the market price in order to sell their product. Because each price taker's output is small relative to the total market, price takers can sell all their output at the market price, but they are unable to sell any of their output at a price higher than the market price.

Primary market The market in which financial institutions aid in the sale of new securities.

Principal-agent problems The incentive problem that occurs when the purchaser of services (the principal) lacks full information about the circumstances faced by the seller (the agent) and cannot know how well the agent performs the purchased services. The agent may to some extent work toward objectives other than those sought by the principal paying for the service.

Private property rights Property rights that are exclusively held by an owner and protected against invasion by others. Private property can be transferred, sold, leased, or mortgaged at the owner's discretion.

Producer surplus The difference between the price that suppliers actually receive and the minimum price they would be willing to accept. It measures the net gains to producers and resource suppliers from market exchange. It is not the same as profit.

Production possibilities curve A curve that outlines all possible combinations of total output that could be produced, assuming (1) a fixed amount of productive resources, (2) a given amount of technical knowledge, and (3) full and efficient use of those resources. The slope of the curve indicates the amount of one product that must be given up to produce more of the other.

Profit An excess of sales revenue relative to the opportunity cost of production. The cost component includes the opportunity cost of all resources, including those owned by the firm. Therefore, profit accrues only when the value of the good produced is greater than the value of the resources used for its production.

Progressive tax A tax in which the average tax rate rises with income. People with higher incomes will pay a higher percentage of their income in taxes.

Property rights The rights to use, control, and obtain the benefits from a good or resource.

Proportional tax A tax in which the average tax rate is the same at all income levels. Everyone pays the same percentage of income in taxes.

Proprietorship A business firm owned by an individual who possesses the ownership right to the firm's profits and is personally liable for the firm's debts.

Proved reserves Specific mineral deposits that have been shown by scientific examination and cost calculation to be extractable and deliverable to the market for use, with current technology and expected market conditions.

Public goods Goods for which rivalry among consumers is absent and exclusion of nonpaying customers is difficult.

Public-choice analysis The study of decision-making as it affects the formation and operation of collective organizations, like governments. In general, the principles and methodology of economics are applied to political science topics.

Pure competition A market structure characterized by a large number of small firms producing an identical product in an industry (market area) that permits complete freedom of entry and exit. Also called price-taker markets.

R

Rational ignorance effect Because it is highly unlikely that an individual vote will decide the outcome of an election, a rational individual has little or no incentive to search for and acquire the information needed to cast an informed vote.

Rationing Allocating a limited supply of a good or resource among people who would like to have more of it. When price performs the rationing function, the good or resource is allocated to those willing to give up the most "other things" in order to get it.

Real earnings Earnings adjusted for differences in the general level of prices across time periods or geographic areas. When real earnings are equal, the same bundle of goods and services can be purchased with the earnings.

Real rate of interest The money rate of interest minus the expected rate of inflation. The real rate of interest indicates the interest premium in terms of real goods and services that one must pay for earlier availability.

Regressive tax A tax in which the average tax rate falls with income. People with higher incomes will pay a lower percentage of their income in taxes.

Renewable resources Those that are renewed in nature, like water flows, or grown, like timber.

Rent-seeking Actions by individuals and groups designed to restructure public policy in a manner that will either directly or indirectly redistribute more income to themselves or the projects they promote.

Repeat-purchase items An item purchased often by the same buyer.

Residual claimants Individuals who personally receive the excess, if any, of revenues over costs. Residual claimants gain if the firm's costs are reduced or revenues increase.

Resource An input used to produce economic goods. Land, labor, skills, natural resources, and human-made tools and equipment provide examples. Throughout history, people have struggled to transform available, but limited, resources into things they would like to have—economic goods.

Resource market The market for inputs used to produce goods and services.

Resource markets Markets in which business firms demand factors of production (for example, labor, capital, and natural resources) from household suppliers. The resources are then used to produce goods and services. These markets are sometimes called factor markets or input markets.

Resource mobility The ease with which factors of production are able to move among alternative uses. Resources that can easily be transferred to a different use or location are said to be highly mobile. Resources with few alternative uses are immobile.

S

Samaritan's dilemma The dilemma that occurs when assisting low-income citizens with transfers reduces the opportunity cost of choices that lead to poverty. Providing income transfers to low-income individuals and discouraging behavior that leads to poverty are conflicting goals.

SAVING Current income that is not spent on consumption goods. Saving makes it possible for resources to be devoted to investments (like the making of tractors or other equipment used in production).

Scarcity A fundamental concept of economics that indicates that there is less of a good freely available than people would like.

Scientific thinking Developing a theory from basic principles and testing it against events in the real world. Good theories are consistent with and help explain real-world events. Theories that are inconsistent with the real world are invalid and must be rejected.

Secondary effects The indirect impact of an event or policy that may not be easily and immediately observable. In the area of policy, these effects are often both unintended and overlooked.

Secondary markets The market in which financial institutions aid in the buying and selling of existing securities.

Secondary mortgage market A market in which mortgages originated by a lender are sold to another financial institution. In recent years, the major buyers in this market have been Fannie Mae, Freddie Mac, and large investment banks.

Security-rating A rating indicating the risk of default of the security. A rating of AAA indicates that the risk of default is low.

Shirking Working at less than the expected rate of productivity, which reduces output. Shirking is more likely when workers are not monitored, so that the cost of lower output falls on others.

Short run A time period so short that a firm is unable to vary some of its factors of production. The firm's plant size typically cannot be altered in the short run.

Shortage A condition in which the amount of a good offered for sale by producers is less than the amount demanded by buyers at the existing price. An increase in price would eliminate the shortage.

Shortsightedness effect The misallocation of resources that results because public-sector action is biased (1) in favor of proposals yielding clearly defined current benefits in exchange for difficult-to-identify future costs and (2) against proposals with clearly identifiable current costs that yield less concrete and less obvious future benefits.

Shutdown A temporary halt in the operation of a firm. Because the firm anticipates operating in the future, it does not sell its assets and go out of business. The firm's variable cost is eliminated by the shutdown, but its fixed costs continue.

Socialism A system of economic organization in which (1) the ownership and control of the basic means of production rest with the state and (2) resource allocation is determined by centralized planning rather than by market forces.

Special-interest issue An issue that generates substantial individual benefits to a small minority while imposing a small individual cost on many other citizens. In total, the net cost to the majority might either exceed or fall short of the net benefits to the special-interest group.

Stock options The option to buy a specified number of shares of the firm's stock at a designated price. The designated price is generally set so that the options will be quite valuable if the firm's shares increase in price but of little value if their price falls. Thus, when used to compensate top managers, stock options provide a strong incentive to follow policies that will increase the value of the firm.

Stocks Ownership shares of a corporation. Corporations raise funds by issuing stock ownership shares, which entitle the owners to a proportional share of the firm's profits. The stock owners are not liable for the debts of the corporation beyond their initial investment. However, there is no assurance that the owners will receive either their initial investment or any return in the future.

Strike An action of unionized employees in which they (1) discontinue working for the employer and (2) take steps to prevent other potential workers from offering their services to the employer.

Subjective An opinion based on personal preferences and value judgments.

Subprime loans A loan made to a borrower with blemished credit or one who provides only limited documentation of income, employment history, and other indicators of creditworthiness.

Subsidy A payment the government makes to either the buyer or the seller, usually on a per-unit basis, when a good or service is purchased or sold.

Substitutes Products that serve similar purposes. An increase in the price of one will cause an increase in demand for the other (examples are hamburgers and tacos, butter and margarine, Chevrolets and Fords).

Substitution effect That part of an increase (decrease) in amount consumed that is the result of a good being cheaper (more expensive) in relation to other goods because of a reduction (increase) in price.

Sunk costs Costs that have already been incurred as a result of past decisions. They are sometimes referred to as historical costs.

Surplus A condition in which the amount of a good offered for sale by producers is greater than the amount that buyers will purchase at the existing price. A decline in price would eliminate the surplus.

T

Tariff A tax levied on goods imported into a country.

Tax base The level or quantity of an economic activity that is taxed. Higher tax rates reduce the level of the tax base because they make the activity less attractive.

Tax incidence The way the burden of a tax is distributed among economic units (consumers, producers, employees, employers, and so on). The actual tax burden does not always fall on those who are statutorily assigned to pay the tax.

Tax rate The per-unit amount of the tax or the percentage rate at which the economic activity is taxed.

Team production A production process in which employees work together under the supervision of the owner or the owner's representative.

Technology The technological knowledge available in an economy at any given time. The level of technology determines the amount of output we can generate with our limited resources.

Total cost The costs, both explicit and implicit, of all the resources used by the firm. Total cost includes a normal rate of return for the firm's equity capital.

Total fixed cost The sum of the costs that do not vary with output. They will be incurred as long as a firm continues in business and the assets have alternative uses.

Total product The total output of a good that is associated with each alternative utilization rate of a variable input.

Total variable cost The sum of those costs that rise as output increases. Examples of variable costs are wages paid to workers and payments for raw materials.

Tournament pay A form of compensation in which the top performer (or performers) receives much higher rewards than do other competitors, even if the others perform at only a slightly lower level.

Transaction costs The time, effort, and other resources needed to search out, negotiate, and complete an exchange.

Transfer payments Payments to individuals or institutions that are not linked to the current supply of a good or service by the recipient.

U

Underground market A market that operates outside the legal system in which either illegal goods or services are sold, or legal ones are sold at illegal prices or terms.

User charges Payments users (consumers) are required to make if they want to receive certain services provided by the government.

Utility The subjective benefit or satisfaction a person expects from a choice or course of action.

V

Value marginal product (*VMP*) The marginal product of a resource multiplied by the selling price of the product it helps produce. For a price-taker firm, marginal revenue product (*MRP*) will be equal to the value marginal product (*VMP*).

W

World Trade Organization (WTO) The new name given to GATT in 1994; the WTO is currently responsible for monitoring and enforcing multilateral trade agreements among its 164 member countries.

Index

Note: Page numbers followed by "*n*" indicate notes and "e" indicate exhibit.

A

B

D

F

H

I

P

Q

R

T

U